UNTYING THE KNOTS IN BUDDHISM

BUDDHIST TRADITION SERIES

Edited by

ALEX WAYMAN

VOLUME 28

Untying the Knots in Buddhism

SELECTED ESSAYS

ALEX WAYMAN

MOTILAL BANARSIDASS PUBLISHERS
PRIVATE LIMITED • DELHI

First Edition: Delhi, 1997

ISBN: 81-208-1321-9

Also available at

MOTILAL BANARSIDASS

41 U.A. Bungalow Road, Jawahar Nagar, Delhi 110 007
8 Mahalaxmi Chamber, Warden Road, Mumbai 400 026
120 Royapettah High Road, Mylapore, Chennai 600 004
Sanas Plaza, Subhas Nagar, Pune 411 002
16 St. Mark's Road, Bangalore 560 001
8 Camac Street, Calcutta 700 017
Ashok Rajpath, Patna 800 004
Chowk, Varanasi 221 001

PRINTED IN INDIA

BY JAINENDRA PRAKASH JAIN AT SHRI JAINENDRA PRESS,
A-45 NARAINA, PHASE I, NEW DELHI 110 028
AND PUBLISHED BY NARENDRA PRAKASH JAIN FOR
MOTILAL BANARSIDASS PUBLISHERS PRIVATE LIMITED,
BUNGALOW ROAD, DELHI 110 007

Foreword

The series editor is happy to present these essays in the same series whose quality standard had the good omen of starting with Professor Hajime Nakamura's bibliographical survey *Indian Buddhism*. Since then the series has maintained a general excellence. Readers of the preceding work of my essays *Buddhist Insight* (ed. by George R. Elder) should appreciate the present collection as a companion volume. The attentive peruser of the present essays may notice that they are more devoted to solving basic problems of Buddhism, even with a restrained type of contention. Scholars who had held that Prof. Wayman's contributions are mainly in the field of Tantra should be surprised to find these numerous well-argued essays in non-tantric Buddhism. They illustrate the range of the author's interests.

New York City — ALEX WAYMAN

Preface

There are two kinds of articles in the present work—ones previously published, and ones not previously published. In the latter group, there are those prepared for special purposes, and those composed especially for the present work.

A. *Articles previously published*
May I thank jointly the various editors and organizations, etc. who or which have given permission for reprinting various articles in the present volume.

Especially must I thank Mariasusai Davamony, editor of the annual periodical *Studia Missionalia* in Rome for the numerous invitations to contribute essays, and permission to reprint certain ones for this volume, namely (with their dates of original publication): "Śākyamuni, Founder of Buddhism" (1984), "Nāgārjuna, Reformer of Buddhism" (1985), "Vasubandhu, Teacher Extraordinary" (1988), "The Guru in Buddhism" (1987), "The Buddhist meaning of death" (1982), "The Position of Women in Buddhism" (1991).

Indian Books Centre, Delhi, India for permission to reprint "Doctrinal Affiliation of Asaṅga," from the Professor P.V. Bapat Felicitation Volume, *Amalā Prajñā; Aspects of Buddhist Studies* (1989), pp. 201-21.

V.C. Srivastava, Dept. of Ancient Indian History, Culture & Archaeology, Banaras Hindu University for permission to reprint "Parents of Buddhist Monks" from *Bharati,* 1966-68, Nos. X & XI.

Philosophy East and West (Hawaii), for reprinting "Tathāgata Chapter of Nāgārjuna's *Madhyamaka-kārikā,*" from its Vol. 38 (1988), pp. 47-57; and for "The Meaning of Unwisdom" [now "The meaning of Nescience" with other corrections], from its Vol. 7 (1957), pp. 21-5.

The American Oriental Society for permission to use my translation of *Madhyamaka-kārikā,* Chap. II, from my article "The gait (*gati*) and the Path (*mārga*)—Reflections on the Horizontal," *Journal of the American Oriental Society,* 105.3 (1985).

The *Adyar Society Bulletin* for permission to use the article "The Vedic Three Worlds in Early and Later Times," from its Vol. 50, 1986.

The Faculty of Asian Studies, The Australian National University, Canberra for permission to reprint "Vedāntic and Buddhist Theory of Nāma-rūpa," from the J.W. de Jong volume *Indological and Buddhist Studies* (Canberra, 1982).

The Central Institute of Higher Tibetan Studies, Sarnath, Varanasi for permission to use the article (cf. my essay No. 13) "A Prajñāpāramitā Scripture within a Tantra," from *Śramaṇa Vidyā* (1987).

Kluwer Academic Publishers, Dordrecht, The Netherlands for permission to reprint (although with a few deletions) my "Studies in Yama and Māra," *Indo-Iranian Journal,* 1959, 3:1. pp. 44-75; 3:2, pp. 112-131.

Genjun H. Sasaki, D. Litt., who gave permission on behalf of the publisher Shimizukobunda Ltd., Tokyo, for reprinting "Purification of Sin in Buddhism by Vision and Confession" from the work he edited *A Study of Kleśa* (1975).

Alex Wayman, since his essay No. 16 "Asaṅga on Food" is from his own *Analysis of the Śrāvakabhūmi Manuscript* (Berkeley, California, 1961) and after this work went out of print, one need not ask the publisher for permission.

B. *Articles not previously published*

Articles prepared for specific purposes: "Aniconic and iconic art of the Buddha" was delivered in a panel of the College Art Association, during its 1989 San Francisco meeting.

"Prophecies for Persons" was delivered as a Faculty lecture at the University of Hawaii, Fall 1992.

"The 'no-self' of Buddhism within Indian Culture" after being written in full extent was reduced for presentation at a meeting of the Society for Asian and Comparative Philosophy at New York City, in Dec., 1991.

Articles written especially for the present volume: "Asaṅga's Three Pratyekabuddha Paths" is based on my published edition of Asaṅga's *Pratyekabuddhabhūmi* in *Journal of Indian and Buddhist Studies,* 7:1 (Tokyo, 1960).

"Core Teachings: suffering, karma, seed consciousness, dharma" was especially composed for the present volume.

The articles "The Buddha date and era" and "Virtue consignment (*pariṇāmana*)" were composed for the present volume, but while in Varanasi a few years back, I allowed Prof. A.K. Narain to include the former one in a seminar volume on the date of the Buddha he was editing; and allowed Prof. N.H. Samtani to include the latter in a seminar volume on Buddhist terminology he was editing, informing both scholars that the two essays were meant for the volume UNTYING THE KNOTS. I have no information as to whether either of those seminar volumes was published.

Also composed especially for the present volume were in essay no. 13, on voidness, the translation from Pāli of the *Cūḷasuññatā-sutta*; in essay no. 14, the 'scripture' part translated from the Tibetan prologue to the *Akṣayamatinirdeśa-sūtra*; in essay no. 20, additions to the Buddhist theory of the three worlds; and in essay no. 24, the part "the meaning of omniscience".

After accounting for the essays in this volume, may I take this opportunity to thank Shree N. Prakash Jain, Director, Motilal Banarsidass, Delhi, India, for undertaking to publish the present work in the Buddhist Tradition Series for which I am the general editor.

New York, ALEX WAYMAN
September, 1994

Introduction

The present volume of twenty-four essays is intended as a companion to the previous volume of twenty-four essays published under the title *Buddhist Insight* that was edited by George Elder and published by Motilal Banarsidass, Delhi (in 1984). The present volume is necessarily edited by myself, since various articles had to be modified from their original forms; and also since there has been a number of article substitutions in the volume as it was originally conceived some years ago. It would have been easier for the author to have used previously published articles to fill up the volume, but the author engaged in a considerable amount of further writing, so as to achieve an integrated volume rather than a collection of miscellaneous essays.

In the final form of this text, the first two groups of essays emphasize the Buddha and his Saṃgha among the three Jewels of Buddhism; the next two groups go with the Dharma-Jewel. The fifth group of essays (Hindu-Buddhist studies) is pursuant to the author's position that Buddhism cannot be divorced from its origin amidst the currents of Indian culture.

The superimposition of the number twenty-four is certified by words of the Sanskrit language: *siddha* (perfect) is a name of the number 24; and the term *parama* in the meaning 'highest point' is in the compound *catur-viṃśati-parama* 'at the utmost 24'.

The title's expression '*untying the knots*' has two applicable interpretations: (1) Solving problems. The author claims to 'untie knots' by trying to solve problems of Buddhism, whether of biography, history, or doctrine. This is a procedure that tacitly opposes the frequent copying of previous theories without evaluation, although admittedly many previous theories about Buddhism are correct indeed. (2) Loosening the previous fixation. Here 'untying the knots' is equivalent to the scripture title *Saṃdhinirmocana,* the basic scripture of the Yogācara school. The title implies the charting of a new course. While the present volume reflects such a procedure to some extent—namely, a new approach—the author admits his own effect cannot compare with that of the named scripture.

The attentive readers will probably notice repetition of some citations in these essays. While the writer tried to suppress such repetitions, some probably remain due to the length of years that separate various essays, as the writer returned to certain problems in a different context. On the positive side it may be an evidence of essay compatibility.

The transcription of Tibetan words should be mentioned. In my early essays I used the system employed by the Russian Buddhologist Obermiller. Later I have adhered to the Library of Congress official transcription system for Tibetan language. More recently, I have used the Wilie system which dispenses with most diacritics. The author must apologize to the reader for such inconsistencies in the present set of essays, but readers of the Tibetan language will find little difficulty in recognizing the words by such transcriptions.

Finally, to elude imitation has been a joyful duty.

September, 1994 ALEX WAYMAN

Contents

SECTION I HEROES OF THE SYSTEM

"Brahmā and the rest of the gods call 'Great Hero', the one who was seated at the bodhimaṇḍa (terrace of enlightenment) and destroyed the four Māras".

"Later, I am the hero gladly pronouncing the words that annul all fear, and am called 'Great Hero'."

—*Vairocanābhisaṃbodhitantra* (Chap. 2)

1

Śākyamuni, Founder of Buddhism

The person and his times of Gautama or Śākyamuni, founder of Buddhism have been the topics of a large Western literature. With the wealth of information at hand, partly archaeological, there is no denying the historicity of Buddhism's founder, even when we grant a certain amount of mythological overlay. One cannot doubt that the attitude of disciples toward the Master, the Buddha, and to his Doctrine (called Dhamma in Pāli, and Dharma in Sanskrit) during his lifetime was greatly altered after his passing. In later times, Buddhist practice was not only based on scriptural precepts, but on the Buddha's life as a model. Accordingly, his life as a 'career' (*caryā* or *caritā*) was divided into well-defined periods,

---

Reprinted from *Studia Missionalia*, Vol. 33. Universita Gregoriana Editrice. Roma. 1984.

generously treated in the texts and the subjects of art depictions.[1]

The Bhikkhu Ñāṇamoli book using Pāli sources where Gautama is regarded as a superior kind of man makes these divisions by way of chapters: I. the birth and the early years; II. the struggle for enlightenment; III. after the enlightenment; IV. the spreading of the Dhamma; V. the two chief disciples; VI. Anāthapiṇḍika—the feeder of the poor; VII. the formation of the order of nuns; VIII. the quarrel at Kosambi; IX. the end of the first twenty years; X. the middle period; XI. the person; XII. the doctrine; XIII. Devadatta; XIV. old age; XV. the last year; and XVI. the first council.[2] The Mahāyāna list found in the *Ratnagotravibhāga*, where the Buddha is depicted as superior to men and gods, presents twelve acts: 1. descent from the Tuṣita heaven; 2. entrance into the womb; 3. rebirth; 4. skill in worldly arts; 5. enjoyment of the harem women; 6. departure from home; 7. arduous discipline; 8. passage to the terrace of enlightenment; 9. defeat of the Māra host; 10. complete enlightenment; 11. the wheel of the Dharma; and 12. departure into Nirvāṇa.[3]

The standard modern dating of the Buddha is for his Parinirvāṇa—complete passing away—at age 80 in 483 B.C., hence birth in 563 B.C.[4] These dates can be shifted by a few years in either direction.[5] According to the story, at the age of 29, Gautama saw four signs that led to his leaving home for the religious life. In the next six years, he sought enlightenment by a fruitless severe asceticism. Then in a short time by a moderate course he became enlightened at the age of 35. He spent the next 20 years in wandering, during which his order (the Saṁgha) was established. Then he had to contend with rivals and with dramatic political changes.

The Buddha directs in the *Mahāparinirvāṇa-sūtra* (the equivalent Pāli in *Dīgha-Nikāya* II):[6]

> O *bhikṣus*, four are the spots on earth to be held in mind during the life of a son of the family or daughter of the family, having faith. What are the four? Here the Bhagavat was born. Here the Bhagavat was completely awakened to the highest right perfected enlightenment. Here the noble wheel of the Dharma, having three turns in twelve parts, was set in motion by the Bhagavat. Here the Bhagavat entered *parinirvāṇa* in the realm of Nirvāṇa without remainder. *Bhikṣus*, after my passing away, those who go circumambulating shrines,

> bowing to shrines, are to speak as follows: "Here the Bhagavat . . ." Among these places, whoever with pure thought will die in my presence, all those belong to heaven (*svarga*), whoever are with remainder.

The four places are Kapilavastu (for the birth); Gayā (for the enlightenment); Sārnāth (for the wheel of the Dharma); Kuśinagara (for the *parinirvāṇa*).[7]

Birth and Early Years

Buddhist tradition states that before becoming the Buddha Śākyamuni, he had the personal name Siddhārtha and the family name Gautama in the Śākya clan. He was born to the royal family of King Śuddhodana and Queen Māyā, the latter dying through childbirth. The kingdom was in the Himalayan foothills, approximately the modern southern Nepal, and had Kapilavastu as the capital city (now referred to as the Lumbinī district).

According to a theory gradually developed in the transition to Mahāyāna Buddhism and contained in full form in the *Lalitavistara*, which is a Mahāyāna biography of the Buddha, in a previous birth long ago he had taken a vow in the presence of an earlier Buddha to become a Buddha himself. In due course of time he was reborn in the Tuṣita—one of the six heavens of the 'passion gods' at the top of the 'Realm of Desire'. At the appointed time for rebirth in a last existence, he made certain examinations to be certain about the time, place, district, family, and type of mother (one who would live for ten lunar months and seven days after the womb entrance); and then in this case having decided, the future Buddha appointed the Bodhisattva Maitreya to remain in Tuṣita and be the next Buddha in a later age.[8] Much of the story is already in a Pāli scripture in the *Majjhima-Nikāya* (the *Acchariyabbhutadhamma-sutta*).[9] The Buddha's faithful attendant Ānanda reports that he heard remarkable details face to face (*sammukha*) with the Bhagavat (the lord), including that the future Buddha, mindful and aware (P. *sato, sampajāno*; in Sanskrit, possessed of *smṛti* and *saṃprajanya*), had passed away from the Tuṣita body (*kāya*) and entered his mother's womb. And that during the ten lunar months he is in that womb, his mother is of perfect virtue. That he exits from her side:

> "As soon as he is born, Ānanda, the Bodhisattva, standing with even feet upon the earth, facing north goes with a stride of seven steps. While a white umbrella is held over him (by the gods), he surveys all the quarters and declares with commanding voice: 'I am chief in the world; I am best in the world; I am eldest in the world. This is the last birth. There is not now a re-gestation.' "

The stride of seven steps toward north implies the future Buddhist path; also the Buddha's friendship with chthonian deities, especially serpents (*nāga*). A Mahāyāna scripture called *Vairocanābhisaṃbodhi-tantra,* Chap. X, has:[10] "I am called Lord of the World; am first of the world, and teach the Dharma that is supreme, quiescent from the outset, and incomparable." Notice the emphasis on 'world'; thus the remark in the Pāli scripture seems to portend the Buddha as the teacher. It also implies the legendary first king of the Buddhist genesis myth.[11]

The Bodhisattva (he is called this prior to becoming a Buddha) upon being born is associated with signs. The Pāli *Sutta-nipāta* and the Mahāyāna *Lalitavistara* represent a seer (P. *isi;* Skt. *ṛṣi*) named Asita to see divine signs; and to be informed by the gods that it means the future Buddha has been born in the world of men in the Lumbinī district. Asita proceeds from his Himalayan dwelling to the residence of Śuddhodana and asks to see the child. When this happens, the seer recognizes in Siddhārtha the marks of the 'great person' (*mahāpuruṣa*). The *Lalitavistara* account details the 32 characteristics and 80 minor marks which are held to be shared by a Buddha and by a 'universal emperor'.[12] In fact, the 32 characteristics are a standard list; while the 80 occur with variants, especially one list emphasizing the great yogin (static) and another list the great king (royal gait). Here I give only the 32 characteristics (*lakṣaṇa*), but in sub-sets: 1-2 'each hair of head curled to the right' and 'head topped by an *uṣṇīṣa*'. 3. 'treasure of hair' (*ūrṇā-kośa*). 4-5. 'eyes dark blue' and 'eye-lashes bovine'. 6. 'jaws leonine'. 7-13. 'tongue long and slender', 'voice pure', teeth very white', 'teeth without gaps', 'teeth 40 in number', 'teeth equal in size', and 'taste perfect'. 14. 'shoulders gently curved'. 15-22. 'standing, not bending himself', 'hands which hang low', 'skin delicate', 'skin of golden hue', 'upper part of body leonine', 'broad-shouldered', 'rounded like a Banyan tree', and 'seven mounds on his body'. 23. 'secret of privities drawn into a recess'. 24. 'legs like those of an antelope'. 25. 'each hair of body turning to the right side'. 26. 'fingers and toes long'. 27-32. 'hands and feet marked by a wheel rim', 'feet well-planted', 'hands and feet soft and tender', 'webs joining (the fingers and toes on) his hands and feet', 'heels broad', and 'ankle joints inconspicuous'.[13]

Since Siddhārtha's mother died a week after his birth, he was in fact raised by an aunt, Mahāprajāpati. The youth is given training in the various arts, especially archery; in composition, languages, and so on. While such lists—very detailed in the *Lalitavistara*—have a stereotyped air, they are consistent with the Buddha's later life, his easy association with the Kings of his day, which is a reasonable consequence of an early training as a prince.

Siddhārtha married Yaśodharā, and had a child Rāhula by name; was surrounded also by many women of the court. It was when his son was an infant that Siddhārtha, now 29 years of age, decided to leave home as a religious wanderer, of which there were apparently quite a number in those days. This seems to violate the responsibility of a father in Indian society; and indeed there are indications of a long-held resentment in his immediate family circle, as will be alluded to later in this chapter.

Departure from Home

Now the story that Siddhārtha, or Gautama, saw four signs through the capital gates—the aged man near the East gate; the sick man near the South gate; the dead man near the West gate; the monk near the North gate—visions prepared by the gods—is too neat. It goes with the presumed effort of King Śuddhodana to prevent such sights of Siddhārtha, but rather to surround him with all sorts of pleasures and loveliness so that his mind would not turn to the religious life but would instead agree to succession to kingship. Thomas quite properly points out that this is a later legend contradicted by earlier accounts.[14] Among the more authentic events that can be pointed to, the one in the *Mahāvastu* is indeed worth mentioning:[15]

> King Śuddhodana along with his women circle and a young boy had gone out to the pleasure grounds. The Bodhisattva, strolling in the pleasure grounds came to a section being tilled. There he saw ploughs being drawn. These ploughs

> tossed up a snake (*dīrghaka*) and a frog (*mamḍūka*). The young boy seized the frog to eat it, but tossed away the snake. The Bodhisattva observed this; and upon seeing (what had happened), experienced an intense agitation. (And he thought:) Pleasure, the body, and life, are equally burnt up. Now I shall attain the ambrosial release from phenomenal life. For I cannot check my striving, which is like the thrust of ocean water on the sea-shore.

It is consistent with various accounts of the Buddha's later life, the legends of relations with serpents that Siddhārtha should experience this shuddering at the despoiling of the underground habitations. The passage continues:

> The Bodhisattva sat in the shade of a rose-apple tree for the forenoon; and as the sun's rays shifted, the shade (miraculously) did not abandon the Bodhisattva. He stayed, dwelling in the First Dhyāna, which is attended with inquiry and with investigation.[16]

Such accounts clarify that the Bodhisattva was extremely sensitive to events of the soil (Witness the celebrated 'touching of earth' gesture, signalling the defeat of the demon Māra). Such events could arouse in him a revulsion from the life of pleasures and would catapult him into the wandering state.

According to the legend, he sped away from the capital on his horse named Kanṭhaka. Then he visited various teachers, but the two main ones are undoubtedly Ārāḍa at Vaiśālī, and Udraka Rāmaputra at Rājagṛha.[17] Here I use the version of Aśvaghoṣa's *Buddhacarita*, Canto XII. Ārāḍa of the Kālāma gotra, said to the Bodhisattva:

> 5. It is known to me, how, dear sir, you have come forth from the palace, having severed the bonds made of affection, like a maddened elephant his thong.[18]
> 10. Even though the *śāstra* is explained in time when the student is able to understand, your honor, by reason of profundity and resolution, need not be examined by me.[19]

Gautama, called here 'the bull of men', responds:

> 13. For I deem your system (*darśana*) like one who wishes to see, would (deem) a light; like one who wishes to travel,

> would a guide; and like one who wishes to ford, would a boat.
> 14. Therefore, you ought to tell it, if you deem it to be told—how this person may be liberated from old age, death, and disease.[20]

And Ārāḍa:

> 16. Listen, O best of listeners. This is our *siddhānta* (doctrinal system) as to how *saṃsāra* develops and how it disintegrates.[21]

Ārāḍa proceeds to expound a Sāṃkhya-like system, discussing 'primary matter' (*prakṛti*) and 'secondary matter' (*vikāra*), down to:

> 41. For when the field-knower has understood this set of four (viz. recognition in each case, non-recognition, the manifest, and the unmanifest), it abandons the coming and going (in *saṃsāra*), and reaches the non-changing (*a-kṣara*) plane.[22]

The king's son (*nṛpātmaja*) inquired as to the approach (*abhyupāya*) and as to the ultimate plane (*naiṣṭhika-pada*). Ārāḍa then resorted to another method of exposition, that of *yoga*, going into the theory of the Dhyāna-type meditations, thus showing Aśvaghoṣa's attitude that the theory of the four Dhyāna states and their associated deities, is a pre-Buddhist teaching. Ārāḍa then speaks of transcending these Dhyāna states and initially passing into the *yoga* conviction that the body is empty:

> 63. But another skilled in the inner self with his self stops the self and observes that there is nothing. This state is declared 'the nothing at all'.
> 64. Then, like the stalk from the Muñja sheath, or the bird from its cage, the field-knower, having slid out of the body is defined as 'liberated'.[23]

Evidently, Ārāḍa had presented what is accepted in Buddhist doctrine as the 'formless' realms (*arūpa-dhātu*), the boundless space, boundless consciousness, and the nothing-at-all.[24] But Gautama does not accept Ārāḍa's portrayal of the ultimate condition:

> 69. I have listened to this subtle knowledge, which is further

and further auspicious; but since the field-knower is not completely abandoned, I understand this to not pertain to the absolute.[25]

The prince continued with various arguments against Ārāḍa's position; and having decided that this system was incomplete, he turned away from there. He proceeded to the hermitage of Udraka. This teacher, according to verse 85, had found a state beyond the 'nothing-at-all' which he called the 'neither ideation nor non-ideation'. This latter state is also preserved in Buddhist accounts of the 'formless' realms.[26] But the Bodhisattva denied that this state constitutes a 'release', since reaching it one returns to the world, just as happens with Ārāḍa's so-called 'release'.

The Bodhisattva took up his abode on the bank of the Nairañjanā river. There he saw five mendicants who had located there before him. As he began his austerities there, these five paid him reverence, and waited upon him:

> 95. Engaging in various kinds of fasting that are difficult for a man to practice, for six years he worked at making himself emaciated, with desire to attain quiescence.[27]

Then he decided:

> 101. "This *dharma* does not serve for passionlessness, for enlightenment, for liberation. That is the sure method which I gained that time at the base of the rose-apple tree."[28]

He recalls that event when he drew strength from the earth, and then passed into the Dhyāna-meditation; and that it was an occasion when he had not been starving himself:

> 107. Accordingly the steadfast one of immeasurable intelligence, with decision that the method had its basis in food, made up his mind in the instrumentality (*karaṇa*) of food.[29]

He bathed and slowly moved away from the bank of the Nairañjanā. Then Nandabālā, daughter of the cowherd chief, exhorted by divinities came there:

> 110. Her arms shining with white shells, she was dressed in blue cloth like Yamunā, best of rivers, its blue water wreathed with wreaths of foam.[30]

Doing obeisance with her head, she bade him accept milk rice. By it, and his *yaśas* (fiery energy) his body completely filled out. Thinking he had reverted (to the condition prior to his austerities) the five mendicants left him:

> 115. Thereupon, his resolution toward enlightenment his inseparate companion, he proceeded to the base of an Aśvattha tree, whose nearby ground was bespread with verdant grass.
> 116. At the very moment, Kāla, best of serpents, mighty as the king of elephants, awakened by the incomparable sound of his feet, understood the great *muni*'s resolution of enlightenment and uttered this eulogy:
> 117. "O muni, since the earth repeatedly roars, as it were, pressed by the feet; and since your light shines like the sun, surely today you will experience the desired fruit."
> 118. "O lotus-eyed, since the flocks of blue-jays, flying about in the atmosphere, circle you to the right; since mild zephyrs blow in the atmosphere, surely today you will become Buddha."
> 119. Having been extolled by the best of serpents , he took clean grass from a reaper, approached the base of the pure great tree; and after taking the vow of enlightenment, seated himself.
> 120. Then he bound his legs in the supreme, unshakeable *paryaṅka* posture, massed together like the coils of a sleeping snake, saying, "I shall not disengage, I shall not leave this seat on the ground until the task is done."[31]

It is inescapable that the poet Aśvaghoṣa emphasizes Gautama's affiliation with the *nāga* (serpent) kingdom. The association here of feet with ground is continued into the Buddhist Tantra of the Far East kind.[32]

The Assault and Defeat of Māra

The various contests with Māra in the traditional biographies of the Buddha are mythological elaborations. Thomas points out that Māra appears at various points of the Buddha's life, starting with the six years of austerities, then at dusk, as here, before the night of enlightenment, and after enlightenment.[33] For this reason, later texts speak of four Māras, 'personal aggregate' (*skandha-māra*), of 'defilement' (*kleśa-māra*). 'son-of-the-gods' (*devaputra-māra*), and 'death' (*maraṇa-māra*). A Mahāyāna commentator Vilāsavajra explains the defeat of the four kinds of Māra in terms of the four Buddhist doctrine kinds of 'flux' (*āsrava*). He says: by erasing the flux of desire (*kāma*), he defeated the son-of-the-gods Māra; by erasing the flux of gestation (*bhava*), he defeated the death Māra; by erasing the flux of nescience (*avidyā*), he defeated the defilement Māra; by erasing the flux of wrong views (*dṛṣti*), he defeated the personal-aggregate Māra.[34] Aśvaghoṣa's *Buddhacarita* evidently intends the assault and defeat of the son-of-the-gods Māra in Canto XIII dealing with the present phase of the Buddha's career:

> 1. When the great seer, offspring of a lineage of royal seers, made that vow for liberation and was seated there, the world rejoiced, and Māra, enemy of the Illustrious Doctrine, felt threatened.
> 2. Him, who in the world they declare the God of Love, the one with variegated weapon, the one with flowery arrows, that same one, lord of the usages of passion, the enemy of liberation, they call Māra.
> 3. His three sons, Vibhrama (perturbation), Harṣa (sexual excitement), and Darpa (vanity); and his three daughters, Arati (boredom), Prīti (pleasure), and Tṛṣṇā (craving), asked him about his glumness; and he answered them as follows:
> 4. "Yonder *muni*, wearing the armor of resolve, drawing the bow of courage with the arrow of intellectual penetration, sits, desirous of conquering my realm; hence my mind's despondency."
> 5. "For if yonder one manages to overcome me, and expounds for the world the path of *apavarga* (final release), then is my realm today a nullity like that of the Videha (king) when he fell from proper usages."
> 6. "Therefore, as long as he has not gained the eye (=divine sight, *divya-cakṣus*), just as long as he remains in my sphere—during that time I shall proceed to break his vow like the swollen thrust of the river (proceeds to break) the embankment."
> 7. Then, seizing his flowery bow and his five world-deluding arrows, he, who causes the minds of creatures to be out of sorts, approached the base of the Aśvattha along with his offspring.[35]

The sequel depicts Māra as failing to disturb the Bodhisattva with the flowery arrow. Māra calls up his army, which assumes all sorts of demonic forms. Nature becomes troubled; the wind blows violently in all directions, and so on:

> 30. The serpents who support the earth and are devoted to Dharma, not tolerating the demonic hindrance to the great *muni*; their eyes turned with fury towards Māra, hissed and stretched out.[36]
> 31. The awaking seers of the Pure Abodes, engaged in the aim of fulfilling the Sublime Doctrine, formed compassion with their minds for Māra, but by reason of their dispassionate state did not become angry.[37]

The mythological account continues that the Bodhisattva remains unmoved by the demonic attack. All hurled weapons fall in their tracks, unable to reach their intended mark. The poet Aśvaghoṣa introduces a mysterious being in the sky who lectures Māra on the futility of his attack:

> 56. Then it transpired that a certain being of invisible body and superiority, stationed in the sky, observing Māra enraged without a feud (*avaira-ruṣṭa*) and trying to harm the *ṛṣi*, spoke to him (Māra) with a commanding voice:
> 57. "Māra, you ought not to engage in this fruitless toil. Give up this harmful nature. Go away happily. For this person cannot be shaken by you, just as the great Mtn. Meru (cannot be shaken) by the wind."[38]

And further down to:

> 67. "For whatever were those deeds committed by him for enlightenment, today is their ordained time. Thus is he seated in this seat in the exact manner as were the former *munis*."
> 68. "For this is the navel of the earth goddess' surface endowed with a *dhāman* (power) by the supreme totality. There is no other spot of earth which can withstand his thrust of intense concentration (*samādhi*)."[39]

The intention seems to be that when the Bodhisattva touches earth in the celebrated subject of art depiction, the place which he touches is the 'navel' of earth. Māra is then represented as recognizing his defeat and going away dejected, his army scattering, with weapons abandoned.

The Night of Enlightenment

In the age of Gautama Buddha the night was divided into three 'watches' (*yāma*). According to the traditional accounts, Gautama had a 'clear vision' (Pāli, *vijjā*; Skt. *vidyā*) in each of the three 'watches'. These are set forth in the *Aṅguttara-Nikāya*, 'Book of Eights' (The Great Chapter), the *Verañjā-sutta*. Here, as the first 'chick' to break the eggshell, Gautama is called the 'eldest':

> "Even so, you should know, brahman, when I, for the sake of mankind which in the condition of nescience is covered over (as it were) within an egg had broken out of the eggshell of nescience, I alone in the world was manifestly awakened to the supreme rightly complete enlightenment. For I, brahman, was the eldest, best of the world."[40]

Gautama then mentions the attainments of the four Dhyānas (divisions of the 'realm of form', *rūpadhātu*) in a standard formula (for later centuries) of which the statement for the First Dhyāna was mentioned above in the episode under the rose-apple tree, viz., "He stayed, dwelling in the First Dhyāna, which is attended with inquiry and with resolution." After passing through these four Dhyānas, but not proceeding to the 'formless realm', Gautama then had his three 'clear visions'. In the first 'watch' of night, he saw his previous lives, in this text said to number into many thousands, in each case recalling his name (*nāma*), clan (Skt. *gotra*), caste (Skt. *varṇa*), food (*āhāra*), individual experiences of happiness and sorrow, and end of life.

> This, you should know, brahman, was my first 'clear vision', attained in the first watch of the night: nescience overcome, clear vision arose; darkness overcome, light arose—as I stayed on it, of few wants, ardent, and of resolute will. This, you should know, brahman was my first hatching like a young chicken's from the eggshell.

According to the information previously given about the four Māra demons, the overcoming of nescience (Skt. *avidyā*) signals the defeat of the defilement Māra. However, the same formula is used for the second and third 'clear visions', changing to second and third also for the 'hatchings'. The implication is that the three 'clear visions' constitute a serial elimination of nescience.

In the second watch, Gautama turned his mind to the sentient beings, observing that after the break up of their bodies at death they proceeded to various destinies according to their volitional deeds; and this was his second hatching from the eggshell.

> With the pure divine eye (Skt. *divya-cakṣus*) surpassing the human eye, I saw the sentient beings dying and being reborn, who were inferior and superior, good-complexioned and bad-complexioned, of good destiny and of bad destiny, matching their deeds.

Finally, in the third watch, Gautama turned his mind to the destruction of the fluxes (*āsrava*), realizing the four Noble Truths and flux-destruction, and this third 'clear vision' was his third hatching from the eggshell:

> I comprehended as it really is, "This is suffering"; as it really is, "This is the source of suffering"; as it really is, "This is the cessation of suffering"; as it really is, "This is the path leading to the cessation of suffering". I comprehended as it really is, "These are the fluxes"; as it really is, "This is the source of the fluxes"; as it really is, "This is the cessation of the fluxes"; as it really is, "This is the path leading to the cessation of the fluxes". Knowing this and observing this, my mind (*citta*) was liberated from the flux of desire; was liberated from the flux of gestation; was liberated from the flux of nescience. There being the liberation, there arose the knowledge, "There is liberation." I comprehended, "Destroyed is birth; lived is the pure life (Skt. *brahmacarya*); done what needed to be done; because there is no further life in these conditions."

In terms of the kinds of Māra, Gautama comprehended that by ending the flux of desire, he had defeated the son-of-the-gods Māra; by ending the flux of gestation ("Destroyed is birth"), the death Māra; by ending the flux of nescience, the defilement Māra.

As to the three 'clear visions' (*vidyā*) which Buddhist legend attributes to Gautama's realizations during the celebrated night of enlightenment, there is a suggestion from a later scripture which has enjoyed great popularity, even to this day in Japan, that they are due to the Buddha's characteristic symbol in the middle of his forehead. This is because this scripture, known in Asia as the *Mahāvairocana-sūtra*, has personified the *ūrṇā-kośa* in that forehead place, by a goddess named Vidyorṇā, a name which means "she the *ūrṇā* of *vidyā*".[41]

The traditions differ concerning the respective visions of the three 'watches' of the night. Thus, the *Mahāvastu* places the remembrance of previous lives in the second 'watch' rather than the first, as above.[42]

This text, the *Mahāvastu*, states that the actual enlightenment took place in a single moment of thought (*ekacittakṣaṇa*) in the last watch of night at the time of dawn's uncovering (or, the revelation of the tawny one) when night had joy on its face.[43]

The title 'Buddha' was translated into Tibetan as *saṅs rgyas* ('awakened and expanded') to accord with the explanation likening the attainment to a lotus, opening up ('awakening' from the sleep of delusion) and expanding (or, expanded by the sun).[44]

According to legend the first words uttered by Gautama the Buddha after the enlightenment were these:[45]

> I have passed through the cyclical flow of many births seeking the maker of the house and finding him not; painful is birth again and again.
> Now you are seen, O builder of the house. You will not build the house again. All your beams are broken, your rafters cut to pieces.

The commentary on the *Udānavarga* interprets the 'house' as defilement (*kleśa*) and the 'rafters' as craving (*tṛṣṇā;* Pāli *taṇhā*).[46] This information enables me to suggest that the 'builder' is *karma*. The '(cross) beams' would be nescience (*avidyā*). Thus craving as the 'rafters' has the role of completing the house by furnishing the roof.

Śākyamuni, Teacher of Gods and Men

According to the Buddhist legend, the Bhagavat stayed by the Bodhi Tree for seven days, during or at the close of which he was occupied with the dependent origination formula (*pratītya-samutpāda*) in twelve members, in the forward and reverse direction, and its cessation.[47] Emerging from this *samādhi*, he went to the base of the Ajapāla Nigrodha tree. After seven days here, he moved to the base of the Mucalinda tree. Now a fierce unseasonable storm arose, lasting for seven days during which the serpent king Mucalinda stayed there with his giant hood spread over the Bhagavat's head and his coils around the Bhagavat's body to protect him against the elements and crawling things.[48]

The *Brahma Suttas* of the *Saṃyutta-Nikāya* tell about the Bhagavat's reluctance to teach his profound doctrine:[49]

> This I understood by painful austerity. Away with now broadcasting it! This Dharma is not easily grasped by those overcome by lust and hate. Subtle, profound, hard to see, and fine, it goes against the stream. Inflamed by lust, covered by a mass of darkness, they will not see it.

The legend now has Brahmā Sahampati, the presiding deity of the Brahmā world, becoming aware of the Bhagavat's attitude, and appearing before him to urge a preaching of the Dharma, since some beings, their eyes hardly dimmed, would profit, saying also:

> Among the Magadhas there arose before thee
> an unclean Dharma, thought up with blemishes.
> Open the gate to the immortal (or, ambrosia).
> Let them hear the Dharma that convinces by lack of blemishes.

The Buddha then surveyed the world with his Buddha-eye. Compassionately he saw beings hard to teach, easy to teach, and so on; and addressed Brahmā with a verse that he would indeed proclaim his Dharma. Brahmā passed round him to the right and disappeared.

It might appear contradictory to identify Śākyamuni as 'teacher of gods and men', since the commentators explain '*muni*' as 'muted in body, speech, and mind'—such a one among the Śākya clan.[50] As to 'teacher of gods and men', the *Mahāprajñā-pāramitāśāstra* explains this epithet to mean he teaches them the good (*kuśala*) and the evil (*akuśala*); thus learning what they should accept and what abandon, they may advance on the path to liberation from defilement (*kleśa*).[51] Thus, they could be as he is, a *muni*.

The Buddha reported in the *Ariyapariyesana-sutta* of the *Majjhima-Nikāya* that he then thought to whom should he first teach his Doctrine. He thinks that Ārāḍa and Udraka, who had given him their instruction would, be worthy; a divinity informs him that Ārāḍa had died seven days before, and he likewise is apprised that Udraka had died the day before. He remembers that the five mendicants had waited on him during his austerities, so decides to teach them. With his divine eye he sees those five dwelling at Varanasi in the Deer Park. Leaving the area of the Bodhi Tree and proceeding along the main road, he was seen by Upaka, the Ājīvika, who impressed by the Buddha's bright appearance asked who was his teacher and what his doctrine. The Buddha's response in *gāthā*-type verses includes some important expressions: He has no teacher (Skt. *ācārya*). He is path-perfected (Skt. *arhat*) and incomparable teacher (*śāstṛ*) in the world. The Buddha said:[52]

> I alone am rightly enlightened; cooled (Skt. *śītibhūta*), Nirvāṇa-attained. To set in motion the Wheel of the Dharma I go to Kaśi City, beating the drum of the deathless (or, ambrosia) in a world that is blind.

Upaka responded with a touch of sarcasm: "You ought to be an eternal victor" ("*arahasi anantajino*" *ti*). Undaunted, the Buddha continued in the same vein:

> "They are indeed victors (*jina*) who, like me, have attained destruction of the fluxes. Vanquished by me are the evil natures. Therefore, Upaka, I am a victor."

Upaka's final remark is rendered by Thomas: "would that it might be so, friend";[53] and Upaka, shaking his head (in disbelief) went off on a by-path (implying a wrong path).

As the Buddha entered the Deer Park, the five mendicants saw him coming in the distance; and according to the much-repeated story, made an agreement between themselves not to get up to greet him, since he had given up his austerity in favour of what they took to be abundant food. But as he neared, something in his appearance—be it a kind of brightness—made them forget their agreement. They sprang up, one offering a seat, another offering water for the feet; and they addressed him '*ayuṣmat*' (venerable one). The Buddha told them, "Monks (as though become *bhikṣus* by being so-called), do not address a Tathāgata as '*ayuṣmat*'!"[54] As to this prohibition, it seems to imply that the term *ayuṣmat* is applicable only when a person still has not destroyed the fluxes.[55] The Buddha gave his first sermon, "Setting in Motion the Wheel of Dhamma" to these five, his original companions during the six years of austerity, called in Pāli—Kondañña, Vappa, Bhaddiya, Mahānāma, and Assaji. The first sermon set forth a Middle Path of eight members that avoids the extremes of sense indulgence and mortification of flesh. And he explained the four Noble Truths, of which the fourth is that Middle Path. Afterwards, since Kondañña first understood (*aññāta*), his name was lengthened to Aññāta-Kondañña.[56] He asked for ordination, and the Buddha gave this by its original form "come. monk (*ehi, bhikkhu*)".[57] Later, the Buddha gave at the Deer Park another sermon to this group, often called (in Skt.) the Pañcabhadravargīya (Fortunate Band of Five). It is famous for being the first statement of the 'non-self' (*anātman*) doctrine of Buddhism that has been so often discussed in later times. It is called the *Pañca-sutta* in *Saṃyutta-Nikāya*, iii, 66, and referred to as the *Anattalakkhaṇa-sutta* (Sermon on the characteristics of non-self), where each of the five personal aggregates (*skandha*) are declared to be non-self.

There follow some incidents where the Buddha resorted to magical tricks. In Pāli these are called *iddhi* (Skt. *ṛddhi*). The first recorded one is when the Buddha made a young man named Yasa invisible to his father who tried to follow him when he fled from home. Because Yasa according to the legend left home in circumstances curiously like those of Gautama—getting disgusted one night by seeing the palace attendants asleep in unseemly postures—it has been theorized that one of the two stories was modelled on the other.[58] Whatever be the case, when the friends of Yasa also entered the Order, the number of monks rose to sixty; and the mother and former wife of Yasa became the two first two female lay disciples.[59]

Another incident of magical powers takes place at Uruvelā, which was a location on the banks of the river where Gautama did his six-year asceticism. Here lived Uruvelā-Kassapa with five hundred disciples. Further down the river lived his brothers Nadī-Kassapa with three hundred and Gayā-Kassapa with two hundred disciples. The Buddha visited Uruvelā-Kassapa and stayed for the night at the dangerous place of the sacred fire inhabited by a fierce Nāga. Although this Nāga and another one both vomited fire and smoke, the Buddha overcame them by his magical powers. Kassapa then arranged for the Buddha to have daily food in a grove nearby, where he is said to have been visited by various gods. During that whole rainy season, the Buddha performed several thousand miracles, especially commanding fire, to split firewood for the sacrifice, heat their stoves, etc. Even so, Kassapa thought this great ascetic was not an arhat like himself. The Buddha decided to startle him by telling him what he was thinking and informing him it was not so that Kassapa was an arhat. Thereupon, Kassapa admitted defeat (presumably because the Buddha could not only read his mind, but was also able to determine his spiritual attainment as it was). Kassapa consulted with his pupils; they cut off their hair and threw it into the river along with their sacrificial utensils. Downstream this was noticed by his two brothers who came to inquire what had happened; and they too were ordained along with their pupils.[60] On the hill at Gayā, they all attained arhatship when the Buddha preached to them the Fire Sermon. This has the original title *Ādittapariyāya Sutta* or *Āditta Sutta.* It has the importance of being the third recorded sermon by the Buddha. It teaches that everything is on fire—the eye, perception based on the eye, the object forms, are all on fire; so also the other senses, the perceptions based on them, and their respective objects, are all on fire. On fire with lust, hatred, and delusion; on fire with birth, old age, and death; with grief, etc. Therefore, the Ariyan disciple is repelled by them; and becoming free of them, is liberated.

The next important conversion was the enrolling of Sāriputta and Moggallāna in the Buddhist Order, since they would become the two chief disciples of the Buddha. They had been fellow students of the same Vedic teacher; and upon 'graduation' from this kind of learning, became followers of an ascetic named Sañjaya at Rājagṛha numbered among his two hundred and fifty pupils. But they were as dissatisfied with Sañjaya's teaching as they had been with the Veda.[61] They made an agreement that the first of them to find a superior teacher would inform the other. Sāriputta encountered the elder Assaji, one of the 'Fortunate Band of Five'; who upon inquiry, gave this statement of the Buddha's doctrine:

> Whatever natures arise from a cause,
> their cause the Tathāgata has told,
> and also their cessation,
> Thus teaches the great ascetic
> (*mahāśramaṇa*).[62]

It was fitting that Sāriputta would contact the Dharma in this form and be won over; in later years he was especially interested in this side of Buddhism, and there are suggestions that he is responsible for the original exegesis later to be called the Abhidhamma (Skt. Abhidharma), stressing ontology. Moggallāna was more interested in supernormal powers (Skt. *abhijñā*). They quickly mastered the Buddha's Dharma, exciting some surprise when they were soon appointed chief disciples over the heads of even the 'Fortunate Band of Five'. According to the story, the Buddha pointed out that this was the fulfilment of a wish in former lives of these two to be chief disciples of a Buddha.[63] Centuries later, various leaders of the Buddhist church were converted brahmins, who had the advantage of the best literary education, so this pre-eminent role of the 'excellent pair' is a presage of the later situation.

The conversion of the Kassapa brothers heralds some political moves. In those days the seat of the Magadha Government was at Rājagṛha (Pāli, Rājagaha). When he came there with a host of followers including the Kassapas, King Bimbisāra invited the Buddha and donated to him and his Order the park near Rājagṛha called Veḷuvana (Bamboo Grove). During his stay here, Sāriputta and Moggallāna joined.[64]

The Buddha was invited to visit his father, Śuddhodana. The messenger was Kāludāyin (Udāyin the black), born the same day as the Buddha to a Śuddhodana courtier and a childhood playmate, who became a convert. When the Buddha arrived at Kapilavastu along with a large group of his Order (the Saṅgha), the Śākyas provided a residence in the Nigrodha park. As his kinsmen refrained from any reverence to the Buddha, he performed the 'miracle of the pairs', starting with rising in the air, flames issuing from the upper part of his body, streams of water from the lower part, with reversals and variations.[65] His father the King then bowed to him, which forced the other Śākyas to do likewise. At the close of the magic exhibition, the Buddha told the group of his immediately preceding life as the King Vessantara. As none of the Śākya chieftains invited him, the next day he and his monks went begging house to house. All the neighbors stared through their windows. The Buddha's wife informed the king, who hastened to the Buddha, reminding him, "Our lineage is the kṣatriya lineage of Mahāsammata, and not one kṣatriya has ever practised begging." "Yours is that royal lineage, O king; mine is the Buddha lineage of Dīpaṅkara, (down to) Kassapa, who gained their livelihood by begging." On the occasion of this visit, there were noteworthy conversions. Not only did his father the king become a follower, but also his aunt Mahāpajāpati (Skt. Mahāprajāpati) who had raised him. Along with his two chief disciples he visited his wife in her chamber; she came quickly and grasped his ankles in reverence. On the day prior to the consecration and marriage of Nanda, his half-brother and son of Mahāpajāpati, at the age of sixteen, he deserted his inheritance and joined the Order. Also his son Rāhula entered the Order. Then the king came to Buddha and requested that in the future the ordination be not conferred on a son without the permission of his mother and father. The Buddha agreed and made it a Vinaya rule. It was also on this occasion that the legend places the conversion of Ānanda who much later became the Buddha's personal attendant, and of Devadatta who later on tried to create a schism in the Order. Many of the Śākya families furnished one son to the Order; of these, worth mentioning is Anuruddha who gained the divine eye, which by seeing beings going to different destinies, is the prophetic eye.[66]

On returning to Rājagṛha, the Buddha stayed in the Sītavana, a nearby grove, where he was met by Sudatta, a wealthy householder of Sāvatthī (Skt. Śrāvastī), who is known in Buddhist stories as Anāthapiṇḍika or Anāthapiṇḍada (giver of alms to the unprotected). He had come to Rājagṛha on business and learned from his sister, the wife of the gildmaster of Rājagṛha about the Buddha. He was converted and invited the Buddha to spend a Retreat at Sāvatthī. The Buddha, in accepting pointed out that the Tathāgatas prefer solitary dwelling places. Anāthapiṇḍika looking for a suitable place in the vicinity of Sāvatthī, decided on the park of Prince Jeta (the Jetavana). Jeta said it was not for sale even for a covering with gold pieces, and rejected Anāthapiṇḍika's offer of just that. After an appeal, the ministers decided it was a bargain, and so it happened that way.[67] This park became a favorite residing place for the Buddha. Since he lived for forty-five years after the enlightenment, there were forty-five rainy seasons of which he is reported to have spent twenty-five in Sāvatthī, hence only twenty elsewhere. Rājagaha accounts for the second, third, fourth, seventeenth and twentieth. Hence numerous *suttas* were preached in Sāvatthī, a total of 871, with this distribution in the four Nikāyas (scriptural collections in Pāli): 6 in the *Dīgha*, 75 in the *Majjhima*, 736 in the *Saṃyutta*, and 54 in the *Aṅguttara*.[68] It appears that Anāthapiṇḍika had much contact with Sāriputta, because when the great patron became mortally ill, as recorded in the *Anāthapiṇḍikovāda-sutta* of the *Majjhima-Nikāya*, he sent a messenger to Sāriputta, asking that he, out of compassion, would come to his dwelling. Sāriputta came with Ānanda as his attendant and gave a sermon to Anāthapiṇḍika the day he died: it was about the constituents of man.

Another chief patron of the Buddha in Sāvatthī was the king Pasenadi (Skt. Prasenajit) of Kośala, which had that city as its capital. And there was the famous laywoman, Visākhā of Sāvatthī, who had the curious title 'Migāra's mother', although she was married to Puṇṇavaddhana, son of Migāra, a gildmaster of Sāvatthī. It happened that Migāra was a follower of the Nigaṇṭhas, opponents of the Buddhists. And since Visākhā had become a lay follower of the Buddha, Migāra wanted to oust her from his household. He submitted his grievances to a householder board, who judged her blameless. She threatened to return to her father, the fabulously rich Dhanañjaya, unless he invited the Buddha and his monks for a meal. He listened to the Buddha's sermon from behind a screen, and realized the error of his ways. He adopted Visākhā as his mother by sucking her breast, thus her name 'Migāra's mother'. Henceforth, they kept their house open for the Buddha and his monks.[69] Once she went to hear the Buddha preach, removing her resplendent head-dress on entering the monastery. It was forgotten when she left, and Ānanda put it aside. She then asked that it be sold for the benefit of the monks, but proved too expensive for purchase, so she applied its assessed amount to building a monastery at Sāvatthī in the Pubbārāma, 'the Eastern Park'.[70] Here the Buddha delivered two scriptures of high importance: the *Aggañña Suttanta* (a book of Genesis) in the *Dīgha-Nikāya*; and the *Cūḷasuññata-sutta* of the *Majjhima-Nikāya*, on 'voidness' (Skt. *śūnyatā*). Horner begins her translation of the later *sutta*:[71]

> Thus have I heard: At one time the Lord was staying near Sāvatthī in the Eastern monastery in the palace of Migāra's mother. Then the venerable Ānanda, emerging from solitary meditation towards evening, approached the Lord; having approached and greeted the Lord, he sat down at a respectful distance.

The fifth year of preaching has some events of great importance, viz., death of Śuddhodana, and establishment of the nun order. In this fifth year, the Buddha was dwelling at Vesālī (Skt. Vaiśālī) in the Hall of the Eaved Palace (Kūṭāgāraśālā). His father Śuddhodana was on his death bed; the Buddha "flew through the air" and preached to his father in Kapilavastu. One account has it that the Buddha persuaded the Śākyas to make peace with their neighbors—the Koliyas—about the irrigation rights of the Rohiṇī river, their mutual boundary. The story that Mahāpajāpati, now widowed, on this occasion asked the Buddha to allow women to leave the world and become nuns in his Order; that the Buddha thrice refused, and returned to Vesālī, followed by Mahāpajāpati who had cut off her hair along with many other Śākya women, their feet swollen; that the Buddha still refused, and only accepted after Ānanda interceded with the imposition of the 'Eight Guru-Dharmas' on them as nuns—this story, which is the official one, has been doubted by some modern scholars.[72] It was pointed out that the story includes Ānanda as the Buddha's attendant, while this appointment was not made until twenty years after the enlightenment.[73] However, there is much in favor of the story as is: (1) the vexation anticipated by the Buddha on account of a nun Order was a genuine concern and prophetic,[74] and recall the vexation he anticipated for teaching the profound Dharma upon the enlightenment; (2) this time Ānanda interceded, not in the role of the Buddha's attendant, but as his Śākya relative and a 'go-between' with other Śākyas, recalling for us the intercession of Brahmā Sahampati on that other occasion; (3) it is reasonable that Mahāpajāpati should be the first nun, and this is only possible when she was widowed.

There have been attempts to pinpoint events for each year of what are called the Buddha's twenty years of wandering.[75] What appears certain is that within a few years after the Buddha began his teaching he had gained a monastery near Rājagṛha, the one called 'Bamboo Grove'; another in Śrāvastī, the one called Jeta's park; and one in Kapilavastu; he had gained the disciples of whom the most legends are told; and had delivered his most characteristic sermons, even though the one on 'voidness' may belong to a later period. After his period of wandering, the Buddha settled at Sāvatthī (Śrāvastī) for his last twenty-five years and alternated his retreats at the Jetavana and the Pubbārāma. From this time on, he had

Ānanda as his attendant. This disciple must have had an extraordinary memory, for at the First Council, held a year after the passing of the Buddha, Ānanda recited all the *suttas*.

The Rival Teachers

Buddhist sources speak of six heretical teachers who were contemporaries of the Buddha. The Pāli source is the *Sāmañña-phala-sutta* in the *Dīgha-Nikāya*, where Ajātasattu, the king of Magadha, tells what he found by visiting the six to be their characteristic doctrines. Basham discusses at length these doctrines and the historical circumstances.[76] Vogel has studied the versions of the *Mūlasarvāstivāda Vinaya*, showing that in the *Mūlasarvāstivāda Vinayavastu*, besides a version with the king (Skt.) Ajātaśatru as informer, Upatiṣya (Sāriputta) and Kolita (Moggallāna) find out the doctrines of these six heretical teachers, prior to becoming followers of the Buddha; while in the *Mūlasarvāstivāda Vinayavibhaṅga*, some one called Dravya Mallaputra goes to where the six teachers are and learns their respective doctrines.[77] There is an air of artificiality in the attributed doctrines. Here, I shall present merely what seems to be main point for each of the 'heretical teachers':[78]

(1) Pūraṇa Kassapa. This 'teacher' apparently does not want any disciples, because he says there is neither good nor bad conduct; neither father nor mother; neither higher nor lower world; the fool and the sage perish alike.

(2) Makkhali Gosāla. Beings do becomes soiled and do become pure, but there is cause for either condition. Hence, there is no human action or human prowess that can affect destiny. He could be a 'teacher' for the world as it is, but can give no counsel for a course of action.

(3) Saṃjayin Vairaṭīputra, as interviewed by Upatiṣya and Kolita, seems so bent on mass murder as to scare away all potential disciples.

(4) Ajita Keśakambalin, as interviewed by Upatiṣya and Kolita, seems to have the doctrine of Pakudha Kaccāyana, as interviewed by king Ajātasattu, namely, there are seven elementary bodies, which are not damaged by a sharp weapon, namely, earth body, water body, fire body, wind body, pleasure, misery, and life itself.

(5) Pakudha Kaccāyana informed Upatiṣya and Kolita that whatever is asked of him whether it be the case, he responds that it is the case.

(6) Nirgrantha Jñātiputra was found by Upatiṣya and Kolita to admit no possibility of 'new' *karma*, because he claimed that whatever is experienced by a man, all of it results from previous deeds as cause; so by using up misery, there is no more misery.

In whatever manner these doctrines are stated in variant form in the other versions, they fail to exhibit the attractiveness necessary for gaining intelligent followers. Presumably, these doctrines are not precisely what those teachers taught, whether individually or in a group. After each interview, Upatiṣya and Kolita are held to have judged the 'teacher' as unworthy to be followed; and in each case they spoke a *gāthā* which I translate from the Tibetan as follows:[79]

> Of evil mind, he teaches waywardly,
> known to be an inferior teacher;
> when his doctrine is like this,
> of what sort would be a bad doctrine for him!

The Buddha's brother-in-law and cousin called Devadatta created the one notable schism in the Buddha's Order during his lifetime. Because of this role, which in Buddhist chronicles is understandably regarded as nefarious, Devadatta is credited with all sorts of mischief directed first at the youthful Bodhisattva, and later on against the Buddha in his old age. The Pāli chronicles especially carry these stories. According to information that Devadatta's father Suppabuddha, fathering as well the Bodhisattva's wife (mother of Rāhula) was also hostile to the Buddha in later years,[80] there is a suggestion that the Bodhisattva's immediate family held a grudge for his abandonment of wife and child, which did not lessen when Rāhula joined the Order. The main antagonistic activities of Devadatta appear to start about ten years before the Buddha's death when Bimbisāra resigned his kingdom to his son Ajātasuttu. About that time Devadatta suggested to the Buddha that he, being old (about 70 years of age), should retire from the Order and allow Devadatta to lead it.[81] In this connection, it should be observed that the Buddha had shown considerable willingness to delegate responsibility—he had long before turned over the ordination process to the senior monks, and had put new trainees in the care of the advanced disciples, such as Sāriputta, Moggallāna, and others in the various centers of Buddhist activities. On this occasion, however, he curtly rejected Devadatta's suggestion.

When the Buddha was aged 72, King Ajātaśatru (his name understood to mean 'an enemy before his birth') murdered his father Bimbisāra. Bimbisāra's wife died of grief; and as she was a sister of Prasenajit, king of the Kośalas, the parricide precipitated a conflict between Prasenajit and his nephew. There was a series of battles, which at first went badly for Prasenajit, but in a later engagement, Ajātaśatru was captured alive and peace terms imposed upon him.

King Ajātaśatru admired Devadatta, and the pair plotted against the Buddha's life. The king sent archers to take posts along the paths which the Buddha walked. The first one to encounter the Buddha became stiff with fear. The Buddha calmed him; he threw down his weapon and confessed the intended crime. The Buddha preached to him, converted him, and sent him off by a different path, by which he returned to Devadatta to report his failure. The other archers fared no better in their mission, and all were converted.[82]

Devadatta then tried rolling a boulder down the 'Vulture's Peak' Hill when the Buddha was walking in its shade, only with the result that splinters of the rock struck his foot and caused it to bleed. The Buddha looked up and proclaimed that there was great demerit in causing a Tathāgata's body to bleed. Next, Devadatta instigated the charge of an enraged elephant along the path by which he was coming; but the Buddha effectively subdued the elephant.[83]

Then Devadatta with three others decided to create a schism in the Order. He announced a set of five ascetic practices; charged that the Buddha was living in luxury, and persuaded five hundred recently-ordained monks from Vesālī to join him in a Posatha meeting. The Buddha sent Sāriputta and Moggallāna to rescue them. Devadatta mistakenly thought the pair was coming to join up with him. They listened quietly while Devadatta lectured far into the night until, tired, he asked Sāriputta to speak. He dozed off, whereupon Sāriputta and Moggallāna convinced the five hundred to return. The Buddha received the five hundred, and required only of them to confess their offence. According to the legend, Devadatta after his defeat was sick for nine months; then sent a message that he wanted to see the Buddha. The Buddha declared that impossible; and although Devadatta was being brought on a litter he died as he approached the Jetavana.[84]

King Ajātaśatru on his part came to the Buddha, with repentance for his folly in killing his pious father.

It is related that two years before the passing of the Buddha, a great disaster befell the Śākya clan. The setting for this was laid years before when King Prasenajit cemented a marriage alliance with the Śākyas, but was tricked in getting a low-caste woman, with whom he had a son Viḍūḍabha. Once on a trip to Kapilavastu to visit with his relatives Viḍūḍabha was insulted for his low birth, and vowed revenge. The old king Prasenajit was deserted by his general, who put Viḍūḍabha on the throne. Prasenajit hurried towards Rājagṛha to get help from his nephew, but died of exposure and was buried by Ajātaśatru. Viḍūḍabha, remembering the insult, organized a massacre of the Śākyas.[85] This, however, did not finish off the Śākyas according to the description that after the death of the Buddha they came for a share of the relics, over which they built a *stūpa*.

The Parinirvāṇa of the Buddha

The final year of Śākyamuni is the topic of the *Mahā-Parinibbāna-Suttanta* of the *Dīgha-Nikāya*; and there are versions in all the languages of Buddhism. There has also been much scholarly work dealing with this period (not to speak of other parts of the Buddha's life).[86] Here there is space to present only a few of the important details.[87]

The Buddha decided to spend the rainy season in Beluva, near Vesālī. And now he had a dire sickness which he held down by force of will until it abated, because he needed time to address the disciples and take leave of the Order. He said to Ānanda:

> What then, Ānanda, does the Order of monks expect of me? I have pronounced the Dhamma in the non-inner, non-outer manner. In respect to doctrines (Skt. *dharma*) the Tathāgata does not have the closed fist of a [Vedic] preceptor (Skt. *ācārya*).

The meaning seems to be that the Buddha preached his Dharma without regard to privilege of caste, thus without inclusion or exclusion of the audience. It has been held by translators from Pāli, that the terms 'inner' and 'outer' meant 'esoteric' and 'exoteric' as kinds of Dharma; however, this is not possible grammatically, because the terms rendered "in the non-inner, non-outer manner" qualify the verb, not the term *dhamma*. Of course, the Buddha regarded his Dharma as profound and said so on various occasions; hence, it could be understood fully, partially, or not at all. But having decided to teach it, he did not separate the disciples into those who were entitled to hear it and those not:

> Therefore, Ānanda, in this world remain lamps of yourselves, refuges of yourselves, not refuges of others; lamps of Dharma, refuges of Dharma, not refuges of others!

And how so remain?

> Ānanda, a monk remains in regard to body, observant of body, strenuous, aware, and mindful; . . .; in regard to feelings, (likewise); . . .; in regard to thought, (likewise); . . . ; in regard to natures, (likewise); . . .

The Buddha here refers to what are called the four 'stations of mindfulness' (Skt. *smṛtyupasthāna*), on bodies (*kāya*), feelings (*vedanā*), thoughts (*citta*), and natures (*dharma*).

The Bhagavat rose early and went into Vesālī for alms. Afterwards he told Ānanda he would spend the day at the Chāpāla Shrine. There he mentioned to Ānanda that the one who has fully mastered the four 'feet of magical power' (Skt. *ṛddhipāda*) could in the same life stay for the rest of the eon; and that the Tathāgata had so mastered it. He said it a second and a third time, but Ānanda did not take the hint to ask the Bhagavat to stay for the good of gods and men.

The Bhagavat announced that in three months hence he would pass away. There was an earthquake; and then this verse of exultation:[88]

> The same and the different arise together;
> and the Muni, having equipoised himself
> with inward ecstasy, abandoned the
> life motivation (Skt. *bhavasaṃskāra* = *ayuḥsaṃskāra*),
> like one born in an egg breaks the eggshell.

According to the teacher Asaṅga, 'the same' is the *rūpakāya* (form body) of the Tathāgata (one come the same way); 'the different' is the *nāmakāya* (name body), because without flux (*anāsrava*). When he enters Parinirvāṇa, he breaks the *rūpakāya* and the *nāmakāya* in the manner of an eggshell.[89]

The Buddha picked Kuśinagara, a rather small town, as the place for his Parinirvāṇa. It would happen in the last watch of the night. The last words spoken by the Tathāgata were:

> Constructed things have a transitory nature.
> Accomplish your aim with heedfulness!

Then the Buddha entered the first Dhyāna, the second, third, and fourth; then passed through the formless realms into the state with cessation of ideas and feelings. Ānanda declared to Anuruddha that the Bhagavat had entered Parinirvāṇa. But Anuruddha who, by previous information had gained the divine eye, denied this, identifying the state as the cessation of ideas and feelings. Then the Bhagavat emerged successively from those states, down to the First Dhyāna, then upward to the Fourth Dhyāna; and at its upper limit he entered Parinirvāṇa.

> The ordinary word for 'died' was not employed; and Ānanda:
> "Then was the awe-inspiring!
> Then was the hair-standing! When he, endowed with every best feature,
> The Complete Buddha, entered Parinirvāṇa!"

Conclusion

The foregoing curtailed treatment of Śākyamuni's life enables me to draw some conclusions. He had deep sympathy with the suffering of mankind, even though much of it—old age, sickness, and death—is the ordinary course of nature; and so revealed a path to surmount it. What did disturb him keenly as a young man was the harm inflicted by men on the animal creatures as well as on other human beings. This attitude was exhibited primarily by his kinship with creatures of the soil, predominately snakes. This friendliness was extended to all creatures. To discount as just mythology the various stories involving snakes and 'king of serpents', effectively spoils an understanding of his life. This is because when we accept this strange kind of kinship, it becomes credible that Gautama would desert his wife and newly-born son—haunted by a sense of lacking the kind of kinship that the Śākya clan deemed he should have. There are indications that Gautama's strange kinship with soil and creatures of the soil, is involved with his meditative success, striking powers, and a charmed life. It agrees with the stress on the feet, such as at birth taking seven steps, having six of the 32 characteristics concerned with feet, having epithets 'best of two-footed ones', 'perfected in clear vision and walking' (*vidyā-caraṇa-sampanna*); and agrees with the Buddhist viewpoint that Devadatta's fate was sealed when he drew blood from the Tathāgata's foot.

In the legend, the steps of feet are goal-oriented ('facing North'), so this 'walking' generates the Buddhist path. Given the path, there follows the fork in the road (double or triple), the right and wrong way to go, thus the Middle Path avoiding the 'extremes' (two wrong ways). The right path is fruitful, with the instrumentality of food in moderation. This food is either begged or through invitation. The food by invitation vivifies the Sūtra (the scripture), so we find that when the Buddha and his monks were invited to a meal, he would follow this with his expression of the Dharma.

REFERENCES

1. Among the many works, there are Anil De Silva-Vigier, *The Life of the Buddha Retold from Ancient Sources* (The Phaidon Press, London, 1955); *The Way of the Buddha* (Publications Division, Govt. of India, on the 2500th anniversary of the Mahāparinirvāṇa [Ceylonese dating); C. Sivaramamurti, "Buddha as a Mahapurusha" (Sir Tashi Namgyal Memorial Lectures), *Bulletin of Tibetology*, IX: 3, 1972, Gangtok, Sikkim.
2. Bhikkhu Ñāṇamoli, *The Life of the Buddha according to the Pāli Canon* (Buddhist Publication Society, Kandy, Ceylon, 1972).
3. Cf. Jikido Takasaki, *A Study of the Ratnagotravibhāga* (Istituto Italiano per il Medio ed Estremo Oriente, Roma 1966), pp. 368-9.
4. Cf. Wilhelm Geiger, *The Mahāvaṃsa* (The Ceylon Government, Colombo, 1950), pp. xxii, ff.
5. Cf. André Bareau, "La date du Nirvāṇa," *Journal Asiatique*, 1953, pp. 27-62. The 2500th Anniversary was celebrated in the years 1956 or 1957 in South Asian countries according to the Ceylonese chronicles which put the Buddha's birth and death each 60 years earlier than the modern dating.
6. Ernst Waldschmidt, *Die Überlieferung vom Lebensende des Buddha*, 1944-48 (Abhandlungen der Akademie der Wissenschaften in Göttingen. Phil.-hist. Kl.. 3. Folge, Nr 29, 30).
7. A. Foucher, *The Beginnings of Buddhist Art* (Paul Geuthner, Paris, 1917), pp. 10-1, theorized that pilgrims to those places would bring back a "small material souvenir"—an impetus to Buddhist art based on this veneration.
8. Cfr. Edward J. Thomas, *The Life of Buddha as Legend and History* (Barnes & Noble, New York, 1952), pp. 28-9.
9. I employ the edition of the Nālandā-Devanāgarī-Pāli-Series: *The Majjhima Nikāya*, Vol. 3.

10. Tibetan Kanjur, Japanese photo ed. (PTT), Vol. 5, p. 256-4-5 ,6:/ṅa ni' jig rten daṅ po yin/'jig rten mgon źes bsgrags pa yin / zla med gzod nas źi ba ni/ mñam pa med pa'i chos bśad do/.
11. Who is called Mahāsammata ('the great assent'); but the Buddha denies this lineage on the occasion of his first return, after the enlightenment, to his birthplace, Kapilavastu (*infra*).
12. Cf. J.W. de Jong, "L'Episode d'Asita dans le Lalitavistara," in *Asiatica; Festschrift Friedrich Weller* (Otto Harrassowitz, Leipzig, 1954), pp. 312-25.
13. Cf. Alex Wayman, "Contributions regarding the Thirty-Two Characteristics of the Great Person," in *Sino-Indian Studies; Liebenthal Festschrift* (Visvabharati, Santiniketan, 1957), pp. 249-55.
14. Thomas, *The Life of Buddha*, p. 58.
15. *Mahāvastu Avadāna*, ed. by Radhagovinda Basak (Sanskrit College, Calcutta, 1964), Vol. II, p. 64.
   I am indebted to the Ph. D. dissertation (Institute of Fine Arts, New York University) of Elizabeth Stone, entitled *The Buddhist Art of Nāgārjunakoṇḍa*, where her figure 273 represents the rare depiction of the Miracle below the Jambu Tree, and significantly shows above it "the great departure", agreeing with our conclusion that Gautama decided upon his departure from homelife on this occasion. The figure was published by Pratapaditya Pal, "South Indian Sculptures in the Museum," *Bulletin of the Los Angeles County Museum of Art*, XXII, 1976, p. 30 f., where Dr. Pal correctly identified the scene but thought the provenance was around the Goli village with Amaravati style. Dr. Stone concludes rather that it belongs to the Nāgārjunakoṇḍa school, which is specifically Gummididurru. C. Sivaramamurti, *Amaravati Sculptures in the Madras Government Museum* (Madras, 1956), pp. 249-50, confirms my interpretation about the Miracle under the Jambu tree, and cites two texts (*Nidānakathā* and *Avadānakalpalatā*), neither of which mention the Bodhisattva's strange feelings about the snakes. The non-moving shade of the Jambu tree is probably equivalent to the symbolism of shade afforded by the serpent hoods (episode of Mucalinda).
16. For the explanation of this dhyāna in Asaṅga's school, cf. Alex Wayman, "Meditation in Theravāda and Mahīśāsaka," *Studia Missionalia*, Vol. 25, 1976, p. 14.
17. For the location of these teachers, see Yogendra Mishra, *An Early History of Vaiśālī* (Motilal Banarsidass, Delhi, 1962), pp. 151-2.
18. viditaṃ me yathā saumya niṣkranto bhavanād asi/
   chittvā snehamayaṃ pāśaṃ pāśaṃ dṛpta iva dvipaḥ//
   This and subsequent citations from the *Buddhacarita* are from the edition of E.H. Johnston, *The Buddhacarita*, Sanskrit text (Baptist Mission Press, Calcutta, 1935).
19. śiṣye yady api vijñāte śāstraṃ kalena varṇyate/
   gambhīryād vyavasāyāc ca na parīkṣyo bhavān mama//
20. didṛksur iva hi jyotir yiyāsur iva daiśikam/
   tvaddarśanam ahaṃ manye titīrṣur iva ca plavam//
   tasmād arhasi tad vaktuṃ vaktavyaṃ yadi manyase/
   jarāmaraṇarogebhyo yathāyaṃ parimucyate//
21. śrūyatām ayam asmākaṃ siddhāntaḥ śṛṇvatāṃ vara/
   yathā bhavati saṃsāro yathā caiva nivartate//
22. yathāvad etad vijñāya ksetrajño hi catuṣṭayam/
   ājavaṃjavatāṃ hitvā prāpnoti padam aksaram//
23. adhyātmakuśalas tv anyo nivartyātmānam ātmanā/
   kiṃcin nāstīti sampaśyan nākiṃcanya iti samṛtaḥ/

tato muñjād iṣīkeva śakuniḥ pañjarād iva/
kṣetrajño niḥsṛto dehān mukta ity abhidhīyate//

24. That is to say, in verses 61, 62, and 63, he serially alludes to what in Buddhism are the first three states of the 'formless realm', for which one may find Asaṅga's position in Wayman, "Meditation . . . " (n. 16, above), pp. 17-8.
25. śrutaṃ jñānam idaṃ sūkṣmaṃ parataḥ parataḥ śivam/
kṣetrajñāsyāparityāgād avaimy etad anaiṣṭhikam//
26. It is called the *naivasaṃjñā-nāsaṃjñāyatana*; cf. Wayman (n. 16, above), p. 19.
27. upavāsavidhīn naikān kurvan naradurācarān/
varṣāni ṣaṭ śamaprepsur akarot kārśyam ātmanaḥ//
28. nāyaṃ dharmo virāgāya na bodhāya na muktaye/
jambumūle mayā prāpto yas tadā sa vidhir dhruvaḥ//
29. tasmād āhāramūlo 'yam upāya iti niścayaḥ/
āhārakaraṇe dhīraḥ kṛtvāmitamatir matim//
30. sitaśaṅkhojjvalabhujā nīlakambalavāsinī/
saphenamālānīlāmbur yamuneva saridvarā//
31. vyavasāyadvitīyo 'tha śādvalāstīrṇabhūtalam/
so 'śvatthamūlaṃ prayayau bodhāya kṛtaniścayaḥ//
tatas tadānīṃ gajarājavikramaḥ padasvarenānupamena bodhitaḥ/
mahāmuner āgatabodhiniścayo jagād kālo bhujagottamaḥ stutim//
yathā mune tvaccaraṇāvapīḍitā muhur muhur niṣṭanatīva medinī/
yathā ca te rājati sūryavat prabhā dhruvaṃ tvam iṣṭaṃ phalam adya bhokṣyase//
yathā bhramantyo divi cāṣapanktayaḥ pradakṣiṇaṃ tvāṃ kamalākṣa kurvate/
yathā ca saumyā divi vānti vāyavas tvam adya buddho niyataṃ bhaviṣyasi//
tato bhujaṅgapravareṇa saṃstutas tṛṇāny upādāya śucīni lāvakāt//
kṛtapratijño niṣasāda bodhaye mahātaror mūlam upāśritaḥ śuceḥ//
tataḥ sa paryaṅkam akampyam uttamaṃ babandha suptoragabhogapiṇḍitam/
bhinadmi tāvad bhuvi naitad āsanaṃ na yāmi yāvat kṛtakṛtyatām iti//
32. Cf. H. Smidt, *Eine populäre Darstellung der Shingon-lehre* (Oesterheld & Co., Berlin, 1918) (Sonderabdruck, *Ostasiatische Zeitschrift*, VII, 1/2), pp. 202-3, where the yellow square stands for earth, as the base of the *stūpa* form of the body, called the *samaya*—form of the lord Vairocana, who is seated in the enlightenment posture of *paryaṅka*. See also J. Ph. Vogel *Indian Serpent-Lore* (reprint of Indological Book House, Delhi, 1972), Plate X, a Stūpa worshipped by Nāgas (Amaravati), reminding us of the veneration shown by the Kāla, best of serpents, in the above verses 116-8 of *Buddhacarita* , Canto XII.
33. Thomas, *The Life of Buddha*, pp. 71, ff.
34. Three of these 'fluxes' (*āsrava*) are mentioned in the Pāli *Mahāparinibbāna-sutta* in *Dīgha-Nikāya* II, when the Buddha addressed the monks at Koṭigāma. They are the first three of those in Vilāsavajra's passage; and these three are mentioned in our next section 'The Night of Enlightenment' under the 'third watch'. The fourth one, the flux of wrong views (*dṛṣṭi*), probably means the 'reifying view' (*satkāyadṛṣṭi*) usually explained in terms of the personal aggregates (*skandha*); so, as here, by erasing it, one defeats the personal-aggregate Māra. This fourth one was added in the Abhidharma treatises. Vilāsavajra's passage is in his commentary, the *Nāmamantrārthāvalokinī*, on the Buddhist tantra, *Ārya-Mañjuśrī-nāmasaṃgīti*, in Tibetan Tanjur, PIT, Vol. 74, p. 199-2-7, 8.

35 tasmin vimokśāya kṛtapratijñe rājarṣivaṃśaprabhave maharṣau/
tatropaviṣṭe prajaharṣa lokas tatrāsa saddharmaripus tu māraḥ//
yaṃ kāmadevaṃ pravadanti loke citrāyudhaṃ puṣpaśaraṃ tathaiva/

kāmapracārādhipatiṃ tam eva mokṣadviṣaṃ māram udāharanti//
tasyātmajā vibhramaharṣadarphās tisro 'ratiprītitṛṣaś ca kanyāḥ/
papracchur enaṃ manaso vikāraṃ sa tāṃś ca tāś caiva vaco 'bhuvāca//
asau munir niścayavarma bibhrat sattvāyudhaṃ buddhiśaraṃ vikṛṣya/
jigīṣur āste viṣayān madīyān tasmād ayaṃ me manaso viṣādaḥ//
yadi hy asau mām abhibhūya yāti lokāya cākhyāty apavargamārgam//
śūnyas tato 'yam viṣayo mamādya vṛttāc cyutasveya videhabharṭuh//
tad yāvad evaiṣa na labdhacakṣur madgocare tiṣṭati yāvad eva/
yāsyāmi tāvad vratam asya bhettuṃ setuṃ nadīvega ivātivṛddhaḥ//
tato dhanuḥ puṣpamayaṃ gṛhītvā śarān jaganmohakarāṃś ca pañca/
so 'śvatthamūlaṃ sasuto 'bhyagacchad asvāsthyakārī manasaḥ prajānām//

36. mahībhṛto dharmaparāś ca nāgā mahāmuner vighnam amṛṣyamāṇāḥ/
māraṃ prati krodhavivṛttanetrā niḥśaśvasuś caiva jajṛmbhire ca//
The nāgas said here to support the earth are presumably the ones called Anavatapta, Muchilinda, and Elapāttra, who came for a share of the relics after the Buddha's Parinirvāṇa, as mentioned by Vogel, *Indian Serpent-Lore,* p. 126. Besides, there is the *Ahirāja-sutta* in the *Aṅguttara-Nikāya* (Book of Fours). Monks came to the Buddha and reported, here in Sāvatthī a monk was bitten by a snake and died. The Buddha explained that it happened because the man was not friendly with the snakes of four royal families, which are called Virūpakkha, Erāpatha, Chabyāputta and Kanhā-gotamaka. So he told the monks to suffuse these snakes with their friendship (or, love) (*metta*; Skt. *maitrī*).

37. śuddhādhivāsā vibudharṣayas tu saddharmasiddhyartham abhipravṛttāḥ/
māre 'nukampaṃ manasā pracakrur virāgabhāvāt tu na roṣam īyuḥ//
By 'Pure Abodes' is meant the five dwellings said in Buddhist Abhidharma to be at the top of the fourth dhyāna the 'realm of form' (*rūpadhātu*); cf. Louis de La Vallee Poussin, *L' Abhidharmakośa de Vasubandhu,* Troisiéme Čhapitre (Paul Geuthner, Paris, 1926), p. 2, the Avṛhas, etc.

38. bhūtam tataḥ kiṃcid adṛśyarūpaṃ viśiṣṭabhūtaṃ gaganastham eva/
dṛṣṭvarṣaye drugdham avairaruṣṭam māraṃ babhaṣe mahatā svareṇa//
moghaṃ śramaṃ nārhasi māra kartuṃ hiṃsrātmatām utsṛja gaccha śarma/
naiṣa tvayā kampayituṃ hi śakyo mahāgirir merur ivānilena//

39. bodhāya karmāṇi hi yāny anena kṛtāni teṣāṃ niyato 'dya kālaḥ/
sthāne tathāsminn upaviṣṭa eṣa yathaiva pūrve munayas tathaiva//
eṣa hi nābhir vasudhātalasya kṛtsnena yuktā parameṇa dhāmnā/
bhūmer ato 'nyo 'sti hi na pradeśo vegaṃ samādher viṣaheta yo 'sya//

40. I employ the edition of the Nālandā-Devanāgarī-Pāli-Series: *The Aṅguttara Nikāya,* Vol. 3.

41. Tibetan Kanjur, PTT, Vol. 5, p.246-3-4: / rig sṅags mdzod spu źes grags pa / (called 'Vidyā-ūrṇā').

42. Cf. J.J. Jones, tr. *The Mahāvastu,* Vol. I, 'enlightenment of Dīpaṃkara', pp. 183-5. My article, "Climactic Times in Indian Mythology and Religion," *History of Religions,* 4:2, Winter 1965, pp. 298-9, used the *Mahāvastu* order (1. divine eye, 2. past lives, 3. flash of insight) to correlate with the three forms of Uṣas, feet of Vāk in the cave, three upper states of Ātman, of the Brahmanical literature. Now I believe that the order given above from the 'Book of Eights' may correlate better. That is to say, for the first, level, that of 'dream' (*svapna*), it would be better to put the seeing of previous lives; and for the second level, that of 'deep sleep' (*suṣupti*), the divine eye seeing the beings passing away to destinies (i.e. prophetic); because in the *Māṇḍūkya Upaniṣad,* this *suṣupti* is a mass of fore-knowledge (*prajñāna*).

43. *Mahāvastu Avadāna,* Ed: R. Basak, Vol. I, p. 282-3; *rātrīye paścime yāme nandīmukhāyāṃ rajanyām aruṇopaghāṭakālasamaye*; and he is awakened to the complete enlightenment by insight conjoined with a single moment of thought (*ekacittakṣaṇasamāyuktayā prajñayā*).
44. Cf. A Wayman, "Notes on the Sanskrit term *Jñāna,*" *Journal of the American Oriental Society,* 75:4, Oct.-Dec. 1955, p. 257.
45. In the *Udānavarga,* ed. by Franz Bernhard (Göttingen, 1968), these are in the chapter on the 'mind', XXXI, 6-7; in the *Dhammapada*—tr. by S. Radhakrishnan(London, 1950), p. 110—in the chapter on 'old age', nos. 153-4.
46. W. Woodville Rockhill, *Udānavarga,* tr. from the Tibetan of the Bkaḥ-ḥgyur (Kegan Paul, London, 1892), p. 164.
47. Cf. André Bareau *Recherches sur la biographie du Buddha dans les Sūtrapiṭaka et les Vinayapiṭaka anciens* (École Française d'Extrême-Orient, Paris, 1963), pp. 93-7.
48. Cf. Bareau, *Recherches,* pp. 101-5, for the Mucalinda episode.
49. I employ the edition of the Nālandā-Devanāgarī-Pāli-Series: *The Saṃyutta Nikāya,* Vol. 1.
50. So Vilāsavajra (n. 34, above), commenting on *Mañjuśrī-nāma-saṃgīti,* VI, 1, the expression *mahāmaunī mahāmuniḥ* ('possessed of great silence, the Mahāmuni'), says PTT, Vol. 74, 195-3-4, "has muted Body, Speech, and Mind; and 'Mahāmuni', because always in equipoise (*samāpatti*)."
51. Étienne Lamotte, *Le Traité de la Grande Vertu de Sagesse,* Tome I (Bureaux du *Muséon,* Louvain, 1944), pp.135-7.
52. I employ the edition of the Nālandā-Devanāgarī-Pāli-series: *The Mijjhima Nikāya,* Vol. 1.
53. Thomas, *The Life of Buddha,* p. 82.
54. Cf. Bareau, *Recherches,* pp. 161-4, where we find the Buddha in the Theravāda account also prohibits the calling him by his clan name; so also in the Sarvāstivādin and Dharmaguptaka sectarian versions. As we shall notice later in this paper, when the Buddha first returned to his birthplace, he denied that he was of Śuddhodana's kṣatriya lineage.
55. According to our previous information that the Buddha, by having 'destroyed birth' also defeated the 'death Māra', this seems behind his repudiation of the title '*ayuṣmat*', which means literally, 'possessed of life, i.e., long life'.
56. The Buddha's first sermon, called the *Dhamma-cakka-pavattana-sutta,* is found in the *Saṃyutta-Nikāya,* v, 240, except for the name.
57. This detail plus the name of the *sutta* is found in the Vinaya. For this ordination legend, cf. Bareau, *Recherches,* pp. 183-9.
58. Thomas, *The Life of Buddha,* p. 90, and n. 1.
59. Cf. Bareau, *Recherches,* pp. 199-207 and following to p. 228 for the legend of Yasa (Pāli) or Yaśas (Skt.).
60. The elaborate account about the Kassapa brothers is fully treated in Bareau, *Recherches,* pp. 257-316.
61. The version of the *Mahāvastu Avadāna,* ed. by R. Basak, Vol. III (1968), pp. 74, ff. includes the phase when they were fellow students of the Veda. The account in Bareau, *Recherches,* pp. 343, ff. begins with their study under Sañjaya.
62. This is perhaps the most repeated verse of Buddhism available in original Sanskrit Pāli and Asian renditions; the Sanskrit form is on slips of paper that were inserted in Tibetan prayer wheels, spun innumerable times.
63. Cf. Thomas, *The Life of Buddha,* p. 95.

64. Cf. Bareau, *Recherches*, pp. 321, ff. for the Buddha's stay at Rājagṛha.
65. Years later, after a monastery was established at Sāvatthī, the Buddha performed this 'miracle of the pairs' again at that city, which has a well-known art depiction.
66. For the above portrayal of the Buddha's visit to Kapilavastu, I mainly follow Thomas, *The Life of Buddha*, pp. 97, ff.
67. Cf. Thomas, *The Life of Buddha*, pp. 104-205.
68. G.P. Malalasekera, *Dictionary of Pāli Proper Names* (Luzac & Co., London, 1960), Vol. II, N-H, p. 1127.
69. Malalasekera, *Dictionary*, Vol. II, pp. 626-7.
70. Thomas, *The Life of Buddha*, p. 106.
71. I.B. Horner, tr., *The Collection of The Middle Length Sayings*, Vol. III (Luzac & Co. London, 1959), p. 147.
72. Thomas, *The Life of Buddha*, pp. 107-8.
73. Thomas, *The Life of Buddha*, p. 110.
74. That is to say, prophetic of the vexations caused by the nun Order, which can easily be seen now by a work, Akira Hirakawa, *Monastic Disciple for the Buddhist Nuns*, an English translation of the Chinese text of the Mahāsāṃghika-Bhikṣuṇi-Vinaya (Kashi Prasad Jayaswal Research Institute, Patna, 1982).
75. See Thomas, *The Life of Buddha*, chap. IX "Legends of the Twenty Years' Wandering", pp. 113-23.
76. A.L. Basham, *History and Doctrines of the Ājīvikas* (Luzac & Co., London, 1951), p. 13, and following.
77. Claus Vogel, *The Teachings of the Six Heretics* (Abhandlugen für die Kunde des Morgenlandes, Wiesbaden, 1970), Appendix, pp. 39-55, from Chinese.
78. Vogel, *The Teachings*, pp. 20-35, the translation from Tibetan.
79. From Vogel's Tibetan text in transcription. Here, Tibetan *chos min* would be the Skt. *adharma* which means 'bad doctrine'.
80. Thomas, *The Life of Buddha*, p. 119 and p. 131.
81. Thomas, *The Life of Buddha*, pp. 132-3.
82. Thomas, *The Life of Buddha*, p. 133.
83. Thomas, *The Life of Buddha*, pp. 133-4.
84. Thomas, *The Life of Buddha*, pp. 134-5.
85. Malalasekera, *Dictionary*, Vol. II, 876-7. The legend has been thoroughly discussed by André Bareau, "Le Massacre des Śākya: Essai d'interprétation," *Bulletin de l'École Française d'Extrême-Orient*, LXIX, 1981, pp. 45-73, who concludes that in probability the massacre was a pure invention around the second century B.C.
86. Here I may signal two of the works: 1) Jean Przyluski, *Le Parinirvaṇa et les Funerailles du Buddha* (Paul Geuthner, Paris, 1920); 2) André Bareau, "La composition et les étapes de la formation progressive du *Mahāparinirvāṇasūtra* ancien," *BEFEO*, LXVI, 1979, pp. 45-103.
87. I employ the edition of the Nālandā-Devanāgarī-Pāli series: *The Dīghanikāya*, Vol. 2.
88. D. ii, 107: "tulam atulaṃ ca sambhavaṃ bhavasankhāram avassaji muni / ajjhattarato samāhito abhindi kavacam ivattasambhavaṃ" // I have translated from the Sanskrit, *Udānavarga*, XXVI, 30, ed. by F. Bernhard.
89. Alex Wayman, "A Study of the Vedāntic and Buddhist Theory of Nāma-rūpa," in present volume, p. 522.

2

Date and Era of the Buddha

It is well-known to students of Buddhist history that the Buddha date is a disputed matter. Geiger, in the introduction to his translation of the Pāli classic *Mahāvaṃsa*, took the text's statement that Aśoka's coronation happened 218 years after the Buddha's Nirvāṇa, to justify a 483 B.C. date for that Nirvāṇa.[1] This is usually referred to as the 'long chronology', involving a 60 or 61 year correction of the Ceylonese tradition, which was the basis for the 2,500-year celebration of the Nirvāṇa in the year 1956. Scholars who accept this 'long chronology' may differ by a year or so; and Bareau in a 1953 article said that in the light of the *Dīpavaṃsa* it could be between 478 and 488 B.C.[2] In the present paper, I shall defend the 'long chronology' and tentatively accept the 486 B.C. Nirvāṇa solution, following the Indian historian Raychaudhuri, who agrees with the assailed "dotted record of Canton".[3]

Besides, various northern Buddhist texts have remarks to the effect that a Dharma-Aśoka sponsored a Buddhist council about 100 years after the Nirvāṇa. Such passages emboldened some scholars to espouse a 'short chronology', variously dated. For example, Hikata in a 1985 essay sets forth a Nirvāṇa date of 400 B.C.[4] Another exponent of the 'short chronology', is Eggermont. At least at one time, he insisted on 368 B.C. for the Nirvāṇa on the basis of comparing certain genealogies of Ceylonese kings with Purāṇic lists.[5]

To my knowledge, Bechert has four articles on the matter: "Die Lebenszeit des Buddha . . ." (1986) expanding an earlier paper (1982);[6] one of 1988;[7] and one of 1989.[8] The last one mentioned also gives a brief run-down of the Symposium "The Date of the Historical Buddha" held in Göttingen in 1988. Bechert fairly presents the differing solutions, while decidedly leaning himself towards the 'short chronology'. He rejects the so-called "dotted record of Canton".[9]

I believe that all the methods which scholars have utilized to arrive at the Buddha era—dotted record of Canton; Jain patriarch lists; Buddhist records whether in Ceylonese, Chinese, or Tibetan; the dates of the Maurya kings, including Aśoka—are appropriate and produce arguments of varied validity. Of course, these sources are not always consistent. If one takes just one method, say the Jain patriarch lists, the researcher can justify to himself any date for the Buddha—so this is not the way to solve the problem. For a solution to the date of the Buddha, one should not evade the pertinent data. Yet, it must be acknowledged that any attempt to write on these matters—and the present one is no exception—may be limited in its sources.

Bechert in the 1988 essay validly challenges the 'long chronology'[10] "The trustworthiness of the long chronology rests on the presupposition that the information about the number of years which have passed from the Buddha's Nirvāṇa to the anointment of King Aśoka, viz., 218 B.C., is exact and correct. Indian tradition has, however, not handed down any other reliable chronological information which pertains to the period before Alexander's campaign in India, which was 327-324 B.C., a date which we know from Greek sources. Thus the question arises: Which is the evidence for the claim that the exact date of the Buddha's Parinirvāṇa has been handed down, while all other chronological information from this period is missing." Even so, it is a challenge not only to the partisans of the 'long chronology', but also to the sponsors of the 'short chronology'.

And then what should we say of the Indian historians who place the Mahābhārata War about 900 B.C.?[11] In partial response, a scholar or so has tried to disprove the historicity of the Mahābhārata War. Both sides agree on the validity of discussing the existence, or nonexistence of an Indian event far anteceding the 327-324 B.C. dating.

And what should we say of a book published 1962 in India: Yogendra Mishra, *An Early History of Vaiśālī*, with sub-title "From the Earliest Times to the Fall of the Vajjian Republic circa 484 B.C.?"[12] Mishra in fact did this work at Patna in a tireless pursuit of truth, while trying to make sense of Purāṇic lists and lists from the Pāli literature. In partial response, granted that Purāṇic lists are treacherous, but so are the Buddhist patriarch lists and so are the Jain patriarch lists.

And what should we say of the work by D.D. Kosambi, *Ancient India: A History of Its Culture and Civilization*, which accepts the Bimbisāra rulership of Magadha and the Pasenadi rulership of Kosala to belong to the sixth century B.C.?[13] And who, referring to Ajātaśatru's taking over of Kosala and some of the tribal areas: "At a date which cannot be later than 470 B.C. and not more than sixty years earlier (which is wonderful accuracy for ancient Indian chronology!), Magadha had become the major dominant though not yet paramount power in the Gangetic basin?"[14] In partial response, since any position about the Buddha's dates requires 'authorities,' let us be happy that there are some good authorities, as we hope Kosambi is, when he places the fall of the Vajjian Republic to be possibly 14 years later than Mishra's tentative date. Of course, the foregoing references to the fall of the Vajjian Republic have a bearing on the date of the Buddha, because the *Parinibbāna-sutta* of the Pāli canon shows that in the last year of the Buddha's life Ajātasattu was planning his attack on the Vajjian Republic.[15] There was presumably a lull in the ominous course as Ajātasattu (Skt. Ajātaśatru) and the Vajjian Licchavis shared in the relics. Then, according to La Vallée Poussin's work on the councils, the first council was held at Rājagṛha immediately thereafter.[16] Then we can see the reason for Mishra to decide on 487 as the date of the Buddha Nirvāṇa, whether or not we agree with him. This allows approximately three years for Ajātasattu and the Vajjian Republic to engage in various provocative acts for the actual hostilities, and then the fall of the Vajjian Republic, if we accept the 484 B.C. date for this fall. The main stipulation is that the Nirvāṇa must precede the Vajjian fall, be it by a few years or more years.

In the following account, I shall try to justify my preference for the long chronology. The argument will proceed along two lines: (a) The Buddha's relations with contemporary kings, and compatibility of legends brought to Tibet with the 'long chronology'. (b) The impact of Buddhism on the religions of India.

The Matter of the Kings

Consistent with the Buddha's being the son of a king, i.e., Śuddhodana, he easily consorted with kings during the years of preaching. At that time there was the King Bimbisāra, who established the town of Rājagṛha, which became the capital of Magadha for a while. As to when Bimbisāra lived, I have already mentioned the position of D.D. Kosambi for the 6th century B.C. Doubtless, historians like Kosambi feel that the long chronology fits the known facts of Indian history. Also the eminent historian H.C. Raychaudhuri, in his contribution to *An Advanced History of India*, takes Bimbisāra's access to fall about 545 B.C.[17] Hence, during most of the Buddha's long years of preaching, Bimbisāra was the king of Magadha, and who according to Raychaudhuri "was anointed king by his father while yet a boy of fifteen".[18] In Bimbisāra's old age he was murdered by his son Ajātaśatru. Soon Ajātaśatru had to face a host of enemies in neighboring states, but he eventually defeated all of them. Both Mahāvīra of the Jaina order, and the Buddha are said to have died early in Ajātaśatru's reign.[19]

Besides Bimbisāra, Buddhist traditions speak of the contemporary king of Kosala in Pali *Pasenadi*, Sanskrit *Prasenajit*. His state corresponds roughly to modern Oudh (which includes the city Ayodhyā).[20] Another contemporary king was Udayana, who ruled the Vatsa territory near the present Allahabad.[21] There is an entry on him by his Pāli equivalent, Udena, in Malalasekera's *Dictionary* with the information that he survived the Buddha.[22] It is barely possible that this Udayana is a name corrupted into Udrāyaṇa for the story in the *Vinayavibhaṅga* of the Tibetan canon that a Wheel of Life was presented to this king.[23] Moreover, King Caṇḍapradyota was king of Avanta with the capital Ujjayinī in the time of the

Buddha.[24] According to Malalasekera, a prominent disciple of the Buddha, Mahākaccāna (Skt. Mahākātyāyana) was son of this king's chaplain.[25]

The foregoing information shows why an Indian historian would be reluctant to agree with the 'short chronology' for the Buddha era. One cannot move the Buddha close to the time of King Aśoka of the Maurya Dynasty without the mentioned contemporary kings. Yet some scholars dare to propose their 'short chronology' for the Buddha, while not mentioning these contemporary kings.

Let us now consider some events subsequent to the Nirvāṇa. We have already pointed out the fall of the Vajjian Republic taking place rather soon after the Nirvāṇa. Raychaudhuri informs us that Udāyi, a son of Ajātaśatru, founded the city Kusumapura, or Pāṭaliputra—the site of the modern Patna.[26] Also, that about a century after the Buddha's Nirvāṇa a ruler of Magadha called Kālāśoka or Kākavarṇa transferred his residence from Girivraja to Pāṭaliputra.[27] Although Kālāśoka is just one of the names by which he is referred to, this similarity to the name Aśoka of the Mauryas led to various wrong statements in Buddhist texts of many centuries later to the effect that the king of a century after the Nirvāṇa is the Dharmarāja Aśoka. Scholars supporting the 'short chronology' have been uniformly fooled by these scriptural passages. Of course, Indian historians were not fooled because it is impossible to take the king contemporaries of Gautama Buddha and put them so close to the Maurya King Aśoka.

As for the 2nd council, La Vallée Poussin shows in his work *The Buddhist Councils*, that this is assigned a hundred years after the Nirvāṇa; while the Tibetan version says 110 years.[28] In any case, the commission of the ten prohibited acts by the Vajjian monks precipitated a big problem for the Buddhist Saṅgha sooner or later after this king came to Pāṭaliputra. According to the Pāli account, a personage Yasa (Skt. Yaśas) along with several hundred followers was visiting Vaiśālī and noticed monks practicing various acts which seemed to violate Viṇaya rules. He sought out in that area the aged Sabbakamin, who was over a hundred years old and had been a personal disciple of Ānanda. This is feasible since Ānanda lived on after the Buddha, although we do not know for how long. A local monk named Revata was put in charge. He invited four senior monks from the East and four from the West to constitute a jury for the trial to take place in Vaiśālī, where the affair had happened. A sponsoring king seems unnecessary; perhaps is mentioned in later works to emphasize the gravity; and helps for the historicity.[29] The matter was of great importance for the history of Buddhism, because that was evidently the time for setting the Vinaya rules.[30] The meeting did not have the significance which the *Mahāvaṃsa* at the outset of its Chap. V on the 'Third Council' alleges, namely, that the heretical bhikkhus, who had been ousted by the aforementioned jury—all 10,000 of them, founded the Mahāsāṃghika school.[31] This is said with theological odium, since the Theravādin would never forgive the Mahāsāṃghikas for the Saṅgha split. For tenacious theological odium, truth is secondary. In fact, all that happened in the 2nd Council is that the erring monks were ousted; and there probably were not many in this group. There were no such persons as Mahāsāṃghika at that time. Comparative studies of the various Prātimokṣa texts of the Theravāda, the Mahāsāṁghika, and others that are available show very little difference in the basic rules. In short, there is no evidence that the Mahāsāṃghika Vinaya authorizes the commission of the ten acts that had been condemned; and Hikata in his monograph admitted this.[32]

I learned long ago about the Tibetan tradition for the actual split in the Saṅgha when F.D. Lessing and myself translated a text by Mkhas grub rje that mentioned the 137-year figure associated with the Nanda king, and constituting the Saṅgha split.[33] But this is in other sources such as Taranatha, so European writers have long taken account of the figure. Thus Lamotte, *Histoire*, acknowledged that if this 137 year figure is accepted and associated with King Mahāpadma of the Nanda dynasty, it demands the 'long chronology' for the Buddha era.[34]

The intervention of the Nandas is difficult to pinpoint historically, as is their "destruction of the Kṣatriyas".[35] According to Raychaudhuri, the first victim appears to be that very king Kālāśoka. As the years went by, there came a barber—a handsome bit of maleness who attracted the affections of the queen, who arranged for him to get the job of guardian for the king's sons. He used the opportunity of being within the court to assassinate the king, murder the king's sons, and then to put his own son in charge.[36] Raychaudhuri inclines to the Jaina tradition that this son was the issue of the barber with a courtesan.[37] Thus began the reign of Mahāpadma Nanda over the extensive Magadha kingdom.

Raychaudhuri uses the classical references to conclude that the Nanda on the throne at the time Chandragupta met Alexander in the Punjab, i.e., 326 B.C., could not be Mahāpadma but was the latter's son or one of them.[38] As the well-known story tells it, Chandragupta overthrew this monarch and took over to be the first of the Maurya kings and in turn the grandfather of King Aśoka. According to Raychaudhuri's calculations, after Chandragupta had gathered a group of mercenaries he came to power around 324 B.C. 162 years after the Nirvāṇa according to a Nirvāṇa date 486 B.C. Raychaudhuri claims that this date of 324 B.C. is not inconsistent with classical accounts, in particular, the author Justin.[39] One promptly notices that this accession date agrees with the *Mahāvaṃsa*'s years of Chandragupta's reign—24 years; his son Bindusāra's reign—28 years; and four years between the accession and the coronation of King Aśoka. These add to 56, which added to 162 years after Nirvāṇa yield the figure 218, which the *Mahāvaṃsa* said was the number of years after the Nirvāṇa to Aśoka's coronation—namely, in 268 B.C.[40] In short, the 218 years seem to be a lot of years to account for and to justify, but the amount is less when calculated back from Chandragupta's accession, because now the amount is reduced to 162 years after Nirvāṇa. And since there is the well-attested story of the 2nd council about 100 years after Nirvāṇa, this leaves only a space of 62 years to account for.

This brings us to consider the inclusive reigns of the Nandas. Buddhist, Jain, and the Hindu Purāṇa amounts attributed to their reign differ markedly, but all agree that there were the Nandas. Without going into their differences, I shall simply refer to Raychaudhuri. He appears inclined to accept the statement in certain manuscripts of the *Vāyu Purāṇa*, which is among the oldest of this class of literature, that the first Nanda ruled for 28 years, his sons for twelve years.[41] His 'sons' are grouped as one person in the Tibetan, e.g. in Mkhas grub rje's work alluded to above, simply copying the previous sentences of Tibetan historical literature—and somewhat awkwardly—alluding to the two kings, "Nanda and Mahāpadma"—in fact, Mahāpadma and his son (or sons) called Nanda.[42] It makes sense for the Nandas to have ruled for no more than about 40 years; indeed the total easily fits within the 62 year period. The small amount of years goes with amassing great wealth by military conquest, while losing the respect of the people; and then a paucity of information about them.

As to pinpointing the Nandas in the 62-year period, Raychaudhuri says that the dynasty could not have come to power before c. 367-66 B.C.[43] This figure agrees with about 40 years for the Nandas, since they immediately precede Chandragupta Maurya, whose accession is put around 324 B.C. Thus, if they ruled exactly 40 years, the Nanda dynasty begins around 364 B.C. For a Nirvāṇa date of 486 B.C., the 2nd council approximately 100 years later, is approximately 386 B.C. This leaves approximately 22 years of reign at Pāṭaliputra for the king Kālāśoka before he was assassinated by the barber. He may have had the importance of establishing the city as the new capital, and so was probably already in his 40's when shifting there. For our argument, it is immaterial whether this king reigned exactly 22 years there, or a few years more or less; whether the 2nd council took place exactly 100 years after Nirvāṇa, 99, 102, etc. or 110 as in the Tibetan accounts. The main thing is that a king of such name was there, that the 2nd council is admitted as an actual event of about 100 years after Nirvāṇa. Hence, the events of approximately 100 years, about 22 years more than the approximately 40 years of the Nandas fall one after another, not overlapping. We may conclude that it was not a fluke or an inflated figure for the *Mahāvaṃsa* to have said that King Aśoka was crowned 218 years after the Nirvāṇa, which is equivalent to saying that Chandragupta Maurya became king 162 years after Nirvāna, where 162 is the sum of the approximate figures 100, 22, and 40.

Furthermore, there is an implication that the Tibetan figure of 110 years for the 2nd council may be correct, on account of a *Mahāvaṃsa* tradition reported by Raychauduri: ". . . the second great Council of the Buddhists is said to have been held in the tenth year of the king's reign when a century had gone by since the *Parinirvāṇa* of the Buddha."[44] If the Tibetan tradition is right, the king transferred his residence to Pāṭaliputra 100 years after Nirvāṇa; the 2nd council took place ten years later; and the king was assassinated about 12 years after that.

It should not be said that the ancient Indians were not interested in history. Indeed, without such interest, we would not even have the 218 year figure. And it seems reasonable to conclude that at the time these old writers put down this 218 figure, they were in a better position to know what was right in this respect than authors like us who come so many centuries later. Hence, I accept the 'long chronology' and reject the 'short chronology'.

Now we can turn to the 137-year figure for the initial schism. It had to occur during the reign of Mahāpadma Nanda. Hence, the Tibetan tradition about this association is proper. The further figure that the argument lasted for 60 years—so in the Mkhas grub rje account[45]—falls short of 21 years even to get to Aśoka's crowning. But probably the figure is approximate for the further divisions in the Buddhist sects to arrive at the traditional eighteen Buddhist schools. However, the differentiated theories attributed to these Buddhist sects must have developed over a long period, even past the Maurya dynasty.

As to the cause of the schism, already in my article "Ancient Buddhist Monasticism"[46] I have agreed with Bareau's arguments that the schism took place about 137 years after Nirvāṇa and was due to five theses about the Arhat, and was not due to difference in interpretation of the Vinaya.[47] Hence, despite the unforgiving attitude of the Theravāda, the split giving rise to the Mahāsāṃghika seems not to have resulted in weakening the Buddhist movement. This conclusion results from considering the effect of the split on the three jewels of Buddhism, the Buddha, the Dharma, the Saṅgha. The attack on the Arhat status was an attack on the Saṅgha, because the Arhat was considered the finest fruit of being in the Saṅgha. The attack left the Dharma-Vinaya intact, and promoted the Jewel of the Buddha. It should be observed in this connection that after the Nirvāṇa, the Buddha could only be present in the absence, while the Dharma-Vinaya and the Saṅgha continued in the presence. It follows that a promotion of the Buddha Jewel had to be conducted along symbolic lines, Akira Hirakawa has well-stated the case in his essay, "The Rise of Mahāyāna Buddhism and its Relationship to the Worship of Stūpas."[48] It had to be the Mahāsāṅghika which made up the theological arguments going with the stūpa worship, with specialized doctrines that the Buddhas are supramundane, and so on. This led to the Jātaka literature on the former lives of the Buddha, while he was a Bodhisattva progressing toward enlightenment. Eventually, this build-up of the Buddha Jewel through the development of the Bodhisattva literature brought on the great movement of Mahāyāna Buddhism. That there were both lay and monk bodhisattvas shows that this movement sometimes supported the monk Saṅgha and sometimes operated outside of it.[49]

The 'long chronology' allows for time, namely, for the sects to divide and subdivide before the age of King Aśoka of the Mauryas; and namely for the Mahāsāṅghika, while itself a group of monks, to gradually come to terms with lay Buddhism with theological tenets. It also allows for time in the proliferation of the Vinayas, most of which are only known now from their Chinese translations. The 'long chronology' allows for the development of philosophical subtlety so that by the beginning of the Christian era there could be the tremendous proliferation of the Abhidharma, and the reaction to this in the remarkable treatises of Nāgārjuna. The 'long chronology' allows for the development of a new Buddhist message, that was suitable for the foreign peoples to become converts to Buddhism in Central Asia, fulfilling a role for which the old Nikāya Buddhism would have been at a loss. In short, there is nothing in Buddhist history or its literature that should puzzle the partisan of the 'long chronology'.

Impact of Buddhism on Indian Religion

Gautama Buddha was born with a given name of Siddhārtha among the Śākyas, a small Republican tribe with Kapilavastu as capital. This was located in the present Gorakhpur district to the west of Darbhanga (anciently part of Videha). Thus, to the East of his birthplace was the state called Videha. One may consult C. Collin Davies, *An Historical Atlas of the Indian Peninsula*, "Ancient India, c. 500 B.C."[50] and probably a number of other works—to see the exact geographical placement.

When Siddhārtha left his birthplace to seek out religious teachers and so on, it is noteworthy that he did not go West. He proceeded east to Videha and south to enter the state of Magadha, which had recently been expanded by seizing Kāśi (now Varanasi). He engaged in meditation at Gaya (now in Bihar) and gave his first sermon at Isipatana, now called Sarnath. He often visited with sermons at Vaiśālī, which was in the present Muzaffarpur district of N.E. Bihar, and which at the time of the Buddha was part of the Vajjian republic.

Now, in the light of the 'long chronology' which I have defended above, what would be the kind of Indian religion which Siddhārtha would encounter as he travelled south in Videha toward Kāśi? It is generally accepted that preceding Gautama Buddha there was the development of the sacrificial cult of the Brāhmaṇas and the composition of the oldest Upaniṣads, notably the *Bṛhadāraṇyaka-Up.* and the *Chāndogya-Up.* There is little likelihood that Siddhārtha encountered anything like the *Chāndogya Upaniṣad.* But that the teachings found in the *Bṛhadāraṇyaka Upaniṣad* would be in the areas travelled by Siddhārtha is quite likely, as will become clear as we proceed. It is known that the *Atharvaveda* belongs to this same area.[51]

The first chapter of the *Bṛhadāraṇyaka* is devoted to the horse sacrifice which is identified with the sacrifice of the deity Prajāpati, who is important for all the sacrificial literature of the Brāhmaṇas, and who is also called the creative lord Brahmā. Prajāpati, or by his other name Brahmā is the main deity throughout the *Bṛhadāraṇyaka.* This deity Brahmā was accepted in Buddhism. His realm is noticed in the first division of the realm of form (*rūpadhātu*); and it is said that when sentient beings are in his realm, they falsely believed they were created by Brahmā. Thus, when Buddhism denies creation by a lord, it treats Brahmā as that lord. Also Brahmā Sahāṃpati appeared to the Buddha when soon after his enlightenment he was reluctant to teach, and Brahmā urged him to teach.[52] The terms *brahmacarya* and *brahmavihāra* are honorable expressions in Buddhism.

The 2nd chap. of the *Bṛhadāraṇyaka* is set in Kāśi, where there must have been many earnest discussions about Brahman, the nature of man, and so forth. At the outset there is the remark, "People indeed run, exclaiming 'Janaka', 'Janaka'." From the sequel, starting Chap. III, the point seems to be that King Janaka of Videha had offered a prize of 1000 cows, with gold coins attached to their horns. i.e. offered to anyone who could explain all about Brahman. A Yajur-Veda specialist, Yājñavalkya of Kāśi, decides to take up the challenge. He may be the person of that name mentioned in the *Śatapathabrāhmaṇa,* 3rd chap., as one who likes to eat beef, while in the *Bṛhadāraṇyaka* he is a bigamist. He makes a settlement with his two wives and bids them farewell. Yājñavalkya appears in Videha along with his disciple and claims the 1,000 cows to the consternation of local brahmins, who ask him somewhat hostile questions, trying to put him on the spot; but he seems on top of it all, able to answer everything.

Long ago, the scholars have noticed and treated the important answers to Jāratkārava Ārtabhāga (III, 2, 1-13) when Yājñavalkya replies that what does not leave a person when he dies is his name (*nāma*), and the two persons talked in private about *karma*. Next, of great importance is his answers (III, 7, 1, ff.) to someone he calls Gautama about "*ātma-antaryāmī-amṛta*", rendered "the self" (*ātma*), "the inner controller" (*antaryāmī*), and "the immortal" (*amṛta*). The Buddha's teachings seem to take all this for granted, as topics upon which Buddhism would offer its own solutions. I am of course far from the first western or Asian author to discuss these matters. To save space, I shall only present my own way of treating them.

The Buddha did not discuss *karma* in private. He broadcast it, to anyone who would listen. But did the Buddha agree with Yājñavalkya about the 'name' continuing? Apparently so, per *Samyutta-nikāya* I, 43: to the question—*kiṃ jīrati; kiṃ na jīrati*, "What decays? What does not decay?" the Buddha answers: *rūpaṃ jīrati maccānaṃ; nāmagottaṃ na jīrati*, "The physical body (*rūpaṃ*) of mortals decays; their name and genus (*nāma* and *gotta*) does not decay."[53] Still, we do not know yet whether Yājñavalkya and the Buddha mean the same by the word '*nāma*'. For the Buddha's usage of these words of India, while it might seem unrelated, I appeal to the *Atharva-Veda* (XIII, 3, 18): *sapta yujanti ratham ekacakram eko aśvo vahati saptanāmā* "Seven harness a one-wheeled chariot; one horse, having seven names, draws [it]." Since we know that seven horses are said to draw the sun's chariot, the one horse must be the genus (Pali, *gotta*: Skt. *gotra*) the seven names the distinct horses. This is an evidence of the usage of *nāma* in Magadha in those times.[54] On the other hand, for the Buddha, the *gotra* is tantamount to the *gati*, the destiny, whether human beings, gods, and so forth: while the *nāma* is the distinctiveness of the being in that destiny. But what did the Buddha mean by this distinctiveness? The Buddha did include the *nāma* in the formula of dependent origination in the fourth member, *nāma-rūpa*. According to Buddhaghosa, his *Visuddhimagga*, dependent origination section, *nāma* means the three 'name aggregates' (*nāma-skandha*)—feelings (*vedanā*), ideas (*saṃjñā*), and motivations (*saṃskāra*).[55] Here *saṃskāra* might be explained as the 'old *karma*', the feelings and ideas metaphysically as the 'suffering' (*duḥkha*). Thus, it appears that the Buddha does agree with Yājñavalkya in part, namely, that when *nāma* means the old *karma* as a distinguishing factor, it does continue.

I shall be rather brief about the series *ātman*, etc. while exposing my conclusion, namely, that the Buddha substituted his own words. For *ātman*, he had *anātman*; for *antaryāmī* he had *śūnya*; for *amṛta* he had *anitya*. Let me explain: the Buddha does not deny *ātman* when stressing *anātman*; nor does he deny an *antaryāmī* when calling it *śūnya*; and he also has an *amṛta*, though prefers to talk about *anitya*. And further about *ātman* and *anạtman*: It has been pointed out by a number of scholars that the Buddha did not deny a self, but usually they do not explain that if such is the case why the Buddha kept talking with the term *anātman*. That the term *anātman* is a qualified negation is clear enough from Vasubandhu's explanation in the *Abhidharmakośa*, *akāmakāri*, 'unable to do as wished';[56] and from Asaṅga's explanation in the *Śrāvakabhūmi*, *asvātantrya*, 'not independent'.[57] Thus, the denial is of a self that is independent and omnipotent. Besides, the Buddha points out that at death one must part from all possessions; so *anātman* also connotes a denial that the self is always an owner or *svāmī*.

In the case of the 'inner controller' (*antaryāmī*), Vasubandhu in his *Abhidharmakośa* explains the aspect 'void' (*śūnya*) as *antarvyāpārapuruṣarahita*, 'devoid of an inner person (*puruṣa*) who operates'.[58] This denial means that the Buddha argues in favor of the Buddhist path. This is because if the beings had an 'inner controller' why do they lack self-control? The Buddha teaches that by a regime of training, one may gain the self-control that was not present as a birthright.

Then, without denying that there is such a thing as the *amṛta*—a term (and notion) that is implied in the genesis myth of Buddhism[59]—the Buddha found it more useful to talk about the impermanent (*anitya*) and to teach that even when one has attained the state of Indra, he will after sometime fall down to lower destinies.[60]

In short, for that set of three—the *ātman*, the *antaryāmī*, and the *amṛta*—so much stressed in the *Bṛhadāraṇyaka-Upaniṣad*, the Buddha instead stressed what became called the 'aspects', (*ākāra*) *anātman*, *śūnya*, and *anityatā*, of the first Noble Truth, of *Duḥkha*. Of course, I would not insist that the Gautama to whom Yājñavalkya was speaking, while repeating his series *ātma-antaryāmy amṛta* is Gautama Buddha, who is possibly contemporary in that region if we accept the 'long chronology'. After all, there are various persons named Gautama. What I do insist upon is that the Buddha seems to have been exposed to the corpus of ideas found in the *Bṛhadāraṇyaka*, and that he agrees with some of them, and also presents an alternate of disagreeing position with other ideas of that *Upaniṣad*.

Now for a different approach to the Buddha's impact, I must probe the general hostility of Hindus to Buddhism, which has continued to modern times, and then conclude that it involves the 'long chronology'.

For this, we must consider that peoples called the Vrātya. Here I refer to the book by Choudhary on the Vrātyas.[61] The Vrātyas are a people who apparently belonged to Magadha, and from there moved further East, North, and South. The remarkable Book XV of the *Atharva-Veda* is devoted to the Vrātya. It starts with a Vrātya evoking Prajāpati, and continues with a vision of this evoked Prajāpati. It seems that there were two main currents of the Vrātya in Magadha, whereby 'Magadha' we mean the state with approximate boundaries of 500 B.C. The first one to mention (but probably not the first in time) is an Aryan group perhaps due to an early invasion through the North-West that by-passed the Indus Valley strongholds and proceeded to the east, settling down in 'Magadha'. Presumably the Buddha's use of the term '*ārya*' in the four Truths stems from this Aryan group. This Aryan group in turn subdivided into followers of the Veda and the Brahmanical cults, and into anti-Veda or non-Veda movements of Buddhism, Jainism, and Ājīvikan. The second current of the Vrātya was from the pre-Aryan period of peoples who especially followed the deity called Śiva. According to Choudhary[62] almost all the sects of Śaivism were the products of the Vrātya order. It might be that a subsequent Aryan invasion from the N.W. destroyed the strongholds of the Indus Valley centers. These Aryans—whether of East or West—had originally a chief deity Varuṇa. Then a war-god Indra came to the fore. Toward the end of the composition of the *Ṛg-Veda*, a new deity Viṣṇu had come into prominence and would practically eclipse Varuṇa and Indra. And the followers of Viṣṇu gradually built up the enormous movement of Vaiṣṇavism. The brahmin upholders of the Vedic culture of these peoples, who had settled in the Punjab were somewhat at odds with their Eastern co-religionists. By that time, there were various kinds of brahmins; and while the followers of Viṣṇu were probably much in the majority, there were probably still some followers of Varuṇa as well as of Indra, and of other deities such as Brahmā. The possibly earlier Aryan group that had settled down in the East must have had considerable intermarriage with local people, so that a sincere follower of the Veda might well have a cousin following strange cults.

With the arising of Buddhism consistent with the 'long chronology' the growing success of the non-Vedic and anti-Vedic groups must have prompted much worry among the defenders of the Vedic religion. Where this distress would happen first is naturally in the Magadha area because this is where Buddhism, Jainism, and other non-Vedic groups were flourishing. I suppose that it forced the leaders of the Eastern block of Vedic followers to turn to the Śaivites with a deal amounting to an upping in status of their Śiva, if they would endorse the Veda. This move would bring under the wing of the Vedic followers—a large group of persons: so there need be no more worry about the proselyting success of the Buddhists, etc. The way in which the Śaivism was made 'Vedic' was by identifying Śiva with the Vedic deity Rudra. This takes place in the *Śvetāsvatāra-Up.*, which Dandekar[63] explains to belong to the end of the 5th century B.C. Hence, this important Śaivitic Upaniṣad at least in its earliest form—appears about 80 years after the Nirvāṇa, when the Nirvāṇa is dated in accordance with the 'long chronology'. When the followers of Viṣṇu, who were pre-eminent in the West realized what had transpired, and that now the deity Śiva would be a serious competitor for the hearts of the people, their antipathy for Buddhism was set in motion. Buddhism, they would feel, not only had a major role in bringing about this success of Śaivism along with its host of strange cults, but also Buddhism was becoming the main anti-Vedic movement. And they never ceased to dislike Buddhism for the reason consistent with the 'long chronology', while the supporters of the 'short chronology' would not be able to account with such a cogent reason for this inveterate antagonism to Buddhism.

Another proof is in terms of the *Atharva-Veda.* It is well-known that the mention of three Vedas occurs in the *Ambaṭṭha Sutta* of the Dīgha-nikāya. The translator of this Part I, T.W. Rhys Davids, points out in his note that the commentator Buddhagosa claimed we have to supply the fourth Veda, the *Atharva.* Rhys Davids, disagreeing, says: "But the older Pāli texts do not acknowledge the *Atharva* as a Veda." Toward the end of his note, he mentions that the four Vedas are referred to in the *Milinda.*[64] The fact is that the Buddhists had no qualms about adding a fourth Veda to the list, if that had been the case. All the evidence agrees that when the Dīgha-nikāya scripture *Ambaṭṭha Sutta* was composed or delivered, the Buddhists knew only of the standard three Vedas, the *Ṛg*, the *Sāma*, and the *Yajur.* So the question arises: when did the *Atharva-Veda* become the 'fourth Veda'?

The answer is suggested in terms of the Upaniṣads that are associated with the *Atharva* as a Veda. S. Radhakrishnan, *The Principal Upaniṣads*, includes with this association the *Praśna*, the *Muṇḍaka*, the *Maṇḍukya*, the *Jabala*, and the *Kaivalya.* The first three are the most important and go into *yoga* theory. Macdonell states that only the *Muṇḍaka* and the *Praśna* are old and legitimate Upaniṣads of the *Atharva.* Of these two, Macdonell takes the *Muṇḍaka* to come in time between the *Śvetāśvatāra* and the *Bṛhannārāyaṇa* of the *Black Yajur-veda.*[65] Therefore, the *Atharva* would gain the status of a fourth Veda—for those who acknowledged it as such—about the same time as the original composition of the *Śvetāśvatāra.* This is reasonable, since the *Atharva* in its present form constitutes a compromise between the two currents of the Magadha Vrātyas—the old Vedic and the pre-Vedic; and thus parallels the syncretic *Śvetāśvatāra.*

It follows that the old Buddhist canon of the four *nikāyas* that do not recognize a fourth Veda is the orally handed-down canon that existed in the circa 80 years from the Buddha's Nirvāṇa in the 'long chronology' down to the *Śvetāśvatāra* and which was committed to writing in the 1st century B.C. Nevertheless, it must be granted that some scholars have averred that there is no proof of the Buddhist canon before it was written down; but they appear to talk this way when criticising some viewpoint that requires the existence of the Pāli canon, while not talking this way when they themselves cite the Pāli canon as though it has existed that way. And one might as well say, there is no proof of the Veda before it was committed to writing! Doubtless, Madan Mohan Singh is worth citing for these remarks: "There is a criticism raised against the authenticity of the Pāli canon, as depicting conditions of the pre-Mauryan period on the ground that they were all recorded in writing in Ceylon and retranslated into Pāli in the 5th century A.D. This is true, but the monks were not the least likely to alter the teachings of the Buddha or the facts connected with his life. Sermons like the *Dhammachakkapavattana-sutta*, the *Samaññaphala-sutta*, and the *Mahāparinibbāna-suttanta* would have been hardly changed. After all, sanctity was attached to the words of the Buddha . . . We need not expect that the Pāli canon is still today in the same Māgadhī dialect which was used by the Buddha. But the meaning has remained the same . . . . Mention of cities and towns lead to the same conclusion, e.g. Rājagṛha is prominent; Pāṭaliputra is always Pāṭaligāma."[66] So also Malalasekera in his entry on "Pāṭaligāma, Pāṭaliputta": "The Buddha visited it shortly before his death. It was then a mere village and was known as Pāṭaligāma."[67] Now, with this information it is apparent that the exponents of the 'short chronology', i.e., that the Nirvāṇa took place a hundred years before the coronation of Aśoka of the Maurya dynasty have an irresolvable dilemma. Since that village had grown into the capital even before the Nanda rule, the last twenty years of the Buddha's wandering would have roughly corresponded with Pāṭaliputra as the new capital; and so Buddhist legends would have featured this city prominently; but in fact it is the old capital, Rājagṛha, which has that role in Buddhist legends. Indeed, no exponent of the 'short chronology'—be he or she ever so eminent, and deservedly so—need be believed in for this version of the facts, because the 'short chronology' is indefensible.

Conclusion

It may be admitted that the Indian historian Raychaudhuri accepts the validity of the "dotted record of Canton" for the same reason as I do. That is to say, he found the 'long chronology' the only acceptable alternative for the facts of Indian history as he knew them—and indeed he knew them well; and then the "dotted record of Canton" is a traditional list with a dating for the Nirvāṇa that accords well with the 'long chronology'. I had to accept the 'long chronology' for a number of reasons: The *Parinibbana-sutta* of Pāli mentioned that Ajātasattu (Skt. Ajātaśatru) was planning his attack on the Vajjian republic; so the Nirvāṇa has to precede the fall of the Vajjian republic. Indian history places in the sixth century, B.C. various kings who are contemporaries of Gautama Buddha; specifically those kings are Bimbisāra and Prasenajit; and possibly Caṇḍapradyota. The Aśoka who sponsored the Second Council about 100 years after Nirvāṇa was a king—one of whose names was Kālāśoka, and who was assassinated by the barber . . .

who started the Nanda rule which lasted for forty or more years; but the Aśoka famous among the Mauryas was not assassinated by any barber. Thus, the 219-year figure was not a fluke, but readily explainable. Besides, the Buddha seems contemporaneous with the *Bṛhadāraṇyaka-Upaniṣad.* His authentic discourses precede the casting of the Atharvan scripture into a 'fourth Veda'. The inveterate hostility of the Hindus to Buddhism begins with the 'long chronology'. And the Tibetan tradition of 137 years after Nirvāṇa for the initial split in the Buddhist Saṅgha requires the 'long chronology'. Then, as to the "dotted record", it does appear that partisans of the 'short chronology' have tried their best to disprove this theory.

REFERENCES

1. William Geiger, *The Mahāvaṃsa* (Colombo, 1950), xxx—xxxvi. Geiger accepts the date 483 B.C. that had been proposed by Fleet.
2. André Bareau, "La date du Nirvāṇa, "*Journal Asiatique*, 1953, p. 34.
3. H.C. Raychaudhuri, in *Ancient India*, Part I of *An Advanced History of India* (London, 1960), p. 58; and points out that the Geiger date, while close to the Cantonese tradition is not explicitly recognized by any tradition.
4. Ryusho Hikata, "On the Period of the Lifetime of Śākyamuni," in his *Studies in Buddhism and Buddhist Culture* (Naritasan Shinshoji, Japan, 1985), p. 15.
5. P.H.L. Eggermont, *Persica*, No. VIII (1979), p. 56; and claims that the 100 years before the Aśoka accession is the early dating, that the 486 B.C. epoch is a Theravādin innovation, which he tentatively puts at ca. 150 B.C.
6. Heinz Bechert, "Die Lebenszeit des Buddha—das älteste feststehende Datum der indischen Geschichte?" Nachrichten der Academie der Wissenschaften in Göttingen; 1. Philologisch-Historische Klasse, 4 (1986), pp. 58.
7. H. Bechert, "Remarks on the Date of the Historical Buddha." in *Buddhist Studies* (*Bukkyō Kenkyū*), Vol. XVII, March, 1988, pp. 97-117.
8. H. Bechert, "The Problem of the determination of the date of the historical Buddha, "*Wiener Zeitschrift für die Kunde Südasiens*," Vol. XXXIII, 1989, pp. 93-120.
9. Cf. Bechert, n. 7, above, p. 108; and also see Bechert, n. 6, above, pp. 137-40; and Bechert's summary, n. 8, above, pp. 101-2.
10. Bechert, n.7, above, pp. 98-9.
11. A.L. Basham, *The Wonder that was India* (Grove Press, New York, from the original 1954 ed.), p. 39.
12. Published by Motilal Banarsidass, Delhi, 1962.
13. "Meridian Book" (World Publ. Co., New York, 1969; reprint of "Pantheon Books", 1965), p. 102; and index, S.V. "Bimbisāra."
14. *Op. cit.*, p. 131.
15. This incident is mentioned at the very outset of the *Parinibbana Sutta*; cf. *Dialogues of the Buddha*, Part II, tr. by T.W. Rhys Davids and C.A.F. Rhys

Davids (London, 1959), pp. 78, ff.

16. Louis de La Vallee Poussin, *The Buddhist Councils* (K.P. Bagchi & Co., Calcutta, 1976), p. 2, ff.
17. Raychaudhuri, *Ancient* (n. 3, above), p. 58.
18. Raychaudhuri, *Ancient*, p. 58.
19. Raychaudhuri, *Ancient*, p. 60.
20. Raychaudhuri, *Ancient*, p. 57.
21. Raychaudhuri, *Ancient*, p. 57.
22. G.P. Malalasekera, *Dictionary of Pāli Proper Names* (London, 1960), two volumes.
23. Alex Wayman, "The Interlineary-type Commentary in Tibetan," in *Tibetan and Buddhist Studies*, ed. by Louis Legeti, Vol. 2 (Akademiai Kiado, Budapest, 1984), pp. 376-8. There I perhaps wrongly theorized that Udrāyaṇa was another name for Prasenajit; but now it seems more likely that it goes with Udayana.
24. Raychaudhuri, *Ancient*, p. 57.
25. Malalasekera, *Dictionary*, Vol. Two, entry, 'Mahā-Kaccāna'.
26. Raychaudhuri, *Ancient*, p. 60.
27. Raychaudhuri, *Ancient*, p. 61. H.C. Raychauduri, in *Age of the Nandas and Mauryas*, ed. by K.A. Nilakanta Sastri (Delhi, 1967), p. 11: "the old capital, Girivraja-Rājagṛha"; so the name means the old capital or a part of it.
28. La Vallée Poussin, *The Buddhist Councils*, p. 30, ff.; and for the 110-year figure, see his appendix, p. 67, ff. for citation from the Tibetan Kanjur.
29. For example, Bu-ston, *History of Buddhism*, tr. by E. Obermiller, Part II (Heidelberg, 1932), p. 96, concluding the exposition of the Second Council, states. "and the alms-giver of the monks was the pious king Aśoka".
30. Cf. Etienne Lamotte, *Histoire du bouddhisme indian* (Louvain, 1958), pp. 181-93, for structure and analysis of the Vinayapiṭaka.
31. Geiger (n. 1, above), p. 26.
32. Hikata (n. 4, above), p. 9.
33. Ferdinand D. Lessing and Alex Wayman, trs., *Mkhas grub rje's—Fundamentals of the Buddhist Tantras* (The Hague, 1968), p. 67.
34. Lamotte (n. 30, above), p. 308.
35. Cf. Nilakanta Sastri, *History of India*, Part I: Ancient India (Madras, 1953), pp. 50-1.
36. Raychaudhuri, *Age of* (n. 27, above), p. 14.
37. Raychaudhuri, *Age of*, pp. 13-4.
38. Raychaudhuri, *Age of*, p. 23.
39. Raychaudhuri, *Age of*, p. 136; and cf. *op. cit.*, p. 137. Granted that it appears ridiculous to the casual reader that Chandragupta should meet Alexander in 326 B.C. as a single person with apparently no soldiers at his command, and then just a couple of years later show up as king of the Magadha kingdom. But when furnished some essential information, one may appreciate that this date of 324 B.C. is reasonable. I appeal first to the researches of Buddha Prakash, *Studies in Indian History and Civilization* (Agra, 1962), Chap. III, "The Home of the Mauryas" (pp. 70-85). After an exhaustive consideration of the various theories for the origins of the Mauryas, he finally decides that the place must be the present railroad stop called More (Mor), 58 miles to the east of Patna (the site of the ancient Pāṭaliputra) and 287 miles from Calcutta. We must assume that there was once an ancient road going straight from this place to Pāṭaliputra. According to legend, Cāṇakya (or Kauṭilya), a learned Brahmin had been insulted by the Nanda king; and to get revenge plotted to replace the Nanda king with Chandragupta. Now, it is feasible

that Chandragupta probably in the company of Cāṇakya travelled back to the place now called More, a travel which may have taken a month or so, if they went by horseback. Next, I suppose he encouraged his clan to overcome the Nanda king and then use the immense Nanda army for ridding his country of the Greek satrapies. To understand what they might have done, one may point to a still remaining section of the old rampart or wall of fortification that was constructed by Ajātaśatru. The present writer witnessed this small section in the year 1978. The way such a wall is constructed is while being erected and widened to take away soil from the side of attack, and put that soil on the side of defence; so that, when the fortification is complete, the attackers find themselves at the bottom of a high wall, while the defenders have a gradual rise of ground so that they can easily get to the top of the wall. Therefore, this side needs little defence. It is the other side with graduated slope which needs to be heavily defended. A thousand years later a similar awesome situation faced the supporters of Shivaji, when he decided to retake the mountain fortress called Sing-garh in Maharashtra. See the booklet *Shivaji and the Rise of the Mahrattas* (Susil Gupta, Calcutta, 1953) by Richard Temple and five others. Shivaji's trusted lieutenant Tannaji executed the attack with just 300 men. Sir Richard Temple explains how they ascended this rock wall that went straight up: "Well, Tannaji had the ladders of rope and the grappling irons with him, and with these rope ladders up they went . . . . Alexander and his Macedonians used to do something of the same kind." Chandragupta had probably observed how Alexander's forces did this. When Udāyi founded the city of Pāṭaliputra, he must have initially placed it behind (i.e. protected by) the rampart wall. Presumably, when it was the capital, the place would also be placed close to the rampart so as to get optimum protection. If it went as I suppose, the plotters had to get the right time for the attack, probably when the nights were longest, the weather was suitable, spies showed that the Nanda king was at the palace, and probably when there had been a banquet for some festival, making the participants drowsy. Given my theory it was not until 324 B.C. that it was possible to mount an attack with the prospect of success. And when the attack succeeded and the Nanda king and his retainers were killed, Chandragupta was installed as king; but then probably needed a couple of more years to consolidate his position, get the loyalty of the army commanders in various parts of the country, and so forth, before he could mount an attack on the Greek satrapies. R.C. Majumdar, *The Classical Accounts of India* (Calcutta, 1960), p. 193, has what the Roman historian Justin says about Chandragupta by his reference of Sandrocottus: "Sandrocottus having thus won the throne was reigning over India when Seleucus was laying the foundations of his future greatness." Raychauduri, *Age of*, p. 137, says of this famous Macedonian general that he "acquired the satrapy of Babylon for the first time in 321 B.C., regained control of the city and founded an era in 312 B.C., and assumed the title of king in 306-5 B.C." This means that Chandragupta was reigning when Seleucus in 321 B.C. acquired the Babylon satrapy; but none of these remarks and observations including Justin's statement, militates against Raychauduri's date of 324 B.C. for the beginning of the Maurya dynasty. Indeed, the date 321 B.C. appears reasonable for Chandragupta to then have sufficient control of all the kingdom's armed forces to be able to start defeating the Greek satrapies. From the classical standpoint, this proves that Chandragupta is surely the monarch. In contrast to the above solution, R.K. Mookerji, in *A Comprehensive History of India*; Vol. Two, The Mauryas and Satavahanas, 325 B.C.-A.D. 300 (Orient Longmans, Calcutta, 1956), p. 3, ff., takes the position that Chandragupta first overthrew the Greek rule, then in a bloody war overcame the large army of the Nanda king. This solution which takes Chandragupta's accession at 323 B.C., appears somewhat mythological. And if it were so, then why was Cāṇakya needed to install him on the throne? Rather than the question of why did Chandragupta become the monarch so soon, perhaps scholars should have asked: Why did it take him so long?

40. Geiger (n.1, above), p. xxiii, ff.
41. Raychauduri, *Age of*, pp. 22-3.
42. Lessing and Wayman, trs. (n. 33, above), p. 67.
43. Raychauduri, *Age of*, p. 23.
44. Raychauduri, *Ancient*, p. 61.
45. Lessing and Wayman, trs. (n. 33, above), p. 67.
46. This article first appeared in *Studia Missionalia*, Vol. 28 (1979), and was reprinted in *Buddhist Insight*, essays by Alex Wayman, Ed: George Elder (Delhi, 1984).
47. Wayman, *Buddhist Insight*, pp. 40-41, note; alluding to André Bareau, *Les premier conciles boudhiques* (Presses Universitaires de France, Paris, 1955), p. 89.
48. *Memoirs of the Research Department of the Toyo Bunko*, No. 22 (Tokyo, 1963), pp. 57-106.
49. For some theory of the lay bodhisattva, cf. Alex and Hideko Wayman, *The Lion's Roar of Queen Śrīmālā* (Motilal Banarsidass, Delhi, 1990), p. 8.
50. This is the edition of Oxford University Press, second edition, 1959.
51. Cf. Radhakrishna Choudhary, *Vrātyas in Ancient India* (Varanasi, 1964), Chap. II, esp. p. 32.
52. Wayman, *Buddhist Insight*, pp. 13-14.
53. I use the edition of the Pāli Publication Board, Bihar, 1959, ed. by Bhikkhu J. Kashyap.
54. Cf. Louis Renou, *Études sur le Vocabulaire du Ṛgveda*, 1st series, (Institute Français d'Indologie, Pondichery, 1958), pp. 11-2, for important observations on the Vedic meaning of *nāman*. It is the reality, never just appearance; and he cites the *Ṛgveda* (VI, 75, 8) for "the name of the sacrificial chariot is 'oblation'", thus making the 'name' equivalent to the continuing *karma*. And he mentions that in the *Atharvaveda* the 'name' got magical associations.
55. *Visuddhimagga of Buddhaghosācariya*, ed. by Henry Clarke Warren and revised by Dharmananda Kosambi (Cambridge, Mass., 1950), p. 477, *nāman ti ārammaṇābhimukhan namanato vedanādayo tayo khandhā* ('name' means the three aggregates, feelings, and so on, by bending toward the sense object).
56. This is in Vasubandhu's commentary on *Abhidharmokośa*, VII, 13a, among comments on the 'aspects' of *Duḥkha-satya*: La Vallée Poussin, tr. of this chapter (Paris, 1925), p. 32.
57. Alex Wayman, *Analysis of the Śrāvakabhūmi Manuscript* (Berkeley, 1961), pp. 130-1; here also on the 'aspects' of *Duḥkha-satya*.
58. *Abhidharmakośabhāṣyam of Vasubandhu*, Ed: P. Pradhan, rev. by Aruna Haldar (Patna, 1975), p. 400.9-10.
59. Cf. Alex Wayman, *The Buddhist Tantras* (Delhi, 1990), essay, "Buddhist Genesis and the Tantric Tradition," pp. 25-7, for the theory that the original 'earth essence' (*pṛthivīrasa* or *bhūmirasa*), which was the first 'food' of the beings in the 'first eon', was ambrosial (*amṛta*). This must be the second definition of *amata* (the Pāli equivalent) in the *Pali-English Dictionary* by T.W. Rhys Davids and William Stede. Their first definition, a noun, takes this *amata* as practically equivalent to *nirvāṇa*.

60. Cf. *Nāgārjuna's Letter to King Gautamīputra,* by Lozang Jamspal, et al (Delhi, 1978), pp. 40-1.
61. R. Choudhary, *Vrātyas* (n. 51, above). He made as much use as possible of Hauer's *Der Vratya* in the German language, which was the only serious study of this difficult topic up to Choudhary's work.
62. Choudhary, *Vrātyas,* p. 55.
63. R.N. Dandekar, "Vaisnavism and Śaivism," in *Ramakrishna Gopal Bhandarkar as an Indologist* (Bhandarkar Oriental Research Institute, Poona, 1976), p. 73.
64. T.W. Rhys Davids, *Dialogues of the Buddha,* Part I (London, 1956), pp. 109-10.
65. Arthur A. Macdonell, *A History of Sanskrit Literature* (Motilal Banarsidass, Delhi, 1962), pp. 202-3.
66. Dr. Madan Mohan Singh, "Authenticity of the Buddhist Pāli canon for the Cultural History of Pre-Maurya Bihar," *The Journal of the Bihar Research Society,* Vol. XLVI, 1960, Parts I-IV (Dr. T.P. Chowdhury Memorial Volume), pp. 64, 67.
67. Malalasekera, *Dictionary,* Vol. Two, entry, S.V.

3

Nāgārjuna: Moralist Reformer of Buddhism

This paper is about an extraordinary and elusive individual named Nāgārjuna, in almost two millenia of Buddhist movements most appealed to as an authority next to the Buddha, and whose life and principal activities fall almost entirely in the second century A.D. This Nāgārjuna should not be confused with one or two, and later, persons having the same name.[1] Much has been written about this personage and his Mādhyamika school of Buddhism;[2] and to write about his life and works requires coming to conclusions about controversial issues. A number of details to be brought out herein are readily available in previous modern works, and

Reprinted from *Studia Missionalia,* Vol. 34. Universita Gregoriana Editrice. Roma. 1984.

there are a few conclusions of my own. To clarify my findings, first there is the time of Nāgārjuna and the major events of his life; then his relation to the Prajñāpāramitā literature, followed by the determining of his role as a moralist reformer of Buddhism. Finally, I will treat the understanding of Nāgārjuna and his works. Along the way I decide that a class of scriptures called *Bodhisattva-piṭaka* in fact preceded the Mahāyāna, but that after the time of Nāgārjuna the rival Yogācāra accepted the *Bodhisattva-piṭaka* as Mahāyāna.

The Time of Nāgārjuna

In order to reconcile the various well-considered theories about dating the Mādhyamika Nāgārjuna, it must be accepted that he lived to a ripe old age in full possession of his faculties. This is the implication of both the Chinese and the Tibetan versions of his life (not devoid of some legendary overlays). See Watters:[3] "Nāgārjuna had the secret of long life, and had attained an age of several centuries with his mental faculties still flourishing, when he voluntarily put an end to his life . . ." We need not believe in this 'several centuries' or the Tibetan version, 'six hundred years',[4] to get the point that he did live uncommonly long, so over 90 years, while maintaining vigor of mental faculties.[5] Therefore, his life covers almost an entire century; and taking this as a fact is helpful for solving certain thorny problems of religious history at a time which poses considerable problems for Indian historians.

Murti is right, I believe, in saying—along with previous writers—that the Mādhyamika system was perfected by Nāgārjuna at A.D. 150, which should be construed "by 150 A.D."[6] Robinson is also right in placing Nāgārjuna around 113-213 A.D.[7] A more recent article by Ruegg agrees with E. Frauwallner and various other scholars on a date c. 150-200,[8] which is also acceptable, n.b., for a period covering Nāgārjuna's activities on behalf of Mahāyāna Buddhism. Therefore, I do not accept a dating put forth by various scholars, e.g. Hikata, dating Nāgārjuna in the latter half of 2nd century to the first half of 3rd century, A.D.[9]

The dating accepted accounts for the general agreement that Nāgārjuna wrote two moralizing verse works to a Śātavāhana king. This king is referred to in Tibetan as his friend Bde Spyod ('joyful practice'), which in Sanskrit would be Udayana or Udayī,[10] thus in the sense of 'prosperity', and associated with a story about grammar, which implicates the South India *Kātantra* grammar by Śarvavarman, who is placed in the Śātavāhana area.[11] One of these two verse works, the *Suhṛllekhā* (Friendly Epistle) presents the early Buddhist ('Hīnayāna') basis of ethical theory.[12] The other, the *Ratnāvalī* (precious garland), presents the later Buddhist ('Mahāyāna') basis of ethical theory.[13] All evidence points to a king of the Śātavāhana line.[14] The one who fits by date and a nickname meaning 'prosperity' is Śrī Yajña Śātakarṇi. The Indian historian Raychauduri may be cited: "Gautamīputra Śrī Yajña Śātakarṇi, who probably ruled towards the close of the second century A.D., was the last great king of his house. After his death, the Śātavāhana empire began to fall to pieces."[15] In agreement, Nilakantha Sastri states, "Perhaps the best known Śātavāhana ruler is Śrī Yajña Śātakarṇi (c. A.D. 170-99)."[16] His son Vijaya is the one referred to by Sarkar and Mishra, mentioning the Prākṛta inscription in the 6th regnal year of Gautamīputra Vijaya Śātakarṇi on the unique lime stone pillar.[17]

Nāgārjuna probably did not long survive the passing of Śrī Yajña Śātakarṇi, who it seems had invited Nāgārjuna in his old age to Andhra Pradesh (his native state ?). But the name Nagarjunakonda—applied to an art center built up by a subsequent empire called Ikṣvāku—is medieval, perhaps employed a thousand years later for the place (the Srī Parvata, 'glorious mountain') which legend associated with Nāgārjuna. Unfortunately, the only inscriptional reference to Nāgārjuna found so far has been at Jaggayyapeta, about 30 miles north-west of the celebrated Buddhist-decorated stūpa Amaravati, and dated in characters of the sixth or seventh century A.D.[18] Still, we cannot categorically deny that what was later called Nagarjunakonda was once Nāgārjuna's retreat-residence in his old age.

Major Events of Nāgārjuna's Life

I. *Early life.* According to the Chinese biography attributed to Kumārajīva, as Nāgārjuna's mother gave birth to him under the tree called 'Arjuna' he received the name Arjuna. Since he received guidance from the serpents (*nāga*), he was called Nāga, and so his name became Nāgārjuna.[19] This account seems quite reasonable. On the other hand, the legend in Tibetan sources that he was born in a Brahmin family, had a birth prophecy that he would live only seven years, and so was placed in the monastery at Nālandā—where he was raised and educated—is suspect.[20] The reason for doubting this account is that it is replete with details and deity names that go with the much later tantric Nāgārjuna. On the other hand, the Tibetan legend about Āryadeva, who was Nāgārjuna's most famous disciple is helpful for speaking of the 'southern *ācārya* Nāgāhvāya' (where 'Nāgāhvāya' means 'the one called Nāga') who, together with Āryadeva, served the Dharma at Nālandā.[21] This supports a conclusion that agrees with other evidence to the effect that Nāgārjuna became a leading monk-teacher at Nālandā, and that later on so did Āryadeva. But there appears no solid evidence as to where Nāgārjuna had his early monastic training, be it in the south somewhere or at Nālandā itself. In any case, his Buddhist education was presumably complete at c. 130 A.D., for a birth c. 105 A.D.; and undoubtedly the young Buddhist savant deeply impressed his peers and elders. So, about that time he presumably became a monk-*ācārya* at Nālandā.

II. *At Nālandā*. It is my theory that Nāgārjuna was a monk-professor here for the approximate period 130-150 A.D. Sankalia reports that the Nālandā University was formalized in the fifth century, A.D.[22] However, debates were a regular feature in the Saṅghārāmas which in time grew into the university.[23] We must presume that Nāgārjuna excelled in these debates in which distinguished Buddhists had participated. Out of these debates must have emerged his treatise *Vigrahavyāvartinī* (Warding off the contention), as well as his *Mūla-Madhyamaka-kārikā* (Fundamental verses on the middle [view]), the *Yukti-ṣaṣṭikā* (Sixty verses on the principles), the *Śūnyatā-saptati* (Seventy verses on voidness), and others. Thus, by 150 A.D., Nāgārjuna had laid the foundation for the Mādhyamika school. As to some of the topics of debate, one should observe that at this time there has grown up a school of Abhidharma (doctrinal exegesis), mainly referred to by the names Sautrāntika (taking the scriptures as primary) and Vaibhāṣika (relying on commentary).[24] The Vaibhāṣika is the continuation of the Sarvāstivādin sect of Buddhism, while the Sautrāntika is a re-evaluation of the old scriptures and a philosophical precursor of the Mahāyāna.[25] The Vaibhāṣika was mainly centered in Kashmir after the time of Aśoka.[26] During the patronage of Kaniṣka, the Kashmir school prospered and attracted quite distinguished Buddhist teachers from elsewhere. Among these Vaibhāṣika teachers,

Dharmatrāta may well have been prominent in the generation just preceding Nāgārjuna.[27] The Sautrāntika school was centered especially in Gandhāra. Dutt explains the name Sarvāstivādin as applied to those with the principal tenet that the 64 real elements of 'name' (*nāma*) and 'form' (*rūpa*) exist forever (*sarvam asti*).[28] We shall see that Nāgārjuna in his most important Mādhyamika treatise, the *Mūla-Madhyamaka-kārikā* (MMK), takes pains to combat the realist position, e.g. of those who speak in terms of "It exists" (*asti*) and "It does not exist" (*nāsti*). Therefore, he seems to combat the Vaibhāṣika point of view, but he also rejects the realist position generally.

III. *Also at Nālandā.* In order to justify the legend that Nāgārjuna had an important role in promoting Mahāyāna Buddhism, one must presume that he turned his mind to various new scriptures that were showing up and which of course would all be available at Nālandā. In those days, these scriptures glorifying a person called the 'Bodhisattva' did not have the expression 'Mahāyāna-sūtra' as part of their titles. To understand how such innovations were possible, one should go back to some centuries. A debate about the status of the Arhat, the old Buddhist hero—who had supposedly purified himself and was therefore liberated from phenomenal life had torn apart the Buddhist monk community, leading to a partition into sects.[29] It seems that the then new sect called Mahāsāṅghika allied itself with the layman activities of constructing and honoring stūpas, and began making theological arguments for these activities, as though the stūpa represented the supramundane Buddha.[30] This sect also pushed an old canonical doctrine that the mind is intrinsically pure but covered with adventitious defilements, which in time would lead to the theory that all sentient beings have the potentiality of Buddhahood.[31] Nāgārjuna's Nālandā period was a volatile era in Buddhist history when Buddhism began to spread in China and when there were great numbers of converts to Buddhism.[32] For these new converts the old canon—whether the four Nikāya in Pāli of Southern Buddhism, or the roughly equivalent four Āgama of Northern Buddhism—seemed not adequate. The new age demanded a new kind of Buddhist literature. Those who did the composing were not beholden to the Arhat ideal, but came up with the Bodhisattva—the new Buddhist hero, who patterned his career upon the Buddha, and so also aimed at enlightenment, while having compassion for people at large. In short, people were told that they too could become Buddha. They should take the Bodhisattva vow and then practice six 'perfections' (*pāramitā*). In time, the scriptures that espoused this sort of practice would be called 'Mahāyāna sūtras'. But it seems that the six that are in these works called 'perfections' occurred first in a list without the word 'perfection' (*pāramitā*). Thus, an enormous scripture that expands upon the early so-called Hīnayāna' materials, called *Saddharma-smṛtyupasthāna-sūtra* and preserved in the Chinese and Tibetan canons contains material on these six. This is in the verse extract from that scripture called *Dharmasamuccaya*, where Chaps. XXII-XXVII have verses devoted to *dāna* (giving), *śīla* (morality), *kṣānti* (forbearance), *vīrya* (striving), *dhyāna* (meditation). and *prajñā* (insight),[33] which in the scriptures that add '*pāramitā*' become the six perfections. However, the compiler of the *Dharmasamuccaya*, Avalokitasiṃha, appears to have rearranged the order of verses from their positions in the original scripture,[34] and so may well have had the Mahāyāna order of the six *pāramitā* as a guide. In any case, in the new scriptures—verse or prose—dealing with the six *pāramitā* was collected, or newly composed in works, called *Bodhisattva-piṭaka*; and I am convinced that one work of this character—the *Bodhisattva-piṭaka-sūtra*,[35] which is preserved in both Chinese and Tibetan, was available at Nālandā in the decade before 150 A.D. This is because a successor work, the *Akṣayamatinirdeśa-sūtra* was apparently translated into Chinese by Lokakṣema in the lost Mahāsamnipāta collection in the later Han dynasty, i.e. in the last quarter, 2nd century A.D.[36] Lokakṣema also made the first translation into Chinese of the *Aṣṭasāhasrikā Prajñāpāramitā Sūtra*, in A.D. 178-9, and it is extant.[37] Below, I shall discuss Nāgārjuna's possible relationship with the latter *sūtra*.

IV. *Old age*. Then in his old age, Nāgārjuna was invited—perhaps invited back—to South India, where a Śātavāhana king may have built a monastery for him, where he wrote two verse works addressed to that king. And finally, where his most famous disciple, the Ceylonese Āryadeva studied with him and in the third century wrote the celebrated *Catuḥśataka*. Nāgārjuna died c. 200-202 A.D.

Nāgārjuna and the Prajñāpāramitā Literature

I. *The legend*. The Tibetan tradition depicts Nāgārjuna as rescuing the 100,000-lined Prajñā-pāramitā scripture from the serpent-spirits

(Nāga).[38] The Chinese version has the Nāgas supplying him with scriptures, but without naming them.[39] These unnamed scriptures must be of the innovative kind, because there was at that time no need to resort to serpent-spirits for the early Buddhist scriptures or for the Abhidharma treatises. For initially evaluating this legend, I shall consider the theories of two modern authors— Robinson and Vetter.

a. Robinson in his section "Nāgārjunism and the Prajñā-Pāramitā-Sūtras" and referring to the MMK as the '*Middle Stanzas*' first cites various modern and ancient authorities who thought that Nāgārjuna systematized in his MMK the central theory of the Prajñāpāramitā literature, stated to be 'voidness' (*śūnyatā*), or that he might even have had more to do with this literature, now difficult to determine. To assess such judgments, Robinson makes a comparison between the *Aṣṭasāhasrikā* and the MMK giving as reason, "since if it [the *Aṣṭa*] is connected with Nāgārjuna, he depends on it, not it on him". Robinson's procedure consists in taking terms such as *prajñā* and *dharmadhātu*, and observing their occurrence in the MMK as contrasted with the *Aṣṭa*. He concludes that "Nāgārjuna and the Sūtra were in fundamental agreement on all topics that they have in common . . . They differ radically in style, though each is systematic in its own way."[40] Notice that Robinson starts with the premise that the *Aṣṭa* and the MMK could not have the same author, and on this basis defends the Mahāyāna tradition, i.e., that Nāgārjuna's Mādhyamika treatises agree with the Prajñāpāramitā texts. However, many persons have noticed authors who employ more than one style in their various writings. Even the present writer with only modest talent has written in contrasting styles and articles with almost completely different bibliographical references.[41] When it comes to a religious genius like Nāgārjuna, it appears only the very human trait of modern writers, however intelligent, to reduce the capability attributed to him down to the amount possessed by the modern writer himself or herself. While I find Robinson's approach to the two texts to be intelligent, it does not appear to solve any problem.

b. Vetter in his article, "A Comparison between the Mysticism of the older Prajñā Pāramitā Literature and the Mysticism of the Mūla-Madhyamaka-kārikās" has a promising approach in terms of the "psychological" mysticism in Meister Eckhart's works. Worth citing is Vetter's remark: "The issue is not so much experience as the abandonment of all finite experience so as to be open thereby for the eternal . . ."[42] We shall see below that the *Aṣṭa* has a comparable statement near the beginning of the scripture. Undoubtedly, this kind of mysticism is to be found in the Prajñāpāramitā literature (PPL).[43] Speaking of "Nāgārjuna's method and aim in the MMK" Vetter says, "Nāgārjuna does not hail from the PPL, yet may have known some of the latter's doctrines." Again worth citing is Vetter's remark: "Nāgārjuna's originality put briefly consists in his demonstrating the doctrine supportive of a mystical goal about the voidness of all entities in *argumentative* fashion." However, when Vetter tries to support his statement that Nāgārjuna may have known some doctrines of the PPL, he can only notice MMK, XXIV, 8 about a lower and a higher truth mentioned only once; and the unique mention of the Bodhisattva path in MMK, XXIV, 32.[44] It is clear that Vetter finds very little to associate Nāgārjuna with the PPL. I find much more.[45]

II. *Introducing the Aṣṭasāhasrikā.* To further evaluate the legend about Nāgārjuna and the PPL, I shall translate a passage from the *Aṣṭa* near its beginning along with my comments. After the traditional opening remark found generally in Buddhist scriptures, this text gets down to business. The Bhagavat (the lord) announces to Subhūti:[46]

> Explain eloquently, Subhūti, to the Bodhisattva great beings, starting with the Perfection of Insight, how the Bodhisattva great beings go unto the Perfection of Insight.

Why "starting with the Perfection of Insight"? This remark implies preceding scripture about the six Perfections, of which the Perfection of Insight is the sixth; but one can start with the sixth. It was pointed out above that the theory of six perfections has been worked up in a preceding literature called *Bodhisattva-piṭaka*, and that one work of this kind, still preserved in Tibetan and Chinese, the *Bodhisattva-piṭaka-sūtra* contains adequate treatment of each of the six. The scripture then introduces Śāriputra, whom the early Buddhist texts had declared to be the chief disciple in 'insight' (Pāli, *paññā*). Upon hearing this announcement by the Buddha, Śāriputra had the thought:[47]

> Will the Venerable Subhūti, the elder, by himself, by his own employment of the power of eloquence about insight, by his

> own foundation of the power of eloquence about insight, expound the Perfection of Insight to the Bodhisattva great beings; or, by the might (*anubhāva*) of the Buddha?

The scripture then mentions that by the might[48] of i.e., empowerment by the Buddha, Subhūti knew what Śāriputra was thinking, i.e., temporarily had the supernormal power of knowing the make-up of Śāriputra's mind. Subhūti pointed out that everything taught by disciples (*śrāvaka*) of the Bhagavat is human work (*puruṣakāra*) of the Tathāgata. This is because, they heard the Dharma from the Tathāgata should hold it in mind, train in it, and realize its true nature (*dharmatā*); so that, as 'sons-of-the-family' (*kulaputras*) expounding the true nature, they will not contradict the true nature. Subhūti's remark shows that all his explanations are claimed to be either what was taught by the Buddha or to be consistent therewith. Hence, it is indeed by the might of the Buddha that Subhūti expounds the Perfection of Insight. Then Subhūti reminded the Bhagavat of his instruction to explain eloquently to the Bodhisattva great beings; and continued:[49]

> As to the Bodhisattva when one mentions a 'Bodhisattva', of what *dharma* is this the designation, to wit, 'Bodhisattava'? Bhagavat, I do not see that *dharma*, to wit 'Bodhisattva'. Besides, I do not see a *dharma*, to wit, 'Perfection of Insight'. Since, Bhagavat, I myself do not find, do not apprehend, do not observe a Bodhisattva or a Bodhisattva-dharma; and do not find, do not apprehend, do not observe the Perfection of Insight, what Bodhisattvas shall I advise and instruct in what Perfection of Insight?

The scripture continues, explaining that it is precisely the Bodhisattva whose mind does not despair, turn off in defeat, and get fearful, at the hearing of it, who should be instructed in the Perfection of Insight; that if he stays this way (i.e., fearless), this is his precept and instruction. Although Conze[50] summed up the Prajñāpāramitā literature by the two principles, including, one should become a Bodhisattva, and there is no such thing as a Bodhisattva—in fact, the scripture here has a somewhat different message. It announces three kinds of 'not finding': (1) One may not find or apprehend a Bodhisattva, or any other being, or any object at all, by an advanced *yoga* state which some Buddhist texts call 'non-constructive insight' (*nirvikalpa-prajñā*), and which is like dreamless sleep that has no object; but which here Subhūti can experience only by the might of the Buddha. (2) One may not find or apprehend a Bodhisattva, or something else, because one is not able to, as Subhūti admits, "I myself (*so 'ham*) do not find; that is to say, Subhūti lacks the 'eye of Dharma' (*dharma-cakṣus*)[51] which perceives in beings their spiritual level, and needs the Buddha's might to make up for the inability. (3) One may not find another Bodhisattva, because one is fearful or closes the eyes through timidity.[52] Subhūti continued:[53]

> Besides, Bhagavat, the Bodhisattva great being who is operating in the Perfection of Insight is cultivating the Perfection of Insight, should so train that he in training would not think in terms of the 'Mind of Enlightenment' (*bodhicitta*) [i.e., not with it as object of thought].[54] Why so? As follows: That citta is not a citta; the true nature (*prakṛti*) of the citta is (transparently) clear.[55]

There started a dialogue between Śāriputra and Subhūti. Śāriputra now asked him:[56]

> Given that the citta is not a citta, does that citta exist?

This was a natural question for Śāriputra to pose, because his insight is a discriminative one (*pratyavekṣaṇā*), hence between alternatives such as 'existence', and 'non-existence', an insight invaluable for ethical problems, such as the 'better' and the 'worse'.[57] But Subhūti refuses to answer the question as so worded and counters with a question of his own:[58]

> Now, Venerable Śāriputra, given a non-citta, can one find or apprehend there in the non-citta an existing thing or a non-existing thing?

This could be said by Nāgārjuna, because he wrote in his MMK, XV, 7:

> / kātyāyanāvavāde cāsti[ti] nāstīti cobhayaṃ /
> / pratisiddhaṃ bhagavatā bhāvābhāvavibhāvinā //
> In the 'Precepts of Kātyāyana' the Bhagavat, who has comprehended presence and absence has rejected both "It exists" and "It does not exist."

Furthermore, the scripture's use of the word 'there' (*tatra*) indicates the realist philosophy (n.b. not the scripture's own-viewpoint, but in the question), because Nāgārjuna's MMK, II, 2, shows the realist position on motion, rejected in that chapter, namely, *ceṣṭā yatra gatis tatra* ("Where there is movement, at that place is the gait"). That is to say, the realist believes that an event must happen in a place.[59] Śāriputra responded to the question only by saying, "Not that" (*na hy etad*), which is ambiguous, namely, by either answering the question's content, or denying the question itself. So Subhūti asked him:[60]

> Venerable Śāriputra, well then, was it a suitable or relevant question for you, to wit, '*Can one find or apprehend there in the non-citta an existing thing or a non-existing thing?*'

Śāriputra, by his own sharp insight, catches on that this drift of conversation has happened, because of the way he framed his original question, i.e., in terms of existence. So, instead of answering Subhūti's question, he asks this:[61] "*Now, Venerable Subhūti, What is this 'non-citta'?*" And Śāriputra is rewarded, because Subhūti helped by the Buddha's might responded:[62] "*A non-citta is changeless, unconstructed.*"

Previously we learned that the 'Mind of Enlightenment' is being referred to as this 'non-*citta*'. This amounts to saying that the Mahāyāna rite, referred to innumerable times in that literature, called 'Generating the Mind of Enlightenment' (*bodhicittotpāda*) does not work as it seems literally by the words. This is because if the Mind of Enlightenment is changeless and unconstructed, one must construe 'generating' consistent with what neither arises nor passes away. This forces the meaning of 'Generating the Mind of Enlightenment' to involve a reaching of it with one's mind. That is indeed the language of the initial announcement to Subhūti when the Bhagavat said: Explain eloquently. . . how the Bodhisattva great beings go unto the Perfection of Insight (*prajñāpāramitāṃ niryāyur*), thus employing a verb of motion (*yā—*). Nāgārjuna did not reject motion in his MMK, Chap. II, but rather rejected the realist notion of horizontal motion, described by locatives in the sense of "at".[63] However, the *Aṣṭa* does here exhibit the mysticism that Vetter referred to; and one must concede that 'reaching' the Mind of Enlightenment, which is 'changeless' is equivalent to what

Vetter mentioned, namely, to be 'open' to it by abandonment of finite experience. But then, is that not what Nāgārjuna was talking about throughout his MMK, and the purport of the 'voidness of all entities'? Thus, no matter if Nāgārjuna did not in his MMK mention the word *prajñā* even once![64] Indeed, that this portrayal of voidness was put in argumentative fashion makes it amount to 'discriminative insight' (*pratyavekṣanā-prajña*), and so Tibetan texts are not wrong in referring to MMK as '*Mūlaprajñā*'.[65] This is explained with illustration in the *Kāśyapa-parivarta*:[66]

> Kāśyapa, it is this way: for example, when two trees are rubbed together by the wind, and fire arises (from the friction), (that fire) having arisen burns the two trees. In the same way, Kāśyapa (when given things are analyzed) by the most pure discrimination (*pratyavekṣaṇā*), the faculty of noble insight is born, and (that fire) having been born, (it) burns up that most pure discrimination itself.

Of course, this language of being 'born' is metaphorical and does not conflict with Nāgārjuna's or the *Aṣṭa*'s language in terms of 'non-arising'. The same proposition can be stated without using such words as 'born'. It means that when one analyzes the *dharmas* in the manner of MMK, this is a kind of 'insight' which is transformed into another kind (Perfection of Insight) which replaces the former kind. In short, it amounts to saying that before someone could write the *Aṣṭasāhasrikā Prajñāpāramitā Sūtra*, he should go through the kind of analysis found in Nāgārjuna's *Mūla-Madhyamaka-kārikā*. According to the purport of that passage of the *Kāśyapa-parivarta*, Robinson was wrong in his theory that if the *Aṣṭa* and MMK are related, MMK depends on the *Aṣṭa*, nor the reverse. It is inescapable that the *Aṣṭa* was composed by someone centuries after Gautama Buddha. Historically and in terms of subject matter, the *Aṣṭa* could be composed by Nāgārjuna himself if the dating presented previously holds up, and since the *Aṣṭa* was not translated into Chinese until A.D. 178-179. Much more study of the *Aṣṭa* in comparison with Nāgārjuna's works is necessary before this can be a firm conclusion. However, as is to be pointed out below, it is consistent with the legend of Nāgārjuna. Probably the biggest stumbling block to this theory of *Aṣṭa* authorship is the usual depiction of the *Aṣṭa* as the 'earliest' Mahāyāna scripture, sometimes placed as early as the 1st century B.C.[67] However, a candid look at the very beginning of the *Aṣṭa*, not to speak of the remainder, shows a situation quite to the contrary, namely, that it implicates a previous literature of the type later to be called 'Mahāyāna scripture'. But the *Aṣṭa* is of supreme importance in the movement that would be called Mahāyāna ('Great Vehicle'). A composition date of mid-2nd century is consistent with this role.

III. *Again the legend.* It is now possible to see more in the legend that Nāgārjuna rescued the 100,000-lined Prajñāpāramitā from the Nāgas. If in his old age, Nāgārjuna was invited by the Śātavāhana[68] king—even more if he had been a native of Andhra governed by the regime—is that why that text is titled in Sanskrit *Śatasāhasrikā Prajñāpāramitā*, why another text attributed to Nāgārjuna is entitled *Prajñāśataka*, why Āryadeva's chief work is entitled *Catuḥśataka*, why Nāgarjuna's grammarian friend Vararuci writes a work entitled *Gāthāśataka*?[69] Someone in high authority must have been at least initially in charge of the expansion of the *Aṣṭa* into the largest, most massive of the PPL. The only candidate in sight for such a role is Nāgārjuna himself. Therefore, I must explain the significance of the genitive form *āryaśāradvatasya* that occurs in his *Ratnāvalī*, Chap. 4, v. 85.[70] The group of monks that expanded the *Aṣṭa* —working, I presume in far north-west India or originally in Kashmir?[71]—had a trademark, to wit, spelling the name of Buddha's celebrated disciple in the form Śāradvatīputra instead of Sāriputra. Śāradvatiputra is the form in the 100,000-lined version; also in the *Aṣṭādaśasāhasrikā* the *Saptaśatikā*, and the *Suvikrāntavikrāmi-paripṛcchā*, among the PPL. The name in this form appears in the Kashgar Manuscript of the *Saddharmapuṇḍarīkasūtra*; and also in two moralistic works: the *Āryakuśalamūla-paridhara-sūtra* and the *Buddhapiṭaka-duḥśīlanigrāhīnāma-mahāyāna-sūtra*. The *Akṣayamatinirdeśa-sūtra* uses this form of the name, which is also found in the story collections *Avadānaśataka* (2nd cent.) and *Divyāvadāna*.[72] If indeed Nāgārjuna is the 'ghost writer' of the *Aṣṭasāhasrikā Prajñāpāramitā*, he would be logically the one to head the group to expand this to the 100,000 lines; and while this activity might not have been completed in his life, the impetus was sufficiently powerful to go to its proper end. For such an endeavor, I suppose that he left Nālandā about 150 A.D. to set into motion this expansion of the PPL. Why such a large scripture, which Conze finds to be full of repetitions?[73] It seems reasonable that the aim was to establish this kind of literature on a firm basis, by making it bigger than other scriptures.

Nāgārjuna as a Moralist Reformer of Buddhism

This involves three questions: How is he a moralist? How is he a reformer of Buddhism? What does this have to do with Mahāyāna Buddhism?

(*a*) Readers of his two treatises addressed, it appears, to the Śātavāhana king, namely, the *Suhṛllekhā* and the *Ratnāvalī*, cannot help noticing Nāgārjuna's heavy stress on morals. Since this stress is ubiquitous in those works, mere citations cannot adequately portray it. However, as a mere indication, I shall cite *Suhṛllekhā* from a recent translation:[74]

> Always practice the path of the ten virtuous deeds (performed) through body, voice and mind; refrain from alcohol; and also delight in a wholesome livelihood.(5)

This treatise also has the usual Buddhist threats directed to the sinner that he will fall to hell. As an indication of the *Ratnāvalī*'s teachings, here is my rendition of Chap. I, verses 12-13:[75]

> The one who, disrespectful of the highway of the Illustrious Doctrine which is bright with giving, morality, and forbearance, wanders along wrong roads of the Daṇḍaka forest with bodily torment; enters the terrible, lengthy wilderness of Saṃsāra (cyclical life), which has uncountable persons as its trees while his limbs are licked by wild creatures, his defilements.

The *Ratnāvalī* is apparently addressed to a king who has expressed his willingness to learn the Buddhist doctrine; so Nāgārjuna defines the enlightened king in a number of verses. He also predicts hell (Chap. II, v. 20) for the fool who deeming himself wise rejects the Dharma; and in other verses brings in the Mādhyamika viewpoint. In terms of our later-mentioned 'viewpoint' and 'context of practice' the *Suhṛllekhā* expounds the 'context of practice' while the *Ratnāvalī* achieves a balance between the two.

(*b*) As to being a reformer of Buddhism, this goes with the testimony of the Tibetan author Tāranātha, whose work as translated has this passage: "After that, *Ācārya* Nāgārjuna nourished the

Law [i.e., Dharma] and spread extensively the Mādhyamika system. He greatly helped also the *śrāvakas,* particularly by expelling from the monastery those *bhikṣus* and *śramaṇeras,* who had violated their discipline and yet became much influential within the *saṅghas.* It is said that they numbered about eight thousand."[76] However, since in his day there were a number of Buddhist sects—in later times the number was said to be 'eighteen'—it is hardly believable that all these Buddhist sects could have accepted him as their head, in the sense of a pope. In order to have had such a role of being instrumental in ousting sinful monks and novices, said to number eight thousand, Nāgārjuna would reasonably have been the abbot of a large monastery of a sect that was later on called 'Hīnayāna' (lesser vehicle), and probably the number of those expelled was inflated. Previously, I have reported Nāgārjuna's strong moralist bent, which is consistent with Tāranātha's exposition. While the information is only sketchy, our previous finding that Nāgārjuna lived a very long life with complete faculties, makes it quite reasonable that in his later years he would be a kind of 'elder statesman' called in for his advice in troubling situations. Another way in which he could be considered a reformer is through his Mādhyamika treatises, especially the MMK, because these set forth a rigorous standard of intellectual examination—a sort of knocking out the cobwebs of the wordy exegesis known as the Vaibhāṣika system with its interminable lists of features (*dharma*) of numerous existing things or situations. I believe that he conducted this massive assault on the realist position, whether Buddhist or otherwise, by his MMK and the several other Mādhyamika treatises. He made contact with early Buddhism by championing the sermon to Kātyāyana, wherein Buddhist Dependent Origination (*pratītya-samutpāda*) was declared to avoid the extremes of "It exists" and "It does not exist"; and he identified this dependent origination with voidness (*śūnyatā*). Therefore, his void is efficient.

(*c*) As to Nāgārjuna's role in the Mahāyāna, if we accept his 2nd century A.D. dating, it is clear, as was already noticed, that certain scriptures, later to be called '*Mahāyāna-sūtra*', preceded his own compositions.[77] But, the usual scholarly writing about the matter, placing the earliest Mahāyāna in the 1st century B.C., confuses the 'Bodhisattva, doctrine' with Mahāyāna. It is as though the scripture's talk of Bodhisattvas, as happens in the *Aṣṭa,* renders it *per se* a Mahāyāna scripture. Yet, observe the opening of the *Aṣṭa*: It sets the scripture at Rājagṛha on the 'Vulture Peak' with 1,250 monks—all of them Arhats, as the auditors of the Bhagavat, the Buddha. These Arhats are described with the usual stock expressions, their 'task accomplished', etc. including calling them 'great serpents' (*mahānāga*). Hence, Subhūti and Śāriputra are counted as Arhats. But there are no Bodhisattvas in attendance. The implication is that Subhūti is given the task of convincing the Bodhisattvas to listen to the teachings. In contrast, when we examine the opening of the 100,000-lined version, we find both the Arhats in the same number and described by the same stock expressions and a large group of Bodhisattvas in attendance. It is as though in the interval between the composition of the two scriptures a reconciliation had occurred, whereby the Arhats and the Bodhisattvas could attend the same meeting. It also shows that the 'ghost writer' of the *Aṣṭa* has scant sympathy for the Mahāsāṅghika downgrading of the Arhat as well as some reservations about the previous theories of the Bodhisattva. Dube's book contains a well-written chapter "The Ideal of the Bodhisattva" alluding to the controversies in the *Kathāvatthu* and the role of the Mahāsāṅghikas and their sub-sects in developing the theory of the Bodhisattva as a forerunner of the Mahāyāna.[78] Indeed, the general recognition that the Mahāsāṅghikas developed this Bodhisattva theory, at least in its early formulations, is undoubtedly correct. This was a movement aiming to pattern one's conduct after the example of Gautama Buddha, who according to tradition had taken a vow to become a Buddha in the presence of a former Buddha several eons prior and had been a Bodhisattva in his various lives, until he became fully enlightened in his last life as Śākyamuni. Gradually building up this theory of the Bodhisattva along with a doctrinal theory of Buddha's potentiality in each sentient being, this movement came to a full blooming with the *Bodhisattva-piṭaka* scriptures. At this time, there was a theory about 'generating' the Mind of Enlightenment (*bodhicitta*) and then attending to virtues, the well-known six 'perfections' (*pāramitā*). In the light of Nāgārjuna's long life, some of such scriptures may have been composed when he was very young. Nāgārjuna, as a reformer may well have aspired to put together the fragmented Buddhist sects by combining the Mahāsāṅghika's Bodhisattva with the Āryasthavira's Arhat. This, the next-best thing to restoring original Buddhism, would require a theory of 'stages' (*bhūmi*)—what was missing from the *Bodhisattva-piṭaka* scriptures.[79] In his *Ratnāvalī* (Chap. 5, v. 41, ff.) he gave the theory of ten Bodhisattva stages with the names used in the subsequent *Daśabhūmika-sūtra*; while the *Aṣṭa* had clarified the distinction of the Bodhisattvas who cannot be turned back, i.e., are irreversible (*avinivartanīya*),[80] in contrast to the beginning Bodhisattvas. Once there are 'stages' there is a path, and it is possible to justify a 'great vehicle' (Mahāyāna). Buddhism in its subsequent literature never tired of working with the theory of ten Bodhisattva stages, even in the tantric period associating tantric attainments at certain stages. This shows that the *Bodhisattva-piṭaka* scriptures precede Mahāyāna, even though one of them, the *Bodhisattva-piṭaka-sūtra* was preserved by being included during the Mahāyāna period in the scriptural collection *Ratnakūṭa*, wherein it is called *Ārya-Bodhisattvapiṭaka-nāma-mahāyāna-sūtra*. This suggests that the primitive *Ratnakūṭa* may have been the original *Bodhisattva-piṭaka* scripture collection.[81] It may well have been the rival Mahāyāna group, called Yogācāra, that upgraded these scriptures,[82] while bypassing the Prajñāpāramitā literature. It had become increasingly difficult to understand Nāgārjuna and his works.

Understanding Nāgārjuna and His Works

I. *The viewpoint and the context of practice.*[83] Native Tibetan works make a distinction of the 'doctrinal part' (*darśana-bhāga*) and the 'practical part' (*caryā-bhāga*) for classifying Buddhist treatises. The 'doctrinal part' can be called the 'viewpoint'; and the 'practical part' can be called 'context of practice'. These Tibetan works apply this classification to what are called the three 'wheels of Dharma', which are: (1) that of early Buddhism, the 'wheel of the four noble truths'; (2) that of the Mādhyamika, the 'wheel of lack of characteristics', i.e., voidness; (3) that of the Yogācāra, the 'wheel of intensive analysis'. In the case of the first 'wheel', the doctrinal part is the Abhidharma, the practical part is the Vinaya. In the second 'wheel', the doctrine part is the 'six sets of Mādhyamika principles'—the first five being Nāgārjuna's *Mūla-Madhyamaka-kārikā, Yuktiṣaṣṭikā, Vaidalya, Śūnyatāsaptati, Vigrahavyāvartanī*. There was a dispute about the sixth, a so-called *Vyavahāra-siddhi* being included in the old lists.[84] Later, it has been held there are only five, i.e., dropping the *Vyavahāra-siddhi*; while in the Gelugpa sect, the *Ratnāvalī* is counted as the sixth. Āryadeva's *Catuḥśataka* is in sixteen chapters, of which the first eight show the 'practical part' by the steps of the path, and the second eight show the 'doctrinal part' or 'viewpoint' by selflessness of personality and of *dharmas*. In the third 'wheel', the *Sūtrālaṃkāra* is said to expound the doctrine and practice in equal measure; while in Asaṅga's *Bodhisattvabhūmi*, the *tattva* chapter teaches doctrine, and the remaining chapters practice.

A celebrated Tibetan savant called Sa-pan in his treatise on the 'three vows' (Tib. *Sdom gsum*) has harsh words for persons who will cite such a passage as "There are no beings or Buddhas" (a frequent sentence of the PPL) and draw inferences therefrom, because this is a 'viewpoint' divorced from the context of contemplation and conduct. And has equally harsh words for persons who cite such a passage as "Faults will arise if you doubt" (a statement in texts on meditation) when lacking the (guru's) view.[85]

Among the six Bo hisattva 'perfections' mentioned previously, the first five are frequently called 'means' (*upāya*), and are supposed to be combined with the sixth 'insight' (*prajñā*). Among the many passages which emphasize this, I shall render just one—the words of the *Kāśyapa-parivarta* (n. 42):[86]

> O Kāśyapa, for example, just as the king who is governed by ministers performs all the duties of king, so also the insight of the Bodhisattva which is governed by the means performs all the acts of the Buddha.

Thus, when Nāgārjuna wrote those treatises, the MMK and so on (the 'sets of Madhyamaka principles') and emphasized 'insight' as the 'viewpoint' (*darśana*), in fact, the view of voidness, he seemingly neglects the practical 'means', but does deal with this in other works, such as the *Ratnāvalī*. Previous writers on the Mādhyamika who mainly concerned themselves with the MMK and identified its subtle dialectical analysis with Nāgārjuna's position (whether or not they thought it was his 'own' position), failed to grasp Nāgārjuna's many-sided genius—just as one cannot appreciate the talents of a master chef from just one of his prepared dishes, even if every dish of the master has his superior touch.[87] Some writers on the Mādhyamika portray his MMK as an intellectual exercise in denying everything.[88] They might be surprised to learn that in the Buddhist path tradition, it is possible to treat 'Perfection of Meditation' as calming (*śamatha*), the 'Perfection of

Insight' as discerning (the real) (*vipaśyanā*); and then Nāgārjuna's Mādhyamika principles can be counted as a kind of discerning to be combined with calming (the mind).[89] Our peers might well ask: Well, then, what is the meditative practice that goes with the Mādhyamika analysis? This appears to be explained in a Mahāyāna scripture, the *Śrī-mālādevīsiṃhanāda*, in our translation:[90]

> When he matures any sentient beings by meditation (*dhyāna*), he matures them by having an undisturbed mind, his mind not straying outside and having no mistake of mindfulness. By not being side-tracked though he acts for a long time or speaks for a long time, he protects and matures their minds. They having been so matured stay in the Illustrious Doctrine. This is his Perfection of Meditation.

Hence, the text of practice of the MMK is that Nāgārjuna does not give up, rather stays with it to the end without straying from his purposeful discourse. The MMK kind of contemplation aims at a fruit; so Āryadeva (*Catuḥśataka*, k. 350 cd):[91] "When he sees the objective domain as selfless, the seed of the phenomenal world ceases."

II. *The role of commentaries.* There is an extensive array of commentaries if besides those on Nāgārjuna's known works, one includes the ones on the PPL and on the summation treatise *Abhisamayālaṃkāra*. Here I must confine myself to those on Nāgārjuna's MMK, and for practical purposes to the Candrakīrti commentary, the *Prasannapadā*, because this has been available in the original Sanskrit language. And here I shall only concern myself briefly with the theories of two modern authors—Stcherbatsky and Streng.

(*a*) Stcherbatsky in his book *The Conception of Buddhist Nirvāṇa*[92] translated Candrakīrti's commentary on MMK, I, 'Examination of Causality', and on MMK, XXV, 'Examination of Nirvāṇa'. His introduction made use of the four 'theory-systems' (*siddhānta*), the Vaibhāṣikas, the Sautrāntikas, the Yogācāras, and the Mādhyamikas. He also made some comparisons with the European and Hindu systems of philosophy. de Jong on good grounds rejects Stcherbatsky's translation of *śūnya* by "relative" and shows that due to this initial error and attempting to defend it, Stcherbatsky departed "from the spirit of Nāgārjunian philosophy".[93] But then it appears that Stcherbatsky's explanations were not helped by having translated those two chapters of the *Prasannapadā* (the 'clear-worded'). Perhaps, after all, the Tibetans who assiduously and devotedly pored over Candrakīrti's commentary, and the Western scholars like Stcherbatsky who diligently applied their philological and linguistic skill to this commentary expected too much if they thought that thereby they could understand Nāgārjuna's MMK better. Candrakīrti, of course, would not hold that the student must read his commentary in order to understand the MMK, for that would imply that no one had ever understood it previously. The precisely opposite seems to be the case: Candrakīrti expected the student to have already understood the MMK in terms of the words of the verses, and to read his commentary for his system, usually called Prāsaṅgika-Mādhyamika. This should have been noticed from his kind of commentary, which is not grammatical, i.e., on the words in their order of occurrence, but the kind of commentary which says more. Furthermore, the *Prasannapadā* has more difficult Sanskrit terms than does the MMK, so if one cannot understand the MMK by its words, it appears useless to go to the more complicated commentaries.

(*b*) Streng in the chapter "Nāgārjuna's Dialectical Structure" of his book[94] attempts to relate Nāgārjuna's language to modern language analysis, such as is done by Ludwig Wittgenstein; and to the theory of two truths. Thus, Streng is not against commentaries, but it should be his own commentary. Streng is strong in formulations from a history-of-religions training, or a philosophical background that apparently frowns on the mere citation, and would be 'on top of' the topic by paraphrases and further explanations. This was a problem that the 'ghost writer' of the *Aṣṭasāhasrikā Prajñāpāramitā* also concerned himself with, because he gave Śāriputra—the role of the disciple who could figure it out by his own keen insight. Conze concluded that the PPL regularly subordinated Śāriputra to Subhūti,[95] but the foregoing extract from the *Aṣṭa* would rather suggest that Śāriputra's insight was subordinated to the Buddha's might which enables Subhūti to explain the Prajñāpāramitā, and that without this help Subhūti's insight would hardly be a match for Śāriputra's. The *Aṣṭa* in fact puts the revelation over human insight; and so it is Nāgārjuna's battle with the Vaibhāṣika, the commentarial exegesis by insightful persons. de Jong, when writing a review article on Streng's book is sensitively appreciative of Streng's accomplishment, but does point out some drawbacks, especially that the book would have profited by taking into account the commentaries.[96] I could add that one does not understand Nāgārjuna better by studying the works of Immanuel Kant or Ludwig Wittgenstein—worthwhile as are these works in their own right as topics of study. Nāgārjuna and his works are understood better, I maintain, by studying these works and the early Mahāyāna scriptures with which he was reasonably familiar, and which, if we accept the Buddhist traditions about this matter, he had a hand is promoting. Even so, I believe Streng deserves congratulations for his intuitive language applied to the discussion of MMK, and I do not deny the feasibility of East-West comparisons. But one can make them in a better and in a worse way.

III. *The theory of two truths.* In that same book, Streng cites his own translation of MMK, XXIV, 10 ab (*vyavahāram anāśritya paramārtho na deśyate*), "The ultimate truth is not taught apart from practical behavior;" and adds: "so, according to Nāgārjuna, the structure of apprehending Ultimate Truth is crucially related to the patterns of thinking available to man-in-existence".[97] Notice that Streng mis-rendered the term *vyavahāra.*[98] Consequently, also when presenting his interpretation he misses the mark. This is because the term *vyavaḥāra* is being employed here for 'conventional terminology', the corpus of human words. The point is that before one can teach the wordless absolute (*paramārtha*) one must have learned human words and then employ certain words for the purpose. According to the native Tibetan commentary by Tsoṅ-kha-pa on Candrakīrti's *Madhyamakāvatāra,* the line constitutes a rejection of the (Yogācārin's) Vijñānamātra theory, i.e. that it is possible to have a pure consciousness free from words.[99] Besides, to understand Nāgārjuna's employment of the 'two-truth' theory, one should know about the teaching of three truths in the *Bodhisattva-piṭaka-sūtra,* previously referred to and its successor scripture, the *Akṣayamatinirdeśa-sūtra.* In a previous article I compared these two scriptures on this matter.[100] Here I shall mention only my findings from the *Bodhisattva-piṭaka-sūtra:*

> On the three truths (*satya*) of the bodhisattva (*saṃvṛti-paramārtha-,* and *lakṣaṇa-*), conventional truth (*saṃvṛti-satya*) is as much as there is of mundane convention; and is expression with letters, speech, and discursive thought. When consciousness does not course, how much less the letters—that is absolute truth (*paramārtha-satya*). Truth of

> characteristics (*lakṣaṇa-satya*) is as follows: all characteristics are one characteristic, and one characteristic is no characteristic. On the bodhisattva's skill in truth: the bodhisattva does not weary of expressing conventional truth; he does not fall into direct realization of absolute truth, but matures sentient beings; he reflects on the truth of characteristics as no characteristic.

In short, it appears that there was circulating in Nāgārjuna time this scriptural theory of a third truth—of characteristics as no characteristic, apparently underlying the other two truths, where 'characteristics' means 'characters of differentiation'.[101] As I pointed out in that same article,[102] this may explain Nāgārjuna's MMK, XXV, 19: "There is no differentiation (*viśeṣaṇa*) of Saṃsāra from Nirvāṇa; there is no differentiation of Nirvāṇa from Saṃsāra." That is to say, Nāgārjuna rejected the 'all characteristics' of the Sarvāstivādin that serves to differentiate Nirvāṇa from Saṃsāra in the way the discriminating mind does. With the 'eye of insight' there is one characteristic, or sameness; because with this 'eye' one sees *dharmas*, e.g., their dependent origination.[103] But Nāgārjuna did not say that Nirvāṇa and Saṃsāra are the same. By insisting that Nirvāṇa and Saṃsāra have no characteristic of differentiation, he pointed to 'no characteristic', perhaps implicating the Mahāyāna Nirvāṇa, called 'Nirvāṇa of no-fixed abode' (*apratiṣṭhita-nirvāṇa*). After the time of Nāgārjuna, the Mādhyamika insisted there were just two truths, thus supporting my conclusion that the three-truth theory preceded Nāgārjuna.[104]

Final Considerations

It is difficult to reconstruct the original circumstances in which Nāgārjuna's Mādhyamika system and the Prajñāpāramitā literature first arose. There is a penchant for attributing greater influence than was actually the case in a great man's lifetime when in later centuries his influence was obviously so enormous. Still, it is possible to state some features of that era, the 2nd century, A.D. spanned by this remarkable religious teacher. Adamantly opposed to the realistic interpretation of the Buddhist Abhidharma, he aspired to mend the original split in the Buddhist ranks over the Arhat attainment by combining their 'best'. He accepted the basic Buddhist tenets held by all the Buddhist sects. From the school of the elders (Ārya-Sthāvira), he especially took the discourse to Kātyāyana and the Arhat attainment. From the school of the Mahāsāṇghikas he took their Bodhisattva teachings. In this sense of taking the 'best' from both sides, he was a reformer of Buddhism. Pursuant to this goal, besides his finely wrought abbreviated works to which he gave his name, he used another side of his genius as the 'ghost writer' of the *Aṣṭa*, probably then put out or arranged for a set of verses based on it, that is called *Prajñāpāramitā-ratna-guṇa-saṃcaya-gāthā*.[105] Then, in agreement with the legend that he rescued the 100,000 version of PPL from the Nāgas, in fact he led a group of monks in the expansion of the *Aṣṭa* to this greatly increased form, using as trademark for this and related scriptures the name spelled Śāradvatīputra for the Buddha's celebrated disciple. He added the theory of Bodhisattva 'stages', ten in number.[106]

But as time went on, and the Mahāyāna became fully blown with a wealth of scriptures and treatises called *śāstra*, it became more and more difficult to understand Nāgārjuna's MMK and what the PPL was aiming at. His own treatises were laconic, resistant to understanding; while the PPL's initial success at being the largest scripture collection made it unrealistic for reading throughout. Because of the difficulty of this kind of discourse, false attributions were made to it, both by Buddhist and Hindu critics. In particular, the charge that the stress on 'voidness' lent a negative character to these treatises, allowing for a neglect of the 'means', the virtues of giving, etc., was probably behind the success, at least for some time of the rival Yogācāra championed by Asaṅga. In this rival tradition, the old *Bodhisattva-piṭaka* scriptures were declared to be Mahāyāna, effectively hiding their pre-Mahāyāna status as regards the Mādhyamika Mahāyāna. The Yogācāra by-passed the bulk of the Prajñāpāramitā literature in favor of the earlier canon and a rational Mahāyāna.

Later, Atīśa arrived in Tibet in 1042 A.D. bringing a lineage of combining the two viewpoints. Tsoṅ-kha-pa (1357-1419) wrote it this way in his *Lam rim chen mo*. The Bodhisattva precepts are the six perfections (going back to the *Bodhisattva-piṭaka* literature), but for 'Perfection of Meditation' (*dhyāna-pāramitā*) one uses Asaṅga's system mainly from his *Śrāvakabbhūmi*; for the 'Perfection of Insight' (*prajñā-p.*) one uses Nāgārjuna's Mādhyamika system, especially the 'set of Mādhyamika principles'; and finally there are the four persuasions (*saṃgraha-vastūni*).[107] This formulation apparently omits the ten Bodhisattva stages as well as the paths in the technical summation of the PPL.[108]

REFERE]NCES

1. The later persons with the name Nāgārjuna are an alchemist and a tantrist. Nāgārjuna's disciple Āryadeva also had his name used by a later tantrist, as did the Mādhyamika Candrakīrti by a later tantrist. The three tantrists were followers of the *Guhysamājatantra* and fall in the eighth and ninth centuries A.D.; cf. A. Wayman, *Yoga of the Guhyasamājatantra* (Delhi, 1977), p. 96.
2. Cf. Chr. Lindtner, *Nagarjuniana; Studies in the Writings and Philosophy of Nāgārjuna* (Copenhagen, 1982); David Seyfort Ruegg, *The Literature of the Mādhyamika School of Philosophy in India* (Wiesbaden, 1981); K.S. Murty, *Nāgārjuna* (Delhi, 1978).
3. Thomas Watters, *On Yuan Chwang's Travels in India* (London, 1905), Vol. II, p. 201.
4. *Tāranātha's History of Buddhism in India,* tr. from the Tibetan by Lama Chimpa and Debiprasad Chattopadhyaya (Simla, 1970), p. 110, where one account says, 600 minus 29.
5. There are other examples in Buddhist history: Śubhakarasiṃha (637-735 A.D.) of Orissa, India, who came to China at the age of 80 and translated for almost 20 years; Rin-chen-bzaṅ-po (958-1055), the great Tibetan translator, who continued translating up to the end; and there are undoubtedly more examples.
6. T.R.V. Murti, *The Central Philosophy of Buddhism* (London, 1955), p. 87.
7. Richard H. Robinson, *Early Mādhyamika in India and China* (Madison, 1967), p. 22. This is actually the Japanese scholar Hākuju Ui's theory, as pointed out by Murty, *Nāgārjuna* (n. 2, above, p. 16).
8. D. Seyfort Ruegg, "Towards a Chronology of the Madhyamaka School," *Indological and Buddhist Studies,* ed. by L.A. Hercus et al (Canberra, 1982), p. 507.
9. Ryusho Hikata, *Suvikrāntavikrāmi-Paripṛcchā-Prajñāpāramitā Sūtra,* ed. with introductory essay (reprint by Rinsen Book Co., Kyoto, 1983), pp. LII-LIII.
10. *Tāranātha's History* (n. 4, above), Introductory, p. 9, n. 22.
11. Cf. *'Kātantra'* entry in K.V. Abhyankar and J.M. Shukla, *A Dictionary of Sanskrit Grammar* (Baroda, 1977), pp. 114-5.
12. Now there is the translation, *Nāgārjuna's Letter to King Gautamīputra,* tr. from Tibetan by Lozang Jamspal, Ngawang Samten Chophel, and Peter Della Santina (Delhi, 1978).
13. Much of the text was recovered and edited by Giuseppe Tucci along with English translation in *Journal of the Royal Asiatic Society,* 1934 (pp. 307-25) and 1936 (pp. 237-52; 423-35). Now there is Michael Hahn, *Indica et Tibetica; Nāgārjuna's Ratnāvalī,* Vol. I, Sanskrit, Tibetan, Chinese (Bonn, 1982). Hahn (p.5) states that the best complete translation is that of Christian Lindtner in the Danish original version of his Nagarjuniana; however, the English version is not in Lindtner's book (n. 2, above).
14. Cf. the list of Andhra Śātavāhana kings in K. Gopalachari's contribution in *A*

Comprehensive History of India; Vol. Two (The Mauryas and Śātavahanas, 325 B.C.-A.D. 300) Calcutta, 1957, pp. 326-7.

15. H.C. Raychaudhuri, in *An Advanced History of India*, Part I (Ancient India) (London, 1960), p. 172.
16. Nilakanta Sastri, *A History of South India*, second edition (Oxford University Press, 1958), p. 92.
17. H. Sarkar and R.N. Misra, *Nagarjunakonda* (Archaelogical Survey of India, New Delhi, 1980), pp. 13 and 74.
18. Debala Mitra, *Buddhist Monuments* (Calcutta, 1971), p. 211. Murty, *Nāgārjuna* (n. 2, above) p. 62, points out that since Nāgārjuna is credited by both Indian and Tibetan sources as having gotten the Amaravati stupa enclosed with a railing, plus the fact of the Jaggayyapeta inscription, it is possible that he first lived in or near Dhanyakataka-Amaravati and later on Sri-parvata.
19. M. Walleser, *The Life of Nagarjuna from Tibetan and Chinese Sources* (reprint in India, Delhi, 1979), p. 25. Murty, *Nāgārjuna* (n. 2, above), pp. 53-4 suggests it might have been a name adopted later, which also makes good sense.
20. Walleser, *The Life of Nagarjuna*, p. 6.
21. *Tāranātha's History*, p.126.
22. H.D. Sankalia, *The University of Nalanda* (Delhi, 1972), pp. 51-2.
23. Sankalia, *The University*, p. 44.
24. According to *Tāranātha's History*, p. 109, a certain Suviṣṇu built 108 temples at Nālandā for preserving the *Abhidharma*. As this is said in the chapter on Nāgārjuna, the implication is that this happened at that time.
25. Cf. Th. Stcherbatsky, *The Conception of Buddhist Nirvāṇa* (Leningrad, 1927; reprinted Shanghai, China, 1940), pp. 27-31, for a brief exposition of the Vaibhāṣikas and Sautrāntikas.
26. Nalinaksha Dutt's essay "Buddhism in Kashmir" in *Gilgit Manuscripts*, Vol. I (Srinagar, 1939), pp. 9-10.
27. Dutt, "Buddhism in Kashmir" pp. 22-3.
28. Dutt, "Buddhism in Kashmir," p. 8.
29. Cf. the theory of Arhat limitation among the theses of the Mahāsāṅghikas in Andre Bareau, *Les sectes bouddhiques du Petit Véhicule* (Saigon, 1955), pp. 64-5.
30. Cf. Akira Hirakawa, "The Rise of Mahāyāna Buddhism and its Relation to the Worship of Stupas," *Memories of the Research Department of The Toyo Bunko*, No. 22 (1963).
31. Cf. Alex and Hideko Wayman, *The Lion's Roar of Queen Śrīmālā*; a Buddhist Scripture on the Tathāgatagarbha Theory (New York, 1974), p. 42.
32. See E. Zurcher, *The Buddhist Conquest of China* (Leiden, 1959), pp. 30, ff. for the Church of Loyang in the latter half of the second century. For the routes taken for the spread of Buddhism in this early period, cf. William Willetts, *Chinese Art*, I (Penguin Books, 1958), Map 4, "The Silk Road from China to the Roman Orient (c. 100 B.C.–200 A.D.)".
33. *Dharma-Samuccaya*, 3e Partie (Chapitres XIII à XXXVI) par Lin Li-kouang; Révision de André Bareau, J.W. de Jong et Paul Demiéville (Paris, 1973), pp. 252-332.
34. Lin Li-kouang, *L'Aide-Mémoire de la Vraie Loi* (Paris, 1949), P. Demiéville's introduction, p. viii.
35. I am indebted to the 1976 doctoral dissertation by Kusumita Priscilla Pedersen at Columbia University entitled "The *Dhyāna* chapter of the *Bodhisattva-piṭaka-sūtra*" for the Japanese views about this scripture and works called *Bodhisattva-piṭaka*.

36. Cf. Alex Wayman, "A Report on the *Akṣayamatinirdeśa-sūtra* (Buddhist Doctrinal History, Study 2)," in *Studies in Indo-Asian Art and Culture*, Vol. 6, ed. by Lokesh Chandra, (New Delhi, 1980), esp. pp. 217-21, for the reasons of assigning priority to the *Bodhisattva-piṭaka-sūtra*. Pedersen in her dissertation (n. 35, above), reports (p. 15) that in an article in *Journal of Indian and Buddhist Studies* (Tokyo), Vol. 22, No. 2, March 1974, pp. 578-86, Jikidō Takasaki decides after finding many correspondences between those two *sūtras* as well as the scripture *Dhāraṇīśvararāja* that the *Bodhisattva-piṭaka-sūtra* is later than the other two. However, I still maintain my reasons as valid, especially that the *Bodhisattva-piṭaka-sūtra* is large, rambling, and loosely knit, because it was earlier and took a long time to get to its present state; while the *Akṣayamatinirdeśa-sūtra* being a tightly-knit, acutely organized version of the same material is later and composed in a relatively short time.
37. Cf. Lewis R. Lancaster, "The Chinese translation of the *Aṣṭasāhasrikā-Prajñāpāramitā-Sūtra* attributed to Chih Ch'ien," *Monumenta Serica*, Vol. XXVIII, 1969, p. 246.
38. Walleser, *The Life of Nagarjuna*, pp. 10-11.
39. Walleser, *The Life of Nagarjuna*, pp. 25 and 29.
40. Robinson, *Early Mādhyamika*, pp. 61-5.
41. Cf. A. Wayman, "The Gait (gati) and the Path (mārga)—Reflections on the Horizontal," *Journal of the American Oriental Society*, 105.3. (1985), containing my translation of MMK, Chap. II (on motion), an essay in philological style.
42. Tilmann E. Vetter, "A Comparison between the Mysticism of the older Prajñā Pāramitā Literature and the Mysticism of the Mūla-Madhyamaka-kārikās of Nāgārjuna," *Acta Indologica*, VI (Naritasan Shinshoji, 1984), p. 498.
43. Robinson, *Early Mādhyamika*, pp. 10-3, provides citations and his own views as to the applicability of the term 'mysticism' to the Mādhyamika. Also V.V. Gokhale, "Gotama's Vision of the Truth," *Brahmavidyā*, Vol. XXX (Adyar, 1966), refers to "Nāgārjuna's mysticism" and p. 116 points out that while Nāgārjuna has mystic appraisal of the "Great Truth" which the Buddha perceived, the commentator Bhavya (or Bhāvaviveka) takes a logical position and that another commentator, Candrakīrti, accordingly scoffs at him.
44. Vetter, "A Comparison," pp. 508-9.
45. So did Robinson, n. 40, above.
46. / pratibhātu te subhūte bodhisattvānāṃ prajñāpāramitām ārabhya yathā bodhisattvā mahāsattvāḥ prajñāpāramitāṃ niryāyur iti/ (from the edition publ. by The Mithila Institute, Darbhanga, 1960), p. 2.1-3.
47. / kim ayam āyuṣmān subhūtiḥ sthavira ātmīyena svakena prajñāpratibhāna-balādhānena svakena prajñāpratibhānabalādādhiṣṭhānena bodhisattvānāṃ mahāsattvānām prajñāpāramitām upadekṣyati utāho buddhānubhāveneti? / p. 2.4-6.
48. The term *anubhāva* is translated 'might' by dint of the context as well as by the Tibetan rendition *mthu*.
49. / bodhisattvo bodhisattva iti yad idaṃ bhagavann ucyate, katasyaitad bhagavan dharmasyādhivacanaṃ yad uta bodhisattva iti? /nāhaṃ bhagavaṃs taṃ dharmaṃ samanupaśyāmi yad uta bodhisattva iti /tam apy aham bhagavan dharmaṃ na samanupaśyāmi yad uta prajñāpāramitā nāma /so haṃ bhagavan bodhisattvaṃ vā bodhisattvadharmaṃ vā avindan anupalabhaṃāno 'samanupaśyan, prajña-pāramitām apy avidan anupalabhamāno 'samanupasyan katamaṃ bodhisattvaṃ katamasyāṃ prajñāpāramitāyām avavadiṣyāmi anuśāsiṣyāmi? / p. 3.5-10.

50. Eqward Conze, *The Prajñāpāramitā Literature*, 2nd ed., revised and enlarged (Tokyo, 1978), p. 7.
51. Cf. the essay of A. Wayman on "vision", first published in *Añjali*, Wijesekara volume (1970), now reprinted in *Buddhist Insight; Essays of Alex Wayman* (Delhi, 1984), pp. 156-7.
52. Cf. *Calming the Mind and Discerning the Real; Buddhist Meditation and the Middle View*, from the *Lam rim chen mo* of Tsoṅ-kha-pa, tr. by Alex Wayman (New York, 1978), p. 394, the citation from *Ārya-Mañjuśrī-vikrīḍita-sūtra*, including: "He does not, as does a timid man, close his eyes."
53. / punar aparaṃ bhagavan bodhisattvena mahāsattvena prajñāpāramitāyāṃ caratā prajñāpāramitāyaṃ bhāvayatā evaṃ śiksitayam / yathā / 'sau śiksyamānas tenāpi bodhicittena na manyeta / tat kasya hetoh? / tathā hi tac cittam acittam / prakṛtiś cittasya prabhāṣvarā / p. 3. 16-18.
54. According to Haribhadra's commentary, the *Āloka*, ed. by U. Wogihara, publ. by the Toyo Bunko, Tokyo, p. 38, the reason is that it (the 'Mind of Enlightenment') is far out-of-sight (*atyanta-parokṣatvāt*), hence not accessible to the mind considered as a 'sixth sense organ'.
55. According to Haribhadra's *Āloka*, p. 38, the term *prakṛti* has the [Sāṃkhya] sense of pre-genetic substance (*svabhāvo 'nutpādatā*); and *prabhāṣvara* has the sense of 'clear', i.e., free from qualification—the darkness of constructive thought completely blown away.
56. / asti tac cittam yac cittam acittam? / p. 3.20.
57. Śāriputra expounded the *Saṅgīti-Suttanta*, included in the *Dīgha-Nikāya* of the Pāli canon. This is a presentation of doctrines by one's, two's three's, and so on, up to ten's of doctrines; hence a discrimination by numbers.
58. / kiṃ punar āyusman śāriputra yā acittatā, tatra acittatāyām astitā vā nāstitā vā vidyate vā upalabhyate vā? / p. 3.21-22.
59. Cf. the article by A. Wayman, "The Gait" (n. 41, above).
60. / sacet āyuṣman śāriputra tatra acittatāyām astitā vā nāstitā vā na vidyate vā nopalabhyate vā, api tu te yukta eṣa paryanuyogo bhavati / p. 3.22-24.
61. / kā punar esā āyuṣman subhūte acittatā? / p. 3.25-26.
62. avikārā . . . avikalpā acittatā / p. 3.26-27.
63. As I show in the article, "The Gait" (n. 41, above).
64. As was pointed out by J.W. de Jong, "Emptiness", *Journal of Indian Philosophy* 2 (1982), p. 13.
65. As is the reference to MMK in the work of n. 52, above.
66. As translated by A. Wayman, in the work of n. 52, above, p. 405.
67. Cf. Har Dayal, *The Bodhisattva Doctrine in Buddhist Sanskrit Literature* (London, 1942), p. 44.
68. The name Śātavāhana probably means 'having a hundred conveyances', where the *śāta*; is the vṛiddhi form of *śata* in composition.
69. Cf. Michael Hahn "Vararucis Gāthāśataka—eine Analyse", in *Documenta Barbarorum*, p. 144.
70. Cf. Hahn's edition of the *Ratnāvalī* (n. 13, above), pp. 124-5.
71. For Kashmir as the state most prominently associated with Nāga-worship, cf. Dutt. "Buddhism in Kashmir" (n. 26, above), pp. 10-1.
72. Cf. A. Wayman, " A Report" (n. 36, above), pp. 212-3. For this spelling of the name in The *Astādaśasāhasrikā*, cf. Edward Conze's edition of this from the Gilgit manuscript, chapters 70 to 82 (Roma, 1974), pp. 85-91. For the same in the *Suvikrāntavikrāmi-paripṛcchā* see the Sanskrit text of this in Hikata (n. 9, above).

73. Cf. Conze, "Literature" (n. 50, above), p. 11.
74. Cf. the translation by Jamspal, et al (n. 12, above).
75. Using Hahn's edition of the *Ratnāvalī* (n. 13, above).
76. *Tāranātha's History*, p. 106.
77. A *Sūtrasamuccaya* (Compendium of Scriptures) has been attributed to Nāgārjuna, and a work of this title with his supposed authorship is preserved in Chinese and Tibetan; see Lindtner (n. 2, above), pp. 172-8, , for the list of scriptures cited therein. However, as the *Laṅkavatāra-sūtra* is cited several times, and the Mādhyamika Nāgārjuna surely precedes this scripture, it is highly unlikely that this *Sūtrasamuccaya* is by Nāgarjuna. Indeed, my own investigation, incorporated in the present essay, lead me to doubt whether he was interested in collecting passages in such manner from these 'Mahāyāna scriptures'. Besides, various titles in the list have as last member the term '*parivarta*', which means 'chapter' or 'section', hence implying scriptures in the Mahāyāna collections called *Mābāsamnipāta, Ratnakūta*, and *Avataṃsaka*. The fourth century, A.D. is the earliest possible period for such a compendium.
78. S.A. Dube, *Cross Currents in Early Buddhism* (New Delhi, 1980), pp. 151-73.
79. Dube, p. 168, refers to *bhūmis* (his fnt. 136 missing). In fact, the Lokottaravādin subsect of the Mahāsānghika is represented by the well-known *Mahāvastu*, but the 'stage' section therein (see J.J. Jones, *The Mahāvastu*, Vol. I, London, 1949, pp. 53, ff.) may be reasonably taken as later than Nāgārjuna's formulation of 'stages'. See Franklin Edgerton, *Buddhist Hybrid Sanskrit Grammar* (New Haven, 1953), p. 5, fnt. 13, agreeing with Winternitz (*History of Indian Literature*, II) that while the *Mahāvastu's* nucleus is as early as the 2nd century, it was later expanded, with additions of 4th century A.D.
80. Cf. Edward Conze, *Aṣṭasāhasrikā Prajñāpāramitā*, tr. into English (Calcutta, 1958), Chap. 17, "Attributes, Tokens and Signs of Irreversibility".
81. A.K. Warder, *Indian Buddhism* (Delhi, 1970), p. 357, makes virtually the same point.
82. Cf. *Saṃdhinirmocana Sūtra*, edition of Tibetan text and French translation by Eienne Lamotie (Louvain, Paris, 1935). Chap. IX (where the interlocutor is the bodhisattva Avalokiteśvara), containing four references to *Bodhisattva-piṭaka*, each time praising it as a corpus to be studied. The *Samdhinirmocana* is the basic Mahāyāna scripture for the Yogācāra, as founded by the master Asaṅga.
83. For this division into two 'parts', cf. Ferdinand D. Lessing and Alex Wayman, *Mkhas grub rje's Fundamentals of the Buddhist Tantras* (The Hague, Paris, 1968), pp. 81-99.
84. Lindtner (n. 2, above), pp. 94-9, refers to the rejection of the **Vyavahāra-siddhi* as one of the 'six sets of Mādhyamika principles' that is in Mkhas grub rje's work (n. 83, above), p. 87; but points out that Śāntarakṣita's *Madhyamakālamkāravrtti* cites six verses which are commented upon by Kamalasīla, who supplies the information that they are drawn from Nāgārjuna's **Vyavahāra-siddhi.* Lindtner then presents the six Tibetan verses and translates them. Kamalaśīla should easily recognize the verses to be from a work by Nāgārjuna, since the tantric Nāgārjuna like Śāntarakṣita and Kamalaśīla belongs to the eighth century, A.D. Since the verses deal with the efficacy of *mantra* (a tantric term), it may be concluded that the **Vyavahāra-siddhi* is by this later Nāgārjuna, and that is why the treatise is not cited in the standard Mādhyamika commentaries.
85. I noticed this when giving some help to Jared Douglas Rhoton, who completed a doctoral dissertation at Colombia University on this text (the *Sdom gsum*) by Sa-pan.

86. I draw this from my translation of the Bodhisattva section of Tsoṅ-kha-pa's *Lam rim chem mo,* namely *Ethics of Tibet* (Albany, 1991).
87. Thus A.K. Warder writes an essay, "Is Nāgārjuna a Mahāyānist?," in *The Problem of Truths in Buddhism and Vedānta,* Ed: M. Sprung (Dordrecht, 1973), with restriction to the MMK as the basis for his argument.
88. Yamakami Sogen, *Systems of Buddhistic Thought*(reprinted from the 1912 edition at Delhi, 1979), states, p. 194: "The fundamental doctrine of the *Mādhyamika* school has been imperfectly understood and grossly misrepresented by the so-called scholars of Buddhism in Europe, and latter-day India. Most of them give the appellation of 'Nihilism' to this school, simply because Nāgārjuna applied the term '*Śūnyatā*', or emptiness to express his conception of human life and truth. Śūnyatā, however, . . . does not imply 'nothingness'; it simply expresses 'the everchanging state of the phenomenal word,'. . ."
89. As in the part of Tsoṅ-kha-pa's work translated by A. Wayman (n. 52, above).
90. Cf. the translation (n. 31, above), p. 74.
91. Wayman, "Calming" (n. 52, above), p. 394.
92. Cf. n. 25, above.
93. J.W. de Jong, "The problem of the Absolute in the Madhyamaka school", *Journal of Indian Philosophy* 2 (1972), pp. 5-6. I may add that Stcherbatsky exhibits a translation fault that is indulged in by a number of other scholars, namely, to substitute a contextual implication of a term for the basic meaning when translating. But to my mind, the translation of *śūnya* by 'empty' is also faulty, since this English term connotes a simple, unqualified negation; but I translate the Sanskrit expression as 'void', because this English expression connotes a qualified negation, i.e., 'void of something' (without denying the rest). For example, in the case of the discourse to Kātyāyana—so important to Nāgārjuna—one could say that dependent origination is void of "It exists" and of "It does not exist". Hence, we can see Nāgārjuna's position that for a *dharma* to arise, this does not mean 'it exists'; and besides, if a *dharma* does not arise, this does not mean 'it does not exist'.
94. Frederick J: Streng, *Emptiness; A Study in Religious Meaning* (Nashville, 1967).
95. Conze, *The Prajñāparamitā Literature* (n. 50, above), p. 6.
96. de. Jong. "Emptiness" (n. 64, above).
97. Streng, *Emptiness,* p. 145.
98. A. Wayman's review article of Streng's book, "Contributions to the Mādhyamika school of Buddhism", *Journal of the American Oriental Society,* 89:1, Jan.-Mar., 1969, p. 148, has pointed this out.
99. Japanese photo ed. of Tibetan canons, Vol. 154, p. 70-4-5. The topic of language, in fact, 'designation' *(prajñapti)*, in the Mādhyamika is too large to treat here; cf. Jacques May, "Mādhyamika Philosophy," *Journal of Philosophy,* Vol. 6, 1978, pp. 240-1.
100. Cf. Wayman, "A Report" (n. 36, above), p. 219-21.
101. Cf. Genjun H. Sasaki, "The three aspects of truth in Buddhist epistemology," *Journal of the Oriental Institute,* Baroda, XIV, 3-4, March-June, 1965, pp. 1-16, for a discussion not treating the two scriptures per n. 100, above.
102. Namely, in Wayman, "A Report" (n. 36, above).
103. For the 'eye of insight' see A. Wayman's essay on 'vision', reprinted in *Buddhist Insight* (n. 51, above), p. 136; and his "Nescience and Insight According to Asaṅga", reprinted there, p. 210. Another scripture in the *Ratnakūṭa* collection called *Arya-pitāputra-samāgama-nāma-mahāyāna-sūtra,* states (Photo ed. of

Tib. canons, Vol. 23, p. 195-1-2): "He sees the profound *dharmas* when his eye of insight is pure [i.e., free from dust]" (*śes rab kyi mig rnam par dag par* 'gyur te / *des kyaṅ chos zab mo rnams mthoṅ bar* 'gyur ro /). Since the PPL is referred to as 'Profound', the eye of insight (*prajñā-cakṣus*) is needed to penetrate the PPL, also the Mādhyamika system.

104. Thus, none of the contributors to the volume on the two truths, edited by Sprung (n. 87, above), shows awareness of the theory of three truths. The *sūtra Pitāputra-samāgama* (n. 103, above) also states (p. 168-4-6): "Those are the conventional (*saṃvṛti*) and the absolute (*paramārtha*) truths; and there is no third truth" (*de ni kun rdsob bden daṅ don dam ste / bden pa gsum pa gaṅ yaṅ ma mchis so* /). Such a scriptural passage is an authority for subsuming the four noble truths under the two standard truths. Besides, the passage appears to reject the 'third truth' theory of the *Bodhisattva-piṭaka* scripture. But Whalen W. Lai, "Non-duality of the Two Truths in Sinitic Mādhyamika: Origin of the "Third Truth'," *The Journal of the International Association of Buddhist Studies*, 2:2 (1979), pp. 45-65, believes that the 'Third Truth' theory arose in China. Of course, it is in the *Akṣayamatinirdeśasūtra* translated within the *Mahāsamnipāta* collection into Chinese twice (first translation lost), as well as in the *Bodhisattvapiṭaka-sūtra* translated by the Chinese pilgrim Hsüan-tsang.

105. The Sanskrit text of the verses was first published by E. Obermiller in *Bibliotheca Buddhica* XXIX, 1937). After this text was furnished with corrections by E. Conze and F. Edgerton, Conze translated it (*Indo-Asian Studies*, Part I, ed. by Raghu Vīra, New Delhi, 1962). This is one of the various publications on the PPL produced by Edward Conze, performing a tremendous service to Buddhism. Later, Dr. Akira Yuyama, Tokyo, published detailed grammatical studies of this text, an outgrowth of his Canberra dissertation.

106. Previously I mentioned that Nāgārjuna's *Ratnāvalī*, Chap. 5, presents the ten Bodhisattva stages that are developed into the *Daśabhūmika-sūtra* (hence by a later 'ghost writer'). This was first translated into Chinese by Dharmarakṣa of the Western Tsin dynasty, A.D. 265-316. I agree with Lindtner (n.2, above), pp. 170-1, that Nāgārjuna is the author of the *Pratītyasamutpādahṛdayakārikā*, which has an organization scheme of the twelve-fold members also found in the *Daśabhūmika-sūtra*, but not with Lindtner's further theory that Nāgārjuna took it from that *sūtra*: the situation is probably the reverse.

107. The four persuasions are the last main topic of the *Bodhisattva-piṭaka-sūtra*, which concludes (at least in the Tibetan version) with a story of the former Buddha Dīpaṃkara. This account of the persuasions (the theory of drawing persons into the Buddhist fold) comes right after the extended treatment of the six 'perfections' (*pāramitā*). The four persuasions are summarized in the *Sutrālaṃkāra* (text edited by Sylvain Lévi); XVI, 72: *Giving* is the same (as "Perfection of Giving"); *Pleasant speech* is the teaching of those (Perfections); *Aim concern* is the inducing (of the candidate to performance); *Common aims* is one's own conformity.

108. This technical summation is the treatise *Abhisamayālaṃkāra*, which is commented upon by Haribhadra's *Āloka* (n. 54, above).

4

Doctrinal Affiliation of the Buddhist Master Asaṅga

This paper deals with controversial matters, because the life of Asaṅga is shrouded in mystery. His thorough use of the Āgamas, the Sanskrit equivalent (roughly speaking) of the Pāli Nikāyas, permits some intriguing, if not fascinating considerations of the old canon. The old identification by Hsüan-tsang of Asaṅga's early school as Mahīśāsaka is here newly discussed.

The first topic is to establish Asaṅga as a brilliant author. The section "Asaṅga and the Mahīśāsakas (first approach)" aims to prove Asaṅga's reliance on the Āgamas. The section "Asaṅga and the Mahīśāsakas (second approach)" deals with specialized tenets at-

Reprinted from *Amalā Prajñā: Aspects of Buddhist Studies,* P.V. Bapat Vol. Indian Books Centre, Delhi. 1989.

tributed to the Mahīśāsakas. The section "Asaṅga and the Mahīśāsakas (third approach)" comes to a conclusion about the name Mahīśāsaka.

Asaṅga, The Brilliant Author

The celebrated Buddhist master Asaṅga (or Āryāsaṅga) is accepted here as the brother (or half-brother) of Vasubandhu, author of the *Abhidharmakośa*, whom Asaṅga converted to the Mahāyāna according to Paramārtha's biography. Years ago, when discussing this matter in my *Analysis of the Śrāvakabhūmi Manuscript* (1961),[1] I decided Asaṅga's dates to be circa 375-430[2]; and his brother Vasubandhu's dates to be circa 400-480.[3] I have not seen any subsequent arguments by scholars to lead me to a different conclusion.

As to teachers, this chapter cannot deal with a controversy argued by older scholars of this generation whether Maitreya was a historical teacher of Asaṅga. To the Buddhists of Tibet and China in the past centuries, Maitreya undoubtedly meant the future Buddha. Tibetan tradition has associated Asaṅga with the "Maitreya books" (five in this tradition), and is correct at least to the extent of denying Asaṅga's authorship of the basic verse works, as is one of them, the *Sūtrālaṃkāra*.

Besides, by this personage Asaṅga, I mean the one who authored the entire bulky *Yogācārabhūmi*. This consists of seventeen *bhūmis* (the *Bahubhūmika*) and four comprisal sections called *saṃgrahaṇī* which in their sum are equal to the preceding seventeen *bhūmis*.[4] Here, two points deserve brief discussion: (1) single authorship of the entire work; (2) attribution to Maitreya in the Chinese canon. As to (1) it is untenable to hold that certain sections of the *Yogācārabhūmi* were written by different persons. It appears rather—and this will be treated below—that different parts of the work were composed at different times and not in the present order. Besides, the basic seventeen *bhūmis* were written in a way to stress *sūtra* (or, *āgama*), down-playing sectarian divergence. The large commentarial section *Viniścaya-saṁgrahaṇī* seems to have a different style simply because this is the last written, when Asaṅga established his own school. (It is a feature in Hinduism as well that such an author as Śaṅkara founded an individual school bv a commentary, in his case on the *Vedānta-sūtras*.) My reading over the years in the *Yogācārabhūmi* has led me to conclude that it is the same person writing throughout. In fact, he told his method of writing in the brief exposition of grammatical science (*śabdavidyā*), as *aṅgāṅgādhikaraṇa*[5] (the topic with its sequence of terms). Asaṅga is prosaic, and limits his own versification mainly to writing summation verses (*uddāna*) of the main terms of a section. (The *gāthā* were not his composition). As to (2) Hsüan tsang, believing that Maitreya had inspired Asaṅga, may have entered the name Maitreya in order to get a hearing for the work to ensure its study in his country, where the Buddhists mainly followed Sūtras, such as the Pure land ones, the *Avataṃsaka*, the Lotus Sūtra, and so on.

Of the five Maitreya books, Asaṅga is definitely associated with the *Mahāyāna-Sūtrālaṃkāra*, because the chapter titles of this work were utilized for chapter headings of the *Bodhisattvabhūmi* in the *Bahubhūmika*; and because Asaṅga explicitly mentions the *Sūtrālaṃkāra* in laudatory terms while explaining the name:[6]

> The commentary giving the meaning, exactly as it is of the *sūtras* expressed by the Tathāgata, is called '*Sūtrālaṃkāra.*' It is so, because, for example, a lotus does not give delight as it would when opened up as long as it is not opened up; . . . for example, a food does not give pleasure as it would when eaten as long as it is not eaten; . . . so also, the meaning of the *sūtras* expressed by the Tathāgata gives delight as it would when exposed (or, 'opened up,' 'analyzed') while it would not that way when (previously) not exposed. For that reason, it is called '*Sūtrālaṃkāra*'.

His terminology here, which I render "when exposed" (Tib. *rnam par phye ba*; S. *vibhajya*) is a bit earlier in his text when presenting the twelve kinds of explanation—said to be the Mahāyāna kind of explanation: "Among them, the exposing explanation is generally any explanation in the Mahāyāna *piṭaka*."[7] Just before this remark he said: "Among them, the secret explanation is generally any explanation in the Śrāvaka *piṭaka*."[8] Asaṅga's striking remarks here in part agree with Tucci's observation about the meaning of the word *alaṃkāra* in these titles, alluding to their authors, "to support their claim that the new ideas were all concealed in these venerable texts."[9] Asaṅga thus explains the word *alaṃkāra* as a pleasing versification of a body of scripture previously not versified. In any case, we cannot expect an author to refer to his own work in this manner; but granted that Asaṅga, like other authors, does make cross references in his *Yogācārabhūmi* with mere title mention and without praise.[10] So those scholars, who accepting Maitreya as a future Buddha and not a historical author, concluded that the *Sūtrālaṃkāra* must have been composed by Asaṅga, are wrong in their attribution on these grounds.

However, even though Asaṅga is not the author of the *Sūtrālaṃkāra* verses, he is associated with the work in the manner already mentioned to which one may add that he is the author of the prose commentary on the verses, that was edited along with the verses by Sylvain Lévi. The oldest extant commentary on the *Abhisamayālaṃkāra*—the one by Ārya Vimuktisena has a long citation from the prose commentary on *Sūtrālaṃkāra* XII, 9, concluding "ity ācārya-Asaṅgaḥ."[11] The catalogs of the Tibetan canon are not helpful for author of the prose commentary.[12] Cordier's catalog says the author is not mentioned. While the Tohoku catalog of the Derge Tanjur enters Vasubandhu as the author, the catalog prepared in Japan for the Peking Kanjur-Tanjur enters Vasubandhu in brackets, admitting that the author was not mentioned.[13] Nagao, *Index*, states that the version in the Chinese canon ascribes authorship of both the verses and commentary to Asaṅga.[14] Taking all these accounts together, there is no doubt that the prose commentary is by Asaṅga.

However, it is hardly acceptable that this *Sūtrālaṃkāra* commentary was his first work. Considering Asaṅga's system of cross-references, I have reconstructed the following order of his writing. First he wrote a manual of *yoga*, the *Śrāvakabhūmi* with its four *yogasthāna*, plus precepts of *yoga* called later the *Samāhitaḥbhūmi*. This may have been written around his 20th year. He conceived the plan of writing a large *Yogācārabhūmi* to include parts on the three levels of *prajñā*, the *śrutamayī*, *cintāmayī*, and *bhāvanāmayī*. For this purpose he collected terms, especially around *prajñā* in a division of his great work now called *Paryāyasaṃgrahaṇī*, and made a collection of *sūtra* material drawn from the four *Āgamas*, *Dīrgha*, etc., arranged in topics or categories like the *Saṃyukta-Āgama*, which is now called *Vastusaṃgrahaṇī*. Then he composed the three *bhūmis*, *Śrutamayī*, *Cintāmayi*, and *Bhāvanāmayī*. Showing such early promise as a shining light in his mid-twenties, whatever the precipitating events he turned to the Mahāyāna and was invited to write the commentary on the *Sūtrālaṃkāra*. He saw this as not interfering with his *Yogācārabhūmi* design, since such works anyway had a Bodhisattva appendix.[15] When he wrote the *Bodhisattvabhūmi* around 410 A.D. It was instantaneously successful, and arrangements were promptly made to translate it into Chinese, starting around 414 A.D. After the *Bodhisattvabhūmi* he completed the other *bhūmis* in the seventeen-*bhūmi* system, and composed the large exegesis section whose title is probably *Viniścayasaṃgrahaṇī.*[16]

Now, it can hardly be gainsaid that Asaṅga was a kind of religious genius, of extraordinary erudition. Hence, it is possible here within the space like the present one to give only a sketchy idea of some of the contents of Asaṅga's vast work. Among the four *saṃgrahaṇīs,* the *Viniścayasaṃgrahaṇī* is a commentary on the preceding seventeen *bhūmis* in their given order, which are: (1) *pañcavijñānakāyasaṃprayuktā bhūmi,* (2) *mano bhūmi,* (3) *savitarkā savicarā bhūmi,* (4) *avitarkā vicāramātrā bhūmi,* (5) *avitarkā avicārā bhūmi,* (6) *samāhitā bhūmi,* (7) *asamāhitā bhūmi,* (8) *sacittikā bhūmi* (9) *acittikā bhūmi,* (10) *śrutamayī bhūmi,* (11) *cintāmayī bhūmi,* (12) *bhāvanāmayī bhūmi,* (13) *śrāvaka bhūmi,* (14) *pratyekabuddha bhūmi,* (15) *bodhisattva bhūmi,* (16) *sopādhika bhūmi,* and (17) *nirupādhika bhūmi.* The *viniścaya* therefore presumes these seventeen and contains numerous controversial matters that Asaṅga either downplayed or did not mention at all in his *Bahubhūmika,* such as a spirited defense of the *ālayavijñāna* doctrine.[17] The part which comments on the *Bodhisattvabhūmi* is one-third of the whole and especially depends on the *Saṃdhinirmocana-sūtra.* The *Vastusaṃgrahaṇī,* which includes the *Vinayasaṃgrahaṇī,* is arranged by categories (*vastu*) such as *saṃskāras, āyatanas, pratītyasamutpāda,* etc. This is smaller in size than the *Viniścaya.* The last two *saṃgrahaṇīs, paryāya* and **vyākhyāna* (rather than catalog "*vivaraṇa*") are very small. Outside of the Bodhisattvabhūmi and the third of the Viniścaya commenting upon it, the rest of the Yogācārabhūmi is either directly based on Āgama Buddhism, or is an exegesis of it, with only rare obvious Mahāyāna elements. For example, in a separate paper, I included from the Paryāyasaṃgrahaṇī—a long list of similes of prajñā; these had no obvious Mahāyāna entries, because Asaṅga, according to the foregoing, wrote this part of his great work prior to his Mahāyāna period.[18] The nature of Asaṅga's prosaic writing—and it is consistent throughout—is such that it can easily become tedious to the reader; on the other hand, Asaṅga's genius exhibits itself in powerful touches, especially in the parts which interested himself the most. In the *Bodhisattvabhūmi,* I believe this is true of his *śīlapaṭala* (chapter on morality), and is why there were two independent commentaries on this chapter, and none on any other single chapter of the *Bodhisattvabhūmi*, translated into Tibetan. In other parts of the *Bahubhūmika*, I believe this power is exhibited in the *Samāhitabhūmi*, the *Śrutamayī bhūmi*, and the *Cintāmayī bhūmi*, none of which are available in edited Sanskrit.

After Asaṅga has completed the whole *Yogācārabhūmi*, it appears he was pressured to produce some smaller, easier works. For the Abhidharmists, he put out the *Abhidharmasamuccaya*; and for the Mahāyānists, the *Mahāyānasaṃgraha*. I suppose that both were dictated within a year, perhaps in much less time! It happens that in later times Asaṅga was mainly known for his *Bodhisattvabhūmi* and *Mahāyānasaṃgraha* due to the domination by the Māhāyāna in the later phase of Indian Buddhism. His whole work is available to readers of the Tibetan and Chinese versions; and through these languages one can get a more balanced picture of Asaṅga's writing.

My thesis about Asaṅga's doctrinal affiliation has a premise of this Āgama importance. So in pursuance of my object, I shall give a sketch of his *Śrutamayī bhūmi.*[19] This amounts to the five sciences (*vidyā* or *vidyāsthāna*), to wit, inner science (i.e. Buddhism), medicine, rules of debate, grammar and the arts; requiring hearing, retaining, rehearsing, and recalling. As to the last four, 'outer sciences', the only generous treatment is the "Rules of Debate" (*hetuvidyā*), with perhaps one original Sanskrit folio devoted to grammar (*śabdavidyā*), and the remaining two sciences dismissed with a mere sentence for each. The 'inner science' or Buddhist doctrine is of course the main subject. Here there are four parts: establishing the representation of topic; terminological variety; the meaning of the teaching in categories; the knowable possibility of the Buddha's promulgations. The first part, the representation of topic is the three—the Sūtra, the Vinaya, and the Abhidharma (called *Mātṛkā*); and the author announces that the extensive treatment of the three amounts to the *Vastusaṃgrahaṇī*. The second part—the terminological variety gives a number of Buddhist terms with varieties, e.g., there are three realms, to wit, realm of desire, realm of form, formless realm; and another kind of three realms, the 1000^3 of those world-realms as single series, 1000^3 of those as single medium series, 1000^3 of those as a single widespread series of world-realms (*lokadhātu*). There are three kinds of *saṃkleśa*, and so on. The Buddhist dictionary *Mahāvyutpatti* has many such lists. Asaṅga gives sufficient hints to show what is meant. The third part—the categories of Buddhist instruction, often involves the word "any"; e.g., "What is a nature (*svabhāva*)? Any character of the *dharmas*—whether individual character (*svalakṣaṇa*), general character (*sāmānyalakṣaṇa*), character of sign (*saṃketa*), character of cause or character of effect."[20] Asaṅga also gives a list of sixteen kinds of category—category of cause, and so on.[21] While he is generous in providing examples, doubtless these could also be treated in much greater amplitude.

The fourth part of this 'inner science' in the *Śrutamayī bhūmi* is the knowable possibilities (*jñeyasthāna*).[22] These are the single doctrines, and then the twofold through tenfold doctrines, as in the Dīgha-Nikāya's *Saṅgīti Sutta* expounded by Sāriputta. When T.W. and C.A.F. Rhys Davids translated this in *Dialogues of the Buddha*, Part III, even with the help of a commentary, they did not know how to handle the words *āhāra* and *saṅkhāra* in the text: *katamo eko dhammo? sabbe sattā āhāraṭṭhitikā; sabbe sattā saṅkhāraṭṭhitikā*, and translated this: "What is a single doctrine? All beings persist through causes. All beings persist through conditions." Now compare with Asaṅga's exposition: "What is a single doctrine? Sentient beings persist for a day, i.e., by food (*āhāra*). Sentient beings persist for a lifetime, i.e., by life motivation (*āyuḥsaṃskāra*). Sentient beings persist in rebirth, there being virtuous natures in their stream of consciousness, i.e., by heeding the virtuous natures."[23] And so on. Asaṅga treats the twofold principles through eightfold doctrines extensively. For the example of a ninefold doctrine, e.g., birthplaces, he directs the reader to his *Vastusaṃgrahaṇī*.[24] Again, for the tenfold doctrine, e.g., 'totality' bases (*kṛtsna-āyatana*), he directs one to the *Vastusaṃgrahaṇī*.[25] It does not take much comparison to conclude that Asaṅga follows the equivalent scripture in the *Dīrgha-Āgama*, adding brief comments. Asaṅga's placement of this treatment under *Śrutamayī bhūmi* helps explain the role of Sāriputta as the expounder, because he was held to be the chief disciple in terms of paññā (S. *prajñā*) and because the name of this *bhūmi* is the first level of *prajñā—śrutamayi* (the next two *bhūmis* being also the names of the second and third *prajñā*). This also implicates the canon *Aṅguttara-Nikāya* (Sanskrit canon being *Ekottara-Āgama*) in *śrutamayī prajñā*, alternatively in Sāriputta's lineage. Finally, the example of a single doctrine may illustrate what Asaṅga meant by assigning the secret explanation to the *Śrāvaka piṭaka*. "Secret" therefore means "not open", concealed like the potentiality of a seed.

The preceding is just one among numerous passages that could be adduced to show how much Asaṅga adheres to the Āgama. His entire *Vastusaṃgrahaṇī* is of this nature. It seems reasonable to conclude—in the face of Asaṅga's vast output in the *Yogācārabhūmi*—that he had no trouble writing his numerous comments in the *Śrutamayī bhūmi* and elsewhere. Therefore he is neither of those we might find in the Twentieth Century, simplistic and avoiding problems, or spinning subtle theories while trying to figure it out as one goes along. Asaṅga appears to write with a terrific memory, a touch of genius, and basing himself on a position, i.e., writing through a Buddhist school.[26]

Asaṅga and the Mahīśāsakas (First Approach)

In that same work of mine (*Analysis*, chapter "Literary History") I mentioned the pilgrim Hsüan-tsang's remark that Asaṅga first belonged to the school of the Mahīśāsakas.[27] As far as Hsüan-tsang and the Tibetan tradition as well are concerned, Asaṅga then turned to the Mahāyāna. But I set forth a theory that Asaṅga did not forget or renounce his "Hīnayāna" foundation; he also became learned in the Mahāyāna. This is consistent with the travels of Hsüan-tsang, reporting monasteries where both Hīnayāna and Mahāyāna doctrines were studied.[28]

My proposed association of Asaṅga with the Mahīśāsakas accepts Bareau's suggestion—his theory of what was very probable—namely that the difference between the Theravāda and the Mahīśāsaka at first was mainly geographical, i.e., that the Theravāda, being in Ceylon evolved slowly, while their counterparts in India, the Mahīśāsakas, being subject to the intellectual currents of India proper, evolved rather swiftly.[29]

The work *Tarkajvāla* by Bhavya (=Bhāvaviveka) has a passage setting forth for the eighteen Buddhist sects what each one was supposed to have recited. This passage is in the Derge Tanjur, Mādhyamika commentary part, Vol. Dza, f. 175a-7, ff. Coming to the Mahīśāsakas (the *śāsaka* portion is translated into Tibetan as "teachers"), he says (f. 178b-6): "Thus the Ārya [Mahī-] Śāsakas recited from the *Tshoms brgyad pa*". Now, *Tshoms brgyad pa* means "chapter (*varga*) of eight"; in Pāli this is well-known as the *Aṭṭhaka-vagga*, which in their canon is in a work called *Sutta-Nipāta*; and which in Sanskrit was known as the *Artha-vargīya*. This is also the *Arthapada-sūtra* which Bapat has translated from Chinese and annotated.[30]

For purposes of the present study I surveyed in the *Yogācārabhūmi* (Peking Tanjur) the *Cintāmayī bhūmi*; and therein the subsection Asaṅga calls *Śarīrārtha-gāthā*.[31] Of the possible meanings of *śarīra* in Buddhist texts—'body', 'skeleton', and 'relics', I believe that the meaning of 'relics' i.e., of the Buddha's speech, fits here; and that the *gāthā* express their meaning (*artha*). They amount to forty-one sets of several *gāthas* or only one *gāthā*, accompanied by Asaṅga's commentary. There are three principal sources for these *gāthās*: (1) the *Saṃyukta-Āgama* in whatever version Asaṅga was using, possibly different from both the versions translated into Chinese in Taishō Vol. 2, Nos. 99 and 100; (2) the *Udānavarga*; (3) a Sanskrit collection something like the *Sutta-nipāta* in Pāli. More specifically, the *gāthā* sets 1 through 15 are from the *Saṃyukta-Āgama*; but No. 15 overlaps the first *Udānavarga* citation, namely *Udānavarga* I,1—the celebrated verse beginning *anityā bata saṃskāra*. The *Udānavarga* citations go down through set No. 38, in each case a single verse, except for No. 25, which is the five verses, *Udānavarga*, XXII, 12-16.[32] The *udāna* were collections of verses by topic, these topics presumably going with the traditional explanation of *udāna* as teachings directed to particular persons in accordance with their propensities.[33] Hence, Asaṅga may have been intending all the *Śarīrārtha-gāthas* to be of the *udāna* type, in which case the traditional distinguishing of *gāthā* from *udāna* in the divisions of *dharmapravacana* (for Asaṅga the twelve of *Mahāvyutpatti*, Nos. 1266-78) does not take *gāthā* and *udāna* as exclusive categories. After the *Udānavarga* citations comes the third group of citations. Here the set 39 is ten *gāthās* equivalent to Sutta-nipāta 1032-39 plus two (Ajita's questions). For set 40, six *gāthās* equivalent to *Sutta-nipāta*, 766-71 (*Kāma Suttas*) are from *Arthavargīya*. And finally set 41, *gāthā* 1 is called "Auspicious Night".

I shall discuss the first three sets of verses to show their character; and the last three sets, because of their relevance to the present topic. Of course, Asaṅga used Sanskrit sources, but we must resort sometimes to the equivalent Pāli.

Asaṅga's first verse set is a single verse:[34]

pāpaṃ na kuryān manasā vacā vā,
kāyena vā kiṃcana sarvaloke /
riktaḥ kamaiḥ samṛtimām saṃprajāna(ḥ),
duḥkhaṃ na seveta / anarthasaṃhitam // iti gāthā /

In all the world one should not do any evil with mind, speech, or body. The one free from desires, who is mindful and aware should not follow the suffering which serves no good purpose.

The equivalent Pāli is in *Saṃyutta-Nikāya*, i, 12, Paradise suttas.

The second verse set has four *gāthās*[35]

ākhyeyāḥ saṃjñinaḥ sattvā ākhyeyesmin pratiṣṭhitā /
ākhyeyam aparijñāya yogam āyanti mṛyyante //
ākhyeyan tu parijñāya ākhyātāraṃ na manyate /
taṃ hi na vidyate tasya vadeyur yena te pare //
samo viśeṣa uta vāpi hīno, yo manyate 'yam vivadeta tena /
vidhātrayesmin na vikampati yaḥ, samo viśeṣaś ca na tasya bhavati /
ucchidya tṛṣṇām iha nāmarūpe, prahāya mānaṃ ca na saṅgam eti /
taṃ śāntadhūpam anighaṃ nirāśam, [na] cākṣus[yaṃ] taṃ devamanuṣyaloke //

Men endowed with naming faculty (*saṃjñin*), having the expressible [here,=five strands of desire], take their stand on the expressible. Not rightly understanding the expressible, they are tied up [in the realm of desire] and die.

Rightly understanding the expressible, one does not give thought to the speaker [an illustrious person], who does not exist for him in the way others would talk.

Whoever, [through "I am" pride] gives thought, "I am equal,

> better, or worse [than the speaker]", might thereby quarrel with that [speaker]. Whoever is one not shaking in those three [proud] ways, it does not occur to him, "I am equal, or better."
>
> Having cut off craving in this world toward nạme-and-form [the five grasping aggregates], and having got rid of ["I am"] pride, he is unattached. He being clear of the smoke [that afflicts the eye of insight], invincible (*anigham*, usually 'sinless'),[36] without expectation is not in sight's range in the world of gods and men.

The equivalent Pāli is in *Saṃyutta-Nikāya*, i, 11-12, Paradise suttas.

The third set has five *gāthās.* It is equivalent to the Pali, *Saṃyutta-Nikāya*, i, 188, Vaṅgīsa Suttas; one *gāthā* for Vaṅgīsa's question and four *gāthās* for Ānanda's reply.

Of course, there is no room here to cite from Asaṅga's masterly commentary, which is responsible for my bracketed interpolations. There is no doubt that Asaṅga draws the *gāthā* from the Sanskrit canon *Saṃyukta-Āgama.*

The last three *gāthā* sets,[37] i.e., Nos. XXXVII-XXXIX, bear more on Asaṅga's affiliation than earlier sets, such as the above first three. No. XXXVII consists of ten *gāthās,* Questions of Brahman Ajita, where the equivalent Pāli is in the *Sutta-nipāta*, 1032-39, eight in number. The two extra in Asaṅga's citation come between *Sn* 1037 and 1038; they are, in my translation:[38]

> (Ajita) "The understanding (*vijñāna*) that operates with mindfulness (*smṛti*), how it is aroused, and how it is free from doubt—pray tell me!"
>
> (The Master) "When one takes no delight in feelings of the inner and the outer, that is how the understanding operating with mindfulness is aroused [and how it is free from doubt]"

The *Sn* set of Brahman Ajita's questions is incorporated into the *Netti* (*The Guide*) with much commentary. In the *Sn* itself it is in the last chapter called *Pārāyaṇa.* One of the verses in the *Sn* set is found in the *Saṃyutta-Nikāya*, ii, 47, namely *Sn* 1038:[39]

> *ye ca saṅkhātadhammāse, ye ca sekkhā puthū idha /*
> *tesaṃ me nipako iriyaṃ puṭṭho pabrūhi mārisā ti //*

"Those who have been well-told the Dhamma, and those who here study separately (P. *puthu*; S. *pṛthag*), among them (what be) the prudent conduct—I have asked. Pray tell me, dear sir!"

Since the *Saṃyutta-Nikāya* verse is preceded by the remark, "It is said, Sāriputta, in the *Pārāyaṇa* in the Question of Ajita" (*vuttam idam, sāriputta, pārāyaṇe ajitapañhe*), the translator Mrs. Rhys Davids claimed in a note the historical priority of the *Sn* set of verses to this part of the *Saṃyutta-Nikāya*.[40] But if this is so, then why in Sāriputta's response to the question does he exhibit no knowledge of the rest of Ajita's Questions in the *Pārāyaṇa* chapter of *Sn*, not to speak of the two extra *gāthās* in Asaṅga's citation! It makes more sense for one verse to have grown to eight and then to ten. Against Mrs. Rhys Davids' contention, one may interpret the word *pārāyaṇa* as "final resort"; the locative *pārāyaṇe* "in the sense of final resort"; whereby the line may be rendered, "It is said, Sāriputta, in the sense of final resort, in the question of Ajita," so possibly the *Saṃyutta-Nikāya* precedes the *Sn*; possibly, the *Sn* took the word *pārāyaṇa* and made it into a chapter heading, expanding the one verse to eight.

At the conclusion of Asaṅga's citation of this verse set, he says (from the Tibetan): "This (i.e., verse set) is the *Ajitaparipṛcchā* in the *pārāyaṇa*."[41] Thus he names this work and indicates that there was a Sanskrit set that had grown out of the Middle Indic version, perhaps as extant in the *Pārāyaṇa* chapter of *Sutta-nipāta*. We shall soon get more evidence of a Sanskrit work that was analogous to the *Sutta nipāta*.

Asaṅga's next set, No. XXXVIII, six *gāthā*, is approximately equivalent to *Sn* 766-71, except that the last *gāthā* has variant content. Upon citing them, Asaṅga says, "This *gāthā* set is taken from the *kāmas* in the *Arthavargīya*."[42] In fact, the *Kāma-suttas* are the first scripture in the *Aṭṭhaka-vagga* in the *Sn*. The final verse variant to *Sn* 771, may be rendered this way from the Tibetan, with the help of Asaṅga's comments:[43]

> Whoever [with pure understanding] having determined those [desires] in cutting-off manner, and has cut them off, he wards off sorrow as does the lotus the water drops.

So we find Asaṅga citing the first *sūtra* of the group which Bhavya said was recited by the Mahīśāsakas. In his

Bodhisattvabhūmi (*Tattvārtha-paṭala*),[44] he cites a *gāthā* equivalent to *Sutta-nipāta* 897 in this manner: *uktaś ca bhagavatā arthavargīyeṣu*, the plural suggesting that each *sūtra* in this set was called an *arthavargīya*. And he insists that these *arthavargīyas* were expressed by the Buddha. Of course, Asaṅga's citations of the *Arthavargīya* proves that he employed this text, presumably in a collection analogous to the *Aṭṭhaka-vagga*. While this does not prove he is a Mahīśāsaka, it is a point to be added to any other evidence about his doctrinal affiliation.

The last *gāthā* set in Asaṅga's section consists of one and a half *gāthā*, contained in two verses repeated in *Majjhima-Nikāya*, iii, numbered discourses 131-4. Asaṅga's citation is translated this way:[45]

> The past [personality aggregates] should not be followed after, the future [ones] not hoped for. According as a *dharma* is present, one should discern it thus. Knowing that it cannot be removed and cannot be disturbed, one should promote it.

The translator, I.B. Horner, of the *Majjhima-Nikāyas* stated that the title *Bhaddekarattasutta* is hard to translate; she rendered it in No. 131, "Discourse on the Auspicious."[46] Therefore she translated the *bhadda* part and omitted any rendition for the *ekaratta*. Fortunately, Asaṅga after his citation gave the name of the *gāthā*: it is called "auspicious night" (Tib. *mtshan mo bzaṅ po* = Skt. *bhadrarajanī*). Hence, the *ekaratta* means "one color," i.e. the color of night. In his *Samāhitabhūmi*, Asaṅga mentions the cognition that shines in the darkness.[47]

Another work in the Sanskrit canon which Asaṅga employed is what he calls in his *Viniścayasaṅgrahaṇī* on the *Samāhitabhūmi* the *Mahākauṣṭhila-sūtra*. Checking in Malalasekera's *Dictionary of Pāli Proper Names* under the entry on Mahā-Koṭṭhita, his name in Pāli, and looking up every one of his references in the canon, usually a discourse where he asks Sāriputta a question and the latter gives the information—I could find no place matching Asaṅga's citation, which runs:[48]

> "There is the expression 'mindfulness (*smṛti*) pertaining to the body' because it involves bodily change and pertains thereto"—is the explanation of the *Mahākauṣṭhilasūtra*.

Besides, in his *Śrāvakabhūmi* he presented a kind of *āgama* about Buddhist meditation going back to a disciple of the Buddha named Revata:[49]

> *Yathoktaṃ bhagavatā/āyuṣmantaṃ revatam ārabhya evam anuśrūyate/*
>
> As it was said by the Bhagavat starting with the venerable Revata, so it is repeatedly handed down.

In these various ways, we see evidence of a Sanskrit collection analogous to the *Sutta-nipāta*, containing the Sanskrit *Arthavargīya* and *Pārāyaṇa* as two chapters and possessing other chapters that can be only a matter of speculation. Was the *Mahākauṣṭhilasūtra* included? Or the Revata meditation lore?

The foregoing should show as much as could be compressed into this limited space how Asaṅga exhibits within his vast learning a control of those matters which are of vital interest to the Theravāda sect of Buddhism, especially as concerns the content of such Pāli works as the *Netti-Pakaraṇa* and the *Sutta-nipāta*. In terms of Bareau's theory that the Mahīśāsaka were the India-based counterparts of the Theravāda, this compatibility of Asaṅga's views with the Theravāda supports a theory that Asaṅga belonged to the Mahīśāsaka, but does not prove it.

Asaṅga and the Mahīśāsakas (Second Approach)

Now turning to specialized tenets attributed to the Mahīśāsakas, it should be pointed out that the Vinaya Mahīśāsaka is not meant (indeed, Asaṅga is said to have become a monk through the Mūlasarvāstivāda Vinaya). That work of mine (*Analysis*, "Literary History") claimed that certain Mahīśāsaka tenets are found in Asaṅga's works, for which I use Bareau's thesis numbers. Appealing to Mahīśāsaka thesis No. 14, that denies a supramundane *dhyāna,* I called attention to Asaṅga's insistence on this in the fourth Yogasthāna of *Śrāvakabhūmi,* namely the passage through the four *dhyānas* of the 'realm of form' (*rūpadhātu*) and then through the 'formless realm' is the mundane path (*laukikamārga*), while contemplation of the four Noble Truths is the supramundane path.[50] Now using Bareau's thesis numbers for the later Mahīśāsaka with an asterisk, I then referred to 4*-5* that *karman* is actually *cetanā,* i.e., conforms to the mind; there is no [independent] bodily *karman* or vocal *karman*; and called attention to Asaṅga's definition of *cetanā* in his *Abhidharmasamuccaya* that it is the agent inciting thought to virtue, non-virtue, and the indeterminate; and further showed that the *cetanā*, which I rendered thinking-volition is what arouses action of body and action of speech, according to Asaṅga.[51]

Some other points I raised at that time long ago need not be mentioned. They are among the subtleties that so many other scholars also engage in to convince themselves, but hardly could convince others. The German scholar Schmithausen had some remarks in an appendix to a paper (1970) about the thesis which he treated as mine. There he labelled as "inconclusive" (*nicht schilüssig)* my identification of Asaṅga's early Buddhist sect as Mahīśāsaka.[52] He makes clear why my arguments in that 1961 publication are not sufficiently strong to command scholarly acceptance. The present article attempts to justify that acceptance. However, I never gave up the thesis of Asaṅga's Mahīśāsaka adherence—which was not mine to begin with: Hsüan-tsang said this was his early school; and no present-day scholar has shown that Asaṅga was converted to a different Hīnayāna school to account for his extensive *āgama* reliance, with samples in the present chapter.

I should like now to discuss some other Mahīśāsaka tenets, insofar as space will allow. No. 1, that the past (*atīta*) and the future (*anāgata*) do not exist, while the present (*pratyutpanna*) and the unconstructed (*asaṃskṛta*) exist; seems to be directly contradicted by No. 1* that the past and the future truly exist.[53] In fact, by regarding No. 1 as a meditative precept, there is no contradiction. Notice from my preceding section, Asaṅga cited the verse called "auspicious night" (in Pāli repeated several times in the *Majjhima-Nikāya*). The meditator in *samādhi* is absorbed in concentrating on the present object, so past and future do not exist for him; but when he emerges from that *samādhi* memory of the past and expectation of the future re-appear, as that same *gāthā* suggests.

No. 2, that one has a clear comprehension of the four Noble Truths at one time; when one sees the Truth of Suffering (*duḥkhasatya*) one may see all the Truths. In his *Viniścayasaṃgrahaṇī* on the *Bodhisattvabhūmi* Asaṅga states:[54] "For what reason does one recognize a truth as the comprisal? He said: Because it establishes the four truths; because it has one name; because it is the truth of suffering."

Nos. 3-4, that the traces (*anuśaya*) are neither *citta* (thought) nor *caitta* (thought derivative) nor provided with object (*ālambana*); their own nature is dissociated from thought (*cittaviprayukta*). That the traces are different from the entrapments (*paryavasthāna*); the own nature of the entrapments is associated with thought (*cittasamprayukta*).[55] *Viniścayasaṃgrahaṇī* on the third *bhūmi, savitarkā savicārā bhūmi*, says: The manifest arising of defilement is entrapment; the retaining and protecting of its seed is traces, also contamination (*dauṣṭhulya*). It is called "traces" because of its sleeping state. There is the "entrapment" because of its waking state.[56] These statements easily go with theses 3-4, because "traces" being asleep are dissociated from thought, which apparently means thought of the waking state; while "entrapment" being awake is associated with the thought. And Asaṅga here and elsewhere always contrasts "traces" and "entrapment". Thesis 9* that the traces (*anuśaya*) remain always present,[57] seems to agree with the same place of *Viniścayasaṃgrahaṇī* saying, "The person who is born in the realm of desire possesses the traces of defilement that range in the three realms."[58] Also, "If one eliminates the entrapment but not the traces, again and again the entrapment arises; while if one eliminates the traces, positively neither the traces nor the entrapment will (again) occur."[59] Much more is said about these two.[60]

Some of the tenets are found in Asaṅga's *Paramārtha-gāthā*.[61] Thus, No. 23, that all the *saṃskṛtas* are destroyed each moment, is in *gāthā* 5, "All the *saṃskāras* are momentary" (*kṣaṇikāḥ sarvasaṃskārā*): while No. 24, that no *citta, caitta*, or *dharma* transmigrates from this world to another, is in *gāthā* 44, 'Neither is there any transmigrator here" (*na veha kaścit saṃsartā*). Also, No. 32, that the person (*pudgala*) does not see, is in *gāthā* 6-7, "Neither does the eye see form; nor the ear hear sound," (and so on).

Perhaps the most important tenet is No. 37, that there is an aggregate that lasts until the end of *saṃsāra*. Bareau mentions that this is a prototype of the "store-consciousness" (*ālaya-vijñāna*) of the Mahāyāna.[62] Asaṅga in his S*acittikā* and *Acittikā bhūmi* says, "Among them, by *paramārtha* establishment there is the *Acittikā-bhūmi* that is Nirvāṇa-realm without remainder (*nirupadhiśeṣa*). Why so? For thus the *ālayvijñāna* ceases (*ālayavijñānaṃ niruddhaṃ bhavati*)."[63] Of course the end of *saṃsāra* is *Nirvāṇa* according to this position.

Tenets about the Arhat are important, No. 17, that entry into the stream (*srotāpanna*) may have a falling back (*parihāṇi*), while the Arhat certainly does not have a falling back[64] is the old view consistent with the Theravāda, where the Arhat is the "worthy one". Asaṅga, coming in the Mahāyāna period after there was much downgrading of the Arhat in favor of the Bodhisattva, has a modification of this tenet in his *Śrāvakabhūmi*, namely, that the Arhat who falls away in the present life (*dṛṣṭadharma*) and pleasant abode (*sukhavihāra*) establishes "falling away" (*parihāṇi*) [i.e., why there is the word], while the Arhat who does not fall away in the present life and pleasant abode establishes "non-falling away" (*aparihāṇi*) [i.e., why there is the word].[65] Asaṅga's statement seems consistent with tenet No. 9 that also among the Arhats there is an accumulation of merit (*puṇyopacaya*). There are many allusions to the Arhat attainment in the *Yogācārabhūmi* and usually in a praiseworthy context—in distinct contrast with the criticisms found in the Mahāsāṇghika tenets. The *Viniścayasaṇgrahaṇī* on the stages Nos. 16 and 17, "with remainder" and "without remainder," i.e., the two kinds of Nirvāṇa, especially treats the Arhat attainment in terms of these two stages.[66] According to Asaṅga, the Arhat is the steadfast place of *dharmatā*.[67] The *Viniścaya-saṃgrahaṇī* on the *Bodhisattvabhūmi* has to face up to why the Arhat attainment is inferior to Buddhahood; Asaṅga points out that the Arhat has not comprehended the knowable entities of the three times, and so does not have unhindered knowledge and vision (*jñāna-darśana)*, while it is by having this that the Tathāgata has the eighteen unshared natures of Buddha.[68] This holds that the Arhat needs more accumulation of knowledge rather than of merit.

While certain other tenets could be discussed in this connection, for my purposes it is not necessary to go on this direction. Granted that some tenets are held in common with other Buddhist sects. For example, the older Mahīśāsakas believed tenet No. 8 that there is no intermediate existence (*antarābhava*), but some other sects believed this too. Then tenet No. 2*, i.e., of the later Mahīśāsakas, that there is an intermediate state has adherents among other sects, and Asaṅga along with his brother Vasubandhu accepts this.[69] It was not my theory that Asaṅga, in going along with the Mahīśāsaka is committed to the full list of tenets ascribed to this sect in the rather brief works devoted to the theories of the eighteen Buddhist sects, and where often the tenets are expressed with too much brevity. There is even a possibility that he holds certain tenets brought in by his Mūlasarvāstivāda Vinaya association, since the *Vinayavibhaṅga* of this lineage does contain a number of doctrines. Even so, Asaṅga's agreement with certain Mahīśāsaka tenets remains.

Asaṅga and the Mahīśāsakas (Third Approach)

There are relevant considerations based on the name Mahīśāsaka. Bareau has collected the various explanations of the name, of which the chief ones are the interpretations "who govern the earth" and "who instruct the earth".[70] The Tibetan translation in the *Mahāvyutpatti* opts for the "instructor" (*ston pa*) interpretation of the word *śāsaka.* In a Vinaya work whose Chinese translation is attributed to Ngan Chekao (late Han) but which Lin Li-kouang thinks is more probably in 4th or 5th century, the Mahīśāsaka are said to penetrate the subtlety of *dhyāna* while pursuing that which is abstract and obscure.[71] Besides, he translates a prophetic passage from the *Mahā-saṃnipāta-sūtra* (whose late Han translation into Chinese has been lost), using the Dharmakṣema translation made between 414 and 421 A.D., attributing a characteristic theory to each of six schools, among them saying:[72]

> "O Kauṇḍinya! After my Nirvāṇa, certain disciples of mine who receive, retain copy and recite the twelve categories of the Tathāgata's teaching will not conceive notions (*saṃjñā*) of the earth, of those of water, of fire, of wind, of space (*ākāśa*), or of consciousness (*vijñāna*). Those persons will accordingly be called Mahīśāsaka."

The list of six, namely the four *mahābhūta, ākāśa,* and *vijñāna,* is mentioned in the *Garbhāvakrāntisūtra* along with a summary statement that man has six elements (*ṣaddhātur ayaṃ bhikṣo puruṣaḥ*). This scriptural passage was appealed to by some Buddhists to deny secondary matter, called *bhautika rūpa,* i.e., that there is only the four great elements; and to deny secondary consciousness called *caitta,*[73] i.e., that there is only *citta* (*cittamātra*), referred to in the scripture as *vijñāna.* But if this passage of the *Garbhāvakṛānti-sūtra* is interpreted along the lines of the prophecy to Kauṇḍinya, one must conclude that it is only notions (*saṃjna*) of earth etc., that are rejected, allowing notions of secondary matter or secondary consciousness, and that those called

Mahīśāsaka, by avoiding notions of six elements, accept *cittamātra*, also accept only the four great elements, plus *ākāśa*, to explain man basically.

Now, Asaṅga has a passage about this matter in his *Viniścaya-saṁgrahaṇī* on the first two *bhūmis*, the *pañcavijñānakāyasaṃprayuktā bhūmi* and the *manobhūmi*:[74]

> It is not valid that there is mind-only (*cittamātra*) in the sense of 'continuous substantiality' (*dravyatas*), because it contradicts scripture. How does it contradict scripture? If the *citta* consisted of lust *upakleśa* and consisted of hatred and delusion, *upakleśa*, it could not become liberated—he said. But what is the objection to that? [Someone] says: Mind-only by itself is invalid, because if there is not two together, when one does not resort to representation (*vijñapti*) of lust, etc., one would be free [of those *upakleśa*] [which we know is not the case]. And there is no particular fault in understanding that there is a preceding representation (*vijñapti*). [In response], there is what was said by Bhagavat, to wit, "concomitant (*sahaja*) feeling (*vedanā*), idea (*saṃjñā*), and thinking-volition (*cetanā*)"; and what was said (by Him), to wit, "These natures (*dharma*) are mingled, not unmingled, so these natures are not objects individually separated out; or when separated out (not objects) for reference as distinct, or clear, or different." To demonstrate the meaning of the mingling he used the simile of the light of a butter lamp. Accordingly, if they were not concomitant, it would also have been improper to say they are mingled. Besides, there is the scripture, to wit, "This man has six elements," and its purport stated, so there is no fault. What is the purport here? He stated, the purport is to be observed as chiefly teaching the place where there is the form (*rūpa*), its changed state, and mental concomitants (*caitta*).

The subtle passage continues in similar vein, but the message, is reasonably clear from the part presented above. The remark "chiefly teaching the place" suggests the "space" (*ākāśa*), which is one of the six elements as permitting the "room" or "place" for the other five elements. In this place where is the person, he has *cittamātra* and the four elements. Here also evolve secondary mind and secondary matter. The point about the mingling of the *dharmas* appears to be that it is not possible to separate them from the substratum six elements, because the *dharmas* operate in the same "place". But one has notions of the derived and concomitant natures. This shows the Yogācāra theory of *cittamātra* in a rather different role than surveys of Indian philosophy regard it. Those modern surveys—and older works as well—take the term *cittamātra* as indicating a denial of the external world. But Asaṅga's opponent does not charge this; rather he doubts that a pure consciousness can account for the continuance of defilement that causes rebirth. The term *cittamātra* as here used implies an ideal man, that it is possible to reach, presumably by *yoga*, a state of pure consciousness (*cittamātra*) free from derived consciousness (*caitta*). As a corollary, one reaches a state of just four elements (*mahābhūta*) free from derived elements (*bhautika*).[75] At that time one would be free of notions (*saṃjñā*).

With the foregoing in mind, we may understand the words "Those persons will accordingly be called Mahīśāsaka" of the prophecy to Kauṇḍinya. The clue is the word 'accordingly': It is because they teach the six elements as constituting man's "earth" they have the name meaning "who teach the earth"—the earth of which one should have no notions—those six elements. And taking Asaṅga's passage into account, it is undeniable that his celebrated theory of *Cittamātra* is bound up with the scriptural passage about the six elements. Is this not, then, a justification for the terminology of seventeen *bhūmis*? The word *bhūmi* means "earth" as does *mahī*. Hence, Asaṅga's *bhūmi* system, involving in a "place" the alternation between the *citta* and the *caitta*, as between the *mahābhūta* and the *bhautika* is not an upward progression, as the very titles of the seventeen show.

In conclusion, it should be granted that the various facts of evidence brought forward in this chapter constitute a more cogent association of Asaṅga with the Mahīśāsaka than was the primitive arguing in my work *Analysis of the Śrāvakabhūmi Manuscript*. Yet it is the pilgrim Hsüan-tsang who deserves the credit for associating Asaṅga with this sect as the preliminary for his Mahāyāna venture. It might be well to mention my chief amplification of the thesis. This was to show Asaṅga's overwhelming reliance on the *āgama* scriptures of early Buddhism; thus he not only was trained in one of the Buddhist sects—Hsüan-tsang said Mahīśāsaka—but continued with consistent stress. Asaṅga cited the first *sūtra* of the group recited by the Mahīśāsakas, as identified by Bhāvaviveka. Asaṅga has a long passage that apparently agrees with the characteristic theory attributed to the Mahīśāsaka in a prophecy of the *Mahā-saṃnipāta-sūtra*, and his passage moreover implicates the characteristic term of his school—*Cittamātra*. The last verse which he cites in his section called *Śarīrārtha-gāthā* clarifies the first thesis in both the Mahīśāsaka and later Mahīśāsaka tenets as consistent, even though they seemed to be mutually at odds. Because the present writer was quite aware of this information, he continued to refer to Asaṅga as a Mahīśāsaka in several published articles; and was happy to put all the data together in the foregoing manner for the honor due Professor P.V. Bapat, to whom he presented a copy of the work *Analysis* in the year 1963 and who commented upon it.

REFERENCES

1. This work (hereafter: *Analysis*) was published in University of California Publications in Classical Philology, Vol. XVII (University of California Press, Berkeley, 1961).
2. I follow rather closely the dates proposed by Sylvain Lévi, *Asaṅga: Mahāyāna-Sūtrālaṁkāra* (Paris, 1911), II, 1-2. Therefore, I do not accept the dates proposed by Prof. Péri, 280-350, followed by N. Dutt, *Bodhisattvabhūmi* (Patna, 1966), intro., p. 4-5.
3. Cf. *Analysis*, pp. 19-24. There is no quarrel among scholars that there is a Vasubandhu with approximately such dates. There has been a theory by Frauwallner (*On the Date of the Buddhist Master of the Law Vasubandhu*, Rome, 1951) that the Kośakāra Vasubandhu is different from the Cittamātra Vasubandhu. I rejected this thesis in my *Analysis*, pp. 19-21 as did P.S. Jaini in an article BSOAS, XXI, 1, 1958, pp. 48-53.
4. Cf. *Analysis*, p. 43, for the calculation.
5. This term is found in an instructive folio in the *Śrāvakabhūmi* manuscript, namely on plate 3A.2. See the entry on *aṅgāṅga* in *An Encyclopaedic Dictionary of Sanskrit*, Vol. One, Part III (Poona, 1978), p. 586B.
6. Peking Tanjur (Japanese photo edition), PTT, Vol. III, p. 22-4 and 5: */ de la de bźin gśegs pas gsuṅs pa'i mdo sde rnams kyi don ji lta ba bźin du rnam par' grel ba ni mdo sde'i rgyan ces bya ste / 'di lta ste / dper na padma kha ma phye ba ni ji ltar kha phye ba de ltar dga' bar byed pa ma yin pa'i phyir daṅ / . . . /' di lta ste / dper na kha zas ma myaṅs pa ni ji ltar myaṅs pa de ltar dga'bar byed pa ma yin pa . . . de bźin du / de bźin gśegs pas gsuṅs pa'i mdo sde rnams kyi don rnam par ma phye ba yaṅ ji ltar rnam par phye ba de ltar dga bar byed pa yin pas / de'i phyir mdo sde'i rgyan ces bya'o /.*
7. PTT, Vol. III, p. 18-5-5: */ de la rnam par phye ba bśad pa ni 'di lta stel phal cher*

ni theg pa chen po'i sde bśad pa yin pa'o /.

8. PTT, Vol. III, p. 18-5-4: */ de la gsan ba bśad pa' di lta ste / phal cher ñan thos kyi sde snod bśad pa gan yin pa'o /.*
9. G. Tucci, *On Some Aspects of the Doctrines of Maitreya nātha and Asaṅga* (University of Calcutta, 1930), p. 11. While he made this remark regarding Mahāyāna scriptures, it would apply also to the earlier Buddhist canon.
10. Cf. Unrai Wogihara, *Bodhisattvabhūmi*, 2 (Tokyo, 1936), appendix called "Inhalt," p.12, listing *Bodhisattvabhūmi* references to *Vastusaṃgrahaṇī, Paryāyasaṃgrahaṇī, Manomayī bhūmi, and Śrāvakabhūmi.*
11. Corrado Pensa, *L'Abhisamayālaṃkāravṛtti de Ārya-Vimuktisena; Primo Abhisamaya* (Roma, 1967), pp. 113-5.
12. The *Sūtrālaṃkāra*, the *Yogācārabhūmi*, and other works of this school are included in the *Sems tsam* (S. *cittamātra*) section of the Tibetan Tanjur. I use these catalogs: P. Cordier, *Catalogue du fonds Tibêtain de la Bibliothèque Nationale; A Complete Catalogue of the Tibetan Buddhist Canons*, ed. by Hakuju Ui, et al; *The Tibetan Tripiṭaka*, Ed: D.T. Suzuki, Catalogue & Index. Cordier's work is on the Peking edition; the Ui one is of the Derge edition; and the Suzuki one is of the Peking edition.
13. Presumably the way Vasubandhu came in these modern catalogs to be added as author is like this: Scholars who thought the legend that Asaṅga received the *Sūtrālaṃkāra* from Maitreya in the Tuṣita, a heaven meant in fact that Asaṅga had written this work, then they had to look for someone else to write the prose commentary and settled on Vasubandhu, especially since Sthiramati, author of the voluminous sub-commentary on the *Sūtrālaṃkāra*, has commented on other works of Vasubandhu.
14. Gadjin M. Nagao, *Index to the Mahāyāna-Sūtrālaṃkāra*, Part One (Tokyo, 1958), intro., p. vi.
15. Cf. Paul Demiéville, "La Yogācārabhūmi de Saṅgharaksa," *BEFEO*, 44 (1954), 339, 362-3, and 395-6 for various works of this title.
16. The catalog reconstruction "*nirṇaya*" is equivalent, according to the *Mahāvyutpatti* to the Tib, *gtan la dbad pa* of the full Tibetan equivalent *rnam par gtan la dbab pa.* The term *viniścaya* is equivalent to the full Tibetan; and Edgerton, *BHS Dictionary*, mentions Pāli *vinicchaya* also as "doctrinal exegesis." In Buddhist Sanskrit *viniścaya* has this usage in N.H. Samtani, The *Arthaviniścaya-sūtra and its Commentary* (*Nibandhana*) (Patna, 1971), and see his p. 311.5.
17. This defense is found especially in PTT, Vol. 110, p. 235-6.
18. Cf. A. Wayman, "Nescience and Insight According to Asaṅga's *Yogācārabhūmi,*" *Buddhist Studies in honour of Walpola Rahula* (Gordon Frazer, London, 1980), pp. 260-2.
19. In the Japanese photo edition, PTT, this is in Vol. 109, p. 285-4-8 to p. 304-3-6.
20. This definition of *svabhāva* is at PTT, Vol. 109, p.286-4-3.
21. The list of Categories (T. *bsdu ba*, S. *Vastu*), begins at PTT, Vol. 109, p. 287-3-1.
22. This part begins at PTT, Vol. 109, p. 288-1-6.
23. PTT, Vol. 109, p. 288-1-6: */ sems can gnas pa gsum ste / ñin gcig bźin du gnas pa dan / tshe'i tshad ji srid pa'i bar du gnas pa dan / tshe rabs rgyud du dge ba'i chos rnams la gnas pa ste / dan po kha zas kyi dban gis byun ba'o / gñis pa ni srog gi dban po'i du byed kyi dban gi byun ba'o / gsum pa ni dge ba'i chos rnams la bag yod pa las byun ba'o /.*
24. PTT, Vol. 109, p. 297-5-6.
25. PTT, Vol. 109, p. 297-5-8.

26. Since this section deals with Asaṅga as an author, it is well to mention a false authorship attribution to him that has been repeated by various modern writers since Benoytosh Bhattacharya, ed. *Guhyasamāja Tantra* (Baroda, 1931), intro. p. xxiv-xxxv, concluded that Asaṅga "who belonged to the 3rd century A.D."—which he didn't—"is the author of the *Guhyasamāja Tantra*"—which he wasn't. Of course, B. Bhattacharya knew a lot about the *Guhyasamāja Tantra*, but his literary history here was quite flawed with non sequiturs. The later repeaters of this false attribution appear to possess two kinds of scarcely any knowledge—scarcely any knowledge of Asaṅga's actual works, such as the *Yogācārabhūmi;* and scarcely any knowledge of the *Guhyasamāja-tantra,* its vast commentarial lore being available principally in the Tibetan language. I have also referred to this matter in my *Yoga of the Guhyasamāja-tantra* (Delhi, 1977).
27. Cf. Thomas Watters, *On Yuan Chwang's Travels in India* (London, 1904), Vol. 1, p. 357: "Asaṅga, he tells us, began his Buddhist religious career as a Mahīśāsaka and afterwards became a Mahāyānist."
28. Cf. Watters, *On Yuan Chwang,* Vol. I, p. 298, the section called Ku-lu-to. probably the present Kulu Valley, where Hsüan-tsang found in twenty Buddhist monasteries over 1,000 monks, mostly Mahāyānists with a few belonging to Hīnayāna schools. Also, Watters, *On Yuan Chwang,* Vol. II (London, 1905), p. 184, the section Pun-na-fa-tan-na, apparently a district in Bengal, where the pilgrim found in twenty Buddhist monasteries over 3,000 monks by whom the "Great and Little Vehicles" were followed. In earlier centuries, when the main Mahāyāna scriptures were written, there must have been important monasteries where study of the two kinds of doctrines was stipulated, since some of the Mahāyāna scriptures, such as the *Bodhisattva-piṭaka-sūtra,* and the *Akṣayamatinirdeśa-sutra,* contain so many early Buddhist doctrines besides the distinctly Mahāyāna ones.
29. André Bareau, *Les sectes boudhiques du Petit Vēhicule* (Saigon, 1955), p. 183.
30. P.V. Bapat, "The Arthapada-Sūtra Spoken by the Buddha," *Visva-Bharati Annals,* Vol. I, 1945, pp. 135-227; Vol. III, 1950, pp. 1-109.
31. The *Cintāmayī bhūmi* contains three sections of *gāthā* with Asaṅga's commentary. two of these—the *Paramārtha-gāthā* and the *Ābhiprāyikārtha-gāthā* (the former edited and translated in Wayman, *Analysis*; the latter has appeared in *Buddhist Insight*; *Essays of Alex Wayman,* published by Motilal Banarsidass, Delhi. The third group, the *Śarīrātha-gāthā* is in Tibetan at PTT, Vol. 110, p. 1-4-3 to 22-1-6.
32. Lambert Schmithausen in his learned study, "Zu den Rezensionen des Udānavargaḥ," *Archiv für Indische Philosophie,* WZKS 14, 1970, p. 47-124 (kindly furnished me by Professor Ernst Steinkellner of Vienna) has identified many of the *Udānavarga* citations in Asaṅga's *Śarīrārtha gāthā.* As there is no need to discuss these verses in the present article, I shall simply present the complete list in order of citation in Asaṅga's section: I, 1(Beckh's numbering); IV, I; III, I; V, 24; IX, 6; VIII, 11; X, 1; XXII, 6; XVII, 12; XXII, 12-16; XVI, 22; XVI, 23; XXVI, 1; XXVI, 30; XXIX, 37; XXIX, 38, XXIX, 51; XXIX, 56; XXVIII, 2; XXVIII, 1; XXXI, 1; XXXI, 51; XXXII, 5; XXXIII, 55, (the remainder, Bernard's numbering).
33. Cf. Asaṅga, *Vastusaṃgrahaṇī* (Part I, *saṃskāra-pravicaya*), PTT, Vol. 111, p. 143-3-3, FF., where the *sūtras* are classified into two kinds, *udāna* and non-*udāna.* the *udāna* are directed to persons in accordance with their display of *saṃskāras* (T. *'du byed' bstan pa'i rnam pa gaṅ*). The non-*udāna* are accordingly not of this type.
34. This gāthā is edited from instrusive folios in the Bihar *Srāvakabhūmi* manuscript,

which contains, mainly on the 3A-3B, and 15A-15B plates a large portion of the *Cintāmayī bhūmi*, including the beginning of the *Śarīrārtha-gāthā*.

35. The four gāthas are edited from intrusive folios in the *Śrāvakabhūmi* manuscript, per n. 34, above.

36. While *nigha* is rendered as 'sin' (T.*sdig pa*) in *Mahāvyutpatti* 7308; and *a-nigha* is here paired with *nir-āśa*, as is frequent in Pāli (cf. *The Pāli Text Society's Pāli-English Dictionary*, two entries *nigha*), and Edgerton, *Buddhist Hybrid Sanskrit Dictionary*, under *anigha* declares the meaning still uncertain, Asaṅga's commentary might clarify the term. The Tib. rendition here *'joms pa med pa* is explained at PTT, Vol. 110, p. 3-3-1 to -8. Here the sense of 'invincible' is that the person is not susceptible of being upset or overcome by attraction to possessions, craving of respect, and so on. If he gets angry, jealous, etc., this is his defeat.

37. These begin at PTT, Vol. 110, p. 20-1-4.

38. PTT, Vol. 110, p. 20-2-1: *l dran pa spyod pa'i rnam par śes l ji ltar'jug' gyur źu lags na l ji bźin the tshom ma mchis par l de ni bdag la bśad du gsol ll naṅ daṅ phyi yi tshor ba la l mṅon par dga' bar mi byed na l de ltar dran pa spyod pa yi l rnam par śes pa 'jug par' gyur ll.*

39. The verse is translated in accordance with the Tibetan version and Asaṅga's comments. Translators from the Pāli, whether of Sn (E.M. Hare, *Woven Cadences of Early Buddhists*, p. 149), or of the *Saṃyutta-Nikāya*, II (Mrs. Rhys Davids, p. 36), or of the Netti (Ñāṇamoli, p. 30), do not come close to my rendition, apparently since the available Pāli-English dictionaries do not inform that the word *saṅkhāta* is equivalent to S. *saṃkhyāta, khyā–* "to tell"; and *saṃ–*, as frequently commented upon in Buddhist works, equivalent to *samyak*. And also because those translators took the Pāli *puthu* as "many" even though the Sanskrit equivalents are *pṛthu* (broad) or *pṛthak* (separate).

40. Mrs. Rhys Davids, *The Book of the Kindred Sayings*, II, p. 36, n. Of course, there are some other canonical passages of similar type, seemingly referring to *Pārāyana* as though it were the chapter name, in connection with a single *gāthā*.

41. PTT, Vol. 110, p. 20-2-3: */ źes bya ba ni pha rol tu sgrol ba las [mi] pham pas źus pa yin no /*. Asaṅga's citation of the Ajita verses of the Sanskrit *Parāyaṇa* recalls the legend that he was instructed by Maitreya (called Ajita); cf. É. Lamotte, *Histoire du Bouddhisme Indien*, pp. 775, ff. for the Maitreya legend.

42. PTT, Vol. 110, p. 21-1-5: */ źes bya ba ni don gyi sde tshan las'dod pa rnams las brtsams pa'i tshigs su bcad pa yin te /.*

43. PTT, Vol. 110, p. 21-1-4: */ de la gtan nas gcad pa ltar / gaṅ gis de ni bcad byas pa / de ni mya ṅan ldog' gyur ba / pad ma la ni chu thigs bźin //.*

44. N. Dutt, ed., *Bodhisattvabhūmi*, text, p. 33 .

45. PTT, Vol. 110, p. 21-4-3: */' das la rjes su' gro mi byed / ma' oṅs pa la re ba med / da ltar byuṅ chos gaṅ yin pa / de daṅ de la rnam lta la / mi' phrogs kun tu mi' khrugs pa / de ni mkhas pas' phel bar byed //*

46. I.B. Horner, tr., *The Middle Length Sayings*, III (London, 1959), p. 233.

47. PTT, Vol. 109, p. 269-3-5: *mun pa la snaṅ bar śes pa' i tshul.*

48. PTT, Vol. 111, p. 12-2-1: */ lus gyur pa daṅ ldan pa daṅ / der gtogs pa yin pa'i phyir lus su gtogs pa'i dran pa źes byo ba'o źes gsuṅs te / gsus po che chen po'i mdo rnam par bśad pa yin no //.* The expression rendered "mindfulness pertaining to the body" is probably equivalent to the kāyagatāsati treated in P.V. Bapat, Vimuttimagga and Visuddhimagga: *A Comparative Study* (Calcutta, 1937), pp. 75-7. For more information on topic, cf. Étienne Lamotte, *Le Traité de la Grande Vertu de Sagesse,* Tome III (Louvain, 1970) (Chapitres XXXI-XLII),

pp. 1151-58.
49. *Analysis*, p. 86.
50. *Analysis*, p. 26.
51. *Analyis*, p. 27.
52. Schmithausen, "Zu den Rezensionen des Udānavargaḥ," 115-9.
53. Bareau, *Les sectes*, p. 183, 187.
54. PTT, Vol. 111, p. 68-4-3: */ rgyu mishan bden pa du dag gis bsdus śes na / smras pa / rnam par bźag pa'i bden pa bźis so / miṅ ni gcig gis te / sdug bsṅal gyis bden pas so /.*
55. Bareau, *Les sectes*, p. 183.
56. PTT, Vol. 110, p. 281-4-1, ff. */ de ñon moṅs pa kun tu 'byuṅ ba mṅon du gyur pa ni kun nas dkris pa źes bya'o / de ñid kyi sa bon ma spaṅs sin yaṅ dag par ma bcom pa ni bag la ñal źes bya ste / gnas ṅan len kyaṅ de yin no / ma sad pa' i phyir ni bag la ñal yin la sad pa' i gnas skabs kyi phyir ni kun nas dkris pa yin no /*
57. Bareau, *Les sectes*, p. 188.
58. PTT, Vol. 110, p. 281-4-3 */ gan zag ' dod pa'i khams su skyes śin byuṅ ba ni khams gsum na spyod pa'i ñon moṅs pa rnams kyi bag la ñal daṅ ldan no /*
59. PTT, Vol. 110, p. 281-5-8: */ kun nas dkris pa las spaṅs la bag la ñal las ma spaṅs na ni yaṅ daṅ yaṅ du kun nas dkris pa 'byuṅ bar' gyur gyi / bag la ñal las spaṅs na ni bag la ñal daṅ kun nas dkris pa gñi ga las gtan 'byuṅ bar mi' gyur.*
60. Cf. Padmanabh S. Jaini, "The Sautrāntika Theory of *Bīja*," BSOAS, Vol. 22, 1959, pp. 236-49, discusses some of the controversies around the *anuśaya* and *paryavasthāna*, but does not treat the topic as does Asaṅga, PTT, Vol. 110, p. 282, namely the *anuśaya* in regard to the Truth of Suffering (*duḥkha-satya*), in regard to the Truth of Source (*samudaya-satya*), the Truth of Cessation (*nirodha-satya*), and Truth of Path (*mārga-satya*).
61. Analysis, p. 167, ff.
62. Bareau, Les sectes, p. 187.
63. Alex Wayman, "The Sacittikā and Acittikā Bhūmi and the Pratyekabuddhabhūmi (Sanskrit texts)," *Journal of Indian and Buddhist Studies* (Tokyo), VIII, No. 1, Jan. 1960, p. (32) (=p.377).
64. Bareau, *Les sectes*, p. 185.
65. *Analysis*, p. 85.
66. PTT, Vol. 111, pp. 118 to 121. Cf. L. Schmithausen, *Der Nirvāṇa-Abschnitt in der Viniścayasaṃgrahaṇī der Yogācārabhūmi* (Osterr. Ak. d. Wissens., 264), Wien, 1969.
67. PTT, Vol. 111, p. 163-1-3: */ ' di ltar dgra bcom pa ni chos ñid kyi gnas brtan yin pa.* This is reminiscent of the well-known passage of the scriptures that whether Tathāgatas arise or do not arise, there remains this *dharmatā*.
68. Cf. PTT, Vol. 111, p. 110-1-4 to -6.
69. I have given the sources for this in a paper, "The Intermediate-state Dispute in Buddhism," *Buddhist Studies in Honour of I.B. Horner* (Dordrecht, 1974), pp. 227-39.
70. Bareau, *Les sectes*, p. 181.
71. Lin Li-kouang, *L'Aide-Mémoire de la Vraie Loi* (Paris, 1949), p. 80.
72. Lin Li-kouang, *L'Aide-Mémoire*, p. 300.
73. Cf. Y. Karunadasa, *Buddhist Analysis of Matter* (Colombo, 1967), p. 34.
74. PTT, Vol. 110, p. 266-3-8 to 266-4-5: */ sems tsam źig rdzas su yod pa ni luṅ daṅ 'gal bas kyaṅ mi ruṅ te / luṅ daṅ' 'gal ba gaṅ źe na / 'dod chags kyi ñe ba'i ñon*

moṅs pa can du 'gyur pa daṅ źe sdaṅ daṅ gti mug gis ñe bar ñon moṅs pa can du gyur pa'i sems ni rnam par grol bar mi 'gyur ro źes ji skad gsuṅs pa' o / de la 'gal ba ci yod ce na / smras pa / sems tsam ste gñis cig char du 'byuṅ ba med pa yin na' dod chags sogs pa rnam par rig pa la mi brten par bral bar 'gyur bas mi ruṅ ba'o / rnam par rig pa sṅon du 'gro ba ñid du rtogs na' aṅ de lta na ñes pa khyad par med pa kho nar 'gyur ro / bcom ldan' das kyaṅ lhan cig skyes pa'i tshor ba daṅ 'du śes daṅ sems pa źes gaṅ gsuṅs pa daṅ / chos 'di dag ni 'dres pa ste ma 'dres pama yin pas chos ' di dag so sor phye źiṅ so sor phye na bye brag gam bsam pa [read: bsal ba]' am / tha dad du bya brjod pa mi dmigs so źes gaṅ gsuṅs pa daṅ / ' dres pa'i don de nid rab tu grub par bya ba'i phyir mar me'i' od kyis dpe mdzad pas na / de'i phyir lhan cig skyes pa med na 'dres pa' i sgra mi ruṅ ṅo / skyes bu ' di ni khams drug daṅ ldan pa'o źes gsuṅs pa'i luṅ gaṅ yin pa de yaṅ dgoṅs te gsuṅs pa yin pas ñes pa med do / de la dgoṅs pa gaṅ źe na / smras pa / dgoṅs pa ni gzugs dan yoṅs su gyo [read: gyur] ba daṅ / sems las byuṅ ba rnams kyi gnas gtso cher bstan pa yin par blta bar bya'o /. In this Tibetan passage, the citation "*skyes bu 'di ni khams drug daṅ ldan pa*" means "This person possesses six elements."

75. This implicates the Buddhist theory of *dharmadhātu*; cf. A. Wayman, "Some Accords with the Sāṃkhya Theory of Tanmātra," *A Corpus of Indian Studies; Essays in Honour of Professor Gaurinath Sastri* (Calcutta, 1980), pp. 115-22.

5

Vasubandhu—Teacher Extraordinary

Vasubandhu is a grand master of Buddhist lore. His treatises in twenty verses and in thirty verses had a set of ten Indian commentaries collected by Dharmapāla, and including his own. This set was brought to China by the pilgrim Hsüan-tsang and translated into Chinese to form the Yogācāra doctrinal manual called the *Vijñaptimātratāsiddhi*. Not many Indian treatises have so many commentaries. In Hinduism—the *Brahmasūtra (=Vedānta-sutra)* and the *Yogasūtras* of Patañjali; in Buddhism—Nāgārjuna's *Madhyamaka-kārikā*—all had a number of Indian commentaries.

[Reprinted from *Studia Missionalia,* Vol. 37. Editrice Pontificia Universita Gregoriana. Roma. 1988.]

The popularity of Vasubandhu's two small texts suggests that this author at one time enjoyed lofty prestige. Indeed, he had a cardinal role in the history of Buddhist religious philosophy.

It might be thought that his life and teachings are already solved by publications in Western languages, including a good number of scholarly articles and two recent books that translate various works attributed to Vasubandhu. And yet we find considerable indeterminacy about his dates and in the attribution of works to his authorship, as well as the purport of his teaching. While the present attempt is of modest length, it is hoped that the approach adopted herein may clarify the role of this Buddhist teacher.

My arguments with supporting data will proceed with these headings—I. Identification with dates, and remarks about the works. II. Vasubandhu on "Representation-only" (*vijñaptimātra*). III. Vasubandhu on "Transmutation of the Support" (*āśrayaparāvṛtti*). IV. The four degrees of Penetration (*nirvedhabhāgīya*) followed by a Postscript.

Identification with Dates and Remarks about His Works

Who is the teacher, whose teachings are described herein and when did he live? These are important questions—because it has been claimed that there are two Vasubandhus differing by era and possibly by doctrine. Buddhist records themselves could place a Vasubandhu in the Fourth century A.D., and a Vasubandhu in the Fifth century A.D., Aside from discrepancies of dates after *nirvāṇa* (of the Buddha), this is because Kumārajīva of the Fourth century translated into Chinese some works by a Vasubandhu,[1] while the translations into Chinese of the works by Asaṅga and his brother Vasubandhu suggest a Fifth century date for this Vasubandhu.[2]

Two textual passages inspired a number of studies. (1) Paramārtha's "Life of Vasubandhu" was translated from Chinese by J. Takakusu.[3] (2) Vasubandhu's *Abhidharmakośabhāṣya* refers to an "older master" (*vṛddhācārya*), and Yaśomitra's commentary in one place expanded it to *vṛddhācārya-vasubandhu*, "older master Vasubandhu". After various articles dealing with the date of Vasubandhu, E. Frauwallner devoted a book to the topic (1951), arguing that the Paramārtha biography mixed up two Vasubandhus, the first—a brother of Asaṅga in the Fourth century; and the second, the Vasubandhu, who wrote the *Abhidharmakośa* in the Fifth century.[4] P.S. Jaini in his 1958 article briefly summarized Frauwallner's theory and then rejected it by the evidence of an Abhidharma work he had edited, and which was soon published thereafter, written by an opponent of Vasubandhu—berating him for having embraced the Mahāyāna (kind of Buddhism).[5] E. Frauwallner responded in his useful article of 1961 that Jaini's point did not set aside his own solution, because the *Abhidharmakośa* author also had evidently embraced the Mahāyāna later in his life.[6]

In my own doctoral dissertation on Asaṅga's *Śrāvakabhūmi,* I accepted the approximate dates 375-430 A.D. for Asaṅga, following Sylvain Lévi (*Aṣaṅga: Mahāyāna-Sūtrālaṁkāra*) and accepted Frauwallner's circa 400-480 A.D. for Vasubandhu, author of *Abhidharmakośa.*[7] Independently of Jaini, I rejected Frauwallner's solution of two Vasubandhus by pointing out that the earlier Vasubandhu was a Mādhyamika and probably also an important figure in the lineage of the "Pure Land" school of Buddhism, thus differentiated from the Yogācāra Vasubandhu. Aside from the Paramārtha biography, my solution was not textually based as was Jaini's, but rather appealed to a logical formulation amounting to this: Since the Chinese and the Tibetan traditions agree that the Vasubandhu, who authored the *Abhidharmakośa* was the brother of Asaṅga, the burden of proof is on any Western scholar who would set aside those two independently agreeing traditions. Thus, I cited Frauwallner's own summary of the main differences between the two Vasubandhus and concluded that his two assertions do not have "significant contrast". Of course, the dates do not count, because they were added by Westerners. Then, if we know the home city for one Vasubandhu, we do not know it for the other; ditto for family, teacher, royal patronage, place of death. Thus, Frauwallner does not present two contrasting persons. My own intuition insists that if the Westerner cannot prove what he believes to be a superior solution, one should continue to accept the Buddhist tradition.

Admittedly, my argument as clarified above was hardly convincing to those who perused it. Now, years later, I can provide a more positive argument. It is certain that the Vaibhāṣika master Saṃghabhadra would not have challenged Vasubandhu to a debate and have written works in refutation of his *Abhidharmakośa,*[8] or that the text which Jaini edited would be so vehemently opposed to the *Kośa* writer,[9] unless this Vasubandhu were indeed the author of texts in Asaṅga's lineage as the brother of Asaṅga and converted to the Mahāyāna. Notice first that the *Abhidharmakośa* was translated into Chinese by the Yogācāra translators.[10] Then recall how the *Abhidharmakośa* was composed. Vasubandhu, a follower of the Sautrāntika type of Buddhist theory-system, had studied *in cognito* in the rival Vaibhāṣika Buddhist theory-system, later wrote his *Abhidharmakośa* verses following this rival school and the commentary following the Sautrāntika. From the standpoint of the Vaibhāṣika masters, the verses would constitute an oversimplification of their position, the Sautrāntika commentary an impertinence or insult. From the standpoint of the Sautrāntika masters, the Vaibhāṣika basic verses are a ridiculous concession to the opponents, not recompensed just by a Sautrāntika-type commentary. In short, Vasubandhu did not please either side by his *Abhidharmakośa* and *Bhāṣya*. In classical times of India, this meant that his manuscript would be ignored, not copied in the Abhidharma schools, whether Vaibhāṣika or Sautrāntika; and so would pass into oblivion. But Asaṅga converted his younger brother to the Mahāyāna. He quickly rose to the helm in this kind of Mahāyāna movement, that is often called the Yogācāra school. As the Mahāyāna prospered, the Abhidharma schools were fading, partly through the destruction of their Gāndhāra institutions by the Hūṇa invasions. Vasubandhu's *Abhidharmakośa* became adopted in some Māhāyāna curricula as an introduction to the Abhidharma, and began to enjoy commentaries. This must have happened during Vasubandhu's lifetime, since among the extant commentaries (at least in Tibetan translation) on the *Abhidharmakośa,* there is one by Dignāga, who appears to have been born when Vasubandhu died.[11] Thus as Vasubandhu became eminent in the Māhayāna, his *Abhidharmakośa* became popular in those currents. So it is reasonable that when it was translated into Chinese, it would be by the Yogācāra translators, as did happen. It is therefore comprehensible that some decades after Vasubandhu, as a young man had composed the *Abhidharmakośa,* attempts would be made by Abhidharma masters, especially Vaibhāṣika, to refute it. This would happen when Vasubandhu himself was rather aged and no longer interested in debating it, as Paramārtha's biography mentioned: "I am now already old. You may do as you please. I formerly composed the *śāstra* to refute the doctrines of the Vibhāṣa." There is an implication of an unspoken reason that Vasubandhu had already won the debate by virtue of being challenged to a debate. These remarks are meant to conclude my proof that the author of the *Abhidharmakośa* is the same person, who was converted to the Mahāyāna and composed various treatises and commentaries, especially under the banner of the Yogācāra school of Buddhism.

Now, a recent book on Vasubandhu's works claims that there is only one Vasubandhu—of course the brother of Asaṅga, and that he lived in the Fourth century with patronage of Chandragupta I.[12] This theory rests on the indefensible procedure of determining a certain king and his era and then placing Vasubandhu accordingly. But see the historical work by Majumdar and Altekar. "The references to Vasubandhu in Buddhist works throw light on the literary patronage of a Gupta king, whose identity cannot be established with certainty".[13] These historians point to two references of royalty in connection with a Vasubandhu: (1) the rhetorician Vāmana said that Chandragupta's son called Chandraprakāśa had appointed the Buddhist scholar Vasubandhu as his minister. (2) the biography of Vasubandhu by Paramārtha brought to China, and available in a translation by Takakasu, informs that King Vikramāditya of Ayodhyā admired Vasubandhu, so the crown prince Bālāditya and the queen began to study Buddhism under Vasubandhu; and that when Bālāditya himself became king, he favored Vasubandhu with patronage.[14] Majumdar and Altekar, although themselves unable to solve this problem of royal patronage have provided the essential data for the solution.

This historical and literary data suggests that both Vasubandhus eventually enjoyed royal patronage. The first Vasubandhu, who wrote a commentary on Āryadeva's Mādhyamika work *Śataśastra*, lived in the fourth century and became a minister of a Gupta king.[15] The second Vasubandhu, author of the *Abhidharmakośa* and Yogācāra treatises, lived in the fifth century and was favored by Narasimhagupta Bālāditya (c. 467-473) after he ascended the throne—thus in Vasubandhu's career of later 60's and early 70's.

This conclusion also enables me to suggest a better explanation than my old dissertation's attempt for the reference in Vasubandhu's own commentary on the *Abhidharmakośa*, III, 15c, to *pūrvācārya*, which Yaśomitra commented upon as *pūrvācārya yogācārā āryāsaṅgaprabhṛtayaḥ*. It would be a reference to Asaṅga's *Abhidharmasamuccaya*, a kind of Sautrāntika work. In the sequence of events as I envisage them, Vasubandhu's elder brother Asaṅga was completing his enormous *Yogācārabhūmi* around 425 A.D. (His *Bodhisattvabhūmi* had been partially translated into Chinese sometime between 412 and 418 A.D.), when he converted Vasubandhu to the Mahāyāna. According to Bu-ston's historical account, Vasubandhu said of Asaṅga's huge work, "He has founded a system so difficult and burdensome that it can be carried only by an an elephant."[16] It is reasonable to accept Bu-ston's further remark that the content of the large compendium is summarized in two short treatises, the *Abhidharmasamuccaya* and the Mahāyānasaṃgraha[17]—indicating the composition of these were partially inspired by Vasubandhu's conversion, and that Vasubandhu took the class in these two texts, while he was being trained in the new lineage and probably being groomed for a leading role. Asaṅga must have encouraged Vasubandhu to write a commentary on the *Mahāyānasaṃgraha*, and he must have composed it while Asaṅga was still alive as Vasubandhu's first Mahāyāna commentary. After the death of Asaṅga, Vasubandhu wrote his commentaries on Mahāyāna scriptures, meaning such ones as the *Daśabhūmika-sūtra.* It must be at this time, ten or more years after he composed the *Abhidharmakośa* and *Bhāṣya,* that in the role of an *ācārya* intending to teach a class in this topic, he looked over his commentary, touching it up here and there. He would add a few remarks about Yogācāra theories, the reference to an "old master", perhaps some of the references to "others" *(apare).*

Some brief remarks about Vasubandhu's works are in order. I presume that the Tibetan and Chinese canons are independent in this matter. So far as is known, the works of the first Vasubandhu (Fourth century) are preserved exclusively in the Chinese canon. Ordinarily, the works of the Fifth century Vasubandhu are those which the Tibetan and Chinese catalogs agree to be by him. Works in the Tibetan canon and absent in the Chinese canon, might have been composed by someone unknown or translated from Sanskrit into Chinese or might have been the native Chinese compositions.

Three Vasubandhu commentaries can be considered together: they are the *Abhidharmakośa-bhāṣya,* commentary on the *Gayāśīrṣa,* and commentary on Asaṅga's *Mahāyāna-saṃgraha.* They have a common style of departing from the text being commented upon with information and interpretations often argumentatively presented and leaving various parts of the basic texts unexplained. In contrast, the commentaries on the *Madhyāntavibhāga* and the *Daśabhūmikasūtra* are straightforward on the words and phrases of these texts, apparently taking everything of the basic texts into account.

There are various incorrect attributions in current literature. For example, sometimes Vasubandhu is credited with the prose commentary preserved in Sanskrit on the *Mahāyāna sūtrālaṃkāra*. but without doubt Asaṅga is the author of that commentary.[18] And while Tucci was confident that the *Kārikāsaptati* on the Prajñāpāramitā is by Asaṅga, its commentary by Vasubandhu, there is good reason to believe, in agreement with Chinese records, that both are by Vasubandhu.[19] The Tibetan canon contains a commentary on the *Akṣayamatinirdeśasūtra* attributed to Vasubandhu and not extant in Chinese; elsewhere I have given reasons for denying this attribution.[20]

Vasubandhu seems disinclined to compose a huge comprehensive work like Asaṅga's *Yogācārabhūmi*. He apparently prefers to write summation works. The Tibetan Paṇḍita Bu-ston, when comparing with the immediately following scholars in Vasubandhu's general lineage mentions the tradition that there were four, who were even more "learned" than himself. These were Sthiramati in the Abhidharma, Dignāga in logic, Vimuktasena in Prajñāpāramitā, and Guṇaprabha in Vinaya.[21] This is said of their learning in specialized fields. There is an implication in the case of Sthiramati that he was better as a commentator in Abhidharma, for we have already noticed that Vasubandhu's style as a teacher was independent of the rules for "good" commentaries.

Thus I have identified the Vasubandhu hereafter to be treated. He is the brother of Asaṅga, and lived in the Fifth century. His first work was the *Abhidharmakośa* and its *Bhāṣya*. After his conversion to the Mahāyāna, he composed the commentary on the *Mahāyānasaṃgraha;* and after the death of Asaṅga composed his other Mahāyāna works. He became famous as a teacher, and died at the age of eighty.

Vasubandhu on "Representation-only"

Scholars who read and believe what is usually written about the Buddhist school called Yogācāra or "Mind-only" (*cittamātra*) or "Representation-only" (*vijñaptimātra*) would credit this school with denial of the existence of the external world, as though consciousness is the sole reality.[22] They may have also read that this Buddhist school has a philosophical position of "Idealism", whatever this means. Yet, two recent books that translate various Vasubandhu's works have denied the validity of this usual attribution.[23] The present writer has also previously rejected the standard attribution.[24] The book by Kochumuttom emphatically rejects previous interpretations of Vasubandhu's position, and says regarding the twenty-verse text, "In short, *Viṃśatikā* is polemics not against realism, but against the realistic theory of knowledge."[25] While agreeing with this author's point as here stated, I find his Chapter Six "Idealism or Realism?" difficult to accept, since my quarrel with calling it "Idealism" extends to calling it "Realism"; in short, I find the trouble in understanding this—or any other philosophical system of India, for that matter—is the identification with any Western philosophical system, as though such identification lends an understanding of the Asian system. I also have reservations about the methodology of trying to establish Vasubandhu's position by the data generated through translating his commentary on the *Madhyānta-vibhāga*, his attributed treatise on the three natures, plus his text of the twenty verses and the thirty verses.[26] This is because, it appears that when he comments upon the *Madhyāntavibhāga* and the *Daśabhūmikasūtra*, he is under an obligation to be consistent with the text being commented upon, which is not necessarily the position of his twenty verses and thirty verses. The following comments should clarify those remarks.

According to the Mahāyāna scripture called *Daśabhūmikasūtra* and Vasubandhu's commentary on its Chapter VI, the Tathāgata, i.e. Buddha, discovered the celebrated formula of Dependent Origination (*Pratītyasamutpāda*) with a single area of mind (*ekāgratā-citta*), so in *samādhi*.[27] And in this very context, this scripture has the famous line, *tasyaivaṃ bhavati / cittamātram idaṃ yad idaṃ traidhātukaṃ*, "This occurs to him: 'This mind-only is this derivation from the three worlds." The *Subhāṣitasaṃgraha* cites it with slight paraphrase: *cittamātraṃ yad uta traidhātukam*, "*Mind*-only is namely, what is derived from the three worlds."[28] Now, this scriptural passage appears to claim that whatever we know about the three worlds was discovered by and in the mind. But Vasubandhu's comments are not of Yogācāra doctrine. A Mādhyamika commentator could be expected to say the same thing, namely, that discovering Dependent Origination in a Buddha-*samādhi* by a "single area of mind" is the purport as well of the Prajñāpāramitā scriptures.[29]

As to rendering the term *traidhātukam* in the above manner, of course, it is a derivative noun like Gautama derived from Gotama. But the sense of the derivation must be clarified, and above all, it is so in terms of knowledge. However, Vasubandhu in his commentary (*vṛtti*) on the Twenty verses, mentions it this way: *mahāyāne traidhātukaṃ vijñaptimātraṃ vyavasthāpyate,* "In the Mahāyāna, it is established that what is derived from the three worlds is representation-only."[30] It has been pointed out that Vasubandhu uses the terms *citta* and *vijñapti* as synonyms,[31] and the present switch would indicate it. However, such conclusion fails to notice that Vasubandhu by this substitution implies that the *sūtra* passage is susceptible of more than one interpretation. That is to say, when commenting upon the *Daśabhūmikasūtra,* he presents the general Mahāyāna; while now he intends to give a different interpretation and signals this difference with the term *vijñapti.* This difference is explained by him in the passage in the light of the Yogācāra, namely, with the two added *vijñānas* and the three "natures" (*svabhāva*).

As to the extra *vijñānas* to the standard six accepted by the Mādhyamika, namely, the five perceptions based on the five outer-directed senses and the mental perception (*manovijñāna*), this Yogācāra school had added the "store-consciousness" (*ālayavijñāna*) and the "defiled mind" (*kliṣṭamanas*). Vasubandhu summarizes in his *Karmasiddhi-prakaraṇa*:[32] "Citta (mind) is of two kinds. Among them, one collects its own seeds (*bīja*) [=*ālayavijñāna*]. The other is diversified by having that [first one] as object [=*kliṣṭamanas*], having images (*ākāra*)[33] [=*manovijñāna*], and having different distinctions [five outer-directed *vijñānas*]." Of these two, the second kind is sometimes (e.g. *Madhyāntavibhāga,* I) called "evolving" or "active" (*pravṛtti-*) *vijñānas.* Vasubandhu further explains the "active" kind in his commentary on Asaṅga's *Mahāyānasaṃgraha,* Chap. II:[34] "As to representations (*vijñapti*) of (i.e. belonging to) body, body-possessor, and the eater—the body has the five places (*dhātu*) of eye, etc.; the body-possessor is the *kliṣṭamanas* (defiled mind); the eater (or, enjoyer) is the *manodhātu* (place of mind)." This formulation is curiously comparable to the Upaniṣadic explanation for the two "birds" of the

Vedic verse, namely, that the "higher" bird (=the *ātman*) witnesses and the "lower" bird (=the *jīva*) experiences or enjoys. The "defiled mind" seems to replace the *ātman*, while the "place of mind" replaces the *jīva*.[35]

So far, this is talking about the subjective consciousness without regard to the object. For this topic, it is necessary to know the Yogācāra theory of three "natures". The three are the imaginary nature (*parikalpita-svabhāva),* the dependency nature (*paratantra-svabhāva*), and the perfect nature (*pariniṣpanna-svabhāva*). The two books devoted to Vasubandhu previously alluded to, both include the treatise on the three natures (*Trisvabhāvanirdeśa*) as though it were a composition by Vasubandhu; in fact, it is just in Tibetan, unknown in the Chinese canon. Therefore, I shall avoid the many subtleties of this text, and refer to Vasubandhu's commentary on *Mahāyānasaṃgraha*, II, 32, 2. Asaṅga's statement uses the theory of the three natures: when one sees the perfect nature, one does not see the imaginary nature, and vice versa.[36] This is because one is observing by way of the dependency nature. According to Vasubandhu:[37]

> One teaches it by the example of the earth with a golden pith. Here, the remark, "There is gold within the earth," refers to the golden seed. The element of earth is solidity. Earth is the experienced formation, i.e. any coloring of earth. Those three are the bases for apprehension. The gold appears in the earth itself. The knowledge that it is the gold of it, happens later on, (namely:) at the time it is enhanced by fire (=*nirvikalpa-jñāna*), it becomes apprehended as gold. Thus, it is proved to be an existing thing.

The point of the example is that the imaginary nature (*parikalpita-svabhāva*) is earth as an experienced coloring. When one sees this false coloring, one does not see the gold (*pariniṣpanna svabhāva*); and when one sees the gold, one does not see the imaginary coloring. Neither the golden seed nor the solidity character of earth is denied. What is denied is the reality of the apprehended earth as its coloring. Here, 'coloring' can be interpreted as any imagined activity. Accordingly, the 'defiled mind' (*kliṣṭamanas*) supported by the 'store consciousness' (*ālayavijñāna*) is what experiences the false coloring and transmutation of the *ālayavijñāna* permits the seeing of the true gold.

In short, this theory interprets the 'three worlds' by the above examples, to wit, the solidity of earth or the gold seed hidden therein. Besides, this school teaches that the water (=the three worlds) is seen one way by men, another way by the gods, still another way by the hungry ghosts (*preta*),[38] so these various ways of seeing one objective thing is "representation-only" which the scripture, as Vasubandhu cited it, says is "derived from the three worlds " (*traidhātuka*). We may refer to the basic scripture of the Yogācāra school, the *Saṃdhinirmocanasūtra.* Vasubandhu cites its Maitreya Chapter in the *Mahāyānasaṃgraha,* Chap. II commentary: "Because these reflected images are only representations, Maitreya, I have explained that the consciousness-support (*ālambana*) of perception is defined as representation-only."[39] And Vasubandhu continues, "Hence . . . this representation-only is a term for 'void of entity.'"[40]

One can refer to the part added by consciousness as the "unreal", as does the *Madhyāntavibhāga* ; it calls imagining it, "imagination of the unreal" (*abhūtaparikalpa).* More fully, at I, 8, it asserts:[41]

> The imagination of the unreal is thought (*citta*) and mentals (*caitta*) that own the three worlds. Among them, thought views the object; mentals view features of it.

That this text explains "imagination of the unreal" to be of two kinds is important in terms of Buddhist dogmatics, but our present exposition cannot go into these technicalities. The main point is that when one calls the representation of the unreal "representation-only" or "void of entity", this is the *yoga* precept of how one is to regard it, as a step toward switching from the imaginary nature to the true or perfect nature.

The foregoing should have made it abundantly clear that the Yogācāra school does not deny an external phenomenon called "three worlds" as various survey books of Indian philosophy or rival schools have reported. Kochumuttom quite properly found various previous authors mistaken in taking *vijñaptimātra* as an ultimate of this system.[42] So far the only ultimate phenomenon noticed is the "three worlds" (*tridhātu*). According to the Yogācāra interpretation of *traidhātuka,* what was derived from the three worlds is an unreal addition. Hence, this theory ties in with the old Buddhist insistence on "non-self", since Vasubandhu declares in *Viṃśikā,* k. 10, that representation-only has the advantage of realizing non-self of person (*pudgala-nairātmya*) and non-self of *dharma* (*dharma-nairātmya*). Thus seeing the true *pudgala* or the true *dharma* is not a denial of either, rather is a divestiture of the respective "selves".

Thus, there are various ways of referring to the part added by consciousness when witnessing an "object." It is the "self", the "representation", the (external) entity (*artha*), the "unreal" (*adbhūta*). Also, the part which men, gods, etc. add to the water (in the example), one may notice as the function (*kriyā*). So I must agree with Falk that in the Dharmadhātu no *kriyās* can take place.[43] In the example, water is the "Dharmadhātu" (natural realm) which leaves out any *kriyā*. A Mahāyāna scripture called *Ārya-Akṣayamatinirdeśa* in its section on the objects of "insight" (*prajñā*) has a subsection: "the knowledge comprehending the *dharmadhātu*". The *sūtra* states that the *dharmadhātu* has the four elements, but none of the characters attributed to them. It has the five sense organs, but none of the functions of seeing, etc. attributed to them. In particular, it has the realm of mind (*manodhātu*), but does not have the character of representation (*vijñapti*). It has the perceptions based on the sense organs but not the discrimination of the respective objects. In particular, it has the realm of perception (*vijñāna*) based on the mind (*manas*) but not the character of discriminating *dharmas*. It has all the sense objects, but not the characters attributed to them by perceptions—named by sense organs. And again for the objects, it has all six objects, but not the character of representation as such.[44] The scripture represents the natural realm as an all-comprehensive realm without any function at all. All functions require this natural realm, because there would be no function of the eye to see in the absence of an eye. This, then, is the Yogācāra meaning of *traidhātuka*, namely, that the three worlds are the natural realm, and what is derived from it is the various functions created by sentient life and its perceptions, which this school has called "unreal", and "representation-only".

Vasubandhu's commentary on *Mahāyānasaṃgraha*, Chap. III, presents a list of the various names of this natural realm (*dharmadhātu*) and includes them in the "perfect nature" (*pariniṣpanna-svabhāva*), as follows: Thus-ness (*tathatā*), True End (*bhūtakoṭi*), Without characteristic (*ānimitta*), Absolute (*paramārtha*), Dharmadhātu, and Voidness (*śūnyatā*).[45] He also has called it 'golden seed'.

VASUBANDHU ON "TRANSMUTATION OF THE SUPPORT"

Here four works of Vasubandhu will be utilized: *Abhidharmakośa-bhāṣya, Mahāyānasaṃgrahabhāṣya, Triṃśikā*, and *Ārya-Gayāśīrṣa-nāma-sūtravyākhyāna* [reconstructed title]. The first and third are accessible in Sanskrit. The second and fourth are consulted by way of the Tibetan translations. I shall present the basic theories using the first three works, and try to avoid prolixity; and then go to the *Gayāśīrṣa-sūtra* and Vasubandhu's commentary.

BASIC THEORIES

The first topic is of course the "support" (*āśraya*), and the next one—its transmutation (*parāvṛtti*). We shall find that the *Abhidharmakośa* (*A.K.*) has much information about the "support" but very little about the "transmutation."[46]

Under *A.K.* I, v. 44c-d, *āśraya* is mentioned as the support for perception (*vijñāna*) and identified as the organ (*indriya*) independent of the object. Under I, v. 45a-b, perception changes according to the organ; and under I, v. 45c-d, *vijñāna* takes its name from the (respective) organs. Hence, we speak of "eye-based perception" (*cakṣur-vijñāna*). Old Buddhism had a set of six organs (*ṣaḍāyatana*), the fifth member of Dependent Origination (*pratītyasamutpāda*). Of these, five are the outer-directed sense-organs; and the sixth is the mental organ (*mana-āyatana=mana-indriya*), hence the support of mind-based perception (*mano-vijñāna*). As was earlier mentioned, the Yogācāra adds a "defiled mind" and a "store consciousness", which should also take their names from their "organs"; to wit, "mind based on defilements" (*kleśa*) and "perception based on the store" (*ālaya*). According to Vasubandhu's *Triṃśikā*, v. 5, this "mind" (*manas*) is supported (*tad-āśritya*) by the "store consciousness" and also has it as "object" (here: *ālambana*). But that the *ālayavijñāna* is supported by the store of seeds is not explicitly stated.

Since these supports are fed by foods, it is necessary to treat these.[47] Vasubandhu's *A.K.*, III, v. 38d, v. 39a, v. 40a-b, v. 41, and his *Bhāṣa* thereon, are useful sources for the four: morsel food (*kavaḍaṃkāra-āhāra*), of two kinds—coarse and subtle, for staying alive. Contactual food (*sparśa-āhāra*) involving the three perception, sense organ, and object enhance the sense organs. Volitional food (*maṇaḥsaṃcetanā-āhāra*), which is the mental *karma* (that of destiny), possessed of intention toward the desired things (and which is the "eater" mindplace of the previous section). And perceptual food (*vijñāna-āhāra*), is the aggregate of perceptions (*vijñāna*). Vasubandhu there says (*A.K.*, III, v. 41) that the first two foods (like the nourishment given to the infant) nourish the being already born; the last two (like the mother) enable the being not yet born to come into existence. "Food" here means food—concrete or metaphorical that is eaten and is subject to digestion; and so is an important feature of the *karma* theory of Buddhism. This verse, III, 41, explicitly mentions the "support" (*āśraya*) and the "supported" (*āśrita*), namely, the body furnished with organs as the "support", and thought plus mentals (*citta* and *caitta*) as the "supported". The first kind of food, the morsel(s), makes the body grow; the second kind, contactual, makes the thought plus mentals grow.

Vasubandhu's commentary on the Mahāyānasaṃgraha (*M.S.*) presents much data on these four foods in comments on Chap. I and IX. The Chap. I comments seem to depend heavily on the *A.K.* treatment. The Chap. IX exposition is especially interesting. Here he states that three foods—contactual, volitional, and perceptual, leaving out the morsel food, create the support (*āśraya*), which is the basis (**upādhi*) of sentient beings (*sattva*).[48] He had been referring to the "Nirvāṇa with no remaining basis" (*nirupādhiśeṣa-nirvāṇa*). He goes on to say that the four foods, including the morsel type, create support which is the "pure basis" (Tib., *dag pa'i rten*) because the *śrāvakas* (auditors), and so on are rightly based therein. Soon he speaks about the wonderous nature of this teaching that at the time (the theory of) those foods was received, it was accepted by the gods from the Buddha and given to other sentient beings, who on account of those attained enlightenment.[49] That report of Vasubandhu agrees with the role of moderation in food adopted by the Buddha as the middle path between mortification and indulgence. But now we can realize that what was meant is the moderation, or self-control, in all four foods.

Having given some data about the "supports", before going to their transmutation, I feel some information should be furnished about these extra *vijñānas* of the Yogācāra school. In his commentary on *M.S.*, Chap. I, Vasubandhu points out that it is defiled *manovijñāna* that is reborn.[50] Since it is supported by the "store consciousness"—a store of habit-energy (*vāsanā*) and (underlying) traces (*anuśaya*)—this store must go along with it. Since the Yogācāra school teaches that this "store consciousness" ceases in "Nirvāṇa without remaining basis,"[51] this is consistent with a passage in the Pāli scriptures, namely Saṃyutta-nikāya, IV, 372, where among the names given synonymously with Nirvāṇa is the name *anālaya,* "without a store". Also in his comments on *M.S.*, Chap. I, he declares that there must be the mind possessed of defilement (Tib. *ñon mons pa can gyi yid)* because that is why one endeavors to get rid of the hindrances of (both) defilement and the knowable (*kleśa*-and *jñeya-āvaraṇa*).[52] The point of Vasubandhu's saying this, is that the Yogācāra school in the works of his brother Asaṅga had set forth two kinds of "nescience " (*avidyā*), namely, the kind in which one does not know what Buddhism claims one should know, e.g. the four Noble Truths—and there is no defilement in not knowing it; and the kind involving deviance or positive wrong, termed "defiled."[53] Vasubandhu also refers to this theory of "unmixed nescience" (i.e. unmixed with defilement) in his comments on *M.S.*, Chap. I.[54] Presumably, it was on account of having two kinds of nescience that this school was forced to divide the old *manovijñāna* into two, the one to be labelled "defiled mind" (*kliṣṭamanas*), the other to keep its old name, but regarded as simply "ignorant" and as was noticed above to be called the "eater" or enjoyer. Hence, it is this "ignorant" mind which needs direction from parents, training in schools, precepts from gurus; and so, hopefully—at least from the standpoint of Buddhism—motivated to counteract the defiled mind.

There should now be sufficient background information for the theory of "transmutation of the support". As to where Vasubandhu treats this topic, we first use de La Vallée Poussin's *A.K.* index that gives references for *āśrayaparivṛtti, parāvṛtti, vikopana,* to the Chap. IV (on *karma*) and the Chap. VIII (on the meditative states called *samāpatti*). The Chap. VIII reference turns out to be only in Yaśomitra's sub-commentary.[55] A Chap. IV note refers to the Yogācāra treatise *Mahāyānasūtrālaṃkāra,* ix, 12, that the expression means the appearance of a new personality, the ordinary person (*pṛthagjana*) becomes a noble (*ārya*) (i.e. hearkens to the Buddhist teachings), a woman becomes a man, a human becomes an animal, etc. The *A.K.* itself seems to have used the term mainly for sex change. It does have an important usage in the comment under *A.K.*, v. 56, where this "transmutation of the support" is shown to be a feature of the "path of vision" (*darśana-mārga*) of the Noble Truths, and involves the transmutation to an Arhat (the early Buddhist saint).[56]

While the *Yogācāra* had inherited the term, it certainly expanded its usage. So Vasubandhu's *Triṃśikā*, k. 29c-d, "Transmutation of the support is of two kinds by destruction of 'contamination' (dauṣṭhulya)" and (*āśrayasya parāvṛttir dvidhā dauṣṭulyahāṇitaḥ*). For the "two", Sthiramati's comment points to the hindrance of defilement and the hindrance of the knowable. One of these two supports is the "store consciousness", support of the "defiled mind". The other one must be the five *skandhas* as per *M.S.* X, 5.[57] Sthiramati was forced to his comment by Vasubandhu's own two in his Sanskrit wording. Thus, 29a-b: "Yonder one is the non-thought, non-perceptual reach; and this knowledge is supramundane" (*acinto 'nupalambho'sāu jñānaṃ lokottaraṃ ca tat*). Vasubandhu continues the contrast in k. 30:

> *sa evānāsravo dhātur acintyaḥ kuśalo dhruvaḥ /*
> *sukho vimuktikāyo 'sāu dharmakhyo 'yaṃ mahāmuneḥ //*
>
> Precisely that is the non-fluxional place—inconceivable, virtuous, constant. Yonder is the happy body of liberation. This one is called the Dharma of the Great Muni.

According to Sthiramati, "happy body of liberation" means the *śrāvaka* (Hīnayāna auditor) goal, eliminating the hindrance of defilement, reaching Nirvāṇa. So, "this one" means the Buddha's Dharmakāya with supramundane knowledge, because eliminating the hindrance of the knowable.[58]

Vasubandhu thought he had compressed the main ideas in his twenty verses and thirty verses. He had not predicted the future readers and translators for whom such expressions as *asāu* and *ayam* are merely "space fillers."

Vasubandhu also goes into the theory of "transmutation" in his commentary of *M.S.*, Chaps. I, III, and VIII. In the comments on Chap. I, he states: "Accordingly, as long as one dwells in the active perceptions (*pravṛtti-vijñāna*), it is not feasible that there will be a transmutation of the support, i.e. the basis."[59] The rationale of this remark is soon stated: "As to the phrase, 'the transmutation is not feasible' (Tib. *'gyur ba ruṅ ba ma yin no źes bya ba ste*), in the phase of *samāpatti* (i.e. meditative trances in the realms of form and formless), the active perceptions are in abeyance, because the transmutation is possible when there are no seeds (i.e. of the "store-consciousness").[60] "Hence, we claim that in this way it is the *ālayavijñāna* itself that gets the transmutation."[61] This agrees with the previous observation that the store-consciousness is the support for the "defiled mind", which is the first of the active perceptions.

In his commentary on *M.S.*, Chap. III, Vasubandhu comments about the "diamond-like *samādhi*" (*vajropama-samādhi*) which manages the difficult task of getting rid of the "contamination" (*dauṣṭhulya*): and adds, "With no interval upon that *samādhi*, one is freed from all hindrance (*āvaraṇa*), and achieves thereby the transmutation of the support, i.e. the basis of that (two kinds, as above)."[62] The second kind is found in Asaṅga's *M.S.*, X, 5, showing that by the "diamond-like *samādhi*" one obtains the Dharmakāya with five kinds of sovereignty, namely by transmutation of each of the five personal aggregates (*skandha*) in order, i.e. corporeal formations (*rūpa*), feelings (*vedanā*), notions (*saṃjñā*), motivations (*saṃskāra*), and perceptions (*vijñāna*). According to the Abhidharma (*A.K.* VIII, v.. 28), this diamond-like *samādhi* occurs in the Fourth Dhyāna of the Realm of Form, but Vasubandhu did not mention the "transmutation" at that place. Also, Asaṅga's *Śrāvakabhūmi*, when defining the "diamond-like *samādhi*", did not mention the transmutation theory.[63] This is another indication of Yogācāra's new interpretations of old Buddhist terms.

M.S. Chap. VIII, is devoted to the topic, "Instruction of Insight" (*adhiprajñā śikṣā*) and goes into the instruction about "non-constructive knowledge" (*nirvikalpa-jñāna*). *M.S.* VIII, 19.3, states that the non-constructive knowledge obtained afterwards (*pṛṣṭhalabdhanirvikalpajñāna*) is of five kinds.[64] Vasubandhu comments that one should decide each one, apparently in sequence; and since the transmutation occurs in his explanation, each of the five stages is now given: (1) deciding the "understanding" means that at the time one understands, one decides, "I am understanding this way." (2) deciding the remembrance means that upon arising (from sleep) one recalls, "I understood the non-construction." (3) deciding the contract (**vyavasthā*) means "I shall teach others what

I have understood". (4) deciding the mixture (*saṃsarga*) means "I see all *dharmas* mixed and taken together with knowledge that has this as meditative object." In this way, there is transmutation of the support, i.e. the basis. (5) after that transmutation of the support, i.e. the basis, one decides the manifoldness (*samṛddhi* or *vibhava*), which means "Whatever I anticipated, it becomes all a manifold;" also, "Just as it is earth and so on, and as I have imagined it, it changes into gold, and so on."[65]

M.S., VIII, 20, then goes to the topic of how beings of different destinies see the object differently, e.g. the animals seeing the water as clean which humans see as dirty. As was mentioned earlier in this chapter, the support has to be the organ or sense organ (*indriya* or *āyatana*), and the difference in destinies is in terms of their organs and then of their foods. Thus, the real change, the "transmutation" is in these, not in the active perceptions based thereon.

This emphasis on the "organ" is exemplified by the supernormal faculties (*abhijñā*) called "divine eye" (*divyacakṣus*) and "divine ear" (*divya-śrotra*). So also the *Saddharmapuṇḍarīka-sūtra*, Chap. 18 (edition of Wogihara and Tsuchida) extolling the aids for the Dharma preacher, which turn out to be abnormally keen senses, including the sense of smell.

The Gayāśīrṣa-Sūtra and Vasubandhu's Commentary

The *Gayāśīrṣa* (Sanskrit form) is in Pāli in the Aṅguttaranikāya, Book of Eights, Chap. on Earthquakes.[66] Vasubandhu's rather small commentary, preserved in both the Chinese and the Tibetan languages, clarifies that the Yogācāra notion of *āśrayaparāvṛtti* is a revelation of what was hidden or obscurely referred to in this early Buddhist scripture. Here the Bhagavat, when staying on Gayā-head at Gayā addressed the monks, "Monks, before my awakening, while not yet completely awakened and only being awakened, I conceived "secondary lights" (Pāli, *obhāsa;* Skt. *avabhāsa*) but saw no [real] forms.[67] Monks, it occurred to me, "If I were to both conceive secondary lights and see the [real] forms, knowledge and vision within me would thus be better purified." In the sequel, the Bhagavat informs the monks that practicing most resolutely he did conceive the secondary lights and see the (real) forms, but did not converse with any of those devas. It occurred to him successively with successive performance most resolutely, to further purify knowledge and vision, by a sequence including the conversation with those devas, then knowing their community, then what deed had brought them to the state, then their foods, and their pleasure and pain, then their length of life; finally, whether he had (ever) dwelt with them. The Bhagavat addressed the monks: "Monks, so long as this eightfold series of knowledge and vision of the higher devas was not fully purified in me, I did not realize as one awakened to the complete enlightenment . . . . But when those two were fully purified I did realize as one awakened to the complete enlightenment . . . . Then knowledge and vision (of liberation) arose in me . . . . I knew . . . this is my last birth."

The portion where the Buddha remembers whether he had ever dwelt among those deities amounts to remembering his past lives. As to what that scripture referred to as the eightfold series of knowledge (*jñāna*) and vision (*darśana*), it is reasonable to accept that it is set forth in the immediately following scripture on the eight bases of mastery (Pāli: *abhibhāyatana*; Skt.: *abhibhv-āyatana*, or *abhibhū*).[68] For the first two, the yogin is conscious of his own body while he sees exterior forms (*rūpa*) lovely or ugly, in the first case limited; in the second case unlimited, thinking in both cases, "Having mastered them, I know, I see them." For the next six, the yogin is unconscious of his own body. For the third and fourth, while he sees exterior forms—lovely or ugly—in the one case limited, in the next case unlimited, he thinks in both cases, "Having mastered them, I know, I see them." For remaining four, i.e. fifth through eighth, while he sees exterior forms as all blue; or as all yellow; or as all red; or as all white, he thinks in each of the four cases, "Having mastered them, I know, I see them." These are the eight bases of mastery.

The Buddhist Abhidharma identifies these colors as "totalities" (P. *kasiṇa*, Skt. *kṛtsna-āyatana*) and so assigns the eight bases of mastery associated with these "totalities" as to encompass the entire "realm of form" (*rūpa-dhātu*) among the three realms or worlds.[69]

If one were to comment on the *Gayāśīrṣa* in an expected manner, presumably one would expand upon the topic of "knowledge" and "vision" explaining their eight actions, touch upon the association with devas, and so on, in terms of what is actually spoken about in the scripture. One could scarcely have predicted Vasubandhu's manner of commenting. Since the Bhagavat spoke about the pair being "better purified", Vasubandhu decided to devote his commentary to the problem of purification and to such an extent that the title is the main indication of being a commentary on that scripture. But, for the theory of getting purified, I suppose one could hardly find a better presentation. Most of his text is given over to expanding four headings, i.e. four surpassing teachings about purification of the cause (Tib. *rgyu,* S. *hetu*), namely, (1) teaching about the purifying path and the collection; (2) teaching the collection of merit (*puṇya*) and knowledge (*jñāna*); (3) teaching the method of comprehending the true end (*bhūtakoṭi*); (4) teaching the concordant praxis. Vasubandhu tells eight ways of teaching the path of accumulation, and eight ways of teaching the path of purification. The third section is the one which elicits the comment about "transmutation of the support". Therefore, this section should be exposed in some detail.[70] He explains that the "true end" is taught in four ways: (1) elimination of faults by (realizing) impermanence [shows "whereby" one dwells]; (2) abiding with "inherent character" (*svalakṣaṇa*) [shows "how" one dwells]; (3) incessant abiding in the own-nature (*svabhāva*) of the "natural realm" (*dharmadhātu*) [shows "for what" one dwells]. (4) the aim of neither rejecting nor keeping [shows "wherein" one dwells].[71]

Before continuing with Vasubandhu's list of thirty-three "knowledge attendants", it is well to explain somewhat those four ways. The *Gayāśīrṣa,* as was noticed, is mainly about the theory of *jñāna-darśana,* 'knowledge and vision". This term occurs in the basic scripture of the Yogācāra school, the *Saṃdhinirmocanasūtra*; and the great commentary on this scripture by Yüan-t'sê, which was translated from Chinese into Tibetan has much information about it.[72] Besides, Asaṅga's *Yogācārabhūmi* contains a list of nine kinds of the pair and explains that each are forms of "insight" (*prajñā*).[73] Employing this data enables me to explain Vasubandhu's four ways in terms of this term. No.1, about realizing impermanence, is a "vision". No.2, about the "inherent character", e.g. of earth's solidity, is the comparable "knowledge". Inferentially, No. 3, about the "own-nature", is a "vision"; and No. 4, about neither rejecting nor keeping is the comparable "knowledge". Then, it seems that the first pair goes with a beginner, while the second pair is very advanced. The fact that Vasubandhu, who must have known all this, would not inform the reader shows another side of him as a teacher. If confronted with such data, we could expect him to retort: "So what? Does anyone purify himself more by being told which of those is a 'vision' and which is a 'knowledge'?" Vasubandhu, right after giving those four, states that these are rendered comprehensible by the list of thirty-three knowledge attendants, as follows.[74]

[Fifteen of personal purification]: (1) to purify the path by purification of mind, and to purify mind by purification of the path; (2) solitariness of the path to, and (solitariness of) visualization with knowledge of, the true end; (3) there being the basis, the single reliance on it alone; (4) transmutation of the support when there is knowledge of the true end and purification of the knowledge by the (seriatim) transmutation of the support;[75] (5) the pair [knowledge and vision] dwelling in the duty done; (6) rightly and fully knowing the knowable entity; (7) fully knowing in conformity with the seed of liberation of the sentient beings subject to beginningless *saṃsāra*; (8) fully knowing in conformity with the maturation of diverse *karma*; (9) fully knowing in conformity with benefit to oneself and benefit to others; (10) rendering the root of virtue (*kuśalamūla*), whether small or immeasurable;[76] (11) pondering virtue and non-virtue; (12) rightly and fully knowing as it really is, the arising of diverse aspects (or, images) (*ākāra*); (13) to insert virtuous natures and track non-virtuous natures; (14) conceiving the timely and the untimely; (15) being based within, after rejecting the two extremes.[77] [Eleven of purification of others]: (16) starting (the sentient beings) on the striving to eliminate the evil acts of body— speech, and mind; (17) to transfer others to the (correct) instruction; (18) to incite (their) attraction after oneself has been based in the cultivation; (19) making (them) give up anger; (20) making them seek the precepts about the improper and non-existent train (of thoughts) and (seek) the error-free hearing; (21) making them give thought to, and set about mastering all the *dharmas*; (22) having made them recognize the traces (*anuśaya*), to teach the Dharma in consistent manner; (23) making them comprehend reality (*tattva*); (24) making them embrace the genuine in the mind, and abandon the fake (therein); (25) making them fulfil the ancillary set for enlightenment; (26) maturing the sentient beings. [Seven of one's abiding in the goal]; (27) conceive the rising and passing away of natures (*dharma*); (28) skilful in all the *dharmas;* (29) wishless as to Nirvāṇa; (30) achieved the four confidences;[78] (31) achieved the self-arisen knowledge of all *dharmas;* (32) not doubting any *dharmas;* (33) not clinging to ostentations, because of entry into the absolute method.

In the light of our remarks just before giving Vasubandhu's long list, it seems reasonable to conclude that he intended the first fifteen to constitute realizations and meditations in expansion of Nos. 1 and 2 of his four. Then would follow the eleven of purifying others. Finally, his seven ways of abiding in the goal would go with Nos. 3 and 4 of his four. His first group, which includes the "transmutation of the support" as 4th among the fifteen is clearly meant to be the "Hīnayāna" goal. The next two groups constitute the Mahāyāna—first the practice on behalf of others, and finally one's own aim of enlightenment.

The Four Degrees of Penetration

The Buddhist Abhidharma,[79] Prajñāpāramitā exegesis[80] and Yogācāra texts[81]—each devote attention to the topic of "degrees of penetration" (*nirvedha-bhāgīya),* standardized as four. Vasubandhu is very familiar with this topic, because of his generous treatment of it in *A.K.,* Chap. VI (on the saint and his path), along with his commentary. The four terms are: *uṣmagata* (warmth), *mūrdhagata* (summits), *kṣāntigata* (forbearance), and *laukikāgradharmagata* (supreme mundane natures). This topic is related to previous sections of this chapter. It involves "representation-only"; and since the Abhidharma calls them also the four "roots of virtue" (*kuśalamūla*); this implicates the 10th of Vasubandhu's list of "knowledge attendants" (preceding section). Since Asaṅga's *Mahāyānasaṃgraha (M.S.),* Chap. III, 13, goes into the theory of the four, naturally I shall use Vasubandhu's commentary on this. There are four searches (*paryeṣaṇā*), and four *samādhis.*

Warmth: In the purport of *M.S.* III, 13 "warmth" is a prognostic of fire, so here is employed metaphorically as a prognostic of the "knowledge of reality" (*tattvajñāna*).[82] This initial "search" or examination is the lesser forbearance (*mṛdukṣānti*) regarding the absence of the *artha*—which we previously explained as the imposition on the object. This state of "warmth" has for support a *samādhi* named "acquisition of light" (*ālokalabdha*). According to *A.K.* VI, 16-17, the Buddhist meditation "station of mindfulness on *dharmas*" (*dharma-smṛtyupasthāna*) is responsible for "warmth", includes the sixteen aspects of the four Noble Truths, and involves "non-self of *dharmas*" (*dharmanairātmya*). Vasubandhu, on *M.S.*

III, 13, explains that the knowledge that the *artha* is absent, is what is called "acquisition of light"; hence, this "light" is a form of insight (*prajñā*).[83] Vasubandhu explains "forbearance" as belief (or, favorable inclination; willingness to admit that it be so). He explains "absence of the *artha*" by a term (in Tib. *bsrabs pa*) meaning "diminishing" or "vanishing". Thus, this initial knowledge that the *artha* is absent is a kind of loosening of the normal realistic imputation so that it "diminishes".

Summits: Asaṅga, *M.S.* III, 13, explains that during the superior "forbearance" regarding the absence of the *artha*, there is a *samādhi* named "spread of light" (*ālokavivṛddhi*).[84] According to *A.K.*VI, 17d, commentary by Vasubandhu, this state also involves contemplation of the sixteen aspects of the Noble Truths; but in this case of "roots of virtue", they are elevated to a high pitch. This state of "summits", like the preceding "warmth", is labelled *cala* (not fixed), i.e. one could still backslide. Vasubandhu, on the *M.S.* explains "spread of light" as intending a great knowledge that the *artha* is absent.[85] It appears that this "search" is differentiated from the previous one mainly by intensity.

Forbearance: The third "search" has decided differences from the preceding two. In the *M.S.*, this is the "entrance into representation-only " (*vijñaptimātratāpraveśa*). There is "recognition as it really is" (*yathābhūtaparijñāna*) with certainty that the *artha* is absent. The supporting *samādhi* is called "directed to one part of the meaning of reality" (*tattvārthaikadeśapraviṣṭa*), because it recognizes only the absence of the apprehensible, i.e., the human superimposition on the object.[86] This "forbearance", or tacit acceptance, is "consistent with truth" (*satyānulomikī*), according to Vasubandhu with the meaning that non-self of *dharmas* is true.[87] He adds that this entrance into the character of the knowable (*jñeya*) is a situation of being directed by much learning, and is a contemplation that is (also) of Mahāyāna nature.[88]

Supreme mundane natures: According to *A.K.* VI, 19c commentary by Vasubandhu, they are supreme mundane *dharmas* because lacking a "cause of the same class" (*sabhāgahetu*), in the case of the human meditator what is called "human acts" (*puruṣakāra*).[89] In the *M.S.* III, 13, the *samādhi* is "without interval" (*ānantarya*), i.e., immediate to introduce the "path of vision" (*darśana-mārga*). This *samādhi* removes the notion of "representation-only."[90] The "path of vision" is treated in *M.S.* III, 14, where it is apparently a kind of "after arisen knowledge" (*pṛṣṭhalabdhajñāna*), with "compressed *dharmas*" (*saṃsṛṣṭadharma*).[91] Vasubandhu on this *M.S.* III, 14, explains that the *dharmas* are not compressed by the "store consciousness". But rather are a "seed" compressed by "right mental orientation" (*samyagmanasikāra*). In the way it is done by the "store consciousness"; and that in the manner that the "store consciousness" is a cause of defiling natures (*saṃkleśa-dharma*) so in that manner (the "right mental orientation") is a cause of purifying nature (*vyavadāna-dharma*).[93] The point of his remarks is that the "supreme mundane natures" are according to *A.K.* VI, 19c comments still "possessed of flux" (*sāsrava*), hence impure, even though the best of such. Asaṅga, exegesis of the *Śrāvakabhūmi*, explains that at the outset of this "degree of penetration", the virtue (i.e. root of virtue) is still "attended with flux" so the person is an ordinary person (*pṛthagjana*) with knowledge of convention (*saṃvṛti*). In sequence, as he enters the "path of vision" he visualizes these defiled natures, and they are eliminated by vision (*dṛṣṭi-heya)*, which happens because the "seed" is pure. He knows that he has entered the stream and is no longer liable for evil destiny (*durgati*). As an "*ārya*" he has the "knowledge gained afterwards" (*pṛṣṭhalabdhajñāna*), which is supramundane; and it is denied that one could have the two (mundane and supramundane) together.[93]

In Mahāyāna Buddhism, this "path of vision" takes place on the first stage (in the ten stage theory). Using this type of language, Sthiramati comments on the *Mahāyāna-Sūtrālaṃkāra*, Chap. XIV, 3, the expression *dharmasrotas* (stream of *dharma*): "The path of attaining the first stage, namely the *samādhi* "supreme mundane natures", is called the *samādhi* "stream of *dharma* .[94] And Sthiramati comments on Chap. XIV, 33, the expression *darśanamārga* (path of vision): "From the transmutation of the *ālaya* [meaning the "store consciousness"] there is the first stage."[95] The colophon to Asaṅga's *Yogācārabhūmi* in the Tibetan canon remarks that Asaṅga, worshipping at the feet of Ajita (i.e. Maitreya Buddha) gained this *Yogācārabhūmi* in the pure *samādhi* "stream of *dharma*" which is the perfection (*pāramitā*) of the ocean of his own and other's "theory systems" (*siddhānta*).[96] Of course, this could lead to a speculation that Asaṅga had attained the first stage of the Bodhisattva. However, in the light of the foregoing, it seems to be a precept about getting counsel of the deity—that one must purify one's nature in order to receive the supramundane guidance.

Something more should be said about the "roots of virtue" (*kuśalamūla*). Dr. Yeh, in an article about the Bodhisattva's "hindrances" (*āvaraṇa*), on the basis of the *Madhyāntavibhāga* and Vasubandhu's *Bhāṣya* thereon stresses the requirement of these "roots of virtue" for manifestation of the Bodhisattva; and points out that the term *sarvakuśalamūla* (entirely good roots) intends the lack of lust (*arāga*), lack of hatred (*adveṣa*), and lack of delusion (*amoha*).[97] It is important to notice, however, that the theory of four degrees of these "roots of virtue" is independent of the Bodhisattva lineage. The meaning of the transmutation is the getting of a new lineage (*gotra*). This new lineage could be that of the Bodhisattva, but clearly something else is stipulated usually stated as the "Bodhisattva vow". But the importance of this topic of the four degrees of penetration is that one cannot become a Bodhisattva just by taking the appropriate vow and practising the "perfections" (*pāramitā*). In other words, unless there is the transmutation of the support, the person does not enter the new lineage whatever the lineage that he is entitled to.

It follows that the voiding of the object, called "representation-only", is a necessary part of this process, since it intends the dissolution of a way of looking at the world, to set the stage for a new way of looking, appropriate to the new lineage. On this account, this theory of "representation-only" cannot be identified with some particular Western philosophy, such as Idealism. In short, this sequence of four degrees is not a matter of philosophy: it is a sequence of *yoga* with the premise that a person can radically change his nature, e.g. from not being a saint to being a saint.

Consistent with the above is the statement in the *Laṅkāvatārasūtra*:

> *cittamātraṃ samāruhya bāhyam arthaṃ na kalpayet/*
> *tathatālambane sthitvā cittamātram atikramet//*
> *cittamātram atikramya nirābhāsam atikramet/*
> *nirābhāsasthito yogī mahāyānaṃ sa paśyati//*
>
> When he relies on "mind-only" he does not imagine the external entity (=2nd stage of yoga). Being stationed in the meditative support of thus-ness, he goes beyond "mind-only" (=3rd stage of yoga). Going beyond "mind-only" he goes beyond the non-appearance (of the external entity).

> Stationed in the non-appearance (of both subject and object) (=4th stage of yoga), the yogin sees in the manner of the Mahāyāna.

In my previous study of those verses with the help of a work by Ratnākaraśānti,[98] it turned out that the first stage of this yoga is a kind of waking state. In the 2nd stage of yoga, all the *dharmas* are "mind-only", because they are all in the mind and not outside, a feature of the dream state. The 3rd stage of yoga is the transfer to the thus-ness extreme—what the present article previously called the "true end"; and the non-appearance of phenomenal *dharmas* is a feature of dreamless sleep. The 4th stage of yoga is a kind of re-awakening from both the dream (negation of external) and the dreamless (negation of internal), but this re-awakening is a "stage of vision" in a new lineage.

Returning to the previous terminology, the 2nd degree, called "Summits", is *cala* (not fixed), because the "mind-only" *dharmas* are phenomenal. When Vasubandhu mentioned for the 3rd degree, that "non-self of *dharmas* is true", he points to the thus-ness end. Then, the 4th degree is a kind of "after-arisen knowledge" limited to "right mental orientation".

The 4th degree was treated in *M.S.* VIII, 19.3, for which Vasubandhu's comments on the five-membered sequence were presented above. There, No. 4 of the sequence is "deciding the mixture". The theory of "mixed" and "unmixed" *dharmas* is presented in the *Saṃdhinirmocana-sūtra*, VIII, 13-16, where it is expounded in terms of calming (the mind) (*śamatha*) and discerning (the real) (*vipaśyanā*). The two kinds of *dharmas*[100] are elaborately discussed in Yüan-t'sê's commentary, where the "mixed" kind is treated by the *Sūtra's* three degrees of lesser, great, and measureless.[101] Of course, the *dharmas* are here the objects of the "calming" and "discerning". Besides, the terminology of the four "degrees of penetration", being independent of this Yogācāra school suggests that the 4th degree's "mixture" is a mixture of the preceding three, namely, of the "degree of penetration", a kind of "three in one", or Vasubandhu's "seed."[102]

Postscript

It appears that the designations for this Yogācāra school such as "Idealism", "Realism", "Nominalism" are a way of classifying it so that the school can be spoken about without too much pain of studying it or—what forebodes even more pain—going through the meditative sequence to realize "representation-only".

One should know why Asaṅga needed Vasubandhu's help just as Vasubandhu needed Asaṅga's. Asaṅga, as is obvious in his "Rules of Debate"—a part of his *Yogācārabhūmi*, was a mild-mannered person, reluctant to enter into quarrels. Vasubandhu is a confrontational writer, not hesitating to enter the fray. Asaṅga's style of communication was to cover the topic by treating it extensively. Vasubandhu was better able to get to the point. Acting in consort they launched a Buddhist school of tremendous vitality and intellectuality without departing from the old Buddhist theory of practice.

The subjective nature of truth sometimes called the "primacy of perception", is pointed to in Vasubandhu's commentary on the *Gayāśīrṣa*, the item No. 15 in his list of 33, namely, "being based within after rejecting the two extremes". The frequent use of the form *parivṛtti* (probably in the meaning "exchange") in place of *parāvṛtti* (which I render "transmutation") goes with various remarks cited in this chapter, stressing the replacement of bad natures with good natures, thus eventually to reach the "supreme mundane natures". This would be a seriatim process.

REFERENCES

1. According to Bunyiu Nanjio, *A Catalogue of the Chinese Translation of the Buddhist Tripitaka* (reprint, San Francisco, 1975), no. 1188, Kumārajīva translated the *Śataśāstra* with *Vasubandhu*'s commentary in A.D. 404.
2. Cf. especially J. Takakusu, "The Date of Vasubandhu, the Great Buddhist Philosopher," *Indian Studies in Honour of Charles Rockwell Lanman* (Cambridge, Mass. 1929), pp. 79-88. Amalia Pezzali, "Vasubandhu, l'autore dell' Abhidharmakośa," *Studia Missionalia,* Vol. 36, 1987, pp. 239-51, provides a number of other references.
3. J. Takakusu, "The Life of Vasubandhu by Paramārtha (A.D. 499-569)," *T'oung Pao*, Ser. II, 5, 269-96.
4. E. Frauwallner, *On the Date of the Buddhist Master of the Law Vasubandhu,* Serie Orientale Roma, III (Rome, 1951).
5. Padmanabh S. Jaini, "On the Theory of Two Vasubandhus," *Bulletin of the School of Oriental and African Studies,* Vol. 21, 1958, pp. 48-53; also, editor, *Abhidharmadīpa with Vibhāṣāprabhāvṛtti* (Patna, 1969).

6. Erich Frauwallner, "Landmarks in the History of Indian Logic," *Wiener Zeitchrift für die Kunde Süd–und Ostasiens,* Band V, 1961, pp. 131-2.
7. Alex Wayman, *Analysis of the Śrāvakabhūmi Manuscript* (Berkeley, 1961), pp. 19-24.
8. Samghabhadra's *Nyāyānusāra* was translated in part by La Vallée Poussin, *Melanges chinois et boudhiques,* 2, 1933-34, pp. 25-180. A Columbia University student, Collett Cox did her doctoral dissertation on a part of this work under the title *Controversies in Dharma Theory; Sectarian Dialogue on the Nature of Enduring Reality.* 1983, from the Chinese; and published it in 1995.
9. Jaini, "On the Theory of Two Vasubandhus", p. 50, points out that the *Dīpa* author made 17 hostile references to the "*Kośakāra*" (without mentioning Vasubandhu by name).
10. The *Abhidharmakośa* was translated into Chinese first by Paramārtha, A.D. 564-7; Nanjio's catalog. no. 1269.
11. I accept the dates 480-540 A.D., proposed by Frauwallner. "Landmarks", p. 137. Now, it is well-known that Dignāga criticized a work called *Vādavidhi* and attributed to Vasubandhu and that scholars who accepted dates for Vasubandhu and Dignāga such that the latter could be a personal student of the former, therefore concluded that Dignāga was criticizing his own teacher. The dates I have accepted for Vasubandhu and Dignāga show that such a conclusion is unwarranted. Cf. Masaaki Hattori, *Dignāga, On Perception* (Cambridge, Mass., 1968), pp. 32-5, for the "Examination of the *Vādavidhi* definition".
12. Stefan Anacker, *Seven Works of Vasubandhu* (Delhi, 1984), pp. 7-28. His historical remarks are thoroughly unreliable. The "linchpin" for the wheel of his argument is a typescript by Le Manh That (see his p. 7 and note 2) asserting that Hui-yüan (344-416) "quotes a verse of Vasubandhu's *Viṃśatikā*". Observe that the verse no. is not identified. Observe also that of the three translations of this work of Vasubandhu's into Chinese (Nanjio Nos. 1238-40), the earliest (No. 1238) is that by Bodhiruci, between A.D. 508 and 535. The Chinese appear to have the best historical records of the ancient world. Apparently misled by Śāstri's ed., p. 444, last line, Anacker claims (p. 25) that La Vallée Poussin mistranslated Yaśomitra's comment (*Kośa,* tr. III, p. 70, n.), in part, "Le Sthavira Vasubandhu professeur du maitre Manoratha". Poussin and Wogihara's ed. p. 289.6 are correct; also his allusions in that note are compatible. In fact, that a sthavira Vasubandhu was the teacher of Manoratha, who in turn was the teacher of Vasubandhu, brother of Asaṅga, is feasible historically (see my n. 15, below).
13. Ramesh Chandra Majumdar and Anant Sadashiv Altekar, *The Vākāṭaka-Gupta Age* (Motilal Banarsidass, Delhi, reprint 1986), p. 155.
14. Majumdar and Altekar, pp. 155-6.
15. As to the possible Gupta king of the Fourth century, cf. Radhakumud Mookerji, *The Gupta Empire* (Motilal Banarsidass, Delhi, 5th ed. 1973). The dating of the first Vasubandhu has three possibilities. 1. If it were at the time of Chandra Gupta I (where Anacker placed Vasubandhu) the royal dates are given: (c. A.D. 319-355?)— in short, it is difficult to place this king. 2. For the early fifth century translation into Chinese of this Vasubandhu's works, the king Samudra Gupta (c. A.D. 355-380) is feasible. 3. But notice if it were Chandra Gupta II Vikramāditya (c. A.D. 375-414). If, upon his accession this king would appoint as his minister an elderly *sthavira* Vasubandhu, the news would quickly spread through the Buddhist community. It was the year of Asaṅga's birth and his mother named him as well as the two later children "Vasubandhu"—as Paramārtha's biography

mentions. In such a case, it would be possible for this *sthavira* Vasubandhu to be the teacher of Manoratha, the teacher of the Yogācāra Vasubandhu. And then Yaśomitra's comment on *A.K.*, *vṛddhācārya-vasubandhu*, would be quite comprehensible. Asaṅga therefore is a religious, not a lay name, while his famous brother kept the name Vasubandhu and the youngest adopted the name Viriñcivatsa.

16. *History of Buddhism by Bu-ston,* translated from the Tibetan by E. Obermiller, Part II (Heidelberg, 1932), p. 143.
17. *History of Buddhism by Bu-ston,* II, p. 140 and n. 1008.
18. Although Corrado Pensa, *L'Abhisamayālaṃkāravṛtti di Arya-Vimuktisena* (Serie Orientale Roma, 1967), on the first Abhisamaya, p. 115, n., attributes this commentary to Vasubandhu, Vimuktiseṇa himself, author of the earliest commentary on the *Abhisamayālaṃkāra*, on the page refers to *ācārya*-Asaṅga as author of the citation, which in fact is part of the commentary on *Mahāyāna-Sūtrālaṃkāra*, XII, 9. Moreover, Nanjio's No. 1190, on the Chinese version shows authorship of "Bodhisattva Asaṅga".
19. During my readings over the years in Asaṅga's *Yogācārabhūmi,* I have never found him using *Prajñāpāramitā* sources. For Giuseppe Tucci's arguments, cf. *Minor Buddhist Texts,* Part I (Serie Orientale Roma, 1956), Section 1.
20. In my essay, "A Report on the *Akṣayamatinirdeśa-sūtra* (Buddhist Doctrinal History, Study 2)," *Studies in Indo-Asian Art and Culture,* Vol 6, ed. by Lokesh Chandra (International Academy of Indian Culture, New Delhi, 1980), pp. 211-32.
21. *History of Buddhism by Bu-ston,* II, p. 147, ff.
22. Cf. Alex Wayman, "The Yogācāra Idealism", [a review article] *Philosophy East and West,* 15:1, 1965, pp. 65-73.
23. These are the Anacker book (n. 12, above) and Thomas A. Kochumuttom, *A Buddhist Doctrine of Experience* (Delhi, 1982).
24. A. Wayman, "Yogācāra and the Buddhist Logicians", *The Journal of the International Association of Buddhist Studies,* II: 1, 1979, pp. 65-78.
25. Kochumuttom, p. 164.
26. Kochumuttom, pp. xiv-xv.
27. Cf. *Daśabhūmikasūtra,* Ed: J. Rahder (Paris, 1926), p. 49, "E". Or, cf. *Daśabhūmīśvaro nāma mahāyānasūtram,* ed. by Ryūko Kondō (Tokyo, 1936), p. 98.8-9. For Vasubandhu's commentary in the Tibetan canon, in the Peking ed. (PTT), it is Vol. 104, p. 105.3-4, and 105.5-5,6. And in the edition reproduced from the Derge Tanjur, Mdo section, publ. by Delhi Karmapae Chodhey, 1976, it is 200.7 to 201.1, and 202.7 to 203.1.
28. Cecil Bendall, ed., *Subhāṣita-saṃgraha,* part I, *Le Muséon,* Nouvelle Série, Vol. 4, 1903, p. 593.23-24.
29. In the case of the Prajñāpāramitā scriptural exegesis, one may refer to E. Obermiller, *The Doctrine of Prajñā-pāramitā as exposed in the Abhisamayālaṃkāra of Maitreya* (reprint from *Acta Orientalia,* Vol. XI, 1932), p. 62, where the terminology is rather the Buddha's "ultimate direct knowledge in one single moment, of all the aspects of existence, absolute and empirical".
30. Sylvain Lévi ed., *Vijñaptimātratāsiddhi* (Paris, 1925), p. 3. Immediately after this, Vasubandhu cites the *sūtra* form, and then states: *cittaṃ mano vijnānaṃ vijñaptiś ceti paryāyāḥ,* which means that those four terms are alternative expressions.
31. Kochumuttom, p. 198. In fact, he says *vijñaptimātra* and *cittamātra* are synonymous. Strictly speaking, these are not synonyms, but are interchangeable in certain contexts. For example, in early Buddhism, *cittaṃ, manas,* and *vijñānam* are found in a set, but are often found in context where it would be unthinkable

to replace one of them by one of the other two.

32. Compare with Anacker, *Seven Works*, p. 112, para 31. I have translated from the Tibetan in Derge edition, Tanjur, Sems tsam, Vol. Śi, f. 141b-3: / sems ni rnam pa gñis te / de la gcig ni de'i sa bon rnams bsags pa yin no / gñis pa ni de'i dmigs pa daṅ / rnam pa daṅ / bye brag tha dad pa dag gis sna tshogs pa yin no /.
33. Cf. Yuichi Kajiyama, *An Introduction to Buddhist Philosophy;* an annotated translation of the *Tarkabhāṣā* of Mokṣākaragupta (Memoirs of the Faculty of Letters, Kyoto University, No. 10, 1966), p. 154, for the theory that the Yogācārins must be *sākāravādins*. i.e., that consciousness must have the image (*ākāra*), because this school denies the existence of the external world. However, this school does not make this denial. The reason the *manovijñāna* is credited with having the image, translating the word *ākāra,* is that this Sanskrit word is used for the reflected image of the external object. This usage of the term *manovijñāna* therefore agrees with the Abhidharma tenet that this is the sixth sense, which has the "realm of dharma" (*dharmadhātu*) as object.
34. Derge edition, Tanjur, Sems tsam, Vol. Ri, f. 143b-4: / lus daṅ / lus can daṅ / za ba po'i rnam par rig pa źes bya ba de la / lus ni mig la sogs pa'i khams lṅa'o / lus can ni non moṅs pa can gyi yid do / za ba po ni yid kyi khams so /.
35. For example, *Śvetāśvatara Upaniṣad,* IV, 6, about the two companion birds, one who eats the sweet fruit, the other who looks on without eating.
36. Etienne Lamottte, *La Somme du Grand Vehicule*(Louvain, 1938), Tome II, p. 134.
37. Derge edition, Tanjur, *Sems tsam,* Vol. Ri, f. 153a-4, 5*: / de yaṅ gser gyi sñin po can gyi sa'i dpes bstan te / de la sa khoṅ na gser yod pa źes bya ba ni gser gyi sa bon no / sa'i khams ni sra ba ñid do / sa ni ñe bar rten pa'i gzugs sa'i kha dog gaṅ yin pa ste / de la gsum po de dag ñe bar dmigs pa yin no / gser ni sa ñid du snaṅ ba'o / de'i gser ñid du śes pa ni phyis 'byuṅ bar 'gyur te / gaṅ gi tshe me daṅ 'phel bar gyur pa na / gser ñid du dmigs par 'gyur pa ste / des na de yod pa ñid du grub par 'gyur ro /.*
38. Later in this paper, *M.S.*, Chap. VIII, v. 20, will be referred to as dealing with this topic. But this is also what Vasubandhu means in his *Viṃśatikā,* 3, "furthermore, like the hungry ghosts (*preta*), so with all, there is no certainty in the stream of consciousness, upon seeing the stream of pus, and so". He means that just because people in general see objects about the same, e.g., the stream of water, this does not certify the truth of their representation, because they are seeing the object with human sense organs, granting of course, the differences introduced by faulty vision (astigmatism, etc.) or other sensory deficiencies. So long as we do not rise above our kind of representation by yoga practices, we do not realize our perceptual limitations. He also means that by yoga practices we, can realize how the "hungry ghosts" see that same stream of water, or how the gods see it, and so on.
39. Derge edition, Tanjur, Sems tsam, Vol. Ri, f. 144a-7, for Vasubandhu's citation. Cf. Etienne Lamotte, *Saṃdhinirmocana Sūtra* (Louvain, 1935), Chap. VIII, p. 91.3-5, for the Tibetan; his translation is at p. 211, sect. 7.
40. Vol. Ri, f. 144a-7: *des na . . . rnam par rig pa tsam ñid de / don gyis ston pa źes bya ba'i tha tshig go /.*
41. Compare the translations of Anacker, *Seven Works,* pp. 214-5; and of Kochumuttom, *A Buddhist Doctrine,* his I, 9, pp. 64-5. For the Sanskrit (ed. by Gadjin M. Nagao, *Madhyāntavibhāga-Bhāṣya*): *abhūtaparikalpaś ca citta-caittās tridhātukaḥ / tatrārtha-dṛṣṭir vijñānaṃ tad-viseṣe tu caitasāḥ //.*
42. Kochumuttom, *A Buddhist Doctrine,* pp. 198-201.

43. Marlya Falk, *Nāma-rūpa and Dharma-rūpa* (University of Calcutta, 1943), p. 185, n. 72.
44. Cf. Alex Wayman, "Some Accords with the Sāṃkhya Theory of Tanmātra", in *A Corpus of Indian Studies; Essays in Honour of Gaurinath Sastri* (Calcutta, 1980), pp. 118-9.
45. Derge edition, Tanjur, Sems tsam, Vol. Ri, f. 158b-2,3. And cf. Louis De La Vallée Poussin, *Vijñaptimātratāsiddhi,* Tome II (Paris, 1929), pp. 748-54.
46. Of course, Louis de La Vallée Poussin's great work on this text is still valuable and indispensable: *L'Abhidharmakośa de Vasubandhu* (Paris, 1923-31). He had available Yaśomitra's commentary called the *Vyākhyā,* edited in part by himself with the help of the Tibetan (cf. his Introduction, *Kośa* tr., 1931, xvii-xxiii), and many of the verses of *A.K.* were extant in Sanskrit. The entire text of the *A.K.* verses was published by V.V. Gokhale, *Journal of the Bombay branch of the Royal Asiatic Society,* Vol. 22, 1946, pp. 73-102. Nowadays, we have P. Pradhan, *Abhidharmakośabhāṣyam of Vasubandhu* (Patna, 1975); and Dwarikadas Shastri edition of the *Kośa,* its *Bhāṣya,* and Yaśomitra's commentary here called *Sphutārthā* (Varanasi, 1970-73).
47. Long ago, I treated this matter of food, Alex Wayman, *Analysis,* Chap. V, "Asaṅga's Views on Food", pp. 135-62; and also in the present volume.
48. Derge, Vol. Ri, f. 181b-7: */ de dag ni khaṁ gyi zas bor ba reg pa daṅ / yid la seems pa daṅ / rnam par śes pa'i zas gsum gyis de'i rten gnas par byed par 'gyur te /.*
49. Derge, Vol. Ri, f. 182a-2,3: / zas de dag pa źes pa'i dus su saṅs rgyas las lha rnams gyis blaṅs nas gźan sems can rnams la sbyin par byed de / de dag kyaṅ rgyu des byaṅ chub thob par 'gyur ro/.
50. Derge, Vol. Ri, f. 135au-, ff. At 135a-5, he mentions that the "defiled mind" kind of *vijñāna* is what witnesses the rebirth place, whereupon the "intermediate state" comes to an end, and that mind "faints" (skye ba'i srid pa la dmigs nas bar ma do'i srid pa 'gag par 'gyur ro / brgyal ba de...). At 135a-7, he explains the name "defiled mind" as possessing the defilements (*kleśa*) of lust (*rāga*), etc.
51. Cf. "The Sacittikā and Acittikā Bhūmi, Text and Translation" (from Asaṅga's *Yogācārabhūmi),* in *Buddhist Insight ; Essays by Alex Wayman,* ed. by George R. Elder (Delhi, 1984), p. 330.
52. Derge, Vol. Ri, f. 129b-2.
53. Cf. Alex Wayman, "Nescience and Insight According to Asaṅga", originally in the Bhikkhu Rahula volume, reprinted in *Buddhist Insight* for the two kinds of nescience, pp. 194-205.
54. Derge, Vol. Ri, f. 128b-7: */ yaṅ ma 'dres pa'i ma rig pa gaṅ źe na / gñen po ma skyes pa na de kho na ñid śes pa la sgrib par byed pa ste /* "Besides, what is the 'unmixed nescience'? Since the adversary does not arise, it is the hindrance to knowing reality." The point is, since it does not involve defilement, it is the other kind of hindrance, that of the "knowable".
55. The *Kośa* tr., Chap. VIII reference to p. 211, is in Yaśómitra's commentary, and applied to the theory of the eight liberations with the term *āśrayaparivṛttitas.* The Index also gives VIII, 81, but this is in Chap. VII, again in Yasómitra's commentary with the term *āśrayaparivṛtti.* The expression *parivṛtti,* often used in this literature instead of *parāvṛtti,* implies "exchange" rather that "transmutation".
56. So *Kośa* tr., Chap. IV, under v. 56, p. 123. In Pradhan's ed. of *Kośa,* IV, 56, commentary, we read: *pratyāgrāśrayaparivṛttiśuddhā saṃtatir vartate /* "There takes place a stream (of consciousness) purified by a new *āśrayaparivṛtti.*" Here, the term *parivṛtti* might mean "exchange" (of support).

57. Lamotte, *La, Somme,* II, tr., pp. 276-9.
58. Levi, *Vijñaptimātratāsiddhi,* p. 44.11-13. Here, Sthiramati states the difference in terms of "contamination" (*dauṣṭhulya*) because he mentioned a few lines previously that there is a "contamination" hindrance of defilement, and a "contamination" hindrance of knowable. But Sthiramati is perhaps unnecessarily expanding the usage of the term *dauṣṭhulya,* since, under k. 29c-d, he had already explained the two kinds (*dvidhā*) by the two "hindrances".
59. Derge, Vol. Ri, f. 141b-5: *'jug pa'i rnam par śes pa la gnas pa tsam gyis rten gnas par gyur par mi rigs pa.*
60. Derge. Vol. Ri, f. 142a-4: */ mñam par gźag pa'i gnas skabs na ' jug pa' i rnam par śes pa dag ñe bar gyur pa ma yin pas na sa bon med par 'gyur pa'i phyir.*
61. Derge, Vol. Ri., f. 142a-5,6: */des na' di ltar gyur pa daṅ ldan pa kun gźi rnam par śes pa ñid' dod par 'gyur ro /.*
62. Derge, Vol. Ri., f. 158a-6,7: */tiṅ ne 'dsin gyi bar mtshams med pas sgrib pa thams cad daṅ bral źiṅ de'i rten gnas gyur pa des thob par 'gyur ro zes bya'o*
63. Wayman, *Analysis,* p. 134, where this kind of *samādhi* is explained as overcoming all defilements and not being overcome by any defilements as may occur (*utpattikleśa*).
64. Lamotte, *La Some,* II, p. 250. For each of the five, there is a decision (*vicāra*). According to Asaṅga (cf. Wayman, *Buddhist Insight, p. 210), this vicāra* is a subtle "insight" (*prajñā*)—the "eye of insight" after supramundane insight, and still involved with speech motivation.
65. Derge, Vol, Ri, f. 180a-5, ff. (at 180a-6): */de la rtogs pa la dpyod pa ni/gaṅ rtogs pa'i dus ñid na bdag 'di ltar rtogs so źes dpyod pa ste/khoṅ du chud pa ni 'dir dpyod pa yin par 'dod do / rjes su dran pa la dpyod pa ni gaṅ laṅs pa na bdag gis rnam par mi rtog pa rtogs so źes dran pa'o / rnam par gźag pa la dpyod pa ni gaṅ pha rol la bdag gis rtogs pa de ston par byed pa'o* (at 180b-1:) *'dres pa la dpyod pa ni gaṅ chos thams cad 'dres śiṅ bsdus pa la dmigs pa'i ye śes kyis mthoṅ ba ste/' di ltar rten gnas gyur pa ñid do/rten gnas gyur pa de ñid las ni 'byor pa la dpyod par'gyur te/gaṅ ci bsams pa de thams cad' byor par 'gyur ro/de yaṅ ji ltar sa la sogs pa yaṅ de ltar brtags na gźan gser la sogs par'gyur ba'o/ The Tibetan term 'byor pa above rendered "manifoldness", presumably also means "plenitude".*
66. I employ the Pāli edition Ed: Bhikkhu J. Kashyap, *The Aṅguttara Nikāya,* Chakkanipāta, Sattakanipāta & Atthakanipāta (Bihar Govt., 1960).
67. My first attempt with this sentence is in "Secret of the Heart Sūtra" (reprinted in *Buddhist Insight,* p. 314). Later, I learned more about the term *avabhāsa* in the article "Nescience and Insight" (n. 53, above, in *Buddhist Insight,* p. 208), where I used the rendition "secondary light". The dualism of "secondary lights" and "(real) forms" reminds us of Plato's celebrated account in *The Republic* about the shadow in the cave as contrasted with true being—a contrast which is consistent with the Yoga schools of India, e.g. the present topic of Yogācāra (cf. A. Wayman, "Some Observations of Dualistic Mirror Symbolism in Western Philosophy and in the Upaniṣads", *Aligarh Journal of Oriental Studies,* II, 1-2, 1985, pp. 113-6).
68. Besides the Pāli form, one may easily consult the Sanskrit and Tibetan equivalents for the eight bases of mastery in the Buddhist dictionary *Mahāvyutpatti* (Sakaki ed.), Section LXXI, Nos. 1519-27
69. Cf. the table in *Buddhist Insight,* p. 94, where it is clarified as well that the Third Liberation goes with the Fourth Dhyāna which is associated with "transmutation of the support". This article on meditation first appeared in *Studia Missionalia,* Vol. 25, 1976.

70. Vasubandhu's commentary on the *Gayāśīrṣa* in the Derge edition is in Mdo 'grel, Vol. Ṅi (or Ngi), f. 71b-76a. At f. 74b 2-3, the eight kinds for teaching the path of accumulation; at f. 74b-3, the eight kinds for teaching the path of purification. But I shall deal only with the part about the "true end", as below.
71. Derge, Mdo'grel, Vol. Ni, f. 74b-7 (end): / *de la yaṅ dag pa'i mtha' ni rnam pa bźis bstan te/ mi rtag pa ñid kyis ñes pa yoṅs su spaṅs pa daṅ/raṅ gi mtshan ñid kyis gnas pa daṅ/rtag tu chos kyi dbyiṅs kyi raṅ bźin du gnas pa daṅ/dor ba med ciṅ gzag pa med pa'i don,* The four bracketted comments are from Vasubandhu's comment at the end of this passage, beginning f. 75a-2, namely: *gaṅ gis ji ltar gaṅ gi don du gaṅ du gnas te.*
72. Cf. Lamotte, *Saṃdhinirmocana Sūtra*, Tibetan text, Chap. VIII, para. 25; and in the great commentary of Yüan-t 'sê, as it was translated into Tibetan, Peking canon (PTT), Vol. 106, p. 218-2, ff.
73. In the Peking Tanjur (PTT), Vol. 111, in the part called *Vastusaṃgrahaṇī*, p. 130. 2-5, ff. That they are all forms of "insight" (*prajñā*) is the teaching of the *Saṃdhinirmocana-sūtra*, per reference of n. 72, above.
74. Derge, Mdo 'grel, Vol. Ni, f. 75a-2, ff. I shall present the Tibetan, from which I translated only for a few cases that go especially with the subject of the present chapter.
75. */yaṅ dag pa'i mtha'i ye śes la gnas' gyur ba daṅ/gnas gyur pas ye śes śin tu rnam par dag par 'gyur ba daṅ /.*
76. */ dge ba'i rtsa ba chuṅ ṅu yaṅ tshad med par byed pa daṅ /.*
77. */ mtha' gnis spaṅs nas naṅ la brten pa daṅ /.*
78. These are the four *vaiśāradya*, as in *Mahāvyutpatti.* Sect. VIII: "confidence of manifest enlightenment about all *dharmas"*; "of knowledge that all fluxes have ended"; "of explanation that is non-altering and determinate about the natures that cause interruptions (to religious practice)"; ''of the correctness of the path which is the way of deliverance for realizing all succeses".
79. One may consult *Kośa*, tr., Index, under *nirvedha-bhāgīya* for various chapter references, starting with Chap. II.
80. Still probably the best source is Obermiller, *The Doctrine* (n. 29, above), where it is identified with the "stage of praxis" (*prayoga-mārga)*, and differentiated for the Śrāvaka and the Bodhisattva.
81. Poussin, *Vijñaptimātratāsiddhi*, Tome II (n. 45, above), devotes two chapters, "Nirvedhabhāgīyas ou Prayogāvasthā" (pp. 575-84) and "Darśanamārga ou Prativedhāvasthā" (pp. 585-605).
82. Cf. Lamotte , *La Somme,* Tome II, p. 169.
83. Derge, Vol. Ri, f. 159a-6: / *don med par ses pa ni snaṅ ba thob pa źes bya ba'i sgras bstan to/.*
84. Lamotte, *La Somme,* Tome II, p. 170.
85. Derge, Vol. Ri, f. 159a-7: / don med par śes pa chen po ni snaṅ ba mched pa źes bya ba'i sgras bstan to /.
86. Lamotte, *La Somme,* II, p. 170, para, 3; Vasubandhu, Derge, Vol. Ri, f. 159a-7 to b-1.
87. Derge, Vol. Ri, f. 159b-1: / *chos bdag med pa ni bden pa źes bya'o /.*
88. Derge, Vol. Ri, f. 159b-2: / *śes bya'i mtshan nid la 'jug pa źes bya ba'i don gźan yaṅ / maṅ du thos pas bsgos pa'i gnas / źes bya ba ste / theg pa chen po yoṅs su bsgom pa'i bdag ñid kyi ṅo bo'o /.*
89. Collett Cox, in her Columbia University dissertation (n. 8, above) shows that these were disputed matters. She renders the expressions *sabhāgatā* and *nikāyasabhāga*

"common lot", and points out that according to Vasubandhu (*A.K.* II, v. 41, and so on) there is both a "common lot" of *dharmas* as of sentient beings. We notice by the present context that Vasubandhu must allow for *dharmas,* because the "supreme mundane *dharmas*" have transcended this "common lot". And probably he must also allow it, because this school teaches "non-self" of *dharmas* as well as of person (*pudgala*). The implication is that the adherence to "self" preserves the "common lot", while the realization of "non-self" of two kinds, destroys it, at least for the time being.

90. Lamotte, *La Somme,* II, p. 170, para 4.
91. Lamotte, *La Somme,* II, 14, p. 171.
92. Derge, Vol. Ri, f. 159b-3, 4: */ kun gżi rnam par śes pas bsdus pa ma yin la źes bya ba daṅ / kuṅ gżi rnam par śes pa ltar tshul bzin yid la byed pas bsdus pa'i sa bon, yin no źes bya ba ni ji ltar kun gżi rnam par śes pa kun nas ñon moṅs pa'i chos rnams kyi rgyu yin pa de bźin du de rnam par byaṅ ba'i chos rnams kyi rgyur 'gyur ro źes bya ba'i tha tshig go /.*
93. Peking Tanjur (PTT), Vol. 111, p. 48.3-3 to 8.1 have summarized the Tibetan text.
94. Peking Tanjur (PTT), Vol. 108, p. 317.2-7, 8 */ sa daṅ po thob par 'gyur ba'i lam 'jig rten gyi chos mchog gi tiṅ ṅe 'dsin la chos kyi rgyun gyi tin ne 'dsin ces bya'o /.*
95. Peking Tanjur (PTT), Vol. 108, p. 321.5-6: */ kun gżi gnas 'phos pa ñid las sa daṅ po źes byaba.*
96. Peking Tanjur (PTT), Vol. 111, p. 253.1-2, 3, 4.
97. Ah-Yueh Yeh, "The Theories of the Bodhisattva's *'āvaraṇa'* and *'kāraṇa'* in the *Madhyānta-vibhāga-bhāṣya*", *Philosophical Review* (Taiwan), January 1987, pp. 33-71, esp. 49-53.
98. Alex Wayman, *Yoga of the Guhyasamājatantra* (Delhi, 1977), Appendix I ("The Laṅkāvatāra-sūtra and the Guhyasamājatantra"), pp. 332-9.
99. Lamotte, *Saṃdhinirmocana Sūtra,* Tib. text, pp. 94-6; tr., pp. 215-7.
100. Lamotte, per n. 99, above, Sanskritized the two as *miśradharma* (mixed *dharma*) and *amiśradharma* (unimixed *dharma*). However, Asaṅga in his summary treatise called *Ābhiprāyikārtha-gāthā* (cf. Alex Wayman in *Buddhist Insight,* p. 354, 9), for "mixed" has *saṃbhinna* and for "unmixed" had *abhinna*). Here, "unmixed" means consistent respectively (*anupūrva*); "mixed" means consistent for the goal (*upaniṣad*). When *dharmas* are considered one after the other, they are "unmixed". When taken together by their underlying nature. They are "mixed".
101. Yüan-t'sê, PTT, Vol. 106, p. 195-5 to p. 197-3.
102. The classical text for the "three in one" theory is, of course, the *Māṇḍūkya Upaniṣad.* The four *nirvedhabhāgīyas* are not stated in terms of the "states of consciousness", waking, etc., but can be considered as equivalent anyway. The yogin passing through these phases is not supposed to fall asleep. His "dream" state is the *samādhi* equivalent, perhaps what Mahāyāna Buddhism means by saying that the world is like a dream, an illusion, the castle in the sky, etc.

6

Parents of the Buddhist Monks

The appreciation of parents in a given culture is indicative of its deep-seated sources of authority and hence of its stability. This appreciation or lack of it is doubtless a prime factor in the preservation of a religion or the ease with which a religion yields converts to other faiths. Ancient Buddhism and much of its later form emphasized its followers leaving home to enter the religious life. When one is so deeply involved with Buddhism he would so to say, turn his back on the worldly life for a life claimed to be superior. However, this rejection of worldly values did not necessarily involve a rejection of family values. If such rejection had been the rule, Buddhism could never have assumed its status as a great religion of the world: it would have provoked too much hostility. Hajime Nakamura[1] cites a scripture in the Chinese Buddhist canon (*Taishō,* Vol. 17, p. 359) that of the persons to whom the Buddhist followers are most indebted, the first four groups are in this order: (1) mother, (2) father, (3) tathāgata, i.e., Buddha, and (4) Buddhist monks. This list has the further interesting feature of placing the mother first of all; and Nakamura observes that in Indian Buddhism and especially in its later developments, the mother is venerated more than the father. Moreover, even if he wished, a monk could not efface the psychological imprint of parents or the early loss of them.

Indeed, the Buddhist practice of taking refuge in the three Jewels (the Buddha, the Dharma, the Saṅgha) while the follower is urged to strive by oneself has its inception in the family. The child necessarily takes refuge in the parents (or persons who substitute for them) and needs a lot of help from them, and yet must grow through its inward resources.

Our relevant material is selected from two sources: Biographies of monks; Scriptural references.

Biographies of Monks

The most eminent of all Buddhist monks is Gautama Buddha. Our employment of his biography involves a presupposition amounting to a suspended final judgment of its value, while avoiding the naive extremes of a wholesale rejection or credulous acceptance. Among the Buddha's legends,[2] our own is the moderate one that it represents a real life with plausible human elements, somewhat overlaid with mythological extravagances, with the real and the overlay still to be finally discriminated. But certainly in the real-life thread of the biography, the parents figure strikingly. Again, it is the mythological overlay that tells of the future. Buddha's prenatal "investigations", while he is in the Tushita Heaven: he investigates the time, the country, the locality, and the family in which he will be reborn. From here on, it is difficult to decide on the genuine elements. The parents turn out to be King Śuddhodana and Queen Māyā. Queen Māyā dies when seven nights have elapsed since Gautama's birth. This presumably provokes the monkish tale of the *Lalitavistara* that in the course of the investigation of the future parents, Gautama picks as mother a queen who is destined to die in ten lunar months and seven days, for it is not proper that the mother of a Buddha should thereafter profane the womb sanctified by a Buddha's presence. Inexorable destiny also plagues the father. Sages interpret the auspicious marks of the new-born child to portend either a Universal Emperor (*cakravartin*) or a Complete Buddha (*saṁyaksaṁbuddha*). King Śuddhodana, wishing to bring to pass the first one of the alternatives, then rears Gautama in a type of palace prison, surrounding him with all possible pleasures including a plethora of female energy. But at the age of four times seven years, the prince escapes from the well-decorated prison to go forth to the religious life, so as to become a Complete Buddha rather than a Universal Emperor. No matter what later Buddhism may say about the father and mother, and no matter what scholars may ultimately decide about the biography, the founder of the Buddhist religion served as the precedent for entering the religious life despite the parents. It also rings true of a real life that Gautama having rejected the authority of his father should establish a doctrine, which rebelled against the older conventional religious practice of India. Even so, it is quite reasonable and consistent with the preserved Buddhist scripture (*infra*), that he should instruct his own parents and relations, especially his father Śuddhodana and aunt Mahāprajāpatī, who served as his foster mother. Again, the old scriptural references to mothers and mother's love are what one would expect of a real person, who honored parents in an abstract sense and never experienced a mother's love.

The biographical tradition preserved in Tibet gives great credit to the mother of the celebrated Buddhist teachers Asaṅga and Vasubandhu. We read this in Bu-ston's *History of Buddhism*, as translated by Obermiller:[3]

> At that time, a woman of the Brāhmaṇa caste called Prasannaśīlā has the following thought—Three times have foes brought harm to the Abhidharma which is the foundation of the Teaching, and no one who would be able to expound it can be found. I, being a woman am likewise incapable of doing it. But, if I give birth to sons, I will make of them propagators (of the Doctrine). Accordingly, from her union with a Kshatriya, (a son named) Asaṅga, and (later on) from another union with a Brāhmaṇa, (a second son named) Vasubandhu were born. The mother drew on their tongues the letter A and performed all the other rites in order to secure for them an acute intellectual faculty.

In any case, the half-brothers, Asaṅga and Vasubandhu, having the same mother—the tradition defended in my *Analysis of the Śrāvakabhūmi Manuscript*[4]—attained the peak of eminence, and probably had a remarkable mother. This example shows the willingness of Buddhist traditions to allow a mother to share the glory of a great son's attainment, to acknowledge her partial contribution to the religious result.

The biographies of Tsoṅ-kha-pa (1357-1419 A.D.), founder of the Gelugpa sect of Tibetan Buddhism set forth certain asupicious dreams which Tsoṅ-kha-pa's father and mother had around the time of conception. One of the father's dreams bears on lay Buddhist worship of the Mahāyāna variety. Thus in my manuscript on Tsoṅ-kha-pa's life:[5]

> Toward the end of the monkey year (the next or bird year began Jan. 21, 1357), his father saw in a dream a venerable who said he had come from the five-peaked mountain of China (the Wu-tai-shan, traditional dwelling place of Mañjuśrī—Mañjughosha). He was wearing an upper religious garb stitched of numerous flower garlands and a lower garment of yellow silk which he said consisted of leaves of the tree (in the heaven) of the thirty-three (gods), and he was carrying a book. He said, "You must provide me a lodging." Thereafter, a light proceeded from the Buddhist altar which was in his home. Hence, it occurred to the father that there had been a magical manifestation of Mañjughosha resulting from his constant recitation of the names of that Bodhisattva.

This passage alludes to a practice of lay Buddhist piety consisting of reciting the 108 names of a particular Bodhisattva. The eight great Bodhisattvas, Avalokiteśvara, Maitreya, Khagarbha, Samantabhadra, Vajrapāṇi, Mañjuśrī Sarvanivaraṇavishkambhin, and Kshitigarbha, all have their 108 names as presented in separate texts preserved in the Tibetan Kanjur (Nos. 634-41 of the Tohoku catalog). The passage as occurring in these biographies suggests a belief that by such recitation a father-to-be might attract into his family a reincarnating entity, who is overshadowed or inspired by a particular Bodhisattva. Furthermore, in the night of the tenth day of the bird year, Tsoṅ-kha-pa's mother had a dream about Avalokiteśvara's golden body entering her body; and this was of course the assumed day of conception (or January 30, 1357). Also the father saw in dream Vajrapāṇi hurl a blazing golden thunderbolt which was absorbed into the mother. In short, Tsoṅ-kha-pa's parents had certain dreams which portended the birth of a son who would be overshadowed by or embody the three Bodhisattvas—Mañjuśrī, Avalokiteśvara, and Vajrapāṇi. Of course, I am in no position to judge the veracity of these accounts. However, as these dreams are constituted, they show that the father had an imposing role. This is further brought out in the biography of Tsoṅ-kha-pa, who seems to have been quite a prodigy, coming to the attention of the Mongol king Togon Temur. The latter sent his religious advisor Karma Rol paḥi rdo rje to visit the child; and Tsoṅ-kha-pa took the layman's vow (*upāsaka*) from that Lama—this when he had reached the age of three, which could be less if calculated in the Chinese way! During his third year, the Chos rje (*Dharmasvāmin*) Don grub rin chen brought many valuable gifts, including horses to the father and commanded, "You must present me this boy of yours!" The father submitted and with enthusiastic delight (so the biography) presented the boy to him; and the Lama Don grub rin chen reared the lad with a Buddhist education.

The example to Tsoṅ-kha-pa's parents shows the importance of auspicious dreams to the lay community as prognostics of sons destined to become eminent in the religious life. We also learn about the economic advantage of having such a son.

Chang Chen-chi's epitome of Zen Master Han Shan's autobiography includes this:[6]

> I was born at Chuan Chiao in the country Nanking. My mother, a pious Buddhist had been a worshipper of the All-merciful Kwan Yin all her life. One day she dreamed that the All-merciful Mother brought into the house a child which she received with warm embraces. As a result, she became pregnant, and on the twelfth of October, 1545, I was born.
>
> In 1545, when I was twelve months old, a serious illness carried me to the point of death. My mother prayed to the All-merciful One and vowed that if I recovered she would offer me to the monastery to become a monk. When I recovered, she duly enlisted my name in the Monastery of Longevity.

Now, the lay parent, believing that the celestial Bodhisattva

Kuan Yin holds the power of life, creates a pact. When the child passes successfully through the crisis, the mother believes that Kuan Yin has fulfilled her part of the bargain. The offering of the child to the monastery fulfills the mother's part.

The celebrated Kōbō Daishi, or Kūkai (8th to 9th centuries) at the age of 18 went to (Nara) to study Chinese classics, in which he became extremely learned. He wanted to become a Buddhist monk, but his father, uncle, and brothers were very much opposed on the Confucian principles that it would be contrary to filial piety and loyalty to the emperor. Kūkai published three volumes comparing Confucianism, Taoism, and Buddhism, and thereby clarified his reasons for wishing to become a monk, whereupon his father consented. This example shows the pre-eminence in Japan of the father's authority and of male authority, generally. We also learn of a leading objection by parents to their sons entering the monastic life; this objection based on Confucian principles was of course very strong and widespread in China. There is also a suggestion in the life of Kōbō Daishi that like the Buddha, he revolted against parental authority as a preliminary for a doctrinal rebellion: he brought to Japan the alien esoteric systems of Tantra.[7]

Some biographical sketches of Japanese monks show that they were orphaned at an early age of childhood. In one case, that of Eison, the death of the mother when he was seven years old precipitated his entry into the religious life. Such examples are consistent with the others in revealing the importance of the parents, whether in a positive or negative way in the decision to become a monk.

Scriptural References

The passage in the Anguttara-Nikāya, Book of Threes seems properly translated by F.L. Woodward (London, 1951): "Monks, those families where mother and father are worshipped in the home are reckoned like unto Brahmā. Those families where mother and father are worshipped in the home are ranked with the teachers of old. Worthy of offerings, monks, are those families, where mother and father are worshipped in the home. 'Brahmā', monks, is a term for mother and father. 'Teachers of old', monks, is a term for mother and father. 'Worthy of offerings', monks, is a term for mother and father. 'Why so? Because, mother and father do much for children, they bring them up, nourish and introduce them to the world." However, it is not clear why the passage is in the Book of Threes. Perhaps by 'three' is meant the father and mother and their children.

The early Buddhist view is also well-stated in Nāgārjuna's "Friendly Epistle" to a Southern King:[8]

> Those families where father and mother are honoured are blessed by (lit. endowed with) Brahmā and the teachers; they (i.e., the children in their turn) will be honoured and finally reach heaven.

The translator Wenzel mentions that Prof. Windisch drew his attention to a similar passage in the Pāli canon, *Itivuttakam* Sutt. 106. The *Aṅguttaranikāya* of the Pāli canon in its section on "twos" contains this sermon:[9]

> I shall name two beings to you, O monks, whose goodness one cannot repay. Which two? Mother and father . . . And why? O monks, parents bestow much good on their children, for they brings them into this world, nourish them, and explain this world to them.
> But, O monks, if a man's parents are unbelievers and if he lead them to perfect faith, stimulate and confirm them therein, or if they are wicked, he lead them to perfect virtue, stimulate and confirm them therein, or if they are miserly, he lead them to perfect self-sacrifice, stimulate and confirm them therein, or if they are without insight, he lead them to perfect insight, stimulate and confirm them therein—then, O monks, he has done well by his parents and has repaid his parents for their benefits, indeed, more than repaid them.

As already mentioned, this text is borne out by the Buddha's own instruction of his father and foster-mother. However, at the request of his father, the Buddha ruled that no person should be ordained without the consent of his parents.[10] This decision may have stemmed from civil law at that time.[11]

A Mahāyāna scripture much to the point is the *Śrīmālādevīsiṁhanāda*, important in China and Japan for its teaching of the Ekayāna ("single vehicle") and Tathāgatagarbha, the teaching that all sentient beings have the embryo of Buddhahood. In Japan this scripture is called the *Shomangyo*, and Dr. Hanayama informs us. "In 606, Prince Shotoku (i.e., Shotoku Taishi) gave a lecture on the *Shomangyo* before Empress Suiko. He also gave a lecture on the *Hokekyo* (i.e., the *Saddharmapuṇḍarīka-sūtra*) in the same year. This was the beginning of giving lectures on Buddhist *sūtras* in Japan."[12] After the traditional opening sentences of Buddhist *sūtras*, this work continues:[13]

> At that time King Prasenajit of Kosala and his Queen Mallikā, being a short time involved in understanding the (Buddha's) Doctrine, engaged in conversation.
> Queen: "O great king, your daughter Queen Śrīmālā is profound and clever. If she were just to see the Buddha she would understand the Doctrine with little difficulty, and she would have no doubts about the Buddha's Teaching."
> King Prasenajit: "We should send a message to Queen Śrīmālā to arouse her interest."
> Queen Mallikā: "Yes, this is the time."
> King Prasenajit and Queen Mallikā composed a letter praising the immeasurable merits of the Tathāgata and sent it by a court official named Chandra, who proceeded to Ayodhyā, then to the palace, bowed to Queen Śrīmālā, and placed the letter in her hands. The Queen, with devotion to her father and mother, raised it with both hands above her head, and then read it. Taking to heart its auspicious meaning she was filled with admiration and spoke these verses to Chandra . . . .

Of course, the Tathāgatagarbha teaching is only one of a number of factors affecting the Mahāyānā type of lay Buddhism. But in the case of this particular *sūtra*, that teaching is undoubtedly a theoretical basis for the striking role of a lay Buddhist, Śrīmālā—a woman moreover—whose vision of the Buddha would be understood in the context of this scripture as representing an awakening and externalization of her own Buddha nature. Later in the work, when Śrīmālā explains the Perfection of Meditation (*dhyānapāramitā*), she mentions that any person who can talk at length without straying from the thread of discourse or can pursue an aim in life without wavering, possesses the Perfection of Meditation: this is indeed the laicization of Buddhist meditation. According to the old Pāli scripture *Saṁyutta-Nikāya*, I, 83, the king was not pleased when Queen Mallikā gave birth to a daughter. The Buddha told him: "A woman child, O lord of men, may prove even a better offspring than a male."

Those passages sufficiently demonstrate the Buddhist attitude of reverence towards parents. It should be of interest to observe how this attitude, especially the attitude toward the mother has affected Buddhist meditative procedures. This topic is elaborately set fourth in the Bodhisattva section of Tsoṅ-kha-pa's Tibetan work usually referred to as the *Lam rim chen mo.*[14] This section includes a lengthy discussion on the process concerned with generating the Mind of Enlightenment (*bodhicittotpāda*). Briefly speaking, when one has generated this mind or resolve, one must then become confirmed or habituated in this way of thinking. This process of confirmation is called the stages of practising the Mind of Enlightenment. Tsoṅ-kha-pa presents two alternate methods of such practice, one which was handed down from Atīśa, the great Indian paṇḍit who came to Tibet around 1040 A.D., and the other found in the texts by Śāntideva (i.e., his *Sikṣāsamuccaya* and *Bodhicaryāvatāra*). The former method is in point now. This method is based on Atīśa's precepts of "Seven causes and effects," constituting a type of dependent origination. The seven causes and effects are as follows: perfected Buddhahood arises from the Mind of Enlightenment; that Mind, from altruistic aspiration (*adhyāsaya*); that aspiration, from compassion (*karuṇā*); compassion from love (*maitrī*); love, from gratitude; gratitude from recollection of kindness; recollection of kindness, from seeing as 'mother'—seven in all. This list of seven steps appears to be associated with the old fourfold group called both the four Brahmavihāras and the four Boundless States, namely, Love (*maitrī*), Compassion (*karuṇā*), Sympathetic Joy (*muditā*), and Equanimity (*upekṣā*).

When Tsoṅ-kha-pa treats of this 'mother' contemplation, he brings in the notion common to Indian thought of uncountable rebirths. In the infinite past and in the infinite future, all these rebirths are possible through the loving care of a mother. Every sentient being has sometime or other served as one's 'mother'. Thus, the meditator first sees vividly his own mother, and through her passes beyond all bounds of love for all the sentient beings. He dwells on his mother's kindness in taking care of all his needs when he was completely helpless. This recollection arouses gratitude; gratitude arouses love. Having gotten into that frame of mind, he recognizes as his 'mother' also his father and friends. He then proceeds to the more advanced task of recognizing as his 'mother' the neutral persons. When he is able to regard the same way as he thinks of his friends, he proceeds to the still more advanced task of recognizing as his 'mother' all his enemies. When the latter can be seen this way, he recognizes all the living beings of the ten directions as his 'mother', expanding his meditation into the boundless state. In this way, he brings on the Boundless State of Love (*maitrī*).

Having come to see all these sentient beings as one's 'mother' in the Boundless State of Love, the meditator then reflects on their manifold sufferings in their subjection to transmigration. The intense realization of suffering by empathy with the loved object—the 'mother'—produces Compassion (*karuṇā*). As applied to all the sentient beings, one enters the Boundless State of Compassion.

Having this compassion through realizing the sufferings of these sentient beings, the meditator then aspires to free them from suffering and to bring them happiness—as one wishes to do this for one's mother. Hence, the next stage called "altruistic aspiration," which expands into the third Boundless State of Sympathetic Joy with all the happiness accruing to those sentient beings. However, the description did not specifically use the terminology of the third Boundless State.

The next stage is the Mind of Enlightenment itself, which has two aims: Enlightenment for oneself and Deliverance for others. Again, the description does not link up this stage with the fourth Boundless State, usually called Indifference (*upekṣā*); but this word seems inadequate as a translation.

The final beyond the seventh stage is of course perfect Enlightenment, the final fruition of the sequence inaugurated by contemplation of one's own mother, according to Atīśa's precepts as expanded upon and discussed by Tsoṅ-kha-pa.

It is well-known that the set of four Brahma-vihāras or Sublime Abodes is often encountered in the Pāli scriptures. An interesting contrast to the 'mother' meditation as developed above is contained in the Pāli *Khuddakanikāya*, which in the "loving kindness discourse" has this verse:[15]

> Thus, as a mother (with her life)
> Might guard her son, her only child,
> Would he maintain unboundedly
> His thought for every living being.

Bhikkhu Ñāṇamoli translates the commentary this way: "*As a mother might guard her son*, the child of her breast born in herself, and that being also her *only child*, might guard it *with her life* by laying down her own life in order to ward off the coming of suffering, *thus would he maintain*, would he generate again and again, would he augment, *his* loving-kindness-*thought to every living being*, and he would maintain it in being *unboundedly* by means of the object (of cognizance) consisting of boundless creatures or by means of remainderless (unreserved) extension (pervasion) in a single being." In this Pāli treatment, however, the reference to the mother is in the form of a simile. In Atīśa's precepts, one actually thinks of the mother. Indeed, the Arhat ideal of early Buddhism sometimes downgraded mother-love. Thus, Burlingame, in *Buddhist Legends*, Part 2 (pp. 358-359) mentions that the nun-mother of Kumāra Kassapa attained Arhatship on the every day she uprooted affection for her son, for thus she established "herself as a refuge for herself." Again, the *Udānavarga* (xviii, 4) reads: "As long as affection toward the kinsmen of a man is not cut off-down to an infinitesimal—that man's mind is bound like the suckling calf to its mother."

The seven stages of precepts that begin with seeing the mother show that Atīśa, and the line of teachers he represents, long ago fathomed the secret of love, which is that love begets love. The great modern expert on child care, Dr. John Bowlby, sets forth a similar view in his book *Child Care and the Growth of Love*. Thus Asaṅga lays stress on "rebirth in a noble home" as a principal factor in personal success;[16] and he writes in the *Saṁgrahaṇī* portion of his *Yogācārabhūmi*: "The *sūtra* texts 'The mother . . .' and 'Protection of the mother . . .' refer to unlawful sexual commerce."[17]

However, a passage of the Mahāyāna scripture *Sāgaramati-paripṛcchā* ("Questions of Sāgaramati") assigns the "mother" role to the Lower Vehicle (Hīnayāna). This is a parable quoted by Tsoṅ-kha-pa in his Bodhisattva section, as already utilized above, and furthermore available in the original Sanskrit as found in the *Ratnagotravibhāga* (pp. 47-48). The latter work is a summary of the Tathāgata-garbha scriptures, and the two texts in which the passage is found testify to its significance.

> For example, *Sāgaramati*, suppose an industrialist-householder (*śreshṭhin-grihapati*) has an only son, agreeable,

> dear, beloved, gratifying, not obstinate upon seeing his father; and that boy, while playing as children do, falls into the latrine pit. Then the mother and kinsmen of that boy see that the boy has fallen into the latrine pit: and seeing this, they gasp, are agonized, and utter lamentations; but do not descend into the latrine pit and lift out the boy. Thereupon, the father of the boy approaches that place. He sees that his only son has fallen into the latrine pit; and seeing this, he hastens with all speed, drawn by his altruistic aspiration and affection for his only son. Without shrinking, he descends into the latrine pit and brings out his only son. Sāgaramati, having given you this parable, I shall tell you its meaning. You will see the connection. The "latrine pit" stands for the triple realm. The "only son" stands for the sentient beings because the Bodhisattva's idea of "only son" dwells in him toward all sentient beings. The "mother and kinsmen" means the persons belonging to the vehicle of the Disciples (*śrāvaka*) and Self-Enlightened Ones (*pratyeka-buddha*), who, seeing the sentient beings fallen into the cycle of transmigration (*saṁsāra*), are agonized and utter lamentations, but are incapable of bringing them out. The "industrialist-householder" means the Bodhisattva, who, with mind entirely free from taint witnesses the unconditioned nature (*asaṃskṛta dharma=Nirvāṇa*), and who, reflecting, relates his thinking to the triple realm so as to mature the sentient beings.

Here the mother symbolizes the Hīnayāna, with its commiseration for the suffering of the phenomenal world. The mother is paired with kinfolk. The father is given the superior role of symbolizing the altruistic aspiration of the Mahāyāna to end the suffering of phenomenal world. But according to this viewpoint the Mahāyāna is higher than the Hīnayāna—only in the sense of adding a further attainment. In Tsoṅ-kha-pa's treatment, the mothers and kinfolk represent the stages beneath altruistic aspiration, i.e., seeing as 'mother', recollection of kindness, gratitude, love, and compassion. According to the cited scripture, these can be assumed as attributes of the Disciples and Self-Enlightened Ones, who constitute the Hīnayāna. The Mahāyāna adds the stages of altruistic aspiration and Mind of Enlightenment.

It is of interest that the *Sāgaramati-paripṛcchā* speaks of the son as belonging to the father. In the *Śrīmālādevīsiṁhanāda*; Queen

Mallikā, when conversing with King Prasenajit refers to Śrīmālā as "your daughter." In the *Saddharmapuṇḍarīka-sūtra*, both the famous "parable of the burning house" and "the prodigal son and the seeking father" disregard the role of the mother. The father in these accounts symbolizes the Bodhisattva. However, in the Mahāyāna as the mother has been elevated to an even higher role: she is *Prajñā-pāramitā*, the perfection of insight, mother of the Disciples, Bodhisattvas, and Buddhas.

Our procedure of compiling data from both biographies of monks and scriptural references is justified by the results. One cannot understand these Buddhist scripture except as having been composed by persons with their inevitable psychological differences. The parents of those monk-authors have deeply influenced the compositions. It is one thing to honor the father and mother, still another to use one of these figures as a meditative object: we have seen why the Buddha would not so use one of them. If a meditator loves his mother, it is possible for him, perhaps preferable for him to engage in the sequence in Atīśa's precepts of the "Seven causes and effects," beginning as 'mother'. If the yogin's relation with his parents is devoid of deep-seated affection, he might be more successful in the alternate method of practising the Mind of Enlightenment, that based on the two works of Śāntideva (this is not meant to allege anything about Śāntideva's relations with his parents).

The picture will become clearer by gathering materials on parents from further Buddhist biographies, amassing more scriptural references, and relating the two sets of data as suggested above.

REFERENCES

1. Hajime Nakamura, *Shakuson no Kotoba* (in Japanese), (Tokyo, 1958), p. 122.
2. Cf. Ét. Lamotte, "La légende du Buddha", *Revue de l'histoire des religions*, Vol. 134 (1948), pp. 37-71.
3. E. Obermiller, *History of Buddhism by Bu-ston* (Heidelberg, 1932), II, 37.
4. University of California Publications in Classical Philology, Vol. 17 (Berkeley and Los Angeles, 1961), 19 ff.
5. A portion of my old manuscript work, The Meditative section of Tsoṅ-kha-pa's *Lam rim chen mo,* but not included in the biographical sketch in A.Wayman, *Calming the Mind and Discerning the Real* from the Lam rim chen mo (New York, 1978).

6. Chang Chen-chi, *The Practice of Zen* (New York, 1959), p. 85.
7. *Butsuzō Zukan*, Hito no maki (Japanese), p. 106.
8. Translated by Heinrich Wenzel, *Journal of the Pāli Text Society*, 1986, p. 8.
9. Maurice Winternitz, *A History of Indian Literature*, Vol. II, Buddhist Literature and Jaina Literature (Calcutta, 1933), p. 63.
10. Malalasekera, *Dictionary of Pāli Proper Names*, Vol. I, p. 796.
11. Dr. Dev Raj Chanana, "The Vinaya Piṭaka and Ancient Indian Jurisprudence," *Journal of the Bihar Research Society*, XLIV (Mar.-June, 1958), p. 27.
12. Shinsho Hanayama, *A History of Japanese Buddhism* (Tokyo, 1960), p. 11.
13. From the translation of this work from Tibetan and Sino-Japanese by Alex and Hideko Wayman, *Lion's Roar of Queen Śrīmālā* (New York, 1974).
14. The following material from this work are drawn from A. Wayman's manuscript translation of the Bodhisattva section. Now this work has been published: Ethics of Tibet; Bodhisattva Section of Tsoṅg-kha-pa's Lam Rim Chen Mo, tr. by Alex Wayman from the Tibetan Original (Albany, N.Y., 1991).
15. The Pali Text Society, Translation Series, No. 32 (London, 1960), pp. 288-9.
16. *Analysis of the Śrāvakabhūmi Manuscript*, p. 60.
17. As cited by Tsoṅ-kha-pa in the *Lam rim chen mo*, Tashilunpo edition, 100-4, and followed by materials based on Aśvaghoṣa's *Daśakuśalakarmapathāḥ*, for which see Sylvain Lévi, "Autour d'Aśvaghoṣa," *Journal Asiatique*, 1929.

SECTION II
THEORY OF THE HEROES

nihīyati puriso nihīnasevī
na ca hāyetha kadāci tulyasevī/
seṭṭham upanamaṃ udeti khippaṃ
tasmā attano uttariṃ bhajethā//
Anguttara-nikāya,—**Book of Threes.**

Puggala-vagga

A Person who follows a lower, descends.
Who follows equals never fails.
Who resorts to the superior soon rises.
Therefore, associate with a superior to thyself!

7

Aniconic and Iconic Art of the Buddha

The writer proposes to bring up to date his views expressed in a 1978 essay "The Role of Art among the Buddhist Religieux"[1] which was reprinted in 1984[2]—this time restricting the discussion to representations of Gautama Buddha. That essay pointed out that he was first represented by symbols—such as the tree for his enlightenment, and that these symbols were images (in Greek *agalma*) of deity, but not likenesses (Greek, *eidon*).[3] My use of the expression "aniconic art" for these symbols is not meant to disagree with anyone.[4] In fact, my use of the term agrees with the entry in *The Concise Oxford Dictionary*, namely, "not shaped in human or animal form". Hence, it does not disallow its complement, something "shaped in human or animal form", since the empty throne (aniconic) could have worshippers (iconic).

But that essay of mine did not explain why these images—instances of aniconic art amount to living embodiments. The clarification can start this way: When the Buddha passed away, his Dharma and the Monk order called Saṅgha continued with the Dharma being memorized by the monks. The remembrance of the Buddha was therefore different, being of one entity, who was absent. Thus he was present in an absence. This absentee-presence proceeded initially along four lines or the four pilgrimage places—where the Buddha was born and where he died, and where he became enlightened and then preached. Foucher theorized that the pilgrims would bring back from each of those four places symbolic mementos, which—I declare—would become four kinds of aniconic art. I could add that the mystery of such presence in an absence was accentuated by the pilgrim's faith, often with hardships of the journey.

After that beginning, the clarification further proceeds in this manner: Elsewhere, I have cited the strange verse from a well-known work of Tibetan Buddhism, *Fifty Stanzas in Praise of the Guru*, the verse 23: "As fearful as the sin of destroying a *stūpa*, is the stepping on a shadow (of your *guru*) Never do it! What need is there to mention a refraining from stepping on his shoes, seat, or his mount!" I learned from Tsoṅg-kha-pa's Tibetan commentary that this precept is not only found in various tantric works, but also in the Buddhist Vinaya.[6] This verse shows an attitude that in the case of presence in an absence, symbolized by the shadow, to step thereon is tantamount to treading upon that person, present in the absence. Hence it is proper to regard the aniconic image of deity as a living embodiment.

The Buddha's historical life itself helps foster the symbolic strength of the aniconic images. For example, the tree represents the enlightenment; but besides the well-known tree called the Bodhi-tree there is the earlier Jambu-tree associated with a miracle of when the Bodhisattva was meditating under it and as the hours progressed the shadow protecting him from the hot sun did not move.[7] Hence, this earlier tree incident adds to the overall vigor of the tree in aniconic art.[8] When the Jātakas are added to the Buddha's life—itself overlaid with some legends—this fosters a kind of iconic art long before Mahāyāna Buddhism. Now, the wheel as the symbol of his setting the Doctrine into motion (i.e. disseminating it) is perhaps fortified by stories emphasizing the chariot wheel; and in the terms of the Jātakas, those when he has the role of a king, as in the story of King Śibi—since the wheel is in India a symbol of royalty.[9] It can be concluded that the Jātakas while being represented with iconic art still serve to promote and fortify the symbolism of the Buddha's presence in the absence.

Besides, the traditional statement about remembering previous lives in which the Buddha is portrayed as recalling the name, clan, caste, food, pleasure and pain, and end of life for a particular previous life[10]—go with the basic pilgrimage sites. That is to say, the name, clan, and caste expand upon the place of birth. The food reminds us that moderation in food preceded the Bodhisattva's passage to the Tree of Enlightenment. Besides morsel food, Buddhism speaks of three other 'foods'—contactual, volitional, and perceptual—and the celebrated Buddhist teacher Vasubandhu in his commentary on Asaṅga's *Mahāyānasaṃgraha* speaks of the wondrous nature of the teaching about the four foods, namely, the Buddha gave the precepts about these to the gods, who gave them to other sentient beings who, on account of those, attained enlightenment.[11] Then the part in the memory of previous lives referred to as "pleasure and pain" goes with the Buddha's doctrine, in particular the four Noble Truths, "There is suffering", and so on. Finally, the end of life of course goes with the pilgrimage site of where the Buddha died.

The expression "aniconic art"—as above explicated—works well for the last three pilgrimage symbols, i.e. the tree for the enlightenment, the wheel for the teaching, the *stūpa* for the death referred to as Parinirvāṇa. Only in the case of the birth symbol would there be a problem with such terminology. Sometimes, Gautama Buddha's birth was linked with Queen Māyā's dream of a white elephant entering her womb. But, generally the birth itself is indicated by representations of Queen Māyā standing up and holding on to the branch of a fig tree, and besides those two (the elephant and Queen Māyā), illustrations of Gautama's seven steps.[12] But whether such depictions can be labelled 'iconic' is dubious. However, in terms of depictions with the Buddha not in the scene, a candidate for the true aniconic symbol is the footprint.[13] This in the legend was the evidence for the prophecy. It is directly tied to his birth, since the Hindu astrological first moment of birth usually is the alighting upon earth, *bhūpatana*;[14] and so the footprint can be regarded as the signature or residue of the seven steps. Sivaramamurti accepts the *pūrṇaghaṭa* (the full pot, i.e. graced with water and plant shoots) to suggest the birth of the Buddha.[15] His alternate solution implicates the "appearance of the head" as the first moment of birth,[16] since mystically this goes with the "full pot" by taking the new birth metaphorically as a shoot.

The basic four pilgrimage sites, namely, Kapilavastu (birth), Bodhgaya (enlightenment), Varanasi (first sermon), and Kuśinagara (death), became gradually enlarged in terms of the great, or decisive events of Gautama Buddha's life. Thus, there were eight great events, on which the textual references and Gupta stele depictions do not always agree.[17] The tradition coming into Tibet later on had a standardization into twelve acts.[18] One way to increase the four events to eight was to add four between the first sermon and the *parinirvāṇa*, namely, the Miracle at Śrāvastī, the Descent from the Tuṣita Heaven, the subduing of the wild elephant Nalagiri, and the monkey offering honey to the Buddha.[19] All of these were also associated with places, i.e., cities of ancient India. It is curious that these numbers—four, eight and twelve, are multiples of four. Such numbers have overtones of other numerical groups of Buddhism. For the first two, one may consult the Aṅguttara-nikāya of the Pāli canon, which goes up to the "Book of Elevens". In Buddhism, for example, there are the four foods, the four postures; and in the Buddha's life, the four legendary sights through the four directional gates of the palace at his birthplace. For the eight, there are the eight liberations, the eightfold noble path, and the eight auspicious symbols of art depiction. For the twelve, there is the well-known formula of Dependent Origination (*pratītya-samutpāda*). This does not mean there should be a match-up of the respective items of numerical lists simply because they agree in the over all number. Certainly, the basic four keep their distance and preserve an individuality. It is the numbers themselves that have a subtle connotation. Thus, the number four has been accepted as "symbolic of completeness", namely, the four quarters.[20] In such a case, one would expect the extension to the number eight to implicate a subsidiary four as "intermediate". And then it would not be readily feasible to extend the multiples to the number twelve. It follows that a purely spatial interpretation leaves us in the lurch, as though the places were 'timeless'.

After this establishment of the kind of art here called "aniconic", it is well to turn to the other kind, the likenesses. This brings up the problem of the role attributed to the Buddha's image and calls attention to the many passages of later times that criticize the iconic representations of the Buddha.[21] The modern authors who quote such passages seem unable to find in the early Buddhist canon (say the Pāli scriptures) a prohibition of depicting the human form, and in particular, that of the Buddha.[22] In ancient times, the art styles were matters of prestigious genre: If one religious group starts something that helps increase their converts, the other religious groups try to follow suit. Sivaramamurti says: "Though according to the story of the life of Buddha, Ajātaśatru got the exact likeness of the Master created for him in *gośīrṣa* wood, there is not a single representation in human form of the Buddha till the first century A.D. All the early representations of the master illustrating various incidents of his life have been symbolic."[23] The Buddha's image apparently hails from the time when in areas like Central Asia there were many converts to Buddhism, including some Greeks or Romans and among these some artisans, who offered to make a Buddha; and the local Buddhist elders, not being aware of any prohibition against it in the texts at their disposal must have deemed it a good idea. And so it started that way and took off. Then some other Buddhist elders began to have misgivings, and in time would write those various objections to physical representations of the Buddha. We shall now observe why they had misgivings.

When one makes a 'likeness' in sculpture or in painting, it is lifeless by dint of being a likeness. This is proved by the methods of prayer, meditation, and the like resorted to, so as to get the presumed original model of the likeness to descend into the sculpture or the painting. As I know from an actual example of a Tārā statue that the Tibetans believed had "spoken",[24] this was an especially precious statue; since by contrast, normally the statues do not speak. Therefore, the terminology "living embodiment" cannot be applied to these iconical likenesses. Even so, these images have a special sanctity in a religion, since they are regarded as "standing for" the divinity, thus with cultural import and reinforcing the faith of the laity—hence the considerable consternation when there is a desecration of them. These statues and paintings came to cost tidy sums of local money. Hence, Buddhist institutions which gathered such items could tempt robbers from outside as well as inside thievery. The aniconic *stūpa* relics had similar problems. As I pointed out in my essay, certain symbols, especially the tree, the wheel, and the *stūpa* in time were rendered banal by appearing on punch-marked coins (the "Buddhist coins").[25] This seems not to have constituted a desecration of the symbols. Still such multiplication on coins of the aniconic images may have created a receptivity for the emergence of a new form of art the iconic, namely, in terms of the Buddha himself.

A classic text of Buddhist ethics, the *Udānavarga*, at 22.11, voices its concern this way: "Those who apprehend me by (corporeal) formation, and follow me by speech—those persons when dominated by passionate craving do not know me." In another chapter, I also cited Asaṅga's explanation for this: "It is like this, the ordinary person (*pṛthag-jana*), who has not completely eliminated his passionate craving, when he sees a Tathāgata possessed of the thirty-two characters of the Great Person, apprehends and thinks, 'Gosh! This Bhagavat is a Rightly Perfected Buddha! His Doctrine is well-stated. His congregation of auditors is rightly installed.' Thereafter, this person relies on unworthy persons, heeds pernicious doctrines . . . and comes to blame the Buddha, his Doctrine and his Congregation."[26] The famous *Diamond Cutter* (*Vajracchedika-prajñāpāramitā-sūtra*) in Price's translation from the Chinese, says (in Section V): "Subhuti, what do you think? Is the Tathāgata to be recognized by some material characteristic? No, World-honored One: the Tathāgata cannot be recognized by any material characteristic. Wherefore? Because the Tathāgata has said that material characteristics are not in fact material characteristics."[27] Possibly the scripture means that the characteristic mankind attributes to him is in fact not the characteristic. In any case, it is clear that these scriptures are in their own way voicing a concern that the iconic representations of the Buddha could mislead persons.

Despite the warnings, the multiplication of the images continued, and the Buddha images are sometimes of remarkable artistic merit.[28] Besides, the Buddha image became one of the approved meditative objects. So in a Mahāyāna scripture, the *Samādhirāja*: "Whoever engages his mind in that meditative object—the Lord of the World, glorious with a body like the color of gold—that Bodhisattva is declared 'equipoised' (*samāhita*)." But Tsoṅ-kha-pa, when citing this has to warn the reader: "Some place an icon in front and viewing it with the eye, make a quick contemplation; this has been elegantly refuted by the teacher Ye-shes-sde: *samādhi* is not accomplished by what the senses are aware of; rather it is accomplished by what the mind is aware of.[29] My earlier essay cited Coomaraswamy with a similar remark: "Thus the artist's model is always a mental image."[30]

The artists must have themselves realized the lifeless character of the icons, because they would try to include some aniconic touches to bring in some vitality. Thus they might include a tree in back; and the hooded serpent who shades the meditating future Buddha is a type of replacement for the shade-offered by the tree.

Our investigation shows that there is a kind of art history going on. First, there was the remembrance of the Buddha, creating a "presence in the absence". Then four kinds of aniconic art appeared. Jātakas arose which fortified the presence in the absence and then were themselves used for sculptural depiction of their Buddhist narrative. The early sculptures, such as at Bhārhut or at Sañchi depict some of these Jātakas and add human-looking *yakṣas* (or their female kind), showing no revulsion at depicting the human body. Sometime around the beginning of the Christian era, the first Buddha image appeared, to be followed by many others; then other Buddhas and Bodhisattvas, and so on. Along with this profusion of iconic art, there were a number of textual passages that sought to discount these depictions. The narrative art continued, with lifeless icons enlivened with traces of aniconic art. That is the situation at Ajanta.[31]

The next episode is alluded to in a work I have prepared for publication by Motilal Banarsidass, called *Enlightenment of Vairocana* by A. Wayman and R. Tajima (Delhi, 1992). I have placed this *Vairocanābhisambodhi* text at mid-sixth century A.D., and composed in Maharashtra; and have advanced the theory that its author was part of a movement to introduce exact measurements in the images, thus a hieratic art, evidenced in the initial hewing of the Buddhist caves at Ellora, and evidenced also at Kanheri near present-day Bombay.

And for purposes of the present chapter, I should point out that the old aniconic art continued, so did the Jātakas with their iconic art, so did the exact-measurement type of hieratic art. When it comes to a matter of Buddhist deities in general—leaving out Śākyamuni—one would have to admit the overpowering influence of Mahāyāna scriptures. But when it comes to representations of Śākyamuni himself, it is quite dubious if the nomenclature of

'Hīnayāna' or 'Mahāyāna' applies.[32] For example, there are representations of Śākyamuni surrounded by the sixteen Arhats; but the Mahāyāna itself includes 'Arhats' in the Hīnayāna. And whatever the words 'Mahāyāna' and 'Hīnayāna' may mean to the persons who freely use these words in modern writing, it is a fact that the term 'Hīnayāna' was an innovation of the Mahāyāna literature; and any attempt to trace the flourishing expansion of later Buddhist literature back to Gautama Buddha is quite speculative and takes much for granted that is not in evidence. The present chapter was able to advance positions about aniconic and iconic art without any pressing necessity to use terms like 'Hīnayāna' and 'Mahāyāna'.

REFERENCES

1. *East-West Dialogues in Aesthetics*, ed. by Kenneth K. Inada (State University of New York at Buffalo, 1978), pp. 2-15.
2. *Buddhist Insight; Essays by Alex Wayman*, Ed: George R. Elder (Motilal Banarsidass, Delhi, 1984), pp. 287-306.
3. In the essay (notes 1, 2, above) I had referred to Francis M. Cornford, *Plato's Cosmology.*
4. Susan L. Huntington in her work *The Art of Ancient India* with contributions by John C. Huntington (New York & Tokyo, 1985), p. 99, mentions "aniconic restrictions in the art" as though disallowing "iconic". Since she employs the term 'aniconic' in this special manner, she may well be right in her remarks in terms of this special usage.
5. A. Foucher, *The Beginnings of Buddhist Art* (Paris, London, 1917), pp. 10-11.
6. Cf. Alex Wayman, "The Guru in Buddhism," *Studia Missionalia*, Vol. 36, 1987, p. 213. This essay is reprinted in the present volume.
7. Cf. Dieter Schlingloff, "Die Meditation unter dem Jambu-Baum," *Wiener Zeitschrift für die Kunde Südasiens*, XXXI, 1987, pp. 111-30.
   Besides, there is H. Durt, "La 'Visite aux laboureurs' et la 'Meditation sous l'arbre *Jambu* dans les biographies sanskrites et chinoises du Buddha," *Indological and Buddhist Studies* (Canberra 1982) pp. 95-120.
8. There is much tree lore in India. Cf. Odette Viennot, *Le Culte de l'Arbre dans l'Inde Ancienne* (Presses Universities de France, 1954). Also, M.S. Randhava, "The Cult of Trees & Tree Worship in Buddhist-Hindu Sculpture" *Roopa-Lekha*, XXXIII, Nos. 1 & 2, pp. 1-42.
9. For some of the wheel lore, see *The Wheel Flag of India; Chakra-Dhvaja*, by Vasudeva S. Agrawala (Varanasi, 1964). And Paul Horsch, "The Wheel: an Indian Pattern of World-Interpretation," *Sino-Indian Studies; Liebenthal Festschrift*, , ed. by Kshitis Roy (Visvabharati, Santiniketan, 1957), pp. 62-79.
10. Cf. Paravahera Vajiranāṇa Mahathera, *Buddhist Meditation in Theory and Practice* (Colombo, 1962), pp. 447-8.
11. Cf. Alex Wayman, "Vasubandhu—Teacher Extraordinary, "*Studia Missionalia*,

Vol. 37, 1988, pp. 263-4. This essay is reprinted in the present volume.

12. Cf. *The Way of the Buddha,* Published by Publication Division, Ministry of Information and Broadcasting, Government of India, "On the occasion of the 2,500th anniversary of the Parinirvāṇa of Buddha."
13. Bonpo Kojima, "Some Thoughts on Buddha's Footprints, "*Journal of Indian and Buddhist Studies",* X:2 March 1962, pp. 47-50, includes plates with three examples of Buddha's footprints.
14. Cf. Alex Wayman, "Climactic Times in Indian Mythology and Religion *History of Religions*", 4:2, Winter, 1965, 309-10.
15. C. Sivaramamurti, "Buddha as a Mahāpurusha" (Sir Tashi Namgyal Memorial Lectures), *Bulletin of Tibetology,* IZ:3, 1972, p. 4.
16. Wayman, n. 14, above, *ibid.*
17. See Patricia Eichenbaum Karetzky, "The Act of Pilgrimage and Guptan Steles with Scenes from the life of the Buddha, "*Oriental Art,* XXXIIII, 1987, pp. 268-74.
18. Cf. *Mkhas grub rje's Fundamentals of the Buddhist Tantras,* tr. by F.D. Lessing and A. Wayman (The Hague, Paris, 1968), pp. 24-5, from *Ratnagotravibhāga,* II, 53-36. The twelve acts are (1) Descent from Tuṣita, (2) Entrance into the Womb, (3) Rebirth, (4) Skill in Worldly arts, (5) Enjoyment of the harem women, (6) Departure from home, (7) Arduous discipline, (8) Passage to the precincts of enlightenment, (9) Defeat of the Māra host, (10) Complete Enlightenment, (11) The Wheel of the Dharma, and (12) The Departure into Nirvāṇa.
19. See Ratan Parimoo, *Life of Buddha in Indian Sculpture* (New Delhi, 1982), pp. 44-57.
20. Karetzky (n. 17, above), p. 269, appeals to A.A. Macdonell, *Vedic Mythology,* for this observation.
21. Dieter Schlingloff, "Die Bedeutung der Symbole in der Altbuddhistischen Kunst," in *Hinduismus and Buddhismus; Festschrift für Ulrich Schneider* (Freiburg, 1987), pp. 309-16, surveys the modern authors and relevant passages for this prohibition of making images of the Buddha. Susan Huntington (n. 4, above). at p. 627, n. 12, reports that John C. Huntington has surveyed the prohibition passages in an article in *Studies in Buddhist Art and Archaeology,* edited by A.K. Narain and Lewis R. Lancaster.
22. See Susan Huntington (n. 4, above), p. 70, for the observation that a search of the Pāli canon does not reveal a single textual prohibition against 'image-making'.
23. Sivaramamurti (n. 15, above), p. 4.
24. In the year 1970 when I was in Dharamaśāla, H.P., of Northern India, the Tibetan lama Gonsar Rinpoche pointed out this Tārā to me with the story. It seems that when the Tibetan party headed by H.H. the Dalai Lama fled Tibet, they took this Tārā along.
25. Wayman (n. 2, above), p. 292.
26. Cf. Alex Wayman, "The Tathāgata chapter of Nāgārjuna's *Mūla-Madhyamaka-kārikā, "Philosophy East and West,* Vol. 38, n. 1, 1988, pp. 53-4.
27. A.F. Price, *The Jewel of Transcendental Wisdom* (The Diamond Sūtra) (London, 1947).
28. One may consult reproductions of many of these masterpieces in Anil de Silva-Vigier, *The Life of the Buddha* (Phaidon Press, London, 1955).
29. A. Wayman, *Calming the Mind and Discerning the Real; Buddhist Meditation and the Middle view,* from the *Lam rim chen mo* (New York, 1978), p. 114.
30. Cf. essay (n.2, above), p. 297, citing Ananda K. Coomaraswamy, *The Transformation of Nature in Art* (New York, 1956).

31. The art of Ajanta is depicted and discussed in numerous works. Since my topic is the representations of Gautama Buddha, I should call attention to the detailed bibliographical account in Dieter Schlingloff, "Ein Zyklus des Buddhalebens in Ajanta," *Wiener Zeitschrift für die Kunde Südasiens*, XXVII, 1983, pp. 113-48.
32. By these remarks, I wish to endorse a position taken by Susan Huntington (n. 4, above), p. 70, where she challenges the use of the terms 'Hīnayāna' and 'Mahāyāna' in many previous writings on the topic, as though 'Hīnayāna' is the aniconic phase, and 'Mahāyāna' introduced the human-looking Buddha images.

8

The Tathāgata Chapter of Nāgārjuna's *Mūla-Madhyamaka-kārikā*

The steady increase of translations and scholarly studies of the Mādhyamika school of Buddhism would lead one to suppose that the topic had become thoroughly clarified. Yet in recent times, articles and studies have appeared that challenge the traditional conclusions. The present writer, for example, wrote an article on Nāgārjuna that even claimed for this celebrated author the role of inaugurating Mahāyāna Buddhism (granting that certain earlier scriptures would later be included in the category) and 'ghost' authorship of the *Aṣṭasāhasrikā Prajñāpāramitā-sūtra*:[1] and the present writer wrote another article that included a new translation

Reprinted from *Philosophy East and West*, Vol. 38. No. 1 (January 1988) by the University of Hawaii Press.

of the *Mūla-Madhyamaka-kārikā* (*MK*), Chapter 2, and rejected the usual conclusion that Nāgārjuna denied motion.[2] Another writer, Kalupahana, has put out a new translation of *MK*, denying therein that Nāgārjuna is a Mahāyānist and deciding that Candrakīrti's *Prasannapadā* commentary on *MK* has departed so far from the intent of *MK* as not to deserve the translation (although European scholars sometime back translated the whole of this commentary).[3]

With such astonishing claims by myself and now by Kalupahana, the matter deserves further attention to sort out some of the relevant evidence. I have chosen a study of the Tathāgata Chapter (Chapter 22) of *MK*, because this chapter dovetails with the Chapter 2 examination of *gatāgata*. The question that needs answering is how does Nāgārjuna construe the term *tathāgata*? Of course, various theories have been offered about this word.[4] We shall soon see that the usual explanations do not face up to this chapter of *MK*, especially the last Kārikā (number 16), which uses the term *tathāgata* along with *jagat*—since both terms have the root *gam*- (to go). Thus Nāgārjuna informs the attentive reader that the problem is not, as Kalupahana opined on *kārikā* 1-2, one of 'agent' but rather whether the realm in which there is *gata* (the gone) or *āgata* (the come) implies a realm in which there is *sthita* (staying). recalling that in Chapter 2. Nāgārjuna set forth that a person either goes or stays. Since Nāgārjuna did not deny motion in Chapter 2 of his *MK*, this helps for understanding *MK* Chapter 23, in which it is clear that the Tathāgata went (*gata*).

Before going further, Kalupahana's striking claims deserve responses. As to Nāgārjuna not being a Mahāyānist, Kalupahana points out that Warder has previously written an article claiming this. If they so understand the *MK*, they should be able to translate the verses correctly. However, Kalupahana on *MK* 24.32 claims that Nāgārjuna criticizes the Mahāyāna *bodhisattva* practice, but fails to translate the *te* (Tibetan *khyod kyi*, "according to you") which shows that the verse represents the opponent's view, not Nāgārjuna's. The reader is invited to compare Kalupahana's (or for that matter, some other translator's) rendition of *MK* Chapter 2 with mine in the article mentioned,[5] or with my rendition of *MK* Chapter 22 in the present article,[6] and decide for himself which of them makes better sense of Nāgārjuna's verses. Besides, Nāgārjuna's *Ratnāvalī*, Chapter 5, portrays the six *pāramitās* and the ten Bodhisattva stages that are characteristic of Māhāyāna

Buddhism.[7] Granted that someone may raise a question, doubting that the *Ratnāvalī* is really by Nāgārjuna. It is a wonderful trait of humans to raise questions that elicit answers provided they do not conclude that their question is itself the answer.

Kalupahana's attitude toward Candrakīrti's commentary may well be due to a disappointment shared by other readers who expected Candrakīrti to help in understanding the *MK*. My article on Nāgārjuna dealt with this matter:

> "Candrakīrti, of course, would not hold that the student must read his commentary in order to understand the MMK [the *Mūla-MK*], for that would imply that no one had ever understood it previously. The precise opposite seems to be the case. Candrakīrti expected the student to have already understood the MMK in terms of the words of the verses, and to read his commentary for his system, usually called Prāsaṅgika-Mādhyamika. This should have been noticed from his kind of commentary, which is not grammatical, i.e., on the words in their order of occurrence, but the kind of commentary which says more. Furthermore, the *Prasannapadā* has more difficult Sanskrit than does the MMK, so if one cannot understand the MMK by its words, it appears useless to go to the more complicated commentaries."[8]

Accordingly, I did not employ Candrakīrti's commentary, but did refer to Buddhapālita's in my translation of *MK* 2—since I was concerned with the words employed by Nāgārjuna. Here also, when rendering *MK* 22, I am concerned with the words and find the commentaries (Candrakīrti's: Sanskrit-Tibetan; Buddhapālita's: Tibetan) useful for more information. In so doing, my own explanation of the verses is along the lines of Kalupahana's by way of the premise that one can comment on the verses by means of one's own background of research, and not have to rely on one of the commentaries, except sporadically. I do not, however, denigrate Candrakīriti's commentary, as Kalupahana does. And admittedly my comments follow a certain school of interpretation, namely, accepting the relevance of canonical Buddhist teachings as concerns the notion of Tathāgata.

The Tathāgata Chapter of *MK* appears to fall into these verse groups: *kārikās* 1-9, Does a Tathāgata Adopt Personal Aggregates (*skandha*)? *kārikās* 10-14, Tathāgata and Voidness (*śūnyatā*); *kārikā* 15, Seeing a Tathāgata; and *kārikā* 16. The Tathāgata and the Moving World (*jagat*). Because of these verse divisions, I have employed two renditions of the term svabhāva;[9] for *kārikās* 1-9, the rendition "one's own origination", and for *kārikās* 10-16, the rendition "own nature". Anticipating a conclusion, the rendition "own-nature" intends that "own-nature" belongs to the unmentioned, but implied world of 'staying' that is complementary to the world of 'going'. My translation of the verse agrees usually with the grammatical interpretation in de Jong's French translation,[10] and diverges accordingly from Kalupahana's rendition.

Does a Tathāgata Adopt Personal Aggregates?

> *skandhā na nānyaḥ skandhebhyo nāsmin skandhā na teṣu saḥ /*
> *tathāgataḥ skandhavān na katamo 'tra tathāgataḥ //1//*
> The Tathāgata is not the personal aggregates (skandha). Nor is he different from them: to wit, the personal aggregates are not in him, nor he in them, nor is he possessed of the personal aggregates. What then is a Tathāgata?

The authority for translating the verse in this manner is Candrakīrti's *Madhyamakāvatāra,* where this very verse is cited under 6.144. That is to say, when contemplating each of the five personal aggregates (*rūpa* and so forth) in four ways to counter what are called the 'twenty reifying views' (Pāli *sakkāyadiṭṭhi*), the four ways amount to one denial of identification and three denials of difference.[11] That Candrakīrti would clarify the structure of the verse in his *M-avatāra,* but not in his commentary on the *MK,* agrees with his assuming the reader's ability in the *kārikās* themselves. What then is Tathāgata? He 'went' (gata) 'that way' (*tathā*). The opening scripture in the Pāli canonical *Samyutta-nikāya* tells that a certain deva, as dawn was approaching, came to the Jeta Grove, where the Buddha was staying and asked how he had crossed the flood. The Buddha responded: "Not staying (Pāli *appatiṭṭham*), friend, and not conjecturing (Pāli *anāyuham*), did I cross the flood."[12] This shows that the Buddha went (*gata*) and avoided wayward views (Sanskrit *dṛṣṭi*), so he is Tathāgata. If he had stayed (*sthita*) it would have been in the personal aggregates, and so he could not be called '*Tathāgata*':

buddhaḥ skandhān upādāya yadi nāsti svabhāvataḥ /
svabhāvatas ca yo nāsti kutaḥ sa parabhāvataḥ //2//
If a Buddha (exists) by adopting personal aggregates, he does not exist by way of his own origination. When someone does not exist by way of his own origination, how can he exist by way of another's origination?

If Buddha exists by adopting the five pure aggregates (*skandha*), morality (*śīla*), intense concentration (*samādhi*), (perfected) insight (*prajñā*), liberation (*vimukti*), and the knowledge and vision of liberation (*vimuktijñānadarśana*),[13] he does not exist by way of his own origination (of these), since they were adopted by previous saints. And just as they were not his own origination as a basis for existence as a Buddha, how can he exist as such by another's origination of these?

pratītya parabhāvam yaḥ so 'nātmety upapadyate /
yaś cānātmā sa ca katham bhaviṣyati tathāgataḥ //3//
When someone exists in dependence upon another's origination, it is not valid to call him a 'self'. When someone is without self, how will he become a Tathāgata?

That 'non-self' (*anātma*) is examined by the sole aspect of 'non-self-dependence' (*asvātantrya*) is taught also in Asaṅga's *Śrāvakabhūmi*.[14] And the *Udānavarga*, its Tathāgata Chapter 21.2, has this celebrated verse about the 'self':

I am the Tathāgata,[15] teacher of gods and men; have comprehended enlightenment as a revealer by myself; having reached omniscience, am endowed with the powers; incomparable and unequalled, who can teach me!
yadi nāsti svabhāvaś ca parabhāvaḥ katham bhavet /
svabhāvaparabhāvabhyām ṛte kaḥ sa tathāgataḥ //4//
If there is not one's own origination, how can there be another's origination? Except for one's own origination and another's origination, who would be the Tathāgata?

For the meaning, notice the definition of 'Tathāgata' in the *Prajñāpāramitāśāstra*:[16] (1) He preaches the character of *dharma* (*dharmalakṣaṇa*) according to the manner (*tathā*) in which he understood it (*gata*). (2) In the manner by which the (earlier) Buddhas have gone on the path of acquirement (*yoga*) and security (*kṣema*), so (*tathā*) the (present) Buddha has gone (*gata*), and there are no more rebirths. That is why he is called 'Tathāgata'.

Thus, the first sentence of *kārikā* 4 can be construed as intending that the Buddha's own attainment shows the way for others to follow the path, while the second sentence intends that the present Buddha followed the course of preceding Buddhas; hence both his own attainment and their attainments are implicated in the name 'Tathāgata':

> *skandhān yady anupādāya bhavet kaścit tathāgataḥ /*
> *sa idānim upādadyād upādāya tato bhavet //5//*
> If someone could be a Tathāgata without adopting personal aggregates, he might adopt them now and later adopting them, be (a Tathāgata).

Candrakīrti's commentary provides a hint of the meaning, giving the illustration that Devadatta existed before he acquired riches, and acquired them later.[17] Therefore, it appears that Nāgārjuna understands the first explanation of the term 'Tathāgata' (given already under *kārikā* 4) to mean a Tathāgata who has not yet advanced to *yoga-kṣema*. Later, this Tathāgata could acquire the five pure aggregates (the *yoga*), and then secure them (the *kṣema*) by way of the ten powers and other Buddha's natures:

> *skandhān cāpy anupādāya nāsti kaścit tathāgataḥ /*
> *yaś ca nāsty anupādāya sa upādāsyate katham //6//*
> A Tathāgata does not exist unless he adopts personal aggregates. Anyone, not adopting them, does not exist. How can he appropriate them?

A Tathāgata, in order to exist, must adopt the ordinary personal aggregates, *rūpa*, and so forth. According to Buddhapālita's commentary, since *saṃsāra* is without beginning or end, there does not exist anyone who has not adopted the aggregates, and how can anyone appropriate them if he had not done so previously.[18]

> *na bhavaty anupādattam upādānaṃ ca kiṃ cana /*
> *na cāsti nirupādānaḥ kathaṃ cana tathāgataḥ //7//*
> No adoption occurs prior to its adoption. No Tathāgata exists without an adoption (of *skandhas*).

The first half appears to deny the Sāṃkhya position that the effect pre-exists in the cause, as though there were a pre-genetic adoption. And a Tathāgata must adopt personal aggregates in order to exist. Nāgārjuna, in his friendly letter (to a king), the *Suhṛllekha*, *kārikās* 59-60, stresses the value of human birth for practice of the Dharma and progress toward enlightenment.[19] Hence, the personal aggregates (*skandha*) of a human beings are meant. The five are formation (*rūpa*), feelings (*vedanā*), ideation (*saṃjñā*), motivations (*saṃskāra*), and perceptions (*vijñāna*):

> *tattvānyatvena yo nāsti mṛgyamānas ca pañcadhā /*
> *upādānena sa kathaṃ prajñapyate tathāgataḥ //8//*
> Who being sought for in five ways does not exist as different from the elements (=aggregates) or as the adoption (of aggregates), how can he be designated a Tathāgata?

The five ways are the five personal aggregates listed under the preceding verse. He can be designated a Tathāgata because the Pāli canon *Saṃyutta-ṇikāya* at 2.25 has a famous remark: "Whether Tathāgatas arise or do not arise, there remains this realm (*dhātu*), the continuance of *dhamma*, the rule of *dhamma*, the having of this for condition." This rule of *dhamma* (Sanskrit *dharma*) means the Dependent Origination of the natures (*dharma*) of which the five personal aggregates are composed. Thus, the continuance of the five personal aggregates is independent of whether there is a Tathāgata:

> *yad apīdam upādānaṃ tat svabhāvān na vidyate /*
> *svabhāvataś ca yan nāsti kutas tat parabhāvataḥ //9//*
> But also this 'adoption' (of aggregates) is not found by way of its own origination. And when something does not exist by way of its own origination, how can it exist by way of another's origination?

Upādāna is the ninth member of the Buddhist formula of Dependent Origination (*pratītya-samutpāda*). It arises dependent on the preceding member, *tṛṣṇā* (craving), and so does not arise by way of its own origination. However, it does not exist by way of *tṛṣṇā*'s origination, since this 'craving' is not the cause of *upādāna* ('adoption'), but only the condition for its arising.[20]

Tathāgata and Voidness

> *evaṃ śūnyam upādānam upādātā ca sarvaśaḥ /*
> *prajñapyate ca śūnyena kathaṃ śūnyas tathāgataḥ //10//*
> Thus, adoption and adopter are completely void (of

> *svabhāva*). How can the Tathāgata be designated as void by what is void?

As recorded in the *Saṃyutta-nikāya*, 4.54. Ānanda asked the Buddha about the saying "The world is void! The world is void!" (*suñño loko suñño loko 'ti*), and the Buddha explained: "Because it is void of self or of what belongs to self, therefore, 'The world is void'." So, here, because it is void of adopter and of adoption, the world is void. As to the ability of words to designate something as 'void', this is a matter dealt with by Nāgārjuna in his *Vigrahavyāvartinī.*

The opponent claimed that words being void (of *svabhāva*) were incapable of denying anything or establishing the voidness of anything. Let us accept K. Bhattacharya's translation of this text, 70, "All things prevail for him—for whom prevails this voidness (*prabhavati ca śūnyateyaṃ yasya prabhavanti tasya sarvārthāḥ*). Nothing prevails for him—for whom voidness does not prevail (*prabhavati na tasya kimcin na prabhavati śūnyatā yasya*)."[21]

> *śūnyam iti na vaktavyam aśūnyam iti vā bhavet /*
> *ubhayaṃ nobhayaṃ ceti prajñaptyarthaṃ tu kathyate//*11//
> One should not say he is void or non-void, both or neither.
> But one may use terms for (such) a designation.

Having insisted that words, although void of own-nature (*svabhāva*), have the power to designate something as 'void', Nāgārjuna does not admit that words are always employed wisely. In order to designate something as 'void', one should add 'void of' (something). Notice in the preceding sentence that simply to say "The world is void" does not convey much comprehension to the hearer, and so the Buddha had to add: "void of self or of what belongs to self". Then, how can a person of ordinary comprehension state what the Tathāgata is void of, when declaring the Tathāgata 'void'? Hence, one should not say he is void and so forth. The *Paṭisambhidāmagga* of the Pāli canon has lofty praise of a Tathāgata in the 'Faculties' chapter:[22]

> *na tassa adiṭṭhaṃ idh' atthi kiñci anho aviññatam ajanitabbam /*
> *sabhaṃ abhinnāsi yad atthi neyyam. Tathāgato tena samantacakkhūti.*
> Here in this world—there is nothing he has not seen, nothing

> not understood, nothing unknowable. He has experienced supernormally all that is knowable. Therefore the Tathāgata is called the All-seer.

Therefore, the Tathāgata is not explained by the word 'void'—how much less by the word 'empty'!

> *śāśvatāśāśvatādy atra kutaḥ śānte catuṣṭayaṃ /*
> *antānantādi cāpy atra kutaḥ śānte catuṣṭayaṃ* //12//
> How can the eternal, non-eternal, and so on.... kind of four alternatives be in the peaceful? How can the finite, non-finite, and so on kind of four alternatives be in the peaceful?

Candrakīrti's commentary[23] points out that these two sets of four alternatives are among the fourteen *avyākṛta-vastūni*, meaning the questions which the Buddha refused to answer. The verse mentions the first set, namely, that the world is eternal, non-eternal, both eternal and non-eternal, and neither eternal nor non-eternal, and the second set, namely, that the world is finite, non-finite, both finite and non-finite, and neither finite nor non-finite. The third set is alluded to in the next verse, number 13: they are: the Tathāgata exists after death, does not exist after death, both exists and does not exist after death, and neither exists nor does not exist after death. The last two of the fourteen are: the self (*jīva*) is identical with the body, and the self is different from the body. As to the question, "How can they be in the peaceful?" the peaceful is apparently a reference to Nirvāṇa, or to a person in whom the phenomenal turbulence has been appeased and so finds these fourteen questions not worth answering:

> *yena grāho gṛhītas tu ghano 'stīti tathāgataḥ /*
> *nāstīti sa vikalpayan nirvṛtasyāpi kalpayet* //13//
> The one attached to the gross positing, imagining that the Tathāgata exists or that he does not exist would also imagine (the alternatives) for one in Nirvāṇa.

This verse may provide a clue to the prohibition which the Bhagavat announced to the first five disciples, namely, that they should not address a Tathāgata as 'long-lived one' (*āyuṣmat*). That is to say, the disciples would be guilty of the 'gross positing'. In other words, that title 'long-lived one' could be relevant for one who 'stays' (*sthita*), but the name 'Tathāgata' means 'one who went that way':

> *svabhāvataś ca 'sūnye smiṃs cintā naivopapadyate /*
> *parāṃ nirodhād bhavati buddho na bhavatīti vā //14//*
> The speculation that the Buddha exists or does not exist after death is not admissible, since he is void of own-nature.

The statement that the Buddha is void of *svabhāva* does not constitute a denial of *svabhāva*, but rather assigns *svabhāva* to a status complementary to the Tathāgata, as in the celebrated remark already cited, "Whether Tathāgatas arise or do not arise, there remains....."[24] The inadmissible speculation is in terms of remaining.

Seeing A Tathāgata

> *prapañcayanti ye buddhaṃ prapañcātītam avyayam /*
> *te prapañcahatāḥ sarve na paśyanti tathāgataṃ //15 //*
> Those who verbally elaborate the incessant Buddha who has transcended verbal elaboration—none of them, impaired by verbal elaboration, can see the Tathāgata.

This verse agrees with Udānavarga, Chapter 22, verse 11. This chapter, on the 'Hearer', immediately follows the 'Tathāgata' Chapter (21). It is a reasonable assumption that Dharmatrāta's *Udānavarga* delighted Nāgārjuna, who was probably very young when it first appeared.[25] *Udānavarga* 22.11 follows, rendered from the Tibetan:

> */ gaṅ dag gzugs kyis ṅes par 'dzin /*
> */ ṅa la sgra yis rjes su 'braṅ /*
> */ 'dun pa'i dod chags dbaṅ gyur la /*
> */ skye bo de dag ṅa mi śes //*
> Those who apprehend me by (corporeal) formation and follow me by speech, those persons when dominated by passionate craving do not know me.

While the message, as originally told is said to be by a certain dwarf (Pāli) Bhaddiya, rendered in the commentary to the *Udānavarga* in the Tibetan canon, *'Phags pa Lan-tshwa-bzaṅ-po*,[26] the application in the present context is certainly to the Tathāgata. Asaṅga, in his *Yogācārabhūmi* in the section on *śarīrārthagāthā* cites the set of five verses *Udānavarga* 22.11-15, and explains:[27]

> It is like this: The ordinary person (*pṛthagjana*), who has not completely eliminated his passionate craving, when he sees a Tathāgata possessed of the thirty-two characters of the great person, apprehends and thinks, "Gosh! This Bhagavat is a rightly perfected Buddha! His doctrine is well-stated. His congregation of auditors is rightly installed." Thereafter, this person relies on unworthy persons, heeds pernicious doctrines... and comes to blame the Buddha, his doctrine, and his congregation (*'di ltar di na so so'i skye bo'i 'dun pa'i 'dod chags ril gyis ma spaṅs pa la las de bzin gśegs pa'i skyes bu chen po'i mtshan sum cu rtsa gñis daṅ ldan pa mthoṅ ba na / kye ma bcom ldan 'das de ni yaṅ dag par rdzogs pa'i saṅs rgyas yin no de'i chos ni legs par gsuṅs pa yin no / ñan thos kyi dge 'dun ni legs par zugs pa yin no sñam du ṅes par 'dzin te / de phyis skey bu dam pa ma yin pa bsñen pa dam pa'i chos ma yin pa thos pa la brten nas /...saṅs rgyas daṅ chos daṅ dge 'dun la yaṅ skur pa debs te /*).

Ancient Buddhism declared that the signs of a Complete Buddha were held in common with the Universal Emperor (*cakravartin*); so one could not know just from those signs that one was looking at a Complete Buddha. According to Nāgārjuna's verse, the ordinary person did not really see this Tathāgata. The *Udānavarga* commentary on this verse points out that the 'passionate craving' is a hindrance to *samādhi* (*tiṅ ne 'dzin gyi sgrib pa*); and commenting upon the part, "Those persons ...do not know me" cites the well-known precept: "The man whose mind is equipoised, sees exactly as it is" (*mñam par bžag na ji lta ba bžin du mthoṅ bar 'gyur ro*).[28] Buddhapālita's commentary on the *MK* verse explains the term *prapañca* (verbal elaboration) as 'existence and non-existence', 'permanence and impermanence', and so forth;[29] hence the term suggests the creation of divisive cross-purposes (*dvandva*), or two things where there are really one, and that it is instigated by the 'passionate craving'.[30] And so one does not see objects exactly as they are.

The Tathāgata and the Moving World

> *tathāgato yat svabhāvas tat svabhāvam idaṃ jagat /*

> *tathāgato niḥsvabhāvo niḥsvabhāvam idaṃ jagat //16//*
> Were the Tathāgata to have own-nature (*svabhāva*), then this moving world would have own-nature. Given that the Tathāgata lacks *svabhāva*, this moving world lacks *svabhāva*.[31]

Nāgārjuna's final verse of the chapter shows what the Tathāgata and the *jagat* have in common—going; and it shows what they both do not have—*svabhāva*. In short, *svabhāva* (own-nature) perforce has no 'going'. Indeed, according to the commentator Buddhapālita, this *svabhāva* is the same for the Tathāgata and the *jagat*. Thus the comment (Derge, ed., f. 266b—1, 2):

> "What be the own-nature of a Tathāgata is the own-nature of the moving world (*jagat*). Since the own-nature of a Tathāgata is the own-nature of the moving world, the examination of Tathāgata is also the examination of the moving world." (*/ de bźin gśegs pa dṅos ñid gaṅ / de ni 'gro 'di'i ṅo bo ñid / gaṅ gi phyir de bźin gśegs pa'i ṅo bo ñid gaṅ yin pa de ni 'gro ba 'di'i ṅo bo ñid kyaṅ yin pa de'i phyir de bzin gsēgs pa brtags pa 'di ñid kyis 'gro ba 'di dag kyaṅ brtags pa yin no /*).

It seems to be a contradiction in terms to speak of the Tathāgata lacking svabhāva, and then to refer to the "own-nature of a Tathāgata". In fact, there is no contradiction. It is almost as when we use an expression like "our world" and then admit that the world is not ours. The point of the discussion is that Nāgārjuna never denied '*svabhāva*'; he never claimed that fire lacks the own-nature of burning; rather he insisted that an actual fire is not due to its own-nature. But, in a manner of speaking, it is necessary to refer to the *svabhāva* of a Tathāgata in order to say that the Tathāgata lacks *svabhāva*. A passage from the ancient Pāli canon should clarify the foregoing in part. This is *Saṃyutta-nikāya* 5.41-42, in the *Tathāgata-sutta*:

> *sattā apadā vā dvipadā vā catuppadā vā bahuppadā vā rūpino vā arūpino vā saññino vā asaññino vā nevasaññīnāsaññino vā, tathāgato tesaṃ aggam akkhāyati arahaṃ sammāsambuddho;*
> Of sentient beings (Sanskrit *sattva*), whether footless, two-footed, four-footed, or many-footed; whether having (material) formation or not having (material) formation; whether ideational, or non-ideational, or neither ideational

nor non-ideational—of these, the Tathāgata, the Arhat, the Rightly Complete Buddha is declared the chief.

Notice that the Tathāgata is counted among sentient beings, agreeing with the Nāgārjuna's verse and its commentary that the same examination can be made for the Tathāgata as for the moving world (*jagat*). The Pāli passage begins with *jagat* language by classifying sentient beings by their number of feet for purposes of locomotion. It then classifies by 'formation', which, as was already mentioned, deceives those who have not equilibrated their minds. Finally, it classifies by ideation, which characterizes a 'sentient being'. Hence, the Tathāgata is a kind of flowering of the sentient world. Whatever is appropriately said of the Tathāgata does not apply to the realm of staying (*sthita*), called the realm of Dharma. But it must also be admitted that the Tathāgata uses this realm of Dharma, and that to see the Tathāgata is to see the Dharma. So it is said in the *Saṃyutta-nikāya* (3.120) and other places that "he who sees the Dhamma sees me, and he who sees me sees the Dhamma".

In conclusion, the annotations which the present writer has brought to bear upon the sixteen verses of this chapter rest on the testimony of ancient Buddhism. It was not necessary to appeal to the special language of the Mahāyāna scriptures, such as the *Samādhirāja-sūtra.* But this is not to deny the applicability of such scriptures, as cited in Candrakīrti's commentary. Each commentator follows his line of comments in accordance with a lineage which he continues. The present commentary is not exempt from this condition. Indeed, there is little purpose to speculating about such matters. If authentic scriptures cannot be alluded to, if one has to guess through it, why add another commentary? Indeed, in common between the preceding approach to this Chapter 22 and the approach to my previously published translation of Chapter 2 is an attitude toward the author Nāgārjuna that he was a religious genius. His *MK* is a kind of relic. It requires of the translator both a command of language, meaning the kind of Sanskrit Nāgārjuna employs, and an evocation of the context of the disputes then current.[32] So it is easy to criticize previous translation attempts, as does Kalupahana in addition to myself. And that does not mean that we necessarily do better.

REFERENCES

1. A. Wayman, "Nāgārjuna: Moralist Reformer of Buddhism." Studia Missionalia 34 (1985), pp.63-95. This essay is included in the present volume.
2. A. Wayman, "This Gait (*gati*) and the Path (*mārga*)—Reflections on the Horizontal." *Journal of the American Oriental Society* 105, no. 3 (July-September 1985): 579-88.
3. David J. Kalupahana, *Nāgārjuna: The Philosophy of the Middle Way* (Albany, New York, 1986), Preface—pp. xiii-xv, and p. 7. At p. 26, he opposes the adulation of Nāgārjuna as a 'second Buddha', which my article (n. 1, preceding) justifies, on the grounds that he inaugurated Māhāyana Buddhism.
4. Cf. *Le Tratte de la Grande Vertu de Sagesse*, as translated by Étienne Lamotte, Vol. 1 (Louvain. 1944), p. 126 for various references.
5. There (article of n. 2 preceding) I showed the usage of *gati* in some other branches of Indian literature and investigated the verb form *gamyate* in Sanskrit grammar, as a preparation for translating *MK* Chap. 2, included in the present volume.
6. Here, for translating *MK* Chap. 22. I assumed that because the *Udānavarga* has a Tathāgata chapter, some verses would be relevant (they were!); I assumed that important teachings about the Tathāgata in early Buddhist literature and later repeated, such as "Whether a Tathāgata arises or not, there remains...." and what the Buddha said to the first five disciples, "Do not call a Tathāgata 'long-lived one' (*āyuṣmat*)," would all be relevant (and they were!); and I assumed that the remark on the first page of the *Saṃyutta-nikāya* about crossing the flood, because that requires 'going', would be relevant (and it was!). Moreover, I thought that the commentaries of Buddhapālita and Candrakīrti, fortunately available to me would be useful for certain verses (and they were!).
7. Cf. Michael Hahn, *Nāgārjuna's Ratnāvalī* (Sanskrit, Tibetan, Chinese), (Bonn, 1982).
8. Wayman, "Nāgārjuna," p. 78, this volume.
9. It should not be surprising that the same work employs the term *svabhāva* in more than one sense: cf Ernst Steinkellner, "Wirklichkeit und Begriff bei Dharmakīrti," *Wiener Zeitschrift für die Kunde Südasiens* 15 (1971): 179-211, for various senses of this term as employed by Dharmakīrti.
10. J.W. de Jong, *Cinq Chapitres de la Prasannapadā* (Paris, 1949), has a translation of both the verses and Candrakīrti's commentary with the Tibetan text for these.
11. Cf. A. Wayman, "The Twenty Reifying Views (Sakkāyadiṭṭhi)," originally in *Studies in Pali and Buddhism* (1979), reprinted in *Buddhist Insight: Essays by Alex Wayman*, ed. by George R. Elder (Delhi, 1984), pp. 215-33, esp. p. 218.
12. I employ the edition in the *Nālandā-Devanāgarī-Pāli-Series* (Bihar Government, 1959).
13. These five are called *jina-skandha* (Aggregates of the Victor); cf. Louis de La Vallée Poussin, *L. 'Abhidharmakośa de Vasubandhu* (1925), under VI, 76c (p. 297).
14. Cf. Alex Wayman, *Analysis of the Śrāvakabhūmi Manuscript* (Berkeley, California: 1961), pp. 130-1.
15. According to Prajñāvarman's *Udānavargavivaraṇa*, ed. [from Tibetan] by Michael Balk [Bonn, 1984], Vol. 2, in comments upon this verse at p. 609, this usage of the term 'Tathāgata' shows having come (*āgata*) for the sake of others, the candidates to be taught. Hence, it is the first kind of Tathāgata, as will be alluded to in the following verse, *MK* 22.4. It is this Tathāgata who needs a 'self'.

16. *Le Traité*, Vol. 1 (n. 4, preceding), p. 126.
17. de Jong, *Cinq Chapitres* (n. 10. preceding), p. 77 and p. 147.
18. I employ the edition of Buddhapālita's commentary in the Tibetan Tanjur, the Derge edition (published in Tokyo, 1977), the Dbu-ma section, Vol. 1, i.e., vol. tsa (here, f. 263a-4ff.), beginning: '*khor ba la thog ma daṅ tha ma med do.*
19. Cf. Lozang Jamspal et al., *Nāgārjuna's Letter to King Gautamīputra* (Delhi, 1978).
20. It is of course quite reasonable that when Nāgārjuna uses the term *upādāna*, it can be construed as the term for the ninth member of Dependent Origination: *MK*, Chap. 26, is devoted to this twelve-membered formula. Again, while *tṛṣṇā* is a condition (*pratyaya*) for *upādāna*, it by no means can be taken as its cause, but Nāgārjuna takes it as concomitant in *MK* 26.6B: *tṛṣyamāna upādānam upādatte caturvidham*, "While craving, one indulges in adoption of four kinds."
21. K. Bhattacharya et al., *The Dialectical Method of Nāgārjuna (Vigrahavyāvartanī)*, (Delhi, 1978), p. 47.
22. Arnold C. Taylor, ed., *Paṭisambhidāmagga*, Vol. 2 (London, 1907), p. 31.
23. de Jong, *Cinq Chapitres* (n. 10, preceding), pp. 82-3.
24. For this kind of 'voidness', cf. *Paṭisambhidāmagga*, Vol. 2, the treatise on voidness (*suññakathā*), p. 179; or the translation by Ñānamoli, *The Path of Discrimination* (London: The Pali Text Society, 1982), pp. 357-8, "What is *voidness by characteristic*?" and so on. Here the type is *lakkhaṇasuññam* and of the examples, naturally the one of two kinds (i.e., of *lakṣaṇa*). The translation of the example: "The characteristic of the fool is void of the characteristic of the wise man, and the characteristic of the wise man is void of the characteristic of the fool." In this case, the rendition 'devoid' may serve better than 'void'. For the case of *MK* 22.14, the characteristic of going is devoid of the characteristic of remaining, and the characteristic of remaining is devoid of the characteristic of going. Here the characteristic of remaining is the *svabhāva*, and the characteristic of going is the Buddha after death.
25. This is by the reasonable dating of Nāgārjuna's life as spanning practically the entire second century A.D., and by the dating of the *Udānavarga* composition at the beginning of that century.
26. *Udānavargavivaraṇa* (n. 15, preceding), p. 634.
27. Photo-reproduction of Peking Tibetan canon, Vol. 110. p. 15-5 to p. 16-1.
28. *Udānavargavivaraṇa* (n. 15, preceding), pp. 634-5.
29. Buddhapālita's commentary (n. 18, preceding), Tsa, f. 266a-4, 5: *yod pa daṅ med pa daṅ rtag pa daṅ mi rtag pa la sogs pa'i spros pa rnams.*
30. An illustration is found in Kālidāsa's Śakuntalā, the incident in which Śakuntalā with two girl friends, with a smallest pot (suitable to her size), and attired in a tight-fitting garment of bark cloth, bends to water the basin of hermitage trees. Unknown to them, she is being observed by the king. As though by sympathetic magic of male-female craving—Śakuntalā asks her friend to loosen her garment; and promptly the discussion shifts to her two breasts. Here, the one water pot is succeeded by two breasts, by the power of craving. Cf. M.B. Emeneau, *Kālidāsa's Śakuntalā*, translated from the Bengali Recension (Berkeley, California: 1962), pp. 6-7.
31. I have noticed several translations of this verse along the same lines adopted by Kalupahana. This is his (p. 310) version: "Whatever is the self-nature of the *tathāgata*, that is also the self-nature of the universe. The *tathāgata* is devoid of self-nature. This universe is also devoid of self-nature." "In fact, de Jong's French translation is similar. Grammatically, the translation is impossible. The

reason is that *svabhāvaṃ ıdaṃ jagat* shows that here *svabhāva* (both cases in the first line) is an adjective, and these translations agree in taking it as the subject of the sentence! Both lines must be construed as nominative absolute, as I have done. Furthermore, the renditions agree that *jagat* means 'universe'. But then the verse is gibberish, and completely fails to render Nāgārjuna's point that the *gata* of Tathāgata agrees with *jagat* in having the same root 'to go'. The way these translators have rendered the verse leaves the reader with the conclusion that Nāgārjuna said that both Tathāgata and world have *svabhāva* and both lack it, as though Nāgārjuna could not make up his mind.

32. Probably *MK* 2 was the most severely misrendered by the translators, who apparently wondered why Nāgārjuna was saying such silly things about motion. Oh, never admit that the translators do not know enough about the words and the contexts to do a competent job!

9

Asaṅga's Three Pratyekabuddha Paths

Many years ago, I had edited the *Pratyekabuddhabhūmi* from among intrusive folios in the *Śrāvakabhūmi* manuscript.[1] Among the 17 *bhūmis* in Asaṅga's *Yogācārabhūmi*, that *bhūmi* comes right after the *Śrāvakabhūmi*. Now I shall again present this text in brief, followed by my translation and explanations.

PRATYEKABUDDHABHŪMIḤ

/ pratyekabuddhabhumiḥ katamā / sā pañcākārā veditavyā / gotrataḥ / mārgataḥ / samudāgamataḥ / vihārataś cāritrataś[2] ca //

/ pratyekabuddhagotraṃ katamat / tatra trilakṣaṇaṃ veditavyaṃ / prakṛtyā pratyekabuddhāḥ prāg evābhisaṃbodhān mandarajaskagotrā bhavanti / ye naiṣāṃ saṃsarge cittaṃ na krāmanty ekārāmatāyāṃ krāma(n)ti / prakṛtyā pratyekabuddhā(ḥ) prāg evābhisaṃbodhān mandakāruṇyā bhavanti / ye naiṣāṃ dharmadeśanāyā(ṃ) sattvārthakriyāyāṃ[3] / cittaṃ na krāma(n)ty alpotsukavihāritāyāṃ krāmanti / prakṛtyā pratyekabuddha(ḥ) prāg evābhisaṃbodhān madhyendriyā bhavanti / mānacaritajātīyāś ca / ye nācāryaṃ niḥpratidvandvam abhisaṃbodham abhilaṣanti //

/ tatra pratyekabuddhamārgo 'pi trilakṣaṇo veditavyaḥ / yathāpīhaikatyaḥ pratyekabuddhagotre vyavasthitaḥ / kalpaśataṃ buddhotpādam ārāgayati / tatra ca santatiṃ paripācayati / yad uta skandhakauśalyaṃ āyatanakauśalyaṃ [dhātukauśalyaṃ pratītyasamutpādakauśalyaṃ] sthānāsthānakauśalyaṃ [satyakauśalyaṃ] ca karoti / yāvad evāyatyāṃ pratyekabodhāyai ayaṃ prathamaḥ pratyekabuddhamārgaḥ // punar aparam ihaikatyo buddhotpādam ārāgya satpuruṣasaṃsevām āgamya saddharmaśravaṇaṃ yoniśomanaskāram utpādita(ḥ) pūrvāṇi nirvedha-bhāgīyāni kuśalamūlāny utpādayati / abhinirharati / tadyathā uṣmagatamūrdhakṣāntir no tu śaknoti / tasmin eva janmani dharmābhisamayaṃ kartuṃ śrāmaṇyaphalaṃ vā anuprāptuṃ skandhakuśalaś ca bhavaty āyatanakuśalo dhātukuśalaḥ pratītyasamutpādakuśalaḥ sthānāsthānakuśalaḥ satyakuśalaś ca bhavati yāvad evāyatyaṃ dharmābhisamayāya śrāmaṇyaphala-prāptaye ity ayaṃ dvitīyaḥ pratyekabuddhamārgaḥ // punar aparam ihaikatyo buddhotpādam ārāgya satpuruṣasaṃsevām āgamya saddharmaśravaṇaṃ yoniśo [manaskāram utpādito] dharmābhisamayaṃ karoti / śrāmaṇyaphalam anuprāpnoti / no tu śaknoti sarveṇa sarvam atyantaniṣṭhatām atyantavimalatām atyantabrahmacaryaparyavasānatām arhat(t)vaṃ prāptum / skandhakuśalaś ca bhavaty āyatanakuśalo dhātukuśalaḥ pratītyasamutpādakuśalaḥ sthānāsthānakuśalaḥ satyakuśalaś ca bhavati / yad uta lokottareṇa mārgeṇāyatyām atyantaniṣṭhatā (vimalatā brahmacaryaparyavasānatāyai arhat(t)vaphalaprāptaye ity ayaṃ tṛtīyaḥ pratyekabuddhamārgaḥ //

/ tatra samudāgamato yathāpīhaikatyaḥ prathamena pratyekabuddha-mārgeṇa paripūrṇakalpaśatasaṃbhāraḥ / kalpaśatasyātyayād asati ca buddhānām utpāde anācāryakaṃ saptatriṃśadbodhipakṣyān dharmān bhāvayitvā pratyekaṃ bodhim abhisaṃbudhyate ca sarvakleśaprahānaṃ arhat(t)vaṃ sākṣāt karoti/ yathāpīhaikatyo dvitīyatṛtīyābhyāṃ pratyekabuddha-mārgābhyāṃ tena hetunā tena pratyayena asaty evaṃ buddhānām utpāde anācāryakaṃ saptatriṃśadbodhipakṣyān dharmān bhāvayitvā dharmābhisamayaṃ karoti / yāvad arhat(t)vaphalam anuprāpnoty anuprāptaśrāmaṇyaphalo vā 'tyantaniṣṭhatām atyantavimalatām atyantabrahmacaryaparyavasānatām agraphalam arhat(t)vaṃ prāpnoti // tatra prathamena samudāgamena pratyekabuddho bhavati khaḍgaviṣāṇakalpaḥ / dvitīyatṛtīyena samudāgamena pratyekajino bhavati / na khaḍgaviṣāṇa-kalpaḥ //

/ tatra vihārato yo 'yaṃ khaḍgaviṣāṇakalpaḥ pratyekabuddhaḥ sa ekārāmo bhavaty ekavihārāṃ gambhīrādhimūkto gambhīrapratītyasamutpāda-pratyavekṣaṇāparamaḥ / śūnyatāpraṇihitānimittamanaskāravihārī // tatra dvitīyatṛtīyabhyāṃ samudāgamābhyāṃ pratyekajinaḥ / naikāṃśena ekārāmo bhavaty ekavihārī / api tu vargavihāri bhavati / śiṣṭo vihāras tasyāpi yathā khaḍgaviṣāṇakalpaś ca //

/ tatra cāritrataḥ[4] / te sarva eva grāmaṃ vā nigamaṃ vā niḥsritya vihārānti / te surakṣitena kāyena susamvṛtair indriyaiḥ sūpasthitayā smṛtyā tam eva grāmaṃ vā nigamaṃ vā piṇḍāya praviśati / te punar hīnadīnānukampamānāḥ kāyenānukampante na vācā tathā hi kāyikī teṣāṃ dharmadeśanā bhavati na vācikī / anekavidham ṛddhiviṣayaṃ / vidarśayanti yāvad eva pratihatacittānāṃ pratyāvartanārtham te ca sarve [kleśa]-śamaikayānā veditavyāḥ / samāptā ca pratyekabuddha bhūmiḥ //

Now for the translation:

> What is the stage of the Pratyekabuddha? It is to be understood by five aspects, namely, by birthright (*gotra*), by path (*mārga*), by arrival (*samudāgama*), by dwelling (*vihāra*), and by wandering (*cāritra*).
>
> A. What is the birthright of the Pratyekabuddha? Here are three characters:[5] (a) The Pratyekabuddhas, having previously been manifestly awakened, have naturally a birthright of negligible defilement. They do not engage their minds in *saṃsarga* (i.e., in tandem),[6] but do engage their minds in the joy of solitude (*eka*). (b) The Pratyekabuddhas, having previously been manifestly awakened, have naturally (a birthright) of negligible compassion. They do not engage their minds in teaching the Doctrine or in acting for the sake of sentient beings, but do engage their minds in the abiding in scarcely any eager attachment. (c) The Pratyekabuddhas, having previously been manifestly awakened, have naturally (a birthright) of middling sense organ. They are in a class of

proudful behavior. Thus, without an *ācārya* (master), and without foes (*pratidvandva*) they claim to have manifest complete enlightenment.

B. Among them, the Pratyekabuddha path also has the three characters. It is this way, (a) In this world there is someone established in the Pratyekabuddha birthright. For a thousand eons took pleasure in becoming a Buddha. And in this situation matured his stream of consciousness, as follows: gaining skill in personal aggregates (*skandha*), in sense bases (*āyatana*), in realms (*dhātu*), in dependent origination (*pratītyasamutpāda),* in the possible and the impossible (*sthānāsthāna),* as well as skill in truths (*satya*). And so forth up to, in the future has a solitary awakening (*pratyeka-bodha*). This is the first Pratyekabuddha path.

(b) Furthermore, in this world there is someone delighting in the arising of a Buddha, depending on an illustrious person, who has aroused the listening to the Sublime Doctrine and the methodical mental orientation. Thus he generates the former virtuous roots conducive to penetration (*nirvedhabhāgīya*) and masters them, to wit, warmth, summits, forbearance (i.e., of the *dharmas*);[7] but is unable in the present life to fully comprehend the Dharma or to win the fruit of the ascetic life; namely, in the future for fully comprehending the Dharma and for winning the fruit of the ascetic life, becomes skilled in personal aggregates, sense bases, realms, dependent origination, the possible and impossible, as well as skill in truth. This is the second Pratyekabuddha path.

(c) Furthermore, in this world there is someone delighting in the arising of a Buddha, depends on an illustrious person, has aroused the listening to the Sublime Doctrine and the methodical mental orientation, then fully comprehends the Dharma and wins the fruit of the ascetic life; but is unable to obtain in every way the ultimate goal, the ultimate purity, the ultimate finality of the pure life, and of Arhatship; namely, in the future by the supramundane path, for the ultimate goal, ultimate purity, the ultimate finality of the pure life, and for winning the fruit of Arhatship, has skill in personal aggregates, in sense bases, realms, dependent origination, the possible and the impossible, as well as skill in truth(s).

This is the third Pratyekabuddha path.

C. As to the arrival, it is this way: (a) In this world, there is someone who by the first Pratyekabuddha path has completed the collection, (i.e. of merit and knowledge) through a thousand of eons; but who at the end of the thousand of eons, there being no arising of Buddhas, then with no master (*ācārya*) cultivates the thirty-seven natures accessory to enlightenment (*bodhipakṣya-dharma*), is manifestly completely awakened to the solitary enlightenment, and realizes directly the Arhat-state with elimination of all defilement (*kleśa*). (b) It is this way: In this world, there is someone who by cause (*hetu*) and condition (*pratyaya*), by the second and the third Pratyekabuddha paths (has completed the collection), but likewise, there being no arising of Buddhas, then with no master cultivates the thirty-seven natures accessory to enlightenment, and fully comprehends the Dharma up to, wins the fruit of Arhatship, or has won the fruit of the ascetic life, and attains the ultimate goal, the ultimate purity, the ultimate finality of the pure life and of Arhatship which is the best fruit. Among them, by the first arrival, one becomes a Pratyekabuddha tantamount to the rhinoceros; by the second and the third arrivals, one becomes a Pratyekajina, not a rhinoceros.

D. Among those, the dwelling is as follows: The Pratyekabuddha, who is tantamount to a rhinoceros has solitary joy, solitary dwelling, is convinced about the profound, has uppermost the discernment of profound dependent origination, and abides in the mental orientations of the voidness, the wishless, and the signless. The Pratyekajina, by the second and the third arrivals, does not have solitary joy and solitary dwelling by way of seclusion (*ekāṃśa),* but does dwell in a group (*varga*), and the rest of his abiding is the same as the rhinoceros.

E. Among them, the wandering is as follows: Whatever the town or city they resort to and stay in, they resort to alms seeking in the town or city with well-guarded body, well-controlled senses, and well-approaching mindfulness. Besides, while sympathizing with lowly and wretched persons, they sympathize with body, but not with speech—because all their teaching of Dharma is corporeal, non-

> verbal. They display various kinds of magical sense objects, and so on up to, so as to counter those of hostile minds. All those constitute the sole vehicle (*ekayāna*) for appeasing all defilement.

And finished is the Pratyekabuddha stage.

The extreme brevity of this *bhūmi* exhibits Asaṅga's mode of writing when he is cautious with every word, granted that he is generally a remarkably careful author. Notice that he distinguishes three kinds of Pratyekabuddha when it is a matter of 'birthright' (*gotra*) or a character (*lakṣaṇa*), and of a path (*mārga*). But when it is a matter of 'arrival' (*samudāgama*), they become two, with the second and third taken together, and this manner of two continues with the 'dwelling' (*vihāra*). Finally, they become one when it is a case of their 'wandering' (*cāritra*). When they are two, the first kind is called the 'rhinoceros' (*khaḍgaviṣāṇa*), the second a Pratyekajina.

According to Asaṅga's treatment, then, the so-called 'rhinoceros' has the first 'birthright', namely, of negligible defilement; the first path, namely maturing his stream of consciousness in various skills; the first arrival, namely, after cultivating the 37 *bodhipakṣyadharma* awakens to the solitary enlightenment; the first dwelling, namely, solitary joy and dwelling, discernment of dependent origination, and abiding in the three gates to liberation called the voidness, the wishless, and the signless. The Pratyekajina has the second 'birthright', namely, of negligible compassion, and the third 'birthright', namely, of middling sense organ; has the second path, namely, depending on an illustrious person for guidance and generating the virtuous roots conducive to penetration, and the third path, namely, advancing beyond the second one with full comprehension of Dharma; a joint second kind of 'arrival', namely, after cultivating the 37 *bodhipakṣyadharma*, wins the fruit of Arhatship; a joint second kind of 'dwelling', namely, dwelling in a group (*varga*), the rest like the 'rhinoceros', namely, discernment of dependent origination, and so on.

Asaṅga's inclusion of the fifth aspect of 'wandering' (*cāritra*), clarifies that the term *saṃsarga*, negated, does not render the 'rhinoceros' "lonely", as generally attributed, since the seeking of alms constantly brings the person in contact with the society. Asaṅga explains: "They do not engage their minds in *saṃsarga*" (i.e., in

FIVE ASPECTS OF THE PRATYEKABUDDHA

Birthright (*gotra*)	Path (*mārga*)	Arrival (*samudāgama*)	Dwelling (*vihāra*)	Wandering (*cāritra*)
1. Negligible defilement [Do not engage their minds in *saṃsarga* (Tib. *'du 'dsi*)]	Gaining skill in skandhas, etc. [no *ācārya*]	As 'rhinoceros' collected (merit and knowledge); with no *ācārya* cultivates the 37 *bodhipakṣyadharma* and gains solitary enlightenment (*pratyekabodhi*), Arhat-state with no defilement.	Has solitary joy, solitary dwelling, discerns dependent origination, abides in voidness, wishless, and signless (gates)	Resort to alms—seeking in towns with well-guarded body and senses, and with constant mindfulness. Sympathize with an unfortunate person by their bodies, not speech. When they teach the Dharma, do it with body, not with speech, displaying magical sense objects. (applies to 1–3)
2. Negligible compassion [Do not engage their minds in teaching the doctrine (*dharma*)]	Depends on good teacher, generates virtuous roots conducive to penetration (*nirvedha-bhāgīya*), 1st 3, warmth, summits, forbearance. (applies to 2–3)	As Pratyekajina, with no arising of Buddhas, no *ācārya*, cultivates the 37 *bodhipakṣyadharma*, up to gains the fruit of Arhatship, the ultimate purity. (applies to 2–3)	Does not have solitary joy or solitary dwelling, dwells in a group (*varga*), discerns dependent origination, abides in the three gates. (applies to 2–3)	
3. Middling sense organ (Proud, they claim to have manifest complete enlightenment)	Depends on good teacher, fully comprehends the *dharma* (=4th *nirvedhabhāgīya* 'supreme mundane natures')			

tandem). Thus the solitude was mental, not physical. There is an immediate light cast on *MK* XVIII. 12:

> *saṃbuddhānām anutpāde śrāvakānāṃ punaḥ kṣaye /*
> *jñānaṃ pratyekabuddhānām asaṃsargāt pravartate //*
> When there is no arising of complete Buddhas, and when there is ceasing of their disciples, the knowledge possessed by the Pratyekabuddhas proceeds 'not in tandem'.

According to Asaṅga's text, Nāgārjuna here intends the 'rhinoceros', in the setting of the first kind of 'arrival' (*samudāgama*), so the term 'knowledge' (*jñāna*) implies the 'solitary awakening' (*pratyeka-bodha*) and of course goes with the mind rather than with the body. It seems to me that Nāgārjuna closes the chapter on 'examination of *ātma*' with this verse to give a message for the entire chapter with the clue in the term *asaṃsargāt.* The Tibetan rendition for this, namely *brten pa med pas* seems due to the Buddhapālita commentary, which I had consulted. Ye-śes-sde translated *saṃsarga* with *'du 'dsi* not only in the *Pratyekabuddhabhūmi* but also much earlier in the *bhūmis* 3-5, hence in the part edited by V. Bhattacharya. In this earlier place, *saṃsarga* is one of the six causes of defilement (*kleśa*), and explained there by Asaṅga as following the instruction of bad persons (*asatpuruṣānāṁ anuśikṣamāṇasya*).[8] Thus, the not relying on another *ācārya* incidentally avoids the *asatpuruṣa.* The negation 'not in tandem' appears to fit each of the preceding eleven verses of that *MK,* Chap. XVIII. For example, verse 1 denies that the self is the five personal aggregates or different from them; so the self is not in tandem with those aggregates. Verse 9 starts with *aparapratyayaṃ* 'without another as condition', so not in tandem with another as condition, etc., Nāgārjuna seemingly supports the theory of this Pratyekabuddha to be able even in the absence of Complete Buddhas or a good *ācārya* to have such a realization which is the dissolution of conventional relations involving 'self', referred to as the "knowledge of the Pratyekabuddhas". Therefore, I conclude when in *MK,* XVIII. 6cd, Nāgārjuna wrote: "The Buddhas have taught neither *ātma* nor *anātma,*" it is because these Pratyekabuddhas live at a time when there are no Buddhas present to teach either *ātma* or *anātma.* And so also, when in XVIII. 8, he mentions a *catuṣkoṭi* as the 'graded teaching' (*anuśāsana*) of the Buddhas, this is also meant in XVIII. 11, when Nāgārjuna speaks of the ambrosial teaching of the Buddhas as neither destroyed (*anuccheda*) nor eternal (*aśāśvata*), so possibly to be learned even when Buddhas do not arise.

There is more information about this 'rhinoceros' in the *Abhidharmakośa* VI. 24a-c, as I translate:

> The Teacher (i.e., the Buddha) and the Rhinoceros up to their (individual) enlightenment at the upper end of (the fourth) Dhyāna have a single basis. Before that, what is conducive to liberation (*mokṣabhāgīya*).

There is more than one way to understand the 'single basis' (*sarvam ekatra*). Vasubandhu's comment includes the *nirvedhabhāgīyas*, as common to the Buddha and the rhinoceros, but of course they have different birthrights (*gotra*). Asaṅga's Pratyekabuddha text did not mention the *nirvedhabhāgīyas* for the rhinoceros, but only the mastery of the first three of the four in the second Pratyekabuddha path, that of becoming a Pratyekajina. When describing the third Pratyekabuddha path, Asaṅga says this person relies on an *ācārya*, has the methodical mental orientation, then "fully comprehends the Dharma and wins the fruit of the ascetic life". This clearly indicates the fourth *nirvedhabhāgīya*, the 'supreme mundane natures', the *agradharma*; thus distinguishing between the two Pratyekajina paths. There is a curious feature to the *Abhidharmakośa* depiction, because prior to the above rendered verse, at VI. 23d, and Vasubandhu's comment, one becomes Pratyeka by mastering the first three *nirvedhabhāgīyas*; and the reader of the *Abhidharmakośa* naturally assumes that the kind of Pratyekabuddha meant is the 'rhinoceros' because the very next verse explicitly mentions the 'rhinoceros'. But with Asaṅga's information, we may theorize that the Pratyekabuddha meant is the Pratyekajina of the second path; and this helps for understanding the *Abhidharmakośa* VI. 24a-c, because if the Buddha and the Pratyekabuddha indicated there are *ekatra* (in the same one) up to top of the fourth Dhyāna, we can expect this 'rhinoceros' to have mastered also the fourth *nirvedhabhāgīya*, the 'supreme mundane natures', as has the Pratyekajina of the third path.

Asaṅga does not include an exegesis for the *Pratyekabuddhabhūmi* in his large *Viniścaya-saṃgrahaṇī* exegesis of the basic *bhūmis*. However, the various skills he mentions, in personal aggregates (*skandha*), etc. are explained at length in the *Srāvakabhūmi* and in various later sections of the *Yogācārabhūmi*. His various remarks about Arhats are relevant, since the Arhat-state figures prominently in the *Pratyekabuddhabhūmi*. His *Śrāvakabhūmi* has a basic statement about "arising of Buddhas", including the generating of goodwill and desire of benefit to all sentient beings, the accumulation of merit (*puṇya*) and knowledge (*jñāna*), and the cultivation of the thirty-seven natures accessory to enlightenment. The Pratyekabuddha also cultivates these thirty-seven natures, but they do not suffice, since they amount to the purification, the *saṅs* of *saṅs rgyas*, Tib. for 'Buddha'. Besides, Asaṅga has an intriguing claim that the third Pratyekabuddha character is to have naturally a "middling sense organ". His *Viniścaya-saṃgrahaṇī* on the *Samāhita-bhūmi* in the Peking edition, p. 13-2-4, speaks of three kinds of sense organs, the usual 'sharp' (*rnon po*), 'middling' (*'briṅ*), and 'weak' (*brtul po*), and immediately says these persons have three kinds of *samādhis*: (1) the *samādhi* operating in *adhicitta* has the meditative object (*ālambana*) in four kinds of sentient beings (listed there). (2) the *samādhi* operating in going to the ultimate (*mthar thug par 'gro ba la brtson pa'i tiṅ ṅe 'dsin*) has the meditative object in *dharma*. (3) the *samādhi* operating in constructive thought (*mṅon par rtog pa*) has only a meditative object on *dharma*. Although the text does not mention the names of the persons, one can easily conclude that the Bodhisattva has the 'sharp' organ, the Pratyekabuddha the 'middling' one, and the Śrāvaka the 'weak' one. The implication of the meditative object on *dharma* is the usual association of dependent origination (*pratītyasamutpāda*) as the special object of the Pratyekabuddha, although Asaṅga expands this to include the 'possible and impossible' (*sthānāsthāna*), and the truths (*satya*) as well as the prior skill in the *skandha, dhātu*, and *āyatana*.

It is well-known to the readers of Buddhist literature that in later times, there was a division into the lesser vehicle (*Hīnayāna*) and the great vehicle (*Mahāyāna*), with the Śrāvakas and Pratyekabuddhas called *Hīnayāna*. It is important to notice that this does not implicate dependent origination itself as a 'lesser vehicle' type meditative object. Tsugunari Kubo's book on the Lotus Sūtra (*Saddharmapuṇḍarīka*) (Tokyo, 1987), claims (English summary, p. 6), "The Lotus Sūtra takes the fundamental philosophical stance that all elucidations of the Buddha's teachings, including the Sūtra itself are a product of *Pratītyasamutpāda,*" and he cites the passage (ed. of Wogihara and Tsuchida, p. 37.24-5) *sarvatraiṣā Śāriputra dharmatā daśa-dig-loke,* in that summary (p. 7) rendered "O, Śāriputra, this is the rule in all the worlds of the ten directions." While *dharmatā* is so rendered 'rule', in my own writings I take it either as 'true nature' or as 'continuum'. Asaṅga, in the second division of his *Vastu-saṃgrahaṇī* on *āyatana,* while treating the topic of 'voidness' (*śūnyatā*) declares (p. 163. 1-3): "Accordingly, the Arhat-state is the steadfast place of *dharmatā*" (*'di ltar dgra bcom pa ni chos ñid kyi gnas brtan yin pa*). This was preceded by the remark (p. 163. 1-2): "There are two places of voidness—the place of voidness that is a steadfast place, and the places of voidness generated thereby" (*stoṅ pa ñid kyi gnas pa ni gñis te / gnas brtan stoṅ pa ñid kyi gnas pa daṅ / des bskyed pa'i stoṅ pa ñid kyi gnas pa'o*); continuing, "And among them, any place of non-self of Arhat-state is a place of voidness that is a steadfast place." The passage reminds us of the celebrated remark, often repeated, "Whether Tathāgatas arise or not, there remains this steadfast *dharmatā,*" which in time was called the void Dharmadhātu. Hence, when Asaṅga in his brief treatise writes, "Thus, without an *ācārya* (master), and without foes (*pratidvandva*) [i.e., Arhat, who has destroyed the foe] they claim to have manifest complete enlightenment," he refers to an argument that continued over the centuries, when persons realized the 'steadfast voidness' and thought they were enlightened, and then this achievement was discounted as the Arhat-state, a Hīnayāna goal, while the arising of the Tathāgata is *Mahāyāna*. Śāntideva in *Śikṣāsamuccaya,* denounced also the so-called Mahāyāna *śūnyatā.*[9] The meaning here can be further explicated by reference to the *Mañjuśrī-nāma-saṃgīti,* Chap. VI 'Pure Dharmadhātu Knowledge', verse 10, the words *khaḍgaḥ pratyekanāyakaḥ,* rendered "rhinoceros, solitary guide".[10] Smṛti jñānakīrti's commentary (PTT, Vol. 75, p. 44-5-7) explains the *pratyekanāyakaḥ* as the *vargacārin* (*tshogs na spyod pa*), while the *khaḍga* (rhinoceros) bathes and swims (*khrus ldiṅ ba*). Thus this rhinoceros symbolizes the process of purification from defilement (*kleśa*) leading to the Arhat-state. The point of having two kinds seems to be that the rhinoceros is doing it all by itself, while the *pratyekajina,* also called *vargacārin* is in a group. But according to the famous story about the name Ṛṣipatana (falling of the *ṛṣis*), exhibiting also their magical ability as in Asaṅga's text (under 'wandering'), there is a suggestion that *vargacārin* means 'acting as a group'. For so, in Mkhas-grub-rje's work which Lessing and I translated:[11]

> Why is the place called Ṛṣipatana? Formally when the time approached for the Buddha Kāśyapa to appear in the world, there lived on that hill five hundred Pratyekabuddhas. They learned from a message given by the devas that the Buddha was to manifest himself. By their magical power, they soared up to the sky and equipoised themselves in the element of fire (*tejo-dhātu*). The fire that issued from their own bodies burned their material bodies, and the ashes fell to earth. It was said, "The Ṛṣis have fallen", and for this reason the place is called Ṛṣipatana.

As to why these Pratyekabuddhas would depart from the scene when a Buddha would appear is not clarified at that place, but the *Mañjuśrī-nāma-saṃgīti* name Pratyekanāyaka suggests that these Pratyekabuddhas were performing some kind of guidance to chosen individuals. They apparently have the function of protecting the Buddhist dharma in the interval between arising of Buddhas, as attributed to the set of Arhats. Ferdinand D. Lessing's article, "The Eighteen Worthies Crossing the Sea,"[12] goes into the function of these *sthavira* who, although not Buddhas, possess the six supranatural powers and in the situation described in his article are attributed the role of bringing Buddhism to China. Perhaps, Asaṅga's division of the Pratyekajina into two kinds is meant to separate them into those who perform this somewhat legendary role and those that do not, because he said for the first Pratyekajina there was negligible compassion, but did not say this in the case of the second Pratyekajina. In any case, we may conclude that the term 'Pratyekabuddha' does not mean a Buddha who is *pratyeka*, but rather was a signal for the state of accomplishment that was sometimes deemed to be that of a Buddha, which was denied as such.

Asaṅga's concluding sentence, "All those constitute the sole vehicle (*ekayāna*) for appeasing all defilement" shows this Arhat attainment as a component for becoming a Complete Buddha, so the full title "Tathāgata, Arhat, Saṁyakṣambuddha". Indeed, the emphasis on Dependent Origination shows the *dharma* path of purification, so the theory of the Pratyekabuddha.

Asaṅga mentioned the 'medium' sense organ for the Pratyekabuddha, so it is of interest that the same attribution is in a Mahāyāna scripture the *Akṣayamatinirdeśa.* The Pratyekabuddha comes in its section of Prajñā-akṣaya, the part on various 'skills' and under these 'the skill in vehicles'. I translate from the Tibetan in PTT, Vol. 34, p. 55-3:

"What is the Bodhisattva's skill in the Pratyekabuddha vehicle? By whatever aspects (*ākāra*) and by whatever conditions (*pratyaya*) the Pratyekabuddhas are delivered, the Bodhisattva rightly and accordingly well knows the aspects and the conditions. What are they? By great longing, striving, and heedfulness, with which the Śrāvaka cannot compare, has merit collections of giving, has merit collections of morality; enterprise of the Doctrine (*dharma*), though with meager hearing; does not flinch at honoring and serving the Buddha Bhagavats; medium sense faculty; continually absorbed in deliverance; delights in retreats with few aims, few actions, without pleasure in entertainments; makes one's bed in isolated places; difficult to be met with, and of great force; delighting in places of charity; uninterruptedly views dependent origination; reflects on the one realm of deliverance; rescued by the self-originated wisdom; attains the 'support-engagement'; is uninterrupted in meditation (*dhyāna*), liberation (*vimokṣa*), deep concentration (*samādhi*), and equipoise (samāpatti); generates the wisdom that is not guided by others; understanding the wisdom of conditions in consciousness-support (*ālambana*) as is feasible; what be the explanation, teaching, and further teaching along those lines is called the Bodhisattva's skill in the Pratyekabuddha vehicle."

As the remark "attains the 'support-engagement' " is obscure, the commentary was consulted in PTT, Vol. 104, at p. 216-1-3. The comment mentions two attainments of *samādhi,* "attainment of the motionless" (T. *mi g'yo ba thob pa*) and "of the continuous mental orientation" (*manaskāra*) (*rgyun tu yid la byed pa thob pa*). And the comment continues that here (for the Pratyekabuddha), the phrase "attains the 'support-engagement' is the *āniñjya-samādhi* (Cf. La Vallée Poussin, *Abhidharmakośa,* III, p. 216, where it is explained as the imperturbable in the fourth Dhyāna). Thus, 'support' means the particular support of consciousness (*ālambana*). This information therefore agrees with the previous citation from *Abhidharmakośa,* the k. VI. 24a-c.

Hopefully, the foregoing commentary clarifies this Buddhist theory of the Pratyekabuddha.

REFERENCES

1. A. Wayman, "The Sacittikā and Acittikā Bhūmi and the Pratyekabuddhabhūmi (Sanskrit texts)," *Journal of Indian and Buddhist Studies* (Tokyo), 7:1, 1960, pp. 375-9.
2. Ms. has *cāratataś*; T. has *rgyu ba*.
3. Ms. has *samanvāgatārtha*.
4. Ms has *vihārataḥ;* T. has *rgyu ba*.
5. Asaṅga coordinates these three characters (*lakṣaṇa*) with three paths (*mārga*) and with three arrivals (*samudāgama*).
6. The term *saṃsarga* is here rendered in Tibetan as *'du 'dsi,* better than the *brten pa* of *MK* XVIII 12; and with the suggestion of Apte's Sanskrit-English dictionary, it appears to mean something like "being in tandem," or next to another.
7. For these "virtuous roots conducive to penetration", cf. my essay "Vasubandhu—teacher extraordinary," *Studia Missionalia,* 1988, pp. 274, ff. The fact that Asaṅga mentions the first three as 'warmth', 'summits', and 'forbearance', shows the standard terminology of the north India Abhidharma that was continued into Mahāyāna literature. In the old Pāli canon, the tenfold series of the Dīgha-nikāya, section on four things mentions the four samādhis that are each a *bhāgiya,* and the fourth one is the title of the 'four degrees of penetration'. But in the *Samgiti suttānta* of the Pāli canon, there are four 'cultivations of samādhi' (*samādhibhāvanā*), which may well represent the original statement of the theory. In the order given, they are: conducing to 'pleasant abode' (*sukha-vihāra),* e.g., the four Dhyānas of the 'realm of form' (*rūpadhātu);* acquisition of knowledge and vision (Skt. *jñānadarśana*), e.g., the idea of light (Skt. *ālokasaṃjñā*); mindfulness and awareness (Skt. *smṛti-saṃprajanya),* e.g., the stations of mindfulness (Skt. *smṛty-upasthāna*); destruction of the fluxes (Skt. *āsrava-kṣaya*), e.g., watching the five personal aggregates (S. *skandha*). Using the information of my article on Vasubandhu, we can reorder these to the four degrees of penetration: (1) the mindfulness and awareness; (2) acquisition of knowledge and vision; (3) the *sukha-vihāra*; (4) destruction of the fluxes. Thus, when Asaṅga states: "but is unable in the present life to fully comprehend the Dharma", it must be the fourth degree of penetration, called usually "supreme mundane natures", so the 'destruction of the fluxes' by watch over the five personal aggregates, referred to by Asaṅga as "skill in personal aggregates" as the first mentioned of the 'skills'.
8. The Tib. is at PTT, Vol. 109, p. 250-4-5 (for *'du 'dsi* in the list), and p. 250. 4-6 (for definition of the term); Skt. in V. Bhattacharya, *The Yogācārabhūmi of Ācārya Asaṅga,* text, p. 164.
9. See the translation by Cecil Bendall and W.H.D. Rouse, p. 99.
10. Cf. A. Wayman, *Chanting the Names of Mañjuśrī* (Boston, 1985), p. 77.
11. *Mkhas grub rje's Fundamentals of the Buddhist Tantras,* p. 41.
12. Published by Statens Etnografiska Museum, Stockholm, 1954.

10

The *Guru* in Buddhism

The present chapter intends to present material in a general manner about the *Guru* in Buddhism, and then to present several cases of Buddhist *gurus*. It will first be necessary to differentiate a *guru* from a saint. The Buddhist *gurus* to be treated are Gautama Buddha, Śāriputra, Asaṅga, Kukai, Nāropā, and Tsoṅ-kha-pa. Certain ones will figure in a *guru-yoga* section.

The Buddhist Guru-Generalities

Differentiation of a guru from a saint. It is necessary to show that a *guru* (literally a "weighty person") may or may not be a saint. One of the Sanskrit terms for a saint is *mahāpuruṣa* ("great

Reprinted from *Studia Missionalia,* Vol. 36. Editrice Pontifica Universita Gregoriana. Roma. 1987.

person"). Saintliness is frequently referred to by an alternate term "holiness", namely, of a person, a religious book or other "sacred" entity, or an edifice. In the case of a person, it might involve certain signs sometimes called stigmata. For example, the Buddha was held to have various characteristics (*lakṣaṇa*) of the "Great Person", including special marks on his foot, so that his footprint was worshipped. In the present chapter, the Buddha is considered only in the role of a *guru*, one who teaches disciples in a lineage—either starting or continuing it. The saintly or holy is either so or not, while the *guru* is a better one or lesser. The holy is incomprehensible; the *guru* comprehensible. The holy is a non-verbal situation of a culture; the *guru* uses words or comparable symbolic activity. However, the biographies of eminent Buddhists—sometimes called "sacred biography" may not distinguish a *guru* from a saint by the above criteria. Such biographies frequently contain stereotyped praises—an understandable glorification of the individual with omission of those faults which would suggest a mere human rank. In the case of the Buddha's biography, the life events have an overlay of legend. Be that as it may, it is possible to treat the topic of the *guru* independent of intimations of the sacred.

Words for a guru. The *guru* is a teacher (*śāstṛ*), friendly guide (*kalyāṇa-mitra*), master (*ācārya*), hierophant (*vajra-ācārya*). The *guru* may be outer, as a living human teacher, or may be inner, as a subjective teacher. The inner is further differentiated (*infra*). The *guru* may also be scripture.

The guru as scripture. Here are three indications that Buddhist scripture might be accepted as a *guru*. Moreover, the literal significance of the term, i.e. "weighty", seems involved with the Buddhist tendency to make collections of scripture, canons of increasing weight.

(1) *The Mahāparinibbāna suttānta* (Pāli version entitled "Book of the Great Decease") has a passage whereby the Buddha tells Ānanda that after his passing what will be their caravan (P. *satthā*, S. *sārtha*), what will be their guide (P. *paneta,* S. *praṇetṛ),* is (respectively) the Doctrine (P. *dhamma,* S. *dharma*), and the Discipline Code (P. and S. *vinaya*) that he (respectively) taught and enjoined.[1] This suggests that the Buddhist Abhidharma collection, in order to be included, must be understood as a specialization of Dharma.

(2) Tsoṅ-kha-pa, a great Tibetan pandit, wrote in his *Lam rim chen mo* that the teaching of "calming the mind" (*śamatha*) and "discerning the real" (*vipaśyana*) is expressed in Asaṅga's *Śrāvakabhūmī* "like the personal delivery (of a *guru*)".[2]

(3) The Buddhist tantric work called *Devendraparipṛcchā*, of which only a few verses are preserved, states:[3]

> *tasmāt surādhipa śakra yadi cet śāśvataṃ padam/*
> *saddharmo guru kartavyaḥ smara māyā dvir akṣaram//*
> Therefore, Indra, master of the gods, if you would have (your) rank be perpetual, let the Illustrious Doctrine be your master (*guru*). Remember that the two syllables (i.e. E-Vam) are the Illusion (*māyā*).

To get the point about the reference to "Illusion", one should observe that each Buddhist scripture begins with *evaṃ mayā śrutam* ("*Thus by me it was heard*"). The expression *mayā* by a mystical nominalization of the instrumental becomes *māyā*, as though "Thus (*evam*) was heard as *māyā*"— the "by me" being negated. When "Thus" epitomizes the Illustrious Doctrine, it is the *māyā*, perhaps as a tantric *sādhana* stated: *jagaddvandvanirvāṇamāyām* ("the *māyā* of liberation from the world's cross-purposes");[4] hence it is the dissolution of oppositions. Here the scripture is a *guru* in Buddhism's best sense—soteriological.

The foregoing claim that a scripture can be a *guru* raises some problems. *Gurus* do not teach everybody; and sometimes such a *guru* needs explaining. There are claims that scriptures need commentaries, as though the commentary were the *guru* rather than the text being commented upon. It probably should be concluded that the sense of calling a scripture a *guru* is that it teaches the chosen individuals who do not need further commentary. Hence the scripture does not explain itself, since it is itself the explanation. But what is an explanation for some persons is not so for others.

The human guru. Early Buddhism and later forms consistent therewith stressed the friendly guide (*kalyāṇa-mitra*). The *Mahāyāna-Sūtrālaṃkāra* XVII. 10, presents the optimum standard:

> *mitraṃ śrayed dāntaśamopaśāntaṃ guṇadhikaṃ sodyamam āgamāḍhyaṃ / prabuddhatattvaṃ vacasā 'bhyupetaṃ kṛpātmakaṃ khedavivarjitaṃ ca //*

> Rely upon the friend who is disciplined, self-controlled, puts to rest (his mental defilements) and leaves the merits (active), strives, is rich in scriptures; comprehends reality, skillful in speech, compassionate by nature, and never wearies (to teach).

As a "friend" (*mitra*) he is equal to the disciple in this religious sense—the person in front of the disciple, but not on a higher or lower seat.

The sense in which the disciple is equal to his friend is stated in the Buddhist classic *Udānavarga* (*Śrutavarga*) XX. 9:

> *dharme tu ye hy āryanivedite ratās carante vacasā yad āhuḥ / te kṣāntisauratyasamādhigocaraḥ śrutasya buddher api parām adhyaguḥ*[5]*//*
>
> Those who delight in the doctrine (*dharma*) taught by the nobles (*ārya*), and then practice what those (nobles) tell by speech, who are happy in the society of the forbearing and restrain their senses, will attain the perfection of hearing and understanding.

There is also the practice of hearing the doctrine by attending eagerly while seated on a lower seat, as stated in Āryaśūra's *Jātakamālā*, "The Story of Sutasoma": "Sitting on a lower seat, awakening the glory of discipline" (*nīcaistarāsanasthanād vibodhya vinayaśriyam*). The relation to the *guru* is not mentioned as that of a friend, but rather as the sick man to the physician's counsel (*bhiṣagvākyam ivāturaḥ*). This reminds us of Buddha in the role of the Medicine Guru (Bhaiṣajyaguru), suggesting the holiness of the teacher; but in fact it must be the sacredness of the scripture that is involved.

The *guru* is also the hierophant of the Buddhist Tantras, called *ācārya* or *vajrācārya* . The treatise *Fifty Stanzas in Praise of the Guru* (*Gurupañcāśikā* of the tantric Aśvaghoṣa), k. 8-9, describes him:[6]

> *dhīro vinīto matimān kṣamāvān ārjavo 'śaṭhaḥ/*
> *mantratantraprayogajñaḥ kṛpāluḥ śāstrakovidaḥ//*
> *daśatattvaparijñātā maṇḍalalekhyakarmavit/*
> *mantravyākhyākṛd ācāryaḥ prasannaḥ syāj jitendriyaḥ*
>
> Steadfast [in body], controlled [in speech], intelligent,

> forbearing, just, and without deceit; skilled in the praxis of *mantra* and *tantra,* compassionate, and learned in the expository text; experienced in the ten categories, expert in drawing the *maṇḍala*; who can explain the *mantras,* is devoted and ruler of his senses, so should be the hierophant.

This kind of *guru* is accorded a respect that traditional teachers of Buddhism did not enjoy, according to the significant passage of the *Vajrapāṇyabhiṣekamahātantra* (from the Tibetan):[7]

> Master of the Secret Folk, how should a disciple look upon his preceptor? As though upon the Lord Buddha. The mind of him so disposed incessantly generates merits; he becomes a Buddha bringing benefit to all the world... One should hold to the preceptor's virtues, and never hold to his faults. If one hold virtues, he attains success; if one hold to faults, he attains failure.

The point of such a respect for the *guru* is that he is a link in the lineage going back either to the Buddha, or to the Buddha in the guise of some deity, who heads the master sequence that is inherited by the disciple, either by "acquiring" it, or better still, by "hearing" it.[8] It is important to distinguish between regarding the *guru* as though the Buddha, and regarding him as the Buddha. One would regard the *guru* as a saint, if he were as the Buddha; but "as though the Buddha" shows that the *guru* is regarded as the preceptor either of doctrine or of the tantric ritual, and as though this *guru* is tantamount to the initial promulgator of that lineage. The link is broken, if the disciple were to criticize or blame the preceptor; hence the *guru* must always be praised. Another way of stating this situation is that there is a "generation of arcane mind" through the continuous, i.e., unbroken, line by "arcane body" (the human *guru*) and directly (at that very time) by "arcane speech".[9] In this sense, the tantric hierophant is held to perform "deeds of a Buddha" without being a Buddha. Therefore, in the course of such rituals there is a phase when the performers make offerings to the gods and then to the *guru*. In the tantras, this *guru* thus given offerings is known as "diamond being" (*vajrasattva*) according to the precept, "Therefore, Vajrasattva prompts by himself his own worship" (*vajrasattvaḥ svayaṃ tasmāt svasya pūjāṃ pravartayet*).[10]

The inner guru. For a basic statement on the inner *guru* in the Buddhist Tantras, I here cite my own published research:[11]

> ... the *Śrī-Mahākha-tantrarāja* (Derge Kanjur, Rgyud 'bum, Ga, 203a-6) states: "It is said that there are two kinds of *gurus*—that external *guru* himself; and the inner *guru*, the presiding deity (*bdag po'i lha*)." The presiding deity is defined by Ānandagarbha in his great commentary, the *Śrī-Paramādiṭīkā* (Derge Tanjur, Rgyud, I, 22a-3): "One's presiding deity is *kāmadeva.* The conviction that his diamonds of body, speech, and mind are one's own—with a praxis that it is really so—is the meaning of *yoga.*" The "presiding deity" appears to mean the same as the "tutelary deity" (*iṣṭadevatā*), or the deity which the disciple serves with daily devotions and enshrines in the heart.

Apparently the intention of the expression *kāmadeva* is that these tantric rituals aim at certain desired fruits, and the inner *guru* is believed to prompt these results—the intention also of the expression *iṣṭadevatā.* It is possible to subdivide the inner *guru* according to the precept "the superior three speakers who teach that way". These *gurus* are called "masters" (*ācārya*), in short: (a) the great basic teacher, who purifies one's own stream of consciousness by practices shared with non-tantric Buddhism, tantric pledges, initiations (*abhiṣeka),* and so on. (b) the conditional teacher, who is the great goddess who purifies the object of consciousness in sixteen parts. (c) the co-natal teacher, who is one's own mind (in the heart) which comprehends the co-natal joy. The theory of these three is that they arise in sequence, namely, that the first kind of inner *guru* purifies the stream of consciousness; the second kind, called the goddess purifies the object of consciousness; and finally, the third kind one's own mind, comprehends the union of the tutelary deity and the goddess as an inner joy.[12]

In short, the human *guru* is usually not the one who started the lineage, but he is accorded the respect as though he had started it, because he carries on the unbroken lineage from the originator. The inner *guru* is held to be superior to the outer *guru,* because commanding the acts of body, speech, and mind that enable their identification with the corresponding three mysteries of the Buddha.

EXAMPLES OF HUMAN GURUS

Gautama Buddha. An earlier essay dealt with the founder of Buddhism as a *guru* , in particular citing his name "teacher (of gods and men)" (*śāstṛ-devamanuṣyānām*).[13] This raises the question of how he would teach gods as contrasted with how he would teach men. According to the opening scriptural passages in the Pāli canonical *Saṃyutta-Nikāya,* the gods put questions to Gautama in the form of riddles, and he would solve the riddles. The very first request in that collection, although stated in the "How did you?" form, is tantamount to a riddle. A certain deva, as dawn was approaching came to the Jeta Grove, where the Buddha was staying and asked him how he had crossed the flood. He responded, "Not staying (P. *appatiṭṭham*), friend, and not conjecturing (P. *anāyuham*),[14] did I cross the flood." And when the deva asked him how by those two avoidances he crossed the flood, he responded: "When, friend, I stayed, I sank (P. *saṃsīdāmi*); when, friend, I conjectured, I was wafted about (*nibbuyhāmi*)." The responses are themselves suggestive of other Buddhist doctrines. Thus "not staying": the Buddha is called Tathāgata (one who has gone, or understood the same way), and so did not stay. The Pāli term *appatiṭṭham* is the Sanskrit *apratiṣṭham* implicating at once the Mahāyāna kind of Nirvāṇa the *apratiṣṭhita-nirvāṇa,* the one of no-fixed abode. Then, "nor conjecturing": absolute truth is beyond human reason and logic.

There are of course numerous examples of how the Buddha would teach men. Thus, in the Pāli canonical collection *Aṅguttara-Nikāya* (Book of Threes): "He proclaims thus: 'Come! This is the Path.' This is the course I announce: I so mastered it that I myself realized directly with supernormal faculty the incomparable yoga-way of brahma-conduct. Come you also! May you so course that having mastered it you too yourselves may directly realize with supernormal faculty the incomparable yoga-way of brahma-conduct, and having acquired it may abide (therein)!"[15] When the Buddha taught men, he showed the path which he himself had trod successfully. He also showed that some *gurus* should not be followed, e.g. Arāda.

Śāriputra. Śāriputra (P. Sāriputta) was the Buddha's foremost disciple in the *guru* lineage, and was praised by the Buddha as having the keenest insight (S. *prajñā,* P. *paññā*) among the disciples. Malalasekera has a fine exposition of Sāriputta from scriptures of the Buddhist canon in the Pāli language.[16] Using this account as a basis, one can easily notice that this disciple exemplified what are called in Buddhist terms the "four sublime abodes" (*brahma-vihāra*), or "boundless states" (*apramāṇa*), which are "friendliness" (*maitrī*), "compassion" (*karuṇā*), "sympathetic joy" (*muditā*), and "equanimity" (*upekṣā*). This is surely why the Buddha entrusted younger disciples to Sāriputta's care. The celebrated account "Conversion of Sāriputta and Moggallāna"[17] starts with the keen friendship between these two, who first studied the Veda under the same Vedic teacher; and afterwards joined a wandering band headed by Sañjaya. Quickly mastering this teacher's doctrine, the two friends sought a better teacher. Sāriputta heard from a Buddhist monk a verse about causality that would in later centuries be copied innumerable times, and decided to follow the Buddha. He reported this to Moggallāna, who thought they should go immediately to the Buddha. But Sāriputta, always grateful to his teachers thought they should first break the news to Sañjaya, which they did. Sāriputta's compassion is evident in his custom to visit sick monks, as the Buddha also did. Sāriputta's sympathetic joy is illustrated in how he congratulated Moggallāna on his attainment of the magical powers called *iddhi* (S. *ṛddhi*). As to the equanimity in one scripture, the Buddha commended Sāriputta for the aloofness of his life; and presumably this faculty helped both him and Moggallāna win back the monks who had seceded with Devadatta.

The Buddha trusted Sāriputta to explain to other monks, as well as to laymen those doctrines, which the Buddha had stated in a concentrated form. Thus, a number of scriptures are preserved wherein Sāriputta is the main expounder. The most famous among these are the *Dasuttara* and *Saṅgiti Suttas*, both concerned with numerical doctrines, arranging them by one's, two's, etc. This style is the same in the *Aṅguttara-Nikāya*, so it may be presumed that Sāriputta's students might have arranged this numerical canon. Centuries later, a work by Asaṅga, the *Yogācārabhūmi* has many such numerical lists; and the author calls them "stage involved with hearing" (*śrutamayī bhūmi*), which ancient Buddhism took as the first education of "insight" (*prajñā*). When Anāthapiṇḍika, the great patron of Buddhism was mortally ill, he sent for Sāriputta, who came together with Ānanda and preached the *Anāthapiṇḍikovāda*

Sutta. This scripture contains the theory of six elements (S. *ṣaḍdhātu*), namely, earth (*pṛthivī*), water (*āpas*), fire (*tejas*), wind (*vāyu*), space (S. *ākāśa*), consciousness (S. *vijñāna*); and that there is a faculty called in Pāli *viññaṇa* (S. *vijñāna*), a kind of perception that can have as objects all six of those elements, including the *vijñāna-dhātu*. This theory of six elements of man is preserved in the Abhidharma literature and early Mahāyāna scriptures. It plays a great role in the kind of Buḍdhist Tantra which Kukai brought from China to Japan and which continues in the Japanese Shingon sect.

Some modern writers on the history of Buddhism have pointed out on the basis of knowing that the first writing down of the Buddhist canon was made in Sri Lanka (Ceylon) in the first century B.C.—that this allows little evidence for what was in the earliest Buddhist canon. Naturally, such writers must suppose that this conclusion is deserving of attention and acceptance. These authors are willing to grant that the Brahmins could memorize their Veda and hand it down with great fidelity before it was committed to writing in India several centuries later than that, but are unwilling to grant that the Buddhists could do the same. Without claiming that the present Pāli canon is exactly what was collected by the monks soon after the passing of Gautama Buddha, one can still conclude that no Buddhist writer in India had to travel to Sri Lanka to get the theory of the six elements of man that Sāriputta preached about in that sermon. Perhaps such modern writers on Buddhist history have not realized the strength of the *guru* tradition in India, among the Buddhists as well as among the Hindus.

Asaṅga. This celebrated Buddhist teacher is also called Āryāsaṅga. He lived *circa* 375-430. He had a younger brother celebrated by the name Vasubandhu, who might have been a half-brother, separated by a generation from his older brother. Vasubandhu, who lived, *circa* 400-480 became surrounded by the best Buddhist disciples of the day in his old age. He told his disciples at that time stories of his older brother Asaṅga who had long since passed away, and who could not have been possibly known personally by any of those disciples. A story that has been handed down by Paramārtha, who brought the life of Vasubandhu to China is to the effect that Asaṅga by meditative power had ascended to the Tuṣita heaven, where dwells the future Buddha Maitreya. There Maitreya taught him the "Sunlight *samādhi*" which enabled him to understand all Buddhist scriptures. Asaṅga then prayed to Maitreya to come down to earth (called Jambudvīpa = India) and expound the Mahāyāna. Maitreya came down at night and with much light. He expounded the theory of the seventeen stages *(bhūmi)* to a large assembly in a lecture hall in a period of four months, always at night. Only the Dharma-master Asaṅga had access to the Bodhisattva Maitreya, while the others could merely hear him from afar.[18] Thus, according to the story told by Vasubandhu, Asaṅga established his school of Yogācāra by direct inspiration of the Bodhisattva Maitreya. Asaṅga himself, in the exegetical portion of his *Yogācāra-bhūmi* by his list of kinds of "insight" (*prajñā*), told the difference between the Buddha as a *guru* and subsequent Buddhist *gurus* in terms of "insight":[19]

> "torch (or meteor) or insight" (*ulkā*) is the one that goes along only with the time of Teaching of the Dharma [i.e., during Gautama Buddha's teaching career].
> "secondary light of insight" (*avabhāsa*) is the one which goes along with subsequent times, when the Dharma is well-considered with insight in this and that way, and it is not directly realized by the body [i.e., after the Buddha's Nirvāṇa].

Asaṅga also illustrates in his life how one can have more than one *guru.* He of course follows the Buddha's Dharma as a *guru* and does it through a so-called "Hīnayāna" school, as the Chinese pilgrim Hsüan-tsang reported and I have defended, namely, the Mahīśāsaka.[20] He also accept the Mahāyāna Dharma as above with the Bodhisattva Maitreya as the *guru*; while he is himself the first *guru* of the Yogācāra lineage. In this latter lineage, he is continued by the celebrated Vasubandhu, who had first followed *gurus* in the Abhidharma lineage, and later took Asaṅga as his *guru* in Mahāyāna Buddhism.

Kūkai. This remarkable Japanese scholar-monk (774-835), also called posthumously Kōbō Daishi, of multi-faceted talent, exemplifies the search for the *guru* in another country (China) and the bringing back of the esoteric Buddhist lineage to Japan. Later, as Hakeda informs us,[21] Kūkai denied that esoteric Buddhism was propounded by the historical Buddha, as Buddhists of his era generally believed. Kukai went to China to find out the meaning of the scripture called *Mahāvairocana-sūtra* which had become available in Japan by a copy in 736 of the Chinese version.[22] This scripture called in the Indo-Tibetan tradition, the *Vairocanābhisaṃbodhi-tantra* has many difficult and obscure passages. The present writer published a work on this reporting that it is a wedding of esoteric doctrine with the Buddhism descended from the historical Buddha and composed circa mid-sixth century A.D. in the area of present-day Maharashtra. This lineage was transmitted to China in 716 A.D. with the arrival of Śubhakarasiṃha, who translated the text into Chinese with the help of I-hsing. When Kūkai returned to Japan after studying the scripture through Sanskrit and Chinese, and having gained the corpus of tantric "secrets", he prepared various works explaining this and associated esoteric texts. But Hakeda reports that his writings were also hard to understand, partly because he wrote in ornate classical Chinese with many Sanskrit terms in Chinese transcription and translation, and partly because of the subtlety of the material.[23] To illustrate the continuity of the *guru* transmissal, we may take the example of the "six elements", since Sāriputta had related these to the dying Anāthapiṇḍika, and the esoteric school of Japan makes much of them. Hakeda translates the lines for the first five of these from the Chinese *Mahāvairocana-sūtra*:[24]

> I have realized that which is unborn;
> It is that which language cannot communicate;
> It is free from all defilements;
> It transcends causality;
> I know that it is void like space.

My own translation is from the Tibetan version and includes the line for the sixth element, *vijñāna*:

> I have comprehended "non-arising", have dropped off the domain of speech, negated all faults, and lack causes and conditions.
> I have the knowledge of voidness like space. I am freed from all darkness.

Here, earth is "non-arising"; water washes away speech; fire negates all faults; wind lacks cause and conditions; space is like voidness; and *vijñāna* (when the Buddha's) is freed from all darkness. Hence, this scriptural way of referring to the six elements is tantamount to the riddles which deities have tested the Buddha within the initial verse section of the Pāli *Saṃyutta-Nikāya*. This scripture, the *Mahāvairocana-sūtra* has many such obscure lines, which prompted Kūkai on his perilous and remarkably fruitful trip to China, for gaining the lineage of the *gurus*, then upon returning, to start the sect called Shingon.

Nāro-pā. This is the eleventh century *yogin* and great adept (*mahāsiddha*). According to the biography, which Guenther has translated,[25] Nāro-pā at the age of eleven, despite misgivings of his parents proceeded to Kashmir and in some Buddhist institution took a range of courses, including training in the *Kālacakratantra* and many other treatises. His parents felt he had studied enough and pressured him to get married. After eight years of marriage, the two convinced their parents that they should separate, and so a divorce was granted, he then being twenty-five. His former wife, Vimalā, became his companion, and would in time also write some tantric treatises. Nāro-pā resumed his studies in Kashmir, and subsequently was appointed to the University of Nālandā. Through a dream said to be a message instigated by a tantric goddess Vajrayoginī, he was exhorted to seek out as *guru* the tantric master Tilopa. Much of the biography is taken up by the relations between Tilopa and his disciple Nāro-pā. The Tibetan Mar-pa on his first trip to India obtained from Nāro-pā what would be called "The Six Laws of Nāro-pā," the basic teaching of the Bka'-brgyud-pa sect which Mar-pa founded in Tibet. Nāro-pā has written a number of important tantric works that were translated into the Tibetan language and preserved in the canon called the Tanjur. The present writer made much use of this author's commentary on the *Hevajratantra* for a translation and study of the *Mañjuśrī-nāma-saṃgīti,*[26] and could not help but admire how Nāro-pā displays a masterful control of such tantric topics. Definitely, he is the hierophant type of *guru*.

Tsoṅ-kha-pa. This celebrated Tibetan teacher (1357-1419) has been the subject of various biographies. I prepared a brief one based upon two Tibetan biographies, including this mention of his first important *guru*: "This was the Reverend Red-mda'-pa (1349-1412), who had such mastery of Vasubandhu's self-commentary on the *Abhidharmakośa* as to excite utmost admiration in Tsoṅ-kha-pa. Red-mda'-pa became his *guru*; and the two traveled together for years, starting, it seems, in 1376. Tsoṅ-kha-pa first gained from this teacher the full comprehension of the Mādhyamika and of Buddhist logic that paved the way for his non-tantric treatises."

The next important *guru* was a young Tibetan named Grags-pa Byaṅ-chub-pa: "Then, having arrived at Gdan-sa, the monastery founded by the lama Phag-mo Gru-pa (1110-1170), Tsoṅ-kha-pa learned from the Spyan-sṅa Grags-pa Byaṅ-chub-pa (1356-1386, died at age of thirty-one) the complete precepts of the Path and the Fruit, the Six Doctrines of Nāro-pā, the collected sayings of Rje Phag-mo Gru-pa and of Chos-rje 'Jig-rten Mgon-po, the precepts in the lineage from Lho-brag Mar-pa to Rje-btsun Mi-la (i.e. Milarepa), and the precepts in the lineage from Lho-brag Mar-pa to Rṅog Chos-sku-rdo-rje."[27] The biography continues with numerous other examples of Tsoṅ-kha-pa's assiduous learning from other eminent teachers while himself instructing a growing number of disciples.

The Guru-Yoga Practice

The practice referred to as "*guru-yoga*" developed in the tantric period, and has as its ethics manual the treatise by an author calling himself Aśvaghoṣa, the *Fifty Stanzas in Praise of the Guru*. The premise is that the *guru* represents the divinity by identification with it and by "serving" that deity, thereby imagined to extend protection to the evoker. This *guru* can bestow upon disciples the "permission" (*anujñā*) to invoke that deity, provided the disciples take certain pledges, lack the kind of dreams that betokens departure and disallowal by the deity. When disciples gain such evocation permission and further receive the "initiation" (*abhiṣeka*) of a certain deity and its circle of attendant deities, the disciple is also told the lineage of masters coming down to their *guru* of that time and place. The disciple, besides honoring his own *guru* is expected to honor the former *gurus* going back to the first one who evoked that deity. Therefore, it is possible to have a *yoga* derived from such honoring. If the performer imagines the *guru* lineage, it is subject to the same rules as any other meditative object of Buddhist meditation. That is to say, one should concentrate on the lineage without wandering of mind to other objects with the aim of achieving a "calming" (*śamatha*) of the mind, after which one may subject the object to a discursive construction sometimes called "discerning" (*vipaśyanā*) of the real.

The Tibetan books preserve much material on such practices; and while it is reasonable that the practice existed in North India, it is undeniable that the Tibetan form is quite elaborate, suggesting a further native development. For the line of *gurus* mentioned above for Nāro-pā and the Tibetan Mar-pa, I shall here edit Evans-Wentz' portrayal, where the human *guru* has Milarepa above him:[28]

> The Line of the *Gurus,* imagined in vertical fashion, is now described.
>
> Above the head of one's "root-*guru*" [of the present time] identified with Vajradhāra [the deity of the line] on a throne consisting of a lunar disk as the center of a lotus is Jetsun Milarepa, colored light blue, his right hand against his right cheek in the *vajra*-gesture, his left hand level on his lap in the gesture of equipoise also holding a human skull bowl filled with ambrosia, his feet in the *bodhisattva*-posture; and robed in white silk.[29]
>
> Above him is Mar-pa, of reddish-brown color, body stout, in monk robes, legs crossed, palm upon the other on the lap in *dhyāna*-gesture while holding a human skull filled with ambrosia, his eyes directed upwards.
>
> Above him is Nāro-pā, light blue in color, hair knotted on his crown, wearing a head-tiara of human skulls, adorned with six bone ornaments, loins clad in the Indian loin-cloth, right hand holding an antelope-horn trumpet, left hand displaying the threatening gesture, resting on a dais behind him, feet in [comfortable] blacksmith-posture.
>
> Above him is the glorious Tilopa, brown, with mien partly angry partly smiling, hair made into a knot on top of his head that is surmounted by a gem with a tiara of white lotus blossoms that are loosely held by a meditation-band, body brightly adorned with human-bone ornaments with an apron on his loins made of tiger-skin, feet in an easy posture, right hand upraised and holding a large golden fish, left hand level on his lap in equipoise gesture and holding a human skull filled with ambrosia.
>
> Above him is the Victor Vajradhāra, blue attired in the garb of a Saṃbhoga-kāya deity, his two hands crossed over the breast, the right hand holding a *vajra* and the left a bell.[30]
>
> Each of the *guru* is [imagined as] seated within a five-colored rainbow.

The identification with Vajradhāra in that lineage of the Bka'-

brgyud-pa *gurus* is consistent with the *Fifty Stanzas in Praise of the Guru,* v. 22 (from the Tibetan):

> Therefore, a disciple equipped with the merits of compassion (*karuṇā*) [the root of Mahāyāna] giving away (*dāna),* morality (*śīla*), and forbearance (*kṣānti*) [the first three perfections (*pāramitā*)] should not regard his master (*ācārya*) as different from Vajradhāra.

This, then, is the manner of identification coming from India to Tibet.

The Gelug-pa sect founded by Tsoṅ-kha-pa starts a native tradition of *guru-yoga* in which Tsoṅ-kha-pa is the *guru* inaugurating the lineage by direct transmissal from the Bodhisattva Mañjuśrī. This is clear according to Tsoṅ-kha-pa, collected works, Vol. Ka, two brief works, the first in which Tsoṅ-kha-pa instructs his disciple Mkhas-grub-rje on taking his own *guru* as the root-*guru* identified with a reddish-yellow Mañjuśrī; the second one in which Tsoṅ-kha-pa similarly instructs Ba-so-chos-rje. In both cases, the Mañjuśrī appears to be the Arapacana variety. Mkhas-grub-rje and Ba-so-chos-rje were both abbots of Galden monastery, founded in 1409 by Tsoṅ-kha-pa. *Guru-yoga* in the later Geluga sect especially employs a set of ten verses referred to as the *Dga' ldan lha brgya ma.* The first two words are the Tibetan name written above as Galden monastery and correspond to the Sanskrit Tuṣita (a heaven). The ninth verse is called the *Dmigs brtse ma,* an expression that occurs twice in the instruction to Ba-so-chos-rje. It does appear that this kind of *guru-yoga* with Tsoṅ-kha-pa as the "root-*guru*" is elaborated by the first abbots of Galden monastery. However, the set of ten verses seems to be composed by Blo-bzaṅ Chos-kyi-rgyal-mtshan, a teacher of the Fifth Dalai Lama and sometimes called the First Panchen Lama. I have consulted the commentary by the Seventh Dalai Lama, in his Collected Works, Vol. Kha. This is verse 9, the *Dmigs brtse ma* (from the Tibetan):

> I pray at the feet of Lozangtakpa (S. Sumatikīrti, a name of Tsoṅ-kha-pa), who is Avalokiteśvara—great treasure of aimless compassion; is Mañjughoṣa (= Mañjuśrī)—the power of undefiled omniscience; is Master of the Secret Ones (i.e. Vajrapāṇi)—subduer of the hosts of Māra without remainder; Tsoṅ-kha-pa—head ornament of the savants of the snowy range.

Notice that the *guru-yoga* based on Tsoṅ-kha-pa has been expanded from the initial Arapacana Mañjuśrī to a triad of Bodhisattvas. According to the commentary, Avalokiteśvara and Mañjughoṣa represent the Mahāyāna Perfection of Insight (*Prajñāpāramitā*), hence the two parts of the Bodhisattva vow by compassion to rescue the sentient beings, and by omniscience to awaken to the complete enlightenment. Vajrapāṇi represents the Mahāyāna Diamond Vehicle (*vajrayāna*); hence, a suggestion the Buddhist Tantra starts at that approach of evening when Gautama defeated the hosts of Māra.[31]

Another approach of Tsoṅ-kha-pa as a *guru*, but not necessarily formalized in *guru-yoga* is that of Dge-'dun-grub (1391-1475), founder of the Tashilunpo monastery and posthumously the First Dalai Lama. This is in his poem called "The Song of the Eastern Snow Mountain."[32] Here, thinking of his *guru*, Tsoṅ-kha-pa, is the first verse as rendered:

> On the peak of the white snow mountain in the East, a white cloud as though hastens in the sky. Upon beholding it, I remember my *guru* (*bla ma*). Again and again reflecting upon his kindness, faith is born in me.

Verse ten (also from the Tibetan) is directed toward the disciple:

> When one does not adopt the means of taming the enemy defilement, what is just a bickering over minutia, he hears as the Teaching. That is as purposeless as when a demon is at the eastern gate to offer an effigy-substitute (*glud*) [into which the demon is drawn and stabbed] at the western gate.

Perhaps, the strangest verse in *Fifty Stanzas in Praise of the Guru* is n. 23 (from the Tibetan):

> As fearful as the sin of destroying a *stūpa*,
> is the stepping on a shadow (of your *guru*). Never do it !
> What need is there to mention a refraining from
> stepping on his shoes, seat, or his mount!

Tsoṅ-kha-pa's comment on the verse (no. p. 353 in Delhi ed. of Tashilunpo ed., Vol. Ka) amounts to citations of various tantric passages that say the same thing. Finally, the learned commentator quotes the Vinaya code for a similar remark. Perhaps the reason for the prohibition is that these given things—the shadow, shoes, and so on are symbols of the *guru*—much as the empty throne, the wheel, the parasol, and the *stūpa* are aniconic symbols of the Buddha—not likenesses, but amounting to living embodiments.[33] There is the suggestion that stepping upon them is tantamount to stepping upon the *guru* himself. Thus, this prohibition is not really the folklore theory that the shadow implicates the "soul" of the person, and so on. It is the respect given to relics of the saint. So this particular verse does not deal with the *guru* in the manner of the present paper, i.e., as a teacher of disciples. But since a *guru* might not be a saint, i.e., when he is serving as a teacher or as a tantric hierophant, it does suggest that he should be treated as a saint, especially in his absence, by way of his symbolic associations.

He is present in his absence—this is the meaning of his shadow cast on humanity.

REFERENCES

1. This is in *Dīgha-nikāya*, Vol. II, R. 154, first paragraph; compare the tr. by T.W. and C.A.F. Rhys Davids, *Dialogues of the Buddha*, Part II, p. 171.
2. Alex Wayman, tr., *Calming the Mind and Discerning the Real; Buddhist Meditation and the Middle View*, from the *Lam rim chen mo* of Tsoṅ-kha-pa (New York, 1978), p. 170.
3. Alex Wayman, *Yoga of the Guhyasamajatantra; the Arcane Lore of Forty Verses* (Delhi, 1977), pp. 181-2
4. Benoytosh Bhattacharya, ed., *Sādhanamālā*, Vol. II, n. 187, the *Kurukullāsādhana* by Karūnābhidhāna, in verse 2.
5. The form *parām* follows the Tibetan translation; the edition of Franz Bernhard, *Udānavarga* (Gottingen, 1968), has the reading *sarām*. The form *adhyaguḥ* is Prākrit; the equivalent Sanskrit verb form is *adhi-gam*—with suitable inflection.
6. For the ten categories—inner and outer, cf. *Mkhas Grub Rje's Fundamentals of the Buddhist Tantras*, tr. by Ferdinand D. Lessing and Alex Wayman (The Hague, 1968), pp. 272-3. For the two sets of ten, cf. also *Fifty Verses of Guru Devotion* by Aśvaghoṣa, prepared by the translation bureau of the Library of Tibetan Works and Archives (Dharmasala, India, 1975).
7. Cf. Alex Wayman, *The Buddhist Tantras; Light on Indo-Tibetan Esotericism* (New York, 1973), p. 49.
8. Professor Thubten Norbu (Indiana University, U.S.A.) explained to the writer during the International Tibetan Conference, Munich, 1985, that a Tibetan author like Tsoṅ-kha-pa himself (with modesty), writes up the lineage lists that have come to him as "works received" (*thob yig*), while his followers after his death, when copying his treatise (to honor him) change the title to "works heard" (*gsan yig*).

9. Cf. Wayman, *Yoga* (n. 3, above), p. 296.
10. Wayman, *Yoga* (n. 3, above), p. 267.
11. Wayman, *The Buddhist Tantras* (n. 7, above), p. 49.
12. Wayman, *The Buddhist Tantras,* pp. 49-50.
13. Wayman, "Buddha as Savior", *Studia Missionalia,* 29 (1980); reprinted in *Buddhist Insight; Essays by Alex Wayman,* Ed: George R. Elder (Delhi, 1984), p. 12.
14. The equivalent Sanskrit term would be a negation of form of *ūh,* hence my rendition "not conjecturing". The translators from Pāli, claiming the term means "not striving" are in direct violation of the Buddhist teachings.
15. Cf. Wayman, *Buddhist Insight,* p. 12.
16. Cf. G.P. Malalasekera, *Dictionary of Pāli Proper Names,* Vol. II (London, 1960), s.v.
17. Franklin Edgerton, *Buddhist Hybrid Sanskrit Reader* (New Haven, 1953), contains an edited text of "The Conversion of Śāriputra and Maudgalyāyana" from the version of the *Mahāvastu.*
18. Cf. Alex Wayman *Analysis of the Śrāvakabhūmi Manuscript* (Berkeley, 1961), pp. 31-2.
19. Cf. Wayman, Buddhist Insight, p. 208.
20. Cf. Alex Wayman , "Doctrinal Affiliation of the Buddhist Master Asaṅga", P.V. Bapat volume. (Elsewhere, in the present volume).
21. Yoshito S. Hakeda, *Kūkai, Major Works* (New York, 1972), p. 63.
22. Hakeda, *Kūkai,* pp. 26-7.
23. Hakeda, *Kūkai,* p. 9.
24. Hakeda, *Kūkai,* p. 228.
25. Herbert V. Guenther, *The Life and Teaching of Nāro-pa* (Oxford University Press Paperback, 1971).
26. Alex Wayman, *Chanting the Names of Mañjuśrī* (Boston, 1985). Herein I gave Nāro-pā's fifty three citations of this text in the order of the *Hevajratantra's* chapters.
27. Wayman, tr., *Calming the Mind,* pp. 18-20.
28. W.Y. Evans-Wentz, *Tibetan Yoga and Secret Doctrines* (London, 1935), pp. 274-6.
29. For this form of Milarepa, see Toni Schmid, *The Cotton-Clad Mila* (Stockholm, 1952), p. 14.
30. Wayman, *The Buddhist Tantras* , p. 52, pl, 4, depicts Vajradhāra in this form.
31. This is not a claim that Gautama Buddha preached what would be later called "Buddhist Tantra". But it does suggest that if one tries to trace later forms of Buddhism to the life of Gautama Buddha, the event on his life most compatible with Tantrism is the defeat of Māra at sundown.
32. For the text, cf. Johan Van Manen , "Minor Tibetan Texts; the song of the Eastern snow Mountain," *Bibliotheca Indica* (Calcutta, 1919).
33. Cf. Wayman, *Buddhist Insight,* p. 291.

11

Prophecy for Persons in Buddhism

Introductory Remarks

Indian religion has long-accepted the possibility of personal prediction, for example, by divination methods like astrology. Buddhism prevalently discourages its monks to use divinatory methods for personal predictions, without denying their possible validity. Buddhism, however, like other Indian religions observed phases of the moon for their periodical religious activities, such as meeting of the saṅgha for confessionals, and so on. And like other religions of India presumably observed lunar positions in the asterisms (*nakṣatras*) for starting the building of a temple. Such observances have a premise that certain lunar phases and certain asterisms protend success or failure for certain activities, such as planting by farmers. This kind of prediction and in ancient times, if it were the right day to start a military campaign was the usual type of divination at the time of the Buddha, in the sense of the long chronology. Personal horoscopy came later with certain Babylonians, who were called Chaldeans by the Greeks. The usual predictions for persons had to do with matters of health, children, and business ventures. In short, such predictions pertain to persons who remain in the world in the sense of family, and so on. At the time of the Buddha, there were certainly predictions of religious success for persons who had abandoned family life.

It seems that many of the predictions, whether for mundane or supramundane pursuits were in response to questions. That must be the reason that the principal words for prophecy also mean explanation. Thus, the Sanskrit word *pradarśana* means 'explaining' and 'prophesying'. The usual term for 'prediction' in Buddhism is *vyākaraṇa* and this term is also used for explanations, especially in answers to questions. When a dream was prophetic, it was referred to as *bhāvika*, which does not mean explaining; but does mean a figure of speech—so vivid regarding the past or future that this appears to be present. But the prophetic dream did elicit explanations from 'dream oracles' or experts in interpretation.

The Prophetic Eye and the Dharma Mirror

Thus, the ancient world looked upon certain individuals as fit for explaining the prediction. In Buddhism, their required talent was called the 'divine eye' (Skt. *divya-cakṣus*). This was the 'eye' which the Buddha used for seeing the beings going to different destinies, hence predictive of destinies such as hell, heaven, or rebirth in the human kingdom. The Buddhist commentator Sthiramati says of this 'eye':[1]

> The divine eye is of two kinds, both seeing forms in past and future: (1) that born of past action (*karma*), the eye of the gods; and (2) that born of contemplation (*bhāvanā*) in the *samādhi* of a yogin, and which sees the sentient beings passing away from here and going to various destinies in accordance with past actions.

Asaṅga, in his exegesis (*Viniścayasaṃgrahaṇī*) of his *Śrāvakabhūmi*,[2] sets forth three degrees of this 'divine eye'. He first explains the scriptural phrase, "with an eye surpassing the human eye" that here "human eye" means that of a *pṛthagjana* (ordinary person), even if a Buddhist *śrāvaka* who does not have the divine eye. The first degree is of the disciple, who has "entered the stream", "will be reborn once more", or "will not be reborn". Next are the Arhats, who have been liberated by insight (*prajñā*), who have the keener kind. The third degree is when someone possesses the three Visions (*vidyā-traya*)—as Gautama had under the Bodhi-tree—and is liberated from both parts, namely, the obscuration of defilement (*kleśa*) and the obscuration of equipoise (*samāpatti*), as Asaṅga explained in the *Śrāvakabhūmi* itself.[3] In the exegesis section, Asaṅga explains these degrees in terms of purification. Thus in the case of the Arhat's attainment of this 'eye', it is called (in Tibetan), *rnam par dag pa* (Skt. *viśuddhi*), 'purity'. In the case of the third and highest degree of this 'eye', it is *śin tu rnaṁ par dag pa* (Skt. *ativiśuddhi*), 'surpassing purity'. This nomenclature shows that there is involved some faculty which is held to be present in human consciousness in an obscured form. For this reason, according to this viewpoint, the ordinary person is not prophetic, because the faculty responsible for prophecy is obscured; and so does not operate, except sometimes in dream. According to Asaṅga in this place of his exegesis, if a person can rise above 'human nature' (*mi'i chos*; Skt. *manuṣya-dharma*)[4] and adopt the life of a monk, this faculty becomes stronger, although still not 'pure', as long as the person has not eliminated his defilement (*kleśa*). The Arhat gets rid of the 'obscuration of defilement' (*kleśa-āvaraṇa*); and so has a 'purity' of this faculty. But the Arhat's ability here cannot compare with the Buddha's according to this tradition. This is because the Buddha not only eliminated the 'obscuration of defilement', but also the 'obscuration of equipoise' which might be what the Mahāyāna calls the 'obscuration of the knowable' (*jñeya-āvaraṇa*). Later, Asaṅga in his exegesis attributes to the 'divine eye of the Tathāgata' the ability to recognize the objective situations of all sentient beings, (1) by seeing (namely, with the divine eye) the sentient beings accomplishing various destinies along with instigation (*abhisaṃskāra*) of consistent *karma*; (2) by seeing all the sentient beings living in a multitude of birthplaces; (3) by seeing all the sentient beings that take birth after dying and passing through an intermediate state; (4) by seeing all the sentient beings that take birth after dying while not passing through an intermediate state.[5] What is intriguing about this passage is the claim—and of course, it rests upon canonical precedence—that the Tathāgata sees the *karma* that gives rise to the various objective situations and destinies.

As to that *karma,* a standard verse, often quoted maintains that one cannot evade this *karma* of destiny (usually stated as mental *karma*), whether its fruit comes in the present or a subsequent life:

> The deeds are not lost even in a hundred eons. One should know (*khalu*) that they come to fruition for mankind when they get complete and at the time of death.[6]

We may ask, what is meant by 'seeing' *karma,* which is basically an action, and yet is said to continue until it gets to its result? In our response, it seems that there are two ways of understanding this. In the first way of understanding, we suggest that the prophetic nature of the divine eye consists of its converting the *karma* into a dramatic representation. Thus, the *karma* is not really 'seen', but the dramatic vision of seeing the sentient beings going to diverse destinies is there. The second way of understanding this, is the way Abhayākaragupta treats this matter in his great commentary, the *Āmnāya-mañjari* on the *Sampuṭa-tantra.*[7] He points out that *karma* is invisible and visible. The practical kind of *karma* is invisible. The *karma* wind is visible. His use of the terminology 'visible *karma*' involves the theory that *karma* creates the visible body. It does this by a series of 'winds', which is not really a tantric notion, since the theory of '*karma*-winds' is in the shorter and longer Buddhist embryological scriptures, the longer one entitled *Ārya-nanda-garbhāvakrānti-nirdeśa,* extant in the Tibetan and the Chinese canons. In any case, it is certain from numerous passages that Buddhism insists on the role of *karma* as effectuating the various destinies. So it must also be the case that prophecy applied to persons must implicate this *karma.*

As to the Dharma-mirror in ancient Buddhism there was a religious substitution for the secular magic mirror of a 'mirror of the Dharma'. Thus, in the *Parinibbāna-sutta:*

> Therefore, Ānanda, in this world I will reveal the representation of the Dharma called 'mirror of the Dharma', possessed of which a noble disciple planning would predict for self or selves: "With no more sojourns in hell, no more animal birth, no more realm of the hungry ghosts, no more disaster, evil destiny, ruin—I have entered the stream, not

> liable to purgatory, assured, proceeding toward enlightenment."[8]

This 'mirror of the Dharma' is then explained as four kinds, to wit, 'faith with understanding' (P. *avecca-pasāda*, S. *avetya-prasāda*)—toward the Buddha, the Dharma, the Saṅgha, and toward the moral rules (S. *śīla*) dear to the nobles. Śamathadeva's commentary on the *Abhidharmakośa,* Chap. VIII, refers to this 'mirror of the Dharma' pointing out that each of those four kinds of 'faith with understanding' constitutes a 'mirror of the Dharma'.[9]

This passage from the *Parinibbāna-sutta* about the Dharma-mirror and the further explanation implicating the nomenclature of 'faith with understanding' clarifies Asaṅga's portrayal of the 'divine eye' in terms of degrees of its strength. He pointed out that the *śrāvaka* (the hearer-disciple) who has entered the stream has the weakest form of the 'divine eye'. That is precisely the message in the scriptural passage on the Dharma-mirror, that the disciple having that kind of mirror could predict for self or selves of avoiding the evil destinies, while having entered the stream, and so on.

If follows that this 'Dharma-mirror' is not a reference to the mind as a mirror, rather it is this very 'faith with understanding' that constitutes the Dharma-mirror. It must be that this kind of faith is metaphorically referred to as a predictive mirror because it initially awakens this faculty of 'divine eye' in humans, whereby there is the religious type of prophecy.

The role of educated faith seems to be intended when this mirror was alluded to in the *Jātakamālā*, XXXI, Story of Sutasoma, v.68:

> Having observed the ugly reflected image of my conduct, and perhaps an arisen stirring [of faith] in the mirror of Dharma, might my mind be eager for the Dharma?[10]

Of the four kinds, presumably the 'mirror of the Dharma' here is the 'faith with understanding' toward the moral rules dear to the nobles.

The Pre-Mahāyāna Type of Prophecy for Persons

In the sources of early Buddhism, we distinguish the prophecies for lay persons and for monks:

A. *Prophecies for lay persons*: Buddhism arose in India where there was prevalent—or so we think—a belief in other worlds than the present one. We could see the present world and had to believe in the other one or ones. And there was a belief in various destinies which Buddhism standardized as five, sometimes six. Of these, mankind could see itself as one of the two good destinies, but could not see the realm of the gods, which is the other one of two good destinies. Mankind could see the animals as a 'bad' destiny; and made remarks like, "It's a dog's life." But mankind could not see the destiny of 'hungry ghosts' (*preta*) or the destiny of the 'hell beings' (*nāraka*), also called 'bad destinies', as was also the sometimes added class of *asuras,* the enemies of the gods. It follows that when ancient Buddhism made its moralistic predictions about which sins would eventuate in which bad destinies; or which virtues would be rewarded by which good destiny—it depended upon the intended listeners' acceptance in their belief outlook of this structure of other worlds and destinies which could not be seen.

Buddhism stressed the value of believing in those destinies. In short, it would appeal to retribution in the after-life as a justification for here-and-now ethics. We get this point in Ārya-śūra's *Jātakamālā,* No. XXIX, 'Story of an inhabitant of Brahmaloka.' The story opens with the Bodhisattva, the future Buddha, in a realm called Brahmaloka, which in Buddhist dogmatics of three worlds (of desire, of form, and the formless one), is in the second of the three worlds, the realm of form (*rūpadhātu*).

From this realm the Bodhisattva looked down with compassion upon the 'realm of desire' (*kāmadhātu*) and noticed there a king of Videha named Aṅgadinna, who disbelieving in another life was given over to vile conduct with ill-will toward religious books. The poet summarizes the situation with Buddhist sentiments:

> He who is imbued with conviction, "Surely there is a world hereafter where good and bad *karma* give rise to happiness and sorrow," having discarded sin, will persevere with virtuous resorts. But by disbelief one will proceed according to his (preverse) will. (v. 2)[11]

The Bodhisattva picked an occasion when the king was in a secluded bower and miraculously appeared in front of him. We need not go into the Bodhisattva's arguments to try to win over the king. The lesson, though, is that it does not help to use rational arguments: these do not sway the king. And before one can speak of the joys of heaven that would result from virtuous conduct, the king must be scared of a possible sojourn in the hells. This must be the rationale of so many frightening predictions in Buddhist *karma* stories. There are various Buddhist scriptures and *śāstras* that list the particular sin that gets one in this or that hell, or that results in this or that kind of 'hungry ghost'. There is a full treatment in Paul Mus, *La Lumière sur les Six Voies*, containing the stanzas of Dhārmika Subhūti.[12] As an example of how to 'fit the punishment to the crime', these stanzas mention the retribution for adultery:

> Demonic women, all fiery with large bodies and tusks of iron embrace the one who has ravished the wife of another and devour him.[13]

The stanzas of Dhārmika Subhūti also have a comprehensive treatment of the 'hungry ghosts' (*preta*); and a *sūtra* called *Saddharmasmṛtyupasthāna* has a list of thirty-six 'hungry ghosts' along with the sins that respectively give rise to them.[14]

For prophecies of the rewards for virtue, it is necessary to mention briefly the cosmological theory of the legendary Mt. Meru, as the center of the 'realm of desire'. This is associated with the dogma of six 'passion deity families' constituting the upper strata of the 'realm of desire'. On four lower tiers of the sacred mountain are the four kings with their heaven. The heaven of the thirty-three gods is on the summit of Mt. Meru. Above that and successively higher are the remaining four 'passion families' of gods, starting with the Yāma ('free from strife') gods, then the Tuṣita ('happy'), the Nirmāṇarati ('whose desire is creative'), and the Paranirmitavaśavartin ('who control others by creations'). By adhering to a virtuous life, it is possible to get reborn among certain ones of the six 'passion families'.

Thus, B.C. Law, citing stories from the Vimānavatthu Commentary, gives a number of illustrations of extraordinary charity and other kindnesses by both men and women (mostly the latter) rewarded by rebirth in either the heaven of the thirty-three gods or the Nirmāṇarati heaven.[15] According to Buddhist legend Mahāmāyā, the mother of Gautama, on her death was reborn in the Tuṣita heaven.[16]

B. *Prophecies for monks*. Previously, we presented the passage about the Dharma-mirror. Besides, Asaṅga states in his *Śrāvakabhūmi*:[17]

> What is the person who has only seven rebirths ahead of him? Whatever person, who through elimination of the three fetters, to wit, of view of the transitory aggregate, of adherence to [anti-Buddhist] rules and usages, and of doubt becomes a 'stream-enterer', possessing a nature not liable to fall [to evil existences], having the set goal of enlightenment, having only seven rebirths ahead of him, seven times spending time, transmigrating among gods and men; puts an end to suffering—that one is called 'the person who has only seven rebirths ahead of him'.

The passage agrees with the Dharma-mirror discussion, namely, that a prophecy is possible for the disciple who has 'entered the stream'; but now the information is furnished that in order to 'enter the stream', the disciple must have eliminated the three fetters—a well-known set in Buddhist doctrine.

Then there is the Buddha's adversary Devadatta. When he attempted a schism in the Buddha's order—an attempt which failed—as I read in Thomas book the Buddha "declared that Devadatta was destined to stages of punishment, to hell, doomed to stay there for a cycle, and incurable".[18] After Devadatta's attempts to assassinate the Buddha—each of which failed, Devadatta died; and it is reported that the Buddha prophesied, "that after 100,000 cycles [in the Avīci hell] he would be reborn as a pacceka-buddha [Skt., Pratyekabuddha] named Aṭṭhissara". Thomas also informs us of a variant of the story in the Buddhist Mahāyāna classic scripture *Saddharma-puṇḍarīka* that the one who had been known as Devadatta would become a Tathāgata (a title of the Buddha) named Devarāja.[19] The point is not whether one version of the story is better than the other; the main thing is that these Buddhist traditions really believed that the Buddha made such predictions.

The Mahāyāna—Types of Prophecy

In the Mahāyāna period, there were predictions for Bodhisattvas, especially four kinds in the *Śūraṃgamasamādhisūtra,* for which there is a French translation and elaborate notes by Lamotte.[20]

1. The prediction concerning the person who has not yet aroused the mind of enlightenment (*anutpāditabodhicittavyākaraṇa*). A person who has taken birth in one of the five destinies, either good or bad has keen faculties and aspires to the noble doctrine. The Tathāgata recognizes this person; and predicts that after eons this person will generate the mind of enlightenment, that after more eons of Bodhisattva practice, while venerating crores of Buddhas he will obtain the perfect enlightenment and with a certain name will establish a Buddha land.

2. The prediction conferred on the person who has just aroused the mind of enlightenment (*utpāditabodhicittavyākaraṇa*). This *sūtra* makes further qualifications of this person, namely, that he has for a long time planted the virtuous roots (*avaropitakuśalamūla*), cannot be turned back, and so on. The Tathāgata predicts that he will reach someday the incomparable complete enlightenment and will have such Buddha name and such a Buddha land.

3. The withheld prediction (*rahovyākaraṇa*). There are Bodhisattvas who, though not having obtained a prediction, always energetically seek the incomparable complete enlightenment. In every possible way they practice giving; despite temptation they do not violate morality; impartially disposed to all the beings, they have the power of forbearance; going about with striving they seek all the virtuous natures (*kuśaladharma*); skilled in mindfulness and awareness (*smṛtisamprajanyakuśala*) they can attain the four Dhyāna states (in the 'realm of form'); promoting their insight (*prajñā*), they exhibit the enlightenment (*bodhi*) of the Buddha. After practicing for a long time, those six perfections (*pāramitā*), they gain the marks of the Buddha (*buddhalakṣaṇa*). Then other Bodhisattvas, besides Devas, Nāgas, Yakṣas, Gandharvas, etc., will think, "A Bodhisattva who goes about with such striving is truly extraordinary. How long will it take him to obtain the incomparable complete enlightenment? What will be his name? What will be his land (*kṣetra*)? How many will be his disciples?" Then the Buddha before the entire assembly will give the answers to all these questions; and thereafter these beings will regard that Bodhisattva as though the Bhagavat (lord) himself. However, by magical force (*adhiṣṭhānabala*) the Buddha had kept that Bodhisattva away from the assembly, and so he does not know whether or not he has obtained a prediction.

4. The prediction made in the presence of the one who has the forbearance toward the non-arising natures (*anutpattikadharma-kṣāntilabdhasaṃmukhavyākaraṇa*). Certain Bodhisattvas have for a long time cultivated virtuous roots, and so on; have contemplated non-self (*anātman*) and the void (*śūnya*); and being convinced that *dharmas* do not arise are not disturbed about the non-arising (*anutpādakṣānti*). The Buddha, recognizing the perfect merits (*puṇya*) and insight (*prajñā*) of this Bodhisattva, before a great assembly of gods and men, ascetics and brahmins, Māra and Brahmā, gives this prophecy, saying to him: "Son of the family, in such-and-such myriads of eons, you will become a Buddha having such name, such land, such number of disciples, and such will be your length of life." When the Buddha was asked, if there are actually Bodhisattvas who have received such predictions, he mentioned some, coming to the main ones:

> Finally, Dṛdhamati, I myself, Maitreya, and the thousand Bodhisattvas of the Fortunate Eon (*bhadrakalpa*) have all received the prediction conferred in the presence of those who have the forbearance toward the non-arising natures.[21]

By "I, myself" the Buddha refers to the prophecy that he would become the Buddha Śākyamuni, after three incalculable eons. By the prophecy of Maitreya is meant the prediction that this Bodhisattva will be the next Buddha.[22]

About historical Buddhists, probably the most well-known is the prophecy of Nāgārjuna, founder of the Mādhyamika school. The *Laṅkāvatāra-sūtra* has this:

> After the passing of the lord (*nātha*), who will carry this [Dharma], pray tell? O Mahāmati, you should know who, sometime after the Sugata's Nirvāṇa, will uphold the [Buddha's] way—in Vedalī of the Southern country, a Bhikṣu illustrious and famous, whose name is pronounced Nāga, destroyer of the one-sided [views] 'being' and 'non-being'. After proclaiming my vehicle, the unsurpassed Mahāyāna to the world and attaining the Joyful Stage [the first Bodhisattva Stage, Pramuditā], he will proceed to the Happy Land (Sukhāvatī).[23]

Even though the *Laṅkāvatāra-sūtra* composed circa 4th century A.D. is later than the presumed date of Nāgārjuna, circa early 2nd century A.D., the point should not be overlooked that such prophecies as these, given that they appear to have been written after the fact, still show the strong belief in them held by the Buddhist, and so have this importance independent of whether they are true predictions.

And there is this somewhat mysterious prophetic language cited from a work *Fulfillment of the Mahāyāna*: "In future times, my sons will be three—one will serve others without stint; one will increase the treasures of the father; one will requite the spiritual lineage of the Lion."[24] The three appear to go with the three 'Jewels'—Buddha, Dharma, Saṅgha. This is because the 'Lion' would refer to the name Śākyasiṁha, epithet or alternate name of Śākyamuni; and the prophecy would apply to the future Buddha Maitreya. Dharma is evidently meant by 'treasures of the father', so this is the prophecy of Nāgārjuna. The prophecy that would apply to the Saṅgha (of monks, nuns and lay followers) may well be indicated by the *Saddharmapuṇḍarīka-sūtra,* Chap. 28, when the Bodhisattva Samantabhadra pledges:

> "O World-Honored, One! If... in the last five hundred years,... a bhikṣu, or bhikṣuṇī, or upāsaka, or upāsikā who...wishes to cultivate and practice this Scripture of the Dharma Blossom, then for three weeks he must single-mindedly persevere with vigor. When he has fulfilled three weeks, I mounted on my white elephant with six tusks, will together with incalculable bodhisattvas personally circumambulate him, appearing before that person in body beheld with joy by all living beings, preaching Dharma to him, demonstrating to him, teaching him, benefiting and delighting him."[25]

What in Man is the Subject of Prophecy? (Part I)

In the foregoing I believe to have gathered enough information to establish that the ancient Buddhists as well as the much later ones accepted prophecy as a fact for religious experience. Besides, I set forth and discussed the theory of the 'divine eye' as the faculty which enables prophecy. It was also clear that the theory of *karma* is involved, since the Indians took *karma* as the cause of destiny. But so far there has been no treatment of what in man is the subject of prophecy. Some scholars might even deny that there is such a subject, since the Buddhists stress 'non-self' (*anātman*). Anyway, this topic is our present task.

The Mahāyāna scripture "Meeting of Father and Son" (*Pitāputrasamāgama*), Chapter on the Tuṣita gods raises the question, "What is the *dharma* for which the Bhagavat (i.e., the Buddha) has prophesied the incomparable, rightly completed enlightenment?[26] The scripture then goes on to give its answer. Śāntideva noticed the passage and cited it with some reduction in his *Śikṣāsamuccaya*.[27] In the English translation, it is not well-rendered.[28] The scripture begins its response by another question asking whether any one of the five personal aggregates (*skandha*) of a person, namely, 'formations' (*rūpa*), feelings (*vedanā*), notions (*saṃjñā*), motivations (*saṃskāra*), and perceptions (*vijñāna*), have been prophesied by the Bhagavat the incomparable, rightly completed enlightenment. And the scripture gives its own response, namely, denying for each of those personal aggregates the incomparable...enlightenment. And then asks, "Why is that so?" Responding: Formation (*rūpam)* is a non-arising (*anutpāda*); enlightenment (*bodhi*) is a non-arising. How can a non-arising (i.e. the formation) be awakened to a non-arising (i.e., the enlightenment)?[29] So also the other four personal aggregates. The scripture continues, declaring each of the five personal aggregates to be a non-passing-away; to be a non-elaboration; to be a non-two; to be a non-shifting; to be a non-apprehension. And declaring enlightenment to be a non-passing-away, a non-elaboration, a non-two, a non-shifting, a non-apprehension. And again raising the rhetorical question: How can a non-passing-away, a non-elaboration, a non-two, a non-shifting, a non-apprehension (as is each of the five personal aggregates) be awakened to a non-passing-away, a non-elaboration, a non-two, a non-shifting, a non-apprehension (as is enlightenment)? And as before, the scripture denies the possibility.

The context of Śāntideva's *Śikṣāsamuccaya* and of this *sūtra* itself clarifies that the 'divine eye', the prophetic eye, is not operating in this situation. There is the other eye, of insight (*prajñācakṣus*), which is not a prophetic eye. The eye of insight here envisages the realm of the five personal aggregates, the enlightenment, Bodhisattvas, the Buddha, prophecy itself, as a realm devoid of function. Hence, here there is no sentient being.

We conclude that the scripture's view of this non-sentient world was brought on by the question itself. That question went this way: "What is the *dharma* for which the Bhagavat (i.e., the Buddha) has prophesied the incomparable, rightly completed enlightenment?" Considering this question, it appears that there is no denial of prophecy here. It seems to give a message that as soon as we inquire "What is the *dharma*?" the divine eye cannot give an answer and we must resort to the eye of insight.

In short, the divine eye operates in the realm of function, of *karma*, of sentient beings; and so cannot answer questions about the non-functioning or non-*karma* realm.

It might be helpful to notice what another Mahāyāna scripture has to say about this matter. This is the scripture called the *Tathāgata-guhya*. In a recently published work, I have referred to its Chap. XVII in the Derge edition of the Tibetan canon, in the following manner:

> The Bodhisattva Śāntamati asked Vajrapāṇi about prophecy. After being told there is no prophecy for a sentient being, for personal aggregates, etc., for one with sin or without sin, one in *saṃsāra*, one in Nirvāṇa; and then told there is prophecy for one who does not analyze into two—Śāntamati wondered what is the prophecy and to whom. The response gave the prophecy as 'the liberation of Tathāgata'; and to whom—those who have attained sameness (*samatā)*, explained as 'dwelling in the (non-two) limit', i.e., the 'limit of sentient being' (*sattvānta*) or 'limit of self' (*atmānta*).[30]

Now, despite the gulf that separates this way of talking from the manner of discourse found in early Buddhism, the theory of prophecy seems to be pretty much the same. Let us recall when Asaṅga gave that passage I cited about the person with seven rebirths ahead, Asaṅga did not intend an ordinary person who has the five personal aggregates, whether with sin or without sin. He intends a person who had 'entered the stream' by eliminating the three fetters, including all the realistic imputations to the five personal aggregates. The passage from the *tathāgata-guhya* scripture of course applies the case to the Bodhisattvas, who have attained sameness (*samatā),* which is 'dwelling in the limit of sentient being'. Thus, in place of the three-fetter elimination of early Buddhism, there is elimination of imputation of differences in function. It follows that the Mahāyāna prophecy is for one with the 'eye of insight', or in Mahāyāna terms, the Perfection of Insight (*prajñāpāramitā*). Thus the prophecy turns out to be for the person who has the vision of voidness of differences, i.e., the sameness as was already expounded for the chapter of the Tuṣita gods in the scripture "Meeting of Father and Son". It follows that while the 'eye of insight' is not itself prophetic, it is an essential preliminary for the prophecy. Accordingly, in the case of a Bodhisattva, it is not necessary for this person to be able to make prophecies to deserve a prophecy.

What in Man is the Subject of Prophecy? (Part II)

There has been much written on Buddhism; and despite this flood of literature doubtless many readers would feel that Buddhism has an irreconciliable contradiction. One can read in the translation by J.J. Jones of the *Mahāvastu,* Vol. One, the story of Abhiya; and read there "Again, you may think that at that time and on that occasion, the two perfume-dealers of the great city of Vasumata were some two others. No more must you think that either. And why? Because at that time and on that occasion you two—Śāriputra and Maudgalyāyana were those two perfume-dealers. The vow you made then was your initial vow."[31] And the readers who have gained their knowledge of Buddhism from such a work as that of Walpola Rahula, *What the Buddha Taught,* can read this author's approving citation of H. von Glasenapp, "The negation of an imperishable Ātman is the common characteristic of all dogmatic systems of the Lesser as well as the Great Vehicle, and, there is, therefore, no reason to assume that Buddhist tradition which is in complete agreement on this point has deviated from the Buddha's original teachings."[32] Rahula goes on to mention that a few scholars have made a vain attempt "to smuggle the idea of self into the teaching of the Buddha...". But somehow, in my own reading of Buddhist texts, I have not found it to be like Rahula describes. I need not repeat the arguments in my other essay, "The 'no-self' of Buddhism within Indian culture."[33] But one passage needs repetition, and as many times as it takes to get the significance across. There I point out, what is well-known to Pāli specialists that five days after the Buddha's first sermon to the five disciples, he gave another to the same disciples called the *Anattalakkhaṇa Sutta,* in which he told them how to contemplate each of the five personal aggregates, to wit, "this is not mine; I am not this; this is not my self".[34] Furthermore, this advice on how to contemplate the five aggregates is found in some other sermons by the Buddha. Yet, it is not alluded to at all in Rahula's book. If we grant that the five personal aggregates are not the subject of prophecy—as was expounded above—how about the contemplator, who contemplates, "this is not mine; I am not this: this is not my self"? This same sermon by the Buddha did set forth non-self as one of a threefold set, 'suffering', 'impermanence', and 'non-self'—a set that continued as a cardinal doctrine of Buddhism in the subsequent centuries.

To resolve the seeming contradiction suggested above, one must notice that Buddhist teaching is in terms of three Instructions, that of Morality, of Mental Training, and of Insight. Buddhaghosa's *Visuddhimagga* is in three parts going with the three Instructions. Also the eightfold noble path is susceptible of being subsumed under the three instructions.[35] Also, the *Mahāyāna-Sūtrālaṃkāra* shows how to subsume the six perfections (*pāramitā*) under the three instructions.[36] Asaṅga's treatise on the three instructions—which I have edited, translated, and published—states that the first one, on Morality, is the basis for the other two.[37] It is the Instruction of Morality that insists on differences, such as the difference between virtue and vice. According to the passage I cited earlier from Sthiramati, the theory of the 'divine eye' for prophecy comes from the Instruction of Samādhi. The contemplation of the five personal aggregates as non-self is in the third Instruction, that of Insight. When the *Tathāgata-guhya* scripture stated as the recipients of the prophecy, those who have attained sameness (*samatā*), it probably means also those mentioned in the Prajñāpāramitā scripture *Saptaśatikā* who have realized the 'sameness wisdom' (*samatā-jñāna*).[38] While this is a Mahāyāna teaching, doubtless it also goes with the third Instruction of Insight. Of course, the 'sameness' of the *dharmas* is not in conflict with Morality's stress on good and bad ones. That is because the disciple is expected to always adhere to Morality; and one contemplates the 'sameness' when one does so, just as one contemplates the five personal aggregates as non-self when one does so. In short, the Morality Instruction is how the disciple is supposed to live; and one is also expected to promote the eye of insight. And neither the first or third Instructions are really in conflict with the second Instruction of Samādhi. Hence, the 'divine eye' making prophecy for some kind of consciousness stream is not negated when one employs the eye of insight.

Concluding Remarks

It appears quite clear that all the Buddhists, starting with the first ones and continuing to the more recent ones—believed in prophecy. Yet when we delve into the sources and try to organize the data, we run into a mess of contradictions. We find modern spokesmen for Buddhism who insist that there is nothing in man that one could make a prophecy for, so why all these prophecies?

The present writer is not indebted or beholden to these modern spokesmen. I do not doubt the validity of the scriptures they cite. It is just that I keep on reading, including those scriptures which these modern spokesmen do not like because they do not bear out what they would like to believe the Buddha taught.

We find out that there is no contradiction between believing in prophecy and the non-self teaching. This is because this talk of 'non-self'—which the modern spokesmen would make the chief teachings of the Buddha—is not the way the Buddha treated the matter. He did not superimpose 'non-self' on the five personal aggregates along with all the other superimpositions that the intellect is prone to make.

That is why the Buddha always employed negative terms. So he told how to contemplate the five personal aggregates: "This is not mine; I am not this; this is not my self." That permitted a prophecy for the one so contemplating.

REFERENCES

1. Alex Wayman, "The Buddhist Theory of Vision," *Anjali; O.H. de A. Wijesekera Felicitation Volume* (Peradeniya, 1970), p. 29.
2. Photo ed. of Peking Tib. canons (PTT), Vol. 111, p. 36-4-7, 8, ff.
3. Alex Wayman, *Analysis of the Śrāvakabhūmi Manuscript* (Berkeley, 1961), pp. 84-5.
4. PTT, Vol . 111, p. 36-5-2.
5. PTT, Vol. 111, p. 53-2-6, 7-8.
6. *Divyāvadanam* (ed. by. P.L. Vaidya, Darbhanga, 1959), No. 2, *Pūrṇāvadanam,* k. 19; and in many other stories:

na praṇaśyanti karmāṇi api kalpaśatair api /
sāmagrīṃ prāpya kālaṃ ca phalanti khalu dehinām //

7. PTT, Vol. 55, p. 203-1-4 to -7. Cf. my separate essay, "Core Teachings," II. Karma.
8. *Parinibbāna-sutta, Dīgha Nikāya,* ii, 95. / tasmāt ihānanda, dhammādāsaṃ nāma dhammapariyāyaṃ desessāmi yena samannāgato ariyasāvako ākaṅkhamāno attano va attānaṃ vyākareyya—'khīṇanirayomhi khīṇatiracchānayoni khīṇapettivisayo khīṇāpāyaduggativinipāto sotāpannohamasmi avinipātadhammo niyato sambodhiparāyaṇo'ti.
9. Śamathadeva's *Abhidharmakośaṭīkopāyikā-nāma,* PTT, Vol. 118, p. 275-2-1.2, 3.
10. Kern, ed. *The Jātaka-mālā,* p. 220:
dṛṣṭva me caritacchāyavairūpyaṃ dharmadarpaṇe /
api nāmāgatāvegaṃ syān me dharmotsukaṃ manaḥ //
11. śubhāśubham karma sukhāsukhodayaṃ dhruvaṃ paratreti virūḍhaniścayaḥ /
apāsya pāpaṃ yatate śubhāśrayo yatheṣṭam aśraddhatayā tu gamyate //
12. Publ. in Paris by Institut d'Ethnologie, 1939.
13. Mus, pp. 232-3: lohadaṃṣṭrā mahākāyā jvalatā [bhairavāṇ striyaḥ tam āliṅgyaiva bhakṣanti paradārāpahāriṇam]
14. Cf. my separate essay "Studies in Yama and Māra" wherein there is a reconstruction of the Sanskrit names of the thirty-six 'hungry ghosts'.
15. Bimala Charan Law, *Heaven and Hell in Buddhist Perspective* (Varanasi, 1973), pp. 36-91.
16. Edward J. Thomas, *The Life of Buddha* (New York, 1952), p. 31.
17. Wayman, *Analysis* (1961), p. 84.
18. Thomas, *The Life* (1973), p. 134.
19. Thomas, *The Life* (1973), p. 135.
20. Étienne Lamotte, tr. *La Concentration de la Marche Héroïque (Śūraṃgamasamādhisūtra)* (Bruxelles, 1965), pp. 202-3, as follows.
21. Lamotte, tr. *Śūraṃgamasamadhisūtra,* pp. 214-5.
22. For the prophecy of Maitreya, see Étienne Lamotte, *Histoire du Boudhisme Indiên* (Louvain, 1958), pp. 775-88. The prophecy of Maitreya accounts for the most famous chapter (no. 22) of *The Book of Zambasta; A Khotanese poem on Buddhism,* ed. and tr. by R.E. Emmerick (London, 1968), pp. 301-42.
23. Bunyiu Nanjio, ed *The Laṅkāvatāra Sūtra* (Kyoto), v. 163b-6:
paścātkāle gate nāthe brūhi ko 'yaṃ dhariṣyati //
nirvṛte sugate paścātkālo 'tīto bhaviṣyati /
mahāmate nibodha tvaṃ yo netrīṃ dhārayiṣyati //
dakṣiṇāpathavedalyāṃ bhikṣuḥ śrīmān mahāyaśāḥ /
nāgāhvayaḥ sa nāmnā tu sadasatpakṣadārakaḥ //
prakāśya loke madyānaṃ mahāyānam anuttaram /
āsādya bhūmiṃ muditāṃ yāsyate 'sau sukhāvatīm //
24. Cited in Vajravarman's *Vyākhya-sundarālaṃkāra-nāma* commentary on the *Sarvadurgatipariśodhana-tantra,* Peking Tanjur, Photo edition Rgyud-'grel, Vol. Khu, f. 6b-3, 4, 5: */ de yaṅ bcom ldan 'das kyis theg pa chen po mṅon par rdzogs pa'i mdo las / dus 'gyur 'di yi phyi ma la / ṅa yi sras ni rnam pa gsum / gcig ni mi thogs gźan gyi bran / gcig ni pha yi gter rnams 'tsheṅ / gcig ni seṅ ge'i gduṅ 'tshab yin źes gsuṅs so /*
25. Leon Hurvitz, tr. *Scripture of the Lotus Blossom of the Fine Dharma* (New York, 1976), pp. 333-4.
26. PTT, Vol. 23, p. 169-3-6: */ gaṅ bcom 'das kyis bla na med pa yaṅ dag par rdzogs*

pa'i byaṅ chub tu luṅ bstan pa'i chos de gaṅ zhig /.

27. *Sikṣāsamuccaya of Śāntideva,* ed. by P.L. Vaidya (Darbhanga, 1961), p. 137.7, ff.
28. Cecil Bendall and W.H.D. Rouse, *Śikṣā-samuccaya, a Compendium of Buddhist Doctrine, compiled by Śāntideva* (London, 1922), p. 237.
29. Ed. Vaidya (n. 27, above), p. 137.10: tat katham anutpādo 'nutpādam abhisambudhyate?
30. Alex Wayman and R. Tajima, *The Enlightenment of Vairocana* (Motilal Banarsidass, Delhi, 1992), p. 52.
31. J.J. Jones, *The Mahāvastu,* Vol. I (London, 1949), p. 38.
32. Walpole Sri Rahula, *What the Buddha Taught* (Bedford, England, 1972 reprint), p. 55.
33. Also included in this set of twenty-four essays.
34. Cf. the entry about this scripture in G.P. Malalasekera, *Dictionary of Pāli Proper Names,* Vol. I, pp. 62-3. I used the edition of the Pāli Saṃyutta-nikāya, iii, wherein it is called the *Pañca Sutta,* named after the five disciples who audited it.
35. Cf. Nyanatiloka, *Buddhist Dictionary* (Colombo, 1950), p. 81, on Magga, 'Path'.
36. Cf. Alex Wayman, tr. *Ethics of Tibet: Bodhisattva section of Tsong-kha-pa's Lam rim chen mo* (State University of New York Press, Albany, 1991), 109-10.
37. Alex Wayman, *Buddhist Insight,* essays, edited and introduced by George R. Elder (Delhi, 1984), p. 358.
38. So far I have not published my studies of this *pāramitā* scripture found in PTT. Vol. 21 with its commentary by Vimalamitra in PTT, Vol. 94.

SECTION III
BUDDHIST DOCTRINE

avyāhṛtaṃ vyāhrtāc chreya āhuḥ
satyaṃ vaded vyāhṛtaṃ tad dvitīyaṃ /
dharmyaṃ vaded vyāhṛtaṃ tat tṛtīyaṃ
priyaṃ vaded vyāhrtaṃ tac caturthaṃ //

Mbh., Śāntiparvan

Silence is said to be better than to say anything; to say the truth is the second best.
To say what is consistent with *dharma* is the third; to say what is agreeable is the fourth best.

12

Core Teachings: Suffering, Karma, Seed Consciousness, Dharma

Since my essays on Buddhist doctrine tend to become technical to limited aspects, I have decided to write an essay on more fundamental points of Buddhist theory, which can be referred to as 'Core Teachings'. And yet also here there occurs considerable technicality, which is inevitable when one rests the case on authoritative sources.

The fundamental positions had to be headed by 'suffering' (*duḥkha*).[1] Then the theory of *karma* as life continuance and destiny. Third, the section on 'seed consciousness' treats matters that occasioned much dispute among the Buddhist sects. Finally, there is the most difficult topic—Dharma.

I. Suffering—A Noble Truth

The rendition 'suffering' is for the Sanskrit work *duḥkha*, and 'truth' is for the word *satya*. This 'suffering' is the first of the four Noble Truths (*ārya-satya*); and 'noble' can be construed as an adjective or a noun. So, it is 'noble truth' or 'truth of the nobles' (followers of the Buddha). This truth of suffering is the basis for the other three, to wit, "There is the source (*samudaya*) of suffering;" "There is the cessation (*nirodha*) of the suffering;" "There is the path (*mārga*) leading to the cessation of suffering." Some authors have challenged the translation to *duḥkha* by 'suffering' or 'pain', claiming that this rendition falsely places Buddhism in the camp of pessimism, and even advised the non-translation of the term. The present writer feels that such authors are self-elected protectors of Buddhism in what they believe to be its vulnerable spot. But since Buddhism spread to Asian countries by its appeal of the Bodhisattva practice, where some person promotes his compassion for the suffering of mankind and aspires to liberate the sentient beings—it seems rather than this being the vulnerable spot of Buddhism, it is indeed its strength. And whether it were its strength or its weakness, the business of translators is to translate, arriving at the best possible rendition in the given context; and so I arrive at the rendition 'suffering' (or 'pain') for *duḥkha*.

Then the question arises, what is this suffering that is the first Noble Truth? There are two ways of answering this question that are prevalent in Buddhism: (1) by a set of alternate terms; (2) where *duḥkha* is equated with the five personal aggregates.

(1) The set of alternate terms is already alluded to in the initial sermon of Buddhism: Setting into Motion the Wheel of the Dharma, as the 'three turnings' (*triparivarta*), multiplying the four truths to yield twelve aspects, whereby the first Noble Truth has itself, *duḥkha*, plus three more aspects to make a set of four alternate terms, namely, *duḥkha* (the painful), *anitya* (the impermanent) *anātmaka* (the non-self), and *śūnya* (the void). The first three (painful, impermanent, non-self) are sometimes referred to as the 'three characters' (*lakṣaṇa*). For a brief explanation of the four terms, I may refer to the *Arthaviniścaya-ṭīkā* (author unknown, Tibetan Tanjur, PTT. Vol. 145,

p. 162-1, 2) in description of the *saṃskāra* (motivation) aggregate:

> It is impermanent, because it perishes in each instant. It is painful, because possessing the nature (*dharma*) of birth, old age, and so on. It is void, because those *saṃskāras* are not the self imagined by the heretics. It is non-self because precisely those are not the own-being (*svabhāva*) of self imagined by the heretics.

However, the questions naturally arise: How can those terms be included in one set? They are not really synonyms, are they? Their answer lies in the section on *dharma*. There is an underlying 'true nature' (*dharmatā*) for the set, such that they are neither synonyms nor mutual causes; yet naturally lead from one to the other.

(2) The other way is to take *duḥkha* as equivalent to the five personal aggregates (*skandha*). This is not explicitly stated in the *Dhammapada*, 277-9: "All *saṃkhāras* (S. *saṃskāra*) are impermanent;" "All *saṃkhāras* are suffering (*dukkha*);" "All *dhammas* (S. *dharma*) are non-self." So also, the four 'aphorisms of the Dharma' (*Mahāyāna-Sūtrālaṃkāra*, XVIII. 80, and commentary): "All *saṃskāras* are impermanent; all *saṃskāras* are suffering; all *dharmas* are non-self; Nirvāṇa is calm (*śānta*)." One should notice in the above that the statement. "All *saṃskāras* are suffering" agrees with my essay on *dharma* that the 72 'constructed natures' can be subsumed in the five personal aggregates. Thus it is through *dharma* that the identification is made. Of course, suffering experience begins with the person, and then by empathy is extended to other sentient beings. However, when *saṃskāras* are said to be 'impermanent', it is by their nature as 'constructions'; and when they are said to be 'suffering', it is by their nature as 'motivations'. Hence, one may render the two aphorisms differently: "All constructions are impermanent" and "All motivations are suffering".

The three kinds of misery (duḥkhatā). The second aphorism, "All motivations are suffering" can be clarified by the theory of three kinds of misery. Asaṅga (*Viniścayasaṃgrahaṇī* on *Cintāmayī bhūmi*, PTT, Vol. 111, p. 28-3, 4) identifies them with the three standard feelings—painful, pleasurable, and neither painful nor pleasurable. The first one is the misery of suffering (*duḥkha*), and as the painful kind of feeling, it is the misery experienced and acknowledged in the world, since the pair 'pain and pleasure' (*duḥkha* and *sukha*) are among the eight worldly *dharmas*, of course comprehended by ordinary persons. This kind of misery is stated in the *Arthaviniścayta-ṭīkā* (Tibetan Tanjur, PTT, Vol. 145, p. 209-2, 3): the pain of birth, old age, and sickness; the pain of guarding, when one has gained (valuables); the pain of not having them (i.e., valuables); the pain due to matters beyond one's control (e.g., in life, fearful agencies; and at death, seizure by Yama and his messengers). And then the pains due to derivatives of the four elements, for which various remedies may be applied. Thus, to dispel the pain (or pangs) of hunger, there is food; to dispel the pain of heat and cold, and the shame of one's body, there are clothes; to dispel the pain of sleepiness and weariness, there is a bed; to dispel the pain of coming and going, there is a vehicle; to dispel the pain of illness, there is a medical prescription. Thus, the misery of suffering (*duḥkha-duḥkhatā*) covers the pains which people can do something about, as well as those recognized to be outside of one's control.

The second misery is the misery of change (*vipariṇāma*), and as the pleasurable kind of feeling, it is not recognized as misery by ordinary persons. So *Saṃyutta-Nikāya,* Part IV (Saḷayatana-Vagga), p. 127: / yam pare sukhato āhu / tad ariyā āhu dukkhato/ "What other, call 'happiness' that the noble ones call 'suffering'." This is the application of the first aphorism, "All constructions are impermanent," and pleasure being impermanent, it is succeeded by sorrow.

The third misery is the misery of motivations (*saṃskāra*), and as the feeling that is neither painful nor pleasurable, it is also not recognized as misery by ordinary persons. Asaṅga explains (*ibid.*, p. 28-3, 4):

> It was in connection with the misery of motivations that the Lord said: "In short, the five grasping aggregates are suffering." What is the misery of motivations? These and those bodies with motivations generated by *karma* and defilement (*kleśa*) arising, and any place subject to thorough-going contamination (*dauṣṭhulya*) consistent with the arising of all the defilement and suffering—that is called contamination and is the misery of motivations (*saṃskāra-duḥkhatā*).

Asaṅga also mentions that this 'misery of motivations' is evidenced by the four waywardnesses (*viparyāsa*), i.e., regarding the impermanent as permanent, the painful as pleasurable, the unclean as clean, the non-self as self; and concludes, "Hence this feeling which is neither painful nor pleasurable is the trace (*anuśaya*) of nescience (*avidyā*)." So Asaṅga includes in his *Paramārtha-gāthā*:[2]

> Whatever the abode that is made, that the noble ones know as suffering. Thereby the immature (*bāla*) always suffer. It is not appeased even for a moment.

The foregoing should have made clear that the first Noble Truth—"There is suffering"—has a portion which anybody can understand, then another part comprehensible to the 'noble' (*ārya*) who hearkens to the Buddhist teachings. The part that is ordinarily not appreciated by someone who does not listen to the precepts is the 'misery of change' and the 'misery of motivations'.

This shows that the term *duḥkha,* which we render 'suffering' or 'pain', does sometimes mean this in a concrete sense; and then sometimes has metaphorical extensions; wherefor, some persons challenge the translation 'suffering'. But to change the translation simply because a word is being employed metaphorically is a wrong principle of translation. Granted that some Sanskrit words are employed differently in various contexts, e.g., the word *bhāva;* and so one must change the translation accordingly. But *duḥkha* does not seem to change its meaning in the various passages in which it is found in Buddhist texts. To illustrate this situation, one may refer to the usage of *duḥkha* in a brief work that is attributed to Nāgārjuna—the *Pratītyasamutpāda-hṛdaya-kārikā.* Here, the author groups the twelve members of the celebrated formula under three headings. Thus, Nos. (1) nescience, (8) craving, (9) indulgence, are the three 'defilements' (*kleśa*). Nos. (2) motivations, and (10) gestation, are the two *karmas.* The seven others are the 'suffering' members, namely, (3) perception, (4), name-and-formation, (5) six sense bases, (6) (sense) contact, (7) feeling, (11) birth, (12) old age and death. Now, the seven 'suffering' members are in some cases, easily comprehended to be suffering in a concrete sense, so 11. birth, and 12. old age and death. But the remainder are not obviously so. Previously, the three kinds of feelings were associated with the three kinds of misery, so member No. (7) is taken care of. When (3) perception, (4) name-and-formation, (5) six sense bases, and (6) (sense) contact, are termed 'suffering' it must be because these are the means by which the world of suffering is evoked and experienced; and so these various means are called 'suffering' metaphorically.

A Māhāyāna scripture, the *Bodhisattva-piṭaka-sūtra* agrees with some of the foregoing observations:[3]

> Furthermore, the personality aggregates are suffering. Any characteristic of suffering (='pain') that the aggregates have is (truth of suffering). Comprehending the characteristic of suffering to be the characteristic of voidness is called 'noble truth of suffering' (or, 'truth of suffering comprehended by the nobles').

Besides, there seem to have been divergent theories as to the Cessation of Suffering' (the third Truth) and Nirvāṇa. A Mahāyāna scripture, now translated with the title *The Lion's Roar of Queen Srīmālā* has a striking solution.

> "Lord, what are the two kinds of explanation regarding the meaning of the Noble Truths? The Create and the Uncreate explanations regarding the meaning of the Noble Truths. The Create explanations of the meaning of the Noble Truths present the four Noble Truths with intellectual limitation. Why so? Because when one depends on another person, one does not seek out all suffering, eliminate all sources of suffering, directly realize the cessation of all suffering, cultivate all the paths leading to the cessation. That being the case, not only are there both the constructed and the unconstructed Saṃsāṛa (cyclical flow), but also there are both the constructed and the unconstructed Nirvāṇa."

This scripture intends that there is an 'unconstructed' (*asaṃskṛta*) Nirvāṇa, the 'Cessation of Suffering', and a 'constructed' (*saṃskṛta*) Nirvāṇa, the Buddha natures; and that there is an 'unconstructed' Saṃsāra, suffering (*duḥkha*), and a 'constructed' Saṃsāra, defilement-stores. Also ancient Buddhism regarded defilement and purification to be an individual responsibility, because 'constructed' by oneself. And the implication that the Bodhisattva could accept the responsibility for rescuing sentient beings from their various sufferings is that it is 'unconstructed' by oneself.

II. Karma

To follow a treatment of 'suffering' with a discussion of *karma* is comparable to the second Noble Truth ("There is the cause of suffering") following the first one ("There is suffering"). This is because *karma* and defilement (*kleśa*) are usually stated to be the causes of suffering. The topic of 'defilement' is treated at length in Buddhist sources, and I have gone somewhat into this matter in my paper on confession and so on.[5] Both these causes are alluded to in the brief treatise called *Pratītyasamutpādahṛdaya*, already mentioned in the foregoing section on 'suffering'. This text includes three members of Dependent Origination (*pratītya-samutpāda*) in the category of 'defilement', namely, (1) nescience (*avidyā*), (8) craving (*tṛṣṇā*), and (9) indulgence (*upādāna*); and two members in the category of *karma*, namely, (2) motivations (*saṃskāra*) and (10) gestation (*bhava*). Here I shall restrict myself to the matter of *karma*.[6]

Of those two members in the category of *karma*, I have elsewhere pointed out that member No. (2) is the 'old *karma*' and No. (10) is the 'new *karma*'.[7] The path of *karma*, usually stated as three of body, four of speech, and three of mind seems to apply to both old and new *karma*. Frequently, the No. (2) is described as virtuous (*kuśala*), unvirtuous (*akuśala*) and indeterminate (*avyākṛta*). The member No. (10) is said to be the *karma* of the three worlds, including the foods eaten.[8] It appears that No. (10) is susceptible of being dramatized,[9] and so when the Buddha is said to remember his previous lives, it would be presumably in terms of this No. (10) and perhaps this is the reason that No. (10) *bhava*, gave its name to the whole cycle, or wheel of life, called *bhavacakra*. The traditional statement of the Buddha's memory goes like this (from the Pāli): "In that one (i.e., life) I had such a name, clan, caste, such sustenance, experiencing such pleasure and pain, and having such end of life."[10] This statement also has an implication of the last two members of Dependent Origination, namely, 'birth' (*jāti*), and 'old age and death' (*jarā-maraṇa*).

I have previously cited the sentiment from the *Jātakamālā*'s "Story of an inhabitant of Brahmaloka,": "He who is imbued with conviction, 'Surely there is a world hereafter where good and bad *karma* give rise to happiness and sorrow,' having discarded sin, will persevere with virtuous resorts. But by disbelief one will proceed according to his (perverse) will."[11] This passage points to the numerous stories of *karma* to keep persons on the moral and ethical path. The literature on this topic, especially with exemplary stories is enormous. There is a large collection in the Tibetan Kanjur canon called *Karmaśataka*. The stories illustrating the routes of *karma* are in collections also called *avadāna,* thus the *Avadāna-śatakam* and the *Divyāvadāna.*[12] The *Jātakas* have their way of setting forth the principles of *karma*. A large scripture preserved in Chinese and in Tibetan, the *Ārya-Saddharmasmṛtyupasthāna* relates the particular sin that results in birth as one of the hungry ghosts (*preta*) or as a hell being among the bad destinies (*durgati*).[13] The theory as it was expressed in the above *Jātakamālā* citation is that the belief in an after-life or in future lives permits a threatening of the evil-doer that he will get his just deserts in an after-life. It may seem to Westerners that this is an unsuccessful kind of threat, otherwise thievery and worse sins would have disappeared in that culture by reason of the threats by religious leaders. However, it is a striking feature of such religious beliefs that they do have the power to dictate various actions by the devotees.

Hence a discussion of *karma* must be careful to distinguish between the admonitions to the followers, and the rationalization of the present state of affairs. It is one thing for a follower to believe that his actions may produce an effect in a future life, and another thing that amounts to an explanation of why people are the way they are in the present life. The Vedic peoples kept the two matters straight, because they believed that Varuṇa was visiting misfortune upon men in the present life by reason of their violations of the law (the *ṛta*), and also believed that Yama or his scribe could decide on the fate after death. But after the theory of *karma* and transmigration took over the minds of the Indian people, it was possible for them to become insensitive to sufferings of persons with the attitude that such dire circumstances are the result of deeds in their previous lives.

Since the present essay is dealing with the Buddhist attitudes, it should be distinguished from the general Indian point of view, now well-acknowledged in the West among followers of the Vedānta,and other Hindu offshoots that one's suffering or present state of affairs is "one's *karma*". Some Buddhist stories of *karma* may give this point of view, i.e., that one's present circumstances are "one's *karma*"—a 'produced *karma*' (*nivartya-karman*), produced by a 'changing *karma*' (*vikārya-karman*), which are the two *karmans* of the grammarians,.[14] Although Buddhism does not seem to use this terminology, it has the equivalent in Dependent

Origination where No. (2) causes No. (10) or vice versa—since these are the two *karmas* of Dependent Origination. But according to Buddhism, suffering (and joy) are the results of *karma* and defilement (*kleśa*), but not themselves *karma* or defilement. Therefore, the way of speaking, "my *karma*", disagrees with Buddhist doctrine.

The Bodhisattva movement in Buddhism that began before the rise of Mahāyāna but especially colors this later form of Buddhism, is in fact an opponent of the hard-hearted *karma* theory. Rather than hold that people are their previous acts and so there is nothing we can do about it—the Bodhisattva must believe that he can change their circumstances. Thus, the theory of the Bodhisattva's 'perfections' (*pāramitā*), for example, the first one, 'giving' (*dāna*), involves a premise that one can improve a person's misfortune of dire need by the act of giving things to him. It intends that by morality (*śīla*), one can set a good example for others to follow, and so they are susceptible to a better course of conduct that is incited by the good example. And so on with the other 'perfections'. This attitude is stated with full coverage in the *Vairocanābhisaṃbodhitantra*, Chap. VI: "Sentient beings can be benefited by the power of one's merit, by the gift power of the Tathāgata, or by the power of the Dharmadhātu." As to this "gift power", it is usually designated by *adhiṣṭhāna* (empowerment). For the power of the Dharmadhātu, see the section below "Three definitions of *dharma*." To the latter explanation can be added the abundant information in my *Study of the Vairocanābhisaṃbodhitantra*, the chapter "Mantra Efficacy per V-A-T, Chap. VI".[15] Here the Dharmadhātu power is explained as implicating the family or *kula*, more generally—the community; hence the scripture declares that *mantra* power is not due to the pronouncer. This implicates the two kinds of *karma* acknowledged by Buddhism—personal and group. These two kinds are intended when, as was mentioned in the preceding treatment of "Suffering a Noble Truth", the "misery of suffering" (*duḥkha-duḥkhatā*) is said to cover that which people have in their own control, e.g., to dispel the pangs of hunger by eating food, and that which is outside one's own control, e.g., fearful agencies such as the state police. The suffering which is outside the control of the individual would be explained as due to 'group *karma*'. The theory of the group being able to bring consequences which the individual cannot manage in fact is exhibited in nature when a large group of trees (a forest) is able to bring down the rain which a solitary tree cannot achieve.

One of the peculiarities of *karma* is its long-lasting character, which is meant of the mental *karma*, on which are based the verbal and corporeal *karma*. So teaches a verse repeated in many stories of the *Divyāvadana*:

> *na pranaśyanti karmāṇi api kalpaśatair api /*
> *sāmagrīṃ prāpya kālaṃ ca phalanti khalu dehinām //*
> The deeds are not lost even in a hundred eons. One should know (*khalu*) that they come to fruition for mankind when they get complete and at the time of death.

Since in Dependent Origination there are two *karma* members, it must be that either No. (2) *saṃskāra*, or No. (10) *bhava*, or both of them, is responsible for this long-lasting attribution. An essay of mine, "Doctrinal Affiliation of the Buddhist Master Asaṅga,"[16] shows that Asaṅga's position about life continuance is in words of the well-known *Saṅgīti Sutta* of the Dīgha-nikāya that the translators T.W. and C.A. Rhys Davids ill understood. The ancient scripture declares: *katamo eko dhammo? sabbe sattā āhāraṭṭhitikā; sabbe sattā saṅkhāraṭṭhitikā.* For the equivalent statement of the Sanskrit version Asaṅga explains: "What is a single doctrine? Sentient beings persist for a day, i.e., by food (*āhāra*). Sentient beings persist for a lifetime, i.e., by life motivation (S. *āyuḥsaṃskāra*). Sentient beings persist in rebirth, there being virtuous natures, unvirtuous natures, or indeterminate natures." Asaṅga's account makes it clear that the ancient Buddhist position was that *karma* provides the continuity, since these continuities go with *saṃskāra, bhava*, or both. The *karma* member No. (10) *bhava*, which I render 'gestation', is credited with the actual act producing rebirth, according to the citation under *Abhidharmakośa-bhāṣya*, Chap. III, on 28ab, a scripture: "Ānanda, the act which produces a new existence, such is the nature of *bhava*." Hence, the expression *punarbhava* (renewal).

But, the *karma*, however long lasting can come to an end. The above-mentioned scripture the *Vairocanābhisaṃbodhitantra* in the chapter called "The Secret Maṇḍala," has this passage, translated from the Tibetan here:[17]

> "As to maturation in this life, the fruit of *karma* matures. At the time *siddhi* ('success', 'occult talent') is attained, it is then

> that the *karmas* are warded off. Because the mind is not self-existent, because causes and effects are abandoned, one is liberated from *karma* and *āyus* (life motivation). Life is like the sky."

Buddhaguhya points out in his commentary that both *āyus* and past merits (*puṇya*) become fulfilled in this very life. One is reborn a *vidyādhara,* who can ascend toward the sky.[18]

The foregoing analysis has not dealt with *karma* in the technical sense of its efficiency, that was subject to much dispute among the Buddhist sects. Tsong-kha-pa's commentary on Candrakīrti's *Madhyamakāvatāra* goes into various of these theories; so in PTT Vol. 154, p. 52-5-7, ff. Here he mentions four theories for establishing the efficiency of karma (Tib. *las kyi nus pa*): (1) Certain Cittamātra followers (i.e., Yogācāra school) imagine it is due to the 'store consciousness' (*ālayavijñāna*). (2) Certain Vaibhāṣika (non-Kashmirian), as the commentator Avalokitavrata explained, take it to be like a debt-document, two acts that have different meaning; not saying it is 'not wasted', they believe it is a *saṃskāra.* (3) The standard Vaibhāṣika accept two *karmas* usually, one mental, the other either verbal or corporeal and deny that the two have different meanings. (4) Source not clear, a view found in the commentary on the *Abhidharmakośa,* believes that it is the stream of consciousness affected by the habit-energy (*vāsanā)* of that *karma.*

Karma shows up also in the Buddhist embryological theory, namely, in the shorter scripture, *Ārya-āyuṣman-nanda-garbhāvakrānti-nirdeśa* and in the longer version, *Ārya-nanda-garbhāvakrānti-nirdeśa.* These are in the Tibetan canon, Kanjur; in the Peking, PTT, Vol. 23, pp. 95-101, and pp. 101-15, respectively. In these scriptures, there is prominent mention of a series of 'winds' called 'wind of *karma'* which are held to show up week by week during the 38 weeks of the full term of pregnancy. These 'winds' are claimed to fashion the forms of foetal progression, eventually the various limbs and sensory organs. A summary of the contents of these scriptures, clarifying the particular 'wind of *karma*' for each of the 38 weeks was published at Dharamsala, H.P., India, in a booklet form entitled *Mdo dkon mchog brtsegs pa ga pa'i nang tshan dga' bo mngal 'jug gi mdo nas legs par btus pa.*

Abhayākaragupta treats this matter in his great commentary, the *Āmnāya-mañjari* on the *Saṃpuṭa-tantra,* in the photo ed., PTT, Vol. 55, p. 203-1-4 to -7:

/ las kho na rlung mthong byed de / des bskul ba ni bskyed pa'o / las kyis bskyed pa yang rlung ngo / rnam pa thams cad du las kho na bskul ba po ste / rlung de yang des byas pa nyid kyi phyir ro / yang na mthong ba dang ma mthong ba dag de ltar bstan pa dag go / de ltar ni las la spyod ces pa 'dis ni ma mthong ba ste / las kyi rlung zhes pa 'dis ni mthong ba 'o /

Only *karma* makes the wind visible. Exhorted by it, (the wind) is generated and the wind is engendered by the *karma*. *Karma* alone is the exhorter in every manner, because that wind is created by it. Besides, it (the *karma*) is shown to be invisible and visible. Accordingly, the practical kind of *karma* is invisible. The *karma* wind is visible.

/ de ltar mthong ba dang ma mthong ba tshogs pa las byung ba ni 'bras bu'o zhes pa'i grub mtha' rjes su mthun par 'gyur ro / las kyi rlung 'di de yang lte ba'i 'og tu gnas te / de skad du yang sngar gsungs pa / sum mdo'i phyogs su gnas pa yi / las kyis byas pa las kyi rlung zhes dang / las kyi rlung bskyed byas pa / lte ba'i dkyil 'khor du 'bar ro zes so /

Accordingly, the result ('fruit') which arises from the coming-together that is visible or invisible agrees with the "theory system" (*siddhānta*). Also, this *karma*-wind abides beneath the navel, i.e., dwells in the triple fork, a terminology previously used. And, the *karma*-wind is created by the *karma* (so dwelling). And when the *karma*-wind gets generated, it blazes in the navel-*maṇḍala*.

Abhayākaragupta clarifies that the term *karma* can be used in two ways—the context in which it is invisible called the practical kind of *karma* and the context in which it is said to be visible, by producing the visible form of the body. His second statement alludes to the two textual sources of these statements. There is a non-*tantric* component, such as is treated in the "theory systems"; and here Vasubandhu's *Abhidharmakośa* would suffice. Also, there is this special *tantric* tradition—the *Saṃpuṭa-tantra* on which he comments; and in this tradition the topic gets related to corporeal centers.

III. Seed Consciousness

There have been many studies—East and West, on the nature of consciousness, and the attempt to deal with what can be called "seed consciousness" in only a few pages may seem presumptious. Of course, the topic is necessarily limited to Buddhism; and here a judicious selection of sources may hopefully cover the main ideas. We start with a verse of the *Dharmasamuccaya,* Chap. XI, k. 101:[19]

> *nāśaṃ prayāti vasudhā sāgaraś cāpi śuṣyati /*
> *cittena yat kṛtaṃ citraṃ tad anubhavanasthitam //*
> The kingdom crumbles and the lake dries up, but the painting created by the mind remains in experience.

There turns out to be a difference of opinion in regard to the nature of this 'painting'. It has been observed by persons examining the nature of consciousness that people are exhibiting only some of their attributes at a given time; that other virtues and vices may stay hidden for a while, to emerge into light under other circumstances of temptation and trial. Where do these other tendencies stay when they are not exhibited? Is it a 'subconsciousness' or an 'unconsciousness'? If we say that they stay in the form of 'seeds', one should appreciate the implication of so calling them. This is because a seed has apparently contradictory features: it does not change, e.g., when it grows into an oak tree. In terms of Dependent Origination, that same work previously alluded to, when grouping the members into 'defilement' ones, *'karma'* ones, and 'suffering' ones, heads the suffering group with *vijñāna* ('consciousness', 'perceptions'). This is what must create the painting that is said to remain.

For explaining the 'painting' itself, a possible solution could accept it under the category of 'defilement' (*kleśa*), and another solution would explain it as a '*karma*'. The pointing to *anuśaya* (kind of defilement) as the *bīja* (seed) is well-discussed in Jaini's article, "The Sautrāntika theory of *bīja*".[20] The trouble with such an identification is that these seeds need not be defiled. It is therefore well to cite some passages with these other kinds of seeds, so that we may arrive at a decision about the nature of these seeds.

Jaini calls my attention to the one cited in the Abhidharma literature (Yaśomitra's commentary) where the Buddha noticed in a certain person who had been discounted for ordination that he had hidden in him the very subtle seed of liberation (*mokṣabījam...*

susukṣmam). In Mahāyāna literature the *Gaṇḍavyūha* has this:

> / *bodhicittaṃ hi kulaputra bījabhūtaṃ sarvabuddha-dharmāṇām*
> Son of the family, the Thought of Enlightenment is the seed, so to say, of all the Buddha natures.

The *Ratnagotravibhāga* (I, 34ab) states:

> / *bījaṃ yesām agrayānādhimuktir mātā prajñā buddhadharma-prasūtyai* /
> Whose seed is the conviction in the superior vehicle; whose mother is the insight for giving birth to the Buddha natures.

Tsong-kha-pa, whose Bodhisattva section of the *Lam rim chen mo* cites these passages however, explains that the Thought of Enlightenment is like the father seed, and that the insight intuiting non-self is like a mother. This is consistent with Indian theory of embryology, wherein the father is given credit for the seed of the child with the mother adding various other essential substances. Finally, Mātṛceta's *Śatapañcāśatka*, k. 19:

> / *samyaksaṃbodhibījasya cittaratnasya tasya te* /
> / *tvam eva vīra sārajño dūre tasyetaro janaḥ* //
> "That seed of right, complete enlightenment, your jewel of mind, only you know its core, O hero! Other persons are in a far-off place (i.e., in a blundering state)."

These examples[21] show that the term 'seed' (*bīja*) is sometimes used in place of 'cause' (*hetu*). But the term 'seed' is employed advisedly with a connotation that the word 'cause' does not have. Besides, what I previously mentioned for the seed, it resists inside inspection by ordinary man, who has to wait for the seed to sprout, etc. before being able to say something relevant about *that* seed.

As to the Buddha's ability to observe the very subtle seed of liberation in a person, this can be credited to two sorts of 'eyes' according to Sthiramati's commentary on the *Mahāyānasūtrālaṃkāra* Bodhipakṣya chapter: "The eye of *dharma* understands without impediment...the stream of consciousness of persons in the sense of discriminating whether it is an ordinary person, or one of the eight classes of disciples (on the four paths or in the fruits of the four paths), or a Bodhisattva and if so, then on which of the ten Bodhisattva Stages...." And, "The eye of a Buddha understands all *dharmas*..., understands the state of Arhat ensuing from the 'diamond-like *samādhi*' and the freedom from fluxes of the Tathāgatas."[22] In terms of our previous terminology, this 'eye of a Buddha' can understand the seed when it has not yet sprouted and is only there in its changeless 'own-nature' (*svabhāva*), while the 'eye of *dharma*' can understand the seed as soon as it sprouts and thus undergoes change. It is presumably for this reason that Sthiramati added for the 'eye of *dharma*' that it sees the *dharmas* in the conventional sense (*saṃvṛtitas*), while adding for the 'eye of Buddha' that it understands all *dharmas,* 'whether with or without flux, whether constructed or unconstructed'.

The foregoing suggests that the explanation of seed as *anuśaya* has the flaw of limiting the seed to defilement. In greater generality, the seed can be referred to as *dharma,* defiled or undefiled. Perhaps it is for this reason that the Yogācāra school adopted the terminology of 'store consciousness' (*ālayavijñāna*).

La Vallée Poussin has many references to *bīja* in his *Vijñaptimātratāsiddhi* and has a whole chapter devoted to the topic.[23] These are technical arguments by the followers of the Yogācāra school, who accept the basic theories of the 'store-consciousness' (*ālayavijñāna*) and the 'evolving perceptions' (*pravṛtti-vijñāna*), but then dispute certain subtle points. The chapter discusses the definition of *ālayavijñāna* as *sarvabījaka* ("all-seeded"). The discussion points out (p. 103-4) that the *Laṅkāvatāra* and other texts state that sentient beings are naturally (*prakṛti*) diversified into five families (*gotra*) involving *dharmatābījas* (seeds of underlying nature), meaning that a given family shares the seed(s). And the *Bodhisattvabhūmi* is cited (p. 104) for an explanation that the Bodhisattva has a natural *gotra,* acquired from the underlying nature (*dharmatā*), which has an uninterrupted lineage from time immemorial. And there are discussions of pure and impure 'seeds'.

Now, the German scholar Schmithausen has recently published a large collection in two parts on the *ālayavijñāna* with a different reason given for the inception of the *ālayavijñāna* doctrine.[24] He starts his reasoning by citing a passage from Asaṅga's *Samāhitābhūmi,* which is one of the 17 *bhūmis* of the *Yogācārabhūmi.* In order not to misrepresent him, I shall repeat his rendition of the passage (p. 18):

> "When [a person] has entered [Absorption into] Cessation (*nirodha [samāpatti]*), his mind and mental [factors] have ceased; how then is it that his mind (*vijñāna*) has not withdrawn from [his] body?— [Answer: No problem;] for [in] his [case] *ālayavijñāna* has not ceased [to be present] in the material sense-faculties, which are unimpaired; *ālayavijñāna* which comprises (/possesses/has received) the seeds of the forthcoming [forms of] mind (*pravṛttivijñāna*), so that they are bound to re-arise in future (i.e., after emerging from absorption)."

This scholar felt that the passage has not received its deserved attention and soon (p. 35) told why: "...as in *nirodhasamāpatti* viz., that without the presence of some kind of *vijñāna* to appropriate, i.e., keep alive, corporeal matter the person entering this state [*asamjñisamāpatti*] would die... ." So Schmithausen believes that the theory of *ālayavijñāna* was introduced to account for the continuance of life when the yogin enters certain higher states that entail a cessation of mental precesses. But on p. 204, he correctly points out from Asaṅga's *Yogācārabhūmi*: "the state of lacking (i.e., having eliminated) *ālayavijñāna* is expressly attributed to Buddhas and to Bodhisattvas not liable to turning back as well as to Arhats and to Pratyekabuddhas." This means that when the Buddha found out this state of *nirodhasamāpatti* to tell his disciples about it; and any of those others going into it, he and they would automatically have died for lack of an *ālayavijñāna*. Observe that this author did not find Asaṅga himself admitting that the *ālayavijñāna*'s introduction into Buddhist doctrine was to furnish a good reason why meditators do not die when they get into certain trances. It was Schmithausen's own conclusion.

In my preceding essay on *karma*, I showed from Asaṅga's *Yogācārabhūmi* that life continuance is due to *karma* in terms of its two members of Dependent Origination. Therefore, Asaṅga reasonably had other grounds for adopting the theory of *ālayavijñāna*.

But the foregoing while indicating Asaṅga's position somewhat still does not address the particular passage which Schmithausen deems so important. It should therefore be pointed out that Vasubandhu has a similar statement in his commentary, *Pratītyasamutpādādi-vibhaṅganirdeśa* on the *vijñāna* member, at

PTT, Vol. 104, p. 285-4-7, ff.:

> */ mdo sde las 'gog pa'i snyoms par 'jug pa sems dang bcas par gsungs te / 'gog pa la snyoms par zhugs pa ni lus kyi 'du byed ma 'gags pa yin zhes bya ba nas rnam par shes pa lus nang ma bral ba yin no zhes 'don pa'i phyir ro / de bas na lhag ma med pa'i mya ngan las 'das kyi bar du rnam par shes pa rgyud chad pa ma yin no /*
>
> According to the *sūtra* it is said that *nirodhasamāpatti* is attended with consciousness, because it annqunces that in *nirodhasamāpatti*, the life-motivation (*āyuḥsaṃskāra*) of the body does not stop, while *vijñāna* is not absent in the body. Hence, there is no break in *vijñāna* up to Nirvāṇa without remainder.

Then Vasubandhu goes into the problem of what is this *vijñāna*. He points out that the claim by some that it is the *manovijñāna* has the difficulty that this *vijñāna* has a *dharma* as its object, and has other difficulties that he mentions. Later in his discussion, he brings up the term *ālayavijñāna* (at p. 288-1-2): "Why is it called *ālayavijñāna*? It is the place of seeds of all the *dharmas*" (*ci'i phyir 'di kun gzhi rnam par shes pa zhes bya zhe na / chos thams cad kyi sa bon gyi gzhi gang yin pa'o*). This shows why the Tibetans translate *ālaya* by *kun gzhi*, to wit, "place for all". At p. 288-3-4 in the Tibetan, Vasubandhu refers to the *Yogācārabhūmi* and the *Saṃdhinirmocanasūtra* (the basic scripture of the Yogācāra) for authority of using the term *ālayavijñāna*. And then he refers to the well-known dilemma of later commentators to explain the ancient Buddhist teaching that although Dependent Origination has 'name-and-formation' (*nāma-rūpa*) arising in dependence on *vijñāna*, it added the puzzling remark that *vijñāna* arises in dependence on 'name-and-formation'. At p. 288-4-4, he states that the *vijñāna* that arises in dependence on 'name-and-formation' is the maturation *vijñāna (vipāka-v.)*, which earlier, at p. 288-1-3, he had given as another name of the *ālayavijñāna*. Schmithausen, p. 174, calls my attention to the line of Asaṅga's *Yogācārabhūmi* text, p. 230-8-9, which Schmithausen correctly interprets as a 'doubling' of *vijñāna*. This is when the *pratisandhi-vijñāna* had entered the womb (and *sammūrchate* had fainted or become unconscious). Here, Asaṅga's text has this: */ tan nāmapratyayaś ca punas tad vijñānaṃ tatra pratiṣṭhaṃ labhate/*

"When there is dependence on *nāma* (the incorporeal personal aggregates), that *vijñāna* is again established there." This *nāma* has to be the three non-*rūpa* personal aggregates, excluding *vijñāna*, as the Pāli commentator Buddhaghosa mentioned.[25] *Nāma* could not include *vijñāna*, or else *vijñāna* would arise from itself, which is a type of causation denied in Buddhism. Thus, the words *tatra pratiṣṭhaṃ labhate* (is established there) indicate that *vijñāna* is added to the three to make four *nāma* personal aggregates (*skandha*). Hence, this position of the Yogācāra school claims that this fourth kind of *nāma* is the entire set of *vijñānas,* starting with *ālayavijñāna* and then the 'evolving perceptions' (*pravṛtti-v.).* Thus, even if one belongs to the Buddhists who reject the notion of *ālayavijñāna* and assert that the *vijñāna*, 3rd member of Dependent Origination, which falls into the womb unconscious, does revive on the basis of other personal aggregates, he should admit that originally the *nāma* were the three, the well-known 'notions' (*saṃjñā*), 'feelings' (*vedanā*), and 'motivations' (*saṃskāra*). It is usual in Abhidharma works to assign four aggregates to the *nāma* part of the 'name-and-formation' (*nāma-rūpa*), because for practical purposes this is the case in the generality of Buddhist discussions.

My paper "Vasubandhu, Teacher Extraordinary"[26] made some use of Vasubandhu's commentary on Asaṅga's *Mahāyāna-Saṃgraha.* This paper already pointed out on the basis of this commentary that the *vijñāna* which is reborn is the defiled *manas* (*kliṣṭa-manas*), which therefore must convey the store of defiled seeds that are comprised by the 'store consciousness'. Then to the problem of certain exalted beings no longer having an *ālayavijñāna,* or of having 'transmuted' it, Vasubandhu in that commentary points out that in the 'Path of Vision' (*darśana-mārga*): in the same way as the 'store consciousness' is a cause of 'defiling natures' (*saṃkleśa-dharma*), so 'right mental orientation' (*samyagmanasikāra*) is a cause of 'purifying natures' (*vyavadāna-dharma*). This shows that the act of creating 'seeds' is a characteristic faculty of human consciousness. One can create defiled seeds and so also pure seeds. Therefore, when those certain beings were said to have eliminated the 'store consciousness' the mere statement did not disallow for them other forms of seed consciousness. Thus, we saw the 'Thought of Enlightenment' being called a 'seed'.

In psychological terms, the speaking of the 'defiled mind' as the one which faints and falls unconscious, and of a 'seed' consciousness as the first revival—is making of this 'seed' consciousness a kind of hypnogogic state, the period between sleep and waking, which forecasts the day. Perhaps with a consistent idea in mind, Śāntideva quotes a Māhāyāna scripture *Siṃhaparipṛcchā* in his *Śikṣāsamuccaya*:[27]

> *bodhicittaṃ na riñcati tena sarvāsu jātiṣu /*
> *svapnāntare 'pi tac cittaṃ kim punar yadi jāgrataḥ //*
> Therefore, in all his lives he loses not the Thought of Enlightenment. Even in dream there is this Thought. Even more in the waking state.

The term 'seed' (*bīja*) is also used in the *Buddhist Tantra* for the syllable kind of *mantra*. There are many illustrations of these in the book Mkhas grub rje's *Fundamentals of the Buddhist Tantras* (tr. by Lessing and Wayman). Thus on p. 209, the text speaks of generating the Victor Śākyamuni from any of the four letters A, Ā, AṂ, AḤ. One first attains the sphere of the Void, which in Mahāyāna literature is the object on non-reflective (*nirvikalpa*) insight (*prajñā*). There one imagines a 'germ-syllable', and then imagines this syllable changing into the body of the deity. This process agrees with the theory of 'seed' as susceptible of developing into something. And the fact that the particular germ syllable is pre-determined or laid-down in the instruction implies that it is the right germ-syllable for the given purpose. This germ syllable as a letter is a kind of mental painting on a blank canvas. This kind of seed reminds us of the verse cited at the outset about the "painting created by the mind".

IV. Dharma

Next to the term Buddha, the term *dharma* is the second most important one of Buddhism. It is not the only Doctrine among the three Jewels (the other two being the Buddha and the monk group called the Saṃgha), but in the plural stands for all the elements of life that are expressible and for certain elements that are inexpressible. Bu-ston, *The Jewelry of Scripture*, in Obermiller's translation cites the *Vyākhyāyukti* for ten different meanings of the term *dharma*. Bu-ston explains the derivation of the word *dharma* as from the verbal root *dhṛ*, to hold, hence holding a character, so when *dharma* is in the plural, intending the 'atoms' of this system out of which is built up the subjective and objective worlds. Th. Stcherbatsky, *The Central Conception of Buddhism* presents the Abhidharma theory of multiple *dharmas*. The literature on *dharma* in all these aspects is truly enormous and here only a few aspects can be presented.

I propose to treat this topic of *dharma* under these headings: A. Good in the beginning, in the middle, and in the end; B. Dharma—The other one; C. Constructed and Unconstructed; D. Three Definitions of Dharma; E. Dharmatā the Continuum.

A. Good in the Beginning, Middle, and End

Akira Hirakawa, in his article on Dharma as one of the three Jewels, cites several scriptural passages that the *Dharma* (or Pāli *Dhamma*), which the Buddha expounded is excellent *in the beginning,* excellent in the middle, and excellent in the end.[28] This is a kind of continuation of *dharma* through three phases. Indeed, this *dharma* establishes the Path (leading to the cessation of suffering). The most prevalent interpretation of the three is the three instructions (*trayaśikṣā*); The instruction of morality (*adhiśīla*), the instruction of mind training (*adhicitta*), and the instruction of insight (*adhiprajñā*), which serve for the organization of Buddhaghosa's *Visuddhimagga*.

According to the Mahāyāna scripture *Akṣayamatinirdeśa,* its section on *Prajñāpāramitā,* subsection of various skills, the part on "skill in the Vehicles" shows that the Bodhisattva must get skilled in all three vehicles, the *śrāvaka-yāna,* the *pratyekabuddha-yāna,* and the *mahāyāna*. Here, for the three instructions of the *śrāvaka-yāna,* the scripture adds to the last one of the three. Explaining the Bodhisattva's skill in the *śrāvaka* vehicle, it states:[29]

> When a Buddha does not arise, there is also no *śrāvaka* vehicle. Why not? The right view (*samyag-dṛṣṭi*) of 'hearers' (*śrāvaka*) follows upon the words of others. Here, hearing is the vow of morality. Proceeding in accordance with the attendant points of instruction, one perfects the aggregate of morality. After perfecting the aggregate of morality, one perfects the aggregate of *samādhi.* After perfecting the aggregate of *samādhi,* one perfects the aggregate of insight. After perfecting the aggregate of insight, one perfects the aggregate of liberation (*vimukti-skandha*). After perfecting

> the aggregate of liberation, one perfects the aggregate of knowledge and vision of liberation (*vimukti-jñāna-darśana-skandha*). The skill in this is called the (Bodhisattva's) skill in the *śrāvaka* vehicle.

While the three instructions are the most usual categories, each of the three constituting a *dharmatā* or underlying nature, it is possible to find other interpretations of the three.

The scripture *Vairocanābhisambodhitantra* declares in its first chapter:

> Master of the Secret Ones, moreover, the Stage of Adhimukticaryā is the cultivation of the three kinds of mind. Because it is the practice of the Perfections and the four Persuasions, the Stage of Adhimukti is incomparable, unfathomable, inconceivable, the source of immeasurable gnosis and attained to by ten kinds of mind.

We learn from this passage and the commentatorial traditions that the ten kinds of mind are expressible in three kinds, and that these three are labelled, 'incomparable,' 'unfathomable,' and 'inconceivable'. There are various solutions possible; and the one which the present writer has set forth takes the ten as the ten Bodhisattva stages in this way: The first mind ('incomparable') covers the first five stages, called Joyful (*pramuditā*), Pure (*vimalā*), Luminous (*prabhākarī*) Radiant (*arciṣmatī*), and Difficult to Conquer (*sudurjayā*). The second mind ('unfathomable') covers the sixth and seventh, Facing (*abhimukhī*) and Far-going (*dūraṅgamā*). The third mind ('inconceivable') covers the last three, Motionless (*acalā*), Good-minded (*sādhumatī*), and Cloud of Doctrine (*dharmamegha*).[30]

Furthermore, what is called 'stage of generation' (*utpatti-krama*) in the Anuttarayoga-tantra class of Buddhist Tantra, is expressible in terms of three *samādhis*, and this terminology constitutes practices shared with the class of Yoga-tantra. The three *samādhis* are called 'preliminary praxis' (*prathamaprayoga*), 'triumphant *maṇḍala*' (*Vijaya-maṇḍala*), and 'victory of the rite' (*karma-vijaya*).[31]

The foregoing should clarify that the *dharma* structure called "good in the beginning; good in the middle; good in the end" is a powerful continuity of the Buddhist Dharma from its earliest formulation to those forms of Buddhism many centuries later on.

B. Dharma—The Other One

Background: It is a feature of numerous Buddhist passages that *dharma* is the other one of two. Probably the reader has seen many times the contrast of the two kinds of selflessness (*nairātmya*), namely, of personality (*pudgala*) and of *dharma*, which Mahāyāna texts urge the disciple to realize. If we take just the term 'selflessness of *dharma*', there is an implicit contrast of *dharma* and *self*, so the motto: "All *dharmas* are selfless," showing that all *dharmas* exclude 'self'. Vasubandhu starts his *Triṃśikā* with the words *ātmadharmopacāro*, which admit the contrast of the terms *ātma* and *dharma*.

The *Mahāyāna-Sūtrālaṃkāra*, XVI, 75, distributes the four Persuasions (*saṃgraha-vastūni*) into two groups, that of 'giving' (*dāna*), namely, of material things;[32] and that of '*dharma*', namely, 'pleasant speech' (*priyākhyāna*), 'aim inducement' (*arthacaryā*), and 'common pursuits' (*samārthatā*), respectively, "*dharma* of consciousness-support (*ālambana*)," "*dharma* of practice," and "*dharma* of applying." Of course, 'giving' (*dāna*) is the first of the six Perfections; and it is basic to this theory that the six Perfections are meant to perfect oneself, while the four Persuasions are meant to mature others.[33]

Self and Dharma. It does appear that the expression 'selflessness of personality' amounts to a denial of self. However, the expression 'selflessness of *dharma*' does not appear to deny self, but rather to make *dharma* other than self. Thus, in the above, 'giving' (*dāna*) pertains to 'self' and is not counted in the group of three *dharmas*. Thus, this contrast seems to be an example of the *dharma* that stays in comparison with the self that attains, comes and goes, and the like. Because of the teaching that each of the six Perfections are fractionally within each one, Abhayākaragupta in *Munimatālaṃkāra*[34] is able to explain two other kinds of 'giving' besides 'gift of material things', namely, that Perfection of Morality (*śīla-pāramitā*) and Perfection of Forbearance (*kṣānti-p.*) are gifts (*dāna*) of non-fear (*abhaya*) or of confidence; and that Perfection of Striving (*vīrya-p.*), Perfection of Meditation (*dhyāna-p.*), and Perfection of Insight (*prajñā-p.*) are gifts of the Doctrine (*dharma*). While 'giving' is in the category of 'self', in fact it is a reduction of the ordinary self by opposing the sense of 'mine' (*ātmīya*) and its stinginess.

That brings us to the initial verse of Vasubandhu's *Triṃśikā*. Sylvain Lévi[35] took the term *upacāra* as meaning 'metaphor', as does Anacker.[36] While Kochumuttom[37] renders it 'usages' this in a way amounts to the same, because such 'usages' would have to be metaphorical extensions of the basic (or 'literal') meanings. Kochumuttom, while properly rejecting the claim of P.T. Raju that this treatise "deals with the process of the evolution of the world", is not much better in asserting that "it is an analysis of consciousness throughout"; nor is he convincing in holding that the terms *ātman* and *dharma* "stand respectively for the categories of subjectivity and objectivity".[38] The word *dharma* is not how Buddhism refers to 'objectivity', since—as is noticed in the section below on three definitions—there are *dharmas* of subjective nature, e.g., *vijñāna* itself, and *dharmas* of objectivity, such as the *rūpa* (formations). Now, the present writer would not wish to fault any translator who interprets the term *upacāra* as applying to the term *ātman* and then to the term *dharma,* since the commentator Sthiramati—as Lévi has edited the Sanskrit[39]—comments: *ātmavijñaptir dharmaprajñaptiś ca,* although differentiating, "representation of self, and deciding of *dharma*". Thus, if the translator is taking account of what Sthiramati says, he should acknowledge that the commentator argues that the term *upacāra* has two meanings here, one for the term *ātman* and another one for the term *dharma*. And neither definition takes one as 'subject', the other as 'object'. And by that remark Sthiramati does not rule out another interpretation of the term *upacāra,* namely, 'approach', suggesting that *ātman* and *dharma* are nearby, not easily separated out, and yet are distinct. Then, for *dharma* as the other of the two, the term *prajñapti,* 'determining' does go with *dharma* as what stays; while the term *vijñapti,* 'representation', does go with *ātman* as what evolves. Hence, *Triṃśikā,* k.1:

> */ ātmadharmopacāro hi vividho yaḥ pravartate /*
> *vijñānapariṇāme 'sau pariṇāmaḥ sa ca tridhā //*
> Certainly the representation of self or the determining of *dharma*, is various. What proceeds, that is in the transformation of perception. And that transformation is threefold.

Thus, Vasubandhu announces that he will talk about two things to repeat, the representation of self, or the deciding, the determining of *dharma*. It may be difficult to keep them apart; and it remains to conclude whether Vasubandhu has succeeded. But one does not face up to this issue by pretending that Vasubandhu is talking about something he is not, or pretending that he is talking about one of the two, and not both.

In the view of the present writer, in the light of Daṃṣṭrasena's definitions exposed below, the 'determining of *dharma'* amounts to the *dharmatā* definition, in the sense of grouping. The representation of self is what we imagine it to be, and this is the 'discursive thought' (*vikalpa*) interpretation.

To get a more profound view of *dharma* as the other one, we may recall the passage of the celebrated *Heart Sūtra*:[40]

> Here, Sāriputra, all natures (Dharma) have the Character of Voidness: are not originated and not destroyed, not defiled and not pure, without subtraction and without addition.

It follows that one cannot do anything to increase or decrease the *dharmas*. It is the 'self' that can improve or deteriorate, can become more generous or more stingy, can be more or less compassionate. As the *Heart Sūtra* states, it is not the *dharmas* that are defiled or pure. And yet in the 'self' those *dharmas* are defiled or pure. My essay "Nescience and Omniscience"[41] mentions the five kinds of nescience and the five kinds of wisdom, but the realm of nescience is not different from the realm of wisdom. It is the ordinary self that experiences it as the realm of nescience, and it is the extraordinary self called the Buddha who experiences it as the realm of wisdom.

C. Constructed and Unconstructed

The rendition 'constructed' is for the *saṃskṛta* kind of *dharmas*, while the 'unconstructed' is for the *asaṃskṛta* kind. The Abhidharma treatises give lists of terms, especially for the *saṃskṛta-dharmas*. Here, the writer will not use such works, but treat the matter more in the religious sense. The *Vairocanābhisambodhi-tantra*, Chap. Two, verses 19-27, expresses the matter well, as Vajrapāṇi speaks to the Bhagavat:[42]

> The Buddha is dissociated from signs (*nimitta*); he abides in the Dharmakāya, resorting to the Dharma that is signless, unconstructed, and unequalled. (19)

> "O great hero, for what purpose do you announce this praxis of *mantras*, a ritual associated with signs, which is not the rule of true nature (*dharmatā*)?" (20)
> So asked, the Bhagavat Mahāvairocana at that time told Vajrapāṇi to listen to this character of Dharma. (21)
> The Dharma is free from (mundane) analysis, rejects all constructive thoughts, avoids the constructions of thought (*citta*) and mental concomitants (*caitta*). (22)
> My Dharma is fully enlightened. It arises from the sky. Foolish beings, who range in wayward imagination, do not know it. (23)
> Persons obscured by darkness believe in time, spatial objects, and signs. So as to help them, this means is expressed. (24)
> Spatial object is not, time is not, there is neither deed nor agent. None of the natures (*dharma*) is real. The *dharmas* are only ephemeral. (25)
> However, Master of the Secret Ones, the beings of feeble intellect, deluded by activity-alone, crave concrete entities and in future time will be reborn. (26)
> Because ignorant of this kind of method they are attracted to the fruits of delusion by the virtuous and unvirtuous signs from spatial objects, time, and activity. So they may become great beings, this rite is expressed. (27)

As the Waymans explain the *Śrīmālā* scripture:[43]

The *Srīmālā* summarizes its view of *nirvāṇa* and *saṃsāra* by positing a constructed and an unconstructed *nirvāṇa* and a constructed and an unconstructed *saṃsāra*. The *Ratnagotravibhāga* (p. 8) explains, 'The "unconstructed" (*asaṃskṛta*) should be understood as the opposite of the "constructed". Here, the "constructed" (*saṃskṛta*) is said for whatever thing one recognizes as having birth (*utpāda*), continuation (*sthiti*), and destruction (*bhaṅga*).' The closest the *Śrīmālā* comes to explaining that passage about *nirvāṇa* and *saṃsāra* is when it reports that the Tathāgatagarbha transcends the constructed realm and is the base of constructed Buddha natures as well as the base of external constructed natures that are defilement stores. This confirms that the constructed *nirvāṇa* is the constructed Buddha natures and that the constructed *saṃsāra* is the constructed defilement stores. The *Śrīmālā*... equates the unconstructed *nirvāṇa* with the Truth

Cessation of Suffering. Only the unconstructed *saṃsāra* is left unexplained in the *Śrīmālā*, although this text implies...the Tathāgatagarbha, which experiences suffering.

According to this terminology, the thirty-seven *bodhipakṣya-dharmas* would belong to the category of 'constructed *nirvāṇa*'. For so in the *Akṣayamatinirdeśa-sūtra*, commentary, PTT, Vol. 104, p. 217-5-5,6: "There are also three kinds of Dharma...The 'Dharma to be understood' (*shes bya ba'i chos*) is the twelve classes of scripture; the 'Dharma to be practiced' (*bsgrub par bya ba'i chos*) is the thirty-seven *bodhipakṣya-dharmas*; the 'Dharma to be attained' (*thob par bya ba'i chos*) is Nirvāṇa." Thus, this Nirvāṇa has been 'constructed' by man's endeavor.

D. Three Definitions of Dharma

The material here to be cited and discussed stems from a large commentary on the three biggest Prajñāpāramitā scriptures—the *Śatasāhasrikā*, the *Pañcaviṃśatisāhasrikā*, and the *Aṣṭadaśasāhasrikā*. The Derge catalog identifies the author of this commentary as Daṃṣṭrasena. Mkhas-grub-rje agrees with this authorship and mentions the nickname for this commentary, *Gnod 'joms*.[44] I shall cite the passage from the Peking Tanjur (PTT, Vol. 93, p. 306-4-3, ff.), and intersperse further information. May I say first that part of it goes back to early Buddhism, and part to the Mahāyāna:

> */ chos nyid dang chos kyi dbyings dang chos gnas pa nyid ces bya ba tshig gsum gyis mtshan nyid rnam pa gsum bstan te / chos kyi mtshan nyid dang / 'byung gnas kyi mtshan nyid dang / gnas pa'i mtshan nyid do //*
>
> The three terms *dharmatā*, *dharmadhātu*, and *dharmasthititā* are shown to have three kinds of definitions, namely, the definition of *dharma*, the definition of source (*udaya*), and the definition of staying.

Thus, the three definitions are respectively assigned to the three terms. The author sets the stage for some truly helpful explanations:

> */ chos kyi dngos po ni chos nyid de kun brtags pa dang rnam par brtag pa'i chos thams cad las gzhan du gyur pa na de dang mi 'dra la brjod du med pa chos kyi dngos por gnas pa*

> *gang yin pa de gnas pa'i phyir chos nyid kyi sgrar brjod do//*
> The given state of a *dharma*, i.e., that *dharmatā*, means all *dharmas* that are conceptualized in groups or are conceptualized separately; or else are otherwise, namely an inexpressible *dharma* different from that (the expressible kind that is conceptualized); plus the fixing of their given state. On account of the fixing of that (*dharma*) we use the expression *dharmatā*.

Here, 'conceptualized in groups' is for a form of the term *saṃkalpa* with the '*sam*' understood in the sense of combination or group; and 'conceptualized separately' is for a form of the term *vikalpa* with the '*vi*' understood in the old sense of 'apart' or 'separate'. Stcherbatsky, *Central Conception,* exhibits the main groups. Thus, the Sarvāstivādin system of *dharmas* amounts to 75. There is the group of 'fluxional natures' (*sāsrava-dharma*) influenced by nescience (*avidyā*), and the group of 'non-fluxional natures' (*anāsrava-d.*) influenced by insight (*prajñā*). There is the group of 72 'constructed' (*saṃskṛta*) natures, and 3 'unconstructed' (*asaṃskṛta*) natures. When grouped by the four Truths (*satya*), the 72 'fluxional natures' are in the truths of suffering and source of suffering, while the 'non-fluxional natures' are in the truths of cessation and path; and the 3 'unconstructed' ones in the truth of cessation (*nirodha-satya*). Sometimes, 'all *dharmas*' is explained as the five personal aggregates (*skandha*); the twelve sense bases (*āyatana*) of which six are personal and six objective; and the eighteen elements (*dhātu*) of which six are the sense organs, six are the sense objects, and six are the perceptions (*vijñāna*) using those organs (*indriya*) to experience those objects (*viṣaya*). When the 72 *dharmas* are included in the five personal aggregates, then 'aggregate of formations' (*rūpa-skandha*) gets-11 *dharmas*, 'aggregate of motivations' (*saṃskāra-skandha*) gets 58 *dharmas,* while 'aggregate of feelings' (*vedanas*), 'aggregate of ideas' (*saṃjñās*), and 'aggregate of perceptions' (*vijñānas.)* are each one *dharma.* Also, *dharmas* can be grouped as past, present and future; defiled and undefiled, and so on. Furthermore, the Abhidharma has the grouping called 'constructions associated with thought' (*cittasamprayukta-saṃskāra*), 'constructions dissociated from thought' (*cittaviprayukta-saṃskāra*); with a third group called 'formations' (*rūpa*), namely the four 'great elements' (*mahābhūta*) and their derivatives (*bhautika*). The 'constructions associated with thought' amount to 46, namely, 10 natures present in every moment of consciousness (*citta-mahābhūmika-dharma*), 10 natures present in every virtuous moment of thought (*kuśala-mahābhūmika-d.*), 6 natures present in every defiled moment of thought (*kleśa-mahābhūmika-d.*) two natures present in every unvirtuous moment of thought (*akuśala-mahābhūmka-d.*), 10 secondary defilements of sporadic occurrence (*upakleśa-parīttabhūmika-d.*), and lastly, 8 irregular natures (*aniyata-bhūmi-d.*) that enter into combinations with the above constructions associated with thought', but in an unregulated manner. Besides, there is a fourth group of 'constructions called 'constructions dissociated from both formations and thought' (*rūpacittaviprayukta-saṃskāra*), which has been the subject of much dispute. In such groupings, a fifth group is allotted to the 3 'unconstructed natures' (*asaṃskṛta-dharma*); and a sixth group of natures in Dependent Origination (*pratītya-samutpāda*), 12 in number. That takes care of the main groups of *dharmas*. One may consult that work of Stcherbatsky for the separate members of the groups or consult Vasubandhu's *Abhidharmakośa* in Asian or Western language translation for these separate natures and with a pool of more information. The separate members may themselves have numerous varieties. For example, among the 10 natures present in every moment of consciousness according to those Abhidharma classifications is the nature called *samādhi*, meaning 'concentration'. i.e., thinking *that* rather than something else. But there are also many named *samādhis* as have been listed and discussed in my article, "The *samādhi* lists of the *Akṣayamatinirdeśasūtra* and the *Mahāvyutpatti*."[45]

As to Daṃṣṭrasena's point about an 'inexpressible *dharma*', this cannot be the three called 'unconstructed natures', viz., space (*ākāśa*), cessation through understanding (*pratisaṃkhyā-nirodha*), and cessation without understanding (*apratisaṃkhyā-nirodha*). This is because all three of these are expressible topics spaced within the body and outside the body, etc.; the first kind of cessation as a kind of 'insight' (*prajñā*); the second kind of cessation through removal of the cause (or causes) of phenomenal life and not through 'insight'. What this author intended by that remark may emerge as we pass to his second and third definitions:

> */chos kyi dbyings zhes bya ba ni 'byung gnas kyi mtshan nyid gsungs pa ste / chos ni stobs bcu dang / mi 'jigs pa dang / ma 'dres pa la sogs pa sangs rgyas kyi chos rnams so / dbyings kyi sgra ni rgyu'i don te sangs rgyas kyi chos rnams kyi 'byung gnas yin pa'i phyir chos kyi dbyings zhes bya ste / chos kyi sku zhes bya ba'i tha tshig go //*
>
> 'Dharmadhātu' is said to be defined as source (*udaya*). (Here:) the natures are the ten powers, the confidences, and the unshared ones as well as the other Buddha natures. '*Dhātu*' means cause (*hetu*). And because it is the source of the Buddha natures, it is called Dharmadhātu; and also is referred to as Dharmakāya.

The remark about the Dharmakāya is important, since this identification with 'source' or 'cause' appears to disallow the Dharmakāya as a result, say of collection as Mahāyāna books say, of merit and knowledge. The statement that *'dhātu'* means cause, agrees with the commentary on the *Madhyāntavibhāga*, I, 14-15, which takes the Dharmadhātu as "cause of the noble *dharmas*", since Vasubandhu says *hetvartho hy atra dhātvarthaḥ* (because here the meaning of 'cause' is the meaning of *dhātu*). The 'unshared' natures means the eighteen *āveṇika* natures of the Buddha which are listed in the Buddhist dictionary Mahāvyutpatti, sect. IX:

> */ chos gnas pa nyid ces bya ba ni gnas pa'i mtshan nyid gsungs pa ste / de bzhin gshegs pa rnams byung yang rung ma byung yang rung chos nyid dang / chos gnas pa nyid 'di ni 'dug pa nyid do / zhes ji skad du gsungs pa lta bu ste / don dam pa brjod du med pas yongs su grub pa'i chos ni sngon dri ma dang bcas pa'i gnas skabs dang phyis dri ma med pa'i gnas skabs na yang dus thams cad du yod pa ni chos gnas pa nyid do //*
>
> The staying of *dharma* is said to be defined as remaining; as was told: "Whether Tathāgatas arise or do not arise, the rule of *dharma*, the staying of *dharma* remains." Being absolute (*paramārtha*) and inexpressible (*anirvacanīya*), (this) *dharma*, which has the former soiled phase and the later unsoiled phase also exists in all times [= past, present, and future]. This is the staying of *dharma*.

This statement answers the point raised in the first of our cited paragraphs, namely, about a *dharma* differing from those that can be conceptualized. The commentator meant this particular *dharma*. The cited passage is well-known. There is a form of it in the Pāli canon, where the 'rule of *dharma*' turns out to be the formula of Dependent Origination. However, Mahāyāna forms of this statement make it equivalent to the Dharmadhātu, which was set forth in the preceding paragraph. As to the two phases, subsequently Daṃṣṭrasena at PTT, Vol. 93, 307-1-4, states per the Tibetan translation:

> */ yang dri ma dang bcas dang dri ma med pa'i gnas skabs nyid ls gzugs dang de bzhin nyid ces bya ba la sogs pa'i sgrar brjod pa'i phyir de skad ces bya'o //*
> Regarding the phases soiled and unsoiled, these are mentioned on account of formation (*rūpa*) and thusness (*tathatā*).

And still later (p. 307-4) when giving a number of reasons for 'backsliding' of the candidate, the commentator clarifies that the "phases soiled and unsoiled" apply to both 'formation' and 'thusness'. These two (formation and thusness) appear to be the two extremes mentioned by Asaṅga in meditation context—the phenomenal and the noumenal extremes of the meditative object.[46] Daṃṣṭrasena's explanations help us to understand a remark in the *Prajñāpāramitā* scripture *Aṣṭadaśasāhasrikā*, as Conze renders it:[47]

> *Subhuti:* Has then the Lord known full enlightenment after having stood in ultimate reality?
>
> *The Lord:* Not so.

And soon thereafter, as Conze renders it:

> *The Lord*: The Tathāgata has known the supreme enlightenment, but he has not stood anywhere in the conditioned or unconditioned element.

Rather than this rendition, I have used above, "constructed or unconstructed" (*saṃskṛta* or *asaṃskṛta*); and the word 'element' is for Sanskrit *dhātu*. The scripture amounts to saying that the Lord stands neither in the 'formation' nor in the 'thusness'. Thus, the

Lord does not stay, but it is the *dharma* which stays. And when someone 'stands' or 'stays' in 'thusness', it does not mean he is enlightened; indeed he could be staying in the soiled thusness. This is close to what I pointed out years ago in my review article of Ashok Kumar Chatterjee's *The Yogācāra Idealism*: "The *dharmadhātu* as voidness is the foundation for objectivity as impressed upon the *dharmadhātu* by the 'imagination of unreality.[48] While the various forms conjured up by that imagination are unreal, the underlying substance, the content of those forms is real." In short, neither the 'formation' nor the 'thusness' are naturally soiled; for the commentator pointed out that what was formerly soiled is later not soiled. So, when either the 'formation' or the 'thusness' is soiled, it must be that imagination has soiled them.

E. Dharmatā—The Continuum

My study of the *Vairocanābhisambodhitantra* has illustrations of *dharmatā* as a continuum:[48] and this was the implication of Daṃṣṭrasena's first definition of *dharma*. What is meant should emerge from a consideration of the ancient category of 'three characters' (S. *trilakṣaṇa*) going with the Truth of Suffering, namely, 'impermanence' (*anityatā*), 'pain' (*duḥkha*), and 'non-self' (*anātman*).[50] Later a fourth term, 'voidness' (*śūnyatā*) was added. The question naturally arises: Why are these put in the same group? Otherwise asked: Are they not really independent? As an initial response, it is clear enough that they are distinct; otherwise, they would not deserve individual terms. The theory that they can be spoken about in one group is that each one implicates the other, but not in the usual causation of *hetu* (basic cause) and *pratyaya* (condition), but in a kind of causation as though they have the same underlying nature, so that given one of them, there are the others. While the underlying nature is independent of time and space, the members of the group show up in time or in space.

Another example should further clarify this theory. The scripture *Bodhisattvapiṭaka* and its successor, the *Akṣayamatinirdeśa* have a number of series that are only explainable by an underlying nature. One of these is cited in Śāntideva's *Śikṣāsamuccaya* from those two scriptures' exposition of 'Resolve' (*āśaya*); so the citation:[51]

> */ sa khalu punar āśayo 'kṛtrimaḥ akṛtakatvāt / akṛtako niḥsādhyatvāt / niḥsādhyaḥ suviditatvāt / suvidito nirmayatvāt / nirmāyaḥ śuddhatvāt / śuddhaḥ ṛjukatvāt / ṛjukaḥ akuṭilatvāt / akuṭilaḥ spaṣṭatvāt / spaṣṭaḥ aviṣamatvāt / aviṣamaḥ sāratvāt / sāraḥ abhedyatvāt / abhedyo dṛdhatvāt / dṛdho 'calatatvāt / 'calitaḥ aniśritatvād ity ādi /*
> (Your honor Śāradvatīpūtra, moreover, the Resolve of the Bodhisattvas is also inexhaustible. Why so?) That resolve, you should know moreover, is not artificial because it is not contrived. Not contrived, because it does not need deciphering. Does not need deciphering, because it is well-understood. Well-understood, because not deceptive. Not deceptive because pure. Pure, because sincere. Sincere, because not devious. Not devious, because clear. Clear, because not obscure. Not obscure because essential. Essential, because not disunited. Not disunited, because firm. Firm, because unswerving. Unswerving, because not dependent (on material things). And so on (as the scripture continues).

In the case of this scriptural passage, one sees one nature being justified by virtue of another nature, and so on and on. Thus, this is the acceptance of *dharmatā* as a continuum.

REFERENCES

1. The reader can get more information about this topic from the Kapil N. Tiwari, *Suffering: Indian Perspectives* (Motilal Banarsidass, Delhi, 1986) and in particular from two of its essays "Suffering in Theravāda Buddhism," by James W. Boyd and "Suffering in Mahāyāna Buddhism," by Harsh Narain.
2. Cf. *Buddhist Insight,* Essays by Alex Wayman, p. 339.
3. Cf. Alex Wayman, "A Report on the Akṣayamatinirdeśasūtra," *Studies in Indo-Asian Art and Culture* (New Delhi, Oct. 1980), Vol. 6, p. 220.
4. Alex and Hideko Wayman, *The Lion's Roar of Queen Śrīmālā* (New York, 1974), pp. 96-7.
5. My essay on confession and so on that appeared in Genjun Sasaki's *kleśa* volume, is reprinted in the present set of essays.
6. Among the essays in Wendy Doniger O'Flaherty, *Karma and Rebirth in Classical Indian Traditions* (Berkeley, 1980; and Delhi, 1983), especially to be recommended for further information on the *karma* theory in Buddhism is the essay by James P. Mc Dermott, "Karma and Rebirth in Early Buddhism".
7. Cf. *Buddhist Insight,* p. 208 (in the Dependent Origination Study), and p. 298 (in the 'Role of Art' study).

8. Cf. *Visuddhimagga of Buddhaghosācariya*, Ed: Warren and Kosambi, Chap. XVII, para 188, *Bhavādisu*...and *Ibid.*, para 194, for the food, but here the food consumed by the mother to nourish the embryo.
9. As I cite the Mahāyāna scripture *Pitāputrasamāgama* in an essay on a fivefold ritual, reprinted in Wayman, *The Buddhist Tantras* (New York, 1973), p. 214; cf. the 'Death' essay in the present volume.
10. Cf. Paravahera Vajiranāṇa Mahathera, *Buddhist Meditation in Theory and Practice* (Colombo, 1962), pp. 447-8.
11. Cited in the essay, "Prophecy for persons in Buddhism," printed in the present set of essays.
12. For these collections, cf. Maurice Winternitz, *A History of Indian Literature* (University of Calcutta, 1933), Vol. II, (Buddhist Literature and Jaina Literature), pp. 284, ff.
13. Cf. Wayman, "Eschatology in Buddhism," *Studia Missionalia*, Vol. 32, 1983, pp. 71-94, the stanzas of Dhārmika Subhūti, and so on.
14. Cf. Patañjali's *Vyākaraṇa-Mahābhāṣya*, Kārakāhnika, P. 1.4.23-1.4.55 tr. by S.D. Joshi and J.A.F. Roodbergen, Poona, 1975, p. 148. I used these two *karmas* in the article Wayman, "The Metaphysics of Cooking in the Satyarth Prakash and Indian Tradition," in *World Perspectives on Swami Dayananda Saraswati*, ed. by Ganga Ram Garg (New Delhi, 1984), pp. 288-97.
15. Cf. A Wayman and R. Tajima, *The Enlightenment of Vairocana*, Table of Contents, Motilal Banarsidass, Delhi, 1992.
16. This essay is included in the present volume.
17. PTT, Vol. 5, p. 263-5-2 (end): / rnam par smin pa 'di nyid la / las kyi 'bras bu smin 'gyur pa / nam zhig dngos grub thob pa na / de tshe las kyang ldog par 'gyur / sems ni ngo bo nyid med phyir / rgyu dang 'bras bu rnams spangs shing / las dang tshe las rnam grol ba / nam mkha' lta bur 'gyur ba yin /.
18. PTT, Vol. 77, p. 183-3-1, ff.
19. *Dharma-samuccaya*, Second part, by Lin Li-kouang, revised by André Bareau and others (Paris, 1969), p. 366.
20. BSOAS, Vol. 22, 1959, pp. 236-49.
21. I have selected these examples from my translation of the Bodhisattva section of Tsong-kha-pa's *Lam rim chen mo*—a section which I have arranged for separate publication because of its size and individual importance under the title: *Ethics of Tibet; the Bodhisattva Section* (Albany, 1991).
22. Cf. Wayman's essay "The Buddhist Theory of Vision" reprinted in the volume of essays *Buddhist Insight*, pp. 156-7.
23. La Vallée Poussin, Vijñaptimātratāsiddhi, pp. 100-23.
24. Lambert Schmithausen, *Ālayavijñāna*, Part I (Text), Part II (Notes, Bibliography and Indices) (The International Institute for Buddhist Studies, Tokyo, 1987).
25. Cf. *Visuddhimagga of Buddhaghosācariya*, Ed: H.C. Warren, rev. by Dharmananda Kosambi (Harvard University Press, 1950), Chap. XVII, para 187, "vedanādayo tayo khandhā" (the three personal aggregates, Vedanā, etc.) as an explanation of *nāma-rūpa*.
26. This essay is included in the present volume.
27. *Śikṣāsamuccaya of Śāntideva*, Ed: P.L. Vaidya (Darbhanga, 1961), p. 33.28-29.
28. Akira Hirakawa, "The Meaning of 'Dharma' in the Concept of the 'Jewel of the Dharma' (Dharmaratna), "*Amalā Prajñā: Aspects of Buddhist Studies*, P.V. Bapat Vol. (Delhi, 1989), pp. 235-49.
29. Photo ed. of Peking Kanjur, PTT, Vol. 34, p. 55-2-2: / sangs rgyas byung ba med

par nyan thos kyi theg pa yang med do / de ci'i phyir zhe na / nyan thos rnams kyi yang dag par lta ba ni pha rol kyi sgra'i rjes su gro ba'o / de la nyan pa ni gang 'di tshul khrims sdom pa ste / ji ltar bslab pa bcas pa'i rjes su 'jug pa ni tshul khrims kyi phung po yongs su rdzogs par 'gyur te / tshul khrims kyi phung po yongs su rdzogs nas ting nge 'dsin kyi phung po yongs su rdzogs par byed pa dang / ting nge 'dsin kyi phung po yongs su rdzogs nas shes rab kyi phung po yongs su rdzogs par byed pa dang/shes rab kyi phung po yongs su rdzogs nas rnam par grol ba'i phung po yongs su rdzogs par byed pa dang/rnam par grol ba'i phung po yongs su rdzogs nas rnam par grol ba'i ye shes mthong ba'i phung po yongs su rdzogs par byed pa ste / gang 'di la mkhas pa 'di ni nyan thos kyi theg pa la mkhas pa zhes bya'o/.

30. Cf. A. Wayman and R. Tajima, *The Enlightenment of Vairocana,* pp. 69, 76.
31. Cf. A. Wayman, *Yoga of the Guhyasamājatantra* (Motilal Banarsidass, Delhi, 1977), pp. 160-2.
32. The *Akṣayamatinirdeśa-sūtra,* PTT, Vol. 34, p. 61-5-3, 4, states that this *dāna* is both of material things and of the doctrine (*dharma*).
33. As is shown in the Bodhisattva section, *Lam rim chen mo* (cf. n. 21, above).
34. Photo ed., PTT, Vol. 101, p. 158-4-3, 4.
35. Sylvain Lévi, *Materiaux pour l'étude du système Vijñaptimātra* (Paris, 1932), pp. 62-3.
36. Stefan Anacker, *Seven Works of Vasubandhu* (Delhi, 1984), p. 186.
37. Thomas A. Kochumuttom, *A Buddhist Doctrine of Experience* (Delhi, 1982), p. 128.
38. Kochumuttom, p. 127, ff.
39. Sylvain Lévi, *Vijñaptimātratāsiddhi* (Paris, 1925), p. 15.
40. A Wayman, "Secret of the Heart Sūtra," in *Prajñāpāramitā and Related Systems,* by Lewis Lancaster (Berkeley, 1977), pp. 143-4.
41. This essay is included in the present volume.
42. Wayman and Tajima, *The Enlightenment of Vairocana,* pp. 115-6.
43. Alex and Hideko Wayman, *The Lion's Roar of Queen Śrīmālā* (New York, 1974), pp. 40-1.
44. Mkhas grub rje's *Fundamentals of the Buddhist Tantras,* p. 97. The long title of Daṃṣṭrasena's commentary is reconstructed—it is the *Bṛhaṭṭīkā,* translated into Tibetan by Surendrabodhi and Ye-shes-sde.
45. A. Wayman's essay, in *Acta Orientalia Academiae Scientiarum Hung.,* Tomus XXXIV (1-3), 1980, pp. 305-18.
46. Cf. Alex Wayman, *Analysis of the Śrāvakabhūmi Manuscript* (Berkeley, 1961), p. 86. For further explication of the two extremes or limits of the meditative object, based on Asaṅga's treatment, see A. Wayman, tr., *Calming the Mind and Discerning the Real,* p. 105.
47. Edward Conze, *The Gilgit Manuscript of the Aṣṭadaśasāhasrikā-Prajñāpāramitā,* Chapters 55-70 (Rome, 1962), pp. 336-7.
48. *Philosophy East and West,* 15:1, 1965, pp. 65-73.
49. *The Enlightenment of Vairocana,* pp. 60-1.
50. Cf. Edward Conze, *Buddhist Thought in India* (London, 1962), Chap. Three—where he calls the three, 'the three marks'.
51. *Śikṣāsamuccaya,* Vaidya, ed., p. 150.31; and I consulted the Tibetan, PTT, Vol. 34, p. 40-3-7, f.

13

About Voidness: Two Scriptures

The two scriptures herein translated are: the *Cūḷa-suññatā-sutta*, translated from the Pāli language, which is in the *Majjhima-nikāya*, part III (Bihar Govt., 1958), pp. 168-73; and the *samādhi* "Great Gate of Diamond Liberation," translated from the Derge edn. of the Tibetan Kanjur, Rgyud 'bum, Vol. Dsa, f. 287a-291a, where it is part of the work *Ārya-Mahāvajrameruśikharakūṭāgara-dhāraṇī*.

In terms of the three Jewels of Buddhism—the Buddha, the Dharma, and the Saṅgha, the first scripture associates the Dharma with the Buddhist monk Saṅgha, while the second one associates the Dharma with the Buddha Jewel. Hence, this is the difference between the early Nikāya type of Buddhism and the later Mahāyāna Buddhism. It is truly remarkable to observe that the first scripture is probably the source of the Yogācāra type of voidness discussion; and that the other, so different in emphasis, is the Mādhyamika discourse.

And yet when we consider our translation of *suññatā* as 'voidness', we may find the second scripture surprisingly consistent with the oldest Buddhism. This scripture states: "Self is void of self," and explains: because it is "an imagination of what is not the case." According to this view (known as a 'right view'), the self that mankind values using letters and words is denied in Buddhism as having that value. Thus, in English idiom, a document is declared "null and void" when the face value indicated by printed letters is nullified and declared void of that stated value. So, this 'voidness' way of speaking is not a denial of existence *per se* — the document is still there—rather a denial of the imputed value. In English idiom, the term 'empty' is regularly used for denying existence. Since there is a Pāli scripture passage wherein the Buddha explains 'right view' to Kaccāyana as that one avoiding the extremes "All exists" and "Nothing exists" and since this 'right view' was adopted by Nāgārjuna in his *Madhyamaka-kārikā,* referring to this disciple by his name in Sanskrit, Kātyāyana, I never use the rendition 'emptiness' in my translations.

Now there is the evidence from the translation of the *Paṭisambhidāmagga* (Pāli Text Society, London, 1982). Buddhist scholars should feel gratitude toward Warder for the labor over a number of years to prepare for publication Ñāṇamoli's typescript, as Warder sets forth in his excellent introduction. Here, Ñāṇamoli always uses the noun 'voidness' and the adjective 'void' in his translation of the chapter called 'Treatise XX'. This chapter is based on the scriptural explanation by the Bhagavat to Ānanda that it is said "the world is void" 'because it is void of self or of what belongs to self'. At the end of the chapter Ñāṇamoli has a wonderful note, including "And the word 'void' for what is non-existent contradicts the blessed one's use of it above for the 'world' and also those words of the books of logic and linguistics (*ñāyasaddagantha*); and it contradicts many logical arguments. Therefore that assertion should be rejected as rubbish. [One hears that] in many such passages in the Buddha word as this: 'Bhikkhus, what sages in the world say is not, of that too I say that it is not; what sages in the world say is, of that too I say that it is.' . . ."

A. Introduction to the Cūḷa-suññatā-sutta

This remarkable scripture was probably delivered by the Buddha in the latter part of his life. The reader will notice a considerable amount of repetition. This type of language is typical of the orally transmitted prosaic scriptures of Buddhism. There is another reason for repetition: teachers who give examinations based on their lectures may well find out that the students imagine that what the teacher considers important is what the teacher repeats.

There are a few terms which need some discussion. So the rendition, "There is only this measure of embrasure: the singleness depending upon the idea of the 'congregation of monks.' In subsequent paragraphs of the scripture, other items are substituted for the 'congregation of monks'; thus: 'forest', 'earth', 'infinite space', and so on. It should be explained why the rendition 'embrasure' was adopted for the Pāli (and Sanskrit) term *daratha*. Pāli reference works claim that the term means 'trouble', 'disturbance', or 'distress'—renditions that clearly do not apply to the present scripture. The Monier-Williams Sanskrit-English Dictionary provides for the term *daratha* the meanings 'cave' and 'taking flight' from Ujjvaladatta's commentary on the *Uṇādi-sūtras.* If we put the two senses together: the one taking flight would like a kind of 'cave' to hide in: so 'cave' can be interpreted as 'making a cave'. I found for this notion the term 'embrasure', which as a verb means 'to widen an opening', and which as a noun was used in a military sense, e.g., widening a hole in a rampart so that the sides flare outwards, enabling a cannon placed therein to be able to swing in various directions. For application to the present scripture, we must remove the cannon and imagine going through this opening to a 'forest' or to 'infinite space' and so on. The way this is taken as a cave is to imagine the empty space outside the opening as a sort of 'mountain' and that the sides which flare outwards continue and create a cave in this 'mountain'. It is this cave which is understood to be void of this or that, and to be non-void of this or that.

Thus, this early *sutta* takes the term *suñña* ('void', S. *śūnya*) in its etymological sense. See Surya Kanta, *A Grammatical Dictionary of Sanskrit* (Vedic), p. 250, associating *śūnya* with the verb *śū*-swell'. This agrees with our rendition 'embrasure' for the word *daratha*. The 'swelling' is productive of a cave, a kind of opening that affords an opportunity for what the *sutta* calls 'abundance'.

Then for the part of the sentence used for illustration: "the singleness depending upon the idea of a congregation of monks"—here the term *ekattam* is rendered 'singleness'. The scripture states that this depends upon an idea. In the case of the military use of the term "embrasure", it depended upon the idea of a cannon. Therefore, this 'singleness' is a resultative notion; and the scripture says it is a 'measure' (of embrasure), where the Pāli *mattā* is Skt. *mātrā*. It follows that the 'singleness' as a kind of measure could vary. And this conclusion agrees with the scripture itself, which assigns a wide variety of 'ideas' (P. *saññā*; Skt. *saṃjñā*) starting with the 'monks', as the basis for the result. The term right after the 'monks' is 'forest', then 'earth'. Since the series then goes into the members of the 'formless realm', namely, 'infinite space' and so on, the scripture suggests that the 'forest' one constitutes the means of transcending the 'realm of desire' and that the 'earth' one is the means of transcending the 'realm of form'. It follows that the 'earth' one is explained as one of the four elements, and that any of the other three, 'water', 'wind', or 'fire' could be used for the purpose.

The actual description of the 'earth idea' speaks in terms of avoiding features of earth such as gullies, hills, and so forth. Thus, it seems to be a kind of advanced meditation in which one holds onto a 'sign' of earth in the cave of the mind, without permitting its modification into any particular mode of earth. This is a kind of 'voidness' aiming at the pure earth, devoid of any earthly features. Presumably, one practicing this to a degree of success would have to hold onto such sign for an entire meditative session, say 24 minutes or as much as 48 minutes.

Now for another point about the scripture. In para No. 1, Ānanda reminds the Bhagavat about an incident when the Buddha was among the Sakyans and had said, "I, Ānanda, by dwelling in voidness, now dwell in abundance." I.B. Horner, in her translation of this scripture has a note referring to M, iii, 294. But in this later scripture, the *Piṇḍapātapārisuddhisutta,* it is Sāriputta, not the Buddha, to whom this 'voidness-abundance' experience is attributed.

As to a possible association of this scripture with the Yogācāra point of view, this is properly claimed by Gadjin M. Nagao, "'What Remains' in Śūnyatā: A Yogācāra Interpretation of Emptiness" in his essay collection *Mādhyamika and Yogācāra* (Albany, 1991). He refers to Vasubandhu's comment on *Madhyānta-vibhāga,* I, 1, as I translate it: "The character of voidness (*śūnyatā-lakṣaṇam*) is rendered correctly when one observes as it really is that according as something does not exist in a place, it is the void of it; and when one knows as it really is that according something remains in this place, it is the reality (*sat*) here." In the *sutta,* what 'remains' is successively, the congregation of monks, a forest, etc.

The *Laṅkāvatāra-sūtra* has a category called *itaretara-śūnyatā* which it criticizes and which seems relevant to the *Cūḷa-suññatā-sutta* type of voidness. I shall deny the relevance. First, let us see what the *Laṅka* (text, p. 75) is talking about. It brings in the logical notion of two kinds of *lakṣaṇa*—the generality one (*sāmānya-l*) and the individual one (*sva-l*). Hence, in the *Laṅka*'s example, that the lecture hall is devoid of animals such as sheep, but is not devoid of monks, it follows that the monks who remain there are the *svalakṣaṇa* because the object of direct perception (*pratyakṣa*), while the absent animals are the *sāmānyalakṣaṇa* because inferred (with *anumāna*). The *Laṅka* scripture properly criticizes this kind of 'voidness'. However, in the case of the *Cūḷa-suññatā-sutta*, the sequence 'monks', 'forest', etc. seems to be *samādhi* objects, which lead upward through the three realms. So the *Laṅka* category is not relevant.

B. Introduction to the Samādhi "Great Gate of Diamond Liberation"

The translation of this tantric extract was first presented in the Prof. Jagannatha Upadhyaya Commemoration Volume, published by the Central Institute of Higher Tibetan Studies (1987). It was found in the *Ārya-Mahāvajrameruśikharakūṭāgāra-dhāraṇi,* among a group of Vajrapāṇi texts in the Kanjur, Rgyud 'bum division. The Tibetan was given in transcription, but is omitted in the present essay, which also omits the Pāli for the first scripture.

As the translator I added numbers to the paragraphs, making 27 in all, thus 3×9, with the first nine paragraphs setting forth Vajrapāṇi's initial discourse, ending with Śāradvatīputra's challenging questions; and with the next eighteen paragraphs devoted to Vajrapāṇi's answers, the last paragraph among them giving the praises.

In para 12, the mention of *manovijñāna* for comprehending Dependent Origination is consistent with the Mādhyamika school, which denies the Yogācāra theory of other kinds of *vijñāna,* such as *ālayavijñāna*. Hence, it is the *manovijñāna* which starts out as "the natural presence of the mind" and is promoted, e.g. by repeated practice of meditation.

There may be a corruption in the text where in para 13 the Dharmakāya is declared "the body secret of the Tathāgata," rather than, as expected, the "mind secret" because in para 11, it is the Sambhogakāya which is attributed the "body secret" and which "is the natural result of great merit"—in fact, the first four perfections, as is also mentioned in para 20. In para 11, the Nirmāṇakāya is attributed the speech (secret). Then, in para 13, the Dharmakāya is said to be what remains as the Middle Path of natures (*dharma*), hence not the result of merit. It appears from para 21 that the last two Perfections, of Meditation and of Insight constituting the collection of knowledge, is how one reaches the Dharmakāya.

Further, as to the Mādhyamika association near the outset of the essay, I called attention to the Kaccāyana discourse of the Pāli canon about the right view of avoiding "All exists" and "Nothing exists," which Nāgārjuna accepted for his *Madhyamaka-kārikā*. This appears consistent with para 6 of this scripture, which warrants repeating here:

> What is the Middle Path, is without one extreme, is without two extremes, without apprehensible, without apprehender, without apprehension, without nihilism, without eternalism, without arising, without ceasing, without constructive thought, without discursive thought, not independent, not dependent on another, not going, not coming, without thorough defilement, without complete purification, without union, without separation. That is discerning (the real).

Finally, this scripture excerpt gives the impression of a text handed down orally and finally recorded in a Vajrapāṇi tantric work.

Cūḷa-suññatā-suttam

(1) Thus have I heard upon an occasion. The Bhagavat was dwelling at Sāvatthī in the Eastern monastery in the palace of Migāra's mother. Then, you should know, the venerable Ānanda, having emerged from his meditative solitude at evening time, approached the Bhagavat. Having approached, he respectfully greeted the Bhagavat and sat down at one side. And, being seated at one side, you should know, the venerable Ānanda spoke thus to the Bhagavat: "Once, revered sir, the Bhagavat was dwelling among the Sakyans.

Nagaraka is the name of a Sakyan market place. While there, revered Sir, face to face with the Bhagavat, I heard, face to face I received (these words): 'I,.Ānanda, by dwelling in voidness, now dwell in abundance.' I hope, revered Sir, that I well-heard, well-received it, rightly oriented my mind, rightly reflected."

(2) "Certainly, Ānanda, you well-heard, well-received it, rightly oriented your mind and rightly reflected upon it. Formerly, Ānanda, as well as now, by dwellng in voidness, I dwell in abundance. For example, Ānanda , this palace of Migāra's mother is void of elephants, cows, horses, and mares; void of gold and silver; void of an assemblage of [lay] women and men; and there is just this non-voidness, to wit, this singleness depending on the congregation of monks. So also, you should know, Ānanda, is the monk paying no attention to the idea of a village, paying no attention to the idea of human beings, and orienting his mind to the singleness depending on the idea of a forest. His mind rejoices in, trusts in, takes the shape of and is convinced of the idea of a forest. He knows this: There are no embrasures depending on the idea of a village; there are no embrasures depending on the idea of human beings. There is only this measure of embrasure: the singleness depending upon the idea of a forest. He knows: This ideation is void of the idea of a village. He knows: This ideation is void of the idea of human beings. And there is only this which is non-void: the singleness dependent on a forest. Whatever is not there, one observes to be the void of it. And whatever remains there, he knows: That being, this is. Thus, Ānanda, this becomes for him a genuine, non-deviant, utterly pure manifestation of voidness.

(3) "And besides, Ānanda, a monk, not paying attention to the idea of human beings, not paying attention to the idea of a forest, pays attention to the singleness depending on the idea of earth. For example, Ānanda, when a bull's hide is well-stretched out with a hundred spikes, its wrinkles are gone. In the same way, Ānanda, you should know, a monk, paying no attention to anything [in particular] on the earth, promontories or gullies, difficult passageways such as rivers, spots with tree stumps or thorns, uneven places like hills; [rather] pays attention to the singleness depending on the idea of earth. His mind rejoices in, trusts in, takes the shape of, and is convinced of the idea of earth. He knows this: There are no embrasures depending on human beings; there are no embrasures depending on a forest. There is only this measure of

embrasure: the singleness depending on the idea of earth. He knows: This ideation is void of the idea of human beings. This ideation is void of the ideation of a forest. And there is only this which is non-void: the singleness depending on earth. What is not there, he observes as the void of it, and whatever remains there, he knows: That being, this is. Thus, Ānanda, this becomes for him a genuine non-deviant, utterly pure manifestation of voidness.

(4) "And further, Ānanda, a monk paying no attention to the idea of a forest, and paying no attention to the idea of earth, orients his mind to the singleness depending on the idea of the base of infinite space. His mind rejoices in, trusts in, takes the shape of and is convinced of the idea of the base of infinite space. He knows this: There are no embrasures depending on the idea of a forest; there are no embrasures depending on the idea of earth. There is only this measure of embrasure: the singleness depending on the idea of the base of infinite space. He knows: This ideation is void of the idea of forest; this ideation is void of the idea of earth. And there is only this which is not void, the singleness dependent on the idea of the base of infinite space. What is not there, he observes as the void of it. And whatever remains there, he knows: That being, this is. Thus, Ānanda, this becomes for him a genuine, non-deviant, utterly pure manifestation of voidness.

(5) "And besides, Ānanda, a monk, paying no attention to the idea of earth, and paying no attention to the idea of the base of infinite space, orients his mind to the singleness of the idea of the base of infinite perception. His mind rejoices in, trusts in, takes the shape of and is convinced of the idea of the base of infinite perception. He know this: There are no embrasures depending on the idea of earth; there are no embrasures depending on the idea of the base of infinite space. He knows: This ideation is void of the idea of earth; this ideation is void of the idea of the base of infinite space. And there is only this, which is non-void, the singleness depending on the idea of the base of infinite perception. What is not there, he observes as the void of it. And whatever remains there, he knows: That being, this is. Thus, Ānanda, this becomes for him a genuine, non-deviant, utterly pure manifestation of voidness.

(6) "And besides, Ānanda, a monk, paying no attention to the idea of the base of infinite space, and paying no attention to the

idea of the base of infinite perception, orients his mind to the singleness of the idea of the base of nothing-at-all. His mind rejoices in, trusts in, takes the shape of, and is convinced of the idea of the base of nothing-at-all. He knows this: There are no embrasures depending on the idea of the base of infinite space; there are no embrasures depending on the idea of the base of infinite perception. There is only this measure of embrasure: the singleness depending on the idea of the base of nothing-at-all. He knows: This ideation is void of the idea of the base of infinite space; this ideation is void of the idea of the base of infinite perception. And there is only this, which is not void, the singleness depending on the idea of nothing-at-all. What is not there, he observes as the void of it. And whatever remains there, he knows: That being, this is. Thus, Ānanda, this becomes for him a genuine, non-deviant, utterly pure manifestation of voidness.

(7) "And besides, Ānanda, a monk, paying no attention to the idea of the base of infinite perception, and paying no attention to the base of nothing-at-all, orients his mind to a singleness depending on the idea of the base of neither-ideation-nor-non-ideation. His mind rejoices in, trusts in, takes the shape of, and is convinced of the idea of the base of neither-ideation-nor-non-ideation. He knows this: There are no embrasures depending on the idea of the base of infinite perception; there are no embrasures depending on the idea of the base of nothing-at-all. There is only this measure of embrasure: the singleness depending on the idea of the base of neither-ideation-nor-non-ideation. He knows: This ideation is void of the idea of the base of infinite perception; this ideation is void of the idea of the base of nothing-at-all. And there is only this which is non-void, the singleness depending on the idea of the base of neither-ideation-nor-non-ideation. What is not there, he observes as the void of it. And whatever remains there, he knows: That being, this is. Thus, Ānanda, this becomes for him a genuine, non-deviant, utterly pure manifestation of voidness.

(8) "And besides, Ānanda, a monk, paying no attention to the idea of nothing-at-all; and paying no attention to the idea of neither-ideation-nor-non-ideation, orients his mind to the singleness depending on the *ceto-samādhi (samādhi* of mind fixation) that is signless (*animitta*). His mind rejoices in, trusts in, takes the shape of and is convinced of the *ceto-samādhi* that is signless. He knows this: There are no embrasures depending on the idea of the base

of nothing-at-all; and no embrasures depending on the idea of the base of neither-ideation-nor-non-ideation. There is only this measure of embrasure—the six sense bases which, depending on the body (*kāya*), follow upon the condition of life (*jīva* = Skt. *āyuḥsaṃskāra*). He knows: This ideation is void of the idea of the base of nothing-at-all, and is void of the idea of the base of neither-ideation-nor-non-ideation. And there is that which is non-void, the six sense bases that, depending on the body, follow upon the condition of life. And that which is not there, he observes to be the void of it. And whatever remains there, he knows: That being, this is. Thus, Ānanda, this becomes for him, a genuine, non-deviant, utterly pure manifestation of voidness.

(9) "And besides, Ānanda, a monk, paying no attention to the idea of the base of nothing-at-all; and paying no attention to the idea of the base of neither-ideation-nor-non-ideation, orients his mind to the singleness depending on the *ceto-samādhi* that is signless. His mind rejoices in, trusts in, takes the shape of and is convinced of the *ceto-samādhi* that is signless. And he knows: This *ceto-samādhi* that is signless is instigated and motivated. He knows: whatever is instigated and motivated is impermanent, has the nature of cessation (*nirodhadharma*). The mind of the one who knows thus and sees thus, is freed from the flux of sense attractions (*kāmāsava*), is freed from the flux of gestation (*bhavāsava*), and is freed from the flux of nescience (*avijjāsava*). When there is liberation, there is the knowledge, '[I] am liberated;' and he knows—'ended is birth; fulfilled is the career in purity; done is the duty; no more is the becoming a such.' He knows: The embrasures that in the three times [i.e. past, present, future] depend on the flux of sense attractions no longer exist. The embrasures that in the three times depend on the flux of gestation, no longer exist. The embrasures that in the three times depend on the flux of nescience, no longer exist. And there is only this measures of embrasure, the six sense bases that, depending on the body, follow upon the condition of life. He knows: What is not there, one observes as the void of it. And whatever remains there, he knows: That being, this is. Thus, Ānanda, this becomes for him, a genuine, non-deviant, utterly pure, ultimate manifestation of voidness.

(10) "And Ānanda, those ascetics (Skt. *śramaṇa*) and brahmans who in past time attained and dwelled in the pure, ultimate voidness, all these did attain and dwell in precisely the pure, ultimate

voidness. And, Ānanda, those ascetics and brahmans who in future time will attain and dwell in the pure, ultimate voidness, all these will attain and dwell in the pure, ultimate voidness. And, Ānanda, those ascetics and brahmans who in present time attain and dwell in the pure, ultimate voidness, all these are attaining and dwelling in precisely the pure, ultimate voidness. Consequently, Ānanda, thinking, 'Attaining, I shall dwell in the pure, ultimate voidness,' this is how you should train, Ānanda."

(11) Thus spoke the Bhagavat. Enraptured, the venerable Ānanda rejoiced in the Bhagavat's words.

The Samādhi—"Great Gate of Diamond Liberation"

Then Vajrapāṇi master of the secret folk, emerged from that *samādhi* "Great Gate of Diamond Liberation". Whereupon, the venerable Śāradvatīputra spoke as follows to Vajrapāṇi, master of the secret folk: Son of the family, in what state were you, displaying this marvel of magical power? What is the name of this *samādhi* in which you induced the sinful Māras to generate the mind of Enlightenment; and also arranged all the evil spirits, ghosts, hindering demons, swerving spirits (*vināyaka*) to take pledges and generate the mind of Enlightenment?[1]

When he had so spoken, Vajrapāṇi, master of the secret folk, spoke as follows to āyuṣmat Śāradvatīputra: Reverend Śāradvatīputra; This *samādhi* cannot be comprehended by name, letters, or words. Why so? It is because whether it be the name, the color, the shape, the place, and whether one is equipoised or has a straying mind, none of these are the natures of the *samādhi*. When it is without name, without color, without shape, without place, without equipoise, without straying, why should it occur to someone, Śāradvatīputra, to ask what is the name of this *samādhi*?"[2]

Besides, reverend Śāradvatīputra, this clarification is neither a clarification to oneself, nor a clarification to another, and neither a clarification to both. Still, one imagines a clarification. Here, a clarification is void of being a clarification. Self is void of self, and the other is void of being another. Also, both are void of being both. This is because, they are an imagination of what is not the case. Whatever two syllables are composed, they are void of being a word; and the syllable is not a syllable.[3]

That way one may understand the meaning of Dependent Origination. Even if that meaning is told, it comes from nowhere and goes nowhere; even so, because of dependency on another, it is also imagined as syllables. Because it is imagined, imagination is also void. Because of Dependent Origination, dependency on another is void. Because, arising from the cause and condition, Dependent Origination is also void. Because generated by cause and condition adventitiously, it is void of being an origination. Here, Dependent Origination is void of its own-character (*svalakṣaṇa*).[4]

What is void of own-character lacks a character. What lacks a character is Thusness (*tathatā*). What is Thusness is error-free Thusness. What is error-free Thusness is not otherwise Thusness. What is not otherwise Thusness is the *samādhi*. What is the *samādhi* is comprehending it. What is the comprehension is voidness (*śūnyatā*). What is the voidness is discerning (the real). What is discerning (the real) is calming (the mind). What is calming (the mind) is liberation (*vimokṣa*). What is liberation is the Middle Path.[5]

What is the Middle Path, is without one extreme, is without two extremes, without apprehensible, without apprehender, without apprehension, without nihilism, without eternalism, without arising, without ceasing, without constructive thought, without discursive thought, not independent, not dependent on another, not going, not coming, without thorough defilement, without complete purification, without union, without separation. That is discerning (the real).[6]

What is discerning (the real) is without personal aggregates (*skandha*), without realms (*dhātu*), without sense organs (*indriya*), without sense bases (*āyatana*), without objective realms, without attaching names to objective realms, without (destiny's) action, without the fruit of (destiny's) action. What is without (destiny's), action and without the fruit of (destiny's) action is the incomparable right-completed Enlightenment. What is the incomparable right-completed Enlightenment is the incomparable right-completed Buddha. What is the incomparable right-completed Buddha is the Dharma. What is the Dharma is not born, does not die. What is not born and does not die should be understood to be the same as the sky.[7]

Reverend Śāradvatīputra replied: Son of the (Buddhist) family, the instruction on *samādhi* which you have expounded is extremely deep. Since it is not in the scope of the *śrāvakas* and the *pratyekabuddhas*, why speak at all of the worldly heretics and adversaries! This Dharma passage is a hard thing to know for all those who have not generated virtuous roots or who have meagre faith. The objective domain of the Tathāgata's eye does not belong elsewhere. That eye of the Tathāgata is without aim and without place.[8]

When he had so spoken, the master of the secret folk, Vajrapāṇi addressed *āyuṣmat* Śāradvatīputra as follows: Reverend Śāradvatīputra, a 'Tathāgata' has the character of Thusness. What is the character of Thusness is voidness. What is voidness is without a Tathāgata, and a Tathāgata is without a character. Śāradvatīputra responded: Son of the family, if a Tathāgata is without a character, then why it is taught that a Tathāgata possesses the thirty-two characters of a great person, and why is his body adorned with the eighty minor marks? How can we make a place for the three bodies of a Tathāgata? How did the Tathāgata become manifestly and fully awakened to the incomparable, right-completed Enlightenment?[9]

Vajrapāṇi, master of the secret folk, explained: Reverend Śāradvatīputra, 'thirty-two characters of the great person' is a term of convention (*saṃvṛti*). 'Adorned' means elaborated letters and speech. 'Minor mark' means the character of illusory and dream formations. 'Right-completed Enlightenment' means the character of sky-formation. 'Making a place for the three bodies' is the character magically manifested by the two collections (of merit and knowledge).[10]

Reverend Śāradvatīputra, besides, there is the objective realm for the body secret of the Tathāgata. Here, 'body secret' is the character which is the natural result of great merit. What is the natural result of merit is the Sambhogakāya of the Tathāgata. Besides, it is the body secret and the marvelous action of the body of the Tathāgata. Reverend Śāradvatīputra, 'speech' is the character of both convention (*saṃvṛti*) and absolute (*paramārtha*). What is the character of both convention and absolute, that is the Nirmāṇakāya of the Tathāgata.[11]

Comprehending that Dependent Origination is without nihilism and without eternalism is a comprehension by way of the understanding proper to mental perception (*manovijñāna*). One may know it by repeated practice of meditation (*dhyāna*), that is, without aim, without any defilement, and void of purification. It is not the objective realm of body, not the scope of speech. What is not an objective realm for the natural presence of the mind is the Dharmakāya of the Tathāgata, rightly united in the realm of sky. That is how a place is made for the three bodies of the Tathāgata [12].

Reverend Śāradvatīputra, besides, what be the body secret of the Tathāgata, that is the Dharmakāya. What be the Dharmakāya, observe as the Middle Path of natures (*dharma*). What be the Middle Path, that is not born, does not die. Whether Tathāgatas arise, or do not arise, this Dharmakāya remains[13].

Reverend Śāradvatīputra, 'natural result of merit' belongs to the terminology of the perfections' (*pāramitā*). Here, also regard a 'perfection' as a natural result of merit. Who so? Reverend Śāradvatīputra, the Perfection of Giving (*dāna-pāramitā*) is allowed to have two kinds—outer and inner things. Among them, the 'outer' is a term of convention (*samvṛti*) and 'inner' is a term of the absolute (*paramārtha*).[14]

Among them, the 'outer' is the giving of food to whoever desires food; the giving of drink to whoever desires drink; likewise, the giving of male servant, female servant, workman, wage earner, elephant, horse, chariot, earth, head, arm, leg, eye, flesh, blood, marrow, fat, and so on, up to bone. Besides, when used with the perfection of (skillful) means (*upāya-pāramitā*) the giving of maturation, (fulfilling of) human hopes, abundance, magnificence, and the paying of respect. All these are 'outer' giving.[15]

By the 'inner' (is meant) the giving of the doctrine (*dharma*), And it is of two kinds: While understanding and absorbed in Dependent Origination, to resort to the Perfection of (Skillful) Means controlled by compassion with tales of giving, tales of morality, tales of forbearance, and tales of (the other perfections) striving, meditation, insight, means, power, aspiration, and knowledge. Moreover, inner giving might resort to the Perfection of Power controlled by sympathetic joy at (anybody's) elimination of the positing of extremes (such as eternalism or nihilism), of the constructive thought and discursive thought of birth and cessation, and of the (dualistic) knowing and knowable. These (two) are gifts of the Doctrine.[16]

The one which controlled by Perfection of Insight (*prajñāpāramitā*), while there is neither lassitude nor over-excitement of body, speech, and mind; and while there is no straying (to improper objects) of body, speech, and mind; or, solely, resorts to the Perfection of (Skillful) means controlled by equanimity (*upekṣā)* while one remains without defilement (*kleśa*)—is the Perfection of Morality (*śīla-pāramitā*).[17]

The one which, disregarding one's own body and life, resorts to the Perfection of Insight controlled by friendship (or, love, *maitrī*), while avoiding (judgment of) merit or demerit, virtue or vice, truth or falsehood, moving or motionless entities—that is here the Perfection of Forbearance (*kṣānti-pāramitā*).[18]

The one enthusiastically enterprising without discouragement for achieving (the perfections of) giving, morality, forbearance, and *samādhi,* while resorting to the Perfection of Insight controlled by friendliness, continual placelessness, and non-aiming at that (goal)—that is here the Perfection of Striving (*vīrya-pāramitā*).[19]

Reverend Śāradvatīputra, this is the collection of merit which accomplishes the secret of the Tathāgata's Sambhogakāya. [20]

Reverend Śāradvatīputra, besides, the collection of knowledge is what understands those four Perfections; analyzes, explains and clarifies the Perfections; and while absorbed in that (pursuit), rightly teaches impermanence, non-self, and voidness; that feeding and collection are non-given things, that all given things are non-given things. In short, what rightly teaches the dispelling of lust, hatred, and delusion, defilements and associate defilements; and is equal to the Dharmadhātu, the base of infinite space; this, aimless, is the Perfection of Meditation (*dhyāna-pāramitā*). What is the self-presence of thusness, voidness, transcendent voidness (*atyanta-śūnyatā*), voidness at the latter end (*aparāntaśūnyatā*), and of the Dharmadhātu, that is here, the Perfection of Insight (*prajñā-pāramitā*). Reverend Śāradvatīputra, this is the collection of knowledge.[21]

Since Nirvaṇa is blissful, the absolute, calm, untroubled, wholesome, without sickness—enroll in the Dharma-text! Get placed on the path with every station (of success)! The Buddha Bhagavat's introspective knowledge realm is equal to the unequalled by reason of equality, (the Tathāgata) adds the omniscient wisdom possessed of all the best aspects (i.e., the Perfections). Hence, one should rightly embrace, rightly extol, rightly rejoice (in that path); and should enroll upon the stage which is delightful, pure, and gladdening. One should not transgress the time and right measure for maturing the sentient beings by distinguished expression (conveying) understanding of the Dharma, and taming them like the great ocean. Thus one acts in obedience to the cause (i.e., the path, etc.) for those (results, i.e., Nirvāṇa, or omniscience).[25]

For the sake of the great assemblage of persons, their benefit and happiness; for the sake of gods and men, one should place them in the series one after another of the incomparable Dharma method of the Mahāyāna. One should confer the scriptures one after another so that there is no interruption in the stream of (consciousness) for the (three) insights, consisting of hearing (the scripture), pondering it, and cultivating it; or in the mental continuum becoming the *yogi* through repeated exercise of wisdom. When there is a fortunate person, but not yet matured, on account of his being worthy of getting matured, I have put forward a single gate of just a side, but have barely explained the entrance.[26]

When he had so spoken, *āyuṣmat* Śāradvatīputra was full of surprise and wonder followed by joy, and said this to Vajrapāṇi, master of the secret folk: Son of the family, excellent, excellent! It is just because such as us have (sorely) limited knowledge, and because you have clarified such a meaning of the profound words to the *śrāvakas* who follow the sermons by others that also you, son of the family, are excellent. Vajrapāṇi replied: Reverend Śārādvatīputra, so it is; as you said it, it is exactly so. Reverend Śārādvatīputra, as to what this *samādhi* is called, it is said that this *samādhi* has the name, "Great Gate of the Diamond Liberation."[27]

14

Going and Not Going: The Scripture and MK, Chap. 2

The following passage is based upon two sources, the prologue to the Mahāyāna scripture *Akṣayamatinirdeśa*, and Nāgārjuna's *Madhyamakakārikā*, Chapter 2. I repeat my previously published translation of Nāgārjuna's second chapter.

Introduction to the Scripture

One may refer to my published article about the scripture *Akṣayamatinirdeśa*, where it is pointed out that this is a re-working of a prior scripture entitled *Bodhisattvapiṭaka*. The prologue of the *Akṣayamati* has a setting of Rājagṛha. Here the Bhagavat was busily proclaiming all sorts of doctrines to the innumerable disciples hearing his promulgations. This initial section concludes with this remark (from the Tibetan): "Thus the Bhagavat rightly taught in extenso this *dharmaparyāya* of the Mahāsamnipāta of final meaning (*nitārtha*) very much along those lines."

The scripture then states: "At that time there appeared in the eastern direction a great golden light." And continues, telling how this golden light spread through the 'three thousand-thousand' world realm down to this world and was not impeded by mountains, and so forth. Then the venerable Ānanda was astonished to see this golden light and array of bejeweled lotuses. He proceeded to where was the Bhagavat and inquired as to what this was a portent. The Bhagavat responded: "Ānanda, in the Eastern direction there is a Bodhisattva called Akṣayamati; he surrounded by sixty myriads of Bodhisattvas will together come in front here. It is a portent of their coming." Shortly after the Bhagavat pronounced those words, the Bodhisattva Akṣayamati along with sixty myriads of Bodhisattvas arrived and gathered in the space in front of the Bhagavat at a height of seven Sāl trees, bowing with folded hands; and praised the Bhagavat with these verses:

> 1. We bow to the compassionate dustless Buddha, the hero who is dustless, free from dust, free of defilement; who has the purified three eyes, whose knowledge is free from caul; who has dispelled the faults, eliminated the three impurities and sin.
> 2. Fearless, you have destroyed the net of delusion; with your ten powers you are unassailable by the host of opponents and frighten the host of opponents who are following a wayward path. Like a lion you go anywhere without timidity.
> 3. Your body, being immaculate and free from the faults of the realm of gods and those of earthlings, dwells within light (Tib. *lam me*). Having eliminated darkness and caul-like nescience, you shine like the sun when free from clouds.
> 4. The best of sentient beings generated love and compassion for these living beings who are protectorless and suffering, are tormented by old age and death, also lack the opportunity (for their aspirations); and arrived to liberate them in the manner of a healing remedy.
> 5. Though it is difficult to cross the phenomenal ocean of nescience and delusion by oneself without listening to other

teachers, you have crossed over the many torrents of defilements and discursive thoughts, and like the lotus which is not adhered to (by water drops) have come (the same way).

6. You, lord of the world have announced for the benefit of the sentient beings that none of these natures (*dharma*) have a self by own-nature and (so) arise in dependence like the sound of an echo; that there is no agent and that there is no feeler.

7. That mundane natures flow like the water of (i.e. down) a mountain, that there is no pith in what unwise persons rely upon. That when one understands all natures to be like the clouds of autumn, one crosses over phenomenal life and reviles all of phenomenal life.

8. Bearing eyes like wide-open petals of the white lotus, you bear a lustre greater than that of the sun and moon. We bow to thee, worthy of being praised and extolled in all the world, who is free of the illness of the undisciplined.

9. We bow with head to the best bull of men, who has gone to the limitless beyond; who has arrived with good qualities (*guṇa*) that are beyond all distinctions; (with head) to the immeasurable good qualities of Sugata, the field of merit (*puṇyakṣetra*) of the Buddha.

The scripture then tells of the Bodhisattva Akṣayamati and his sixty myriads of followers descending from the air in front, bowing with their heads to the feet of the Bhagavat, then circumambulating the Bhagavat seven times, then seating themselves in lotus posture in a group. This should suffice for the introduction to the scriptural extract.

Extract from Akṣayamatinirdeśasūtra Prologue

Then, by the Buddha's power, venerable Śāradvatīputra arose from his seat, adjusted his upper robe, placing his right knee-cap on the ground, bowed with folded hands in the direction where was the Bhagavat, and inquired of the Bhagavat with these words: "Bhagavat, from where did this Bodhisattva Akṣayamati come? What is the name of his Tathāgata? What is the name of his world realm? And how far is it from that world realm to here?" The Bhagavat replied: "Śāradvatīputra, for that you should ask this Bodhisattva Akṣayamati.

He will inform you." Thereupon, the venerable Śāradvatīputra spoke as follows to Bodhisattva Akṣayamati: "Son of the family, where have you come from? What is the name of your Tathāgata? What is the name of that world-realm? How far is it from that world-realm to here?" Akṣayamati spoke: "Venerable Śāradvatīputra, do you now have the idea (*saṃjñā*) of coming and going?" He responded: "Son of the family, I well know that it is an idea." The other said: "Venerable Śāradvatīputra, the one who well knows that it is an idea still does not understand the notion that there are the two. Why is it that in this way you ask, 'Where have you come from'? Consider this:

(1) 'Coming,' venerable Śāradvatīputra, is a term for joining. 'Going,' venerable Śāradvatīputra, is a term for ouster. Where there is neither the term for joining nor the term for ouster at that place, there is neither coming nor going. No-coming, no-going is the 'going' of the nobles.

(2) 'Coming,' venerable Śāradvatīputra, is the character of action (*karma*)-nature. 'Going,' venerable Śāradvatīputra, is the cessation character of action-nature. Where there is neither the character of action-nature, nor the cessation character of action-nature at that place, there is neither coming nor going. No-coming, no-going is the 'going' of the nobles.

(3) 'Coming,' venerable Śāradvatīputra, is the character of fervent aspiration (*praṇidhāna*). 'Going,' venerable Śāradvatīputra is the cessation character of fervent aspiration. Where there is neither the character of fervent aspiration nor the cessation character of fervent aspiration at that place, there is neither coming nor going. No-coming, no-going is the 'going' of the nobles."

[Nos. (4) through (10) have a similar pattern, namely: (4) 'Coming'—character of arising (*utpāda*); 'Going'—character of cessation (*nirodha*); (5)—the character of gateway to worldly information (*vijñapti*);—the cessation character, to wit, the gateway to liberation (*vimokṣa*); (6)—the domain (*viṣaya*) of coming;—the domain of going; (7) the character of condition (*pratyaya*);—the cessation character of condition; (8) the character of dependent origination (*pratītyasamutpāda*); —the cessation character of dependent origination; (9)—character of arising from a cause (*hetu*); —cessation character of arising from a cause; (10)—conventional sound (Tib. *tha snyad kyi sgra*), letters (*yi ge*), a sign (*brda*);

—the experience (*parijñana*) of conventional sound, letters, signs.]

Then the venerable Śāradvatīputra said this to the Bodhisattva Akṣayamati: "Son of the family, your eloquence does not apply, inasmuch as I asked to hear about matters not heard before. Son of the family, it is like this, for example: A customs official is deciding the state tax and customs duty. Somebody comes along the road carrying incense sticks or a burden;, and the official asks him, 'What are you carrying?' And he insists, 'Give me the state tax and the customs duty! In the same way, son of the family, we, the Śrāvakas, follow the speech of another. Being convinced through hearing (the teaching) from another, there is no interruption in these (teachings) staying present in our streams of consciousness. It is through such illustrious persons as yourself that the Śrāvakas and the pratyekabuddhas arise. Since you have embraced this Mahāyāna, you should be asked. Hence, son of the family, please explain where you come from; what is the name of your Tathāgata; what is the name of the world realm, and how far is that world realm to this place!" "Śāradvatīputra, since the Tathāgata is here in front of you, you should ask him. Were he to give reply, the entire retinue would have no doubts." Thereupon, the reverend Śāradvatīputra questioned the Bhagavat with these words: "Bhagavat, as to where bodhisattva Akṣayamati came from, the name of his Tathāgata, the name of the world realm, and how far is this world realm to here—innumerable sentient beings, upon hearing the name of the Tathāgata in this case and the name of that Buddha field, would seek the armor for enlightenment. Would the Tathāgata please tell us. O Bhagavat, Sugata, please tell us!" The Bhagavat said: "Śāradvatīputra, alright, listen well, hold it in mind, and I shall tell you. Being told the virtues of that world realm, having heard the names of those Bodhisattvas and of that Tathāgata, may they with faith and conviction not be afraid of the unattached, unhindered wisdom of the Tathāgata; may they have no doubts." The venerable Śāradvatīputra exhorted the Bhagavat, saying, "Excellent!" and waited expectingly. The Bhagavat spoke as follows: "Śāradvatīputra, in the direction East of this Buddha field there are Buddha fields more numerous than the sands of the Ganges, and past them there is a world realm called Unwinking (*mi 'dzums*). There the Tathāgata, Arhat, Samyaksambuddha called Samantabhadra presently dwells, lives, tarries, and teaches the Dharma. The Bodhisattva Akṣayamati came from there." [The

Bhagavat in the words of the scripture then dwells upon the virtues of that world realm. After a lengthy portrayal, the Bodhisattva Akṣayamati in a *samādhi* "Revelation of all Buddha fields" and with help of the group's 'roots of virtue' (*kuśalamūla*) enabled Śāradvatīputra and the entire retinue to have a vision of the world realm Unwinking. This had the result of producing a miraculous rain of flowers in that world realm called Unwinking. The Bodhisattvas there asked the Tathāgata Samantabhadra, the reason for the rain of flowers and was told it was because the Bodhisattva Akṣayamati had gone to the world realm where the Buddha Śākyamuni was teaching and had presented flowers to him. At the supplication of those Bodhisattvas, the Buddha Samantabhadra drew light from his body, which light passed through the various Buddha fields and revealed to his own Bodhisattvas the world realm where Śākyamuni was teaching this assembly.] All those Bodhisattvas (in the retinue of Samantabhadra) arose from their individual seats, folded their palms, saluted this Bhagavat Tathāgata Śākyamuni and these Bodhisattvas, and then spoke as follows: "Bhagavat, considering that those Bodhisattvas amount to no more than what could be placed on the tip of a hair in this world realm, from where were this many Bodhisattvas assembled? That Bhagavat (i.e. Śākyamuni) responded: "Sons of the family, these Bodhisattvas have assembled from the ten directions of innumerable Buddha fields in order to hear the Dharma." (That sentence concludes the prologue of this scripture.)

Remarks on the Foregoing

There is little doubt that this *Akṣayamatinirdeśasūtra* aims in its prologue chapter to present the Buddhist theory of coming and going. The nine verses of praise of the Bhagavat Śākyamuni set the stage. Thus, vs. 2, "Like a lion you go anywhere without timidity;" vs. 4, "have arrived;" vs. 5, "have crossed over" and "have come" vs. 7, "one crosses over;" vs. 9, "who has gone to" and "who has arrived with." The verses exemplify the two meanings of the title *tathāgata*, namely, *tathā+gata* and *tathā+āgata*, "who has thus gone and "who has thus come".

Then, when Śāradvatīputra asks the Bodhisattva Akṣayamati to tell where he had come from, the Bodhisattva seemingly sidesteps the question by detailing ten different significations of 'coming' and of 'going' beginning with 'coming' as a term for joining, and 'going' as a term for ouster. The Bodhisattva announces that the negations of both the 'coming' and the 'going' in each of those ten cases as applied to a particular place is a 'going' to the nobles. We may conclude that the 'going' of the nobles is independent of the place. But Śāradvatīputra is dissatisfied with this exposition by the Bodhisattva; and points out that when he had asked the question of where the Bodhisattva had come from, he meant in the usual meaning of the words as used in normal conversation and communication, just as, for example, when a customs official declares the tax to be paid. Śāradvatīputra means that explanations with veiled intentions are not suitable for Śrāvakas, who depend on others for instruction.

So the Bodhisattva sends Śāradvatīputra back to the Buddha to get the answer to the question. Then Śākyamuni tells the answer in clear, unambiguous language; but now there is an appeal to faith, since the answer strains credulity, when it announces that a group of Bodhisattva has been able to come here from an immensely distant world realm in the east, and do it practically in an instant. But one must also concede that if they are to succeed in the remarkable visitation, it must be in an instant, for if it had to be done in ordinary time of past, present, and future, there would be insufficient time for them to arrive.

In Buddhist dogmatics, this ability of 'going' is attributed to the 'body made of mind' (*manomayakāya*) which is treated in the Buddhist genesis accounts. The *Mahāvastu* (I, 339), speaking of men of the 'first eon' describes them as living in this 'body made of mind' and "going where they wish" (*yenakāmagatāḥ*), with the implication that wherever they wish to be, they are there; and yet if indeed such can happen, the 'body made of mind' must be independent of here and there.

Śāradvatīputra—here the early disciple Śāriputra reacting to new-fangled Mahāyāna formulations—does not care for a sentence like "No-coming, no-going is the 'going' of the nobles." He prefers the difficulty in lie in profundity of the statement. The hearer finds no trouble in understanding Śāradvatīputra's example as far as the words are concerned. But what if the 'incense sticks' are the person's virtue, the burden his vices; and what if the official is the scribe of Yama (lord of the dead)? In such an interpretation, the 'state tax' is the judgment rendered for the virtues, and the 'customs duty' the one for the vices; and then the road is the path to the other world.

INTRODUCTION TO MK, II

I approached the second chapter of *Madhyamakakārikā* in a different way in a published article. There I claimed that the desperate unintelligibility of translations of this chapter was in part due to not recognizing that the form *gamyate,* passive in appearance is in fact sometimes employed reflexively in the context of that chapter. While I still maintain this position, I need not here cite the various passages from Indian sources about 'going' that I cited in that essay, since I have preceded with scriptural materials. Even so, it is necessary to face up to some grammatical points.

The form gamyate. Vasu's work on Pāṇini gives the illustration of 'Causal Passive': *rāmo grāmaṃ gamyate* (Rāma is caused to go to a village). But he provides no example of the reflexive use of *gamyate* in the manner of the grammatical example *odanaḥ svayam eva pacyate* ("the rice cooks of itself"), where the *karman* functions as the agent; and of course the words *svayam eva* did not have to be expressed (they would be understood). On the occasion of the orientalist conference in Japan in early September, 1983, two Sanskritists native to India discounted my suggestion that *gamyate* could be employed reflexively, claiming the denial was Pāṇini's. At that same meeting I discussed the matter with Dr. Ram Karan Sharma, who has had a distinguished career in India in terms of the Sanskrit language. He laughed and explained that the denial was not Pāṇini's; and that in fact the passive of any verb can be employed reflexively; and is, if one can find authentic examples in the literature. Therefore, to validify my contention about this use of the form *gamyate,* it was incumbent upon me to find other examples than just attributing the usage to the *Madhyamakakārikā,* chapter II. Since its author Nāgārjuna was a Buddhist, it seems preferable to find such examples in Buddhist literature in particular, because these authors especially relied on the grammar called *Kātantra Vyākaraṇa,* which is a post-Pāṇinian system of Sanskrit grammar. In my published article I cited Dharmakīrti's *Pramāṇavārttika,* Svārthānumāna chap., k. 17:

> *na ca nāstīti vacanāt tan nāsty eva yathā yadi /*
> *nāsti sa khyāpyate nyāyas tadā nāstīti gamyate //*

> Not just by saying, "It is not," is it not. If a rule is expressed, to wit, how it is not, one (easily) understands that it is not.

In this case the reflexive use of the passive is an example where the verb *gam-* has the sense 'to understand'. I have now found an example where *gam-* means 'to go'. The passage is from Nāropa's *Sekoddeśaṭīkā,* where the author comments on a citation from the *Vimalaprabhā* (an exegesis of the *Kālacakratantra*). This is the *Vimalaprabhā* passage:

> *ekaṃ padaṃ vajramaṇāu rajo 'rka uṣṇīṣaśukre śaśini dvitīyam /*
> *abhyastaṃ sadā 'cchedyam abhedyam iṣṭam bhartus trilokasaṃhitaṃ śirasā praṇamya //*
> Bowing with head to the one foot of the Lord that is always unbroken, undivided, desired; placed upon the three worlds; and is focussed upon (*abhyasta*) when the solar discharge is in the diamond gem and the second one is in the moon, i.e. in the *uṣṇīṣaśukra* . . .

I cite Nāropa's commentary only for the part needed to support my contention:

> *bhartur bodhicittavajrasya śrīkālacakrasya /*
> *padyate gamyate yena tat padaṃ jñānam akṣaram //*
> [Bowing with my head] to that (one) foot i.e., to the incessant wisdom of the Lord, i.e., of the diamond of Bodhicitta, i.e., of Śrīkālacakra by which he proceeds, i.e., goes (easily) ...

That is to say, the term *padyate* (he proceeds) is not the passive, for which there is *pādyate*. Therefore, when the commentator adds *gamyate* this cannot be construed as the passive in meaning, although it is the passive in form, but rather as the reflexive in meaning.

But as various Sanskritists may still not be convinced, I shall try my hand at an example outside of Buddhist literature, namely, in the *Nirukta* etymological and lexicographical tradition. Admittedly, Mehendale, in his fascinating essay *Nirukta Notes,* Series 1, the "Etymology of the Word Artha," tried to justify the passive interpretation of the two 'going' terms *aryate* and *gamyate*. He points out that Yāska (Nirukta 1-18) has two possible etymologies for artha, from *r-* 'to go' or from *araṇa* + *stha-* 'to remain in a distant place'; and that the commentators took the primary sense of *artha* to be 'wealth' or 'meaning'. The Durga commentary opts for 'wealth'. For Durga's second etymology Mehendale properly translates the comment: "because when the owner of the wealth goes from this world to another, it does not go with him to the next world, but stays behind". But for the first etymology—he translates the comment *aryate hy asäv arthibhiḥ* with the passive interpretation of the verb; "because wealth is sought (lit. gone to) by those desirous of it". But if this comment is translated consistently with the second comment (above), it may be rendered with reflexive interpretation of the verb: "because it (the wealth) (easily) goes (*aryate*) yonder (*asāu*) along with those who own the wealth (*arthin*)". Granted that the interpretation of *arthin* as 'desirous of' is a prevalent usage of the term in Sanskrit; but this employment of *artha* in the sense of 'goal' suits neither of the primary meanings, 'wealth' or 'meaning'; and either of these two would have to be on hand somewhere before one of them could be (secondarily) an aim or goal. Mahendale then takes up the commentary ascribed to Skanda-Maheśvara, which accepts the primary sense of *artha* to be 'meaning', with 'wealth' secondary; and comments on each for both 'going' and 'staying', a word when pronounced disappears but its meaning stays; the wealth stays when the owner goes abroad. In the case of the first etymology of 'going', the secondary 'wealth' is illustrated: "because in business it goes from one person to another". But for the 'meaning' interpretation *yas tāvac chabdasyārthaḥ sa tasmād gamyate,* Mahendale renders it: because the meaning (of the word) is understood (lit. gone to, *gamyate*) from it, the word. Of course, *gamyate* is employed countless times in Sanskrit in this passive sense. However, to adopt the passive sense here defeats the intention of the commentator, who employs this form of the verb *gam-* 'to go' to illustrate the 'going' etymology of the word *artha;* wherefore the secondary sense of *gam-* 'to understand' is irrelevant. It follows that the way to bring out the commentator's intention is to adopt the reflexive interpretation of *gamyate* while rendering the comment: "What is meanwhile (*tāvat*) the meaning of the pronounced word (*śabdasyārtha*), that (easily) goes from it (the pronounced word) [to another pronunciation of that word]."

The foregoing argument completes my proof that sometimes

gamyate was employed reflexively, while acknowledging that the form is usually quite correctly interpreted as a passive.

The So-called Denial of Motion

It will be noticed in my translation of the MK, II verses that the adoption of the reflexive interpretation of *gamyate* in certain places effectively spoils the theory that Nāgārjuna denied motion. In any case, he certainly did not deny it to the Tathāgata, who has the term *gata* or *āgata* in the name, in his chapter on the Tathāgata in MK. Granted that Nāgārjuna gives the impression of having denied motion in MK, II. But I cited the commentator Buddhapālita on this very chapter. He starts his commentary with the union remark (*pratisaṃdhi*): "You have taught (i.e. in chap. I) in successive manner the principle of non-arising. We are thrilled to hear about voidness. Pray explain how the 'gone' (*gatam*) and the come' (*āgatam*) according to mundane perception in not valid." Thus, the commentator disagrees that Nāgārjuna denies motion; rather that he rejects the ordinary notions of what motion amounts to.

In fact, Nāgārjuna rejects the realist notion of horizontal motion. This realist position is described by locatives in the basic grammatical sense of "at". That is to say, the realist insists that the goer starts *at* some point; at each successive time he is again *at* some place on the road. The realist opponent's position is presented in MK, II, k. 2, with the expression *yatra* ("where") and *tatra* ("there"). The scripture cited in the foregoing section says the same but in a negative way. The Bodhisattva Akṣayamati in ten statements each time uses a formula involving the same locative expressions, there rendered "where" and "at that place". Thus, the very first one of the list: "Where there is neither the term for joining nor the term for ouster at that place there is neither coming nor going. No-coming, no-going is the 'going' of the nobles." Akṣayamati tells it with a sort of veiled intention. He is speaking to a realist, Śāradvatīputra, who insists that the Bodhisattva speak in ordinary terms, as when a traveller comes along a road and the customs official stops him, since the realist requires a road for the motion to work. It was with this realist position that some previous translators of MK chapters, including chapter two, tried to introduce an 'understood' (but not expressed) "road" in their renditions of MK,

II, k. 1. That is why such translators are dismayed at my 'reflexive' interpretation of *gamyate*—when the *karman* is the agent—because with my interpretation, it is not that Nāgārjuna was making silly statements, and those translators were correct—but it is simply that those translators did not know grammar sufficiently, and they were more willing to attribute inappropriateness to Nāgārjuna than to admit their own incapacity in this matter. In Akṣayamati's way of stating the case, the noble's way of going is with no-coming and no-going in the realist sense of "where" and "at that place"

A Reading in MK, II, k. 11

Regarding my correction of a reading in k. 11 of Nāgārjuna's *Madhyamakakārikā*, second chap., J.W. de Jong challenges this in a brief communication in *JAOS*, Vol. 106.4, 1986. He said: In a note he [Wayman] rejects the readings *cājyate* and *yayājyate*, because the verb *aj-* means 'to drive, propel' (*JAOS*, Vol. 103.3, p. 586, n. 35). It is therefore perhaps not superfluous to point out that *ajyate* is the third person singular present passive of the root *añj-*. Wayman refers to p. 62, n. 45 of Jacques May, Candrakīrti: *Prasannapadā Madhyamakavṛtti* . . . (Paris, 1959) in which Jacques May not only cites Walleser's *Tibetische* version, but also mentions the root *añj-* and not the root *aj-*. I may add that the manuscript R leaves no doubt about the correctness of the reading *cājyate* and *yayājyate*, cf. *Indo-Iranian Journal*, Vol. XX (1978), pp. 37-38." I admire de Jong's scholarship for his splendid translation into French of six chapters of the *Prasannapadā*, Paris, 1949; for his edition of the *Mūlamadhyamakakārikā* (The Adyar Library, Madras, 1977); and for his useful "Text Critical Notes on the Prasannapadā"—which is meant by his reference to the *Indo-Iranian Journal*. But when he says, "It is therefore perhaps not superfluous . . ," I would respond that it is indeed superfluous. This is because neither J. May nor any other competent translator could have rendered that verse using the *añj-* ("to anoint"); J. May in fact accepted the reading *ucyate*. It was in William Dwight Whitney, *The Roots. . . of the Sanskrit Language* (reprint, New Haven, 1945) that I noticed the form *ajyate* as the passive for both *aj-* and *añj-*; but in my published essay I mentioned *aj-* which was the only possibility for de Jong's readings to be correct. I rejected his suggested solution because the Tibetan translation *mngon* apparently disagrees with him. Now I have more information on that Tibetan term. There is available the three-volume Tibetan-Chinese dictionary called *Bod rgya tshig mdzod chen mo.* Under *mngon* it gives two meanings: (1) *gsal cha 'am mtshon pa* "clarification or showing"; (2) *mdun nam thad ka,* "in front or straight ahead". Only the first meaning can apply since the Tib. *mgnon pa* in k. 11 represents a finite verb. Jampa Chogyal, *A Tibetan Dictionary* [by syllables] (Delhi, 1969), has a well-developed entry, and the set *mngon rgyu mngon bzhin mngon pa* seems applicable. Here *mngon* as *rgyu* (Skt. *hetu)* has the sense to be motivated'; *mngon bzhin,* in the light of other entries: 'to envisage'; so *mngon pa,* either 'be motivated' or 'to envisage'. This supports neither La Vallée Poussin's *ucyate* nor de Jong's *ajyate* (whether from the root *añj-* or the root *aj-*). It does support my suggestion of *ūhyate,* probably as 'be motivated' (agreeing with both *ūh-* roots), almost the 'resolves' in my previous translation—both solutions indicating a mental component to the 'going', i.e., a person is motivated to go or 'resolves' to go. Buddhism stresses the mental component as decisive for acts of speech or body.

Sthiramati (*Pañcaskandha-prakaraṇa-vaibhāṣya,* PTT, Vol. 114, p. 21-1-7, 8) probably also intends *ūhyate* for *mngon* as a verb, but in the meaning "is proved": "How is it proved that there exists an *ālaya-vijñāna* other than, i.e., not belonging to the six *pravṛtti-vijñāna?* It is proved by scripture (*āgama*) and by reason (*yukti*)." (*'jug pa'i rnam par shes pa drug po ma gtogs par gzhan kun gzhi rnam par shes pa yod par ci mngon zhe na / lung dang rig pas mngon no /*).

Madhyamakakārikā, Chap. II

In the foregoing, the term *gamyate* was explained as possibly to be construed as a reflexive.

Besides, MK, II, 1 has the term *gatam, agatam,* and *gamyamānam.* Some scholars, according to their understanding of the Candrakīrti's commentary, thought that these terms agree with an unexpressed word for road, although *gatam* and the others are neuter in form and there is no word for 'road' normally in Buddhist texts that would fit, since *mārga, patha,* and *adhvan* are all of masculine gender.

It should be pointed out for MK, II, 1 that the term *tāvat* serves as the 'how' for the initial negation. The *na. . . tāvat* reminds me of the compound *atāvat* ('not equal to them in number); adapting this significance to a sentence dealing with going or the lack of same, *atāvat* would mean according to information from Bhoja and the *Nāṭyaśāstra,* not equal in quickness, slowness, in resolute nature, or in abundance of steps.

The last bit of necessary information is from the Tibetan translation of MK, II, 1, which interprets the *gamyate* of the second hemistich with the 'understanding' sense. This then is MK, II, 1:

> *gataṃ na gamyate tāvad agataṃ naiva gamyate /*
> *gatāgatavinirmuktaṃ gamyamānaṃ na gamyate* //1 //
> What has already gone (or moved forward) does not of itself go to that extent. What has not yet gone does not of itself go at all. One is led to misunderstand a present-going (or treading) excluding both the 'already gone' and the 'not yet gone'.

In short, I construed the first two *gamyate* as reflexives, and the last *gamyate* as the 'causal passive'. The expressions "does not of itself go" agree with Nāgārjuna's initial verse in MK, I that a *hetu* (here, 'motive') is required. In the last half, Nāgārjuna does not deny a present-going (or treading): he charges that one is led to misunderstand it, namely, if one believes the realist account to be given in MK, II, 2:

> *ceṣṭā yatra gatis tatra gamyamāne ca sa yataḥ /*
> *na gate nāgate ceṣṭā gamyamāne gatis tataḥ* //2 //
> Where there is movement, at that place is the gait. And that movement is at the treading, but neither at the already gone nor at the not yet gone. Therefore, there is a gait at the treading.

The realist requires a road on which to go. That is why he uses the expressions *yatra, tatra*. Nāgārjuna's first retort is in MK II, 3:

> *gamyamānasya gamanaṃ kathaṃ nāmaopapatsyate /*
> *gamyamāne dvigamanaṃ yadā naivopapadyate* //3 //
> How can it be valid that there is a going of the treading? At the time it is at the treading, there is no validity for two kinds of going (i.e., both treading and going).

The realist imagines that the treading moves forward, increasing the 'already gone' and decreasing the 'not yet gone', and thus requires both the *gamyamāna* ('treading') and the *gamana* ('going') as though the *gamana* is pushing the *gamyamāna* onward. According to Nāgārjuna, this is ridiculous. And II, 4:

> *gamyamānasya gamanam yasya tasya prasajyate /*
> *ṛte gater gamyamānaṃ gamyamānaṃ hi gamyate* // 4 //
> For whom the treading possesses going, there is entailed a treading in the absence of a gait, for the treading goes by itself.

Another person thinks the treading possesses the going, so without the goer's gait, it goes by itself (*gamyate* again as a reflexive, implying *svayam eva*). And II, 5:

> *gamyamānasya gamane prasaktaṃ gamanadvayam /*
> *yena tad gamyamānaṃ ca yac cātra gamanaṃ punaḥ*/ /5//
> When there is going of the treading, two goings are entailed—the treading by someone and the going in that place.

Nāgārjuna modifies the previous attack by introducing the role of the goer by the term *yena*. Many of the subsequent verses deal with this goer, as does the next group, II, 6-11:

> *dvau gantārau prasajyete prasakte gamanadvaye /*
> *gantāram hi tiraskṛtya gamanam nopapadyate* // 6 //
> When two goings are entailed, two goers are the logical consequence; for in the absence of a goer, a going is not valid.

> *gantāram cet tiraskṛtya gamanaṃ nopapadyate /*
> *gamane 'sati gantātha kuta eva bhaviṣyati* // 7 //
> If in the absence of goer, the going is not valid—how on the other hand, is there a goer when there is no going?

> *gantā na gacchati tāvad agantā naiva gacchati /*
> *anyo gantur agantuś ca kas tṛtīyo tha gacchati* // 8 //
> A goer does not go so much. A non-goer does not go at all. What third other than a goer or a non-goer goes?

> *gantā tāvad gacchatīt katham evopapatsyate /*
> *gamanena vinā gantā yadā naivopapadyate* // 9 //

How is it valid to say that a goer goes so much, when a goer is not cogent in the absence of going?

pakṣo gantā gacchatīti yasya tasya prasajyate /
gamanena vinā gantā gantur gamanam icchataḥ // 10 //
When someone espouses the logical case (*pakṣa;* or 'thesis'), "A goer goes," claiming a going of the goer—(in fact,) the goer is outside the going [i.e., the *gamana* is not in the *pakṣa*].

gamane dve prasajyete gantā yady uta gacchati /
*ganteti *cohyate*[35] *yena gantā san yac ca gacchati* // 11 //
Besides, two goings are entailed if a goer goes: who resolves[36] to be a 'goer', and the goer who goes.

The important k. 11 shows the interior, or mental, going; and the exterior, or obvious, going. The mental kind of going as a category sets the stage for the next three verses dealing with starting:

gate nārabhyate gantuṃ gantuṃ nārabhyate 'gate /
nārabhyate gamyamāne gantum ārabhyate kuha // 12 //
One does not start to go at the already gone. One does not start to go at the not yet gone. One does not start to go at the treading. How does one start to go?

na pūrvaṃ gamanārambhād gamyamānaṃ na vā gatam /
yatrārabhyeta gamanam agate gamanaṃ kutaḥ // 13 //
Before going has started, there is neither a treading nor an already gone where one starts the going. How is there a going on the not yet gone?

gataṃ kiṃ gamyamānaṃ kim agataṃ kiṃ vikalpyate /
adṛśyamāna ārambhe gamanasyaiva sarvathā // 14 //
As long as the start of the going is not envisaged at all—What is imagined as the already gone? What as the treading? What as the not yet gone?

Then three verses dealing with staying:

gantā na tiṣṭhati tāvad agantā naiva tiṣṭhati /
anyo gantur agantuś ca kas tṛtīyo 'tha tiṣṭhati // 15 //
A goer does not stay so much. A non-goer does not stay at all.

What third other than a goer or a non-goer stays?

gantā tāvat tiṣṭhatīti katham evopapatsyate /
gamanena vinā gantā yadā naivopapadyate // 16 //
How is it valid to say that a goer stays so much, when a goer is not cogent in the absence of going?

na tiṣṭhati gamyamānān na gatān nāgatād api /
gamanaṃ saṃpravṛttiś ca nivṛttiś ca gateḥ samā // 17 //
One does not stay via the treading, via the already gone, or via the not yet gone. Going, advancing, and retreating are the same as a gait.

Four verses on identification of the goer:

yad eva gamanaṃ gantā sa eveti na yujyate /
anya eva punar gantā gater iti na yujyate // 18 //
It is not valid that whatever be the going, the goer is precisely it. It is not valid that the goer is precisely other than the gait.

yad eva gamanaṃ gantā sa eva hi bhaved yadi /
ekībhāvaḥ prasajyeta kartuḥ karmaṇa eva ca // 19 //
For, if the going were precisely the goer, it would entail an identity of the agent and the action.

When agent and action are identified, it amounts to the reflexive verb; so if this were always the case, it would not be possible to have any of the three possibilities which Vasu gives, by calling them 'primitive', 'causal active', and 'causal passive':

anya eva punar gantā gater yadi vikalpyate /
gamanaṃ syād ṛte gantur gantā syād gamanād ṛte // 20 //
On the other hand, if the goer is imagined as other than the gait, there would be both going without a goer and the goer without a going.

ekībhāvena vā siddhir nānābhāvena vā yayoḥ /
na vidyate tayoḥ siddhiḥ kathaṃ nu khalu vidyate // 21 //
Of which two, there is no proof either by identity or by separateness, I should like to know[37] how there is their proof.

Four final verses on the three ways of going:

gatyā 'yayohyate gantā gatiṃ tāṃ sa na gacchati /
yasmān na gatipūrvo 'sti kaścid kiṃcid dhi gacchati //22//

Who resolves per gait—the goer: he does not approach that gait.[38] This is because when anyone goes somewhat, he does not precede the gait.

*gatyā *yayohyate gantā tato 'nyāṃ sa na gacchati /*
gatī dve nopapadyete yasmād eke tu gantari // 23 //
Who resolves per gait—the goer: he does not approach one (i.e., gait) different from that. This is because when there is one goer, two gaits are not cogent.

sadbhūto gamanaṃ gantā triprakaraṃ na gacchati /
nāsadbhūto 'pi gamanaṃ triprakaraṃ na gacchati // 24 //
An actual goer does not go (as per) three ways of going. Also an unreal goer does not go (as per) three ways of going.

gamanaṃ sadasadbhūtaḥ triprakāraṃ na gacchati /
tasmād gatiś ca gantā ca gantavyaṃ ca na vidyate // 25 //
One who is actual or is unreal does not go (as per) three ways of going. Hence, there is neither the gait nor the goer nor the to-be-gone upon (a road).

The *gantavyam* in the final verse of this chapter is Nāgārjuna's only reference to the road as such. The verb, 'to go' does not have a ***karman*** object, "ways of going."

NOTE

The reader who observes my extensive use of the *Akṣayamatinirdeśasūtra* at the outset of the present essay on 'going' and elsewhere in the present volume, should be advised that after all these 24 essays had been assembled in their present form and presented for publication by Motilal Banarsidass, I received in the latter part of 1994 the work by Jens Braarvig, *Akṣayamatinirdeśasūtra*, Vol. I and Vol. II (Oslo: Solum Forlag, 1993)—a monument of scholarship. The reader can derive more information therefrom.

15

The Meaning of Death in Buddhism

Buddhist texts are rich in allusions to death, both in its literal sense and in metaphorical extensions. It happens that Buddhism shares many of the positions about death with other Indian religions. This is so with the myth of death, treated first; and it is also true of my next section, definition and signs of death; so also of the mind at death, the third part. The section "mindfulness of death" deals with a special concern of Buddhism. Brief sections on suicide and on the treatment of the deceased allow for other aspects. Indeed, all these topics could be exposed in much greater amplitude. Still, compressing the subject-matter in the given manner, thus surveying the main points may permit an understanding of the Buddhist attitude.

Reprinted from *Studia Missionalia*, Vol. 31, University Gregoriana Editrice. Roma. 1982.

One could hardly overestimate the importance of the topic. This is where the technical doctrines of the monks overlap the popular legends and stories. It is the basis of the moral injunctions as well as the razor-edge path of *yoga*. In the symbolism, it goes with the day's dusk and the year's autumn. However, it is possible to treat this matter in scholarly fashion; and this is what I propose to do.

The Myth of Death

There are two sources for the myth of death in Buddhism: (1) the genesis story found in ancient Buddhist works; (2) the theory of Yama as lord of the dead descended from the fearful form of the Vedic deity found in the *Atharva-Veda* and later Indian literature. May I take these up individually with brevity?

The Buddhist genesis story of the Pāli and northern Buddhist scriptures is contained in each of the three main divisions called Sūtra, Vinaya, and Abhidharma. This involves a theory of periodical destruction of the world systems, and with loss of lower receptable worlds, (the *bhājana-loka*) the retreat of sentient beings to higher realms. At the outset of the new evolution, the sentient beings are called "first eon" (*prathama kalpa*) men. As the lower receptable worlds re-evolve, these beings are said to be subject to a kind of birth called "transformation" (*upapāduka*), which is the kind of birth among the gods and hell beings, as well as among disembodied men in the so-called "intermediate state" (*antarābhava*) between death and rebirth. This kind of birth means a succession of deaths, i.e., death from a higher state and rebirth in a successively lower state until those beings are born "here" in our world, and begin to be born from wombs. The men of the first eon have a beautiful form (*rūpin*) and are made of mind (*manomaya*); are self-luminous, feed on joy and go where they wish. Death as known to modern era was not then possible. It was not until the body became heavier and more substantial due to the intake of food, progressively more coarse, that it became possible to have the present-day dramatic kind of death. Hence the early kind of death, the mythic kind, is analogous to the present-day stages of life, wherein we cease to be children, then cease to be adolescents, and so on. That the first eon men had a life preceding death is implied in that the reverse current towards Nirvāṇa arrives at a state called "deathless" (Pāli, *amata*; Sanskrit, *amṛta*; also to be rendered "ambrosia").[1]

Scholars long ago noticed that in the *Ṛg-Veda* Yama was the first mortal, who chose death and became "King of the dead" (*paretarāj*). In the *Atharva-Veda,* he had a messenger Mṛtyu (death personified), and sometimes Yama was identified with Mṛtyu, accounting for a later name Antaka (the ender). It was this more fearful form of Yama prevalent at the time Buddhism arose, that was adopted by Buddhism. In an article of my own, I cited a passage from the later Abhidharma that all four theory-systems (*siddhānta*) of Buddhism, namely the Vaibhāṣika, Sautrāntika, Yogācāra, and Mādhyamika agreed that the Yama of Hell is a person (*pudgala*).[2] This use of the word *pudgala* is consistent with the Pāli Abhidhamma treatise *Puggala-paññatti*.[3] In its various classification of human types, there is no classification in terms of death or types of death, implying that the *pudgala* is mortality itself.[4] The well-known depictions of the Buddhist "Wheel of Life"—the Tibetan temple-banner form being now the most disseminated—show the wheel held in the claws of a demonic being, usually called Yama. There are indications that this is Yama as Mṛtyu.[5] Besides, the Indian mythology places Yama in the underworld. There are variant descriptions of his residence there. The old Buddhist scripture *Majjhima-Nikāya* III has this description in Horner's translation:[6]

> Four-cornered and with four gates,
> It is divided into equal portions,
> Encircled by an iron wall, with a roof of iron above;
> Its incandescent floor is made of glowing iron;
> All round it stands a hundred *yojanas* square.

In the later period of Indian Buddhism, the *Kālacakra* work called *Vimalaprabhā* referred to three kinds of Yama in this verse:[7]

> The departed spirit (*preta*) dwelling in the place;
> The lord of death (*mṛtyu*) dwelling in the body;
> The defilement (*kleśa*) dwelling in the mind;
> These three are the *karmic* Yama to be tamed.

Of these three, the one "dwelling in the place" means the Yama of the underworld. The one "dwelling in the body" is assigned to the heart. The one "dwelling in the mind" appears to be responsible for the death vision (*infra*). The three have individualized depictions in Tibetan iconography and are respectively called "external", "personal", and "concealed". One of the most popular of the Buddhist tantra deities is Yamāntaka (destroyer of Yama), and there are three forms of this deity to go with the three kinds of Yama.

One of Yama's names is *kālarūpa,* meaning "the form of death-time".[8] This term seems associated with an old Buddhist term, the Pāli *kālakiriyā,* Sanskrit *kālakriyā,* meaning something like "the possible activity at death-time". One of Asaṅga's explanations of the term is: "slaying, an act of Māra" (*māraṇam mārakarma*).[9] We shall see that there is both the "death-time act" and the "form of death-time".

When we consider together the Buddhist genesis account and the foregoing information on the three kinds of Yama, it is clear that the theory of generating a deity Yamāntaka to defeat Yama has the aim of overcoming dramatic death in favor of the kind of death whereby the birth is called "transformation". And this as though one is aiming to re-become one of those "first eon" men.

The prominent role of food in the myth helps explain the fasting rites. The fact that these become life-threatening (Sanskrit *viṣama or bhīṣma*) is not a deterrent to the cult followers, who believe that such practices might enable them to control a situation which is inevitable anyway, since everybody becomes subject to something that is life threatening. However, the Buddha rejected the extreme of severe austerity as well as the extreme of sense indulgence, and announced a Middle Path of moderation and gradual progress. This is a hint that the Buddhist practice does not simply aim to re-become a "first eon" man, since this being is not free from the cyclical flow (*saṃsāra*), but only temporarily free from temptation.

Definition and Signs of Death

Perhaps the oldest formulation in Buddhism of death is the canonical explanation of "old age and death" as the last member of the Dependent Origination formula (*pratītya-samutpāda*). For the death portion of this member the old scripture said:[10]

> Whatever of this and that sentient beings in this and that group is falling or passing away, break up and disappearance,

> death as concrete death, the act of death-time, collapse of personal aggregates, laying down of corpse, severance of life faculty (*jīvitendriya*), this is called death.

According to the Buddhist master Asaṅga, "falling or passing away" (*cyuti-cyavanatā*) means abandonment of body; "breakup" (*bheda*), i.e., of the set of formations (*rūpakāya*); "disappearance" (*antardhāna*), i.e., of the set of names (*nāmakāya*); "severance of life faculty" (*jīvitendriya-nirodha*) means "whose time is up;" "death as concrete death" (*mṛtyu-maraṇa*) means the conscious principle (*vijñāna*) has departed from the heart; "act of death-time" (*kālakriyā*) means starting with death, one or two, or three, or seven days.[11] Some of these expressions need further explanation. The name-set is explained in the Pāli canonical work *Paṭisambhidāmagga* to include feelings (*vedanā*), ideas (*saññā*), volitions (*cetanā*), sense contacts (*phassa*), mental orientations (*manasikāra*), and any mental motivations (*cittasaṅkhāra*). The formation-set is explained in the same work to include the four great elements (*mahābhūta*) and their derivatives, exhalation and inhalation, and any corporeal motivations (*kāyasaṅkhāra*).[12] As to the heart placement of consciousness by the word *vijñāna*, this appears to be Upaniṣadic influence on Buddhism in the Gupta Dynasty, since the old Buddhist canon was silent on the matter and we find such statements by Asaṅga and by the Pāli commentator Buddhaghosa.[13] The personal aggregates (*skandha*) are the well-known five (see below).

In another place Asaṅga presented some alternate definitions. "Falling or passing away" means rupture of a mortal spot (*marmaccheda*); disappearance is the stopping of the formal sense organs (*rūpiṇām indriyāṇām nirodhaḥ*); loss of life (*āyus*) is rattle-breathing (*hikkā-śvāsa*); loss of warmth (*ūṣman*) is an immobile state (*niśceṣṭāvasthā*); abandonment of personal aggregates and stopping of life organ is timely death (*kālamaraṇa*); act of death-time is a state when death cannot be postponed (*asannā ciramṛtāvasthā*), and in other terminology, it is slaying—an act of Māra (*māraṇaṃ mārakarma*).[14]

The traditional signs of approaching timely death were in the description of old age (*jarā*), the first term of the compound "old age and death" (*jarā-maraṇa*), constituting the last member of the Dependent Origination formula. This need not be repeated here.

Other passages had descriptions of severe and life-threatening illnesses. Most famous is the story of the young prince Gautama going out through the various gates of the palace, where he had been leading a sheltered life. Passing through one gate he saw a sick man, through another an old man, and through a third—a corpse being carried on a stretcher. Finally, through the fourth gate he saw a person in the attitude of a pious monk. These visions, in graphic detail are traditionally said to have been instigated by the gods to turn Gautama's mind toward the religious life.[15]

In the medieval period, after the rise of the Buddhist tantras, there is mention of death omens, such as one's face, or a part of it, disappearing in the mirror;[16] and there were rituals called "cheating death" (*mṛtyuvañcana*).[17]

The *Guhyasamājatantra* literature contains omens for the dissolution of the personal aggregates (*skandha*). Thus the mirage goes with the dissolution of the aggregate of formation (*rūpa-skandha*); smoke, the feeling aggregate (*vedanā-skandha*); fire-flies, the aggregates of ideas (*saṃjñā-skandha*); a changeable lamp, the aggregate of motivations (*saṃskāra-skandha*); the three lights (white, red and black), the aggregate of perceptions (*vijñāna-skandha*).[18]

The Mind at Death

Buddhism accepts the general Indian view that the state of mind at death determines one's destination after death.[19]

Asaṅga summarizes this matter in his *Yogācārabhūmi*:[20]

> How does one happen to die and transfer? It is by way of life fully meted. And one should know about death that it is of someone with virtuous mind, with non-virtuous mind, or with indeterminate mind, at proper time or untimely, through exhaustion of life, through exhaustion of merit, or through not avoiding the dangerous (or, threatening).
> How through exhaustion of life? How someone here fulfills life as it was cast and having exhausted it, dies; and this is also "timely death."
> How through exhaustion of merit? Now someone here dies penniless. How through not avoiding the dangerous? It is as the Bhagavat said: "There are nine causes and nine conditions for death-time act (*kālakriyā*) when life is not exhausted. What are the nine? (1) eating food in improper measure; (2)

eating unwholesome food; (3) eating without digesting; (4) being unable to stand the uncooked, while thinking it cooked; (5) refusing medicines; (6) not discriminating what agrees and what disagrees with one's constitution; (7) [not discriminating what one is used to and not used to]; (8) travelling at the wrong time; (9) having impure conduct." And this is also "untimely death".

What is dying with virtuous consciousness? Now, someone here, while dying, remembers previous (virtuous) natures; or, again, someone else makes him remember—whereby in his mind virtuous natures, faith and so on, range; as long as a rough idea operates. When a subtle idea occurs, the virtuous mind is warded off and an indeterminate mind takes place. It is this way: At that time, he is unable to bend (his mind) to the previously repeated virtuous (nature), nor can someone else make him remember.

What is dying with unvirtuous consciousness? Now, someone here while dying remembers by himself previously repeated unvirtuous natures, or others make him remember. At that time in him unvirtuous natures, craving, and so on range; as long as a rough idea operates. And so on, as in the case of the virtuous consciousness (i.e., the indeterminate).

Among them, the one dying with virtuous consciousness dies with a pleasant death, i.e. especially painful feelings do not befall his body at the time of death. The one dying with unvirtuous consciousness dies with a painful death, especially painful feelings befall his body at the time of death. Furthermore, the one dying with virtuous consciousness sees forms that are non-delusive. The one dying with unvirtuous consciousness sees forms that are delusive.

What is dying with indeterminate consciousness? Whether it be engaging in virtuous or unvirtuous (natures), he does not engage in it by himself remembering, or being made to remember by others. He is dying neither with virtuous consciousness nor with defiled consciousness. He dies neither with a pleasant death nor with a painful death. Furthermore, it is a person (*pudgala*) dying while engaging in (both) virtue and unvirtue, either that he by himself remembers the previously repeated virtuous and unvirtuous natures, or is made to remember by others.

The alternative, several times mentioned, "or is made to remember by others", points to the value of death sermons, which grew into *The Tibetan Book of the Dead* and smaller treatises in Tibet that were read to the dying person.

Asaṅga points out that the experience at the time of death is fruitional (a *phala*) being governed by two causes, delight in elaboration (of sense objects) (*prapañcābhirati*) and *karma* good and bad (*śubhāśubhakarma*).[21] This shows that if one wants the proper kind of consciousness to be present at death, he must prepare for it. This is the message of a scripture in the Pāli canon *Aṅguttara-Nikāya* (Book of Sixes), the *Bhaddaka-sutta*. Sāriputta, the celebrated Buddha disciple tells the monks how they fashion their lives to an unfortunate death (*na bhaddakaṃ maraṇaṃ*), and then how they fashion their lives to a fortunate death. In each case, the fruitional state is called "death-time act" (*kālakiriyā;* Skt. *kālakriyā*). Just as in Asaṅga's terminology, the one who delights in elaboration (*prapañcābhirata*) has an unfortunate death. While this particular *sutta* does not mention the "*karma* good and bad," Asaṅga in the same place cites the Bhagavat with such a passage, specifically about the sinful, unvirtuous action (*pāpakam akuśalaṃ karma*).[22] Asaṅga refers to the death experience as a vision of form (*rūpadarśana*) comparable to a dream, especially due to the causal *karma*,[23] and this reminds us of Yama's name *kālarūpa*.

Of course, it is because Buddhism, like most Indian religions generally, believed in rebirth, that it paid particular attention to this death experience, attributing to it a forecast of the next destination or destiny. A Mahāyāna scripture, the *Pitāputrasamāgama-sūtra,* may be cited: "So, great King, a 'first *vijñāna*' arises having two conditions pertaining to birth—by reason of the 'last *vijñāna*' as predominant condition (*adhipati-pratyaya*) and by reason of *karma* as support condition (*ālambana-pratyaya*).[24] Hence, death has both a 'death consciousness' and a 'death vision.' Combining this information with Asaṅga's, the last *vijñāna* seems due to the preceding elaboration' (*prapañca*), while the death vision, tantamount to a dream is due to the preceding *karma* good and bad. These can be matched up presumably with "death-time act" and with the "form of death-time". And these two serve as two conditions to determine the next life.

This emphasis on the preceding life is also the theme of a scripture in the Pāli canon *Majjhima-Nikāya*, III, No. 125, "Discourse on the Tamed State" (*Dantabhūmisutta*). This scripture has the message that one cannot understand the state of death without distinguishing between the "tamed" (*danta*) and the "untamed" (*adanta*), and to get the point across the Buddha uses the simile of the tamed elephant, horse, or oxen, as compared with the untamed ones. The scripture concludes with the information that just as an untamed elephant dies untamed, so in the case of the monk, if he dies "not having exhausted the fluxes" (Pāli,, *akhīṇāsava*) he has the "untamed death" (*adantamaraṇa*); and in the opposite case he has the "tamed death".[25] Asaṅga continues this theme in his *Yogācārabhumi* while discussing six kinds of death: (1) *past death,* which is any death between the (time of) transfer of past motivations (*saṃskāra*) and the (time of) cessation of the life organ (*jīvitendriya*); (2) *present death,* which is any death between the (time of) transfer of present motivations and the (time of) cessation of the life organ; (3) *tamed death* (a long explanation); (4) *untamed death;* (5) *similar death,* e.g., in past time died untamed, also this time; (6) *dissimilar death,* i.e., in past time died untamed, this time tamed; or in past time died tamed, this time untamed.[26] The importance of these kinds of death should be more obvious by Asaṅga's other passage, when he comments on a well-known verse:[27]

> *apramādo hy amṛtapadaṃ pramādo mṛtyunaḥ padam/*
> *apramattā na mrīyante ye pramattāḥ sadā mṛtāḥ//*
> Heedfulness is the situation of non-death; heedlessness is the situation of death. The heedful do not die; the heedless always die.

While the verse seems to use "death" in a metaphorical way, Asaṅga takes it quite literally, explaining the "heedfulness" (*apramāda*) as four kinds of guarding: (1) guarding one's life, (2) guarding one's strength, (3) guarding against defilement of the mind, and (4) guarding right praxis. Hence the monk is progressing toward Nirvāṇa, the "deathless" situation. The opposite is called "situation of death", because the person does not guard his life or his mind, thus is prone to untimely death and certainly is not progressing toward the "deathless". Here, Asaṅga mentions five kinds of death: (1) tamed death, (2) untamed death, (3) past death, (4) present death, and (5) future death. Summarizing the points: The heedful person has a "tamed death", and repeating this for a certain number of lives, he achieves the "deathless" Nirvāṇa. The heedless person has the "untamed death," and so must in that way die again and again.[28] This shows that in this way of talking the meaning of "death" is whether it is tamed or untamed. Accordingly, we can understand this verse from the *Dharmasamuccaya* (XXII, 46):[29]

> A person lacking knowledge and morality, who shuns the jewel of giving, though living is called dead.

Using Asaṅga's explanations, this person is "called dead" because he is headed toward the untamed death. But this introduces a difficulty for those believing in rebirth, and so also in re-death—of which Asaṅga seems well aware by virtue of his list of six kinds of death—that one may speak meaningfully about past death and present death—since they can be said to be "tamed" or "untamed". But, since a pair of deaths are similar or dissimilar in this sense, a future death is indeterminate in this way of judging. This helps to explain a problem about the Buddhist formula Dependent Origination, namely, about its last member "old age and death", a consideration of which is probably irrelevant to this essay, although of great importance in the history of Buddhist doctrine. It has to do with the usual Buddhist explanation of "old age and death" as a kind of suffering (*duḥkha*), to be experienced at the end of a present life, to be inferred of a previous life, and which is indeterminable of a future life.[30]

Mindfulness of Death

The preceding considerations are in topics shared by general Indian religion, although Buddhism has its own contributions to make, as was indicated. The present topic, in contrast, appears to have been a special development in Buddhism starting from its beginnings and continued in numerous passages in subsequent literature of this religion. We should start with the scripture devoted to the topic in the Pāli canon *Aṅguttara-Nikāya* (Book of Sixes), i.e., the First and Second *Maraṇasati-sutta*. The Buddha announces to the monks that mindfulness (P. *sati;* Skt. *smṛti*) of death, when made to expand, may serve for exhausting the fluxes (P. *āsava;* Skt. *āśrava*) and culminate in the "deathless" (*amṛta*). By "made to expand" is meant that this mindfulness is carried on while breathing in and out, while eating, and so on. The second *sutta* clarifies how this mindfulness is to be carried out. In the evening, the monk is to reflect that there are many chances of death from stings of poisonous creatures, bad food (recall the first four of the nine causes as cited by Asaṅga in the foregoing section), the three *doṣa* (bile, phlegm, and wind) going wrong, and so on. Suppose he were to die that very evening. Had he sufficiently rid himself of wickedness that brings the just deserts at death? He must strive as though his days were predictably numbered. Doing the right thing as though his life depended on it, he lives with zest and delight.[31]

The canonical *Saṃyutta-Nikāya,* V, expresses the idea in a verse:[32]

> Who, desiring merit, established in virtue,
> cultivates the path to reach the deathless;
> he, attaining the essence of the Dhamma,
> rejoicing in the exhaustion (of the fluxes),
> does not tremble to think: The King of Death is coming.

The large canonical verse collection called *Dharmasamuccaya* has numerous verses of such type, especially in the first published volume.[33] Here there is a series of verse, Chap. IV, 33-44, each with the first half the same: "Having enjoyed, they look forward to the lord of death, persons deluded by desires (*bhuktvā mṛtyuṃ pratīkṣante te janāḥ kāmamohitāḥ*), and with different second halves:

33. who, having learned the tradition, the discipline, and austerity do not apply themselves to truth or giving.
34. who neither knows the maturation of *karma*, nor wish to destroy their vices.
35. who being encircled by the fire of craving, do not know about the cyclical flow (*saṃsāra*).
36. who do not see that the suffering created by separation is terrible.
37. their hearts attached to women, who do not recognize the gestation again.
38. who never shrink from troubles, maladies, and sorrows.
39. who, associating with sinful companions create a great evil.
40. whose minds are not cultivated, and who do not tell the truth.
41. who do not fear, in any circumstance, the danger of cyclical flow.

42. who never tell according to truth what should and what should not be done.
43. who never, with cognition of reality, wish for the benefit of creatures.
44. who, deluded, injure the Dharma in the aim of their body's pleasure.

On the other hand, *Dharmasamuccaya,* X, 50:[34]

> The persons who spurn the intoxicating drink,
> who with the nature of Dharma have equipoised (their minds), they go toward the supreme place
> where death does not exist.

And *Dharmasamuccaya,* XXIII, 10:[35]

> The person who is moral,
> and who relies just on morality,
> he proceeds toward the Nirvāṇa
> where death does not exist.

Such verses abound in Buddhist literature. They stem from the numerous stories, sometimes well-written, sometimes crudely stated, aiming to keep the Buddhist layman and monk on the right virtuous course by pointing out the blissful state he could thereby attain, whereas various sinful acts would land him in this or that cold or hot hell. This was technically expressed in terms of destinies (*gati*), the good ones (*sugati*) of men and gods, the bad ones (*durgati*) of 'hungry ghosts' (*preta*), animals and hell beings. Sometimes the good destiny was split with a separate group of *asura*, the fighting gods, to make a total of six destinies.[36]

My further references come from the Tibetan work by Tsoṅ-kha-pa called *Lam rim chen mo*. In an earlier section, he treats "mindfulness of death" in a manner consistent with the foregoing. The value of such mindfulness is shown by a citation from the Mahāyāna version of the *Parinirvāṇa-sūtra*:[37]

> Among all ploughings of fields, the best are those at the return of autumn. Among all tracks, the best is the track of a bullock [= Godānīya, the Western Continent, place of sundown]. Also, among all ideas (*saṃjñā*) the best are the ideas of impermanence and death. These dispel all the lust, nescience, and pride of the three worlds.

The well-known collection *Udāna-varga* devotes its first chapter to impermanence (*anityavarga*). One verse shows the omnipresence of death (I, 25):

> Not in the atmosphere, not in the midst of the ocean, not in the clefts of mountains is there a place to live where the lord of death would not seize (you).

Striking verses use similes of the spider, the danger-surrounded animal, the river, writing on the water, and cowherd to show lack of independence (I, 13-17):[38]

> It is with the life of mortal man (*martyasya jīvitam*) as with the spider. It stretches its thread here and there, spins a web and becomes small [itself trapped]. It is with the life of mortal man as with the doomed (animals). Whichever way he takes a step, he comes closer to death.
>
> As a river that flows turbulently and does not turn back, so goes away the life of men and does not return.
>
> Joy is fleeting and mixed with pain. It quickly disappears like the writing with a stick on water.
>
> As a cowherd with his staff brings his cattle to the stable, so old age with its sickness brings the life on men to the lord of death.

Typical of numerous passages about impermanence is a verse from the Mahāyāna biography of the Buddha, the *Lalitavistara*:[39]

> The three spheres are as unstable as a cloud in autumn; birth and death of the living beings is like a glimpse of a dancer's arena. The time the living beings have to live is as lightning in the sky, and passes by as quickly as rivulets down a steep mountain side.

Such contemplations are said to help keep the person in the pure life, as in the *Udānavarga*, I, 26:

> Whatever men have been or will be, all abandon this body and depart. The wise man, having recognized the universal destruction, stays in the Dharma and practices the pure life (*brahmacarya*).

Besides, one might be able to escape the lord of death's implacable gaze (*Udānavarga*, XVIII, 17):

> He who has recognized that this body is (empty) like a pot, and also knows natures (*dharma*) as mirages (*marīci*), destroys here the flowery weapons (*puṣpaka*) of Māra, and escapes the view of the death-king.

It is held as an unparalleled spur to getting things done, as Mātṛceta says it in his *Mahārājakaniṣkalekha*, 58-9:[40]

> The lord of death, with whom is he not acquainted? Since he suddenly alights, may you, not waiting with the thought, "tomorrow I will do it", apply yourself hastily to the illustrious doctrine (*saddharma*)?
>
> "Tomorrow, not today I will do it", saying this is not a good auspice in a man. That *tomorrow* will doubtless come, but *you* will not be.

And when one applies himself to the illustrious doctrine today, rather than tomorrow, how he thinks is stated, among various places, in Ārya-Śūra's *Jātakamālā*, No. 32, *The Story of Ayogṛha*, verses 7-9:[41]

> "Alas," (he thought), "piteous is the state of the world and disagreeable in its inconstancy. This glorious Kaumudī-day will exist just in memory.
>
> "And such being the condition of the world, it is astonishing how fearless are men, in that they chase after enjoyment with untroubled minds, while all their paths are supervised by the lord of death.
>
> "Disease, old age, and death—enemies of irresistible strength stand by, wishing to slay. And since one will surely go to the dreadful world hereafter, how can an intelligent person have occasion for merriment in this (fix)!"

By Kaumudī-day is meant the full moon day of Aśvina—in India the second month of autumn, but that day is possibly close to the autumnal equinox. And this goes with the previous citation mentioning the return of autumn.

The foregoing should suffice for citations from the *Lam rim chen mo* section. The reason for giving these points by way of verses is that the verses themselves were memorized for purposes of being mindful of death.

Mindfulness of death can be even more formulized as is done

in Buddhaghosa's *Viśuddhimagga*, where the meditator goes through a sequence of eight considerations of death.[42]

In conclusion of this matter, it should be clear that the teachings about this mindfulness of death take for granted or state explicitly, that mankind does not ordinarily think this way. Therefore, it was necessary to state a positive value in so contemplating. This value was in the presumed fostering of righteous conduct and in combatting procrastination. Even more, there is implied a kind of conversion of the mind, a "death" from previous ways of thinking by way of contemplating death.

Regarding Suicide

A monk who incites another to commit suicide is in the Pāli Vinaya (disciplinary code) declared Pārājika, i.e., must have permanent expulsion.[43] The same is stated in the Chinese Vinaya work by Saṅghabhadra. This work also states: "The Buddha has said to the Bhikkhus: 'Do not commit suicide'. One who commits suicide, even to the extent that he abstains from food, becomes guilty of a Dukkaṭa offence."[44] This Dukkaṭa offence, in Sanskrit *duṣkṛta,* one needing a sort of expiation, would mean, according to earlier information in this essay that he would have an untamed death. However, the same Chinese work continues with an exceptional case, where a Bhikkhu afflicted with an incurable disease and by contemplation realizing that he would not live long, and regretting the great trouble being caused for others to care for him, incurs no sin in refusing food or medicines. The exceptional case is the topic of the *Channovādasutta* in the Pāli canon *Majjhima-Nikāya,* III. Sāriputta tried to dissuade the monk Channa, who was desperately ill with intense pain from stabbing himself; but the Buddha declared Channa blameless since he was not attached to his body. In adding that the person who is attached to body does incur blame (hence the untamed death) with suicide, the Buddha shows the position that suicide in itself does not mean a person is unattached to his body. The Buddha's middle path avoiding both the self-torture and self-indulgence indicates the general condemnation of suicide. Still the example of Channa shows the acknowledgement of exceptional cases, where suicide was justified.

Still there have been many cases of "religious" suicide. Jan says, "The means of this self-immolation also varies from death by fire, to drowning, jumping from a height, self-inflicted wounds, fasting, or being devoured by animals."[45] Indeed, whatever the reason advanced for the self-immolation, it is not the reason itself that could ever justify the suicide, according to the Buddhist position mentioned above and in other places. Indeed, one would have to inquire whether the suicidal person is or is not attached to his (or her) body, hence whether there is a "tamed death".[46]

As to the numerous cases of suicide by fire, it has been claimed in the cases of Chinese monks, that they were inspired to this action by the example in the *Bhaiṣajyarāja* chapter of the Lotus Sūtra (*Saddharmapuṇḍarīka-sūtra*). There was in India another celebrated story of self-burning. Why is the Deer Park (now called Sarnath, just north of Varanasi) called Ṛṣipatana (Pāli: Isipatana)? When the former Buddha Kāśyapa was due to appear in the world, five hundred Pratyekabuddhas, who lived on a hill there, learned about it from the devas. By magical power they rose up in the atmosphere and equipoised themselves in the element of fire. The fire burned their material bodies and the ashes fell to earth. It was said, "The Ṛṣis have fallen," and so the place is called Ṛṣipatana (the falling of the Ṛṣis).[47]

Those legendary personages might serve as excuses for suicides, but not by reason of emulation, since the monks practicing this kind of self-immolation could not by any stretch of our imagination be as Bhaiṣajyarāja or be able to levitate to a height, there to magically evoke the fire.

Treatment of the Deceased

The ancient Buddhist formula of Dependent Origination usually has an appendage of five terms after the last one of the standard twelve, i.e., No. 12, 'old age and death' (*jarā-maraṇa*). These five terms are concerned with the unhappiness of relatives and friends over the demise of their loved one. Asaṅga in his discussion[48] calls them evolutes of the basic suffering. The first is 'grief' (*śoka*). As a result, there are utterances called 'lamentation' (*parideva*). The next term, 'misery' (*duḥkha*) is explained as chest-beating, meaning more generally the applying of force or some substance to a part of one's body. The following term refers to the inner sorrowing, called 'dissatisfaction' (*daurmanasya*), but this term can also mean a mental castigation. The last term 'perturbation' (*upāyāsa*) is 'irritations', apparently referring to an intrusion into daily affairs by the requirement to do services for a given number of days in regard to the deceased.

There is much material available on Buddhist treatment of any services for the dead, because these could be readily observed, even if an observer were not himself grounded in the doctrinal premises. Here there is room for some samplings of the data.

When Buddhism spread in China, the monks brought from India the custom of cremation, and monasteries were provided with a crematorium a short distance outside the precincts. Yetts informs us that the Confucianists conducted crusades against this custom, but that not until A.D. 1370 did they succeed in getting it banned by imperial edict. At the approach of death many monks adopted the well-known meditative posture of crossed legs, with hands in the lap. For cremation purposes, the hands may be tied together, palm to palm; or a rosary is put in one hand, the fly-whisk in the other. Often the head was crowned with the ceremonial head-dress. Sandal-wood was the ideal fuel, if it could be afforded. In the case of a particularly saintly monk, the body might be kept for a week of more in a special air-tight box, while special masses were conducted. Besides, it was believed by the Mahāyāna Buddhists that the corpse of a true saint was incorruptable. Actual burials of the clergy and laity did not differ.[49]

Tambiah[50] mentions from modern observations in Thailand that the crematorium was located on the west side of the monastery, and that the corpse is laid with the head pointing west. Of course, from our previous citation attributed to the Mahāyāna *Parinirvāṇa-sūtra,* this is because the direction of the setting sun symbolizes death and impermanence generally; but Tambiah's native informants did not hit upon this, saying: "This means he has already gone to the new world."[51] Again when they close up the eye and mouth orifices of the deceased with wax, this should be to remove these as possibilities for exerting an evil influence,[52] but the informants are here more irrelevant: "This is to prevent the living members of the family from losing interest in life. For, they know that finally they too will die in the same way."[53] Later, when during the funeral procession, the coffin is so carried that the feet of the deceased are pointing west, this should be for the reason that the informants gave in the first instance for the contrary direction, namely that the deceased has gone to the other world ('east'), but now the villagers say that "the coffin also is carried to the cemetery pointing 'west'"—which is only stating the obvious and not explaining anything.[54]

Ashikaga has written on the Japanese *Bon* festival for the spirits of the dead.[55] This is celebrated for three days, the thirteenth to the fifteenth of the seventh month ('moon') of the lunar calendar. Of course, this points to the three-day occultation of the moon;[56] and probably this is the intention of Naciketas' three-day stay without food in the house of death, as told in the *Kaṭha Upaniṣad.* This festival, during which a special meal is offered to the spirits of the dead is traced to a scripture called the *Ullambanapātra-sūtra,* with a story of when the Buddha's disciple Maudgalyayana tried to bring some food to his mother who was in the 'hunger-hell.' The lighting of lanterns ('welcoming fire') throughout the cemeteries to light the way for the spirit guests reminds one of the Indian festival of lights, Divālī.[57]

Lessing[58] has a fascinating article, based on Tibetan and Mongolian practices about a ceremony named "calling the soul (*bla*)" or "ransoming from death" (literally, "cheating death"). This involves making an effigy (*glud*) from dough-mixed with slops, which is placed in the middle of a wooden board. By 'slops', it is apparently meant impurities and the washwater from the body of the human being for whom the effigy is a substitute in the ceremony. If available, the valuable substances are added to the dough. Eyes, ears, nose, etc. are entered in the effigy. The dead person's worn clothes, or a piece of them is placed in front of the effigy. Food offerings, gems, silks, and so on, are arranged around it. The ceremony involves the making of certain frames with colored threads to catch the demons and make them remain during the ritual, deceived by the effigy. Various spirits are invited to enjoy the effigy as a substitute. At the right time, the soul of the deceased is called back by a bystander with appropriate remarks:[59] "Soul and life of such and such a person, of such and such a family, of such and such an age, bearing such and such a name, whether thou hast come to a royal palace,... or an island or islet,... a place noisy with human activities, or a place inhabited by malignant spirits... or whether thou art traveling or drifting in the wind floating on the water, or scattered about, whether thou art snatched away or carried off, I bid thee come back." Meanwhile, the officiant in deep concentration imagines that the soul-life of the person has returned.

CONCLUDING REMARKS

When one collects material of the foregoing type, gradually one may come to notice that the Indian theory of transmigration and rebirth, plus a rich literature about the heavens and hells, not only invests death with peculiar subtle meaning beyond dying *per se*, but also renders the "other world" nearby, especially in folk belief. While this essay could not go into the enormous topic of demonology, it is well to mention at least that there are many stories about the departed, using the Pāli term *Peta* or the Sanskrit *Preta*. These stories go back to Vedic times in India with the legend of Yama, who upon dying became king of the (later) deceased (*preta-rāja*). A bulky scripture intermediate between early and later Buddhism called the *Ārya-Saddharmasmṛtyupasthāna* sets forth thirty-six classes of these *Pretas*, starting with the "Limbless-trunk *Preta*".[60] Oriental art depicts these frustrated spirits as wandering among men unseen. That is, normally unseen, but the Pāli stories called *Peta-vatthu* in the minor part of the canon have numerous accounts of when these Pretas appear to men and converse with them.[61] In all Buddhist countries, there were these sorts of "ghost stories". These "materializations" of the deceased provide opportunities for them to do mischief as well as to be instructive.

We see by these considerations that death was regarded as a transit in a cyclical course rather than as a decisive final event.

REFERENCES

1. Cf. Alex Wayman, "Buddhist Genesis and the Tantric Tradition," *Oriens Extremus*, 9:1, 1962, pp. 127-31; mostly reprinted in Wayman, *The Buddhist Tantras; Light on Indo-Tibetan Esotericism* (New York, 1973).
2. A. Wayman, "Studies in Yama and Māra" *Indo-Iranian Journal*, III (1959, nos. 1-2), p. 53. See the present volume for this essay.
3. Cf. Bimala Charan Law, *Designation of Human Types (Puggala-Paññatti)* (London, 1922).
4. The word *puggala* (Skt. *pudgala*, also *puṃgala*) is used by both the Buddhists and Jains, but differently; cf. Padmanabh S. Jaini, *The Jaina Path of Purification* (Indian edition, Delhi, 1979), pp. 101-2, where it stands for matter. In Buddhism it contrasts with soulless matter (*jāḍa*) and is employed like the *jīva*, a kind of soul so that *pudgalavāda* "espousing the *pudgala*- soul" was a well-known heresy.
5. Cf. Alex Wayman, tr. *Calming the Mind and Discerning the Real* (New York, 1978), p. 453, n. 164, suggesting that the demonic creature is Māra, but this would

be the variety called Mṛtyu-Māra, "death Māra."

6. I.B. Horner, tr. *The Collection of the Middle Length Sayings (Majjhima-Nikāya)*, Vol. III (London, 1959), p. 227, in the *sutta* on the Deva-Messengers.
7. Wayman, "Studies in Yama and Māra," p. 126, ff.
8. This name is not found in standard reference works. It occurs in *dhāraṇīs*, or mantra formulas, normally transcribed rather than translated into Tibetan. The name occurs several times in a native Tibetan text in my possession devoted to the evocation of Yāma as a protective deity, called *Drug bcu pa* (The Rite of Sixty), e.g., *Oṃ Kālārūpa zhal du Oṃ Āḥ Hūṃ* ("Oṃ, as the Kālarūpa-face, *Oṃ, Āḥ, Hūṃ*").
9. Vidhushekhara Bhattacharya, ed., *The Yogācārabhūmi of Ācārya Asaṅga*, Part I, (University of Calcutta, 1957), p. 212.1.
10. This is the version in *Saṃyutta-Nikāya*, II, 2, using the edition by Bhikkhu J. Kashyap, 1959.
11. These explanations are in Asaṅga, *Paryāya-saṃgrahaṇī*, in Japanese photo. edition of Peking Kanjur-Tanjur, Vol. 111, p. 239-4-7 to 239-5-2. Cf. N.H. Samtani, *The Arthaviniścaya-sūtra and its Commentary (Nibandhana)* (Patna, 1971), pp. 154-6, for a treatment in Sanskrit of death and its synonyms, according to Buddhism.
12. Bhikkhu J. Kashyap, ed. *The Paṭisambhidamagga* (Pāli Publication Board, 1960), p. 212-10-15.
13. For this theory of heart basis in Pāli commentarial works, cf. Y. Karunadasa, *Buddhist Analysis of Matter* (Colombo, 1967), p. 62.
14. V. Bhattacharya, ed. *The Yogācārabhūmi*, Part I, p. 211.9 to 212.1.
15. Hermann Oldenberg, *Buddha: his Life, his Dorctrine, his Order* (translation from the original German by William Hoey, 1882, reprint of 1971 by Indological Book House), p. 103, claimed that the narrative was concocted by later tradition.
16. Cf. Alex Wayman, "The Mirror as a Pan-Buddhist Metaphor-Simile," *History of Religions*, XIII: 4, May 1974, p. 264.
17. There are four evocation rituals (*sādhana*) of such title given in the index to the Tibetan canon, especially with evocation of the goddess Tārā.
18. Cf. Alex Wayman, *Yoga of the Guhyasamājatantra; the Arcane Lore of Forty Verses* (Delhi, 1977), pp. 278-9.
19. Cf. P.V. Kane, *History of Dharmaśāstra*, Vol. IV (Poona, 1953), p. 185, f.; and Franklin Edgerton, "The Hour of Death," *Annals of the Bhandarkar Institute*, Vol. VIII (1927), pp. 219-49.
20. V. Bhattacharya, *The Yogācārabhūmi*, Part I, p. 15.7 to 16.20. I have used the Tibetan translation along with the Sanskrit original, enabling me to supply cause no. 7 (missing in the Skt. text), and further down to render the Skt. *avyākulaṃ* and *vyākulaṃ* respectively as "non-delusive" and "delusive."
21. *The Yogācārabhūmi*, Part I, p. 17.2-3.
22. *The Yogācārabhūmi*, Part I, p. 17.6.
23. *The Yogācārabhūmi*, Part I, p. 17.4-5.
24. As cited in Śāntideva's *Śikṣāmuccaya*, ed. of Mithila Institute, p. 135.12-13.
25. This sutta is available in English: Horner, *The Collection of the Middle Length Sayings*, IIi, pp. 175-83.
26. Asaṅga, *Vastusaṃgrahaṇī*, Photo. ed. Vol. 111, p. 125-5 to 126-1.
27. Asaṅga, cites the version, i.e., the one with the reading *sadā*, as in the *Apramādavarga of the Udānavarga*, IV, 1 (Ed: Franz Bernard, Band 1, Göttingen, 1965, p. 126); and of the *Dharmasamuccaya*, IV, 4, (ed. by Lin Li-Kouang, second

part revised by A. Bareau, J.W. de Jong and Paul Demiéville, Paris, 1969). The *Dhammapada,* II, 1; *The Gāndhārī Dharmapada,* ed. by John Brough (Oxford University Press, 1962), VII, 6; and The Buddhist Hybrid Sanskrit Dharmapada, ed. by N.S. Shukla (Patna, 1979), II, 1 have the reading *yathā* (Gāndharī *yadha*) in which case the translation would read: "the heedless are as dead".

28. Asaṅga, *Cintāmayī bhūmi,* Photo. ed. Vol. 110, p. 12-2 and -3.
29. This is the third part, Ed: Lin Li-Kouang, revised by A. Bareau, J.W. de Jong, and Paul Demiéville (Paris, 1973).
30. The problem came to my attention when preparing the article "Dependent Origination—The Indo-Tibetan Tradition," *Journal of Chinese Philosophy* 7 (1980), pp. 275-300. I gave three ways of interpreting the formula according to Tibetan tradition that especially follows Asaṅga (his *Abhidharmasamuccaya* and *Yogācāra-bhūmi*), and in each case the last member "old age and death" is understood as belonging to the present life. Yet the Pāli *Abhidhamma* takes the last two members ("birth" and "old age and death") as belonging to a future life.
31. Cf. E.M. Hare, tr., *The Book of the Gradual Saying (Aṅguttara-Nikāya),* Vol. III (London, reprint of 1952), pp. 217-20.
32. Translated from the Pāli as ed. by Bhikkhu J. Kashyap, *The Saṃyutta Nikāya (5. Mahāvagga)* (Pāli Publication Board, 1959), pp. 343-4.
33. *Dharma-Samuccaya,* 1st part, Ed: Lin Li-Kouang (Paris, 1946), pp. 91-9. Among the language versions of this text edited by Lin, namely, Sanskrit, Tibetan, two Chinese versions, plus his French translation—I have used the Sanskrit and Tibetan and occasionally his French.
34. 2nd part, Paris, 1969.
35. 3rd part, Paris, 1973.
36. Cf. Paul Mus, *La Lumière sur les Six Voies* (Paris, 1939).
37. Tshoṅ-kha-pa, *Lam rim chen mo* (Tashilunpo edition), f. 60b-2.
38. For this set I have adopted some of the renderings in W. Woodville Rockhill, *Udānavarga,* tr. from the Tibetan (London, 1892), but use the Sanskrit, missing only in I, 14, as Ed: Franz Bernhard along with the Tibetan in *Lam rim chen mo* context.
39. S. Lefmann, ed. *Lalita Vistara* (Halle, 1902), XIII, p. 173.13-14; also cited in *Śikṣāmuccaya,* from which the *Lam rim chen mo* citation is probably drawn.
40. The letter in verse form written to the great king Kaniṣka was translated by F.W. Thomas from the Tibetan in *Indian Antiquary,* 32, 1903, pp. 345, ff.
41. Hendrik Kern, ed., *The Jātaka-Mālā* (The Harvard University Press, 1943), p. 226.19-24.
42. Cf. George D. Bond, "Theravada Buddhism's Meditations on Death and the Symbolism of Initiatory Death," *History of Religions,* 19:3, Feb. 1980, pp. 243-7.
43. Cf. Edward J. Thomas, *The History of Buddhist Thought* (London, 1963 reprint), pp. 16-7.
44. P.V. Bapat and A. Hirakawa, *Shan-Chien-P'i-P'o-Sha; a Chinese version by Saṅghabhadra of Samantapāsādikā* (Bhandarkar Oritental Research Institute, Poona, 1970), p. 327.
45. Jan Yün-hua, "Buddhist Self-immolation in Medieval China," *History of Religions,* 4:2, Winter 1965, p. 246.
46. Jaini, *The Jaina Path of Purification,* p. 229, expresses it differently in the case of the Jaina who fasts himself to death, i.e., it is an "impure" suicide if there is an increase in the passions, and "pure" if he preserves "inner peace". Jaini mentions that numerous Jainas of both sexes have fasted to death with inscriptions glorifying

their act. This contrasts with the Buddhists who do not glorify suicide.

47. Cf. F.D. Lessing and Alex Wayman, *Introduction to the Buddhist Tantric Systems* (tr. from Mkhas grub rje's *Rgyud sde rnam gžag pa*), New York, 1980, p. 41.
48. Photo edition of the Tibetan Kanjur-Tanjur, Vol. 111, p. 144-1-4 to 144-2-2.
49. Cf. W. Perceval Yetts, "Notes on the Disposal of Buddhist Dead in China," *Journal of the Royal Asiatic Society,* 1911, pp. 699-725.
50. S. J. Tambiah, *Buddhism and the Spirit Cults in North-east Thailand* (Cambridge, University Press, 1970), pp. 179-94.
51. Tambiah, *Buddhism,* p. 180.
52. Cf. Clarence Maloney, ed., *The Evil Eye* (New York, 1976), the editor's own contribution, "Don't Say 'Pretty Baby' lest You Zap It with Your Eye—The Evil Eye in South Asia," pp. 131-3, for the combination of evil mouth with evil eye.
53. Tambiah, *Buddhism,* p. 180.
54. Tambiah, Buddhism, p. 182.
55. Ensho Ashikaga, "The Festival for the Spirits of the Dead in Japan," *Western Folklore,* IX:3, July, 1950, pp. 217-28; also, Ensho Ashikaga, "Notes on Urabon," *Journal of the American Oriental Society,* 71:1, 1951, pp. 71-5.
56. Cf. a Dawn hymn of the Ṛg-Veda (X, 55; trans. R.T.H. Griffith), 5. The old hath waked the young Moon from his slumber who runs his circling course with many round him. Behold the God's high wisdom is in its greatness: he who died yesterday is living today".
57. In the case of the Indian festival, there are five days including the last three days of Āśvinā, i.e., thirteenth, fourteenth, and fifteenth of the dark half of the moon; formerly on the fourteenth day, there was satiation (*tarpana*) of Yama; cf. A. Wayman, "Climactic Times in Indian Mythology and Religion," *History of Religions,* 4:2, Winter 1965, p. 307.
58. F.D. Lessing, "Calling the Soul: a Lamaist Ritual," *Semitic and Oriental Studies,* University of California Publications in Semitic Philology, XI, 1951, pp. 263-84.
59. Lessing, "Calling the Soul," p. 273.
60. Wayman, "Studies in Yama and Māra," in this essay collection, for the thirty six classes. From the *Ārya-Saddharmasmṛtyupasthāna* is extracted the verse work called *Dharmasamuccaya;* cf. above, notes 33-5.
61. Cf. *The Minor Anthologies of the Pāli Canon,* Part IV. *Vimāna Vatthu*: Stories of the Mansions; and *Peta Vatthu*: Stories of the Departed, translated by Jean Kennedy and Henry S. Gehman, respectively (London, 1942).

SECTION IV
BUDDHIST PRACTICES

akāraṇaṃ vyākaranaṃ tantrīśabdo 'py akāraṇam /
akāraṇaṃ trayovedās taṇḍulās tatra kāraṇaṃ //

Śukasaptati (Seventy Tales of a Parrot)

In this case, grammar is not the means; the sound of strings is not the means; the three Vedas are not the means; piling the threshed grain is the means.

16

Asaṅga on Food

Background

The oldest Upaniṣads, which precede Buddhism, contain many passages about food in a metaphysical way.[1] The *Bṛhadāraṇyaka Upaniṣad* says (V, 12.1): *pūyati vā annam ṛte prāṇāt; . . . śuṣyati vai prāṇa ṛte 'nnāt,* 'Food becomes putrid when apart from life;. . .life dries up when apart from food.' Asaṅga appears to have a similar idea in his *Yogācārabhūmi* in the section *Viniścaya-saṃgrahaṇī,* while developing a passage that begins: "Furthermore, the varieties of natures (*dharma*) that accomplish the abode are established by five kinds."[2] He goes on to state that the first four are the four kinds of foods, which will be discussed below, and that the fifth is the 'life organ' (*jīvitendriya:* T. *srog gi dbaṅ*

Reprinted from Alex Wayman, *Analysis of the Śrāvakabhūmi Manuscript* (Berkeley, 1961.

po). His presentation brings out that both food in a concrete as well as a metaphorical sense, and the life organ are necessary to accomplish the abode of sentient beings (*sattva*). Vasubandhu clarifies the term 'life organ'.[3]

> Qu'est-ce que l'organe vital (*jīvitendriya*)?
> 45 a. Le *jīvita,* c'est la vie (*āyus*).
> En effet, l'Abhidharma dit: ((Qu'est-ce que le *jīvitendriya* ?— L'āyus des trois sphères d'existence.))
> Quelle sorte de *dharma* est l'*āyus?*
> 45 a-b. Le support de la chaleur et de la connaissance (*ādhāra uṣmavijñānayor hi yaḥ/)*

This last verse is consistent with the teaching of certain Buddhist Tantras that the Prāṇa wind located in the heart supports the personality aggregate (*skandha*) called 'perception' (*vijñāna*),[4] as well as with the fact that *vijñāna* is one of the four foods.

The oldest Buddhist scriptures, now represented principally by Pāli, have a number of passages about food, some of which will be detailed below. Such passages, in the comparable Sanskrit form in the four *āgamas* are undoubtedly the basis for Asaṅga's presentation. The Pāli of the *Dīgha-Nikāya* (III, 84 ff.) has a story that might be termed "Genesis According to Buddhism," for which a Sanskrit version exists in the *Mahāvastu* under the title *Rājavaṃśa,* and of which a similar version was translated from Tibetan by Csoma de Körös.[5] According to this story, at the time of a new evolution of the world most of the beings are in a heaven called Ābhāsvara.[6] In the *Mahāvastu* (I, 338-9, ed. Senart), 'beings' (*sattva*), 'self-luminous' (*svayaṃprabha*), 'range in space' (*antarikṣacara*), 'made of mind' (*manomaya*), 'feed on joy' (*prītibhakṣa),* 'abide in pleasure' (*sukhasthāyin*), 'go wherever is desired' (*yenakāmaṃgata*). The various versions agree that by eating foods of increasing coarseness, the bodies of these beings became more and more coarse, and these beings lost their original attributes. I do not know whether Hindu texts have a similar account, which may provide a rationale for the frequent Indian *yoga* practice of drastically curtailing food. Presumably, by reversing the process, one could gradually refine the body and ultimately re-attain the primordial state. Even assuming that such a goal is thereby reached, does this constitute the highest goal, or in Buddhist terms, would one be a Rightly Accomplished Buddha (*samyaksambuddha*)? The life of the Buddha shows that Gautama could not succeed in his aim by years of mortification. Consequently, he taught the avoidance of the extremes of mortification and indulgence. The application of this teaching in terms of food is well-shown by Asaṅga's extended treatment of *bhojane mātrajñatā* ('knowing the required amount in food'), where we find that the important thing is the attitude with which one eats food.

The Four Foods

Asaṅga's extended *bhojane mātrajñatā* section alludes to four foods: morsel food (*kavaḍaṃkāra-āhāra*), contactual food (*sparśa-āhāra*), volitional food (*manaḥsañcetanā-āhāra)*, and perceptual food (*vijñāna-āhāra*), but it discusses only morsel food, and in fact only the coarse morsel food. The teaching about four foods for consumption is ancient in Buddhism. According to the *Saṃyutta-Nikāya,* Part II (*Nidāna-Vagga*), 98, there is: *Cattaro me bhikkhave āhārā bhūtānaṃ vā sattānaṃ ṭhitiyāsambhavesinam vā anuggahāya // Katame cattāro // Kabaliṃkāro āhāro aḷāriko vā sukhumo vā // phasso dutiyo // manosāncetanā tatiyā // viññāṇaṃ catutthaṃ //* 'Four, my brethren, are the foods for maintaining the sentient beings (*sattva*) who have been born or for aiding those who wish to come forth. Which are the four? Morsel food, coarse (*audārika*) or subtle (*sūkṣma*); contact is the second; volition is the third; perception is the fourth.' The Pāli passage goes on to give examples of each food. The reason for the standard order of the four foods is at least partially explained by the information in the *Abhidharmakośa* that the first two foods nourish the being already born—extend its life—and that the last two foods enable the being not yet born to come into existence.[7]

The four foods in the same order as above are concisely mentioned in the *Abhidharma-samuccaya* of Asaṅga: "Food (*āhāra*) is to be seen not only as the transformed increment from transformation, but also as the sensory deposit from the sensory domain, the derivatives of intention from intention, and the holdings from taking."[8] In the Tibetan native sub-commentary by Rgyal tshab rje,[9] the first or morsel food involves the three 'sense bases' (*āyatana*) of smell, taste, and the tangible. The second or contactual food is the contact attended with 'flux' (*sāsrava*) that enhances the 'senses' (*indriya*) and the 'great factor elements' (*mahābhūta*).

The third, or volitional, food is the 'volition' (*cetanā*) possessed of 'intention' (*āśaya*) toward desired things. The fourth or perceptual food implies the set of six 'perceptions' (*vijñāna*), because the text says 'of eleven realms' (*ekādaśānāṃ dhātunāṃ*), as well as the chief perception, the 'store-consciousness' (*ālayavijñāna*).

Asaṅga says in his *Yogācārabhūmi*:[10]

> Among those, this is the enjoyment of food: namely, the sentient beings born and originated who range in the three worlds have maintenance of life to whatever extent by means of four foods. Among those, not all the sentient beings who range in the three worlds stay alive by three kinds of food—contactual, volitional, [and perceptual]: the sentient beings, who only range in the world of desire-stay alive also by morsel food. Among those [latter], the sentient beings born as hell beings have subtle morsel food of wind that blows in their insides; thereby they stay alive. The animals, hungry ghosts (*preta*), and men have coarse morsel food, which they render in morsels and eat. Moreover, the sentient beings dwelling in [the embryonic states of] *kalala,* and so on,[11] and the gods ranging in the realm of desire (*kāmāvacara-deva*)[12] have just the subtle kind. For thus, no sooner is their morsel food eaten than extending throughout all the members of the body, it undergoes digestion; and no excrement or urine takes shape in those beings.

It is of interest that Asaṅga views the food of a hell being as a wind, since Buddhist theologians once argued about what food is eaten in the hells.[13] The Mahāsaṃghikas taught that suffering is a kind of food, "Because those beings in the infernal regions [are said to] subsist on lumps of heated iron, [but] still retain their lives."[14] Asaṅga's meaning here may be deduced from an explanation in Vasubandhu's *Abhidharmakośa,* where the name Avīci (of a certain hell) is said to mean 'without interruption (*vīci*) of suffering.' But: "La souffrance est interrompus dans les autres enfers. Dans la Saṃjīva, par exemple, les corps sont d'abord brisés et réduits en poussière; ensuite un vent glacé revivifie les êtres et leur rend le sentiment. . ."[15] Judging from this passage, it may well be that Asaṅga is mentioning the wind food merely as an example. His attitude seems to be that whatever serves to revive the hell being from the ghastly nightmare and thus restores the sensations so that he may again suffer the same torture constitutes his food. In Saṃjīva, the food is an icy wind. However, this view has the difficulty that the denizen of Avīci is without food.

The intermittent character of the food in most of the hells does justify calling it 'morsel' food. This is the implication of *kavaḍaṅkāra-āhāra;* cf. *kavalaḥ* in Mayrhofer.[16]

It may be of interest to introduce at this point Asaṅga's conception of the passage way of food, which is always the 'realm of space' (*ākāśadhātu*). Thus he writes in the *Śrāvakabhūmi* (MS 8A.8-2c, end, to -3c, middle).[17]

> / ākāśadhātuḥ katamaḥ / yac cakṣuḥ-sauṣiryaṃ vā śrotra-sauṣiryaṃ vā ghrāṇasauṣiryaṃ vā mukhāsauṣiryaṃ vākaṇṭha-sauṣiryaṃ vā/iti yena vābhyavaharati/yatra vābhyavaharati/ yena vābhyavahriyate/adhobhāgena pragharati/iti yo vā punar anyo 'py evaṃ-bhāghīyaḥ ayaṃ ucyata ākāśadhātuḥ/
> What is the 'realm of space'? Either the hollow of the eye, the hollow of the ear, the hollow of the nose, the hollow of the mouth, or the hollow of the throat; that by which one ingests; the place where one ingests; or the lower part by which what is ingested flows out,[18] furthermore, any others of the same category. This is called 'realm of space'.

Because Asaṅga adheres to the teaching of four kinds of food, it is reasonable to conclude that his remarks about ingesting do not refer exclusively to morsel food. Contactual food through the hollow of the eye, for example, passes through the 'realm of space'.

Bhojane Mātrajñatā, Concise Statement

In the first part of the *Śrāvakabhūmi*, Asaṅga makes concise statements on various topics with which he will later deal extensively. Thus he writes (MS 1B.6-8b through-9c; and 1A.2-1a, b).[19]

> /bhojane mātrajñatā katamā/sa tathā saṃvṛtendriyaḥ pratisaṃkhyāyāhāram āharati/na dravārthaṃ[20] na madārthaṃ na maṇḍanārthaṃ na vibhūṣaṇārthaṃ yāvad evāsya kāyasya sthitaye (yāpanāyai jighatsoparataye brahmacaryānugrahāya,[21] iti/paurāṇā(ṃ) ca vedanā(ṃ) prahāsyāmi navā(ṃ) ca notpādayiṣyāmi yātrā ca me bhaviṣyati/balaṃ ca sukhaṃ cānavadyatā ca sparśavihāratā ceyam ucyate bhojane mātrajñatā/

> What is 'knowing the amount in food'? When he has thus restrained senses after detailed consideration[22] he eats food not for sport, not for intoxication, not for smartening, and not for embellishment, but simply[23] to keep his body alive, to maintain it, allay its desire of food, and promote its chastity with the thought, "I shall eliminate the old feeling, and not give rise to new; and I shall have sustenance, strength, delight, no reproach, and an agreeable condition [euphoria]." This is called 'knowing the amount in food.'

An equivalent passage in Pāli is in the *Saṃyutta-Nikāya* (ed. Feer), Part IV (*Salāyatana-Vagga),* 104:

> /kathaṃ cāvuso bhojane mattaññū hoti // idhāvuso bhikkhu paṭisaṅkhāyoniso āhāram āhāreti // neva davāya na madāya na maṇḍanāya na vibhūsanāya yāvad eva imassa kāyassa ṭhitiyā yāpanāya vihiṃsūparatiyā brahmacariyānuggahāya iti purāṇaṃ ca vedanam paṭihankhāmi navaṃ ca vedanaṃ na uppādessāmi yātrā ca me bhavissati anavajjatā ca phāsuvihāro cā ti//

Pāli has *vihiṃsuparatiyā,* for which the expected Sanskrit would be *vihiṃsoparataye* but is actually *jighatsoparataye*. Buddhaghosa's *Visuddhimagga* (ed. Warren and Kosambi) comments (p. 26): *Vihiṇsūparatiyā ti, vihiṇsā nāma jighacchā ābādhaṭṭhena* ('allay its pangs [of hunger and thirst]:' desire for food is called 'pangs' in the sense of oppression). The Sanskrit word is not known to have the meaning of 'pangs' and presumably for this reason was replaced by *jighatsā*.[24]

Minor differences are the addition of *bala* and *sukha* in the Sanskrit, and the change of prefix **prati* to *pra,* for Pāli *paṭihankhāmi,* S. *prahāsyāmi*.

It is feasible to suppose that Asaṅga has reproduced without alteration except for initial question and final declaration, the paragraph as it occurs in the Sanskrit recension *Saṃyukta-āgama* used in his school. Dr. Waldschmidt[25] has recently discussed a fragment of this lost work that includes a reference to the four foods in a manner equivalent to the Pāli passage cited above.

Bhojane Mātrajñatā, Extended Statement (Edited Text)[26]

/bhojane mātrajñatā katamā / yathāpīhaikatyaḥ pratisa-

ṃkhyāyāhāram āharati / na dravārthaṃ na madārthaṃ na maṇḍanārthaṃ na vibhūṣaṇārtham iti vistareṇa pūrvavat //

/kathaṃ pratisaṃkhyāyāhāram āharati / pratisaṃkhyocyate prajñā[27] *prajñayā kavaḍaṃkārasyāhārasyādīnavaṃ samanupaśyaty ādīnavadarśanena vidūṣayitvābhyavaharati //*

/tat punar ādīnava-darśanaṃ katamat / yad uta yasyaiva kavaḍaṃkārasya paribhogānvayo vā vipariṇāmānvayo vā paryeṣaṇānvayo vā //

/tatra katamaḥ paribhogānvaya ādīnavaḥ / yathāpīhaikatyo yasmin samaya [MS: samaye] āhāram āharati varṇasaṃpannam api gandhasaṃpannam api rasasaṃpannam api supraṇītam api tasya kavaḍaṃkāra āhāraḥ samanantarakṣipta eva āsye yadā dantayantra-vicūrṇitaś ca lālā visarati klinnaś ca bhavati/lālā-pariveṣṭitaś ca bhavati/sa tasmin samaye kaṇṭhanālī-praluṭhitaś ca bhavati/sa yāsau pūrvikā purāṇā manāpatā tāṃ sarveṇa sarvaṃ vijahāti parāṃ ca vikṛtim āpadyate/yasyāṃ ca vikṛtau vartamānaś charditakopamaḥ khyāti/tad-avasthaṃ cainaṃ saced ayaṃ bhoktā puruṣapudgalaḥ saced ākārato manasikuryāt samanusmaren nāsya sarveṇa sarvam anyatrāpi tāvad avipariṇate praṇīte bhojane bhoga-kāmatā saṃtiṣṭheta/kaḥ punar vādas tatra tadavastha iti ya ebhir ākārair anekavidhair anayānupūrvyā bhojana-paribhogam adhipatiṃkṛtva yāsau śubhā varṇanibhā antardhīyate/ādinavaś ca prādurbhavati aśuci [MS: aśūci]-saṃgṛhītaḥ ayam ucyate paribhogānvayaḥ/ādīnavaḥ/yad uta āhāre//

/tatra katamo vipa[ri]ṇāmānvaya ādīnava āhāre/tasya tam āhāram āhṛtavata ā[? śitava]taḥ[28] *yadā vipariṇamati rātryā madhyame vā yāme paścime va yāme tadā sa rudhira-māṃsa-snāyv-asthi-tvag-ādīny aneka-vidhāni bahu-nānā-prakārāṇi/ asmin kāye 'śuci-dravyāṇi vivardhayati saṃjanayati . . . -at*[29] *pariṇataś cādhobhāgībhavati/yad asya[ikasmi]n*[30] *divase śodhayitavyaṃ ca bhavati/tena ca yaḥ spṛṣṭo bhavati/hasto vā pādo vānyatamānyatamad vāṅgapratyaṅgaṃ tad vijugupsanīyaṃ bhavaty ātmanaḥ pareṣāṃ ca tan-nidānāt [MS: tan-nidānāś]*[31] *cāsyotpadyante/kāye bahuvaḥ kāyikā ābādhāḥ/tadyathā gaṇḍaḥ piṭakaḥ dardrū vicarcikā kaṇḍū kuṣṭhaḥ kiṭibhaḥ kilāso jvaraḥ kāsaḥ śoṣo 'pasmāra [MS: śoṣaḥ śoṣāpasmāra] āṭakkaraṃ pāṇḍurogaḥ rudhiraṃ pitta(ṃ) bhagaṃdara itīme cānye'py evaṃbhāgīyāḥ*[32] *kāye kāyikā ābādhā utpadyante/bhuktaś cāsya vipadyate/yenāsya kāye visūcikā saṃtiṣṭhate/ayam ucyate/*

vipariṇānvaya ādīnavo yad uta āhāre//

/tatra katamaḥ paryeṣaṇānvaya ādīnava āhāre/paryeṣaṇānvaya ādīnavo 'nekavidha(ḥ) samudānanā-kṛtaḥ/ārakṣā-kṛtaḥ/ snehaparibhraṃśa-kṛtaḥ/atṛpti-kṛtaḥ/asvātantrya-kṛtaḥ / duścarita-kṛtaś ca //

/tatra katamaḥ ādīnava āhāre / samudānanā-kṛtaḥ yathāpīhaikatya āhārahetor āhāranidānaṃ śīte śītena hanyamānaḥ uṣṇe uṣṇena hanyamānaḥ utsahate ghaṭate vyāyacchate/kṛṣiṇā vā gorakṣyeṇa vā vaṇijyena vā lipi-gaṇanā-nyasana-saṃkhyā-mudrayānekavidhena śilpasthāna-karmasthānenāpratilabdhasya vā āhārasya pratilabdhāya upacayāya vā yathā āhārasyaivam [MS: āhārasyevam] āhāranidānasya tasyaivam utsahato ghaṭata vyāyacchata/sacet te karmāntā vipadyante/sa taṃnidānaṃ śocati kṛpyati paridevate/ uras tāḍayati/krandati/saṅgo vā saṃpadyate [MS: sāpadyate]/moho bata me vyāyāmo nisphala [MS: ti phala] iti/ayam udānanā-sahagata [MS: sahagateḥ] ādīnavo yad uta āhāre//

sacet saṃpadyate sa tasyārakṣādhikaraṇahetos tīvram autsukyam āpadyate/kaccid me bhogā [MS: bhogā na] rājñā vāpahriyeraṃś caurair vāgninā vā dahyeran udakena vohyeyuḥ [MS: vā uhyeyuḥ] kunihitā [MS: kunihatā] vā nidhayaḥ praṇaśyeyuḥ kuprayuktā vā karmāntāḥ pralupyeran apriyā [MS: apriyo] vā dāyādā adhigaccheyuḥ/kule vā kulāṅgāra utpadyeta/ yas tān bhogān anayena vyasanam āpādayet [MS: āpādayeyus] ārakṣā-sahagata ādīnavo yad utāhāre/

/ katama ādīnavaḥ [MS: ādīnavaṃ] snehaparibhraṃśa-kṛtaḥ /yathāpi tad āhāranidānam āhārādhikaraṇahetor mātā putrasyāvalguṃ bhāṣate putro mātuḥ [MS: mātyaḥ] pitā putrasya putraḥ [MS: putro] pitur [MS: pituḥ] bhrātā bhaginyā bhaginī / bhrātuḥ sahāyakaḥ /sahāyakasya prāg eva jano janasya te / cānyonyaṃ vigṛhītā bhavanti vivādam āpannās tathodārā [MS: tathā udārā] brāhmaṇa-kṣatriya-gṛhapati-mahāsālā āhārādhi-karaṇahetor evaṃ vigṛhīta-vivādam āpannā [MS: āpannāḥ] anyonyaṃ pāṇinā praharanti / loṣṭenāpi daṇḍenāpi śastreṇāpi praharanty ayam ucyate snehaparibhraṃśa-kṛta ādīnavaḥ //

/tatra katamaḥ / atṛpti-kṛta ādīnavaḥ / yathāpi tad rājānaḥ kṣatriyā mūrdnābhiṣiktāḥ sveṣu grāma-nigama-rāṣṭra-rājadhāniṣu asaṃtuṣṭā viharanta ubhayato vyūhakāni saṃgrāmānīkāni pratisaranti / śaṃkhai (ḥ) kasyamānaiḥ[33] *paṭahair vadyamānair [MS: vadyamāṇaiḥ] iṣubhiḥ kṣipyamānair viveśus [MS: viveṣes]*[34] *te*

tatra bhrāntenāśvena sārdhaṃ samāgacchanti / bhrāntena hastinā rathena vāhinā [MS: vahinā] sārdhaṃ samāgacchanti /iṣubbhiḥ śaktibhir va apakṛttagātrā maraṇaṃ vā nigacchanti / maraṇamātra[ka]ṃ vā duḥkham ayam ucyate / atṛpti-kṛta ādīnava iti yo vā punar anyo' py evaṃbhāgīyaḥ//

/tatra katamaḥ /asvātantrya-kṛta ādīnavaḥ / yathāpi tad rājñaḥ pauruṣeyā āvarodhikāni nagarāṇy anupraskandataḥ / taptenāpi tilenāvastīryante [MS: tilenāvasinyante][35] /taptayā vasayā taptayā gomaya-loḍikayā[36] taptena tāmreṇa taptenāyasā iṣubhiḥ śaktibhiś [MS: saktibhiś] cāpakṛttagātrā maraṇaṃ vā nigacchanti / maraṇamātrakaṃ vā duḥkhaṃ / ayam ucyate asvatantrya-kṛta ādīnava iti yo vā punar anyo 'py evaṃbhāgīyaḥ //

/ tatra katamo duścarita-kṛta ādīnavaḥ /yathāpi tad ekatyenāhāra nidānaṃ prabhūtaṃ kāyena duścarita-kṛtaṃ bhavaty upacitaṃ yathā kāyenaivaṃ vācā manasā sa ca ya [smin sama]ya [MS:-ye][37] ābādhiko bhavati / duḥkhito bādhaglānaḥ tasya tat pûrvakaṃ kāyaduścaritaṃ vāg-mano-duścarita(ṃ) parvatānāṃ vā parvatakūṭānāṃ vā sāyāhne yac chāyā [MS: chayā][38] avalambate / adhyāvalambate /abhipralambate /tasyaivaṃ bhavati/ kṛtaṃ bata me pāpaṃ na kṛtaṃ bata me puṇyaṃ kāyena vācā manasā so 'haṃ yā gati(ḥ) kṛta-pāpānāṃ gatiṃ pretya gamiṣyāmīti /vipratisārī kālaṃ karoti/ kālaṃ [MS: akālañ] ca kṛtvā' pāyeṣūpapadyate /yad uta narakeṣu tiryak-preteṣu ayam ucyate duścarita-kṛta ādīnavaḥ//

/ tasyaivaṃ bhavati/ ity ayam āhāra-paryeṣamāṇo 'pi sādīnavaḥ paribhujyamāno' pi sādīnavaḥ paribhukto 'pi pariṇāma ādīnavaḥ/

/evam asti punar asyāhārasya kācid anuśaṃsa-mātrā sā punaḥ katamā/ āhārasthitiko 'ya[ṃ kāya] āhāraṃ niśritya tiṣṭhati / nānāhāra iyam asyānuśaṃsa-mātrā / evam asyāhārasthitiko' yaṃ kāyaḥ [MS: kāyāṃ] suciram api tiṣṭhan vā [MS: va] varṣa-śataṃ vā tiṣṭhati / kiṃcid vā punar bhūyaḥ samyak paribhriyamāṇaḥ asti cāsyārvāg uparatiḥ/ tatra ye kāyasthitimātre pratipannāḥ na te supratipannā ye kāyasthitimātrakeṇa saṃtuṣṭā na ca te susaṃtuṣṭā na ca punas ta [MS: te] āhārakṛtaṃ paripūrṇam anavadyam anuśaṃsaṃ pratyanubhavanti /ye punar na kāyasthitimātrakeṇa saṃtuṣṭā na kāyasthitimātrake pratipannā te supratipannāpi tu tām eva kāyasthitiṃ /niśritā [MS: niścim][39] brahmacaryaṃ samudāgamāya pratipannās te supratipannāḥ ta eva ca punaḥ paripūrṇam anavadyam anuśaṃsaṃ pratyanubhavanti /ye punar na kāyasthitiḥ[40] *tan na me pratimaṃ*

syād yad ahaṃ [MS: avāṃ] pratyavareṇa āhārānuśaṃsamātrakeṇa saṃtuṣṭo vihareyaṃ /na me pratirūpaṃ syād yad ahaṃ bālam abhāgatāṃ bāla-saha-dhārmikatām adhyāpadyeyan evaṃ āhāre sarvākāraṃ paripūrṇam ādīnavaṃ jñātvā sa itaḥ pratisaṃkhyāyādīnava-darśī niḥsaraṇānveṣī cāhāra-niḥsaraṇārtham eva putra-māṃsopamam āhāram āharati //

/ tasyaivaṃ bhavati /evam ete dāyaka-dānapatayaḥ kṛcchreṇa bhogān samudāyīna mahāntaṃ paryeṣaṇa-kṛtam ādīnavaṃ pratyanubhavantaḥ prapīḍya prapīḍya tvag-māṃsa-śoṇitam asmākam anuprayacchanti /yad utānukampās upādāya viśeṣaphalārthinaḥ tasyāsmākaṃ tathā pratilabdhasya piṇḍāpātasyāyam evamrūpo ta rūpaḥ paribhogaḥ syād yad ahaṃ tathā paribhūtam ātmānaṃ / sthāpayitvā paribhuṃjīya[41] *yathā teṣāṃ kārāḥ kṛtā atyarthaṃ mahāphalāni*[42] *mahānuśaṃsā mahā dyutayo mahāvistārāḥ candropamaś ca kulāny upasaṃkrameyaṃ vyavakṛṣya kāyam vyavakṛṣya cittaṃ hrīmān apragalbhaḥ anātmoddhatvī aparakutsī [MS: aparapansī]*[43] *yathā svena labhena citta(ṃ) syāṃ sumanā [MS: sumanāḥ] evaṃ parasyāpi labhena citta(ṃ) syāṃ sumanā evaṃ cittaṃ ca punaḥ kulāny upasaṃkrameyaṃ /tat-kṛta etal labhyaṃ pravrajate na parakuleṣu yad-vad atra me pare mā na dadatu / satkṛtya mā asatkṛtya prabhūtaṃ mā stokaṃ praṇītaṃ mā lūhaṃ tvarita(ṃ) mā (?) baddhaṃ [MS: gatvaṃ]*[44] */evaṃ caritasya me kulāny upasaṃkrāmataḥ sacet pare na dadyus tenāhaṃ na teṣām antike āghāta-cittatayā pratigha-cittatayā vyavadīyeyaṃ/na ca punas tan-nidānaṃ kāyasya bhedād apāyopapattyā vighātam āpadyeya/ yad uta tām evāghāta-cittatāṃ pratigha-cittatām adhipatikṛtvā saced asatkṛtya na satkṛtya sacet stokaṃ na prabhutaṃ /sacel lūhaṃ na praṇītaṃ / saced (?)baddhaṃ na tvaritaṃ dadyuḥ / tayāhaṃ [n]āghāta-cittatayā pratighacittatayā ca vyavadīyeyam iti vistareṇa pūrvavat / [evaṃrūpaḥ paribhogo me pratirūpaṃ syād yad ahaṃ tathā ātmānam / sthāpayitvā paribhuñjeya]*[45] *imaṃ cāhaṃ kavaḍīkāram*[46] *āhāraṃ niśritya tathā tathā pratipadyeya tāṃ ca mātrāṃ pratvedyeyaṃ / yena me jīvitendriyanirodhaś ca na syān na ca piṇḍakena klāmyeyaṃ/ brahmacaryānugrahaś ca me syād evaṃ ca me śramaṇa-bhāve pravrajita-bhāve sthitasyāyaṃ piṇḍapāta-paribhoga(ḥ) pratirūpaś ca /pariśuddhaś cānavadyaś ca syād ebhi[rā]kāraiḥ sa pratisaṃkhyāyāhāram āharati //*

/ āhāraḥ punaḥ katamaḥ / catvāra āhārāḥ / kavaḍaṃkāraḥ

sparśo manaḥsaṃcetanā vijñānaṃ cāsmiṃs tv arthe kavaḍaṃkāra āhāro 'bhipretaḥ /sa punaḥ katamas tadyathā manthā vāpūpā vā odana kulmāṣaṃ vā sarpis tailaṃ madhu phaṇitaṃ[47] māṃsaṃ matsyāṃ vallūrā lavaṇaṃ kṣīraṃ dadhi navanītam itīmāni cānyāni caivaṃ rūpāṇy upakaraṇāni yāni kavaḍāni kṛtvābhyavahriyante /tasmād kavaḍaṃkāra ity ucyate //

/ āharatīti bhuṅkte / pratiniṣevaty avaharati khādati bhakṣayati svādayati pibati cūṣatīti paryāyāḥ//

/ na dravārtham iti yaś caite kāmopabhogina ity arthaḥ / ya āharanti yad vayam āhāreṇa prīṇita-gātrāḥ saṃtarpita-gātrāḥ pratyupasthite sāyāhna-kāle samaye abhikrāntāyāṃ rajanyāṃ maulībaddhikābhiḥ sārdham alābu-romaśa-bāhubhiḥ kanduka-stanibhir naribhiḥ sārdhaṃ krīḍa[n]to ramamāṇāḥ paricārayan-[t]a auddhatyaṃ dravaṃ prāviṣkariṣyāma iti drava eṣa ārye dharmavinaye yad uta kāmarāgopasaṃhitā maithunopasaṃhitā pāpakāḥ akuśalādharmā vitarkayair ayaṃ khādyamāno bādhyamāna uddhatendriyo bhavaty uddhatendriyaś ca drutamānasaḥ plutamānasaḥ asthitamānaso 'vyupaśāntamānasaḥ te punar atyartham āhāram āharanto dravārtham āharantīty ucyate //

/ śrutavāṃs tv āryaśrāvaka(ḥ) pratisaṃkhyāna-balika ādīnava-darśi niḥsaraṇaṃ prajānan paribhuṅkte / na tu tathā yathā te kāmopabhogino bhuñjante /tenāha na dravārtham //

/ na dravārthaṃ na madārthaṃ na maṇḍanārthaṃ na vibhūṣaṇārthaṁ iti/ yathāpi ta eva kāmopabhogina ity artho ya āhāram āharanti / adya vayam āhāram āhṛtavanto yad uta prabhūtaṃ ca tṛptito yathā śaktyā balaṃ snigdhaṃ ca vṛṣmaṃ ca bṛṃhaṇīyaṃ ca varṇasaṃpannaṃ gandhasaṃpannaṃ / rasasaṃpannam endhībhūtam [MS: endhābhūte] nigatāyāṃ rajanyāṃ śaktā bhaviṣyāmaḥ / pratibalā vyāyāmakaraṇā [MS: karaṇo] yad uta ātatīkriyayā[48] vā nirghaṭṭena [MS: nirghātena] vā vyāyāma-śilayā vā ulloṭhanena pṛthivi-khātena vā bāhuvyāyamena vā /pādāvaṣṭambhanena vā plavanena vā laṅghanena [MS: alaṃghanena] vā tatra vyāyāmena vā taṃ ca punar vyāyāmaṃ niśritya balavanto [bhavi] ṣyāmaḥ /vyāyata [MS: avyāyata] -gatrā dīkṣaṃ cārogāḥ cirakālaṃ cāsmākaṃ 'sau balam anuvartakaṃ bhaviṣyati no tu tvaritaṃ / virūpakaraṇ[ān]i jarādeham abhibhaviṣyantīti / cirataraṃ ca jīviṣyāma iti / prabhūtabhakṣaṇe ca pratibalā bhaviṣyāmaḥ /bhuktaṃ ca[49] samyak pariṇamiṣyati / doṣānām cāpacayaḥ kṛto bhaviṣyati/ ity

ārogya-madārthaṃ yauvana-madārthaṃ jīvita-madārthaṃ paribhuñjate//

/teṣāṃ punar evaṃ bhavati / kṛtavyāyāmā vayaṃ snātra-saṃvidhānaṃ kariṣyāmo / yad uta śucinā toyena gātrāṇi prakṣālayiṣyāmaḥ prakṣālitagātrās ca keśāni ca prasādhyaiṣyāmaḥ /vividhena cānulepanena kāyam anulipya [MS: anupalipya] vividhair vastrair vividair mālyair vividhair alaṃk [āraiḥ] kāyaṃ bhūṣayiṣyāmaḥ / tatra yat snānā-prasādhanānulepanam idam ucyate / teṣām maṇḍanaṃ //

/tathā maṇḍana-jātānāṃ yad vastra-mālyābharaṇa-dhāraṇam idam ucyate /vibhūṣaṇam iti / maṇḍanārthaṃ vibhūṣaṇārthaṃ paribhuñjā[n]t[asta?][50] *evaṃ madamattā maṇḍanajāti-vibhūṣitagātrāḥ / pratyupasthite madhyāhna-samaye sāyāhna-samaye vā bhakta-samaye tṛṣitā bubhukṣitāś ca pareṇa tarpeṇa parayā nandyā pareṇāmodena / anādī nava-darśino niḥsaraṇam aprajānanto [MS: aprajānanta] yathopapannam āhāram āharanti / yāvad eva punaḥ punar dravārthaṃ maṇḍanārthaṃ vibhūṣaṇārthaṃ ca śrutavāṃs tv arya-śrāvakaḥ /pratisaṃkhyāna-balika ādīnava-darśi niḥsaraṇaṃ prajānan paribhuṅkte / na tu tathā yathā te kāmopabhoginaḥ paribhuñja[n]te / nānyatremam asaṃniṣevaṇaṃ prahātavyam āhāraṃ pratiniṣevamāṇa eva prahāsyāmīti//*

/ yāvad evāsya kāyasya sthitaya [MS: sthitaye] iti bhuktvā nābhuktvā yaś ca jīvati tasya kāyasthitir ity ucyate / so 'ham imam āhāram āhṛtya jīviṣyāmi na mariṣyāmīty āharati / tenāha [MS: tenāhaṃ] yāvad eva kāyasya sthitaye //

/ kathaṃ yāpanāyai āharati / dvividhā yātrā asti kṛcchreṇa yātrā asty akṛcchreṇa kṛcchreṇa yātrā katamā yad rūpam [āhāram] āharato jighatsā daurbalyaṃ vā bhavati / duḥkhito vā bāḍha-glānaḥ / adharmeṇa vā piṇḍapātaṃ paryeṣate na dharmeṇa / raktaḥ paribhuṅkte sakto gṛddho grathito mūrchito 'dhyavasito 'dhyavasāyamāpannaḥ /guruko cāsya kāyo bhavaty akarmaṇyaḥ aprahāna-kṣamaḥ yenāsyātvaritaṃ cittaṃ samādhīyate [MS: samādhiyate] /kṛcchreṇa vā āśvāsa-praśvāsāḥ pravartante / styāna-middhaṃ vā cittaṃ paryava[na]h[at]īyam ucyate kṛcchreṇa yātrā //

/ akṛcchreṇa yātrā katamā yathāpi tad rūpam āhāram āharato yathā jighatsā daurbalyaṃ vā na bhavati / <u>*nābhyadhiko bhavati*</u>[51] *duḥkhito vā bāḍhaglānaḥ / dharmeṇa vā piṇḍapātaṃ paryeṣate na vādharmeṇa / arakto vā paribhuṅkte 'sakto 'gṛdhro grathito*

'nadhyavasito 'nadhyavasāyamāpannaḥ / na cāsya kāyo guruko bhavati / karmaṇyo bhavati/ prahāṇa-kṣamo yenāsya tvaritaṃ cittaṃ samādhīyate / alpa-kṛcchreṇāśvāsapraśvāsāḥ pravartante / styāna-middhaṃ cittaṃ na paryavanahatīyam ucyate alpakṛcchreṇa yātrā//

/tatra yā kṛcchreṇa yātrā tayā jīvita-sthitir bhavati / kāyasya yāvad ya sa-saṃkliṣṭā tatra ye 'yam alpakṛcchreṇa yātrā tayā jīvita-sthitir bhavati / kāyasya sā ca punar anavadyā /asaṃkliṣṭa tatra śrutavān āryaśrāvakaḥ /sāvadyāṃ saṃkliṣṭāṃ yātrāṃ parivarjayati / anavadyām asaṃkliṣṭāṃ yātrāṃ gacchati / pratiṣevate / tenāha yāpanāyai //

/ sā punar anavadyā asaṃkliṣṭā yātrā ya pūrvam uktā / taṃ kathaṃ kalpayati / āha yady ayaṃ jighatsoparataye brahmacaryānugrahāya iti paurāṇām ca vedanāṃ / prahāsyāmi navāṃ ca notpādayiṣyāmi/ yātrā ca me bhaviṣyati / balaṃ ca sukhaṃ cānavadyatā ca sparśavihāratā ceti / evaṃ pratiṣevamāṇaḥ anavadyām asaṃkliṣṭāṃ yātrāṃ kalpayati //

/ kathaṃ ca punar jighatsoparataya [MS:-taye] āharati pratyupasthite bhakta-samaye utpannāyāṃ kṣudhāyāṃ yadā paribhuṅkte tasyaiva kṣut-parya[va]sthānasya jighatsā-daurbalyasya ca prativigmāya tāṃ ca mātrāṃ paribhuṅkte / yathāsya bhuktavataḥ akāle punar jighatsā daurbalyan na bādhate / yad uta sāyāhna-samaye vā abhikrāntāyāṃ vā rajanyāṃ śvo-bhūte pratyupasthite bhakta-samaye evaṃ jighatsoparataye āharati/

/ kathaṃ brahmacaryānugrahāyāharati / tāṃ mātrāṃ paribhuṅkte / tad rūpam āhāram āharati / yenāsya kuśalapakṣe prayuktasya dṛṣṭa eva dharme bhukta-samanantaraṃ tasmin eva vā divase 'gurukaḥ kāyo bhavati / karmaṇyaś ca bhavati / prahāṇa-kṣamaś ca yenāsya tvarita(ṃ) tvaritaṃ cittaṃ samādhīyate [MS: samādhiyate] /alpakṛcchreṇāśvāsa-praśvāsāḥ pravartante / styāna-middhaṃ cittaṃ na paryavanahati / yenāyaṃ bhavyo bhavati / pratibalaś ca / kṣipram evāprāptasya prāptaye 'nadhigatasyādhigamāyāsākṣātkṛtasya sākṣātkriyāyai/ evaṃ brahmacaryānugrahāyāharati //

/ kathaṃ paurāṇām vedanāṃ prahāsyāmīty āharati /yathāpi tad atītam adhvānam upādāyāmātrayā vā paribhuktaṃ bhavaty apaśyaṃ vāpariṇate vā yenāsya vividhaḥ kāyika ābādhaḥ samutpanno bhavati / tadyathā kaṇḍū kuṣṭha(ḥ) kiṭibha(ḥ) kilāsa iti vistareṇa pūrvavat / tasya cābādha-nidānā utpadyante śārīrikā vedanā-duḥkhas tīvrāḥ kharā kaṭukā amanāpā

tasyābādhasyopaśamāya tāsāṃ ca tan-nidānānāṃ duḥkhānāṃ vedanānām upaśamāya hitaṃ paśyam anukūlam ānulomikaṃ vaidyopadiṣṭena vidhinā bhaiṣajyaṃ pratiṣevate sāṃpreyaṃ cāhāram āharati / yenāsyotpannasyābādhasya tannidānānāṃ ca duḥkhānāṃ vedanānāṃ prahāṇaṃ bhavaty evaṃ paurāṇāṃ vedanāṃ prahāsyāmīty āhāram āharati //

/ kathaṃ navāṃ vedanāṃ notpādayiṣyāmīty āhāram āharati / sa vartamānam adhvānam upādāya sukhi arogo balavān nāmātrayā vā paribhuṅkte / apaśyaṃ vāpariṇate vā yenāsy[ān]-āgatam adhvānam upādāya śvo vā uttaraśvo vā visūcikā vā kāye saṃtiṣṭheta / anyatamānyatamo vā kāye kāyika ābādhaḥ samutpadyeta / tadyathā kaṇḍū kuṣṭha(ḥ) kiṭibha(ḥ) kilāsa iti vistareṇa pūrvavat / yan-nidānā utpadyerañ chārīrikā [MS: utpadyeran cchārīrikā] vedanā pūrvavat / evaṃ ca navām vedanāṃ notpādayiṣyāmīty āharati //

/ kathaṃ yātrā me bhaviṣyati / balaṃ ca sukhaṃ cānavadyatāṃ ca/ sparśavihāratā cety āharati / yat tavad bhuktvā jivatīty evaṃ yātrā bhavati / yat punar jighatsā-daurbalyam apanayati / evam asya balaṃ bhavati/ yat punaḥ paurāṇāṃ vedanāṃ prajahāti / navāṃ notpādayaty evam asya sukhaṃ bhavati / yat punar dharmeṇa piṇḍapātaṃ paryeṣṭyāraktaḥ paribhuṅkte 'sakta iti vistareṇa pūrvavad evam asyānavadyatā bhavati / yat punar bhuktavato na gurukaḥ kāyo bhavati karmaṇyaś ca bhavati / prahāṇa-kṣamo vistareṇa pūrvavad evam asya sparśavihāratā bhavati / tenāha pratisaṃkhyāyāhāram āharati / na dravārthaṃ na madārthaṃ/ na maṇḍanārtham iti / vistareṇa pūrvavad ayam tāvad bhojane mātrajñatāyā vistara-vibhāgaḥ//

/ samāsārthaḥ punaḥ katama āha / yaṃ [MS: yaś] ca paribhuṅkte / yathā ca paribhuṅkte / ayaṃ samāsārthaḥ so[52] *kaṃ paribhuṅkte / yad uta kavaḍaṃkāram āhāra(ṃ) manthā vāpūpā vā odana kulmāṣa(ṃ) vā vistareṇa pūrvavat / kathaṃ paribhuṅkte / pratisaṃkhyāya paribhunkte / na dravārthaṃ na madārthaṃ na maṇḍanārtham iti vistareṇa pūrvavat //*

/ punar aparaṃ samāsārthaḥ pratipakṣa-parigṛhītaṃ ca paribhuṅkte / kāmasukhallikānta-[vi]varjitaṃ ca / ātmaklamathānta-vivarjitaṃ ca / brahmacaryānugrahāya ca / kathaṃ pratipakṣa-parigṛhītaṃ / yad āha pratisaṃkhyāyāhāram āharati / kathaṃ kāmasukhallikānta-vivarjitaṃ ca / yad āha / na dravārthaṃ na madārthaṃ na maṇḍanārthaṃ na vibhūṣaṇārtham iti/ katham ātmaklamathānta-vivarjitaṃ / yad

āha jighatsoparataye paurāṇāṃ ca vedanāṃ prahāsyāmi navāṃ ca notpādayiṣyāmi / yātrā ca me bhaviṣyati / balaṃ ca sukhaṃ ceti / kathaṃ brahmacaryānugrahāya paribhuṅkte / yad āha / brahmacaryānugrahāyanavadyatā ca / sparśavihāratā ca me bhaviṣyatīti //

/ punar aparaṃ [MS: aparaḥ] samāsārthaḥ dvayam idaṃ bhojanaṃ cābhojanaṃ ca / tatrābhojana(ṃ) / yat sarveṇa sarvaṃ sarvathā kiṃcin na paribhuṅkte / abhuñjaṃś ca mriyate / tatra bhojanaṃ vividhaṃ / sama-bhojanaṃ / viṣama-bhojanaṃ ca / tatra sama-bhojanaṃ/ yan nātyalpaṃ nātiprabhūtaṃ / nāpaśyaṃ nāpariṇate na saṃkliṣṭaṃ/ tatra [vi]ṣama-bhojanaṃ /yady atyalpam atiprabhūtaṃ ca / apariṇate vāpaśyaṃ vā saṃkliṣṭaṃ vā paribhuṅkte / tatra sama-bhojane nātyalpa-bhojane jighatsā-daurbalyam anutpannaṃ / notpādayati / utpannam prajahāti / tatra nātiprabhūta-bhojane (MS: bhojanena] samabhojane na gurukaḥ kāyo bhavaty akarmaṇyaḥ / aprahāṇa-ksamo vistareṇa pūrvavat /tatra pariṇata-bhojanena samobhojanena paurāṇāṃ ca vedanāṃ prajahāti / navāṃ ca notpādayiṣyaty evam asya yātrā bhavati / balaṃ ca sukhaṃ cāsaṃkliṣṭa-bhojanena / samabhojanenānavadyatā ca bhavati / sparśavihāratā ca //

/ tatrātyalpa-bhojanaṃ / yena jīvati / jighatsā-daurbalya-parītaś ca jīvati / atiprabhūta-bhojanaṃ / yenāsya guru-bhārādhyākrāntaḥ kāyo bhavati / na ca kālena bhaktaḥ pariṇamati/ tatrāpariṇata-bhojanena visūcika kāye saṃtiṣṭhate / anyatamānyatamo vā kāye kāyikas tu bādhaḥ / samutpadyate / yathāpariṇatabhojanenaivam apaśyabhojanena tatrāyam apaśyabhojane viśeṣaḥ doṣaḥ pracayaṃ gacchati / kharaṃ cābādhaṃ spṛśati / tatra saṃkliṣṭa-bhojanenādharmeṇa piṇḍapātaṃ paryeṣya raktaḥ paribhuṅkte / sakto gṛddho grathita iti vistareṇa pūrvavat //

/ iti yaḥ sama-bhojanaṃ ca / paribhuṅkte / viṣama-bhojanaṃ ca parivarjayati / tasmād bhojane samakārīty ucyate / bhojane ca samakāritaiṣā ebhir ākārair ākhyātā uttānā vivṛtā saṃprakāśitā / yad uta pratisaṃkhyāyāhāram āharati / na dravārthaṃ na madārthaṃ na maṇḍanārthaṃ na vibhūṣaṇārthaṃ /iti / vistareṇa pūrvavat / tatra yat tāvad āha / pratisaṃkhyāyāhāram āharati / na dravārthaṃ na madārthaṃ na maṇḍanārthaṃ na vibhūṣaṇārthaṃ / yāvad evāsya kāyasya sthitaye yapanāyai anena tāvad abhojanaṃ pratikṣipati [MS: na pratikṣipati] / yat punar āha /jighatsoparataye brahmacaryānugrahāya vistareṇa yāvat /

sparśavihāratāyai anena viṣama-bhojanaṃ pratikṣipati//

/ kathaṃ ca punar viṣama-bhojanaṃ pratikṣipati / yat tāvad āha / brahmacaryānugrahāyānenātiprabhūtabhojanaṃ pratikṣipati / yad āha / paurāṇām ca vedanāṃ prahāsyāmi / navāṃ ca notpadayiṣyāmīty anenāpariṇata-bhojanatām apaśyabhojanatāṃ ca pratikṣipati / yad āha / yātrā ca me bhaviṣyati / balaṃ cānen[a n]ātyalpabhojanatāṃ prabhūtabhojanatāṃ ca darśayati / yad āha / sukhaṃ ca me bhaviṣyatīty anena pariṇatabhojanatāṃ paśyabhojanatāṃ ca[53] *darśayati / yad āha / anavadyatā ca me bhaviṣyati / sparśavihāratā cety anenāsaṃkliṣṭa bhojanatāṃ darśayati //*

/ yo 'sāv adharmeṇa piṇḍapātaṃ paryeṣya raktaḥ paribhuṅkte / sakto vistareṇa pūrvavat / sa-saṃkliṣṭaś ca paribhuṅkte sāvadyatā cāsya bhavati / tasyaiva kuśalapakṣa-prayuktasya pratisaṃlayane yoge manasikāre uddeśa-svādhāye 'rtha-cintāyāṃ ta eva pāpakākuśalā vitarkāś cittam anusravanti / ye 'sya tāṃ [MS: taṃ] nimnāṃ tatpravaṇāṃ tatprāgbhārāṃ cittasaṃtatiṃ pravartayanti / yenāsya sparśavihāro na [MS: sparśa-vihāreṇa] bhavati //

/ sā ceyaṃ dvividhā sparśavihāratātiprabhūta-bhojanaparivarjanāc ca yenāsya na gurukaḥ kāyo bhavati / akarmaṇyaḥ / aprahāṇa-kṣama ima iti vistareṇa pūrvavat / āhāre cāsvāda-karaṇād yenāsya vitarka-saṃkṣobha-kṛtāṃ asparśavihārata na bhavati //

/ tad evaṃ sati sarvair ebhiḥ padair bhojane samakāritā vyākhyātā [MS:vyākhyā cā] bhavati //

/idam ucyate bhojane mātrajñata / vistarataḥ saṃkṣepataś ca/

Translation of the Text

What is 'knowing the amount in food'? A case in point: Someone here after detailed consideration eats food, not for the purpose of sport, not for the purpose of intoxication, not for the purpose of smartening, and not for embellishment and so forth, as previously.[54]

How does he eat food after detailed consideration? Detailed consideration is explained as insight (*prajñā*). By insight, he observes trouble[55] of morsel food. Having become averse[56] by seeing the trouble, he ingests [food].

Furthermore, what is that seeing of trouble? It runs as follows: [the trouble] associated with enjoyment, associated with transformation, or associated with search of [*or* for] whatever morsel [food].

[Among those] what is the trouble associated with enjoyment? A case in point. At the time that someone here eats food that has perfect color, perfect odor, perfect taste and is well-prepared immediately upon the morsel food being cast into his mouth, when it is ground up by the teeth apparatus, saliva flows and it becomes wet and imbued with saliva and at that time is rolled along the gullet. Whatever was the former (*pūrvika, purāṇa*)[57] agreeability, it entirely abandons that and undergoes a thorough change. And it, being engaged in that change is explained as comparable to vomit. If the eating person (*puruṣa, pudgala*) would have paid attention to it, having that state from the standpoint of its appearance, and would remember it, in no case on another occasion would desire of enjoyment take shape for him while the food is untransformed and excellent—how much less when it has that state [of transformation]! When he has mastered the enjoyment of food by means of that succession [of steps in eating] and those multiple appearances [of that state], whatever was the seeming good color disappears, and the trouble involved in the unclean becomes apparent. This is called 'trouble associated with enjoyment,' namely, in regard to food.

Among those, what is the trouble in regard to food, associated with transformation? Of him having eaten and ingested that food, when it is transformed at night, whether in the middle or last watch, at that time it increases, generates, makes flourish in that body by numerous kinds and many different sorts of unclean substances, such as blood, flesh, sinews, bones, skin; and he transforms some of them into the substance of urine and ordure; and what is transformed goes into the lower part. He should purge that each day. And whatever is touched by that—whether hand, foot, or major or minor limb, as the case may be, becomes repulsive for oneself and for others, and from that cause there arise many bodily ailments in his body, as follows: boils (*gaṇḍa, piṭaka*), cutaneous eruptions (*dardrū, vicarcikā*), itching (*kaṇḍū*), leprosy (*kuṣṭa*), febrile eruptions (*kiṭibha*), white leprosy (*kilāsa*), fever (*jvara*), cough (*kāsa*), consumption (*śoṣa*), epilepsy (*apasmāra*), pathological hunger (*āṭakkara*),[58] jaundice (*pāṇḍuroga*), (?) bleeding (*rudhira*), unbalance of bile (*pitta*), fistula in the sex organ or anus (*bhagaṃdara*). Those and other bodily ailments of the same category arise in the body. And what is eaten goes wrong for him. Thereby indigestion attended with purging in both directions occurs in his body. This is called 'the trouble associated with transformation', namely, in regard to food.

Among those, what is the trouble in regard to food, associated with search? The trouble associated with search of food is of multiple kinds: created by acquisition, created by protection, created by breakdown of affection, created by dissatisfaction, created by servitude, and created by evil action.

Among them, what is the trouble, in regard to food, created by acquisition? A case in point: Someone here, owing to food as cause, on account of food, being oppressed by cold when it is cold, being oppressed by heat when it is hot, struggles (*utsahate, ghaṭate, vyāyacchate*) with agriculture, with tending cows, with commerce of various kinds—writing, measuring, arranging, counting, sealing; or with arts and crafts; either in order to obtain food that has not been obtained, or to store it. When he has struggled (*utsahata, ghaṭata, vyāyacchata*) for food, on account of the food, if those works go wrong, that is the primary cause that he grieves, laments, bemoans, beats his breast, weeps; or attachment turns to bewilderment, with his cry, "Alas, my effort is fruitless!" This is the trouble associated with the acquisition, that is, in regard to food.

If he prospers, he is reduced to fierce effort because of its protection. "Suppose my goods would be seized by the king or by robbers, or burnt by fire, or carried away by water; or stores badly stored would be lost; or works badly done would be destroyed; or unfriendly kinsmen would take charge; or a 'family firebrand' [a ruiner of the family] would arise in the family, who by wrong method would reduce those goods to ruin." [Such is] the trouble associated with its protection, that is, in regard to food.

What is the trouble created by breakdown of affection? A case in point: Because of that food, on account of food, a mother speaks in a nasty way to son; the son to mother; the father to son; the son to father; the brother to sister; the sister to brother; a companion to his companion. How much more so, person [at large] to another person! They become mutually hostile and fall into quarrels. In the same way, noble 'great Sāl trees'[59] of Brahmans, Kṣatriyas, or Householders, because of that food, thus fall into hostile quarrels, strike one another with their hands, and strike with clod, with club, with sword, This is called 'trouble created by breakdown of affection.'

Among those, what is the trouble created by dissatisfaction?[260] A case in point: Some kings—warriors consecrated on their heads—dwelling unsatisfied regarding their own villages, towns, realms, capitals, attack the military arrays, the forces of troops, on both sides. They begin with conch shells being blown, drums being sounded, and arrows being shot. They approach together with horses moving to and fro. They approach together with elephants, chariots, and (?) infantry moving to and fro. They with bodies wounded by arrows or spears, incur death or suffering as great as death. This or anything else of the same category is called the 'trouble created by dissatisfaction'.

Among those, what is the trouble created by servitude? A case in point: Hirelings of a king storming well-fortified cities are bestrewn with boiling sesame oil, boiling fat, boiling cow-dung watery mixture, boiling copper, boiling iron; and with their bodies wounded by arrows and spears incur death or suffering as great as death. This or anything else of the same category is called 'trouble created by servitude.'

Among those, is the trouble created by evil action? A case in point: Someone, because of food, has accumulated much evil action committed by body; and just as by body, so also by speech and by mind. And at the time he becomes sick, suffers, has severe illness, when at eventide a shadow descends toward, hangs over, alights upon mountains or mountain peaks, it occurs to him regarding his former evil action of body, evil action of speech and mind: "Alas, I have done evil; alas, I have not done good, with body, speech, and mind. Whatever be the destiny belonging to sins committed, dying, I shall go to the destiny." He with regret, dies, and having died goes to evil states, among hell beings, among animals and hungry ghosts. This is called 'trouble created by evil action'.

It occurs to him as follows: "Searching for food I have trouble; I have trouble in enjoying it, and also when it has been enjoyed, the transformation is trouble."

Still, food has some modicum of benefit. And what is that? This body lives by food. Based on food, it abides, but does not when without food. This is the modicum of benefit. Also this body of some, thus living by food, having abided for a long time, abides for a hundred years, or still a little more, when cared for properly.

Also that person could die early. Here, those who are engaged in mere life of body are not well-engaged. And those who are satisfied with mere life of body are not well-satisfied. Moreover, they do not experience the perfect, irreproachable benefit created by food. Moreover, those who are not satisfied with mere life of body, not engaged in mere life of body are well-engaged. Further they, based on just that life of body, who are engaged to accomplish chastity are well-engaged. Also just those experience the perfect, irreproachable benefit. "Therefore, it is not my mental picture[61] that I should dwell satisfied with the mere base benefit of food. It is not my mental picture that I should incur the law associated with fools—the foolish misfortune." When one has thus completely understood the trouble with all its aspects in regard to food, he from this point onward after detailed consideration, seeing the trouble and seeking the way of deliverance, eats food like 'the flesh of a son'[62] just for the purpose of deliverance from food.

It occurs to him: "Thus, these donors and patrons, attaining goods with difficulty, experiencing great trouble created by search, oppressing skin, flesh, and blood, present [those goods] to us, taking into account (*upādāya*)[63] that they have compassion toward [us] and desire special fruit, those alms thus received by us involve actions done by those (donors) that are exceedingly of great fruit, great benefit, great splendor, great extent; and [so] I should go to homes like the moon.[64] And I should go to homes withdrawing body, withdrawing thought, with modesty, without pride, not extolling myself, not reviling another; and with the thought that just as I should be pleased according to thought because of my own receipts, so I should be pleased according to thought because of another's receipts." On that account, this is allowable—he goes as a monk to others' homes not as follows [thinking]: "May others not fail to give to me; and with respect, not without respect; much, not a little; good, not bad; speedily, not delayed." [It occurs] to him so practicing:

"When I have gone to homes, if others do not give to me I should not in their presence sever [good relations][65] with malicious thoughts and with hostile thought. I would not fall upon an obstacle through occurrence of evil states. That is to say, when I have mastered precisely that malicious thought and hostile thought, if they should give without respect, not with respect; a little, not much; bad, not good; delayed, not speedily, I would not sever [good relations] with malicious thought or with hostile thought." And so forth, as previously. "Enjoyment of such kind would be my mental picture that having based myself, I should enjoy so. And having taken recourse to this morsel food, in such way should I behave and know that measure, whereby there would be no cessation of my life organ and I would not be weary with alms; [whereby] I would have promotion of chastity, and thus I, dwelling in ascetic state and in monk state, would have enjoyment of alms—that is the mental picture, pure and irreproachable." After detailed consideration by means of these aspects, he eats food.

Furthermore, what is food? There are four foods: morsel, contact, volition, and perception. In the present context, the purport is morsel food. Again, what is the latter? As follows: mixed beverage (*manthā*), rice or barley cakes (*apūpa*), cooked rice (*odana*), sour gruel (*kulmāṣa*), ghee (*sarpis*), oil (*taila*), honey (*madhu*),[66] molasses (*phaṇita*), meat (*māṃsa*), fish (*matsya*), dried meat (*vallūrā*), salt (*lavaṇa*), milk (*kṣīra*), curds (*dadhi*), fresh butter (*navanīta*). Having rendered in morsels those and whatever others are thus forms sustaining life, they are ingested. Therefore, the term 'morsel' is used.

'He eats, (*āharati*) has as synonyms: enjoys a meal (*bhuṅkte*), attends upon in each case (*pratiniṣevati*),[67] ingests (*avaharati*), chews (*khādati*), eats up (*bhakṣayati*), relishes (*svādayati*), drinks (*pibati*), sucks (*cūṣati*).

'Not for the purpose of sport' means those with enjoyment of passions, who eat thinking: "We have bodies delighted, bodies satisfied by food. When eventide is at hand, as night progresses, playing, enjoying ourselves, amusing ourselves among women girt with diadem, arms like [stems of] gourds, breasts like play-balls, we will indulge in unrestrained sport."[68] This sport is in the noble doctrine and discipline as follows: Those addicted to sensuous passion, addicted to carnality,[69] possess sinful, unvirtuous natures; the one eating, being oppressed with discursive thoughts has dissolute senses, and he who has dissolute senses has a coursing mind, a swaying mind, an unstationed mind, an unpacified mind. Furthermore, it is said that they, eating food excessively, eat 'for the purpose of sport'. The noble disciple possessed of hearing, with the power of detailed consideration, seeing the trouble, eats knowing the way of deliverance, but not as those with enjoyment of passion eat. Therefore it is said, 'not for the purpose of sport'.

'Not for the purpose of intoxication, not for the purpose of smartening, not for the purpose of embellishment' means—a case in point—those with enjoyment of passions, who eat food thinking: "Today we are eating food that is of large quantity, has oily power as satisfying as possible, is nourishing, nutritious, has perfect color, perfect odor, perfect taste, is heated. When night is past, we shall be capable, be powerful, have the skill of athletic exercise, namely, for drawing [the bow], rubbing [the body], lifting the contest stone, digging the soil, contesting with arm, running, swimming, jumping, or contesting there; and, furthermore, having taken recourse to that athletic exercise, we shall be strong, have athletic bodies, be free from illness for serious purposes (*dīkṣam*); and for a long time that strength will cleave to us, and not speedily will disfigurements overcome the body of old age; and we shall live for a very long time, and we shall be able to eat much; and there will be proper transformation of what is eaten, and there will be effected a reduction of faults." Thus one eats for the purpose of intoxication with freedom from illness, intoxication with youth, intoxication with life.

Furthermore, it occurs to them: "Having done the athletic exercise we shall go through the bathing procedure, namely, we shall wash our bodies with clean water; and with our bodies washed we shall comb[70] our hair; and anointing the body with various anointments, we shall adorn the body with various clothes, various garlands, various ornaments." Whatever be here the bathing, combing, and anointing, this is called their 'smartening'. The wearing of clothes, garlands, and ornaments by those who are characterized by smartening in that way is called 'embellishment'.

When they eat for the purpose of smartening, for the purpose of embellishment, they thus are intoxicated with intoxication, and have bodies of the smartening class and embellished. When midday or eventide is present at the time of eating, having become thirsty and hungry, with exceeding satisfaction, exceeding delight, exceeding joy, not seeing the trouble, not knowing the way of deliverance, eat food according as it is provided, simply again and again for the purpose of sport, of smartening, and of embellishment. The noble disciple, possessed of hearing, having the power of detailed consideration, seeing the trouble, eats knowing the way of deliverance, but not as those with enjoyment of passion eat. and he thinks, "Just never again resorting to this food which should not be resorted to, which should be renounced, I shall renounce [it]."

'Simply to keep his body alive' means that he who lives by eating, not by not eating, has life of the body. He eats thinking, "Eating this food, I shall live, not die." Therefore it is said, 'simply to keep his body alive.'

How does one eat for maintenance? There are two kinds of sustenance: sustenance with difficulty and without difficulty.

What is sustenance with difficulty? Whatever food of such material he eats, there is desire for food, or weakness; or he suffers with severe illness; or he seeks alms in an unlawful, not in a lawful, manner. He eats with clinging, attachment, desire-fettered, infatuated, coveting, fallen into covetousness. His body is heavy, inefficient; he is without patience for the elimination-exertion (*prahāṇa-kṣama*)[1] for which reason his consciousness (*citta*) is not speedily concentrated. Or the breathing in and breathing out proceed with difficulty. Or torpor and sleepiness enwrap his consciousness. This is called 'sustenance with difficulty'.

What is sustenance without difficulty? In particular (*yathāpi*), how, when he eats food of such material, there is no desire for food, or weakness. He does not suffer with severe illness. He seeks alms in a lawful, not in an unlawful manner. He eats without clinging, without attachment not desire-fettered, not infatuated, not coveting, not fallen into covetousness. His body is not heavy. It is efficient. He has patience for the elimination-exertion, for which reason he speedily concentrates his consciousness. Breathing in and breathing out proceed with little difficulty. Torpor and sleepiness do not enwrap his consciousness. This is called 'sustenance with little difficulty'.

Among those, whatever is sustenance with difficulty, thereby there is continuation of life of the body, that is to say, with stain. Among those, whatever is sustenance with little difficulty, thereby there is continuation of life of the body, and that, moreover, is irreproachable without stain. Among those, the noble disciple, possessed of hearing entirely casts away that sustenance attended with reproach and with stain. He proceeds, resorts to the sustenance without reproach, without stain. Therefore it is said 'for maintenance'.

Furthermore, that irreproachable, unstained sustenance which has been mentioned above—how does one conceive that? It is said that if he resorts [to food: 'attends upon in each case'] to allay [the body's] desire for food and to promote chastity with the thought, "I shall eliminate old feeling, and not give rise to new; and I shall have sustenance, strength, delight, no reproach, and an agreeable condition," then he conceives the irreproachable, unstained sustenance.

And how does he eat to allay [the body's] desire for food? When eating time is present and hunger has arisen, and he eats, and he eats that [particular] amount for dispelling his possession by hunger and his weakness through desire for food. As further, the weakness through desire for food does not oppress the one who eats out of proper time, that is, when the time of eating is eventide, or night as it progresses, or the next day, thus he eats to allay the desire for food.

How does he eat to promote chastity? He eats that [particular] measure. He eats food so formed. Thereby, the one practicing in the virtuous side in this very life has a light body immediately after eating or on that very day. And he has an efficient body, and patience for the elimination-exertion, for which reason his consciousness is very speedily concentrated. His in- and out-breathing proceed with little difficulty. Torpor and sleepiness do not enwrap his consciousness. Thereby he has the fortune and is able quickly to attain the unattained, comprehend the uncomprehended, see in immediacy what has not been seen in immediacy. Thus he eats to promote chastity.

How does he eat with the thought, "I shall eliminate old feeling?" A case in point: In the past he had eaten in improper measure, or something unwholesome,[72] or there was wrong transforming, that thereby numerous bodily illnesses have arisen in him, that is, itching, leprosy, febrile eruptions, white leprosy, and so forth, as previously; and that in him arise intense, harsh, fierce, unpleasant corporeal feeling-sufferings which have the illness as their cause, [then] in order to allay that illness, and in order to allay those feeling-sufferings caused by it, he takes recourse through a procedure indicated by a physician, to a medicament that is beneficial, wholesome, favorable, suitable; and eats wholesome food. Thereby there is elimination of that illness that has arisen and of the feeling-suffering caused by it. Thus he eats food with the thought, "I shall eliminate old feeling."

How does he eat food with the thought, "I shall not give rise to new feeling?" At the present time, happy without illness and strong, he does not eat with improper measure, or something unwholesome, or when there is bad transformation, [in such a way] whereby in the future, tomorrow or the following day, indigestion attended with purging in both directions would take shape in his body, or one or another bodily illness occur, that is, itching, leprosy, febrile eruptions, white leprosy, and so forth, as previously, from which cause corporeal feelings would arise, as previously. Thus he eats with the thought, "I shall not give rise to new feeling."

How does he eat with the thought, "I will have sustenance, strength, delight, no reproach, and an agreeable condition?" When he thinks, "One, having eaten that much, lives," thus arises his sustenance. When, "One dispels the weakness through desire of food," thus arises his strength. When, "One eliminates old feeling, and does not give rise to new," thus arises his delight. When, "Seeking alms in a lawful manner, one eats without clinging, without attachment ... [so forth, as previously]," thus arises his state of non-reproach. When, "Having eaten, one's body is not heavy and is efficient, and he has patience for the elimination-exertion ... [so forth, as previously]," thus arises his agreeable condition.

Therefore, he said: "After detailed consideration, he eats food, not for the purpose of sport, not for the purpose of intoxication, not for the purpose of smartening," and so forth as previously. That much is the extensive analysis of 'knowing the amount in food.'

Furthermore, what is the meaning in short? He said: "What he eats, and how he eats—this is the meaning in short." What does he eat? As follows: morsel food—mixed beverage, rice or barley cakes, cooked rice, sour gruel, and so forth, as previously. How does he eat? After detailed consideration, he eats not for the purpose of sport, not for the purpose of intoxication, not for the purpose of smartening, and so forth, as previously.

Moreover, the meaning in short is that he eats in a manner governed by the antidote, in a manner shunning the extreme of indulgence in desires, in a manner shunning the extreme of mortification of self,[73] and in order to promote chastity. How in a manner governed by the antidote? As he said: "After detailed consideration, he eats food." How in a manner to shun the extreme of indulgence in desires? As he said: "not for the purpose of sport, not for the purpose of intoxication, not for the purpose of smartening, not for the purpose of embellishment". How in a manner to shun the extreme of mortification of self? As he said: "to allay desire of food; and with the thought, 'I shall eliminate old feeling and not give rise to new; and I shall have sustenance, strength, delight.'" How does he eat to promote chastity? As he said: "to promote chastity; and with the thought, 'I shall have no reproach, and an agreeable condition.'"

Moreover, the meaning in short is this pair: food and no food. Among those, no food means that someone eats nothing whatsoever and not eating, he dies. Among those, food is of two kinds: moderate food and immoderate food. Among those, moderate food is that which is not too little, not much, not unwholesome, not when there is bad transformation, not stained. Among those, immoderate food is if he eats too little, too much, when there is bad transformation, the unwholesome, the stained.

Among those, when there is moderate food, that is not too little food he does not give rise to weakness, through desire for food, that has not arisen, and he eliminates it if it has arisen. Among those, when there is moderate food that is not too much food, his body does not become heavy and inefficient, he does not lack patience for the elimination-exertion, and so forth, as previously. Among those, by means of moderate food that is transformed food, he eliminates old feeling and will not give rise to new. Thus there is his sustenance, strength, and delight. By means of moderate food that is unstained food, the state of no reproach arises, as well as an agreeable condition.

Among those, too little food—whereby he lives, and lives possessed by desire for food and by weakness; too much food—whereby his body is attacked by a heavy weight and his food is not transformed in due time. Among those, by reason of untransformed food, indigestion attended with purging in both directions takes shape in his body; or bodily illness, one or another, arises in his body. Just as by reason of untransformed food, so by unwholesome food. Among those, when there is unwholesome food, a special fault (*doṣa*)[74] builds up, and he comes upon harsh illness. Among those, by reason of stained food, seeking alms in an unauthorized manner, he eats with clinging, attachment, desire-fettered, and so forth, as previously.

That being so, one eats moderate food and shuns immoderate

food. Because of that, he is said to be 'with moderation in respect to food'; and that moderation with respect to food is by these aspects completely explained (*ākhyāta, uttāna,*[75] *vivṛta, saṃprakāśita*); namely, after detailed consideration he eats food, not for the purpose of sport, not for the purpose of intoxication, not for the purpose of smartening, not for the purpose of embellishment, and so forth, as previously. In that passage, the part where he says, "After careful consideration, he eats food, not for the purpose of sport, not for the purpose of intoxication, not for the purpose of smartening, not for the purpose of embellishment, but simply to keep his body alive, to maintain it," with that he rejects the lack of food. Again, the part where he says, "[to] allay [the body's] desire for food and to promote chastity" and so forth down to "an agreeable condition" with that he rejects immoderate food.

And how [in particular] does he reject immoderate food? The part where he says, "To promote chastity," with that he rejects too much food. The part where he says, "and I shall eliminate old feeling and not give rise to new", who with that he rejects untransformed food and unwholesome food. The part where he says, "and I shall have sustenance and strength", with that he indicates neither too little food nor [too] much food. The part where he says, "and I shall have delight", with that he indicates transformed food and wholesome food. The part where he says, "and I shall have no reproach and an agreeable condition", with that he indicates unstained food.

The one who, seeking alms in an unlawful manner eats with clinging, attachment, and so forth, as previously, and eats with stain, also has reproach. Those sinful, unvirtuous discursive thoughts flow according to the consciousness of precisely that person who has applied himself to a virtuous category in introspection, *yoga,* mental orientation, recitation of the exposition, and pondering of its meaning. They set in motion his 'stream of consciousness' (*cittasaṃtati*) which is so headed, so inclined, so bent. Thereby he does not have an agreeable condition. Also, that agreeable condition is of two kinds: As a consequence of shunning too much food, thereby he does not have a body that is heavy and inefficient, he does not lack patience for the elimination-exertion, and so forth, as previously. And by reason of having no relish for food, thereby he does not have a disagreeable condition caused by the commotion of discursive thought.

That being so, all these words have elucidated moderation regarding food. This is called 'knowing the amount in food', in extension and briefly.

REFERENCES

1. Robert Ernest Hume, *The Thirteen Principal Upanishads* (London, 1934, reprint). See, e.g., "General Index," 574.
2. Derge T., *Sems tsam*, Zi, 211b-3 ff.:/ gnas pa sgrub paḥi chos rnams kyi rab tu dbye ba yaṅ rnam pa lṅas rnam par gźag ste/: Ch. trans. *Taishō*, 30.664a-9 f.
3. Louis de La Vallée Poussin, trans., *L'Abhidharmakośa de Vasubandhu; Premier et deuxième chapitres* (Paris, 1923), 214-5.
4. Alex Wayman, "Studies in Yama and Māra," *Indo-Iranian Journal*, 3 (1959), No. 1 and No. 2, n. 155. This essay (reduced) is herein.
5. Alexander Csoma de Körös, "Origin of the Shakya Race Translated...," reprinted in E.D. Ross, ed., *Tibetan Studies* (Calcutta, 1912), Appendix to *Journal of the Asiatic Society of Bengal*, 1911.
6. In the Buddhist cosmogony of three realms—*kāmadhātu, rūpadhātu,* and *arūpadhātu*—the Ābhāsvara *devas* are located in the realm of form *(rūpadhātu)*, in the division Second Dhyāna, which consists of Parīttābhāḥ, Apramāṇābhāḥ, and Ābhāsvarāḥ. The immediately lower or First Dhyāna is the Brahman world. The being in both the First and Second Dhyānas has joy (*prīti*) and pleasure (*sukha*). Cf. Louis de La Vallée Poussin, trans., *L'Abhidharmakośa de Vasubandhu: Troisiéme chapitre* (Paris, 1926), 2; and Nyanatiloka, *Buddhist Dictionary* (Colombo, 1950), 62.
7. La Vallée Poussin, *L'Abhidarmakośa...Troisiéme chapitre*, 126.
8. Prahlad Pradhan, ed., *Abhidharma-samuccaya of Asaṅga* (Santiniketan, 1950), 30: pariṇatito 'pi pāriṇāmikaḥ viṣayato 'pi vaiṣayikaḥ āśayato 'py āśi-(? śayi)-kaḥ upādānato 'py upādānikaḥ āhāro draṣṭavyaḥ.
9. Collected works (Labrang ed., Vol. Ga), *Chos mṅon*, 101a-6 f: khams kyi zas ni/ dri ro reg byaḥi skye mched gsum gyi bdag ñid yin la/reg paḥi zas ni/dbaṅ poḥi ḥbyuṅ ba chen po rgyas par byed paḥi zag bcas kyi reg paḥo/sems paḥi zas ni/ ḥdod pahī dṅos po la re ba daṅ ldan paḥi sems paḥo/rnam par śes paḥi zas ni/rnam par śes paḥi tshogs drug kyaṅ yin te/ khams bcu gcig ces ḥbyuṅ baḥi phyir daṅ/ gtso bo ni kun gźiḥi rnam par śes paho/For *khams kyi zas* read *kham gyi zas;* for *dbaṅ poḥi ḥbyuṅ ba* read *dbaṅ po ḥbyuṅ ba*.
10. Vidhushekhara Bhattacharya, ed., *The Yogācārabhūmi of Ācārya Asaṅga*, part 1 (Calcutta, 1957), 99-100; Tib. trans., Derge T., *Sems tsam*, Tshi, 51b-1 to -4; Ch. trans., *Taishō*, 30.300a-13 f. Bhattacharya's reading of the passage (100.3): *tatra narakopapannānāṃ sattvānāṃ sūkṣmaḥ kāvaḍīkārāhāragarbho vāyur vāti* should be corrected to: *kāvaḍīkārāhāro garbhe...* according to the Tibetan translation of the passage: */de la sems can dmyal bar skyes paḥi sems can rnams kyi khoṅ na ni/rluṅ rgyu baḥi kham gyi zas cha phra ba yod do/*. The words (100.7) *jarām āpadyate* are translated 'it undergoes digestion' on the authority of

both the Tibetan (*źu bar ḥgyur te*) and the Chinese. Also (100.5) correct *sūkṣma to sūkṣmaḥ*.

11. The embryonic states are *kalala, arbuda, peśin, ghana,* and *praśākhā*; see La Vallée Poussin, *L'Abhidharmakośa......Premier et deuxième chapitres,* 255.
12. There are six groups of these gods; for their names, *cāturmahārājika,* etc., see Franklin Edgerton, *Buddhist Hybrid Sanskrit Dictionary,* 270. Cited hereafter as Edgerton, *Dict.*
13. La Vallée Poussin, *L'Abhidharmakośa.....Troisième chapitre,* 128.
14. Jiryo Masuda, *Origin and Doctrines of Early Indian Buddhist Schools* (Leipzig, 1925), 25.
15. La Vallée Poussin. *L'Abhidharmakośa....Troisième chapitre,* 149.
16. Manfred Mayrhofer, *Kurzgefasstes etymologisches Wörterbuch des Altindischen,* I, 186-7.
17. Tib. trans., Derge T., Dzi, 83a-7ff.; Ch. trans., *Taishō,* 30.430b-26 f.
18. *Pragharati* is translated 'flows out' in agreement with Tibetan *ḥdzag par byed pa* and with the entry in Edgerton, *Dict.*, 357a.
19. Tib. trans., Dzi. 56g-4; Ch. trans., *Taishō,* 30.397b-1.
20. MS *darpārtham.* Asaṅga's extended treatment always has *dravārtham.*
21. The portion in parentheses was mutilated in the MS at this point; but the fact that the same words recur in the extended treatment by Asaṅga makes possible their presentation here with no doubt that they are correct. The mutilation cut off also the *anusvāra* marks for the immediately succeeding words.
22. *Pratisaṃkhyāya,* ger.: Edgerton, *Dict.* 371-2.
23. *Yāvad eva*: Edgerton, *Dict.* 447b.
24. Such a replacement represents a procedure contrary to that which produced much of the vocabulary of Buddhist Hybrid Sanskrit as explained by Franklin Edgerton. BHS constitutes a Sanskritization of Prakrit texts, and Prakrit words would be given an equivalent Sanskrit form, whose meaning would then be different often from such a Sanskrit word, if existent in classical Sanskrit.
25. Ernst Waldschmidt, "A Fragment from the Saṃyuktāgama," *The Adyar Library Bulletin,* Buddha Jayanti Issue, 20 (December, 1956), 223.
26. Bihar MS 1B.4-2c through -7c (end of folio side); 5A.7-5B (mid) through -7C; 5B.7; 5A.8, 5B.8; 5A.9; 5B.9; 6A.1; 6B.1; 6A.2; 6B.2 through 6b.2-3c. Tib. trans., Derge T., Dzi, 29b-5 to 38b-1; Ch. trans., *Taishō,* 30.408a-14 to 411b.
27. MS *yamā* is a corruption somehow for *prajñā*. The latter word is attested by the translation T. *so sor rtog pa źes bya ba ni śes rab ste / =pratisaṃkhyocyate prajñā.*
28. The word is disfigured in the MS. The missing portion is restored by T. *mid par gyur nas,* suggesting a verb meaning 'to ingest', which in the present *sandhi* situation should begin with *ā* (the visible *akṣara* could be so interpreted), with two or three syllables in the hiatus.
29. The word *saṃjanayati* ends folio 1B.4 *-ati pariṇataś* is the resumption of the food section in the middle of a folio on plate on plate 5A, in fact 5A.7-5b, where the expression (?) *arthataś ca/ati pariṇataś* without warning ends the intrusion of the *Cintāmayī Bhūmi.* The hiatus amounts to the Sanskrit original for T. *brta bar ḥgyur ba daṅ /de dag las la ni bśaṅ ba daṅ/gci baḥi dṅos por yoṅs su ḥjug par ḥgyur ṣiṅ/.* Now, T. *yoṅs su ḥju bar ḥgyur ba* translates the word *vipariṇamati,* above. This indicates that the *ati* of the MS is the residue of the word *vipariṇamati.* The Tibetan passage may be translated into Sanskrit as follows: *utkarṣayati/teṣām ekatyāni ca viṇmūtra-vastunā vipariṇamati.* The form *ekatyāni* is based on the BHS pronoun *ekatya,* for which see Edgerton, *Dict.*

30. The reading *ekasmin divase* is justified by T. *ñin gcig*.
31. T. *gźi de las* shows the ablative.
32. *py evaṃbhāgīyāḥ* is corrupted in the MS to *bhairaṃ bhagaṃ yāḥ*.
33. Possibly to be emended to *kaśyamānaiḥ*.
34. The correction to perfect of *ıiś*- (here) 'begin' is supported by T. *chas śin* 'started'.
35. The correction is supported by T. *gtor cin* 'strewn'.
36. Here *loḍikā* is translated by T. *thug pa* 'soup, broth'.
37. The portion within brackets is covered by a tack that was used to hold the folio straight during photography in Tibet. The solution is the only feasible one for the time reference in the translation T. *gaṅ gi tshe na*. The *-ma-* of *samaye* is partly visible.
38. The T. *grib ma bźin du* 'like a shadow' appears to be free translation.
39. The correction is suggested by T. *brten nas* 'based on.' For the BHS from *niśrita*, see Edgerton. *Dict*. 307.
40. The italicized phrase seems to be an intrusion and will not be translated.
41. The italicized phrase is an intrusion and apparently belongs later (see note 45), where it will be used to reconstruct a missing passage.
42. MS ending of this word is partly illegible, and concludes with *ur*.
43. The correction is based on T. *gźan la mi smod pa* 'not reproaching others.'
44. The next MS occurrence iș? *batvaṃ*. The T. *ḥgyaṅs te* means ,'delayed'.
45. T. *de ltar bdag ñid bźag ste/yoṅs su loṅs spyod par byed na /de ltar yoṅs su loṅs spyod par byed pa de ni/ bdag gi tshul daṅ mthun pa yin te/*. The MS at this point did not show any corresponding Sanskrit term, but it is obvious that the preceding intrusive passage (note 41) corresponds in great measure with the Tibetan. A Sanskrit reconstruction has been attempted within the brackets to utilize as much as possible the intrusive passage alluded to, and simultaneously to constitute a model that could have given rise to the Tibetan translation.
46. The spelling here is close to the Pāli *kabalimkāra*, as cited above. But in the list of four foods and earlier, Asaṅga spells the word *kavaḍaṃkāra*, according to the MS. However, cf. note 10, above, containing a citation of the reading *kāvaḍīkāra* from part 1 of the *Yogācārabhūmi* as edited by V. Bhattacharya.
47. Girija Prasanna Majumdar, "Food [Man's Indebtedness to Plants]," *Indian Culture*, January, 1935, 417, spells the word *phānita*, remarking, "sugarcane juice boiled down to one-fourth; it can be drawn out in threads". A.F. Rudolf Hoernle. ed., "The Bower Manuscript," in *Arch. Survey of India*, n.i.s., Vol. 22. General Sanskrit Index, 300, enters "Phāṇita, molasses, in *sa-phāṇita*, q.v."
48. MS is obviously corrupt with a reading *atar* [?] *kayā*. The emendation is based as far as possible on the MS reading as well as on the translation T. *gźu dgaṅ ba* 'stretching the bow'.
49. MS adds another *bhuktaṃ* by mistake after the ca.
50. The portion within brackets was covered by a thumb-tack.
51. The italicized phrase is an intrusion, as can be seen by comparison with the preceding paragraph.
52. The syllable *śo* is an intrusion.
53. Although the MS has *ca* here, it omitted *paśya-bhojanatāṃ*, and then repeated the sentence with the latter expression. According to the Tibetan, there is only one sentence.
54. By "and so forth, as previously", Asaṅga refers to the paragraph presented above on p. 139.
55. BHS *ādinava*, for which see Edgerton, *Dict*. 94, where the possibilities "misery,

evil, danger, mishap, wretchedness" are suggested.

56. *vidūṣayitvā* a BHS, form. Edgerton, *Dict.* 487, gives for *vidūṣaṇā*, 'self-denunciation'.

57. Asaṅga uses a sequence of two or more virtually synonymous terms to show emphasis, here 'former' (*pūrvika, purāṇa*). Later in this section, he employs the same device to mean 'person' (*puruṣa-pudgala*), 'struggles' (*utsahate, ghaṭate, vyāyacchate*), 'struggled' (*utsahata, ghaṭata, vyāyacchata*), and 'compeletely explained' (*ākhyāta, uttāna, vivṛta, saṃprakāśita*).

58. Edgerton, *Dict.* 91, enters 'āṭakkara, m., = aṭakkara, q.v.; Bhik 17a.2, in list of diseases'. He is referring to *Bhikṣuṇī-karmavācanā*, ed. Ridding and La Vallée Poussin, *BSOS,* Vol. 1, part 3 (1920), 123-43. The list of diseases (pp. 131-2) contains the sequence *śoṣo 'pasmāraḥ/āṭakkaraḥ/pāṇḍurogaḥ*. By comparison with Asaṅga's list, this supports the reading *apasmāra* rather than *śoṣāpasmāra* for 'epilepsy'; cf. MS reading *śoṣaḥ śosāpasmāra,* p. 141.

59. Asaṅga is referring to families of the three upper castes; cf. *Mahāvyutpatti,* 3862-4: *kṣatriya mahāsāla kula, brāhmaṇa mahāsāla kula, gṛhapati mahāsāla kula*.

60. This and the next paragraph are of obvious anti-war sentiment. But see the remarks by Asaṅga referred to in Paul Demiéville, "Le Bouddhisme et la guerre," *Mélanges publiés par l'Institut des hautes études chinoises,* XI (Paris, 1957), I, 379-80, where we find that a *bodhisattva* is exhorted to kill another who was on the point of killing many others. Presumably a contemporary of Asaṅga, Kālidāsa has a much higher opinion of kingship, as can be seen from B.S. Upadhyaya, *India in Kālidāsa* (Allahabad, 1947), 105 f.; for the descriptions of warfare in Kālidāsa's works, see pp. 157 f.

61. The expression 'mental picture in this sentence translates S. *pratima*; and, in the following one, S. *pratirūpa*. Asaṅga apparently employs *pratima* and *pratirūpa* in a technical sense of Buddhist meditation. Both are approximately synonyms of *pratibimba*. This is an important concept in the *Śrāvakabhūmi*. The meditative object is the *ālambana*. The reflected image in the mind of that object is the *pratibimba*. There are two *pratibimba, savikalpa-pratibimba* and *nirvikalpa-pratibimba,* as is shown in my chap. iv, *Analysis*.

62. Bhikkhu Ñāṇamoli, trans., *The Path of Purification* (*Visuddhimagga*) *by Bhadantācariya Buddhaghosa* (Colombo, 1956), 33, has a note: *"Child's flesh (putta-maṃsa)* is an allusion to the story (S. ii, 98) of the couple who set out to cross a desert with an insufficient food supply, but got to the other side by eating the flesh of their child who died on the way." This is a reference to the passage of which the first part was quoted on p. 136, above. However, the story actually has the parents slaying their child in order that they may survive. It goes on, "Now what do you think monks? Would they eat the food for sport?" (*taṃ kiṃ maññatha bhikkhave api nu te davāya vā āhāraṃ āhareyyuṃ*) and so forth with 'intoxication', 'smartening', and 'embellishment', ending with the reply, "Not so, your honor" (*no hetam bhante*). The *Laṅkāvatārasūtra* (246) converts the simile to an argument against eating meat: the *bodhisattva* has the "idea that all sentient beings are his sole child" (*sarvasattvaikaputra-kasaṃjñā*). Apparently, according to this *sūtra,* a *bodhisattva* is not allowed to eat meat even in a situation as exceptional as that of the couple alluded to above. At least in his *Śrāvakabhūmi* Asaṅga opposes this extreme view, and certainly he does not oppose meat-eating, as can be seen from his list of foods, soon to be detailed. Tapo Nath Chakravarty, "Food and Drink in Ancient Bengal," *Journal of the Department of Letters,* University of Calcutta, n.s., Vol. 2, part 2 (1958), 235, cites the views of the ancient Indian Hindu

Smṛti writer Manu: "There is thus nothing wrong *(Nāsti doṣaḥ)* in the act of partaking [of] fish and meat (matsya-māṃsabhakṣaṇe) .... Nivṛtti or complete abstinence from the aforesaid natural habits ... is thus characterised as being of inestimable value."

63. The translation of *upādāya* is based on Edgerton, *Dict.* 145, where a lengthy entry on this word is found.
64. Cf. the line in *Dhammapada, Brāhmaṇa-Vagga* 31: *candaṃ va vimalaṃ suddhaṃ vippasannam anāvilam* '(who) like the moon is undefiled, pure, serene, unmuddled . The equivalent verse is in the BHS *Udānavarga, Brāhmaṇa-Varga,* numbered 39 in H. Beckh's edition of the Tibetan text.
65. The optative form *vyavadīyeyam* is based on the root ²dā–'divide. share' according to T. *rnam par ḥbyed pa,* the usual translation of S. *vibhakti.* Accordingly, the rendition 'sever [good relations]' was adopted as satisfying the context as well as the root. While Edgerton's *Dict.* does not have the form, it does enter *vyavadāna* 'purification', which is presumably based on the root ⁴dā- 'clear But Whitney. *The Roots....* remarks after this particular root. "Only with *ava*; certainly no separate root, and probably a specialization of meaning of the participle of / ²dā."
66. Regarding the three immediately preceding entries, the *Carakasaṃhitā, Vimānasthāna,* I, 13, says that oil, ghee, and honey are the substances which serve to calm (respectively) wind, bile, and phlegm (*tailasarpirmadhūni vātapittaśleṣmapraśama-nārthāni dravyāṇi bhavanti*). These last symptoms are often called the three *doṣas* in Indian medicine.
67. Edgerton, *Dict.* 363, enters-*pratiniṣevaṇa* (-*tā*), "cultivation (of) adherence (to), severally, in each case (*prati*) ...," but does not associate this with eating.
68. Hajime Nakamura, "The Influence of Confucian Ethics on the Chinese Translations of Buddhist Sutras," Liebenthal Festschrift, *Sino-Indian Studies,* Vol. 5, parts 3 and 4 (Santiniketan, 1957), 156 f., esp. 159, shows that passages of this type were modified by pre-Tang translators to eliminate vulgarity; but (160), "In the Tang period, however, this bashfulness had gone..." The *Śrāvakabhūmi* was translated in the Tang period, but some translators at least had not become sufficiently sophisticated: as my wife translates for me the Chinese version in *Taishō,* 30.309b-5, 6, this sentence has shrunk to: "When night comes we will play with beautiful ornamented women, enjoy and amuse [ourselves], [and] indulge in unrestrained sport."
69. The word *maithuna* is here translated as 'carnality' to accommodate the eight varieties mentioned in Johann Jakob Meyer, *Sexual Life in Ancient India* (New York, 1953), 251 n., though the author translates the word as 'copulation': "Maithuna (copulation), indeed, is according to old Indian eightfold teaching: smaraṇa (thinking of it), kīrtana (speaking of it), keli (dallying), prekṣaṇa (viewing), guhyabhāṣaṇa (secret converse), saṃkalpa (firm will to copulate), adhyavasāya (resolve to do it), kriyānishpatti (the actual accomplishment). Each is in itself maithuna."
70. 'We shall comb' translates *prasādhayiṣyāmaḥ* on the authority of the Sino-Japanese renditions, *Kokuyaku Daizōkyo,* Rommbu, VI, 665. The dictionary of Monier-Williams does not enter this meaning for the verb, but does have *prasādhana,* m. a comb' (lexical) and *keśa-prasādhanī* (from *Suśrutasaṃhitā*).
71. 'Patience for the elimination-exertion' (*prahāṇa-kṣama*) refers to meditative practice. The translation of *prahāṇa* is discussed in my chap. iv, *Analysis.*
72. BHS *apaśya.* The meaning is assured by T. *mi ḥphrod pa* 'unwholesome'. This

BHS word, = *adṛśya*, reflects the use of the root *paś*- in places where Sanskrit uses only, or generally, the root *dṛś*-.

73. These are the two extremes to be avoided, according to the teaching of early Buddhism; the celebrated Middle Path is the course to follow. In BHS, the two are *kāmasukhallikā* and *ātmaklamatha*; in Pāli they are *kāmsukhallikā* and *atthakilamatha*.
74. It is possible that Asaṅga is referring here to the *doṣa* theory of Indian medicine. See note 66, above.
75. Cf. the entry in Edgerton, *Dict.*, s.v.

17

The Position of Women in Buddhism

The position of women in Buddhism is a vast topic, and much has been written in ancient and modern times on this matter. In the present essay, the topic will be exposed along two lines: I. What the Buddhist texts have to say about women. II. The role of women themselves in Buddhism.

I. What the Buddhist Texts Say?

Now the material will be treated under these headings:

(a) Pseudo and vertitable references to women. (b) Position of women in society, and specifically in Buddhism. (c) Theory of

Reprinted from *Studia Missionalia,* Vol. 40. Editrice Pontificia. University Gregoriana Roma. 1991.

mother's love. (d) The imputed ability or lack of same for religious attainment of women.

(a). *Pseudo and veritable references to women.* As a kind of pseudo reference is the much-quoted passage from the Pāli *Parinibbāna-sutta* in the Dīgha-nikāya, Vol. II. Here Ānanda questions the Buddha, who responds:[1]

> Q: How, lord, are we to conduct ourselves in regard to womankind (P. *mātugāma*)?
> A: As not seeing them, Ānanda.
> Q: If we should see them, what are we to do?
> A: No talking, Ānanda.
> Q: If they should speak to us, lord, what are we to do?
> A: Remember me, Ānanda.

The passage gives no information about women. The advice is directed to the male monk, who is supposed to adhere to celibacy.

So also in a brief text reputed to have been the first Buddhist scripture translated into Chinese, namely, "The Sūtra of 42 sections," where the translation reads:[2]

> 29. The Buddha said: "Take care to avoid looking on the beauty of women and do not converse with them. If you do (have occasion to) converse with them, control the thought which runs through your minds. When I was a Sramana and came in contact with the impure world, I was like the lotus which remains unsullied by the mud (from which it grows). Think of old women as of your mothers, those older than yourselves as of your elder sisters, of those younger than yourselves as of your younger sisters, and of very young ones as your daughters. Dwell on thoughts of Enlightenment and banish all evil ones."

Our third pseudo reference to women was directed to laymen, and is found in the Pāli Vinaya. Here, I repeat the story as it was presented by Horner and Coomaraswamy:[3]

> On his way from Benares to Uruvelā, the Buddha fell in with a party of young men picnicking with their wives. One of them being unmarried had brought with him his mistress; but she had run off with some of the young men's belongings. They were all looking for her and asked the Buddha, if he

> had seen her. The Buddha replied: "What think ye? Were it not better ye sought the Self (*attanaṃ gaveseyyātha*), rather than the woman?"

From this rather remarkable passage we may conclude that this Self is neither male or female, since the Buddha is addressing persons who have either male egos or female egos; and we may infer that this Self is devoid of possessions, since it was on account of 'stolen' goods that they were looking for the 'woman'. It follows that either a man or a woman could seek this Self, according to this Buddhist tenet. Even so, the *Āṭānāṭiya-sutta* of Dīgha-nikāya, Vol. III, speaks of men in this role by the line, *manussā tattha jāyanti, amamā apariggahā,* "There men live, without a 'mine', or without a 'my wife'.[4] The remark does apply as well to women, who like men live with a 'mine', and with 'my spouse'. So the question is raised, did those men really live without a 'mine', and can women do likewise? A partial response will be attempted as we continue. In the meantime, the claim that Gautama Buddha was without property (P. *nibbhoga*) is explained in the "Book of Eights" in the Aṅguttara-nikāya as that he had abandoned all the objects of the five senses.[5]

For veritable references to women, we also refer to the "Book of Eights". Elsewhere, I have shown that the number eight is especially associated with women.[6] In this part of the Pāli canon, there is a passage on how women bind men.[7]

> Monks, a woman binds a man in eight ways. What eight? A woman binds a man by weeping (P. *ruṇṇa*), by laughter (P. *hasita*), by speech (P. *bhaṇita*), by attire (P. *ākappa*), by presents of wild fruits and flowers (P. *vanabhaṅga*), by perfume (P. *gandha*), by delicacy (P. *rasa*), by touch (P. *phassa*).

The eight are easily grouped by the sense objects. Thus, the weeping, the laughter, and the speech are objects of hearing. The attire—passive—and the presents of wild fruits and flowers—active—are objects of seeing. The perfume is the object of smelling. The delicacy (of limbs)—and suggestion of fine sensibilities—are mystically the objects of tasting. Finally, touch is the object of handling.

Besides there is the Jewel of Woman among the seven jewels

of the universal emperor who turns the wheel (*cakravartin*) according to the scripture *Mahāsudassana-sutta* of Dīghanikāya, Vol. II. She is described this way: lovely, a sight to see, serene, endowed with special beauty of complexion; not too tall or too short, not too fat or too lean, not very dark or very whitish; surpassing human looks she has attained the looks of the gods. It is also said that a close contact with the body of that precious woman was as the touch of cotton or cotton wool. When it was cold, her limbs were warm; when it was hot, her limbs were cool. The body of that jewel of woman disseminated the odor of sandalwood, her mouth the perfume of the *utpala*-lotus. She would rise up before King Mahāsudassana and retire after him; and was always willing to do his bidding; of pleasing conduct and sweet speech. Even in mind, she did not transgress against Mahāsudassana. How much less could she with body![8]

In contrast, ordinary women—so also men—come in for various criticism in Buddhist texts. However, such passages have to be carefully considered, especially by consultation of the original language when available. A case in point: The Pāli "Book of Fours" has a criticism which Woodward translated this way:[9] "Womenfolk are uncontrolled, Ānanda. Womenfolk are envious, Ānanda. Womenfolk are greedy, Ānanda. Womenfolk are weak in wisdom, Ānanda." This translation has been cited in some present-day articles on the position of women in Buddhism. I consulted the Pāli in the Aṅguttara-nikāya[10] and found that this criticism answers a question which contains the term in the title of this scripture called *Kamboja-sutta*. Ānanda had asked the Buddha for the cause (P. *hetu*) and the condition (P. *paccaya*) that womanfolk (P. *mātugāma*) do not sit in a *sabhā*, courtroom, or engage in a *kammanta* (a business), or reach *Kamboja*. Woodward had much trouble with this name, which means a certain country. The commentary did not help, only adding "in search of wealth". So this translator decided to render 'kamboja' as "essence of the deed", a guess not attested in any reference work. But if we take the equivalent Sanskrit as Kāmboja (a derivative form), the Monier-Williams Sanskrit-English Dictionary explains this term as a native of Kamboja, a race which shave the whole head. In this light, it appears that Ānanda asked in a conditional manner, i.e., asking for the condition when women do not do those things, forcing the response to also be conditional, wherefore, I would translate the response this way:

"When womenfolk are given to angry outbursts (*kodhanā*), are envious (*issukī*), are greedy (*maccharī*), and are weak in wisdom (*dupaññā*)—that is the cause, that is the condition that..." Here, I accept the "weak in wisdom" as the cause, and the other three as the respective conditions. In this solution, the "angry outbursts" make for unsuitability in the courtroom; "being envious" spoils the engaging in a business; when "greedy" a woman would be reluctant to have her head shaved to be a nun.[11] And I presume that being "weak in wisdom" goes with all three cases. It could not be seriously held that women never engaged in those activities, because as to the *kammanta* it is usually agreed that women have the oldest profession of all. And see below, Horner on the woman worker.

So far I have noticed the main denigration of women to consist of their being a kind of danger for the monks' celibacy. So, in the *Utpatha-sutta* of the Saṃyutta-nikāya comes the line: *itthī malaṃ brahmacariyassa,* "Woman is the stain of the pure life."[12] This kind of danger is illustrated in the *Cātuma-sutta* of the Majjhima-nikāya, Vol. II.[13] This scripture sets forth four dangers to the person—in this case the male—who has gone forth from his home to enter the religious life. The person has entered a kind of stream in which there are dangers called 'waves', 'alligators', 'whirlpools', and 'dolphins'. It is the fourth one, the danger of 'dolphins' (P. *susukā*),[14] that brings in women. A young man, bearing his begging bowl and religious robe has entered a village for almsfood, while being unguarded in body, speech, and mind with senses uncontrolled. He sees there a woman perversely unclothed (P. *dunnivattha*) or purposely without upper covering (P. *duppāruta*). His mind is assailed by passion; he abandons his training and turns to base conduct.

(b). *Position of women in society according to Buddhist texts.* Here, I mainly use Horner's book, Part I, devoted to the topic of laywomen. She treats in order, the mother, the daughter, the wife, the widow, and the woman worker.[15] There are surely some historical layers in these Buddhist texts, so they should not be used to determine society at the time of Gautama Buddha. Even so, the large corpus of Buddhist literature that is extant for the B.C. period is an invaluable source of information. The position of women as depicted in these texts evinces an easier lifestyle for them than was increasingly the case in Indian society generally, with its lowering of the age of daughter marriage. This shows that the old Buddhist canon is conservative in its content, i.e., resistant to including contemporary events, or to taking account of presumably contemporary Brahmanical texts. It should be remembered that the early Buddhist texts are a product of North India; and there are strong indications that women had more opportunities in South India.

Horner's section on the Mother points out—as is well-known—that at one time, during the Vedic period, the wife would engage in the sacrificial cult along with her husband; but that as this role for the wife was gradually lost, the wife was allowed in Indian society chiefly a child-bearing role. Horner informs us that Buddhist texts accorded women in general a greater respect, with the mother included. It was usual in Buddhist literature when mentioning the parents to give the word for mother first. The crime of either matricide or patricide was viewed with special horror by the Buddhists. See below on "mother's love".

The Daughter is given a higher status in Buddhist literature than previously in the Vedic period or later on, when the girl-child was looked upon as a burden until she was married. There are a number of passages where the married couple wishes for an offspring, without specifying the boy. Horner refers us to the Saṃyutta-nikāya story of when King Pasenadi of Kosala was not pleased when his Buddhist Queen Mallikā had given birth to a daughter. But the Buddha pointed out to him that a girl "may prove even a better offspring" than a boy.[16] Horner seems discouraged that this view was not repeated in the texts. However, in the early period of Mahāyāna Buddhism there appeared—in the Andhra region of India, according to the translators—a scripture translated with title *The Lion's Roar of Queen Śrīmālā* with a setting of precisely a conversation between King Pasenadi (Skt. Prasenajit) and Queen Mallikā about their daughter, Queen Śrīmālā, who is the interlocutor of the Buddha in this scripture.[17] Although, the author of the Tamil classic *The Anklet Story* is known to be a Jain, this work may be cited to show how women were able to express themselves in India. Speaking of one of those daughters:[18]

> Oh foolish swan compete not with her
> You cannot match her gait.
> She is stalking men on the seashore like a hunter
> Oh foolish swan do not compete with her
> You cannot match her stately gait stalking youths.

Horner treats the topic of Wife at length. She concludes from her reading of the Pāli classics that monogamy prevailed under Buddhism, while various kings contemporaneous with the Buddha were practicing polygamy, and polyandry was practically nonexistent. She cites the *Sigālovāda-sutta*, verse 30 for the ideal relations between the husband and wife as follows:[19]

> In five ways should a wife as western quarter be ministered to by her husband: by respect, by courtesy, by faithfulness, by handing over authority to her, by providing her with adornments.
> In these five ways does the wife, ministered to by her husband as the western quarter, loves him: her duties are well-performed, by hospitality to the kin of both, by faithfulness, by watching over the goods he brings, and by skill and industry in discharging all her business.

There is a longer treatment of the exemplary wife in the Uposatha-vagga of the "Book of Eights", and therein the *Anuruddha-sutta*.[20] During his noonday rest Anuruddha had a vision of a group of lovely divinities (P. *devatā*), who could take on any color of body, garments, and ornaments as desired; some of them dancing, some performing sweet music, and so on. Anuruddha kept his senses under control, and the group promptly vanished. At eventide Anuruddha approached the Buddha and inquired as to what natures (P. *dhamma;* S. *dharma*) womankind (P. *mātugāma*) requires so as to reach such a condition after break up of the body. The Buddha explained that such a woman has eight natures: (1) To whatever husband she is betrothed, she is gentle, loving, and obedient while rising before and retiring after him. (2) Whomever her husband respects and honors, so does she. (3) Whatever her husband's trade, she is interested in it and is nimble at assisting him. (4) She manages the husband's household, including hired workers, judging who is ill and apportioning foodstuffs. (5) Any valuables brought home by her husband she keeps secured and wastes nothing. (6) She has taken refuge in the Buddha, Dhamma, and the Saṅgha. (7) She observes the five lay vows of a Buddhist, not taking life, etc. (8) Devoid of stinginess, she is active in charities.

Of course, the ideal relations between the husband and the wife often were not the case. Horner cites some examples of this and rightly points out that usually the wife was subservient to the husband.[21]

When it comes to the topic of Widow, there are not many references in Buddhist literature. Yet, it is rather easy to establish that in contrast to her miserable lot in Hinduism, where she was virtually a non-person, the widow in Buddhist circles still has her place in the social structure. Even so, she was by virtue of widowhood in an unprotected condition, and so has to be protected by family members, her clan, or else by becoming a Buddhist nun. Horner furnishes some evidence that a widow in Buddhist communities could inherit her husband's property.[22] The texts are silent on the matter of widow-remarriage. Yet, there appears to be an historical example of this in the mother of the celebrated Buddhist teachers Asaṅga and Vasubandhu. Long ago I wrote, "In Bu-ston's history of Buddhism, we read that a woman of the Brāhmaṇa caste had a son Asaṅga from her union with a Ksatriya, and later a son Vasubandhu from her union with a Brāhmaṇa."[23] The only conclusion in this case is that this mother was widowed and later remarried.

Finally, Horner goes into the matter of the Woman Worker. In Buddhist India, the women of the better classes were supported by their own families and their work consisted in household tasks. There are various records that women of the poorer classes were engaged in trades and became self-supporting.[24] Among the trades that were mentioned included being the keeper of a paddy-field, keeper of burning-grounds, acrobats, and domestics in the households of wealthy persons. There were also female musicians. And there were some famous courtesans. Doubtless other occupations unrecorded.

(c). *Theory of mother's love.* There is no doubt that in the role of mother, the Indian woman attains her recognized eminence and strength. She is responsible for the growth of love or friendliness (P. *metta*; S. *maitrī*) in the family. There was a limitation on this love, since the mother applies it to her 'own' family, especially her 'own' children. Therefore, the meditative exercises of friendliness to all sentient beings has its inception in mother's love. This is the message of the *Metta-sutta* in "The Chapter of the Snake" of the *Sutta-nipāta*, in particular, these two verses:[25]

> Just as a mother guards her own son, her only son with her life, in the same way cultivate a boundless mind toward all creatures.
> Cultivate a boundless loving mind toward the entire world, upwards, downwards, and across—(a mind) unhindered, free of hatred and rivalry.

When Mahāyāna Buddhism treats this topic, it admits that there is this boundless love—and also boundless compassion—as a meditation in the 'lower vehicle'; but not the aspiration (*adhyāśaya*) to rescue the sentient beings.[26] Thus, mother's love—wonderful as it is—is not a rescue mentality. The latter role is credited to the father. This is the message of a passage from the Mahāyāna scripture *Sāgaramati-paripṛcchā* that is cited in a Buddhist work available in Sanskrit, and which I render as follows:[27]

> For example, Sāgaramati, a certain merchant-householder had one son, desired, loved, favorite, gratifying, without anything adverse to the sight. That boy, while playing in the mode of a child fell into a cess-pit. Thereupon, the mother and kinsfolk of that boy saw that the boy had fallen into the cess-pit: and seeing that, sighed deeply, were sorrowful, and uttered lamentations, but they did not enter the cess-pit and bring out the boy. Then, the father of the boy, having approached, saw that his only son had fallen into that cess-pit. And seeing that, hastening swiftly, drawn nearby his affection of aspiration for the only son without nausea, he descended into that cess-pit and brought out his only son. There, the cess-pit is a metaphor for the threefold realm; the boy, a metaphor for the sentient beings; the mother and kinsfolk [are the Śrāvakas and Pratyekabuddhas] who, seeing the sentient beings fallen into the cyclical flow are sorrowful and utter lamentations, but are incapable of bringing them out; and the merchant-householder is a metaphor for the Bodhisattva.

The passage does not deny that a woman can also do some rescuing. It means that her mother love plus her compassion do not succeed in rescuing; that if she does manage to rescue, it requires an aspiration and action pursuant to that aspiration. The passage also shows that those followers of Mahāyāna Buddhism who reject something they call 'lower vehicle' (*hīnayāna*) display an abysmal ignorance of Buddhism. This is because such a contemplation as is presented above from the *Sutta-nipāta* and a comparable one to expand compassion are also mandatory in the practice of the Bodhisattva. So, much of this started with mother's love, even though it was applied just to her 'own' family.

(d). *The imputed ability or lack of same for religious attainment of women.* It is a well-known attitude of the Buddhist scriptures that it takes a male to get to enlightenment. Two Pāli scriptures (Majjhima, iii, 65, and Aṅguttara i, 28) have the same statements, having to do with skill in various topics, here, skill in the possible and the impossible (*sthāna* and *asthāna,* in Skt.). According to this scriptural statement, both a man and a woman could be Arahants, but the woman cannot be a rightly awakened one (S. *samyaksaṃbuddha*) or a universal emperor (S. *cakravartin*) while a man could be.[28] A woman could not be a Sakka (S. Sakra = Indra), a Māra, a Brahmā, while a man could be any of those. These claims are curious; and the ladies need not feel discriminated against in the case of Sakka, etc. since these are mythological attainments anyway. As to getting enlightened, since the usual Buddhist depiction is that it takes at least three incalculable eons of lives striving toward this goal, in order to succeed—it appears out of reach for both men and women. Perhaps some early monks—themselves as far from enlightenment as were the nuns—entered these remarks in the canon pursuant to a current cultural bias in favor of the boy-child over the girl. Mahāyāna Buddhism has a different attitude and produced a legend about a queen, who took a vow that in all her lives she would be reborn a woman and attain enlightenment in that body; she is deified as the Green Tārā.[29]

It should be acknowledged that despite that legend of Tārā, there continued a strong current of bias against women with stories about how a certain woman was able to change her physique into a male body, as though this was a marvellous accomplishment. In recent times, as various women were trained in Buddhist scholarship, lady scholars have written articles on these matters, collecting and discussing those passages that come to their notice.[30] The present essay cannot go into the theories of such essays, since my emphasis is on the Buddhist literature itself. Therefore, I shall present the Buddhist teachings of how such a change is possible.

There is a theory of four *abhisaṃdhi* ("veiled intention"), of which the fourth is a special meaning of the term *pariṇāmana*, namely, "change-over". The Buddhist commentator Ratnākaraśānti gives the illustration "change over to a lion" (Tib. *seng ge rnam par bsgyur ba*) and he explains the meaning that the change takes place in the mind (Tib. *blo;* Skt. *buddhi, mati,* or *dhī*).[31] This situation is referred to in an old scripture of the Dīgha-nikāya, Vol. II, in the *Sakka-pañha-sutta* (Questions by Śakra). This is the way the two Rhys Davids' translated.[32] "There was at Kapilavatthu, a daughter of the Sākyans named Gopikā, who trusted in the Buddha, the Dhamma and the Order, and who fulfilled the precepts. She, having abandoned a woman's thoughts and cultivated the thoughts of a man was at the dissolution of the body after her death, reborn to a pleasant life into the communion of the Three-and—Thirty gods, into son-ship with us. And there, they knew her as 'Gopaka of the sons of the gods'." I consulted the Pāli in the Bihar edition,[33] which has commentarial notes at the bottom of the page; and the edition (p. 202. 16-7) confirms that the term *itthi-tta* ('*tta'* of a woman) means *itthi-citta* or *itthī-citta,* while the term *purisa-tta* ('*tta*' of a man) means *purisa-citta*. However, the term *citta* does not really mean "thoughts", as was translated, for which one would expect *cittāni.* Here, it means "mind", as above with the words buddhi, etc. Hence, this is the Buddhist theory of *karma*—that the mind eventually determines the body. But the commentators do not enlighten us on the supposed difference of a woman's mind from a man's mind; and the obvious sexual difference is presumably not intended here.

Perhaps, then, we should revert to the discussion I started early in the essay, about the concept of 'mine'. The *Dhammapada*, 62, chapter on the Fool, asserts (S. Radhakrishnan's translation):

> The fool is tormented thinking 'these sons belong to me', 'this wealth belongs to me'. He himself does not belong to himself. How then can sons be his? How can wealth be his?

The statement "He himself does not belong to himself" is apparently the qualified negation of the Buddhist 'non-self' doctrine of realization, i.e., 'lacking independence' (*asvātantrya*) as the Buddhist master Asaṅga explains;[34] thus in the vernacular, "not his own man". But the mother and the father do not mean the same when saying, 'these children belong to me', although the

Dhammapada calls both of them 'fools'. The father means only: 'these are my children'. The mother means: 'these are my children: they came out of my body'. While the term 'fool' sounds harsh for the situation, the verse evidently is a precept about understanding, to wit, that by regarding the children as 'my children' this amounts to a barrier in the understanding of those children. And that by regarding the wealth as 'my wealth', this amounts to a barrier in using it wisely or even in sound predictions about it. That passage cited above from the *Sutta-nipāta* with the advice: "Cultivate a boundless loving mind toward the entire world," probably requires a renunciation of the 'my children' fixation. While it might be more difficult for the mother than for the father to give up this kind of 'mind' (*citta*), there does not seem any good reason to deny that she and he could do it. About this topic, there is the *Kassaka-sutta* (on the ploughman) among the Māra-suttas of Saṃyutta-nikāya, Vol. I.[35] The point of this scripture is that as long as one thinks in terms of 'it is mine', one is in the power of Mārā.

As to the woman changing her mind of woman to the mind of a man—whatever that entails, it seems not necessarily a worthy goal. After all, if her mother's love could be meditated upon by a man and expanded to all the sentient beings, why can't she do the same with his rescue mentality and contemplate that she will rescue all the sentient beings?

II. The Role of Women Themselves in Buddhism

Here there is (a) The role of laywomen in Buddhism; (b) The position of women as Buddhist nuns. Under laywomen, there is the role of laywomen in general, and the role of specific women. Under the Buddhist nuns, there is the topic of Ānanda and the beginning of the nun order, the topic of the eight guru-dharmas, and a brief reference to the psalms of the sisters.

(a). The Role of Laywomen in Buddhism

Generalities. To become a laywomen (*upāsikā*), one takes refuge in the Three Jewels (the Buddha, the Doctrine, and the Congregation). So in the *Verahaccāni-sutta* of Saṃyutta-nikāya, Vol. IV (the *Saḷāyatana* book):[36]

Having been so addressed, the Brahmin lady of the

> Verahaccāni clan said to the venerable Udāyin: "Wonderful, Sir! Wonderful, Sir! Just as one makes stand up a person lying face down, or unveils what was covered over, or describes the path to a person wandering confused, or holds a lamp in the darkness so that those with eyes may see the forms,—even so in various ways the Dhamma has been revealed by the noble Udāyin. I myself, reverent Udāyin, do go to the Bhagavat (i.e., Buddha) for refuge, likewise to the Dhamma and the congregation of monks. May the noble Udāyin accept me as a lay-disciple who, from this day henceforth while endowed with life, has so taken refuge."

Accordingly, it must be subsequently that the lay disciple is enjoined to adhere to five vows, to not take life, or steal, engage in lusting behavior, tell lies, or take intoxicating liquors. The same volume of Saṃyutta-nikāya states that the woman so avowed with these five rules (*sīla*) lives at home with confidence (also, meaning 'non-fear', P. *visārada*).[37] This volume continues with a *sutta* on 'growth' (or 'increase') (P. *vaḍḍhī*; S. *vṛddhi*) in five things on the part of the laywoman. The noble woman disciple (P. *ariyasāvikā*; S. *āryaśrāvakā*) takes on the essential (P. *sāra*) and takes on the better (P. *vara*) in the sense of an aggregate (P. *kāya*) and grows in the noble manner, when she grows in (or, increases) faith (P. *saddhā*), virtue (P. *sīla*), generosity (P. *cāga*), learning (P. *sutta*), and insight (P. *paññā*).[38] In Buddhism, 'faith' in this sense usually means an acceptance of religious teachings on the effect of *karma*, for example, that virtue (*sīla*) leads to heaven (S. *svarga*). 'Learning' means here a devoted listening to religious discourses.

In every place where Buddhism penetrated, the laywomen helped enormously, probably to a greater degree than their husbands (if married), perhaps because they had more time to do so. The Pāli scriptures—as a kind of closed corpus—could not show this in a general way, although there is abundant evidence in special cases, as is described in the next sub-section. When Buddhism entered its phase of the Mahāyāna, since new scriptures were composed, this role of the laywomen could be entered in the next era. This was done by the terms 'daughter of the family' (*kuladuhitṛ*), where the term *kula*[39] is employed in the abstract sense of the 'Buddhist family'. For example, the *Saddharmapuṇḍarīka*, Chap. 18, speaks of the many virtues (*guṇa*) to be gained by any 'son of the family' or any 'daughter of the family' by accepting this particular scripture, studying it, copying it, and so forth. This terminology of son and daughter of the family is frequent in the Mahāyāna scriptures. While the terminology presumably applies to monks and nuns, it surely applies to the laymen and laywomen.

The role of specific women. Naturally, it is impossible in this essay to do full justice even to the situation in ancient India, let alone the role of specific women in other Asian countries which have experienced the strength of Buddhism in various centuries. A few examples should suffice to suggest the important contribution of women.

Of the wealthy women, the most famous was Visākhā.[40] When sixteen years old, she heard the Buddha preach for the first time. She approached the Buddha with proper etiquette; and she and her attendants became converts. Later, when the enormously wealthy family was living in the territory ruled by King Prasenajit, Visākhā, who is said to have been a handsome woman, also athletic and strong, was chosen in marriage by Puṇṇavaḍḍhana, son of Migāra, a great merchant of Sāvatthi (S. Śrāvastī), said to have been situated in the present Gonda district of Uttar Pradesh, India. In her new home, Visākhā missed the Buddhist atmosphere of her father's dwelling, because her husband favored the Nirgranthas (in Pāli, Nigaṇṭha)—a kind of ascetic order,[41] whose doctrine her husband's father Migāra also somewhat accepted. When the Buddha came to stay at Sāvatthi, she asked permission to invite him and his fraternity to the house, and her husband assented, since he did not want to anger her influential family. She received the group the next day and sent word twice to her father-in-law to come. Finally, despite the Nirgrantha attempt to dissuade him, he came. The Buddha's sermon converted Migāra and soon Migāra's own wife was converted to Buddhism. Thereafter, Visākhā was lavish in her alms support to the Buddha's monk congregation. Visākhā has been referred to as Migāra's mother.[42] Thus, when Visākhā built a great Vihāra for the Buddha and his monks, it became known as the Eastern Monastery in the palace of Migāra's mother; where the Buddha delivered some important sermons, alternating his sojourn here and on the other side of Sāvatthi at the Jetavana of Anāthapiṇḍika.

Various courtesans became converts to Buddhism and benefited the Order of monks. The most famous of them is Ambapālī. She offered her mango-grove "to the fraternity of almsmen with the Buddha at its head". The Buddha could not refuse her, since she was in the process of regeneration; and it is said that she finally attained arahant-status.[43]

The influence of queens has been decisive in the successful march of Buddhism. King Udena (S. Udayana) was converted by his queen Sāmāvatī; and King Pasenadi (S. Prasenjit) was converted by his queen Mallikā.[44]

And I have cited Nilakanta Sastri: "The reign of his [i.e., the Īkṣvāku founder's] son Vīrapurisadata formed a glorious epoch in the history of Buddhism and in diplomatic relations. He took a queen from the Śaka family of Ujjain and gave his daughter in marriage to a Chutu prince. Almost all the royal ladies were Buddhists; an aunt of Vīrapurisadata built a big stūpa at Nagarjunikoṇḍa. Her example was followed by other women of the royal family and by women generally as we know from a reference to one Bodhisiri, a woman citizen."[45]

One cannot leave out the contribution of mothers. That mother of both Asaṅga and Vasubandhu—both religious geniuses in Buddhism—had a fantastic success of her faith.[46]

(b). The Position of Women as Buddhist Nuns

Ānanda and the beginning of the nun order. There are various scholarly disputes about the relation of Ānanda to the beginning of the Buddhist nun order. The accounts of the 'First Council' held in the year after the Parinirvāṇa of the Buddha are well-treated by La Vallée Poussin. He points out that the Buddha had temporarily united rather diverse and ordinarily incompatible persons. Kassapa (S. Kāśyapa), the president of the 'First Council' represented the ascetics, the kinds of persons who would fast, meditate in caves and so on. Ānanda represented those who took account of worldly matters and accepted the Eightfold Noble Path which avoids the extremes of ascetic mortification and sensory indulgence. And there was Upāli, concerned with monastic discipline, which had monks drawn from the upper classes of society and also from lower classes.[47] The 'First Council' appears to have been composed entirely of men. Since this council was meant to preserve the Buddha's Dharma and Vinaya (the Doctrine and the Discipline), it was necessary to utilize Ānanda's and Upāli's talents. As to Upāli, there was no doubt that he was perfectly sound for reciting the rules of the disciplinary code. Ānanda had travelled together with the Buddha for years, and had an extraordinary memory for the sermons, so he was the logical person to give out with all these sermons so they could be taken in memory by the other attendees. But Ānanda was suspect, since he had commited some 'sins'; and in the minds of the Kassapa group probably his greatest 'sin' was convincing the Buddha to start the nun order. Thus, how could he be trusted to recite the scriptures without error? In accordance with the Buddhist theory of confession of minor sins, that the person is freed of them by dint of confessing them.[48] Ānanda was first made to confess five sins, after which he was declared to be an Arahant, and so could properly recite the sermons.

There was a precedent for the Buddhist nunnery, since the Śvetāmbara Jains, believing that both men and women could attain release (*mokṣa*) had enrolled a large amount of women as nuns.[49]

Horner describes the events leading to the Buddhist nun order. Five years after he had attained enlightenment, the Buddha is reported to have received a group of women led by Mahāprajāpati Gotamī including some relatives of his own from the Sākya clan and who were mostly widows. Three times they asked for admission into the Order, each time refused. The Buddha was then about to proceed to Vesāli (S. Vaiśālī)—which was close to where is now the Bihar town of Muzaffarpur. The ladies, undaunted, cut off their hair, donned saffron-colored robes, and also proceeded to Vesāli, arriving with travel stains and very dejected. They were met there by Ānanda, who was shocked to see them in such a condition and was impressed by their determination, so he agreed to plead their case with the Buddha.[50] Ānanda at this fifth year was not yet the permanent attendant of the Buddha—a post which he was appointed to in the twentieth year, having then recently become a monk,[51] so at this time Ānanda seems to have been a novice in the Order, having begun in the second year of the Buddha's ministry.[52] His authority for approaching the Buddha on this mission was especially as a first cousin in the Sākya clan; and it might be that the Buddha foresaw something about this Ānanda. Ānanda asked the Buddha three times to grant the request of the ladies, each time met with silence. Then Ānanda tried a different approach; and, in Horner's words, "got him to admit that women were as capable as men of leading a contemplative life and of treading on the paths of arahantship."[53] This became the source of the position in Buddhism that women like men are capable of attaining liberation from *saṃsāra*. Then, like Ānanda's critics at the time of the 'First Council', we can fault Ānanda for not asking the Buddha if women can attain enlightenment. The Buddha therefore agreed to Ānanda's petition on behalf of the ladies, but laid down as the condition for entering the Order that the women should accept the 'eight chief rules (*gurudhamma*)', as spelled out. The leader of the lady group joyously accepted the terms as relayed by Ānanda. Ānanda then returned to the Buddha with the news of their acceptance of the terms. The Buddha now announced (as Horner states it):[54]

> If, Ānanda, women has not received permission to go out from the household life and enter the homeless state, under the doctrine and discipline proclaimed by the Tathāgata, then would the pure religion, Ānanda, have lasted long, the good law would have stood fast for a thousand years. But since, Ānanda, women have now received that permission, the pure religion, Ānanda, will not last so long, the good law will now stand fast for only five hundred years.

Of course, we do not know if this statement were actually made by the Buddha or inserted later by monks, who begrudged the nun order. If the statement be accepted as a true utterance of the master, then in terms of the 'long chronology' for the Buddha, whereby he enters *Parinirvāṇa* in the 480's B.C., five hundred years takes us to the first century, A.D. Then a seemingly new kind of Buddhism arose, in which a person called a Bodhisattva is both seeking enlightenment and working to rescue sentient beings in general. A new kind of literature emerged to be called Mahāyāna-sūtras. The 'Nikāya-Buddhism' was sometimes labelled 'lower vehicle' (*hīnayāna*).

As to why women in the Order would have anything to do with it, the only valid reason that occurs to me is that it was not a matter of the particular group of ladies that first wanted to enter the Order, but of the motivations of later women who would go through the stages called novice and so on. That is to say, when women entered the Order to escape desperate and hopeless situations in their social lives, their faith might well not be as strong as that present in that first group of ladies. Then, once the hopeless situation from which they fled begin to recede in their mind, they may become increasingly irked with the monasterial discipline. The work by Hirakawa[55] on the Buddhist nuns suggests that often these women came from disadvantaged families, which gave them insufficient training in ordinary etiquette or in matters of cleanliness, so that they became guilty of a great number of offenses which had the effect of adding more and more injunctions to their rules. If the question is raised: Would not those faults also be present in the male members of the Order?—One may respond that because the male was better treated in Indian society, he would be much less likely to enter the monastery to escape from society; and when army deserters tried to escape to the Buddhist monastery they were turned away, so as not to offend the civil authorities.

In short, while the laywomen made tremendous contributions to Buddhism, Buddhism did much for the Indian women by allowing them to become trainees and then nuns in the Buddhist monasteries, but got a lot of 'headaches' over these women who had left the home.

During Ānanda's lifetime thereafter, he was a kind of hero to the nuns and naturally would always get their appreciative smiles. This posed a kind of problem for him; and so from time to time he would question the Buddha about women, eliciting the responses which are preserved in the canon, two of which have been cited in the present essay.

The eight guru-dharmas. For the present exposition, necessarily brief, there are two sources: in Horner's work, Chap. II, "The Eight Chief Rules for Almswomen;" in Hirakawa's work, Chap. I, "The Practices of the Bhikṣunī (Bhikṣunī-dharma)."

A weighty reason for the eight rules is that the monasteries, besides the times for doing this or that, the robes, and so forth, were places of instruction in the Dharma. In India, the books had been practically all composed by men, i.e., the Vedas down to the Buddhist Dharma itself; and the explainers of those books had been almost always men. Therefore, the monks would not only have to give instruction to the male members of the congregation; but would also have to give instruction to the almswomen, until such time as they would be sufficiently learned in the Dharma that they could be trusted to carry on such teaching practices by themselves. It follows that the nunneries had to be reasonably close to the monk establishments. These reasons should clarify why certain ones of the eight rules were stated as they were. There is some difference in the ordering of the rules, and here I follow the order in Hirakawa's book—a Mahāsāṃghika text. Here we find that the Buddha has appointed Mahāprajāpati Gautamī as the first Superior (Sthavirā) and has described the eight rules to her.

The first Gurudharma is stated this way: When a bhikṣuṇī, even though she has been ordained for a hundred years meets a bhikṣu who has newly entered the Order, she ought to rise, venerate, and pay obeisance to him... Ali bhikṣuṇīs ought to rise, venerate, and pay obeisance to the elder, the middle-aged, and the young bhikṣus. Whenever a bhikṣuṇī comes to monastery of bhikṣus, she ought to pay obeisance to all the bhikṣus by touching their feet one by one with her forehead. (If she is sick or infirm from age, there is a fitting modification of the rule.) Whenever a bhikṣu comes to the nunnery, all bhikṣunīs ought to rise and pay obseisance at his feet. (They should not make slighting remarks, such as "He is a fraud.")

The second Gurudharma (No. 6 in Horner's list) states that when a woman wants to be ordained as a bhikṣuṇī she must be ordained in the bhikṣuṇī congregation and then in the bhikṣu congregation; and must precede this ordination by two years of study. More technically as a lay believer, she has taken the three refuges and accepted the five precepts. As a novice (*śrāmaṇerikā*) she takes the ten precepts. Then at the lower age of eighteen, she takes the *śikṣamānā* precepts, remaining in this student status for two years. Horner explains the benefit of two years as that some women may have left home for the monastic life on a whim or perhaps motivated by a certain disagreeable event in their life; or perhaps had a leaning to the ascetic life and then find no scope for it in the monastic life; or for such other reasons.[56]

The third Gurudharma is entitled: "A bhikṣuṇī cannot admonish a bhikṣu for either real or unreal offenses, but a bhikṣu can admonish a bhikṣuṇī for real offenses." This seems to cover both No. 7 and No. 8 in Horner's list.

The fourth Gurudharma in the *Mahāsāṃghika* list is not to receive donations before the bhikṣus receive them. This item is missing in Horner's list.

The fifth Gurudharma is the half-month penance (*māṇatva*) in both the Order of bhikṣus and the Order of bhikṣuṇīs, when she has transgressed one of the other Gurudharmas or certain other Vinaya rules. This is No. 5 in Horner.

The sixth Gurudharma is reporting the *Uposatha* (Observance Day) and seeking instruction every half-month. All the bhikṣuṇīs or a proxy representative go to the monastery of the bhikṣus. Horner (No. 3) reports that already in the time of the Buddha, a difficulty arose on abiding with this stipulation, because on this day there was the confessional. Finally, the Buddha had to allow the confessional of the nuns to take place in the nunnery, just as the confessional of the monks was taking place before the other monks.[57]

The seventh Gurudharma states that an almswoman is not to spend the rainy season in a district where there is no almsman. This is Horner's No. 2.

The eighth Gurudharma states that when the rainy season is over, the bhikṣuṇīs should observe the ceremony of repentance of their offenses (the *pravāraṇā*) in the two Orders—Horner's No. 4.

From a standpoint outside India and in more modern times, it appears that the rules were demanding too much humility from the almswomen. But there seems to have been an unending supply of nuns. Altekar said:[58] "The institution of nunnery in Jainism and Buddhism and the instances of several grown up maidens taking holy orders against their parents' desire and some of them later falling from their high spiritual ideal must also have strengthened the view of those who favored marriages at about the time of puberty. If a girl is married before her personality is fully developed, there was no danger of her joining a nunnery. We may therefore conclude that during the period 400 B.C. to 100 A.D. the marriageable age was being gradually lowered and the tendency on the whole was to marry girls at about the time of puberty." Altekar apparently blames the institution of nunnery for the deplorable lowering of the marriage age for girls. It would be difficult to prove the connection, but it certainly indicates that the nunnery was a viable and attractive option for many women.

The Psalms of the Sisters. These psalms have been translated in a separate volume.[59] Also Chap. V of *Saṃyutta-nikāya*, Vol. I, is devoted to *suttas* of the sisters, which I consult for the present purpose. The second *sutta* is on the sister Somā, which is sufficiently brief to present here:[60]

> Thus have I heard upon an occasion. The Bhagavat was staying at Sāvatthi in the Jeta Grove, Anāthapiṇḍika's Park. The sister Somā dressed herself early, and bearing the begging bowl and robe, entered Sāvatthi for alms. And having gone about Sāvatthi for the purpose, after her meal returning, she entered Blind Wood (*andhavana*) for a noonday session. And going deep into this Wood, she sat down at the base of a certain tree. Then Māra, the evil one, desirous of arousing fear, stupefaction, and 'gooseflesh' in sister Somā, and desirous of diverting her from equipoise, approached sister Somā and addressed her with a verse:
>
> That station reached by the seers (P. *isi*; S. *ṛṣi*) is difficult to gain. With her two-finger wisdom [in the kitchen],[61] that (station) a woman cannot obtain.[62]

Then sister Somā thought: "Who is this, a human or a non-human that speaks a verse? It must be Māra speaking a verse, desirous of arousing fear, stupefaction, and 'gooseflesh' in me, and desirous of diverting me from equipoise." And sister Somā, having recognized that it was Māra the evil one, replied to Māra with verses:

> What is there for woman's nature to do,
> when the mind is equipoised, when higher
> knowledge operates, when one rightly discerns
> the Dhamma?
> There is no doubt of it;
> for whom the thought arises, 'I am a woman,'
> or 'I am a man,' or 'I am otherwise,'
> to such a one, Māra ought to speak.[63]

Then Māra the evil one thought, 'Sister Somā knows me!'. And pained and dejected, right on the spot he vanished.

Horner states: "Dwelling in complete solitude was not feasible for women; and dwelling at the foot of a tree was interdicted... Almswomen... had instead to seek the safe shelter of the Vihāra."[64] By Horner's discussion in another place[65] it is clear that 'dwelling' means taking up residence in the forest, where the women might be attacked by men or animals. In the case of sister Somā, she is not taking up residence in the forest, but simply going there for a meditative session. Mrs. Rhys Davids informs us of Buddhaghosa's information that the Andhavana (Blind Wood) was a *gāvuta* (perhaps about 1½ miles) south of Sāvatthi and so-called because once it was the haunt of 500 bandits who gouged out the eyes of their victims; but now it was guarded by royal custodians.[66] Thus it was a kind of protected sanctuary, often visited by a brother or sister in quest of solitude. All ten of the *suttas* of the sisters included in this first volume of the Saṃyutta-nikāya are based on their entry into this particular wooded area. It is of course wonderful that this place was available for the purpose. Yet, it is a dismal conclusion that nowhere else was such a place available, which is of course not the fault of the women. It is rather than each of the ten taunts of Māra were the attitudes of men[67] toward the women who preferred the ascetic life. When those men denied that a woman can endure severe discipline, it is because they did not want her to do it—it was not part of their ideal of womankind.

It remains to settle what was the attainment aimed at by sister Somā. Māra was denying that she could reach that station which the seers attain. Buddhaghosa explained this station as Arahantship.[68] Previously, it was pointed out that the Buddha agreed that both men and women could attain such status, so this is what must be meant in the case of sister Somā.

REFERENCES

1. I follow here the translation given by the two Rhys Davids' in *Dialogues of the Buddha*, Part II (4th edition, London, 1959), p. 154, except for the last line which they render 'Keep wide awake, Ānanda.' The Pāli term here is *upaṭṭhāpetabbā*. The solution to the meaning is by taking the virtually equivalent Skt. *upasthāpana*, for which the Monier-Williams Sanskrit-English Dictionary provides a meaning "causing to remember"; and under the non-causal form *upasthāna* provides such a meaning as a sanctuary. The advice is to keep the mind as a sanctuary, remembering the guru or the lord.
2. Chu Ch'an, *The Sutra of 42 Sections and Two Other Scriptures of the Mahāyāna School* (London, 1947).
3. *The Living Thoughts of Gotama the Buddha*, presented by Ananda K. Coomaraswamy and I.B. Horner (London, 1948), p. 5.
4. Pāli line from *Dīghanikāya*, Vol. III (Bihar Government, 1958), p. 153.20. For the interpretation, "without a 'my wife'" see T.W. and C.A.F. Rhys Davids, *Dialogues of the Buddha*, Part III (London, 1957), p. 192 note, citing the commentator Buddhaghosa, 'no woman property'. Under the term *parigraha*, the Monier-Williams dictionary has a meaning, 'takes (a wife)'.
5. Cf. E.M. Hare, tr., *The Book of the Gradual Sayings*. Vol. IV, pp. 118-9.

6. Alex Wayman, "The Mathurā Set of Aṣṭamaṅgala (Eight Auspicious symbols) in Early and Later Times," in Doris Meth Srinivasan, ed., *Mathura: The Cultural Heritage* (American Institute of Indian Studies, New Delhi, 1988), esp. p. 236.
7. *The Aṅguttara Nikāya* (Bihar Government, 1960), Vol. III, p. 306. This scripture is followed by another brief detailing exactly the same means for how men bind women. The former one appears to be the basic list, or the prototype.
8. *The Dighanikāya*, Part II (Bihar Govt., 1958), p. 134.13-24.
9. F.L. Woodward, tr., *The Book of the Gradual Sayings*, Vol. II (London, 1952), pp. 92-3.
10. *The Aṅguttaranikāya*, Vol. II (Bihar Govt., 1960), p. 87.
11. I.B. Horner, *Women Under Primitive Buddhism* (Motilal Banarsidass, Delhi, 1975), p. 322, informs us: "Greed was looked upon as an unsuitable thing, unworthy of almspeople and not to be tolerated in them." On p. 323 she points out that monasticism, Buddhist and others, by suppression of certain bodily appetites gets an accentuation of greed. Her explanation may be better than mine.
12. *The Saṃyuttanikāya*, Vol. I (Bihar Govt., 1959), p. 36.4.
13. *The Majjhimanikāya*, Vol. II (Bihar Govt., 1958), pp. 144-7, with the fourth danger on p. 147.
14. The Sanskrit equivalent appears to be the *śiśumāra* in the feminine—the female porpoise or dolphin.
15. Horner, *Women*, pp. 1-94.
16. Horner, *Women*, p. 20.
17. Alex and Hideko Wayman, trs., *The Lion's Roar of Queen Śrīmālā; a Buddhist Scripture on the Tathāgatagarbha Theory* (Columbia University Press, New York, 1974); Indian edition by Motilal Banarsidass, Delhi, 1990, with a new foreword by Alex Wayman.
18. *The Anklet Story: Silappadhikaaram of Ilango Adigal*, rendered from the Tamil by Ka. Naa. Subramanyam (Agam Prakashan, Delhi, 1977), p. 38.
19. Horner, *Women*, pp. 41-2. I have accepted her translation.
20. E.M. Hare, tr., *The Book of the Gradual Sayings*, Vol. IV (London, 1955), pp. 175-8; *The Aṅguttara Nikāya* (Bihar, 1960), III, pp. 358-61.
21. Horner, *Women*, pp. 56-7.
22. Horner, *Women*, pp. 75-6. For more information of inheritance rights of widows, cf. A.S. Altekar, *The Position of Women in Hindu Civilization* (Motilal Banarsidass, Delhi, 1962), pp. 250-70.
23. Alex Wayman, *Analysis of the Śrāvakabhūmi Manuscript* (University of California Press, Berkeley, 1961), p. 23.
24. Horner, *Women*, esp. pp. 83-4.
25. Edition by Bhikshu Samgharatna (Varanasi, 1951) p. 30: / māta yathā niyaṃ puttaṃ āyusā ekaputtam anurakkhe / evaṃ 'pi sabbabhūtesu mānasaṃ bhāvaye aparimaṇam // 7 / mettaṃ ca sabbalokassiṃ mānasaṃ bhāvaye aparimāṇaṃ / uddhaṃ adho ca tiriyaṃ ca asambādhaṃ averaṃ asapattaṃ // 8 /.
26. This is well-explained in Alex Wayman, tr., *Ethics of Tibet; The Bodhisattva Section of Tsong-kha-pa's Lam rim chen mo* (State University of New York Press, Albany, 1991), under the heading "The Stages of Exercising the Thought of Enlightenment, Part I."
27. The translation of this scriptural passage is as found in the same place of the work just mentioned (n. 26, above), which also furnishes the Sanskrit as it was found in the work *Ratnagotravibhāga Mahāyānottaratantraśastra*, ed. by E.H. Johnston (Patna, 1950), pp. 47-8.

28. This denial to women is also in *The Clarifier of the Sweet Meaning (Madhuratthavilāsinī)*; Commentary on the Chronicle of Buddhas (Buddhavaṃśa) by Buddhadatta Thera, tr. by I.B. Horner (The Pali Text Society, London, 1978), pp. 132-3.——
29. For Tārā's vow to gain enlightenment, see Giuseppe Tucci, *Tibetan Painted Scrolls* (La Liberia dello Stato, Roma, 1949), pp. 389b-390a. For the color green as the mind of enlightenment, see A. Wayman, *The Buddhist Tantras* (Motilal Banarsidass, Delhi, 1990), pp. 74-6.
30. For a good survey of these matters, see Janice D. Willis, "Nuns and Benefactresses: The Role of Women in the Development of Buddhism," in *Women, Religion, and Social Change*, ed. by Yvonne Yazbeck Haddad and Ellison Banks Findly (State University of New York Press, 1985), pp. 59-85.
31. This is in his *Prajñāpāramitopadeśa*, extant in Tibetan, consulted in the Peking Tibetan canon (PTT), Vol 114, pp. 238-3-1.
32. The volume of n. 1, above, p. 306.
33. The volume of n. 8, above.
34. Wayman, *Analysis* (n. 23, above), pp. 130-1.
35. The volume of n. 12, above, pp. 114-5.
36. *The Saṃyuttanikāya* (Bihar Govt., 1959), Vol. IV, p. 113.24 to 114.2.
37. The volume of n. 36, above p. 222.1-6.
38. The volume of n. 36, above, p. 227.7-10.
39. By consultation of the *Pāli Tripitakam Concordance*, Vol. II, K-N (Pāli Text Society, London, 1973), under entry 'kula', one gets the impression that the word meaning 'family, clan' was employed in the Pāli canon in the concrete significance.
40. Horner, *Women*, pp. 345-61.
41. Various scholars have identified this group as Jains. However, this identification will be shown to be false by a dissertation completed at Columbia University by Lozang Jamspal on a Buddhist text in which a Nirgrantha is a chief interlocutor.
42. Horner, *Women*, p. 348, states: "Visākhā is sometimes referred to as Migāra's mother from the fact that she converted her father-in-law. 'From this day forth, you are my mother,' he had exclaimed in gratitude." She says this, apparently not liking the other explanation found in G.P. Malalasekera, *Dictionary of Pāli Proper Names*, Vol. II (London, 1960), p. 627: "At the conclusion of the sermon, Migāra became a *sotāpanna* ['entered the stream,' i.e., the Eightfold Noble Path], and, realizing the error of his ways, adopted Visākhā as his mother by sucking her breast. Henceforth Visākhā was called Migāramātā." It was the Buddha who converted Migāra.
43. Horner, *Women*, pp. 88-94.
44. Horner, *Women*, p. 370.
45. The Waymans, *The Lion's Roar* (n. 17, above), p. 2.
46. Wayman, *Analysis* (n. 23, above), same page 23.
47. Louis de La Vallée Poussin, *The Buddhist Councils* (Calcutta, 1976), p. 25.
48. Cf. Alex Wayman, "Purification of Sin in Buddhism by Vision and Confession," in G.H. Sasaki, ed., *A Study of Kleśa* (Tokyo, 1975). pp. 58-79.
49. Horner, *Women*, pp. 101-2.
50. Horner, *Women*, p. 103.
51. Here I accept Edward J. Thomas, *The Life of Buddha as Legend and History* (New York, 1952), pp. 122-3.
52. Malalasekera, *Dictionary of Pāli Proper Names*, Vol. I, 1960, pp. 249-50, accepts the tradition (denied by Thomas, n. 51, above) that Ananda entered the Order in

the second year of the Buddha's ministry, the same time as Devadatta. If we accept Thomas, Ānanda might have became a novice at this time, perhaps when Devadatta became a *bhikṣu*.

53. Horner, *Women,* pp. 103-4.
54. Horner, *Women,* pp. 104-5.
55. Akira Hirakawa, *Monastic Discipline for the Buddhist Nuns* (Jayaswal Research Institute, Patna, 1982).
56. Horner, *Women,* p. 251.
57. Horner, *Women,* pp. 124-5.
58. Altekar (n. 22, above), pp. 54-5.
59. Mrs. Rhys Davids, *Psalms of the Early Buddhists;* I. Psalms of the Sisters (London, 1909, with later reprints).
60. The volume of n. 12, above, pp. 129.9.
61. Mrs. Rhys Davids, *The Book of the Kindred Sayings,* Part I (London, 1917), pp. 161-2, note, refers to her separate work (n. 59, above), p. 45, for Dharmapāla's explanation that the women, already from the age of seven or eight, learn to test if the rice is cooked by taking a few grains with a spoon and pressing them between two fingers. It also occurs to me that the lady holds the needle steady with two fingers so she can 'thread' it with fingers of the other hand which would also be used to hold the spoon. There is a suggestion that the women were being 'put down' as unable to rise above duality (the two fingers) to attain the non-two realization of the seers.
62. "yaṃ taṃ isīhi pattabbaṃ, thānaṃ durabhisambhavaṃ/
    na taṃ dvaṅgulapaññaya, sakkā pappotum itthiyaā" ti/.
63. "itthibhāvo kiṃ kayirā, cittamhi susamahite//
    "ñānamhi vattamānamhi, sammā dhammaṃ vipassato//
    "yassa nūna siyā evaṃ, itthāhaṃ puriso ti vā/
    kiñca vā pana aññạsmi, taṃ māro vattum arahatī" ti//
    Buddhaghosa's commentary took the term *nūna* as sign of the interrogative, accounting for Mrs. Rhys Davids' translation, which I do not follow. Here, *nūna* means something like "There is no doubt of it;" cf. *Sanskrit Studies of M.B. Emeneau; Selected Papers,* ed. by B.A. van Nooten (Center for South and Southeast Asia Studies, University of California, Berkeley, 1988), p. 143.
64. Horner, *Women,* p. 259.
65. Horner, *Women,* pp. 155-6.
66. Mrs. Rhys Davids, the translation of n. 61, above, Part I, p. 160, note.
67. In the first part of the present paper, section on ability of women for religious attainment, it was pointed out that a man could be a Māra. Our present context provides a kind of confirmation of this.
68. Mrs. Rhys Davids, cf. n. 61, above, and nn. 66, above, p. 161, note.

18

Purification of Sin in Buddhism by Vision and Confession

The topic of defilement (*saṃkleśa*) and purification (*vyavadāna*) is so central to Buddhism that even specialized studies of this religion must somehow relate to this issue in order to be ultimately relevant. Then it should be exceedingly proper to deal directly with this central topic. However, in this case there is the basic Buddhist theory about defilement of sentient life and the differentiated lists of defilements, sin, and faults. Besides, there are various means employed for the purification or elimination of these defilements. Sometimes, there are divergent premises about the

---

Reprinted from *A Study of Kleśa* ed. by G.H. Sastri, Shimizukobado Ltd., Tokyo 1975.

nature of mind as the entity, which is defiled and purified. Among the means, this paper will deal principally with the role of vision and confession "face to face," in particular before the thirty-five Buddhas of Confession, and will lead up to a tentative solution of the number "thirty-five".

Generalities of Defilement and Purification

Early Buddhism believes in three basic defilements or affictions (*kleśa*)—lust, hatred, and delusion. They are man's animal nature, symbolized respectively as a cock or dove, a snake, and a pig, in the central circle of the "Wheel of Becoming" (*bhavacakra*). They are not simply the absence of good, but a positive defilement, which in the words of the *Dhammapada* (Dh. 121) "the fool gathers little by little, just as the wise man gathers good deeds by little. Those defilements or afflictions are called poisons, the residues of sin. According to the *Dharmasamuccaya* (Vii, 50):[1] "For, while the poisonous flower is enjoyable, when touched it is a source of burning. Likewise, is the joy produced by lust. When transformed, it is like a poison."

In the *dharma* theory of Buddhism, there are six universal defiled natures (*kleśa-mahābhūmika*) in every defiled consciousness: delusion (*moha*), heedlessness (*pramāda*), laziness (*kausīdya*), lack of faith (*āśraddhya*), torpor (*styāna*), arrogance (*auddhatya*). There are two universal unvirtuous natures (*akuśala-mahābhūmika*) in every unvirtuous consciousness: lack of shame for oneself (*āhrīkya*) and lack of conscience for others (*anapatrāpya*).[2] Moreover, there are shorter and longer lists of defilements and sins, and faults for the monk and yogin, that are not faults for the ordinary person.[3]

According to Asaṅga's *Ābhiprāyikārthagāthā* (*gāthā* No. 6) and his own commentary:

> */sikṣāpadeṣu vidyante catasro gatayas triṣu/*
> */vivarjayitvā dvigatī dvigatī samudānayet//*
>
> When there are the three *śikṣāpadas*, (*adhiśīla, adhicitta,* and *adhiprajñā*), there are four destinies to wit, having warded off two destinies (*sugati* and *durgati* of the realm of desire), one should acquire two destinies (the upper destiny of the form and formless realms, and the *nirvāṇa* destiny).

In the same place, Asaṅga explains that good destiny (i.e., of men and gods) in the realm of desire (*kāmadhātu*) is the fruit of the training in morality (*adhiśīla-śikṣāpada*), and that bad destiny (i.e., of animals, hungry ghosts, and hell beings) in the realm of desire is the fruit of violation of morality (*adhiśīla-vipatti*). The *deva* destiny in the form and formless (*rūpārūpyadhātu*) is the fruit of training in meditation (*adhicitta-śikṣāpada*) by way of the mundane path (*laukikamārga*). The *nirvāṇa* destiny, which is not included in the three realms (*tridhātukāparyāpanna*), is the fruit of training in insight (*adhiprajñāśikṣāpada*) by way of the supramundane path (i.e., knowledge of the four kinds of each of the four Noble Truths.[4]

The Buddha, having taught these three *śikṣāpadas*, has shown how to counteract and eliminate the poison of defilement. Thus, eventually, he became the "Healing Buddha" (Bhaiṣajya-rāja) in the Mahāyāna cult.

In Buddhist meditation theory, the defilements are like weeds in the mind: The visible tops are removed by "calming (the mind)" (*śamatha*)—a concentrated meditation on the defilement's opponent, capable of temporarily displacing the defilement from the field of consciousness, thus cutting off merely the top of the weed. Its roots are extirpated by "insight" (*prajñā*) led up to by the training in "discerning (the real)" (*vipaśyanā*).[5] Thus, *prajñā* was symbolized as a sword, sometimes as a fire. It is prevalently associated with vision[6] and is said to "see voidness (*śūnyatā*)", i.e., seeing an entity as it really is, devoid of its mental impositions—whether usual or unusual.

The Buddhist scriptures frequently state that it is consciousness (*citta*), which is defiled and purified.[7] But then the disagreements start, because the Yogācāra school—except for the Buddhist logicians—identifies the *citta* with the "store consciousness" (*ālayavijñāna*); and some other Buddhist movements, especially the Mādhyamika, deny the existence of this *ālayavijñāna*.

The sect called the Mahāsāṅghika inaugurated a special development of the theory by their doctrine that the mind (*citta*) is intrinsically pure, but covered by adventitious defilements. The Yogācāra school, especially following the brothers Asaṅga and Vasubandhu, expands philosophically upon a theory of the mind as a mirror. Consistent with this symbolization of the mind as a mirror, it could be "wiped off" and "washed". Readers of Ch'an or Zen Buddhism will recall the controversy in China over whether or not there is a mirror from which the dust can be wiped. Later, in Buddhist Tantrism, Paṇḍita Smṛti explains four kinds of washing with voidness, and correlates them respectively with the Buddhist follower called śrāvaka, pratyekabuddha, yogācārin, and Mādhyamika. He even regards the four classes of Buddhist Tantra to be so correlated, but this is certainly not the orthodox explanation of the four Tantras.[8] However, it is not necessary to discuss the removal of defilement—using the distinct terminology of "mirror" and "washing". Indeed, the Prajñāpāramitā school avoids this kind of discourse.

Defilements—Seen and Unseen

There is no doubt of the Buddhist theory that the dark forces of the mind must be brought into the light and there examined and that the evil withers when so exposed. But it must not be concluded that defilements cease merely by being seen: indeed, the theory demands that the seeing of them takes place under controlled, or yoga, circumstances. Of course, when the Māra (the evil one) and his host appeared to the meditating Gautama, Māra was not vanquished simply by being seen; rather, vanquished because Gautama (his left hand in the *samāpatti* gesture) was unmoved by the spectacle, and because (his right hand in the earth-touching gesture) mythologically the earth goddess appeared.

What does the seeing? Already we have been introduced to *prajñā,* the kind of eye which "sees" the void. But ordinarily the perception principle is indicated by the word *vijñāna* (not, as frequently mistranslated, by *saṃjñā,* which is the set of ideas and notions). In Buddhist Dependent Origination, perception is indicated first explicitly by No. 3, *vijñāna,* and then implictly in No. 6, *sparśa,* which is the trisection of the world into sense organ (*āyatana*), object (*viṣaya*), and perception (*vijñāna*). On the basis of No. 6, arises No. 7, *vedanā* (feeling), and the scripture says, "What one feels, one notices (i.e., has a notion of)."[10] The Buddhist logicians replaced the word *vijñāna* with *pratyakṣa* (direct perception).[11] As is well-known, the Abhidharma identifies the three terms, *citta, manas,* and *vijñāna*. Therefore, the "sixth" *vijñāna,* the *manovijñāna,* (the other five being the outer or sense *vijñānas*), can be construed either as the "perception based on the mind" or as the "*manas* kind of *vijñāna*". This *manovijñāna* has the function of perceiving the *dharmas* (the natures or features).

Ordinarily, *vijñāna* does its perceiving in situations of bondage. Thus, the *Pitāputrasamāgamasūtra* states that a "first perception" (*prathamavijñāna*) pertaining to birth has for its two conditions, the "last perception" (*caramavijñāna*) as predominant condition (*adhipatipratyaya*) and the *karma* as support condition (*ārambanapratyaya*). In fact, these two conditions are respectively the basic cause (*hetu*) and condition (*pratyaya*), which the Vaibhāṣika tradition stipulates as necessary for a thing to arise.

These conditions then enter into the initial members of Dependent Origination, the series beginning (1) nescience (*avidyā*), (2) motivations (*saṃskāra*), (3) perception (*vijñāna*), which are labelled by the *Daśabhūmika-sūtra* and by Nāgārjuna as respectively (1) defilement (*kleśa*), (2) action (*karma*), and (3) suffering (*duḥkha*).[13] Here, No. 3, perception as the birth vision (of the parents in sexual union) is explained as perceiving No. 2, motivations (of the past).[14] Thus, the "last perception" (death) is the predominant condition for this "first perception" (birth), while *saṃskāra* is the support condition. That makes more comprehensible the verse in the *Lalitavistara*: "By the wrong procedure engendered by the constructions of imagination, nescience arises, and there is no one who is its producer. It furnishes the cause of motivations and there is no transmigration. Perception arises with transmigration in dependence. On perception, name and form have origination."[15] That is to say, the *Lalitavistara* considers the "predominant condition" of *vijñāna* moment to control the transmigration, while the "support condition" of *karmas* is not the transmigration, yet is necessary for such transmigration.

But No. 2, *saṃskāra,* arises having No. 1, *avidyā,* as condition. Tsoṅ-kha-pa's *Lam rim chen mo* (section on Dependent Origination) cites part of the *Abhidharmakośa* III, 28, for *avidyā*: "the contrary of wisdom (*vidyā*), like enmity and untruth." That is to say, *avidyā* is not just an opposite or something different from *vidyā*, but actively opposes *vidyā*.[16] There Tsoṅ-kha-pa alludes to the work of Dharmakīrti (*Pramāṇavartika*) for the Buddhist interpretation of *avidyā* as *ātmagrāha* of *pudgala;* and to the brothers Asaṅga and Vasubandhu for the position that it is the discrimination (*buddhi*) which misunderstands, i.e., has deception about the right meaning. Tsoṅ-kha-pa refers to Asaṅga's

Abhidharmasamuccaya about two kinds of deception and their results: The deception about *karma* and its fruit amasses the *saṃskāra* that sends one to bad destiny; the deception about the meaning of reality (*tattvārtha*) amasses the *saṃskāra* that sends one to good destiny. Both the positions of Dharmakīrti and of Asaṅga and Vasubandhu agree in allowing the chief opponent to *avidyā* to be the insight (*prajñā*) which understands the selflessness (*nairātmya*).

The above is rather technical, but necessary to clarify the Buddhist positions. Of course, it was not the intention of the Buddha's biography to suggest that he had attained the complete enlightenment by defeating Māra at dusk, because he had still before him the "three *vidyā*" of the night to accomplish the supreme awakening. It is helpful for my sequel to mention those *vidyā* (Pāli, *vijjā*). A standard source is the *Bhayabherava Sutta*[17] which states the three as the knowledge of previous lives, the knowledge of the passing away and rebirth of sentient beings and the knowledge of the destruction of the fluxes. These take place in that order in the three watches of the night of enlightenment.

In the theory of the four Māras, the Māra defeated at dusk was the "Son-of-the-gods" Māra from among the Paranirmitavaśavartin deities at the top of the realm of desire, the Māra which manifests to keep the ascetic from conquering the other Māras.[18] This is not an impediment to rising from the realm of desire to the *dhyānas* of the realm of form, because the Buddha according to legend had already passed through the four *dhyānas*, when meditating by the Nairañjanā River.[19] Therefore, this Māra manifests to swerve the ascetic from full-enlightenment. Furthermore, since the Buddha defeated the "*skandha*" and "*kleśa*" Māras during the three watches of the night, it follows that with the first two *vidyā*,[20] he defeated the "*skandha*" Māra, and with the third one defeated the "*kleśa*" one.

Therefore, if one correlates the foregoing with Dependent Origination, one must take into account all the first seven members, according to my suggestions elsewhere.[21] To be explicit: The defeat of the "Son-of-the-Gods" Māra requires surmounting the members Nos. (4) through (7)—in reverse order, to wit, (7) feelings, (6) sense contact, (5) six sense bases, and (4) name-and-form. Perhaps, this can be done by a meditation operating on any one of the four, as with four Brahma-vihāras (friendliness, compassion, sympathetic joy, and equanimity), which Vasubandhu said was the way the Buddha overcame this Māra; since this apparently operates on No. (7), feelings. Then, instead of (3) perception, witnessing (2) motivations in bondage thereto the Arhat understands the selflessness of *pudgala,* thereby defeating the *skandhamāra,* and is no longer deceived about *karma* and its fruit, thus avoiding the evil destiny.

But then Gautama went beyond this to the last watch of night, when he directed his mind to the destruction of the fluxes (S. *āsrava*), the defiling elements, and so defeated the *"kleśa"* Māra. Now, precisely this achievement gave rise to heated arguments about the status of the Arhat, because some Buddhist sects (such as the Theravāda) held that the Arhat also gains this knowledge of the destruction of the fluxes. However, others (such as the Māhāsāṅghika) denied that the Arhat had achieved this much, which amounts to overcoming No. (1) nescience. In the latter camp, the Mahāyāna scripture *Śrīmālādevīsiṃhanāda-sūtra* denies that the Arhats and the Pratyekabuddhas have ended the fluxes, because they "are obscured and preve..ted, are enwrapped and blinded by the nescience entrenchment".[22] Because they have not eliminated the deception about the meaning of reality, they have—in the words of that *sūtra*—"neither eliminated all defilements nor avoided all rebirth." Hence they have a remainder of rebirth in good destiny.

Face to Face

The foregoing analysis enables us to place certain passages in proper focus from Mahāyāna scriptures about the passing away of sin. Dutt[23] reports from the *Mahāsannipāta-Ratnaketu-dhāraṇī-sūtra* that "At the sight of the Buddhas, the three impurities of attachment (*rāga*), hatred (*dveṣa*), and delusion (*moha*), etc. of all beings subsided and their minds became calm and serene." This is a statement concerning the temporary displacement of defilement from the field of consciousness through calming of the mind.

Śāntideva[24] quotes the *Trisamayarāja*: "Closing his eyes meditating on Buddhas and Bodhisattvas, he should recite the hundred Syllables 8,000 times; as soon as he shuts his eyes, he beholds the Buddhas and Bodhisattvas, and his sin passes away." Concerning the "Hundred Syllables", Śāntideva cites this formula in the same work, presumably from the basic Tantra.[25] Besides, the

Trisamayarājasādhana (the first one in the *Sādhanamālā* collection) cites the formula in this context:[26]

> Then, so as to destroy all the hindrance of *karma*, he should recite 8,000 times with that rite the Hundred-Syllable heart of all the Tathāgatas. All obstruction of *karma*, such as the reviling of the Illustrious Dharma and what ensues directly therefrom is effaced. And this is it: "Homage to the Tathāgatas of the three times (past, present, and future), everywhere engaged in the true nature of unimpeded attainment. OM. Oh, the teaching of the attainment, unequal and equal,[27] universal without end! Bring it, bring it! Remember and make remember! May thy passionless Buddha-dharma flow on, flow on. May she[28] of equal strength laugh, laugh; rescue, rescue! Oh, thou lady, whose character is the great boon of the sky! Burn it, make it burn, in the ocean! Svāhā."

Also in the tantras, as related in Mkhas-grub-rje's *Fundamentals of the Buddhist Tantras,*[29] it is held that just to behold the *maṇḍala* (the fane and deific residents) will purify the mind from sins accumulated for aeons. According to a native Tibetan general *maṇḍala* ritual of the three families:[30] "Now you must proceed to open your eye as the Venerable Mañjuśrī. When it is open, the incomparable diamond eye will see everything. Uttering Hevajra Paśya, remove your eye band you who have been introduced to see the *maṇḍala*, and observe this auspicious *maṇḍala*." Naturally, if one has first developed the pride of identification with Mañjuśrī, he sees the *maṇḍala* with different eyes than if he merely gazes with his ordinary state of mind.

In short, the three statements (cited by Dutt, Śāntideva, and from Mkhas-grub-rje's work) about the cessation of sin, refer to the various degrees of overcoming the "Son-of-the-gods" Māra from among the gods in the realm of desire, and so of temporarily overcoming the power of members 4 through 7 of Dependent Origination. The beings, who thus see the Buddhas and Bodhisattvas and who thus behold the *maṇḍala* may or may not be of Arhat status; but with only that much, they are certainly not Buddhas! However, if these statements can be extended to constitute a vision at death, then the theory would demand that the being would be reborn in a good destiny, and so perhaps as an Arhat. This is the rationale of the speed-up methods of achieving

Buddhahood, to wit, by premature evoking of the death vision with control of the circumstances, so one may eliminate the deception about *karma* and its fruit, and hopefully also the deception about the meaning of reality. This can be called a "symbolic death".

A feature of those passages is the seeing of Buddhas, Bodhisattvas, or deities, but there was no requirement of a mutual facing. The latter-type of facing occurs in the priestly confessional (below), where the Pāli *Mahā-Vagga* uses the phrase *mukham pamukham*. *Sammukha* is the equivalent single word used in the legend of the Buddha's death, when the Buddha asks the disciples to put questions and says, "Do not have later regret, remarking 'The Teacher was face to face with us but we who were face to face with the Bhagavat did not venture to ask him.' The word occurs in the *Visuddhimagga,* Chap. XII:[31] "That day, it seems, was called the day of the Revelation of the Worlds (*loka-vivaraṇa*). Human beings saw deities, and the deities saw human beings. And in doing so, the human beings did not have to look up or the deities down. They all saw each other face to face." This seeing "face to face" is mentioned in the very title of a Mahāyāna *sūtra* that was important in the Chinese Amita cult—the *Prātyutpanna-buddha-sammukhāvasthita-samādhi-sūtra,* "Sūtra of the *samādhi* in which the Buddha is present, stationed face-to-face." In the theory of *sādhana,* or evocation of deities as practiced in Tibet, the Gelugpa school insists that first the performer must generate himself into a deity and then generate the deity in front.[32] If one merely generates the deity in front, then this again amounts to a meditation on a par with contemplation of friendliness (*maitrī*) as the opponent of hatred (*dveṣa*), meditation on corpses and other unpleasantries as the opponent of lust (*rāga*), and so on: it can serve to temporarily void the mind of defiling evidence. But if one first generates himself into deity (as above, with the pride of Mañjuśrī), then he belongs to the class of deities; the deities see him as well as them; and in this case it is claimed that he obtains various occult powers (*siddhi*) from those deities, perhaps even the supramundane *siddhi* of Buddhahood, and frequently a new scripture.

Therefore, to see a Buddha 'face-to-face" is quite an achievement. To see five Buddhas—the usual number in the Mahāyāna Buddhist texts—according to the exact instructions of the rite is of course more a strain on the imagination than seeing one Buddha. As is well-known, such imagery is heightened by fasting and isolation. A candidate with still keener power of imagery is necessary for evoking the thirty-five Buddhas of Confession. For these differences in native capacity, the Buddhist books use words like "weak sense organ" (*mṛdv-indriya*) and "keen sense organ" (*tīkṣṇendriya*). Besides, the *Śrīmālādevīsiṃhanāda-sūtra* mentions the kind of disciple who by his humility obtains the mental presence of the Lord.

Generalities of Confession

The old confession is related in the Pāli *vinaya* text *Mahā-Vagga*. Here we learn that confession called *pāṭimokkha (prātimokṣa* in Sanskrit) became a fast-day duty, that is, held on Buddhist sabbath days, called Poṣadha, on the 8th, 14th, and 15th days in both the increasing and decreasing phases of the moon.[33] The days could be decreased to four by omitting the two "fourteenth" ones and reduced to two by then omitting the two "eighth" days. In the Hindu law book *Manusmṛti,* these days are among the traditional non-study (*anadhyāya*) days, based on the theory that on such days adverse influences are afoot, harassing either the teacher, the student, or the subject-matter. This establishes a temporal limitation for the confession in terms of the luni-solar calendar. Besides, there were specified places and laid-down procedures. Warren[34] reprints the 1874 observations of a J.F. Dikson at such a confessional in Ceylon, who wrote: "After we were seated the priests retired two and two together, each pair knelt down face to face and made confession of their faults, one to another, in whispers." The *Mahā-Vagga* (Nalanda ed., 106.23) even attempts a false etymology of the word *pāṭimokkha* as "mutual facing" or "confrontation". In the ancient Buddhist confessional, the one-faced was not a god. It was believed that by confession of violating any of the numerous *pāṭimokkha* rules, the monk was thereby purified. Of course, when a grave offense was committed, the monk was ousted from the order in any case.[35] The Tibetan translation of the *Prātimokṣa* title is liberation one-by-one," implying some sort of release from the acts stated with verbal truth. It seems that the solemnity of the ritual, the special days chosen for it, the attendant fasting, the mutual trust and concord thereby engendered among the monks—all combine to create a situation, where the monk with the right attitude, we might say "insight" (*paññā*), feels liberated from the acts committed. But, since Buddhism always placed the burden of purification on meditative practices, it must at least here agree with western psychoanalysis that what the ordinary mind can reveal is important to be sure, while the therapeutic procedure must rest its case on the deep-seated impulses of the mind.

Naturally, the confession involves the ethic that it is better to tell the truth. In a way, this is a special example of the precept in *Manusmṛti* (II, 83): *maunāt satyaṃ viśiṣyate,* "Truth is superior to silence." The fact that the *Laws of Manu* mentions this in connection with the efficacy of the Vedic mantra does not nullify its application here, because the theory that confession in appropriate circumstances can absolve from sin involves a premise of ritual magic.

Mahāyāna Buddhism developed the ritual context of confession with a seven-membered rite, itemized in *Dharmasaṃgraha* (No. 14):[36] praises (*vandanā*), worship (*pūjanā*), confession of sins (*pāpadesanā*), sympathetic joy (*anumodanā*), solicitation for the Buddha to instruct (*adhyeṣaṇā*), generating the Mind of Enlightenment (*bodhicittopāda*), and turning over of one's merit to others (*pariṇāmanā*). The confession member is in a *sādhana* of the orange Mañjughoṣa called Arapacana:[37]

> "Whatever sins I have commited from time immemorial under the influence of *karma* and *kleśa*—the nature of which are by way of body, speech, and mind; and the violations of the three vows [the Prātimokṣa, the Bodhisattva, and the Mantra (=Tantra)]; with repentance for the entire aggregate of faults, I confess them in the presence of the worthy ones with my mind set on amends."

Another Tibetan text mentions that the defilement will be purged:[38]

> Furthermore, there are omens for the purging of sin and defilement, that, speaking generally, are superior when concrete, middling when mental, and inferior when in dream; to wit, the good omens that the body emits much filthy matter, or bleeds blood and pus, or that one is bathed

and in white clothes. And so long as they do not occur one should continually trust (that they will).

The Thirty-five Buddhas of Confession

The special form of confession done before the thirty-five Buddhas is a Mahāyāna development that combines the procedure of confession with that of meditation, and so perhaps does reach the deep-seated impulses of the mind.

Both in China and Tibet, the oldest textual sources for the names of the thirty-five Buddhas is the *Upālipariprcchā*, a rather brief scripture of the *Ratnakūṭa* collection; and the names are known in Sanskrit by Śāntideva's quotation of this scripture in his *Śikṣāsamuccaya*. Chinese Buddhist books describe all thirty-five Buddhas iconographically. In Tibet, Tsoṅ-kha-pa visualized and described the thirty-five, and I have studied his little treatise on these.[38]

In the section just prior to the part Śāntideva quoted, the *Upālipariprcchā*[40] speaks of the three great abandonments (*tyāga*, T. *gtoṅ ba*) to be done by the Bodhisattva, who has attained the "forbearance of unoriginated natures" (*anutpattika-dharma-kṣānti*), namely, abandonment (T. *gtoṅ ba*)—that of kingdom (T. *rgyal srid*); great abandonment (T. *gtoṅ ba chen po*)—that of wife, son, and daughter; exceeding abandonment (T. *śin tu gtoṅ ba*)—that of head, eye, skin, etc. The "exceeding abandonment" is the symbolic death previously alluded to and is referred to in the *Śrīmālādevīsiṃhanāda* (also in the *Ratnakūṭa*) this way: "renouncing his body, thus obtaining the body of a Buddha". Besides, the "forbearance of unoriginated natures" is a feature of the Eighth Bodhisattva Stage. The *Upālipariprcchā* continues with discussion of the three basic defilements: lust leads to rebirth, hatred to evil destiny, delusion to falling into the eight great hells. This is again consistent with death's *karma* vision constituting a cause of a new destiny. Then the text presents the famous confession passage that Śāntideva quotes as follows:[41] "Śāriputra, for Bodhisattvas there are two most objectionable sins. What are the two? That associated with hatred and that associated with delusion. Of these, Śāriputra, the first is to be confessed straight-forwardly in a group of ten monks. The sin of the hand is to be confessed as serious in a group of five monks, namely, the holding of a woman's hand. The transgression of wicked thought, while seeing a woman he should reveal as serious to one or two persons. Sins associated with the five of immediate retribution, sins concerning women, maidens, the hand, the shine, the order of monks, and such-like sins, these the Bodhisattva, while alone must reveal day and night as serious in the presence of the thirty-five Buddha lords." Agreeing with the seven-membered rite, the confession formula is preceded by the worship: "I, named so and so, take refuge in the Buddha; I take refuge in the Order of Monks. Homage to Śākyamuni, the Tathāgata-Arhat-Samyaksambuddha. Homage to Vajrapramardin. Homage to Ratnārśiṣ. Homage to Nāgeśvararāja. Homage to Vīrasena. Homage to Vīranandin. Homage to Ratnaśrī. Homage to Ratnacandraprabha. Homage to Amoghadarśin. Homage to Ratnacandra. Homage to Nirmala. Homage to Vimala.[42] Homage to Śūradatta. Homage to Brahma. Homage to Brahmadatta. Homage to Varuṇa. Homage to Varuṇadeva. Homage to Bhadraśrī. Homage to Candanaśrī. Homage to Anantaujas. Homage to Prabhāsaśrī. Homage to Aśokaśrī. Homage to Nārāyaṇa. Homage to Kusumaśrī. Homage to Brahmajyotir-vikrīḍitābhijña, the Tathāgata. Homage to Dhanaśrī. Homage to Smṛtiśrī. Homage to Suparikīrtitanāmadheyaśrī. Homage to Indraketudhvajarāja. Homage to Suvikrāntaśrī. Homage to Vijitasaṃkrama.[43] Homage to Vikrāntagāmin. Homage to Samantāvabhāsavyūhaśrī. Homage to Ratnapadmavikramin. Homage to Ratnapadmasupratiṣṭhita-Śailendrarāja, the Tathāgata-Samyaksambuddha. As many Tathāgata-Arhat-Samyaksambuddhas stay, support, and nourish in all the realms of the world, so facing (*evaṃpramukha*), may those Buddha lords take heed of me!" He now confesses his sins, beginning: "In this birth, or in other births, whatever by me circling in the cyclical flow (*saṃsāra*) of birth without beginning or end was the sinful deed done, caused to be done, or sympathised in while being done;[44].... [Confesses his various sins]. All those obscuring deeds, in front of those Buddha lords, knowledgeable (*jñānabhūta*), witnessing (*sākṣibhūta*), authoritative (*pramāṇabhūta*), who know (*jānant*), I reveal, uncover, do not hide, and guard against in future." [He then states that just as the Buddha turn over their merit, so does he, and continues:] "I sympathetically delight in all (their) merit; I solicit all the Buddhas (to instruct)." ...."Thus, Śāriputra, with thirty-five Buddhas facing him, the Bodhisattva must purge his sins by mental orientations directed to all the Tathāgatas. To him, thus purged of all sins, the Buddha lords reveal their faces, so as to liberate the sentient beings; and reveal their various marks so as to mature the confused, immature ordinary persons."[45]

A significant element of this account is that the Buddhas do not reveal their faces until after the confession. Up to that point, the performer of the rite only imagines the Buddhas, i.e., visualizes them in the phase of calming the mind. The revelation of their faces creates the "face-to-face" situation; and since the faces are seen as they really are, the performer could be said to have the "perfection of insight" (*prajñāpāramitā*) which sees things as they really are.

The thirty-five Buddhas are also associated with the worship of the Bodhisattva Ākāśagarbha. De Visser has rendered the contents of the *Kwan Kokūzo Bosatsu kyō,* including the following:[46]

> Then the Buddha prescribed the following rites of repentance. "There are thirty-five Buddhas whose great compassion saves the world; you must revere and worship them. When doing so, you must put on clothes of shame (*zangi-i*). Full of shame, like a patient with sores upon his eyes, from one to seven days you must worship Buddhas and especially the name of the Great Compassionate Bodhisattva Ākāśagarbha, and you must wash your body and burn several kinds of incense. When a bright star appears, you must kneel down, join your palms and with tears of sorrow invoke Ākāśagarbha saying: 'Oh Bodhisattva of Great Virtue and Great Compassion. Pity me and appear on my behalf.' Then you must think as follows: 'On the top of Ākāśagarbha's head, there is a *cintāmaṇi,* emitting a purple golden color. If one beholds this jewel, at once he sees the Bodhisattva's heavenly crown. The images of the thirty-five Buddhas appear in that crown, and those of the Buddhas of the ten quarters are visible in the *cintāmaṇi*.... Out of compassion with sinners, this Bodhisattva in all kinds of shapes appears in their dreams or in *samādhi,* and with the cintāmaṇi seal stamps their arms, thus removing the marks of crime. After having obtained this sign they must return to the congregation of the monks and explain the commandments as before."

The description makes it evident that the penance is the one called in Pāli *mānatta* and in Sanskrit *mānatva,* ordinarily for the suspension types of offense, to wit, the thirteen cases entitled Saṅghādisesa in Pāli and Saṃghāvaśeṣa in Sanskrit.[47] The "clothes of shame" are often rendered "sack-cloth". The "bright star" might be Venus as the evening star. However, it should not be concluded that the confession before the thirty-five Buddhas is limited to persons guilty of offenses, requiring suspension from the monk order. It is hard to believe that monks like Tsoṅ-kha-pa (founder of the Gelugpa sect of Tibetan Buddhism) were trying to erase heinous offenses, such as the five of immediate retribution, by confession before those Buddhas.[48] The meaning is given in the *Upālipariprcchā* passage as cited by Śāntideva: "In this birth, or in other births...." The confession here implies the memory, or possibility of former lives. Thus it is equivalent to a *karma* vision in the yoga state of symbolic death as the first *vidyā* of the night.

The actual visualization is given in several places. I take the following from Tsoṅ-kha-pa's treatise:

Śākyamuni (yellow) has his right hand in earth-touching and left in *samāpatti* (mudrās). Like Śākyamuni is Ratnaśrī (red), Ratnacandraprabha (white), Brahma (yellow), Candanaśrī (white), Brahmajyotirvikrīḍitābhijña (yellow), and *Padmajotis (red).

Vajrapramardin (yellow) has both hands in teaching the Law (*dharmadeśanā*) (mudrā). Also only teaching the Law: Vīranandin (yellow), Ratnacandra (white), Śūradatta (yellow), Brahmadatta (red), Varuṇadeva (white), Anantaujas (red), Prabhāsaśrī (dark blue), Nārāyaṇa (yellow).

Ratnārśiṣ (red), both hands in *samāpatti.* Likewise Nirmala (dark blue), Varuṇa (white), Aśokaśrī (orange), Dhanaśrī (dark blue), Smṛtiśrī (yellow).

Nāgeśvararāja (white from neck up, and dark blue below neck) with his two hands makes a *vajra* near his chest by extending the two forefingers their tips not quite touching, with the other fingers bent inward and the thumbs up close.

Vīrasena (yellow) has his right hand in refuge-giving (*mudrā*), and the left at the chest with the thumb close to the fingers of the palm and the palm exhibited. Likewise is Amoghadarśin (green), Bhadraśrī (yellow), and Kusumaśrī (yellow).

Suparikīrtitanāmadheyaśrī (white) has his right hand in teaching the Law (*mudrā*) and his left in *samāpatti.*

Indraketudhvajarāja (dark blue). With right hand has a banner raised toward his left side; left hand in *samāpatti.*

Suvikrāntaśrī (dark blue). With right hand holds a sword at his chest; left hand in *samāpatti.*

Vijitasaṃkrama (dark blue). With both hands holds yellow coat of mail with helmet.

Vikrāntagāmin (dark blue). Both hands in earth-touching (*mudrā*).

Samantāvabhāsavyūhaśrī (red). No *mudrā* mentioned in Tsoṅ-kha-pa's text.[49]

Ratnapadmavikramin (orange). Right hand in refuge-giving; left in *samāpatti.*

Śailendrarāja (yellow). Holds a mountain upon his two hands in *samāpatti.*

Moreover, in the case of Nāgeśvararāja, which Tsoṅ-kha-pa gives first, the description says, "wears the garb of an idol" (*na bza' gos 'khyud pa*), and the implication is that the same is understood for all the other Buddhas. Tsoṅ-kha-pa's treatise did not present an explanation for the number "thirty-five" nor any list of thirty-five sins that would go respectively with the thirty-five Buddhas. The great Japanese Buddhist encyclopaedia by Mochizuki does not state a thirty-five sin list corresponding to the thirty-five Buddhas. There is a fascinating, but admittedly remote possibility that this group is a Buddhist recasting of the Egyptian group of forty-two gods, each associated with a negative confession in Chap. CXXV of *The Book of the Dead* (Budge translation). The negative form is of the type, "I have never...." or "I no longer...." but there is no evidence that this negative form was employed in the Mahāyānist confessional.

However, it is possible to advance a theory of the system's origin that closely adheres to the obvious breakdown of the thirty-five list into the first twenty-eight—ending with *Suparikīrtitanāmadheyaśrī*—followed by four military figures, and three miscellaneous. It appears to me that the first twenty-eight Buddha figures were substituted for the twenty-eight *nakṣatras*,[50] the next four for the four world protectors (*lokapāla*)[51] and the last three for the sun, moon, and Dhruva (the pole star).[52] The previous passage about repentance associated with the Bodhisattva Ākāśagarbha is consistent with this hypothesis, because that name means "sky-womb" and the thirty-five Buddhas are seen in his crown after the penitent sees the bright star. Such contemplation would also be consistent with the old Buddhist meditation practice of staying awake in the former and latter parts of night.[53]

If my hypothsis is correct, the situation may be reconstructed this way: The penitent fixes his attention on the evening star as a device for focussing of mind, imagining it to be the Bodhisattva Ākāśagarbha. Then as the evening advances and the numerous stars appear, the zodiacal belt is imagined as Ākāśagarbha's crown. As the star clusters called the *nakṣatras* arise in the east and set in the west, he visualizes them as Buddhas, who are the witnesses and confesses to them. Eventually, the contemplation was formalized with the twenty-eight *nakṣatras*, the four world protectors, plus sun, moon, and pole star, all visualized as Buddhas, making thirty-five in all.[54] Once the system of visualization was established, it could be abstracted from the stellar background which had been its inception; and thereafter could be contemplated without actually observing the sky.

Conclusion

My paper so far should have made it clear that defilement in man has to be removed by man himself; no one else can do it for him. This is the prevalent position of Buddhism from early times, and all the data here collected bears this out. Since this point deserves repetition, it can hardly be better stated than by a verse which Tsoṅ-kha-pa cites in his *Lam rim chen mo,* now translated along with the Tibetan annotational commentary:[55]

> The Munis do not wash away the defilements (of the streams of consciousness of the sentient beings) with water (as though it were a matter of washing away dirt). And do not remove the suffering of beings with a hand (as though it were a matter of pulling out a thorn). They do not shift to another the (features of) comprehension of reality (as though it were a matter of shifting a tool from the right to the left hand). (But rather) they liberate (the beings from the cyclical flow) by the teaching (provided the beings meditate on its meaning) of the truth of real nature (or absolute truth).

REFERENCES

1. *Dharmasamuccaya,* 2° Partie, par Lin Li-Kousang, Révision de André Bareau, J.W. de Jong et Paul Demiéville (Paris, 1969), p. 127 (my own translation from the Sanskrit given here).
2. Cf. Louis de La Vallée Poussin, tr., *L'Abhidharmakośa de Vasubandhu,* II, pp. 161-62; 164; 171; and Th. Stcherbatsky, *The Central Conception of Buddhism* (Calcutta reprint), pp. 87-8.
3. For example, there are the ten sporadic defiled natures (*parīttakleśabhūmika)* of *Abhidharmokośa,* II, verse 27 anger (*krodha*), grudges (*upanāha*), guile (*śāṭhya*), jealousy (*īrṣyā*), contentiousness (*pradāsa*), hypocrisy (*mrakṣa*), greed (*matsara*), deceit (*māyā*), conceit (*mada*), harmfulness (*vihiṃsā*). These are among longer lists called "secondary defilements" (*upakleśa*). The most defilements ever mentioned (but no detailed list is given) is the set of 84,000 defilements, to wit, 21,000 practices in which lust predominates in the candidates, a like number with predominating hatred, and again with predominating delusion, and 21,000 of practicing with the three in equal proportions (i.e., with none of the three poisons sufficiently strong to predominate); cf. F.D. Lessing and Alex Wayman, trs., Mkhas grub rje's *Fundamentals of the Buddhist Tantras* (The Hague, 1968), pp. 57 and 221, n. In the multiple *dharma* system, lust, hatred, pride (*māna*), and doubt (*vicikitsā*) are among the indeterminate (*aniyata*) group and are considered to be exclusive, that is to say, one of them present in consciousness excludes the others. Of these, doubt is not particularly faulty for the ordinary person, but constitutes a hindrance for the person progressing in Buddhist meditation.
4. This material is taken from the Bihar Research Society's manuscript of the *Śrāvakabhūmi,* and is not in my *Analysis of the Śrāvakabhūmi Manuscript* (Berkeley, 1961), where I included Asaṅga's *Paramārthagāthā* which directly precedes the *Ābhiprāyikārthagāthā* in the *Yogācārabhūmi.*
5. These roles of *śamatha* and *vipaśyanā* are treated extensively by Tsoṅ-kha-pa in his *Lam rim chen mo (ži gnas = śamatha,* section). I have made a translation of the last two sections of the *Lam rim chen mo—śamatha* and *vipaśyanā* under the title *Calming the Mind and Discerning the Real.*
6. Dr. Fred Underwood, Department of Religion, Columbia University, expanded upon this visionary implication of the Pāli word *paññā* in his doctoral dissertation Buddhist Insight: The Nature and Function of Pañña in the Pāli Nikāyas.
7. See the section 'Saṃkleśa and Vyavadāna' in Louis de La Vallée Poussin. *Vijñaptimātratāsiddhi* (Paris, 1928), I, pp. 214-20.
8. Cf. Table 1 in my *The Buddhist Tantras: Light on Indo-Tibetan Esotericism* (Samuel Weiser, Inc., New York, 1973).
9. For a judicious study of Māra as a symbol of evil, see James W. Boyd, "Symbols of Evil in Buddhism," *The Journal of Asian Studies,* XXXI, No. 1 (Nov. 1971), pp. 63-75.
10. *yaṃ vedeti taṃ sañjānāti,* in the *Madhupindikasutta* of *Majjhima Nikāya,* I, 111-2. Of course, *sañjānāti,* is the finite verb form for the noun *saññā,* Sanskrit *saṃjñā.*
11. This is clear enough from Masaaki Hattori, *Dignāga, On Perception* (Cambridge, Mass., 1968), p. 26.
12. Śāntideva's *Śikṣāsamuccaya* (Darbhanga, 1961), p. 135. 12-3.
13. Cf. A Wayman, "Buddhist Dependent Origination," *History of Religions,* Feb. 1971, p. 188; and *Śikṣāsamuccaya* (*op. cit.*), p. 123. 21-2.

14. The evidence for this point is too lengthy to go into here. It is developed in my article contributed to *Philosophy East and West,* 46: 4 (October, 1996), entitled "A Defense of Yogācāra Buddhism," wherein I present my more recent views on these and affiliated matters.
15. As given in Franklin Edgerton's *Buddhist Hybrid Sanskrit Reader,* p. 21: *saṃkalpakalpajanitena a noniśena/ bhavate avidya na pi saṃbhavako 'sya kaścit/saṃskārahetu dadate na' ca saṃkramo'sti/vijñānam udbhavati saṃkramaṇaṃ pratitya/.* I have also translated this verse in a different centext in my "Buddhist Dependent Origination," p. 203.
16. Cf. Genjun H. Sasaki, "The Time Concept in Abhidharma," (Proceedings of the Twenty-Sixth International Congress of Orientalists, Vol. III, Part I, pp. 474-5), for a like theory of *avidyā* from Saṃghabhadra's *Nyāyānusāraśāstra.*
17. This is a scripture in the *Majjhima Nikāya,* I; cf. in translation, I.B. Horner, *The Middle Length Sayings I* (London, 1967), pp. 28-9.
18. Cf. the summary of the multiple Māras according to theories of Asaṅga and Vasubandhu, in my "Buddhism", *Historia Religionum* II (Leiden., 1971), p. 447. The last Māra to be defeated, the "Killing" Māra, was not defeated during the night of enlightenment, but rather at Vaiśālī, three months before the Buddha's passing when he repressed the "life motivation" (*āyuḥ-saṃskāra*).
19. See, for example, the Mahāyāna legends set forth in Mkhas grub rje's *Fundamentals of the Buddhist Tantras,* pp. 21, ff.
20. For the supernormal faculties associated with the first two *vidyā* as constituting the inner directed and outer directed functions of the same faculty, see my "The Buddhist Theory of Vision," *Añjali; O.H. de A. Wijesekera Felicitation Volume* (University of Ceylon, 1970), pp. 27-8, also based here on a passage from a Vasubandhu commentary.
21. "Buddhist Dependent Origination," Table 3, p. 196. and the article generally.
22. See Alex Wayman and Hideko Wayman, translators and annotators, *The Lion's Roar Of Queen Śrīmālā* (Columbia University Press, New York, 1974).
23. N. Dutt, *Gilgit Manuscripts,* Vol. IV (Calcutta, 1959), p. xi.
24. C. Bendall, and W.H.D. Rouse, trs., *Śikṣā-samuccaya,* Compiled by Śāntideva (London, 1922), pp. 168-9.
25. The translators (Bendall and Rouse, *op. cit.,* p. 136, n.) say, "Some of the words have no meaning." It would be more proper to have said that they failed to find the meaning.
26. B. Bhattacharya, ed., *Sādhanamālā*, Vol. 1 (Baroda, 1968 reprint),/ *tataḥ sarvakarmāvaraṇakṣayārthaṃ sarvatatathāgatahṛdayaṃ śatākṣaraṃ tenaiva vidhinā aṣṭasahasraṃ japet/saddharmadūṣaṇān antaryādikaṃ karmāvaraṇaṃ prahīyate/idaṃ ca tat—*
namas traiyadhvikānāṃ tathāgatānāṃ sarvatrapratihatāvāpti-dharmatāvalīnāṃ OM asama sama samantato 'nantatāvāptiśāsani hara hara smara smaraṇa vigatarāga buddhadharma te sara sara samabalā hasa traya traya gaganamahāvaralakṣaṇe jvala jvalana sāgare SVĀHĀ/
27. For the "unequal and equal mantra" of the Heart Sūtra, cf. Wayman, "The Buddhist 'Not This, Not This,'" *Philosophy East and West,* XI:3 (Oct. 1961), pp. 112-33. Besides, the complete Buddha could be said to be equal to a Bodhisattva of the Tenth Stage (honored by all the world) and unequal (possessed of the eighteen exclusive features).
28. The goddess suggested by the "hundred-syllable heart *mantra*" is easily Tārā. Cf. Alex Wayman. "The Twenty-One Praises of Tārā, a syncretism of Śaivism and

Buddhism," *Journal of the Bihar Research Society*, XXXXV, Pts. I-IV, Mar.-Dec.-1959, pp. 36-43. The following selections from the verse (vs.) praises obviously apply to the *mantra* indications: vs. 21, "O Lady endowed with the Power (*śakti*):" vs. 10, "who domineers the world of Māra with the laughing, mocking sound Tuttāre"; vs. 11, "who liberates all in distress"; vs. 2, "who blazes with the laughing beams of a thousand starry clusters"; vs. 13, "who lives amidst the garland blazing like the fire at the aeon's end". For the meaning of the word "ocean", I mention there (p. 39, n.), "She is the Gaṅgā in heaven, or the Milky Way."

29. Previously cited (n. 3), p. 149.
30. "Rigs gsum spyi'i dkyil 'khor gyi cho ga phrin las lhun grub," by 'Jam-dbyaṅs Mkhyen-brtse'i dbaṅ po, in *Sgrub thabs kun btus; a collection of sādhanas and related texts of the Vajrayāna traditions of Tibet* (Dehradun, 1970), Vol. II (Kha), f. No. 35: /rje btsun 'jam dpal deṅ khyod kyi/mig 'byed par ni brtson par mdzad/ phye bas thams cad mthoṅ 'gyur ba'i/rdo rje mig ni bla na med/he badzra pā śya źes pas mig ras bsal te dkyil 'khor bltar gzug/dkyil 'khor bzaṅ po 'di la ltos/. The three tantric families are the Tathāgata, Padma, and Vajra, for which see *Mkhas grub rje's*, pp. 103, ff.
31. Bhikkhu Ñāṇamoli, tr., *The Path of Purification (Visuddhimagga) by* Bhadantācariya Buddhaghosa (Colombo, 1956), p. 429.
32. *Mkhas grub rje's*, Index, under the word "Generation".
33. For another reference, see *Aṅguttara Nikāya*, Book of Threes, No. 37.
34. Henry Clarke Warren, *Buddhism in Translations* (Cambridge, Massachusetts, 1947), pp. 406-7.
35. Cf. P.V. Bapat and A. Hirakawa, *Shan-Chien-P'i P'o-Sha, a Chinese version by Saṅghabhadra of Samantapāsādikā* (Poona, 1970), p. 545, "The one which regret cannot mend is the Pārājikā."
36. The *Dharmasaṃgraha* in Sanskrit is included in P.L. Vaidya, ed., *Mahāyāna-sūtra-Saṃgraha* (Darbhanga, 1961).
37. *Sgrub thabs kun btus* (*op. cit.*), Vol. Kha, "Chos rje sa skya paṇḍita daṅ'jam dbyaṅs dmar ser sbags te sgrub pa'i thabs byin rlabs daṅ bcas pa'i skor," f. no. 318: /bdag ni thog med dus nas su/las daṅ ñon moṅs dbaṅ gyur pas/lus daṅ ṅag daṅ yid sgo nas/ruṅ bźin sdig pa ci bgyis daṅ/sdom pa gsum daṅ 'gal gyur pa'i/ñes pa'i tshogs kun rab 'gyod pas/mchod 'os rnams kyi spyan sṅa ru/slan chad bsdam pa'i sems kyis bśags/
38. *Sgrub thabs kun btus (op. cit.)*, Vol. VI (Cha), "Rdo rje mkha' 'gro la brten pa'i sdig sbyoṅ sbyin sreg gi cho ga sgrib gñis kun 'joms" by Koṅ-sprul Blo-gros-mtha'-yas, f. no. 282: /de'aṅ sdig sgrib dag pa'i rtags spyi daṅ mtshuṅs par rab dṅos/'briṅ ñams/tha ma rmi lam du lus las dri ma maṅ po 'am khrag rnag don pa daṅ/ khrus byed pa daṅ/gos dkar gyon pa sogs ltas bzaṅ yid ches pa yaṅ ma byuṅ gi bar du bya ba yin no/.
39. "Saṅs rgyas so lṅa'i mṅon rtogs daṅ/lha sku'i phyag tshad," Tsoṅ-kha-pa collected works, Lhasa edition, Vol. Da.
40. I used the edition with title *Ārya-vinayaviniścaya-upāli-paripṛcchā-nāma-mahāyāna-sūtra*, in the Japanese photographic edition of the Tibetan Peking canon (PTT), Vol. 24.
41. *Śikṣāsamuccaya*, 94.12-18:/bodhisattvānāṃ śāriputra dve mahāsāvadye āpattī/ katame dve? dveṣasahagatā mohasahagatā ceti/tatra śāriputra prathamā āpattir daśavarge ṛjukena deśayitavyā/hastāpattiḥ pañcavarge gurvī deśayitavyā/striyā hastagrahaṇaṃ cakṣurdarśanaṃ duṣṭacittāpattir ekapudgalasya dvayor vā śāriputra tām gurvī darśayet/pañcānantaryasamanvāgatāpattir bodhisattvena

stryāpattir dārikāpattir hastāpattiḥ stūpāpattiḥ saṃghāpattiḥ/tathā anyāścāpattayo bodhisattvena pañcatriṃśatāṃ buddhānāṃ bhagavatāmantike rātriṃdivam-ekākinā gurvyodeśyitavyāḥ/.

42. Tsoṅ-kha-pa's text omits an equivalent to "Vimala" and adds an equivalent to Padmajyotis just prior to Dhanaśrī. Likewise, in the little Chinese text on confession to the thirty-five Buddhas that is in my possession from the late F.D. Lessing manuscript remains. It was published in 1931, no city mentioned, but probably Peking.
43. Vicitrasaṃkrama, the reading in the *Śikṣāsamuccaya,* is obviously a scribal corruption for Vijitasaṃkrama, the reading accepted by the translation in Tsoṅ-kha-pa's text as well as in the Chinese text (n. 42, above), "who has won the battle".
44. *Śikṣāsamuccya,* 94.30-31:/yan mayā asyāṃ jātau anyāsu vā jātiṣu anavarāgre jātisaṃsāre saṃsaratā pāpakaṃ karma kṛtaṃ syāt kāritaṃ vā kriyamāṇaṃ vā anumoditaṃ bhavet/.
45. *Śikṣāsamuccaya,* 95. 21-3: /iti hi śāriputra bodhisattvenemān pañcatriṃśato buddhān pramukhān kṛtvā sarvatathāgatāgatānugatir manasikraiḥ pāpaśuddhiḥ kāryā/tasyaivaṃ sarvapāpaviśuddhasya tatra ca buddhā bhagavanto mukhāny upadarśayanti sattvavimokṣārtham evà/nānāvyañjanākāram upadarśayanti vibhrāntabālapṛthagjanānāṃ paripācanāhetoḥ/.
46. M.W. De Visser, *The Bodhisattva Ākāśagarbha (Kokūzō) in China and Japan* (Amsterdam, 1931), pp. 31-2.
47. I.B. Horner, *The Book of Discipline,* Vol. I (London, 1949), translates the Pāli term Saṅghādisesa as "formal meeting", i.e., of the Saṃgha.
48. Note that in the Mahāyānist *Laṅkāvatāra-sūtra* (text, pp. 138-40) the five sins incurring immediate retribution are explained symbolically: craving is the mother, nescience the father; thus "matricide" and "patricide" have the immediate retribution of liberation from the world.
49. In the depiction of this Buddha among the thirty-five iconographical representations in the Chinese text (n. 42, above), the mudrā of the right hand and appearance of left hand appear the same as that of Vīrasena; and the Chinese description assigns a golden color to this Buddha. The Tibetan-Mongolian blockprint (Peking edition) of the "300 Buddhas", depicts this Buddha in agreement with the Chinese text.
50. The 28-system of nakṣatras is preserved in the Buddhist scripture narrative *Śārdūlakarṇāvadāna,* which is included in the *Divyavadāna* collection. Cf. Sujitkumar Mukhopadhyaya, ed., *Śārdūlakarṇāvadānam* (Santiniketan, 1954), pp. 45, ff., for the description of the twenty-eight, divided into four groups of seven asterisms, each alloted to the four directional gates, eastern gate (*pūrvadvāra*), and so on.
51. For an elaborate discussion of the four great kings and lamaist iconography for these, see F.D. Lessing, *Yung-Ho-Kung: An Iconography of the Lamaist Cathedral in Peking* (Stockholm, 1942), pp. 38-52. Lessing's table (p. 11) gives them in the traditional order, starting with Vaiśravaṇa, holding a banner as does the Buddha Indraketudhvajarāja: then Virūpakṣa, who holds in his right hand a serpent, but alternately a drawn sword—as does, in the case of a sword. Suvikrāntaśrī; then Dhṛtarāṣṭra, who holds and plays the *vīnā,* and Virūḍhaka, who holds a sword or club in the right hand—presumably corresponding, in either order to Vijitasaṃkrama and Vikrāntagāmin. The four Buddhas constitute a sub-set of the thirty-five, by reason of all being dark blue in color, and all demonstrating the military in their names.
52. Of course, Dhruva entered prominently in the ancient marriage ceremony of India,

because at a certain point of the ritual, the bridegroom would show the polar star to the bride, for steadfastness, progeny, and so on. Cf. P.K. Narayana Pillai, *Non-Ṛgvedic Mantras in the Marriage Ceremonies* (Trivandrum, 1958), pp. 292-300. The association with the Buddha Śailendrarāja is transparent, because the latter holds a mountain, and the mountain stands for immovability and steadfastness.

53. The practice of staying awake according to watches of the night is called *jāgarikānuyoga;* cf. A. Wayman, *Analysis of the Śrāvakabhūmi Manuscript,* pp. 60, 71-3.

54. Naturally this hypothesis applies to India especially where the stars often show up brilliantly, particularly in South India. The present author and his wife notes this during their 15,000 miles of travel on the floor of India during 1963 under the auspices of the American Institute of Indian Studies and with special remembrance of the town of Dhar near Ujjain.

55. The basic verse is cited in the *Lam rim chen mo* (Tashilunpo ed.) at f. 21b—3:/ thub rnams sdig pa chu yis mi 'khru ziṅ/ 'gro ba'i sdug bsṅal phyag gis mi sel la/ ñid kyi rtogs pa gźan la spo min te/chos ñid bden pa bstan pas grol bar mdzad. The annotational expansion is made with the help of the *Mchan bu bźi* commentary, a reprint of which by the Tibetans has appeared in north India.

19

The Buddhist Theory of Virtue Consignment (*Pariṇāmana*)

INTRODUCTION

The present writer had to decide how to translate the term *pariṇāmana* (or its alternate spelling) because it occurred a number of times in important contexts he has completed and which has been published at Albany, New York: *Ethics of Tibet: the Bodhisattva section of Tsong-kha-pa's Lam rim chen mo*.[1] The frequent translation of the verb by 'transfer', as though a person on the Buddhist path can 'transfer' his so-called "roots of virtue" (*kuśala-mūla*), did not satisfy some modern translators. One can easily see why: the older translators did not explain how such transfer can be effected—the *modus operandi*—as by mysterious particles through the air; and did not explain how it would accord with the Buddhist theory of *karma,* in which it is expected that persons are responsible for their own merit and vice. So more recently translators have resorted to a rendition 'dedicate' as though this person would 'dedicate' his roots of virtue (and so keep them), much as a person dedicates his book and it is still his book.

However, the various passages in the Bodhisattva section of Tsong-kha-pa's *Lam rim chen mo* wherein this term occurs as a noun or as a verb, and whether in citations or in the native Tibetan discussions made it clear that neither of those two renditions (transference or dedication) is suitable. I finally decided on a translation 'consignment', as though some other person or religious goal is intended as a recipient, meanwhile the person who so consigns can use those "roots of virtue" or use those objects intended to be given, while not regarding them as his own or belonging to himself. The person thus following the Buddhist path by this attitude toward his "roots of virtue" or toward more physical possessions cuts down his sense of 'mine' (*ātmīya*) and is headed toward a realization of his 'true self'. This observation agrees with a story preserved in the Pāli canon. A young man's mistress had run off with some of his belongings. He and his friends looking for her happened to meet the Buddha and asked if he had seen her. But the Buddha replied: "Were it not better that you sought the self (Pāli, *atta;* Skt., *ātman*)."[2] Here, 'self' means the one that is stripped of its belongings.[3] However, this does not necessitate an actual detachment of all possessions. It is a profound change of attitude. The mistress was guilty of theft, but when one seeks the true self, one is not dismayed by a reduction in possessions.

Various commentaries are utilized here, because the scriptural sentences with this term have been noticed for a long time and yet resisted satisfactory rendition. Franklin Edgerton under the word in his *Buddhist Hybrid Sanskrit Dictionary* gave four meanings: (1) change, alternation; (2) ripening; (3) development; and (4) diversion. Presumably, various previous translators have consulted this dictionary and did not find the renditions helpful, since none of these seem to have been adopted, viz., the prevalent 'transference' and 'dedication'. In fact, Edgerton's fourth definition 'diversion' or the gerund form 'diverting' does get the significance of the scriptural term in a literal sort of way; and I believe that my rendition 'consignment' agrees with this 'diverting', but furnishes a better communication of the contextual significance. This is said for the term *pariṇāmana* when it applies to the "roots of virtue", which is the prevalent discourse with the term. In such a case, it is rendered into Tibetan by *yongs su bsngo ba*. But there is another rendition into Tibetan for the term, when it has the first of the four meanings given by Edgerton, namely, *bsgyur ba* ("change-over"). The term *pariṇāmana* has this meaning, when it is the fourth of the four *abhisaṃdhi* ("veiled intention"), for then the Buddhist commentator Ratnākaraśānti gives the illustration "change-over to a lion" (Tib. *seng ge rnam par bsgyur ba*), and further explains that the change takes place in the mind (Tib. *blo;* Skt. *buddhi, mati,* or *dhī*).[4] Thus, this kind of *pariṇāmana* applies to the 'self' (*ātman*). Our discussion of the term *pariṇāmana* will also dwell upon the usage when it involves the "roots of virtue" or other possessions and so applies to what belongs to the self (*ātmīya*).

Granted though, my rendition 'consignment' for the possessions' case should be justified by the scriptures[5] and/or the commentaries. Besides the materials in the Bodhisattva section mentioned above, I have utilized the *Akṣayamatinirdeśa-sūtra,* and its commentary, both in the Tibetan canon; Vimalamitra's commentary on the *Saptaśatikā-prajñāpāramitā-sūtra* also in Tibetan; and a commentary on the well-known verse set *Bhadracaryā*, as well as the *Saṃcaya-gāthā*. I append a note about Śāntideva's tenth chapter. These are all Mahāyāna Buddhist works, as are of course the mentioned Bodhisattva section. But before going to the material from these traditions, it is well to consider the situation in what might be termed the "Śrāvaka vehicle", or called "Nikāya Buddhism", and which has been referred to as "Sinhalese Buddhism".

The Position in Sinhalese Buddhism

A work of Mahāyāna Buddhism, Nāgārjuna's *Ratnāvalī* (IV, 90) states:[5]

> In the Vehicle of the Śrāvakas there is no mention of the vow of the Bodhisattva or of his consignment to others of his career. How, then, is one a Bodhisattva through that (vehicle)?

This verse does not deny this 'consignment' generally in the Śrāvaka vehicle, but in terms of the Bodhisattva's career, namely, of the practice of six Perfections (or ten) in ten Bodhisattva stages.

It is known that the Theravāda of Sri Lanka does have a theory rendered as "merit transference" but as the topic is discussed by G.P. Malalasekera a different term is utilized, namely the Pāli *parivaṭṭa* (*sic.*).[6] The Pāli Text Society's *Pāli-English Dictionary* writes the term *parivatta* and gives the verb form *parivattati* and under the meaning 'change' refers to *Peta Vatthu,* II,10, where the commentary has glossed the verb as *pariṇamati*. The particular story is that of Uttara's mother.[7] Because of her imprecation involving blood, after her death she became a "hungry ghost" (*petī*, Skt. *Pretā*), for whom the river became full of blood which she could not drink. Once this spirit saw a certain monk and related her sad story.[8] According to the translation: "Then the venerable Revata gave water to the Order of monks in the name of the petī; he went on his round for alms, and having taken food, he gave it to the monks. Then he took some rags from a rubbish heap, and having cleansed and sprinkled them and having made bark-clothes, he gave it to the monks. Because of this, the petī attained deva-bliss . . ." The passage concludes with this petī informing that certain monk of her happiness. Now, it is difficult to justify the rendition "merit transference" for what has happened in this particular story. Where is the "merit" and how the "transference"? It seems that the instance exposed above as the "change-over" meaning of the Skt. term *pariṇāmana* fits the situation, to wit, that the petī has had a change in her stream of consciousness. It seems that the venerable Revata, while in a kind of *samādhi* has employed a kind of sympathetic magic.

Malalasekera also mentioned that the term *patti* (Skt. *Prāpti*), while etymologically 'acquisition', gets extended senses, eventually, "gift of merit that was acquired".[9] These extended senses are accepted in the *Pāli-English Dictionary*. This author also gave his theory of how the transference takes place: "The method of such transference (the Pāli term for which is *parivaṭṭa*) is quite simple. The doer of the good deed has merely to wish that the merit he had thereby gained should accrue to someone in particular, if he so wishes, or to 'all beings'. The wish may be purely mental or it may be accompanied by an expression in words. This could be done with or without the particular beneficiary being aware of it."[10] But while Dr. Malalasekera calls this the 'method', in fact it is simply a well-stated exposition of the procedure without explaining how this merit can be given to others, or without presenting a criterion for judging the success of this giving in terms of the recipient. Indeed, when the recipient is a *petī* (female hungry ghost), it is normally out of the question to ask such recipient about the effect of the giving.

R. Gombrich wrote a subsequent article on the topic, referring to Malalasekera's.[11] Gombrich cites the continuation of the above-cited passage by Malalasekera: "The fact of 'transference' does not in the slightest degree mean that the 'transferer' is deprived of the merit he had originally acquired by his good deed. On the contrary, the very act of 'transference' is a good deed in itself and therefore enhances the merit already earned."[12] Gombrich goes on with his own observation: "One might add that the classical simile for this act of transfer, *patti* in Pāli is the lighting of one lamp from another." Here Gombrich shows that some remark about the *modus operandi* is called for.

Gombrich's article is on the whole more sophisticated than Malalasekera's. Yet both scholars appear to labor under the limitation of taking the 'transfer' or 'transference' (of merit) as unassailable; and so taking this 'transfer' for granted, they structure their articles around these English words.

Gombrich makes the point that this 'transference of merit' is fully developed in Theravāda Buddhism of Ceylon, independently of the notion of the Bodhisattva which is of paramount importance in Mahāyāna Buddhism. He also believes that the later position—presumably of that very Bodhisattva practice—can be rationalized to conform to the earlier canonical doctrine. But while so declaring, he evidences no knowledge of that later position, as it will be developed in the present paper. Gombrich discusses the two pieces of evidence which Malalasekera had pointed to for attributing the 'transference of merit' theory to early Buddhism; and finds both of them—one from the *Milindapañha,* the other from an ordination ceremony—to be late. Gombrich himself attributes the early evidence of the theory to be in the *Mahāparinibbāna Sutta,* hence canonical. To be fair to Gombrich, I must present his main statement. He points out that the Buddha received a meal from two ministers and thanked (*anumodi*) them with verses, including:

> Wherever a wise man dwells he should feed the virtuous and restrained ascetics there, and dedicate the gift (*dakkhiṇaṃ ādise*) to whatever deities are there; when worshipped they worship, when honored they honor him..

Gombrich then cites the commentary on the verse, namely, that on the words *dakkhiṇaṃ ādise* the commentary says: *pattiṃ dadeyya* rendered by him, "One should give the merit." He also considers it significant that on the words "when worshipped they worship" the commentator should say: "they think, these people are not even our relatives, and even so they give us merit".[13] Gombrich presumably knows, though not mentioning it, that he was preceded in this interpretation of the canonical verse by T.W. and C.A.F. Rhys Davids, who when translating this scripture of paramount importance in the series Sacred Books of the Buddhists, used these expressions: "And give the merit of his gifts to the deities who haunt the spot."[14]

But how does the term *ādise* justify the renditions 'dedicate' and 'give the merit'? Helmer Smith, in his work on the *Saddanīti,* says for the verb *ādisati* that it is equal to *uddisati.*[15] And the equivalent Sanskrit verb *ā-diś* has such a meaning as "to point out", but no suggestion of such meanings as 'dedicate' and 'give the merit'. The fact that the commentator glossed *dakkhiṇaṃ* as *pattiṃ* is quite proper, since both terms here mean 'gift', but hardly 'merit'.

The present writer believes that in the zeal of the translators T.W. and C.A.F. Rhys Davids, and later of R. Gombrich, to pin this notion of "merit transference" on the *Mahāparinibbāna Sutta,* they failed to notice the real significance of the canonical passage, which was to show that certain actions (*karma*) in the 'seen' (Skt. *dṛṣṭa*) world have a reciprocal action in the 'unseen' (Skt. *adṛṣṭa*) world. Although Sunidha and Vassakāra were chief ministers of Magadha, when by invitation the Buddha with Saṅgha members partook of good food at the residence of these two ministers, these two personally served the food and waited upon them. Then when the Buddha had finished his meal, the ministers sat on a lower seat at his side, whereupon the Buddha expressed sympathetic joy (*anumodi*) with these *gāthā:*[16]

> *yasmiṃ padese kappeti, vāsaṃ paṇḍitajātiyo /*
> *sīlavantettha bhojetvā, saññate brahmacārayo //*
> In whatever place a wise person makes his abode, there he should feed the virtuous and self-controlled brahmacārins.

yā tattha devatā āsuṃ tāsaṃ dakkhiṇaṃ ādise /
tā pūjitā pūjayanti, mānitā mānayanti naṃ //
And point out the gift to whatever deities live there. Worshipped, they will worship him. Honored, they will honor him.

tato naṃ anukampanti, mātā puttaṃ va orasaṃ /
devatānukampito poso, sadā bhadrāni passati //
Then they are compassionate toward him, as is a mother toward her own son. The man who has the sympathy of the gods will always behold good auspices.

The suggestion of the verbal form *ādise* is that the 'pointing out' is verbal, whether orally expressed or said in the mind, and amounts to something like: "All you local deities, observe this gift!" Hence, the passage advises some form of the rite which has been treated by various articles with name in Sanskrit *satya-kriyā* (the act of truth).[17]

It seems remarkable that two fine scholars as are Malalasekera and Gombrich would write articles on the transference of merit in Sinhalese Buddhism and not even mention a word for 'merit' in the Pāli language. Of course, there is the Pāli term *puñña*, which means 'merit'. In Mahāyāna Buddhism, the equivalent term *puṇya* stands for one of the two kinds of Bodhisattva 'collection' (*sambhāra*), namely, of merit and knowledge.[18] Since it is acknowledged as something that can be amassed, it would appear reasonable to associate it with *pariṇāmana,* as do the Prajñāpāramitā scriptures (*infra*), but other Mahāyāna scriptures apparently do not employ *puṇya:* instead they allude frequently in this connection to the "roots of virtue" (*kuśala-mūla*). This term in its Pāli form, *kusala-mūla,* stems from the old Nikāya Buddhism, and the three kinds there given are the same found in their Sanskrit equivalents in Vasubandhu's *Abhidharmakośa,* namely, 'lack of greed' (*alobha*), 'lack of hatred' (*adosa,* Skt. *adveṣa*), 'lack of delusion' (*amoha*).[19] While all three kinds consist of 'lacks', they are acknowledged to have a positive content, namely, 'lack of greed' includes liberality; 'lack of hate' is a name for kindness (P. *mettā*); 'lack of delusion' amounts to wisdom (P. *paññā*).[20] As even animals exhibit such traits toward their young, there is no need to transfer such traits, rather to promote them.

I do applaud Gombrich's position that the later Bodhisattva

approach to the topic may well have a forerunner in early canonical Buddhism. While the *Mahāparinibbāna Sutta* connection was suspect, it is more promising that the canonical connection is in terms of the notion of "roots of virtue" (P. *kusala-mūla*). The topic is well-treated in Majjhima-nikāya I, 26, the Discourse on Right Views (*sammādiṭṭhi-sutta*), on one of the eight members of the path. Here the previously-discussed type of *pariṇāmana* that means 'change-over' seems to apply, because the premise is that it is possible to change from greed to non-greed, from hatred to non-greed, from hatred to non-hatred, and from delusion to non-delusion. The other kind of *pariṇāmana* involving an operation on the "roots of virtue" themselves seems more elusive to locate in the old nikāyas.

Even more promising for the canonical connection is the term *vossagga-pariṇāmi* which occurs at Saṃyutta, I, 88, and at Dīgha. III, 226. Mrs. Rhys Davids translation "maturity of surrender" is abject, after she presents Buddhaghosa comment demanding the *dvandva* interpretation: ejection of the defilements (Skt. *kleśa*) and leap into Nirvāṇa. In the case of the Saṃyutta account,[21] the term *vossaga-pariṇāmi* occurs in the discussion of the first member of the "eightfold path", namely, 'right views'. Here, the context suggests that the term is construable as 'elimination' (*vossaga*) of the bad and 'change-over (*pariṇāmi*) to the good—agreeing with our above observations based on the Majjhima-nikāya; and that in this manner the 'right views' set the stage for the rest of the "eightfold path".[22] This *sutta* is about the 'friendly guide' (Skt. *kalyāṇa-mitra*), who in the present context amounts to 'friend' (*mitra*) of the 'virtuous' (*kalyāṇa*).[23]

In the case of the Dīgha account,[24] it involves the seven 'ancillaries of enlightenment' (*bodhyaṅga*), namely, meaning dismissal (*vossagga*) of defilements, and consignment (*pariṇāmi*) (of the seven ancillaries) to enlightenment, since Gautama chose enlightenment over universal royalty, recalling the legend that his marks at birth portended either. The following correlation shows the ancillaries chosen by the future Buddha and the jewels chosen by the universal emperor:[25]

1. Analysis of the Dharma (*dharmapravicaya*)	conquering wheel
2. Equanimity (*upekṣā*)	gem

3. Cathartic (*praśrabdhi*) queen
4. Striving (*vīrya*) magical horse
5. Deep Concentration (*samādhi*) elephant
6. Exultation (*prīti*) general
7. Mindfulness (*smṛti*) treasurer

The foregoing division clarifies the early Buddhist notion of what I render 'consignment'. It was especially a concern of 'right views' as the foundation of the 'Noble Path', and then especially a matter of 'right effort'. In Mahāyāna Buddhism, the topic was especially treated under Perfection of Giving.

The Position in the Bodhisattva Section

Tsong-kha-pa treating the Bodhisattva's first Perfection, that of Giving (*dāna*), cites Śāntideva's *Caryāvatāra*, V, 9-10:[26]

> If the Perfection of Giving is in making the world wealthy—and the world is today impoverished—how could former saviors have had that Perfection? The Perfection of Giving has been explained as the mind of abandoning to all people everything, together with the fruits. Hence that (Perfection) is precisely the mind (of that abandoning).

The Tibetan author explains: "Hence, the path-procedure of the Perfection of Giving is not the giving of materials to others in a concrete sense: it is the volition of giving, with the giving generated in many directions and in ever increasing measure."[27] This means that whether or not there is a concrete giving, the main thing is the volition of giving. Otherwise, there could be the situation of giving without really wanting to give, which is surely not counted as Perfection of Giving! Tsong-kha-pa introduces that citation from the *Caryāvatāra* by saying: "Accordingly, one should cut off the covetous grasping towards body, possessions, and roots of virtues as all belonging to one's own wealth; and should tie one's resolve to others and give those away. And that is not all: Also the fruits are renounced, because the Perfection of Giving arises from the complete making part of one's nature the mentality of consignment to sentient beings."[28] Tsong-kha-pa refers to various disputes about the meaning. Some persons claimed that if one believes that one's apparent possessions really belong to others, but meanwhile uses them as one sees fit, this amounts to a defiled fall. Tsong-kha-pa follows the position of Śāntideva's *Śikṣāsamuccaya* which states:[29]

> But if one thinks that one's embodiment is the servant of sentient beings and it is protected by usages as a servant of sentient beings, there is no fault. For a servant always busy with the master's work (*karma*) does not own what he/she busies oneself with.

Tsong-kha-pa explains that passage with the illustration: "The person who thinks, 'I am making use of what belongs to that sentient being, and thus perform his aim,' incurs no fault in so practicing."[30] Besides, what is called "the lustre of consignment" is one of the six "lustres" which Tsong-kha-pa includes according to the explanations in Asaṅga's *Mahāyāna-saṃgraha*.[31] These six turn out to be the way in which all six Perfections of Mahāyāna Buddhism are taken as fractions of a given one of the six. Thus, the Perfection of Giving has among its six fractions (those of Giving, Morality, Forbearance, Striving, Meditation, and Insight) the 'lustre' of consignment, defined as the consignment of virtues given away for complete enlightenment; and explained as the meditation (fifth Perfection) which, "by a single-area thought having nothing in common with the lower vehicle, consigns the virtues, for complete enlightenment".[32] In short, this theory of consignment, emphasizing the mind that has the resolve of giving away is further clarified by the information that this kind of mind is meditational, i.e. the person is in a kind of *samādhi*. In the tradition of the Pure Land School of China and Japan, according to the commentary on the *Sukhāvatī-vyūha*, the *samādhi* has fractions of both Meditation and Insight by requiring both *śamatha* (calming the mind) and *vipaśyanā* (discerning the real).[33] This is the commentary by a Vasubandhu, who is probably a little earlier in time than the Vasubandhu who is the brother of Asaṅga.

Returning to the Bodhisattva section, a further consideration is that the various stories illustrative of the Perfection of Giving, such as those in Ārya-Śūra's *Jātakamālā*, show that the giver must try to meet the requests of supplicants, But then, sometimes such requests could be for items which it is not lawful to give, for example, the monk's religious garments. The Bodhisattva is supposed to use skillful means to fend off such requests. Tsong-khapa shows such a procedure:

> At the beginning, the Bodhisattva consigns with a pure resolve all his property to the Buddhas and Bodhisattvas of the ten directions. Just as, for example, a monk having considered the religious garments and so on, consigns them to the teacher and his disciples, who wear them. Because of consigning that way, the property accumulates, and the 'Bodhisattva living in the Noble Family' increases his merit unfathomably. Thereby, those property items are held as though in trust by the Buddhas and Bodhisattvas. If a solicitating person comes, one should give the property item to that person, if it is lawful to do so, thinking, 'There is no property not given to the sentient beings by the Buddhas and Bodhisattvas,' and give it. And if it is not lawful to do so, using his consideration he should consign it ritually to those (Buddhas and Bodhisattvas); and based thereon, one should inform (that petitioner) with mild words, 'O dear one, this belongs to others, so it cannot be given to you.'[34]

The above passage clarifies that this practice did not necessarily involve an actual transfer of anything—although of course it could; and clarifies that the frequent present-day rendition of 'dedication' does not get at the meaning. It was believed that this feature not only increases the 'roots of virtue' but protects the stock of goods from unlawful requests. It thus becomes an essential ingredient of what is called 'skillful means'. So far the only rendition that seems to work in such contexts is 'consignment'.

In the preceding part, the discussion of this term *pariṇāmana* and its meaning took place as a topic under the Perfection of Giving (*dāna-pāramitā*). I have found a different kind of inclusion in the theory of the four Persuasions (*saṃgraha-vastūni*), which are in Mahāyāna Buddhism the means of benefitting others. They are (1) Giving, which is the same as Perfection of Giving; (2) Pleasant speech; (3) Aim inducement; and (4) Common pursuits, which is one's own conformity. It was under this fourth one that long ago I noticed in the *Bodhisattvapiṭaka-sūtra* near its end the explanation, "'Common pursuits' is consignment to the Mahāyāna."[35] This is consistent with Tsong-kha-pa's information in treating this fourth one near the end of his Bodhisattva section: "In this case, those who have newly entered and those who have already entered, will be steadfast in not backsliding."[36] If such words go with the theory of entering the Bodhisattva path, they implicate a usage of 'consignment' as creating a Mahāyāna family. Perhaps with the same meaning, Tsong-kha-pa in an auto-biographical sketch called *Mdun legs ma* showing how he mastered the Buddhist texts, writes: "The third phase, taking into experience throughout day and night, and consignment of all for the sake of spreading the Teaching, was completed."[37] While agreeing that all his personal attainment can be consigned to others, in fact it is the author's actual composition that constitutes the 'consignment'.

In short, this 'consignment' is basically in the mind of the performer where it seems to agree with the old Buddhist category of 'right views' (*samyag-dṛṣṭi*), and then involves others with a kind of 'right effort' or in Mahāyāna language, a fraction of striving (*vīrya*).

Commentary on the Bhadracaryā

The treatment here concerns a list referred to in this literature as the 'seven members'. The *Dharma-saṃgraha*, list XIV, "The seven kinds of highest worship" (*saptavidhānuttarapūjā*), presents them as praise (*vandanā*), offering (*pūjanā*), confession of sins (*pāpadeśanā*), sympathetic joy (*anumodanā*), asking for instruction (*adhyeṣanā*), arousing the Thought of Enlightenment (*bodhicittotpāda*), and consignment (to another) (*pariṇāmanā*).[38] This list appears to stem from the celebrated verse set called the *Bhadracaryā*, which concludes the Mahāyāna scriptural collection *Avataṃsaka*. In 1958 the International Academy of Indian Culture, New Delhi, published the edition by Sushma Devi of the *Samantabhadracaryā-praṇidhānarāja* with other Asian equivalents, such as Tibetan; and concluded with a Sanskrit-Tibetan word list. This list shows that the Tibetan *bsngo ba* which regularly renders *pariṇāmana*, also renders the shorter form *nāmana*, while *bsngo* can render the verbal form *nāmayami*. This Sanskrit stem must be of the verb *nām-*, to bend, so here metaphorically, to bend to a different purpose. In 1961, the Namgyal Institute of Tibetology, Sikkim published the Sanskrit and Tibetan versions under the title *Āryabhadracaripraṇidhānarāja* with introduction and notes by Sunitikumar Pathak. In 1963, the Namgyal Institute of Tibetology published the Tibetan work Lcang skya Khutukhtu Lalitavajra's Commentary on the Samantabhadracaryāpraṇidhānarāja, edited with an Introduction by Lokesh Chandra. Besides the foregoing, I also have Professor Ferdinand Lessing's typescript translation of the text also taking into account the Chinese and Mongolian versions. I do not have now the essay of Peter Asmussen, "The Khotanese Bhadracaryādeśanā," apparently a thorough study, published in 1961 in Denmark.

There are five Tanjur commentaries on the *Bhadracaryā*.[39] But here I use the native Tibetan commentary, above mentioned, by the Lcang skya Khutukhtu. He explains the seventh member, 'consignment' as "consignment of the roots of virtue". The second half of his commentary is an analysis of one of the Indian commentaries that of Dignāga.[40] In the case of 'consignment' sixteen kinds are set forth: (1) purification of resolve; (2) not forgetting the Mind of Enlightenment; (3) untainted practice; (4) benefit to the sentient beings; (5) attiring in armor; (6) consorting with Bodhisattvas of like good fortune; (7) pleasing the spiritual guides (*kalyāṇamitra*); (8) facing the Tathāgatas; (9) embracing the Illustrious Dharma; (10) gaining the inexhaustible store; (11-15) entering power(s), operating with the adversary (to defilement), works (*karma*), understudy; (16) compilation (*saṃgraha*). Some of these are described with further sub-varieties. It would take too much space to present these minutely. Enough will be presented to clarify the terminology.

1. Purification of resolve,[41] is shown by three verses of the *Bhadracaryā*:

> (1) As many as be the lions of men as exist in the past, present, and future in the ten quarters of the universe, all of them without exception I revere in purity with body, speech, and mind.
>
> (2) I bow to all the Victors (*jina*) by the power of the Bhadracaripraṇidhāna (vow of auspicious conduct), with mind directly perceiving all the Victors, while bowing with body as many times as be the sands of the (Buddha) fields.
>
> (9) Whatever the merit (*puṇya*) in the ten quarters of the universe, whether of the moving beings (*jagat*), of those in training (*śaikṣa*), those beyond training (*aśaikṣa*), self-victors (*pratyekajina*), (Bodhisattva) sons of the Buddha, or of all the Jinas (=Buddhas), I rejoice in all (of that merit).

2. The wish to not forget the Mind of Enlightenment,[42] has six

parts: The first, the wish to remember former lives; and the second, the wish to (again) be a monk, constitute the first cause for not forgetting the Mind of Enlightenment:

> (16) As I practice the *bodhi*-career, may I recall the lives in all the destinies. In each of my lives, dying and being reborn, let me always become a monk.

The third, the wish to not violate morality is the second cause for not forgetting the Mind of Enlightenment:

> (17) May I emulate all the Victorious Ones, completely fulfilling the good conduct. May I always course in the practice of morality that is unbroken and unflawed.

The fourth, to teach the Dharma with the diverse languages of living beings is the third cause for not forgetting the Mind of Enlightenment:

> (18) I shall teach the Dharma in all languages—the language of the devas and the nāgas, the language of the yakṣas, kumbhaṇḍas, and humans; in however many the voices of all living beings.

The fifth, the wish to enterprise the six Perfections with a pliable (*peśala*) stream of consciousness is the fourth cause for not forgetting the Mind of Enlightenment:

> (19A) When one is pliable (or, adaptable), enterprising the Perfections, the Mind of Enlightenment is never forgotten.[43]

The sixth, the wish to eliminate the hindrance of sin, is the wish to avoid the discordant side to arousing the Mind of Enlightenment:

> (19B) Whatever sinful hindrances there are, may they all be completely destroyed.

3. Untainted practice,[44] is shown by one verse:

> (20) May I practice in the destinies of the world free from *karma*, defilement, and the acts of Māra, like the lotus, which is not adhered to by the water; and like the sun and moon, which are not hindered in the sky.

Skipping down, 8. wish to face the Tathāgatas,[45] is the wish to meet and to please the best Nirmāṇakāya:

> (25) May I constantly behold face to face all the Victorious Ones surrounded by the Sons of the Buddhas. May I do munificent homage to them untiringly in all future eons.

No. 11, Entering,[46] is of eight kinds. Of these, the first two are the beholding and then the entering into Buddha fields:

> (28) May I, practicing in the career of enlightenment, behold on a single grain of dust as many fields as there are grains of dust; and in each field inconceivably many Buddhas seated in the middle (i.e. surrounded by) the Sons of the Buddhas. (29) So may I, within a single tip of hair, enter and move through oceans of Buddhas, oceans of fields, and oceans of eons to the whole extent of all the ten quarters of the universe and in all three times.

Enough of those *Bhadracaryā* verses have been cited along with commentarial explanation to give a fair idea of the contribution of this tradition to the theory of *pariṇāmana*. I believe that the rendition 'consignment' holds up throughout these discussions; that is to say, if what is ordinarily considered to be the self or to belong to the self, namely, one's body, speech, and mind, can be consigned to this purpose of enlightenment. Thus, this search for the 'true self' is perhaps the true meaning of the Buddhist teaching of 'non-self'.

The Akṣayamatinirdeśa-sūtra

The *Akṣayamatinirdeśa-sūtra* is a topic amounting to eighty *akṣaya* ('inexhaustibles'). In the Chinese Buddhist canon, it is included in the *Mahāsaṃnipāta* collection. In the Tibetan canon, it is among the miscellaneous *sūtras* in the Kanjur, and besides has a commentary in the Tanjur, that is dubiously attributed to Vasubandhu. For both the scripture and its commentary, I employ the Peking version of the Tibetan canon.[47]

In a survey of the scripture, I noticed references to 'consignment' in seven of the *akṣaya*, namely, in No. 3, praxis (*prayoga*); No. 5, giving (*dāna*); No. 8, striving (*vīrya*); No. 10, insight (*prajñā*); No. 18, knowledge of remembering previous lives (*pūrvanivāsānusmṛtijñāna*); among the four Persuasions, No. 23, common pursuits (*samānārthatā*); No. 32, collection of merit (*puṇya-sambhāra*). I may have overlooked some, but the ones found should suffice for information from this scripture.

I. *The passage in 'Praxis'*: In a list of four kinds of "unsatiated praxis", the fourth kind is the praxis unsatiated (*atṛpta*) with realizing the consignment to enlightenment. The commentary explains it as the praxis of "skill in the means" (*upāya-kauśalya*); and that the skill of consigning all the roots of virtue to the incomparable enlightenment is the "realizing the consignment to enlightenment". Also, that having consigned that way, even if the root of virtue be small, there is no intermediate state up to attaining the incomparable enlightenment. And the commentator refers to the passage given under III, below.[48]

II. *The passages in 'Perfection of Giving'*: There is no gift (*dāna*) without consignment to the mind (*citta*) of omniscience (*sarvajñatā*). The commentary explains that there is no consignment for the sake of (more) property; that when one has completed the collection of giving, there is no consigning except to omniscience—that is the meaning of the scripture text.[49] The scripture also states: One consigns the gift to the non-construct realm (*anabhisaṃskṛta*). The commentary explains the 'non-construct' as the true end (*bhūtakoṭi*), the *dharma* not arisen by cause and condition; and one so consigns in order to attain that realm.[50] And the scripture states: That gift is the right consignment. The commentary explains "right consignment" as the consignment there, where one should consign.[51]

III. *The passages in 'Perfection of Striving'*: "There is no loss of the root of virtue that has been consigned to enlightenment until one is seated at the precincts of enlightenment (*bodhimaṇḍa*). In the same way, your honor Śaradvatīputra, there is no loss of a water drop fallen in the great ocean up to the end of the eon."[52]

IV.. *The passages in 'Perfection of Insight'*: Under the large treatment of *prajña pāramitā* there, is a section on *prajña*'s eight objects. No. 6 is "skill in the three times": The remembrance (*anusmṛti*) of the virtuous thoughts (*citta*) and mental concomitants (*caitasika*); and having remembered them, the consignment to enlightenment—this is skill in the past. The anticipation (*nidhyapti*) of future roots of virtue and the *karma*-attentiveness (=virtuous *cetanā*) directed to enlightenment, to wit, "Whatever the virtuous thought-generations that will occur for me, I shall consign to the incomparable right complete enlightenment"—this is skill in the future.[53] The *sūtra* does not include the term *pariṇāmana* for "skill in the present", explained as the methodical practice with thoughts and mentals concomitants, discriminating between the virtuous and the unvirtuous ones—the warding off of the unvirtuous ones, etc.[54] According to the commentary, the *karma*-attentiveness of consigning to enlightenment shows that there is no consigning toward the 'good destinies' (*sugati*) of gods and men.[55]

V. *The passages in 'Remembering Previous Lives'*: Remembering one's own root of virtue and the root of virtue of other sentient beings along with the (respective) causes from which they arose; and having remembered one's own root of virtue, one consigns it to enlightenment.[56] Also in present time, even for one's life, one would not do what shouldn't be done and consign the former roots of virtue to enlightenment.[57] Also, one's presently arisen roots of virtue, one consigns as shared with all sentient beings.[58] One purifies the consigning that is discordant with oneself, [to wit] one consigns so as not to interrupt the lineage of the Buddha, the lineage of the Dharma, the lineage of the Saṅgha, and for omniscience.[59] The commentary construes this non-interruption of the Three Jewels as not consigning for birth as a *śrāvaka*, a *pratyekabuddha*, or among the gods or men.[60]

VI. *The passages in the Persuasion of Common Pursuits*: When there is the mind (*citta*) possessed of equanimity (*upekṣā*) without (discriminating) high and low, there should be the mind consigning to omniscient knowledge (*sarvajña-jñāna*). When one gives the gift of Dharma, one should rightly engage and consign (the gift) to the incomparable right complete enlightenment.[61]

VII. *The passages in the Collection of Merit*: The scripture poses the question. What is the Bodhisattva's inexhaustible collection of merit? There follows a long list in which there is the item: consignment to enlightenment of the entreated collected roots of virtue, with accompanying meritorious entities.[62] The commentary on the item partially clarifies, namely, that one should have sympathetic joy in the roots of virtue of others and should preach the Dharma at others' entreaty or exhortation; that it is the resultant collection of roots of virtue that one consigns for attaining the incomparable enlightenment, and which is said to have accompanying merits.[63]

Definitely, the above scriptural passages do advance the topic of consignment.

VIMALAMITRA'S COMMENTARY ON THE SAPTAŚATIKĀ

So far there has been set forth various types of consigning. The *Prajñāpāramitā* scripture approach has a limitation on this activity, as is noticed by Vimalamitra in his commentary on the half portion of the *Saptaśatikā* that is available in Sanskrit. Vaidya mostly copies Masuda's edition.[64] Vimalamitra's cited passage is in Vaidya, p. 342, 2nd half page. In the scripture the Buddha asks Mañjuśrī a question: When he contemplates the Perfection of Insight do his 'roots of virtue' increase or decrease? And Mañjuśrī responds that at that time they neither increase nor decrease.[65] And a few lines later, Mañjuśrī points out that it is a contemplation of the Perfection of Insight when one neither rejects the natures (*dharma*) of the ordinary person (*pṛthagjana*) nor gains Buddha natures.[66]

Vimalamitra's commentary is employed in the Peking Tanjur edition (photo. ed.). Previously, we had noticed that there is a manner of 'consigning' that greatly increases one's merit.[67] It must be with this thought in mind that Vimalamitra states: "Now should be mentioned the consigning to enlightenment of giving and the other (Perfections), so that all those who have entered (the vehicle) may gain what they wish for and avoid what they do not wish for. And this consigning to enlightenment of giving and the other (Perfections) is so that one may attain Buddhahood and drop off the condition of an ordinary person. Accordingly, one should imagine it."[68] Vimalamitra continues pointing out, when one contemplates the Perfection of Insight, no natures arise.[69] It follows that this teaching about 'consignment' of Perfection is only the case when one is not contemplating the Perfection of Insight.

To validate his commentarial remarks, Vimalamitra cites a series of verses without mentioning the source. They happen to be in the *Abhisamayālaṃkāra*, Chap. II, which has several allusions to *pariṇāmana*, Vimalamitra's citation concludes with these two verses:[70]

> *nirvāṇagrāhaśāntatvaṃ buddhebhyo rakṣaṇādikam /*
> *aprāṇivadham ārabhya sarvākārajñatānaye* //15//
> *svayaṃsthitasya sattvānāṃ sthāpanaṃ pariṇāmanam /*
> *dānadīnāṃ ca saṃbodhāv iti mārgajñatākṣaṇāḥ* //16//[71]
>
> The moments (16 in number) in supernal realization of the Path, namely, ... (13) the peacefulness of seizing Nirvāṇa; (14) the protection, etc. by all the Buddhas; (15) the maintenance

> of oneself who after starting with non-killing (and the other layman vows) had become fixed in the way of knowing all the modes and maintenance of sentient beings (who after starting with the layman vows, also in the way of knowing all the modes); (16) the consignment of the (five) Perfections, beginning with Giving, to Complete Enlightenment.

It appears from Obermiller's published researches that all 16 are a kind of subsequent realization; hence the *pṛṣṭhalabdhajñāna* (wisdom subsequently obtained). They succeed the four '*nirvedha-bhāgīya*' of the Path of Praxis.[72] Besides, right after Vimalamitra gave the verses for the sixteen 'moments', he says in agreement with the previous citation of the commentary on the *Sukhāvatī-vyūha* that—"One should understand those (i.e. the sixteen) as 'limits of the entity' (Tib. *dngos po'i mtha*'; Skt. *vastu-paryantatā*) in terms of meditative objects for 'calming' (*śamatha*) and 'discerning' (*vipaśyanā*)."[73] By 'limits of the entity' is meant the phenomenal and the noumenal limits.[74] This theory of two limits for each authorized meditative object is basic to the *Saptaśatikā* where the noumenal end is the true limit (*bhūtakoṭi*) and the phenomenal end is the imputed self or the five personality aggregates. It must be at the noumenal end that there is no arising. It follows that consignment must take place at the phenomenal end.

According to Vimalamitra, the *Saptaśatikā* here expounds the 'Path of Vision' (*darśana-mārga*),[75] which in the formulation of ten Bodhisattva stages is held to be equivalent to the first Bodhisattva stage. While Giving, the first of the Perfections, is held to be predominant on the first stage, the other Perfections are there fractionally. According to Tsong-kha-pa's *Gser phreng,* his great commentary on the *Abhisamayālaṃkāra,* the consignment listed as the sixteenth moment has to be last of all, because there must already be the cause of omniscience by dint of resorting to the 'mother' *prajñāpāramitā* with the desire of becoming enlightened and after installing oneself in the cause installing other candidates therein. Then, given a desire to render inexhaustible the virtue-roots of Giving and the other Perfections, and by dint of mindfulness (*smṛti*) and friendliness (*maitrī*), one may consign the Perfections, and so on, to the right complete enlightenment.[76] It follows that this sort of consignment is the culmination of the first Bodhisattva *bhūmi*. It also follows that the old definition of the 'roots of virtue' in terms of three lacks, which had been credited with positive content, was now enlarged to include the first five Perfections.

The Right and the Wrong Way to Consign

The Tibetan author Bu-ston, in his small treatise "Explaining the distinct powers (*guṇa*) of *pariṇāmana*" (in his collected works, Vol. 26, or LA), says that 'consignment' can apply to vices as well as to virtues: "When consigning, a hating person would consign for the purpose of harm to his enemy; a craving person would consign for the purpose of obtaining a craved object" (*bsngo ba na/ zhe sdang can dgra bo la gnod pa'i don du bsngo/ chags pa can chags yul thob pa'i don du bsngo ba*). And, referring to virtuous roots, "One should consign for the sake of all sentient beings" (*sems can thams cad kyi don du bsngo dgos te*).

Bu-ston cited an early work of the *Prajñāpāramitā* literature called *Ratnaguṇasañcaya-gāthā*. This scripture considers right and wrong consignment in Chap. VI, 5-9, which I shall therefore present together with my translation:[77]

> *pariṇāmayantu yadi vartati cittasamjñā*
> *tatha bodhisaṃjñā-pariṇāmana-sattvasaṃjñā/*
> *saṃjñāya dṛṣṭisthitu citta tisaṃgayukto*
> *pariṇāmitaṃ na bhavatī upalabhyamānam //5//*
>
> If when consigning there should be notions (*saṃjñā*) in the mind, to wit: (1) the notion of enlightenment [as the object to attain], (2) consignment [as the procedure], (3) notion of a sentient being [doing it]—while one has (such) notions, the mind stays in 'views', clinging to the three.[78] Apprehending [in that manner], consignment does not take place.
>
> *saci eva jānati nirudhy imi kṣīṇadharmā*
> *taṃ caiva kṣīṇu pariṇāmyiṣyāmi yatra/*
> *na ca dharmu dharmi pariṇāmayate kadācit*
> *pariṇāmitaṃ bhavati eva prajānamāne //6//*
>
> As one who realizes that the dharmas ceasing, come to an end; then in whatever I consign, that also comes to an end,[79] nor is ever a dharma consigned to a dharma[80]—then when wisely considering that way, it is (indeed) consigned.

> *saci so nimitta kurute na sa mānayāti*
> *atha ānimitta pariṇāmita bhoti bodhāu /*
> *viṣasṛṣṭabhojanu yathaiva kriyā-praṇito*
> *tatha śukladharma upalambhu jinena ukto //7//*
>
> When one creates a 'sign' [of the hated, craved, or delusive object], there is no consigning [in the present sense]. But when there is the 'signless', one (indeed) consigns to enlightenment. The Jina has declared that (the former case) is just like taking the food-mixed with poison to be good to eat and that (the latter case) depends on pure dharmas.
>
> *tasmā hu nāma pariṇāmana śikṣitavyā*
> *yatha te jinā kuśala eva prajānayanti/*
> *yaj jātiyo ya prabhavo yadlakṣaṇaṃ ca*
> *anumodamī tatha tathā pariṇāmayāmi //8//*
>
> Hence, thus should one train in a consigning, as the Victors wisely consider its class, its origin, and its character to be virtuous (*kuśala*). Just as I sympathetically rejoice, so do I consign.
>
> *evaṃ ca puṇya pariṇāmayamāna bodhāu*
> *api so na buddhu kṣipate jina-uktavādī/*
> *yāvanti loki upalambika bodhisattvā*
> *abhibhonti sarva pariṇāmayamāna śūro //9//*
>
> And thus consigning merit to enlightenment, the one who repeats the words of the Jina does not reject the Buddha. As many the Bodhisattvas who overcome the world while remaining in it, they are the hero consigning all.

This particular scripture does use the term 'merit' (*puṇya*) as the substance of the consignment, implicating the enlargement of the 'roots of virtue' to include the "collection of merit" (*puṇya-sambhāra*). Bu-ston, in that small essay on *pariṇāmana*, when citing the *Sañcaya-gāthā*, VI. 7 (translated above), also cites the *25,000 Prajñāpāramitā* to similar effect.

Those verses of the *Sañcayagāthā* seem to be a development based on Chap. 6 of the *Aṣṭasāhasrikā Prajñāpāramitā*, which is entitled *Anumodanā-pariṇāmanā* (Sympathetic rejoicing and Consignment). The first paragraph of this chapter declares that the 'given thing' (*vastu*) of meritorious work (*puṇyakriyā*) consisting of Sympathetic rejoicing and Consignment of a Bodhisattva Mahāsattva is superior to the 'given thing' of meritorious work consisting of giving (*dāna*), morality (*śīla*), and [other] cultivation (*bhāvanā*) of all the sentient beings.[81] Hence, this scripture may well be the first in Mahāyāna Buddhism to associate the theory of merit by the word *puṇya* with the theory of consignment.

A Note on Śāntideva's Tenth Chapter

Previously the data was drawn from Buddhist scriptures and sometimes from commentary thereon. When we look at Śāṇtideva's *Bodhicaryāvatāra* written after the *Mahāyāna-sūtra* corpus was complete, we notice that he names his last chapter, the tenth, Pariṇāmanā.[82] The language of his verses follows the lead of the *Bhadracaryā* and the placement of the chapter follows the position of the *Abhisamayālaṃkāra* exegesis of the Prajñāpāramitā. As to the style of language, it is the verbal declaration, in fact 'aspiration' (*adhyāśaya*); and the placement right after the Prajñāpāramitā, the ninth chapter, agrees with our pervious information that consignment is the sixteenth 'moment' following the resort to the 'mother' Prajñāpāramitā as the cause of omiscience and then aspiring to install other candidates in that cause. Śāntideva's chapter is written at a time when the 'roots of virtue' had been expanded to include the 'collection of merit' (*puṇya-sambhāra*), so he can refer either to 'merit' or to 'virtue' (*kuśala*) in the situation of consignment. All the verses of this tenth chapter are of this type; so verse 1:[83]

> Whatever good thing is mine from thinking out this Entrance to the Career of Enlightenment (Bodhicaryāvatāra), by it may all creatures be ornaments of the career of enlightenment.

Śāntideva's way of talking makes salient the Buddhist theory of *karma*. In the Mahāyāna theory of the Bodhisattva, he is disallowed to think that the sufferings of the sentient beings are their 'retribution' for past sins.[84] Thus he resolves to relieve their sufferings—as though he could do it. As I have elsewhere pointed out, suffering is due to varied causes; there are those within one's own power to evade, and those outside of one's control. There are sufferings due to one's heedlessness, and suffering by virtue of having been born.[85] But as one reads Śāntideva's tenth chapter, one can gather that the Bodhisattva is not thinking in terms of Buddhist *abhidharma* classifications of suffering. It is as though by virtue of his aspirations, the sentient beings could be relieved of their sufferings, no matter what caused their sufferings. While it is true that despite the Bodhistatva's aspirations to help the sentient beings, perhaps, many would not be helped—this does not matter for the aspirations, since when such aspirations are accompanied by skillful means, some, perhaps many, would be helped. Thus, it is claimed that the practice of 'consignment' does work; and the Bodhisattva must practice on the basis that it works, whether or not it does.

Indeed, it is not only the Bodhisattva in the formal sense of taking the 'mind of enlightenment' and so forth, but also it is the Buddhist practice at all times. For example, the emphasis on medical remedies in Buddhist monasteries had a premise that it could help persons, i.e., their illness was not a retribution, a *karma* fruit for which nothing could be done. Even if it be conceded that some illnesses are due to one's sins, the physician cannot be expected to have the supernormal faculty of knowledge of other persons' minds to detect this situation. So he must present remedies on the theory that they might help persons over their illness; and if such remedies do not 'work' then perhaps some other remedies would 'work'. And if, despite his intelligent attempts to cure someone's illness, if he does not succeed, this does not prove that the illness was a retribution.

CONCLUSION

We notice that this topic of *pariṇāmana* is traceable to early Buddhist scriptures, although authoritative writers on Sinhalese Buddhism did not recognize the importance of the *dvandva* expression found in the Saṃyutta and in the Dīgha of the Pāli canon. Here, 'right views' and 'right effort' among the members of the eightfold noble path are the main places for the discussion.

In Mahāyāna Buddhism, the practice of 'consignment' becomes a way of approaching 'non-self' (anātman) through 'non-self-belonging' (*anātmīya*). One of the surprising results of collecting this material is the evident use of the term to apply to verbal declarations, such as those in the *Bhadracaryā* and in Śāntideva's tenth chapter of his treatise. The verbal part also was expressed as "sympathetic rejoicing" (*anumodanā*).

The main content of the 'consignment' according to these texts is the 'roots of virtue' (*kuśala-mūla*), initially defined by three 'lacks', in Pāli Buddhism given positive content, and later in Mahāyāna Buddhism expanded to include the accumulated 'merit' (*puṇya*). To have the "roots of virtue" in their minimal form is what any good parent, whether in the animal or human kingdoms, would have in order to take care of the young. Thus, simply to have them is not noteworthy. The Mahāyāna aim is to expand these 'roots', so that they apply to all the sentient beings.

In particular, the commentary on the *Akṣayamatinirdeśa-sūtra* on the passage in 'praxis' has the remarkable hint that the way to control one's rebirth on the way to incomparable enlightenment is by this very consignment, i.e., attaining the self without possessions.

Thus, the present writer joins others, who have found this topic worthy of writing about.[86]

REFERENCES

1. This work has been published by State University of New York Press with date of 1991 in their Buddhist series.
2. Cf. Ananda K. Coomaraswamy and I.B. Horner, *Gotama the Buddha* (London, 1948), p. 5.
3. The present essay cannot concern itself with the Buddhist teaching of "non-self". However, it may be worth mentioning a conversation some years ago with H.H. the Dalai Lama in Dharamsala, H.P., India. We were talking about "non-self". He laughed and exclaimed: "If there is no person, who would practice Buddhist meditation?" Otherwise stated, when one has the worldly clinging, one is in the state of "non-self"; when one is practicing Buddhist meditation, one is the person so doing, and is seeking the true self.
4. The Peking Tibetan canon (PTT), Vol. 114, p. 238-3-1; and cf. Shoryu Katsura, "A Synopsis of the Prajñāpāramitopadeśa of Ratnākaraśānti, "*JIBS,* XXV, No. 1, Dec, 1976, pp. 484-7.
5. Cf. Michael Hahn, *Nāgārjuna's Ratnāvalī,* Vol. 1 (Bonn, 1982), for the extant verse: *na bodhisattvapraṇidhir na caryāpariṇāmanā / uktāḥ śrāvakayāne 'smād bodhisattvaḥ kutas tataḥ //*
6. G.P. Malalasekera, " 'Transference of Merit' in Ceylonese Buddhism," *Philosophy East and West,* XVII, 1-4, pp. 85-90.
7. For the story in English translation, see *The Minor Anthologies of the Pāli Canon,* Part IV; Vimāna Vatthu and Peta Vatthu, tr. by Jean Kennedy and Henry S. Gehman, respectively, Ed: Mrs. Rhys Davids (London, 1942), pp. 194-6.
8. The monk (p. 195 of the translation) in fact was an elder named Kaṅkhārevata, sitting for his midday rest on the bank of the Ganges.
9. Malalasekera, p. 85.

10. Malalasekera, pp. 85-6.
11. Richard Gombrich, " 'Merit Transference' in Sinhalese Buddhism: A Case Study of the Interaction between Doctrine and Practice, "*History of Religions,* 11:2, 1971, pp. 203-19.
12. Gombrich, pp. 204-5.
13. Gombrich, p. 207.
14. T.W. and C.A.F. Rhys Davids, *Dialogues of the Buddha,* Part II (London, 1959), p. 94.
15. Helmer Smith, *Saddanīti,* V.1 (Lund, 1954), Tables, 2nd Part, p. 1238.
16. I use the edition of the *Dīghanikāya* in the Nālandā-Devanāgarī-series; here 2. Mahā Vagga, publ. 1958, p. 71.
17. Cf. A. Wayman, "The Hindu-Buddhist Rite of Truth—an Interpretation, *Studies in Indian Linguistics*(Poona, 1968), pp. 365-9. This essay was reprinted in *Buddhist Insight; Essays by Alex Wayman* (Delhi, 1984).
18. There is considerable material on the two kinds of 'collections' in the text which A. Wayman, "A Prajñāpāramitā-type scripture within a Tantra," includes in *Śramaṇa Vidyā; Studies in Buddhism,* Ed: N.H. Samtani (Sarnath, Varanasi, 1987), pp. 287-303. (This is reprinted in the present volume).
19. Louis de La Vallée Poussin, *L'Abhidharmakośa de Vasubandhu,* Chap. II, p. 160.
20. Cf. Nyanatiloka, *Buddhist Dictionary* (Colombo, 1950), p. 90, pointing out that the three virtuous roots "though being negative in form, nevertheless possess a distinctly positive character, . . " and presenting the three positive attributions.
21. See in translation, *The Book of the Kindred Sayings,* Part I, tr. by Mrs. Rhys Davids (London, 1917), pp. 112-5. The setting is at the court of King Pasenadi (Skt. King Prasenajit). The Buddha repeats a former discussion with Ānanda.
22. Some years ago when the writer attended an orientalist meeting in San Francisco, a speaker stated that Nāgārjuna rejected all 'views'. In the question period, I challenged the speaker to tell where in Nāgārjuna's writings he had rejected the 'right views' of the eightfold path. The speaker was unable to respond. It seems that the nomenclature "all views" excludes "right views".
23. Curiously, Mrs. Rhys Davids heads the *sutta* with the title "Diligence (2)" instead of rendering the Pāli title, *Kalyāṇamittasutta.*
24. It is in a celebrated scripture of the Dīgha, the *Saṅgīti-sutta;* and therein under 'fourfold doctrines', viz., the theory of the four 'elimination-exertions' (Skt. *prahāṇa),* wherein the first is to avoid bad natures, the second to eliminate bad natures, the third to develop good natures and the fourth to preserve good natures. The term *vossagga-pariṇāmi* occurs under the third of these.
25. This way of correlating the seven jewels with the seven *bodhyaṅgas* (ancillaries of enlightenment) is found in a commentary ascribed to Buddhaguhya on the *sarvadurgatipariśodhana-tantra* (PTT edn. of Tibetan canon, Vol. 76, p. 288-1, 2).
26. *adaridraṃ jagat kṛtvā dānapāramitā yadi/jagad daridram adyāpi sā kathaṃpūrvatāyinām//phalena saha sarvasvatyāgacittāj jane 'khile/ dānapāramitā proktā tasmāt sā cittam eva tu//*
27. *Lam rim chen mo,* Tashilunpo edition, fol. 220b-4: */des na sbyin pa'i phar phyin gyi nyams len ni/* . . . See the work of n.1, above for the context.
28. *Lam rim chen mo,* Tashi ed., fol. 220b-1:*/'di ltar rang la bdog pa'i lus dang longs spyod dge rtsa thams cad* . . . See the work of n. 1, above for the context.
29. *Sikṣās.,* Vaidya ed., p. 79, 12-3: */sattvasvāmikais tu bhogaiḥ sattvasvāmika svātmabhāvaḥ saṃrakṣata ity adoṣaḥ/na hi dāsasya nityaṃ*

svāmikarmavyāvṛtasya svadravyam asti yena varteta/

30. *Lam rim chen mo*, Tashi ed., fol. 223 b-4: */ sems can kho rang gi longs spyod spyad la* . . See the work of n. 1, above for the context.
31. *Lam rim chen mo,* Tashi ed., fol. 224a-3, ff.
32. *Lam rim chen mo*, Tashi ed., fol. 224b-1,2: *theg dman dang ma 'dres pa'i sems rtse gcig pas dge ba de rdzogs byang du bsngo ba'i bsam gtan.*
33. *Amitāyus-Sūtropadeśa*, in *Selected Texts of Shin Buddhism* (Honpa Hongwanji, Kyoto Japan, 1953), p. 42.
34. *Lam rim chen mo*, Tashi ed., fol. 231b-4, ff.: *byang sems kyis dang po nas phyogs bcu'i sangs rgyas byang sems la yo byad* . . . See the work of n. 1 above for the context.
35. The Peking Tibetan canon (PTT), Vol. 23, p. 89-2-8: *don 'thun pa ni theg pa chen po la bsngo ba' o/*
36. *Lam rim chen mo*, Tashi ed., fol. 279a-4: *gsar du 'jug cing zhugs zin pa rnams kyang mi ldog par brtan par ' gyur bas.*
37. I have included this auto-biographical sketch in the introduction to the work of n. 1, above.
38. *The Dharma-Saṃgraha*, by Kenjiu Kasawara and F. Max Müller (reprint, New Delhi, 1981).
39. In the Tibetan canon, the five attributed authorships are those of Nāgārjuna, Vasubandhu, Dignāga, Ratnabhadra, and Śākyamitra.
40. This is the commentary *Samantabhadracaryā-praṇidhānārthasaṃgraha.*
41. *bsam pa rnam par dag pa*, in the 1963 Namgyal Institute publication p. 30.
42. *byang chub kyi sems mi brjed pa'i lam*, Namgyal, p. 32.
43. I follow the numbering in *Āryabhadracaripraṇidhānarāja* (Namgyal Institute of Tibetology, Gangtok, Sikkim, 1961), where the first words were corrupted. The edition of Sushama Devi, numbering this v. 20, is correct; *peśalu pāramitāsv abhiyukto bodhiyi citta ma jātu vimuhyet/*. The commentary states: " Besides, it is the wish to dwell in the good qualities of the family—it being explained that there are many good qualities of the Mahāyāna family" (*de yang rigs kyi yon tan la gnas par smon pa yin te / theg pa chen po' i rigs kyi yon tan mang du bshad*). Then the commentary mentions the chief thing for the "pliable stream of consciousness" is that it has a predominance of loving kindness (*gtso bo ni byams brtse shas che ba'i rang rgyud' jam pa*).
44. *ma gos pa'i sbyor ba,* 1963. Namgyal, p. 33.
45. *de bzhin gshegs pa mngon du gyur par smon pa*, 1963, Namgyal, p. 36.
46. *'jug pa,* 1963, Namgyal, p. 38.
47. For the structure of this Mahāyāna scripture, cf. Alex Wayman, "A Report on the *Akṣayamatinirdeśa-sūtra*," in *Studies in Indo-Asian Art and Culture*, ed. by Lokesh Chandra (New Delhi, 1980), pp. 211-32.
48. The *Akṣayamatinirdeśa-sūtra* is in vol. 34, Peking Tibetan canon, PTT edn.; commentary is in Vol. 104 of that canon, PTT edn. Here, Sūtra at p. 41-3-8 to 41-4-1; Comm. at p. 163-3-8 to 163-4-1, 2.
49. Sūtra, p. 43-2-6; Comm., p. 165-3-5, 6.
50. Sūtra, p. 43-2-8; Comm., p. 169-4-8 to 169-5-1.
51. Sūtra, p. 43-3-3; Comm., p. 169-5-8.
52. The passage is cited from the scripture by *Śikṣāsamuccaya*. Vaidya ed., p. 88-6-8:*/na hi bodhipariṇāmitasya kuśalamūlasyāntarā kaścit parikṣayo yāvad bodhimaṇḍaniṣadanāt/ tadyathāpi nāma bhadanta śāradvatīputra mahāsamudrapatitasyodakabindor nāntarāsti kṣayo yāvan na*

kalpaparyavasānaḥ //

53. The passage is cited from the scripture by *Śikṣāsamuccaya;* Vaidya ed., p. 22-19-22 (with a necessary correction):/ *kuśalānāṃ ca cittacaitasikānām anusmṛtir anusmṛtya ca bodhipariṇāmanā, idam atītakauśalyam/ yo 'nāgatānāṃ kuśalamūlanaṃ nidhyaptir bodher āmukhi-karma- samanvāhāraḥ, ye me utpatsyante kuśalās cittotpadāḥ, tān anuttarāyāṃ samyaksambodhāu pariṇamayiṣyāmīti, idam anāgatakauśalyam //* For *karma-samanvāhāra,* Tib. has *las sems te,* p. 54-5-2. See entry 'samanvāhāra' in Edgerton, *Buddhist Hybrid Sanskrit Dictionary*; here it is equivalent to *cetanā* (thinking-volition).
54. Sūtra, p. 54-5-4, 5.
55. Comm., p. 208-1-8.
56. Sūtra, p. 61-1-2, 3.
57. Sūtra, p. 61-1-8 to 61-2-1.
58. Sūtra, p. 61-2-1.
59. Sūtra, p. 61-2-1, 2.
60. Comm., p. 237-1-2.
61. Sūtra, p. 62-2-1, 2.
62. Sūtra, p. 65-1-7: / *gsol ba gdab pa' i dge ba'i rtsa ba bsags pa rnams byang chub tu bsngo ba dang ldan pa' i bsod rnams bya ba'i dngos po*
63. Comm., p. 249-3-1, 2, 3.
64. P. L. Vaidya includes the *Saptaśatikā* in his collection, *Mahāyāna-sūtra-saṃgraha* (Darbhanga, 1961), pp. 340-51.
65. *bhagavān āha—yasmiṇ samaye tvaṃ mañjuśrīḥ prajñāpāramitāṃ bhāvayasi, katarat [=kataraṃ] te kuśalamūlaṃ tasmin samaye upacayaṃ gacchati apacayaṃ vā? mañjuśrir āha—na me bhagavan tasmin samaye kiṃcit kuśalamūlam upacayaṃ gacchati apacayaṃ vā /*
66. *sā bhagavan prajñāpāramitābhāvanā yā naiva pṛthagjanadharmān jahāti, nāpi buddhadharmān upādatte?*
67. The passage with note 34, above.
68. PTT edn., Vol. 94, p. 176-3-3, 4: /*da ni sbyin pa la sogs pa byang chub tu yongs su bsngo ba brjod par bya ste / rab tu 'jug pa thams cad kyang 'dod pa dang mi 'dod pa thob pa dang yongs su spang ba' i ched yin la / sbyin la sogs pa byang chub tu yongs su bsngos pa 'di yang sangs rgyas nyid dang so so skye bo gnyis go rim bzhin du 'thob dang / yongs su spang ba'i ched yin no zhes de ltar rnam par rtog pa skye'o/.*
69. PTT edn., Vol. 94, p. 176-3-4, 5.
70. PTT edn. Vol. 94, p. 176-4-8 to 176-5-1.
71. Sanskrit from Th. Stcherbatsky and E. Obermiller, eds., *Abhisamayālaṃkāra-prajñāpāramitā-upadeśa-śāstra* (1970 reprint of 1929 edn.).
72. Cf. E. Obermiller, "The Doctrine of Prajñā-pāramitā as exposed in the Abhisamayālaṃkāra of Maitreya," *Acta Orientalia*, XI (reprint, 1932), pp. 37-41, on the *darśana-mārga* of the Bodhisattva saint.
73. PTT edn., Vol. 94, p. 176-5-1: / *de dag ni zhi gnas dang lhag mthong gi dmigs la dngos po'i mtha' yin par rig par bya'o/*
74. For these two limits, see Alex Wayman, tr., *Calming the Mind and Discerning the Real* (New York, 1978; or Indian reprint, Delhi, 1979), p. 105.
75. PTT. Vol. 94, p. 176-5-2.
76. The separately printed Dharamsala volume, *Bstan bcos mngon rtogs rgyan 'grel pa dang bcas pa'i rgya cher bshad pa legs bshad gser phreng,* 1970, p. 567.
77. For the Buddhist Sanskrit verses, there are the editions. (1) *Prajña-Pāramitā-*

Ratna-Guṇa-Sañcaya-Gāthā; Sankrit and Tibetan text, ed. by E. Obermiller; reprint with a Sanskrit-Tibetan-English index by Edward Conze (S-Gravenhage, 1960); (2) (same title), (Sanskrit Recension A), ed. by Akira Yuyama, along with a Tibetan version from Tunhuang (London, 1976) (3); a translation by Edward Conze (International Academy of Indian Culture, New Delhi, 1962)—but for the set now translated I do not accept Conze's renderings.

78. The three seem like the standard triad of giver (the sentient being), the gift (here the consignment), the recipient (here the object of consignment). The three are called *trimaṇḍala* (three spheres).
79. This remark agrees with my above conclusion that consignment takes place at the phenomenal limit.
80. Presumably, if a *dharma* can be consigned to a *dharma* this amounts to a positing of *dharma*-self. Mahāyāna Buddhism recommends realizing both the non-self of personality (*pudgala*) and of *dharma.*
81. I employ the edition by P.L. Vaidya, *Aṣṭasāhasrikā Prajñāpāramitā with Haribhadra's Commentary called Āloka* (Darbhanga, 1960). Edward Conze, in his translation of the scripture (The Asiatic Society, Calcutta, 1958), p. 43, rendition of first paragraph renders the term *anumodanā* as "rejoicing at the merit of others". Of course, this is an accepted interpretation, as was shown by my essay citing the *Akṣayamatinirdeśa-sūtra* and commentary for the passage in the "*Collection of Merit*". Nevertheless, the part "at the merit of others" should have been bracketed as an interpolation—which it is.
82. I employ the edition by P.L. Vaidya, *Bodhicaryāvatāra* (Darbhanga, 1960).
83. *bodhicaryāvatāraṃ me yad vicintayataḥ śubham / tena sarve janāḥ santu bodhicaryāvibhūṣaṇāḥ//*
84. I learned this from the Bodhisattva section, *Lam rim chen mo* (cf. n. 1, above), in the sub-section on Perfection of Giving, exposition of the varieties of "giving's bare nature", under a citation of the *Guṇāparyantastotra.*
85. So in my essay on Core Doctines, sub-section 'Suffering'.
86. Now there is the essay by Y. Krishan, "*Puṇyadāna* or transference of merit—a fiction," *Journal of Indian Council of Philosophical Research*, VII 2, Jan.- April, 1990, pp. 125-37, which refers to some further essays on the topic; and in fact, there are still others which he doesn't mention. I agree that in terms of *English words,* e.g. "transference of merit"—this is a fiction. But, *pariṇāmana* is not an English word. I claim that in terms of what that Indic word means—it is not a fiction.

SECTION V
HINDU-BUDDHIST STUDIES

na jalāt samam anyat syān nānyad vātāt pramā bhavet/
nānyad dūraṃ bhramād ūrdhvan nāṅyat sūtrād ṛjur bhavet//

Kātyāyana Śulba Sūtra

There is nothing so uniform as water... Nothing so creative as wind... Nothing so far flung or so elevated as error... Nothing so correct as measuring cord.

20

The Three Worlds, Vedic and Buddhist

The Vedic Three Worlds in Early and Later Times

Readers of Indian literature frequently see the expression 'three worlds' sometimes as the epithet of a god, as 'Protector of the Three Worlds', or perhaps a cliche in poetry, as 'Honored of the three worlds'. Thus, there is a general awareness among such readers of this basic division in Indian cosmogony. The details, when one delves into the relevant texts, become revelatory of Indian religion, especially of its mythological side. The three have been referred to by various names throughout the history of the Indic language, starting from Old Indic of the Vedic language, at the latest 1000 B.C. For a summary of the Vedic theories of the world and its origin, see Macdonell.[1]

NAMES AND SYMBOLIC COLORS OF THE THREE WORLDS

Sky and earth amount to a pair with intermediate space added in between. The intermediate region is usually called *antarikṣa.* V.K. Rajavade says while annotating his edition of Yāska's *Nirukta* (p. 342): '*Antari* may be the loc. sing. of *antar; kṣa=kṣeti=nivasati*; the aerial region dwells (*kṣa=kṣeti*) between (*antari*) heaven and earth; very likely this is the real derivation of *antarikṣa*.' In the basic pair, a frequent name for the sky is *Div*, for earth, *Pṛthivī*. According to the Vedas, the sky is a masculine deity, the earth the mother. The Veda occasionally calls the sky 'heavenly-father' (*Dyaus-pitṛ*).[2] It is agreed that the name *Pṛthivī* means 'the broad or extended one, which accounts for its use to signify the earth. When the three elements are listed in a group, the usual order is sky, intermediate space and earth. When the three worlds are regarded as objects of mastery or *yoga,* the order is reversed. The *Śatapatha Brāhmaṇa* referring to Prajāpati (the Creative Lord), says: 'he uttered the word *bhūr*, which became this earth: *bhuvaḥ* which became this firmament; and *svah*; which became that sky.'[3] This arrangement was inherited by later Indian literature. Even the Buddhist tantra accepts it, since I found this passage in a Tibetan work of this type the *Sṅags rim chen mo* of Tsoṅ-kha-pa:[4]

> *Bhūr* is the underworld (*pātāla,* sa 'og) accompanied by the circles of the wind disk (*vāyu-cakra*) and so forth. *Bhuvaḥ* is the perishable receptacle (*loka*) of the 'upon-world' (*bhūmi,* sa steng). *Svaḥ* is the ultimate pinnacle of existence, the 'bright' (*svarga,* mtho ris).

Thus we can see the terminological relations:

svaḥ (svarga)	< *Div* ('Heaven')
bhuvaḥ (bhūmi)	< *Antarikṣa* ('the intermediate dwellings')
bhūr (pātāla)	< *Pṛthivī* ('Earth')

Besides, the five elements can be put into this arrangement. This is because earth and water are counted as the 'heavy' elements and so go with *Pṛthivī*. Fire and wind are counted as the 'light' elements and so go with *Antarikṣa.* Space (*ākāśa*) also means 'sky' and so goes with *Div.*

There is a theory that various other triads can be put into correspondence with the basic three worlds. A champion of this theory was Professor V.S. Agrawala of Banaras Hindu University. In May-June, 1960, he conducted a Summer School of Vedic Studies, whose proceedings were published as *Vedic Lectures*. To explain the Veda as a coherent system, he used a series of triadic formulas, each called a 'Form' (*tanū)*. This word *tanū* occurs in a celebrated name of Agni, *tanūnapāt* (descendant of the *tanū*, himself), because the Father Agni is in the sky, his son in the middle region: and grandson on earth. Agrawala (p. 126) lists twelve of these 'Forms', the most important for our present considerations being his 'Trideva Form' (*adhipativatī tanūḥ*) namely, Brahmā, Rudra, Viṣṇu. It is more usual to mention Śiva rather than Rudra in this triad. The associated colors come from the accepted consorts of the *'trimūrti'*. Thus Brahmā has Sarasvatī, normally colored white. Viṣṇu has Lakṣmī, the yellow goddess. Śiva is associated with the night-time goddess with the old name Rātri, who is the prototype of the demon-destroying goddess, a type of Raudra fire. It easily follows that the 'preserving' lord Viṣṇu goes with earth; that the 'creative' lord Brahmā goes with the intermediate space; and that the 'destructive' lord Śiva goes with the night-time sky.

And Bhāskararāya in his commentary on *Lalitā-Sahasranāman* has to explain why the goddess is called Tripurā. In short, because the goddess dwells in everything that is threefold, she is called Tripurā. This commentary tells a story (translation publ. by S. *Anantakrishna Sastri,* Adyar, p. 275) that a threefold vision appeared to the triad of Brahmā, Viṣṇu and Śiva: from that sight sprang a maiden of divine form. They asked her: 'Who are you?' And that maiden of three colors responded: 'Don't you know me, the beautiful Śakti born from your gaze?' Then the triad of gods, pleased, asked her to make her body threefold according to the three colors, which were white, red, and black. And it is explained: 'The supreme energy endowed with the *Sāttvika* quality remaining with Brahmā becomes white; the same endowed with the *Rājasa* quality and remaining with Viṣṇu becomes red; the same endowed with *Tāmasa* quality and remaining with Rudra is said to be black.' Our previous conclusions are supported by this passage, the only difference being that the Śaivite earth goddess is red, while the Vaiṣṇava one is yellow.

Granted that the dark night-sky was alluded to above. Well, then, how about the day-time sky? The hymn to Sūrya, *Ṛg-Veda*,

1.50.6, appears to make Varuṇa the day-time sky with the roving sun his shifting eye, for it says: *yenā pāvaka cakṣúsā bhuraṇyantaṃ janām anu/ tvaṃ vāruṇa paśyāsi//* 'With which bright eye, you Varuṇa look at the one who is busy among mankind.' And in H.D. Velankar's translation of *Ṛgveda Maṇḍala VII,* hymn 49, to the Waters, verse 3, 'in whose midst (i.e., of the divine Waters) Imperial Varuṇa moves about watching the truth and the falsehood of men'. Thus he watches by means of the sun.

Separation of the Worlds; Mid-space as Death

The mythological elements of the three worlds in Indian literature are extensive. Here are a few details about the world separation. The *Agni-Purāṇa,* Chap. 18, has an account of the golden egg. Mahāviṣṇu thinking to create a diversity of living things, first created water and put his whole energy into it. That energy grew into a golden mass of an egg, and Brahmā (the creative lord) was born from that egg when Mahāviṣṇu broke it, making one half heaven and one half earth. Thus Brahmā is located in the middle region, as was observed previously.

In the *Ṛgveda* it is Indra, who according to several hymns is the generator of heaven and earth, stretches out heaven and earth like a hide, supported the earth and propped the sky, and holds asunder heaven and earth as two wheels are kept apart by the axle. But it is well-known that later on Viṣṇu eclipsed Indra, and this function was therefore taken over by Viṣṇu. But while Viṣṇu apparently won this contest for popularity, it may well have been a goddess named Uṣas (the 'Dawn Goddess') who after all should be credited with the feat, according to *Ṛgveda* 4.52.7, from the hymn addressed to her: *ā dyāṃ tánoṣi raśmibhir āntarīkṣam uru priyam/uṣāḥ śukreṇa śociṣā/* 'Uṣas, you stretch (*tanoṣi*) with beams—the broad, favorite intermediate space to the sky, along with your bright radiance.' As I mention elsewhere,[5] the Dawn Goddess is mystically credited with stretching between sky and earth, the lengthwise threads (the 'beams') called the warf (*tantu*) of the loom—as the intermediate space—and then is credited with being a kind of shuttle that puts in the crosswise colorful threads (the 'bright radiance').

Apparently the sky and earth come closest together on moonless nights, and so the role of Uṣas in separating them is most noticeable after such a night.

The theory that the intermediate space represents death is ancient in Indian mythology and is apparently due to the myth that earth and heaven were together and had to be separated to create the intermediate space which is therefore transitory. N.J. Shende summarizes in his monograph, *The Foundations of the Atharvanic Religion* (p. 256):[6] 'Gods....having attained immortality....went to the heaven or *svarga*. This path leading to the heaven is called *devayāna*. While men, mortal as they are had to die prematurely.... or naturally owing to old age (*jarāmṛtyu*). They after death went also to *dyauḥ* or *svarga*. But their path is called *pitṛyāna*.' The alternate tradition, probably more influential is that Yama, the first man to die found a place in the middle region (*antarikṣa*); afterwards all deceased persons went there.[7] Yama, as their lord is called Pitṛpati, Pretapati, and Paretarāj. Apparently the intermediate realm is referred to in *Ṛgveda* X, 135, 1, *yasmin vṛkṣe supalāśe devaiḥ sampibate yamāḥ*, 'the tree of beautiful foliage within which Yama drinks with the gods.' In later texts, such as the *Mahābhārata*, Yama has his kingdom in the South, in the sub-earth, and is more fearful. Thus V. Fausboll, *Indian Mythology* (1902), p. 137: 'His person is described as being dark, *śyāma*, with red eyes... holding a noose in his hands.' It is a simple procedure for Yama to have moved from the intermediate space to the underworld, because it appears that when the sun sets, it carries some elements of the mid-space along with it. This seems to be the conclusion to be reached from considering the strange case of the winds called Marut.[8]

The wind gods of the intermediate space called Maruts are devoted a hymn, *Ṛgveda Maṇḍala* VII, 56, (H.D. Velankar's translation: '(1) Who are these distinguished sons of Rudra, having a common home and good horse. (2) None indeed knows the births of these, (but) surely, they mutually know their origin.' And *Ṛgveda Maṇḍala* VII, hymn 58, to the Maruts, stanza 1 (Velankar's translation):

> Sing aloud in honor of the Host (of Maruts) which grow together and is the Strong one of the divine race. And they pound (i.e., press asunder) the two worlds by their greatness; from the beamless (world) of Nirṛti they rise up to the firmament.

So these wind gods rise up from that deep chasm, the Vedic hell called Nirṛti (the Truthless). How is this possible? Unless, strange to say, when the sun set and went to the underworld, he took the Maruts along and so that place down there is their mysterious 'origin', from which they rise up with the sun.

Macdonell's *Vedic Mythology* cites the *Atharvaveda* of Rudra's 'wide-mouthed, howling dogs, who swallow their prey unchewed'. That shows the relevance of *Ṛgveda,* 1.161.13. containing the word *śvānam,* meaning 'wind', but it is well-known that the word *śvāna* can mean 'dog', 'hound'. This suggests that the kind of winds that amounts to Rudra's 'howling dogs' are the ones already alluded to as the winds in the nether world.

Some further insight into this intermediate realm, where the Maruts blow can be gained from the list of deities ascribed to this realm in the section devoted to it in Macdonell's *Vedic Mythology.* They are pre-eminently Indra, then Trita Āptya; the Maruts aided these two in their victory over the demon Vṛtra. Then Apām Napāt and Matariśvan (both being forms of Agni). Ahirbudhnya (serpent of the deep) may well apply to the baleful middle region of the nether world. And Aja ekapāda, mentioned in association with Ahirbudhnya is said to rise in the East—which also shows the coming up from the lower realm. Rudra was mentioned somewhat above. Then the Maruts, one of whose functions is to shed rain. Then the wind god proper called Vāyu and Vāta. Parjanya as the rain-god is identified with the rain-cloud. Āpam are the Waters, which cleanse and purify.

It is even possible to find a name of the intermediate state suggesting death. This is in the *Hevajratantra* as cited in Nāro-pa's *Sekoddesa-ṭīkā* (Gaekwad ed.), p. 71: *svargamartyaiś ca pātālair* ...meaning the realms of heaven, of mortals, and of the nether layers. Here *martya* substitutes for the term *bhūmi,* hence the mortal stages.

Another approach is to take into consideration the epic theory of creation as given in the *Anugītā* portion of the *Mahābhārata,* or as found in the first chapter of the *Manusmṛti.* In such literature one can distinguish the three phases: (1) A pre-creation phase of darkness and no sound, i.e., non-two. (2) A first creation of Mahat, the initial two, but unseparated. (3) A second creation of Ahaṃkāra, the separation of the two to make room for creatures. Thus what is called the 'second creation', (*dvitīya-sarga*) is the origin of death.

The 'first creation' is non-life.

The Three Agnis and Viṣṇu's Three Strides

There are well-attested details about Agni. The Fire God is called Trivṛt in the *Taittirīya-Brāhmaṇa* and in the *Śatapatha-Brāhmaṇa*, and is treated as such in the *Ṛgveda*. This term Trivṛt means 'one that exists in the three', namely heaven, middle region, and earth. Usually, Agni is identified with the sun in the sky, with lightning in the intermediate space, and with the ordinary sacrificial fire on earth. Besides, Agni is called Śuci in the heaven, where it is the solar, Saura fire, called Pāvaka as the lightning or flash, Vaidyuta fire in the middle region and Pavamāna as the one excited by friction, Nirmathya on the earth. Or the Fire God is called Agni on earth, 'offspring of the waters' (*apām-napāt*) in the middle realm and *sūrya* the sun in the sky.

Usually the sequence is stated in the order from sky to earth. But Agni does not cease to exist on any level simply through manifesting on another level. In the fire sacrifice he is piled up, thus symbolically establishing the layers in all three divisions. This also agrees with the building of the Hindu temple, even though the usual descriptions of the temple do not mention this. Thus, Stella Kramrisch in *The Art of India* (p. 22) says: 'Although the plan of the temple is, as a rule, based on the square, the monumental architecture usually rises in curved planes in the shapes of hemisphere or dome, vault and tower or *śikhara.*' In such a structure, the square base represents the earth; and of course it contains the 'womb-house' (*garbha-gṛha*) in which is placed the deity icon. The curved planes above this square go with the middle realm, the *antarikṣa* and can be referred to as a world mountain. The small structure on top, frequently in the form of a small dome surmounted by a spire, represents the sky, and Kramrisch does mention this.

Turning to Viṣṇu, J. Gonda, *Aspects of Early Vishnuism* (1954), well summarizes (p. 63) the character of the Vedic Viṣṇu:[1]

> 'By striding Viṣṇu, in fact, obtained for the gods the all-pervading power which they now possess, called *vikrānti*: ŚB.... whilst explaining the significance of the Viṣṇu strides observes that Viṣṇu, being the sacrificer obtained this *vikrānti;* by his first step he gained the earth, by the second the aerial

> expanse, by the last the sky. This same pervading power, the text adds is acquired by the god, as the sacrifice, for the sacrificer.'

We may notice about these strides that they are vertically oriented. Hence, they symbolize the yogic ascension—starting with profane time, to ascend to heroic or great time, finally to reach no-time. Now, Viṣṇu is compared with the sun, hence is not the sun. The sun indeed seems to rise to the sky and then to set in the West, but Viṣṇu typifies the winning of the three worlds in upward motion, so does not set, as does the sun. A.A. Macdonell, *The Vedic Mythology,* p. 38, discusses the two interpretations of Viṣṇu's three strides—(1) The 'naturalistic', in which the three steps mean the rising, culminating, and setting of the sun; (2) the non-naturalistic, where Viṣṇu's three strides are the progress of the solar deity through the three divisions of the world. Macdonell sides with the latter interpretation, which traditional Vedic interpretation generally does, and as I do above. We also find Viṣṇu's Sudarśana-cakra the discus-weapon, compared with the sun, implying the sun as a weapon. And the Veda itself supports the non-naturalistic interpretation of Viṣṇu's three strides, because it alludes to Viṣṇu's non-setting head in *Ṛgveda* IX, 113,8, when the poet prays, 'Make me immortal (in heaven) where dwells king, Vaivasvata, where the sun is confined (i.e., where it never sets) and where the divine waters flow.'

This remark 'where the divine waters flow' brings us back to Agni, because the Agni in the mid-space can be called 'offspring of the waters (*apām napāt*). The Agni there is the offspring of the Agni in the sky. Therefore, the expression 'divine waters' is a reference to the sky. As to a possible meaning, I may refer to the three aims of Hinduism, namely, *dharma, artha, kāma.* To relate these three to the three realms as they have been treated above, I would have to conclude that *kāma* (whether love or lust), because it preserves life goes with the earth; that *artha,* the climbing paths of self-interest goes with the middle realm; and that *dharma,* the duty from above goes with the sky. And the *Iśa Upaniṣad* tells us: 'The face of truth is covered with a golden bowl. Uncover it, O Pūṣan, so that the true *dharma* amy be seen.' Here, 'uncover' must mean 'reveal', because the golden bowl—of the vault of sky—cannot be removed: it can only be revealed.

Further Divisions in the Three Worlds

Readers of the Indian literature of philosophic and religious types are fully aware that such traditions make divisions in the worlds that appear to be of mythological nature, e.g., the seven divisions of earth called the *pātālas* as found in the *Purāṇas*. Further divisions of the three worlds are already to be found in the Vedic literature. Stella Kramrisch tried to figure out the system in a lengthy article that was published in two parts in *History of Religions* (Chicago), Vol. 2:1 (Summer 1963) and Vol. 2:2 (Winter 1963). She points out on the basis of the *Ṛgveda* hymn 3.56 that there is a trebling of the three realms. She disagrees with the usual solution accepted by Macdonell, *Vedic Mythology*, and by others that earth, atmosphere, and sky are each subdivided into three, with the triple earth beneath the triple sky. She claims that each of the three earths lies beneath its own heaven.

Such matters are difficult to decide, especially since they involve rationalization of myths.

The Buddhist Three Worlds

When we pass to the Buddhist scriptures, we notice that such traditions speak of three worlds, viz., of desire (*kāmadhātu*), of form (*rūpadhātu*), and of formless (*arūpadhātu*, or *arūpya*) realms.

The standard subdivisions of the Buddhist three worlds are found in various modern works. Kloetzli presents the lists with various cosmological associations.[9] It should be explained that the Buddhist theory of three worlds is especially involved with meditative praxis. Briefly speaking, 'calming the mind' (*śamatha*) comes through a *samādhi* on an appropriate meditative object, while avoiding faults of meditation. Staying this way, say for a minimal twenty-four minute period, one may gain 'serviceability' (a lightness in body and mind) (*karmaṇyatā*) and the 'cathartic' (*praśrabdhi*). According to the theory, one may thereby surmount the 'realm of desire' and arrive at the threshold of the 'realm of form'. For this theory of 'calming' in Asaṅga's school, see the "Calming the Mind" part of a translation by the present writer.[10] Once one has entered the 'realm of form' there are yoga exercises called bases of Mastery and bases of Totality that are associated with one or another of the four *Dhyānas* of the 'realm of form'; and eight 'Liberations', three in the 'realm of form', four in the 'formless realm' and the eighth 'Liberation' going with cessation of ideas and feelings'.[11] Besides, the Genesis Myth of Buddhism starts with the beings dwelling in a level of the 'realm of form'; and according to the *Parinibbāna-sutta,* the Buddha entered *parinirvāṇa* at the top of the 'realm of form'.

The listing of the meditative states of the Formless Realms occurs in a number of Pāli *suttas,* e.g., the *Cūḷa-suññatā-sutta* of the Majjhima-nikāya. In the invariable sequence, they are: 'base of infinite space', 'base of infinite perception', 'base of nothing-at-all', and 'base of neither idea nor no-idea'.

However, the Buddha tantras usually accepted a formulation of the three worlds much like the ancient Brahmanical divisions, such as my above citation from Tsong-kha-pa's tantric writings. I have presented more illustrations in an article on the 'messengers'.[12] It appears that the *Vairocanābhisaṃbodhi-tantra* uses this division in its Chap. 2 on a *maṇḍala* in three ranks.[13]

The Dispute Over the 'Formless Realm'

Having presented above an abbreviated account of the facts as I understand them, I might as well admit that some scholars have argued that the 'formless realm' (*arūpa-dhātu*) was brought into Buddhism after the time of Gautama Buddha. Of course, there is some truth to the claim that there was a modification of, and additions to the so-called 'original canon'. There are various major and minor differences between the four *nikāyas* in the Pāli language and the four *āgamas* that were translated into Chinese from forms of Buddhist Sanskrit. For example, the very first *sutta* of the Pāli Majjhimanikāya has a list of *dhammas* (S. *dharma*) including the four formless states. Dr. Minh Chau has compared this *sutta* with the equivalent one of the Madhyama Āgama, where it is No. 100, and observes various differences in list items between the two versions; but despite these divergences, the version in Chinese also has the four formless states and in the standard order, as does the Pāli.[14]

Still, Thomas, referring to the unusual depiction of Gautama Buddha's passing through these various stages and ending up at the Fourth Dhyāna, according to the Pāli *Parinibbāna-sutta,* says: "The reason of this order of the stages is probably that the attaining of Nirvāṇa from the fourth stage of trance was the original form of the legend, and that when the other stages were added this circumstance of the fourth trance coming last was still preserved in the above way."[15]

Now two rather recent works have also claimed that the 'formless realm' is a later addition to the canon. These are: Johannes Bronkhorst, *The Two Traditions of Meditation in Ancient India;*[16] and Tilmann Vetter, *The Ideas and Meditative Practices of Early Buddhism.*[17]

First may I cite Vetter (p. 67, n. 7): "This refers to the famous episode in which the Buddha before his enlightenment reaches the sphere of nothingness, when he is with Ārāda Kālāma and the sphere of neither apperception nor non-apperception with Udraka Ramaputra, but does not become realized. Philological arguments (see Bareau 1963, 13-27; Bronkhorst, *Two Traditions,* 80) bring the authenticity of the story into doubt." Suppose we grant the point Vetter makes here. Is it not still a fact that the Buddhist, by believing the story and including those two states among the four 'formless realms' have the authority to deny that attaining either of those two states confers release from *saṃsāra*? In short, Vetter's point in no way indicates a non-presence of those two states among four in a theoretically 'earliest' Buddhist canon. Vetter in his Chap. Twelve speaks of certain persons who "no longer had access to the old dhyāna-meditation, but they knew of states of meditation (originally practised by non-Buddhists)" and these states turn out to be the four 'formless' stages. He continues, alleging that these persons (not specified) added them to the system of four dhyānas (the 'realm of form').[18] Thus, the argument is not whether the set of four is found in *an* early canonical work (since it is found in many *suttas*). Nor whether any of the four is original with the Buddhists. The argument turns merely on whether the set of four formless states was added later to the four dhyānas of the 'realm of form'. But Vetter, although speaking of 'younger' *suttas,* sets forth no criterion for determining which of the *suttas* is 'younger' or 'older'. Bronkhorst, on p. 82, argues that the set of formless states "entered Buddhism from Jainistic or related circles". He supports this by considering certain scriptures, especially the *Mahāsaccaka Sutta* (pp. 10, ff.). He accepted Jacobi's identification of the Nigaṇṭhas of the Pāli canon as Jainas; hence, identifies the Nigaṇṭha son, i.e. Saccaka of this *sutta,* as a Jaina. Accordingly, Bronkhorst researched some Jaina sources for meditation in that tradition. A seemingly consistent account is given in Paṇḍita Sukhlalji, *Essence of Jainism*, Chap. 3, "Hoary Past of Nirgrantha Cult", especially pp. 42-3 '*Nirgrantha Cult in Jainism: Some Proofs*'. Here, 'Nirgrantha' is the Sanskrit equivalent to the Pāli Nigaṇṭha (or Niggaṇṭha). However, Sukhlalji explains this in a manner that deserves repetition. He points out that the Nirgranthas were a kind of Śramaṇa, a general name for anti-Vedic cults. These cults were known from the words used for the preceptor or the recluse; but originally (i.e., when Gautama began his ascetic meditation, according to tradition, by the Nairañjanā river) only the Jainas and Gautama used the name Nirgrantha (in its Middle Indic form) for a preceptor.[19] Gautama went on his separate way when he announced his Middle Path. However, the name 'Nirgrantha' continued to be used in Buddhist circles for a preceptor. This is clear from a scripture composed early in the Mahāyāna period, cited as the *Satyaka-parivarta* (chapter of the truth-teller), but known by a different title in the Tibetan and Chinese canons. The entire scripture has been translated as a doctoral dissertation by Lozang Jamspal at Columbia University; and the principal preceptor (to a king) is in the scripture called Satyaka, son of the Nirgrantha; and here definitely not a Jaina.[20]

The point is that Gautama may well have tried out various teachers, and so was reasonably familiar with ascetic practices of his day and aware of the theories about which supranormal states would be reached by which ascetic or meditative practices: I conclude that Gautama Buddha himself promulgated that set of formless states as a veritable sequence.

The Six Elements

The theory that man is composed of six elements is mentioned a few times in the Pāli canon; but in the Mahāyāna period, becomes an important way of describing man. The six are the four elements, earth, water, fire, and wind; plus the fifth element, space (*ākāśa*), and *vijñāna* (perception or understanding). There is a lengthy citation on the six in Śāntideva's *Śikṣāsamuccaya* from the Mahāyāna scripture *Pitāputrasamāgama*.[21] Their importance in *yoga* is featured in the *Vairocanābhisambodhi-tantra,* Chap. 5.[22]

The point of mentioning this set of six elements is that the 'formless realm' starts with space and *vijñāna*. This implies that the preceding four *dhyānas* may be associated with the four elements. The standard *Abhidharma* discussions do not mention this association.

However, there is a *gāthā* in Asaṅga's *Mahāyānasaṃgraha,* for which the original Sanskrit is preserved because it has been cited in the *Bhāṣya* on Asaṅga's *Abhidharmasamuccaya:*

> *bodhisattve vaśiprāpte 'dhimuktivaśād yataḥ./*
> *tathābhāvaḥ pṛthivyādau dhyāyināṃ copalabhyate/*
> When the Bodhisattva has obtained the power (= attained Eighth Stage) through the power of *adhimukti*, and also in the case of the meditators (*dhyāyin*, i.e., in the four Dhyānas), the entity as it (really) is, is apprehended, i.e., (the elements) earth, and so on.

The verse gives authority for associating elements with the *dhyānas,* without telling how to do it.

However, it is easy to assign an element to each of the four. We can start with the given order. The first *dhyāna* has to go with water, because the standard three parts all involve the deity Brahmā. See Dowson: "As the waters (*nara*) were 'the place of his movement, he (Brahmā) was called Nārāyaṇa.' "[23] So this is the pure water. The second *dhyāna* is governed by the Ābhāsvara deities. As this name means the 'shining deities', it implicates the pure fire. As to the third *dhyāna,* Vasubandhu (*Abhidharmakośa,* VIII, 32c) gives the Abhidharma tradition that this *dhyāna* is shaken by its excellent pleasure. Hence, here is the pure wind. It is the fourth *dhyāna* where there is cessation of breathing (no wind); and Vasubandhu (*Kośa,* VIII, 28) puts here the 'Diamond-like *samādhi*' (*vajropama-samādhi*). Hence, the pure earth is assigned here.

It follows that the first two members of the 'formless' set should be treated differently from the next two members. The 'nothing-at-all' and 'neither ideation nor non-ideation' states were the ones which were explicitly denied for liberation from *saṃsāra.* However, it is reasonably inferred that the disallowance is extended to the first, two, 'infinity of space' and 'infinity of perception' since 'release' here would cancel the next one. Asaṅga, in his *Śrāvakabhūmi,* explains the attainment of the base of infinite space as the transcendence over a host of ideas (*saṃjñā*) of diversity.[22] It seems from the discussion here that it was from the very abatement of those many ideas (*saṃjñā*) that the next stage, the base of infinite perception is possible.

May I speak briefly of the last two? The next stage, the base of nothing-at-all is a kind of idea, namely, that there is nothing at all. As to how Asaṅga explains the next stage in *Śrāvakabhūmi* (Bihar MS. 13A. 8-2a; PTT edn. of the Tib. text, p. 119-4-7): "Regarding the idea of the base of nothing-at-all, one has the idea that it is coarse (*audārika-saṃjñin*), so turns away from the idea of the base of nothing-at-all and transcends it. Therefore, there is no idea (*naivasaṃjñā*) [of the base of nothing-at-all]. But also, one proceeds in a subtle manner (*sūkṣmayā*) in an idea whose object-support (*ālambana*) is without sign (*animitta*). Therefore, there is no lack of an idea (*nāsaṃjñā*). Being convinced that it is a base (*āyatana*), one accomplishes and dwells in the base of neither-ideation-nor-nonideation."

Our foregoing exposition of the states of the *Dhyānas* and then of the 'formless realm' means that the yogin realizing all these states does not have to go anywhere; but, as I have written elsewhere, the yogin's body takes on varied appearances while his mind has these adventures.[25]

Then the Sandhis

Now it is time to turn to the sandhis for further understanding. Long ago I wrote an article "Climactic Times in Indian Mythology and Religion,"[26] and pointed out that yoga experiences were especially at the sandhis. It is therefore reasonable that both the four states in the 'realm of form' and the four states in the 'formless realm' are assignable to the sandhis, if the correlations can be figured out with a minimum of speculation.

It is known that in the Vedic period there were two Sandhis, namely, of sundown and sunrise. In the post-Vedic period, a third sandhi of noon was added; and that is why the Gāyatrī has been practiced at the three sandhis. A fourth sandhi of midnight came to be used in tantra, especially for cemetary rites. However, a midnight period was recognized in the days of the Buddha and somewhat later by the division of the night into three watches. The above-mentioned article points out, "In the *Bṛhad-devatā*, which calls night and morning the divine doors (*devyo dvāraḥ*), the goddess Uṣas or personified dawn is said to have three forms (III, 10): in the beginning of the night she is Doṣā, in the middle of the night she is Tamasvatī, and before the rising of the sun she is Uṣas by name."[27] And in the Buddhist practice, according to Asaṅga's *Śrāvakabhūmi*: "Among those, what is perfection of dignified posture? That when by day he spends time both by walking and by sitting—doing likewise in the first watch of the night; when in the middle watch he takes rest on his right side; and when in the last watch he quickly rises and spends time by walking and sitting; ...."[28]

The Buddha's biography stresses the two old sandhis. Thus, under the bodhi-tree at dusk when the evil Māra appeared, the future Buddha touched earth "as his witness". This associates earth with dusk. Then when the meditating Gautama became enlightened just before dawn as the sky was reddening for the approach of the sun, this is the symbolism of fire for the morning sandhi.

When I associated the four elements with the four states of the 'realm of form', namely, in the preceding subsection, I had no idea of the enormous importance of doing so. Notice that I put the pure earth with the fourth *dhyāna*, and put the pure fire with the second *dhyāna*. Then, in order to put the four *dhyānas* in accordance with the four sandhis, it is necessary to do it with the sandhis in *reverse order*. Thus, taking the four *dhyānas* in their given order:

water	first	*dhyāna*	noon
fire	second	*dhyāna*	sunrise
wind	third	*dhyāna*	midnight
earth	fourth	*dhyāna*	dusk (sundown)

Suppose we do the same with the four formless states:

base of infinite space (*ākāśa*)	noon (*div*)
base of infinite perception	sunrise
base of nothing-at-all	midnight
base of neither ideation nor nonideation	dusk (sundown)

Asaṅga's *Samāhita-bhūmi* brings in members of the 'four immeasurables' namely, friendliness (*maitrī*), compassion (*karuṇā*), sympathetic joy (*muditā*), and equanimity (*upekṣā*). There he says that the base of infinite space is the best place for compassion, "since compassion seeks to free the sentient beings from their manifold sufferings". That the base of infinite perception is the best place for sympathetic joy "because here one can perceive whatever beings are happy, have attained, and so on and have sympathetic joy with them". That the base of nothing-at-all is the best place for equanimity, which usually means not favoring one object over another.[29]

Asaṅga mentioned that each of the four *dhyānas* is "one's partial *nirvāṇa*" (*aṅganirvāṇa*), "because it eliminates only the side of defilement and lacks the side of certainty".[30] He does not so credit the 'formless realms'.

Whether or not the reader accepts the correlation to the four sandhis (as surprising to the present writer as it is to the reader), I hope that the reading person will agree that there is no reason to deny that Gautama Buddha himself announced the yoga sequence of four states in the 'realm of form' and four states in the 'formless realm'.

REFERENCES

1. A.A. Macdonell, *The Vedic Mythology* (Varanasi, 1963), pp. 8-15.
2. See Dowson, *A Classical Dictionary* under *'Dyaus'*.
3. See Dowson, *A Classical Dictionary*, under '*Vyahṛtis*'.
4. Peking ed., 311b-41 *bhūr ni rlung gi dkyil 'khor la sogs pa 'khor dang bcas pa' i sa 'og go/ bhuvaḥ ni sa steng gi' jig rten no/ svaḥ zhes pa ni mtho ris te srid rtse mthar thug pa'o/*
5. In *The Enlightenment of Vairocana; Study of the Vairocanābhi-sambhodhi-tantra and the Mahāvairocana-sūtra*, by A . Wayman and R. Tajima (Motilal Banarsidass, Delhi, 1992).
6. *Bulletin of the Deccan College Research Institute*, IX, 3-4.
7. Shende, *The Foundations*, p. 249.
8. Concerning these names 'Maruta'—they are the Maruta (i.e., the wind gods) themselves (ṚV 14, 39, 4, and elsewhere). Laksman Sarup's work on the *Nirukta* (II, 13) gives the suppose etymology of these deities: '*Ma-rutaḥ* of measured sound (√*mi* + √*ru*) or of measured brilliancy (√*mi* + √*ruc*), or they run very much (*mahad* + *dru*). 'Another theory is that the name Maruta involves the root mṛ-to die, thus differentiating the Maruts from the Wind-god Vāyu. Narayan Aiyangar, *Essays on Indo-Aryan Mythology*, Part II (Madras, 1901), thinks the real derivation of Maruta is from the root *mar-* 'to crush, pound, destroy by friction', but refers (pp. 299-300) to both the *Rāmāyaṇa* and the *Bhāgavatapūraṇa* for a story that Indra's step-mother Diti to get revenge for Indra's conquering of her Daitya sons was growing in her womb a warrior to conquer Indra; that Indra, learning of it entered her womb and cut the garbha into seven or seven times seven pieces; emerged with them to be called Maruts because he said to Diti, *'mā ruda, mā ruda,* ('Don't cry, don't cry'). This story seems related to the name Rudra, since Macdonell's entries on Rudra and the Maruts in *The Vedic Mythology* show that Rudra is taken

as the father of the Maruts, who are several times called Rudras or Rudriyas. He is said to have generated them from the shining udder of Pṛśni—a cow, meaning a cloud charged with rain and lightning. Hence, the name Maruta implicates the 'howler' (Rudra).

9. Randy Kloetzli, *Buddhist Cosmology* (Motilal Banarsidass, Delhi, 1983), pp. 33-9.
10. Alex Wayman, tranl., *Calming the Mind and Discerning the Real; Buddhist Meditation and the Middle View* (Columbia University Press, New York, 1978), pp. 172.
11. Cf. A. Wayman, "Aspects of Meditation in the Theravada and Mahīśāsaka," *Buddhist Insight; Essays of Alex Wayman,* Ed: George Elder (Motilal Banarsidass. Delhi, 1984), Table, p. 94.
12. A. Wayman, "Messengers, What Bring Ye?" *Indo-Tibetan Studies,* Ed: Tadeusz Skorupski (The Institute of Buddhist Studies. Tring, U.K., 1990). pp. 305-22.
13. Wayman and Tajima (n. 5, above), pp. 86-9.
14. Bhikṣu Thich Minh Chau, *The Chinese Madhyama Āgama and the Pāli Majjhima Nikāya* (Motilal Banarsidass, Delhi, 1991), pp. 34-5.
15. Edward J. Thomas, *The Life of Buddha as Legend and History* (New York, 1952), p. 153 and note.
16. Published by Franz Steiner Verlag Wiesbaden GmbH, Stuttgart, 1986.
17. Published by E.J. Brill, Leiden, 1988.
18. Vetter, p. 63.
19. This work is translated from Hindi by R.S. Betai (L.D. Institute of Indology, Ahmedabad, 1988).
20. The scripture is catalogued as *Ārya-Bodhisattvagocaropāya-viṣayavikurvāṇanirdeśa-nāma-mahāyānasūtra.* The dissertation on it was defended in 1991.
21. For the six elements, see Louis de La Vallée Poussin, *L'Abhidharmakośa de Vasubandhu* (Paris, 1923). pp. 49-51, and p. 49, note 2, for references to the literature.
22. *The Enlightenment of Vairocana* (n. 5, above), "10. Chapter V and the Preliminary Service," pp. 157-67.
23. John Dowson, *A Classical Dictionary of Hindu Mythology and Religion* (London, 1950), p. 57.
24. I presented the list of these *saṃjñā*-s according to Asaṅga in my essay "Aspects of Meditation in the Theravāda and Mahīśāsaka" which was first published in *Studia Missionalia* and reprinted in *Buddhist Insight* (n. 11, above), pp. 86-7.
25. The essay of n. 24, above pp. 83, 88-9.
26. This article appeared in *History of Religions,* Vol. 4, No. 2, 1965, pp. 295-318.
27. A. Wayman, article of n. 26, above, p. 298.
28. A. Wayman. *Analysis of the Śrāvakabhūmi Manuscript* (Berkeley, 1961), p. 108.
29. A. Wayman, *Buddhist Insight* (n. 11, above), p. 87.
30. A. Wayman, *Buddhist Insight,* p. 86.

21

Studies in Yama and Māra

These studies utilize pre-Buddhist, Hindu, and Buddhist sources. Granted that it would be easier, but probably less illuminating, to stay within a single tradition and appear consistent. Here there are I. the names; II. the pantheon; III. the Māras; IV. three Yamas. Once the writer tried his hand at this.

I. The Names of Yama

Ehni[1] points out that in the Vedas there is a word *yā́ma* (accent on initial) meaning "tamer, guider (especially of the carriage horse)", and another word *yamā́* (accent on final) meaning "twin". This latter word is the name of the deity Yama. The *Taittirīya Saṃhitā* gives this explanation:[2] "The gods and Yama were at strife over

---

Reprinted and reedited from the version in *Indo-Iranian Journal*, Vol. III, 1959, Nos. 1 and 2.

this world; Yama appropriated (*ayuvata*) the power and strength of the gods; therefore Yama has his name." The *Bṛhaddevatā* has this:[3] "He giving (*prayachan*) offspring here, and gathering (them) goes forth (to the other world): therefore the seer Yama calls him, the son of Vivasvat, Yama." In the epic, "He is called Yama, it being he who keeps mankind in check."[4]

Both the learned and popular idea of Yama among Hindus and Buddhists in India of the first millenium, A.D. are succinctly presented by one and one-half *ślokas* of the *Amarakośa (Svarga-varga,* 53 and 54A of *Bibl. Ind.* edn.), in the form of fourteen names of Yama, for which both the Sanskrit and Tibetan equivalents are given here:

King of the Law (*dharmarāja, chos kyi kgyal po*)
Lord of the Fathers (*pitṛpati, pha gśin bdag*)
Impartial Judge (*samavartin, mtshuṅs ḥjug*)
King of the Dead (*paretarāj, gśin gyi rgyal po*)
Ender (*kṛtānta,*mthar byed)
Brother of Yamunā (*yamunā-bhrātṛ, ya-mu-na yi spun*)
Destroyer (*śamana, źi byed*)
King of the Yamas (*yamarāj, gśin byed rgyal po*)
Yama (*yama, gśin*)
Destructive Time (*kāla, groṅs can*)
Club Bearer (*daṇḍadhara, dbyug ḥdzin*)
God of Rites for Deceased Relatives (*Śrāddhadeva, mtshun gyi lha*)
Son of Vivasvat (*Vaivasvata, ñi maḥi bu*)
The End (*Antaka, mthaḥ can*)

A longer list is included in a lexicon of perhaps the twelfth century, A.D. by the Buddhist Śrīdharasena and available in Tibetan translation.[5] The lexicon presents first the names of Yama (interlinear Tibetan note: "The Lord of the Southern District has twenty-six names"[6]). It is immediately apparent from the Tibetan that this list overlaps the one above in these names: *Dharmarāja, Pitṛpati, Yamarāja, Śamana, Yama, Samavartin, Paretarāj, Kṛtānta, Daṇḍadhara, Vaivasvata,* and *Śrāddhadeva*. Then it is transparent that *antaka* is present with alternate Tib. translation (*byas mthaḥ*), and that T. *graṅs can* is a textual corruption of *groṅs can,* so that *kāla* is also present. Hence, this list omits only *yamunābhrātṛ*. However, it has the equivalent in the "Brother of

Kālindī" (Kālindī is a name of Yamunā), because T. *lto bcas ka-li-ndī* necessarily translates *kālindīsodara*. In effect, the entire *Amarakośa* list is incorporated.

The name *Kālindīsodara* is also found in Hemacandra's *Abhidhānacintāmaṇi* (Ed: O. Boehtlingk and C. Rieu, 1847, p. 32). Other names from our list overlaps Hemacandra's names, and thereby the original Sanskrit is made certain: "Lord of the Southern District" (*dakṣiṇāśāpati*, T. *lho phyogs bdag po*); "Ploughman" (*kīnāśa*, t. *kī-nā-śa*);[7] "Who has the buffalo as his emblem" (*mahiṣadhvaja*, T. *ma-heḥi rgyal mtshan*); "Robber" (*hari*, T. *ḥphrog byed*); and "Lord of the Departed" (*pretapati*, T. *yi dags bdag*). Another name is in Hemacandra's "Addendum" (*śeṣa*, verse 35), "Whose presence is ancient" (*purāṇānta*, T. *rñiṅ gnas*).

Two other names are in the *Mahābhārata:* "Who has the punishment" (*daṇḍin*, T. *chad pa can*);[8] "Who holds or wields the punishment" (*daṇḍadhāra, chad pa ḥdzin*).[9] Then, assuming the Tib. *ḥtshe baḥi dbaṅ phyug* is a textual corruption of *ḥtsho baḥi°*, it translates S. *jīviteśa* "Master of Livelihood".[10] Various Sanskrit possibilities for two expressions did not lead to names of Yama: T. *kun ḥdod*, probably "who has everything he wishes", T. *dgaḥ byed*, "gladdening".

There is one name left in the list of twenty-six: T. *dus ḥdzin*, which appears to mean "holding, or holder of time". Now, there is a name of Yama, *kālakuṇṭha*, in the lexicon *Śabdakalpadruma*.[11] Mayrhofer[12] gives the meaning "blunt, dull" for *kuṇṭha*, but "Nicht sicher erklärt". The Monier-Williams dictionary, p. 289, lists *kuṇṭha* under the "root" *kuṇṭh* "to be lame or mutilated or blunted or dulled". These dictionary meanings convey no obvious sense in construing a compound of which the first member is *kāla*, "time". The same dictionary lists under the passive participle *kuṇṭhita*, besides the expected "blunted, dulled", meanings from Wilson, "grasped, held, encircled". If Wilson is right—but has his contributions to this dictionary ever been evaluated?—we would be justified in interpreting *kālakuṇṭha* as "holder of time", which suits Yama, and certainly this Sanskrit word is the origin for the T. *dus ḥdzin*. However, the latter conclusion cannot be accepted even tentatively, because further on we shall see that Yama has a name indicating that he is a cripple. Thus, it is conceivable that *kālakuṇṭha* means "Time's Cripple", i.e., "Cripple throughout Time". Is Yama's Vedic foot-fetter (*paḍbīśa*)[13] his own shackle as well? The hobbling of a horse was expressed by *paḍbīśa,*[14] and further on Yama is shown to be associated, or identified with the sacrificial horse.

The entry by Śrīdharasena concludes with associated names, which are also in Hemacandra except for the "judgment seat" and the "register of human actions".

> His consort is Dhūmorṇā. His city is Saṃyamana.[15] The name of his doorkeeper (*pratīhāra*) is Vaidhyata.[16] Kaṇīcī[17] is his judgment seat (*vicārabhū*). Pañjikā is his register of human actions (*agrasaṃdhānī*).[18]

Citragupta is his scribe. His servants are Caṇḍa and Mahācaṇḍa. Hemacandra has some names of Yama that are not included by Śrīdharasena: "Death (personified)" (*mṛtyu*); "Having shrivelled feet" (*śīrṇāṅghri*)[19] (cf. the previous reference to Yama as a cripple); "Son of the Sun" (*arkasūnu*)—a substitute for Vaivasvata; and in the "Addendum" (*śeṣa*), "Foremost of Time" (*kālakūṭa*); "Great Truth" (*mahāsatya*); and "Born from the Yamugra" (*yamugraja*). Some other Sanskrit names were found by Scheftelowitz in late Brahmanical passages.[20] "The indigo-colored one" (*nīla*); "Righteousness (personified)" (*dharma*); "Who is victorious over death" (*mṛtyuṃjaya*); Citra—an appearance of Yama;[21] Citragupta—identification with his scribe; "Coming from the Udumbara tree" (*audumbara*); "Coagulated Milk" (*dadhna*); "Wolf-bellied" (*vṛkodara*); "Destroyer of all Creatures" (*sarvabhūtakṣayakāra*);[22] "Standing at the head" (*parameṣṭhin*); and "Who shatters" (*vihantṛ*).

Some of those names of Yama stem from the Vedic literature. In the RV, he is called by his patronymic Vaivasvata. The names "Brother of Yamunā" and "Brother of Kālindī" derive later from the RV story that Yama and Yamī are twins. Yama has a name in the RV, "Lord of Settlers" (*viśpati*),[23] and this seems consistent with the names "Ploughman" (*kīnāśa*) and "Master of Livelihood" (*jīviteśa*). " 'Yama hath given the settlement on earth (to this sacrificer);'..."[24] The RV legend that he was the first mortal seems behind the names "Foremost of Time" (*kālakūṭa*) and "Whose presence is ancient" (*purāṇānta*). Also in the RV, he is said to have chosen death, finding out the path for many, and from this tradition doubtless come such names as "Lord of the Fathers" (*pitṛpati*), "King of the Dead" (*pretarāja*), and "God of Rites for Deceased Relatives" (*śrāddhadeva*).[25]

The AV concept of Yama and related deities is summarized by

Shende.[26] We find here an increasing emphasis on his role as "Lord of the Fathers" and ruler of the other world. Since he is a stern ruler, we see the tradition that later gave rise to the all-important names "King of the Law" (*dharmarāja*), as well as to the name "Impartial Judge" (*samavartin*). Death personified (*mṛtyu*) is Yama's messenger (*dūta*), and he is more fearful than Yama; but since Yama is now sometimes identified with *Mṛtyu*. Yama also becomes more fearful.

Macdonell writes,[27] "In the later Saṃhitās, Yama is mentioned beside Antaka, the Ender..." This Antaka is one of Yama's names in the *Amarakośa*. Thus, by the time of the later Saṃhitās, he is sufficiently fearful as to be called in the course of time, the various names showing him as a destroyer. The spirit involved in identifying him with time is demonstrated by a passage in the *Mahābhārata*:[28] "Time, which brings to pass the destruction of all creatures is passing on." However, the concept of time in the beautiful "Hymn to Time" in the *Atharva-Veda* has a different spirit.[29]

Regarding the name, "Who has the buffalo as his emblem" (*mahīṣadhvaja*), Yama has the mount of buffalo in post-Christian Indian iconography, but in Vedic times he had a horse. Thus Bloomfield translates,[30] "With the blood of the brown horse of Yama, thou hast verily been sprinkled." Bergaigne[31] shows that Yama (among others) is identified with the sacrificial horse.

The names "Coming from the Udumbara tree" (*audumbara*) and "Coagulated Milk" (*dadhna*) must be discussed together. Bloomfield observes:[32] "A tree as the seat of the gods occurs in RV X, 135, 1, *yásmin vṛkṣé supalāśe devaiḥ sampībate yamáḥ*. 'the tree of beautiful foliage within which Yama drinks with the gods'." Eggeling translates,[33] "They [the gods] said, 'Come, let us lay into the Udumbara tree whatever pith, whatever vital sap there is in these trees:'....hence that (tree) is always moist, always full of milky sap..." For the latter phrase, the *ŚBr.* (Mādhyandina, edn. A. Weber) VI, 6, 3, 3, has *tasmāt sa sarvadārdraḥ sarvadā kṣīrī.* The word *kṣīrin* means it possesses *kṣīra,* 'thickened milk'. The word *dadhi* ("coagulated milk") is an explanation of *soma* in Kau. Br.[34] Coomaraswamy states,[35] "There are in fact many texts identifying the *soma* with the essence in the waters, sap in trees, and seed in man and animals." He goes on to give examples, one of which is especially pertinent now: "In AV., XIX, 31, 12, an amulet of *udumbara* wood is called virile (*vṛṣan*)." An amulet of that wood answers to the name "Coming from the Udumbara tree". Consequently, this name shows Yama in the aspect of virility. Moreover, the foregoing theory suggests that the milky sap of the Udumbara tree symbolizes semen or its vital essence. Yama, in order to be the first human, must start out this way.

It is necessary to discuss, even if briefly, the name "God of Rites for Deceased Relatives" (*śrāddhadeva*). Kane has recently provided an indispensable coverage of the subject.[36] He quotes[37] an early explanation that the gods went to heaven owing to sacrifices, and that the men who duplicate those sacrifices will come to dwell with those gods and Brahman. It is also held in Hinduism that the flavor of the sacrificial material pleases the *pitṛs* and that they respond with benefits to men.[38] The factor of the merit of nourishing the *pretas* seems to be the main reason for the Buddhist offerings.[39] The basic point in the pre-Buddhist period is that the Fathers (*pitṛ*) dwell in Yama's heaven, and a dead man may or may not arrive at that Heaven to be one of the Fathers. Since Yama first showed the way, he must have been the first human to perform the sacrifice.[40] His brown horse was the external sacrifice. He himself was the personal sacrifice. But it was also held that the state of mind of a dying man determines his destination after death.[41] It appears that opponents of ritualism, i.e., the Upaniṣadic sages and the Buddhists stressed the latter factor. Of course, a devotee of Śrāddha could maintain a consistency of the two factors by saying that the person who performs the rites will naturally have the proper state of mind as he dies. The name *śrāddhadeva* also settles one point: Yama is called a *deva,* (in connection with certain rites). He is also the *deva* in the *Devadūtasutta,* as shown by Mus.[42] The MBh. names of Yama, *deveśa* and *sureśa,*[43] both meaning "master of the gods", show that Yama consorts freely with the gods, but do not necessarily show that he is one of them. Certainly, Bergaigne is right in considering Yama "*un personnage de nature équivoque, tantôt dieu tantôt homme*".[44] But since the latter judgment was made for the Vedic literature, it probably involves an inference; as Apte says for the Ṛg,[45] "In the case of Yama, for example, it is only *implied* that he is a *devā*!"

The name "Lord of the Departed" (*pretapati*) concerns a subject much treated in Buddhist texts. Oriental art shows the *pretas* as the frustrated spirits wandering among men unseen. They dwell in the 'Realm of Desire' (*kāma-dhātu*) without the means of gratifying their desires, and so usually the word *preta* is translated (inexactly) "hungry ghost". Mus gives a comprehensive treatment based on the verses of Dhārmika Subhūti.[46] Another treatment is in the *Ārya-Saddharmasmṛtyupasthāna*, exposed briefly by Lin.[47] It so happens that the present writer investigated the latter Buddhist source independently of Lin's work, learning about the *sūtra* list from a native Tibetan *abhidharma* work, then locating it in the *sūtra* itself, ascertaining that the Sino-Japanese translations preserve most of the Sanskrit names in transcription; and then attempting to restore these names in Sanskrit by utilizing the Japanese reading of the Chinese logogram transcriptions, the Tibetan translation of the names, and the contexts.[48] This prior study enabled the writer to maintain completely independent judgment and later to read Lin's exposition somewhat critically. In the following, after the English translation, the parenthesis will include first the restored Sanskrit, and next the Japanese reading in those cases, where the solution differs from Lin's. Also it must be said that his solutions were invaluable in a number of instances.

> 1. "Limbless-trunk Preta" (*kapāli-* or *kabandha-preta, kabari*),[49] 2. "Needle-mouth P." (*sūcimukha-°*), 3. "Vomit-eater P." (*vānta-bhakṣa-°*), 4. "Ordure-eater P." (*viṣṭhābhakṣa°*), 5. "Foodless P." (*abhakṣa-°*), 6. "Odor-eater P." (*gandhabhakṣa-° = gandharva*), 7. "Doctrine-eater P." (*dharmabhakṣa-°*), 8. "Water-eater P." (*salilahakṣa-°*),[50] 9. "Hopeful P." (*āśaka-°, ashaka*),[51] 10. "Spittle-eater P." (*kheṭabhakṣa-°*), 11. "Garland-eater P." (*mālābhakṣa-°*), 12. "Blood-eater P." (*raktabhakṣa-°, rakitta*), 13. "Flesh-eater P." (*māṃsabhakṣa- = piśāca*), 14. "Incense-eater P." (*sugandhabhakṣa-°*) 15. "Malevolent-conduct P." (*abhicāra°-abhishara*),[52] 16. "P. looking for the opportinuty" (*avatārapreksin, tendara*),[53] 17. "Under-world P." (*pātāla°*), 18. "P. of great magical power" (*ṛddhi-° = maharddhika*), 19. "Blazing P." (*jvalita-°, jabari*)[54] 20. "P. looking for the opportunity regarding human infant" (*manuṣyaputra-avatārapreksin, tendara*),[55] 21. "Taking any desired form" (*kāmarūpin, kama*), 22. "Seashore P." (*samanantaradvīpa-* or **samudratīra-°, sammudarateiba*), 23. 'Yama policeman" (**yamadaṇḍin = yamarākṣasa, enra*) 24. "Child-eater"

> (*bālabhakṣa*), 25. "(Human) vital heat eater P." (*uṣmabhakṣa* °), 26. "Brahman demon" (*brahmarākṣasa*), 27. "Health P." (*kuṇḍa*-°), 28. "P. of unpleasant street" (*aśubharathyā*-°), 29. "Wind-eater P." (*vāyubhakṣa* °), 30. "Ember-eater P." (*aṅgārabhakṣa*-°), 31. "Poison-eater P." (*viṣabhakṣa* °), 32. "P. of forest" (*aṭavi* °), 33. "P. of charnel ground" (*śmaśāna*-°), 34. "P. of tree" (*vṛkṣa*-°), 35. "P. of crossroad" (*catuṣpatha*-°), 36. "Member of Māra group" (*mārakāyika, maragaya*).[56]

Because of some relevance to what will follow in this or a subsequent section, three of the families should be described; only essential points of the text will be given: No. 18 "Of Great Magical Power" is god of the evil spirits and lives on a lofty mountain or at the seashore; alone has supreme pleasure; is surrounded by innumerable suffering *pretas* who observe his pleasure. No. 23 "Yama policeman" is ordered by Yama to record the wrongdoings of persons; of fearsome aspect, he ties up the deceased wrongdoer and drags him to Yama's palace for sentencing. No. 36 "Member of Māra group" is tortured in the three evil destinies (*durgati*); especially visits *bhikṣus* at training, meal time and brings them nightmares.

While the text here gives no hint that the *preta* "Of great magical power" is Yama himself, this *preta* is outstanding as being the only one, who enjoys himself. Mus[57] gives information that Yama is the variety of preta *maharddhika* ("of great magical power"). The fact that this is a family of *pretas* is also consistent with the multiplicity of *yamas* implied by the name "King of the Yamas" (*yamarāja*). Mus[58] explains this multiplicity in connection with the different hells. So far the writer cannot determine if the *Ārya-Saddharmasmṛtyupasthāna* regards Yama as a *maharddhika-preta*.

Concerning the messengers, Dkon mchog ḥjigs med dbaṅ po writes in his *Rin po cheḥi gru gziṅs* based on Vasubandhu's *Abhidharmakośa*, as follows:[59]

> Now, are the 'Policemen of Yama' (*yamarākṣasa*) sentient beings (*sattva, sems can*) or not?[60] The Vaibhāṣika maintain they are persons (*pudgala*).[61] The Sautrāntika maintain they are unconscious substances (or, "soulless matter") (*jāḍa, bem po*) produced from the differentiations of elements (*bhūta*) and their derivatives (*bhautika*). Both the

> Mādhyamika and the Cittamātra maintain the same as the latter. All [four doctrinal schools (*siddhānta*) of Buddhism] maintain that the Yama of Hells is a person (*pudgala*).

The description of these "Policemen of Yama" (tragically modern) leads to the consideration of Yama's two servants, Caṇḍa and Mahācaṇḍa. The policemen ("die Schergen") Pracaṇḍa, Caṇḍaka, among others unnamed, have in the *Garuḍa-Purāṇa* the function of Yama's policemen.[62] It appears that Yama's servants are the epic substitution for the two dogs of Yama, sons of Saramā (*sārameya*), his regular messengers in the Vedas. "Delighting in lives (*asutṛp*) they watch men and wander among the peoples as Yama's messengers....Their functions therefore seem to consist in tracking out among men those who are to die, and in keeping guard on the path over those who enter the realm of Yama."[63] Bloomfield writes,[64] "The 'four-eyed bitch' is Saramā the mother of the two four-eyed dogs of Yama, Śyāma and Śabala, which I have explained as the sun and the moon; see Journ. Amer. Or. Soc. XV, 163 ff." Hariyappa makes forceful reply,[65] "If the hymns contemplated any mythical motive that the Hounds of Heaven are the Sun and the Moon, or that Saramā is the Storm-Goddess or Vasiṣṭha is the Sun, one wonders why the Veda would not state it: what harm? On the other hand, what harm is there to believe that there were two real hounds in the service of Yama;....." It seems to the writer that the solution lies in the connotation of the word for "dog" in a particular culture. Even today in Japan the word for "dog", *inu,* is used disparagingly to refer to a "spy" or "secret police". Because dogs are noted for ability to track out by scent, a person of analogous occupation might reasonably come to be called, at least colloquially, a "dog". The same word could be employed metaphorically for a function. In terms of word usage, we can arrive at a position mid-way between Bloomfield and Hariyappa. Of course, there were two real hounds in the service of Yama, but this is only true mythologically. Likewise, in accordance with the well-known Buddhist doctrine of *karma,* the Sautrāntika, Mādhyamika, and Cittamātra are of course indicating that our own wrong actions become the "policeman" (in psychological terms, the "super-ego" or punitive self) that drags us away to retribution. Vasubandhu tells us in de La Vallée Poussin's translation.[66] "*Les seize enfers sont crées par la force des actes de tous les êtres...*" What is called the Vaibhāṣika viewpoint here is merely the popular objective representation.

The name "death personified" (*mṛtyu*) of Hemacandra's list is sometimes identified with Yama (Dharma) in the Mahābhārata.[67] Still, not only the *Amarakośa,* but also the more comprehensive list by the Buddhist Śrīdharasena fails to include it. The expression is frequent in Buddhist passages of an admonishing type of which a number are collected in Tsoṅ-kha-pa's *Lam rim chen mo* in the section devoted to meditation on suffering (*duḥkha*). For example, the *Kaniṣkalekha* of Mātṛceṭa has this verse, translated by Thomas.[68] "60. Uncompassionate, the lord of death slays accomplished persons without reason: with the slayer close at hand, what wise man busies himself with cherishing vanities?" The *Udānavarga* has this, translated by Rockhill.[69] "I, 17. As a cowherd with his staff gathers his cattle into the stable, so disease and old age bring mankind to the lord of death." As will be shown in a later section, *mṛtyu* is one of the four kinds of Māra, or metaphorical death. Māra has built up an evil connotation in Buddhist literature, while Yama is "King of the Law" (*dharmarāja*), a model of justice. Perhaps for this reason, some sections of Indian Buddhists did not follow the general Indian identification of Mṛtyu with Yama. But in the *Devadūtasutta,* Yama is the Deva and *mṛtyu.*[70] Shende tells us from the AV:[71] "The gods, like men, were mortals first, and as such were subjected to *Mṛtyu.* But they overcame death by means of celibacy and penance (11.5.19)." As will be seen, likewise the Buddhist ascetic's aim is to overcome the *Mṛtyu*-māra. If this implies overcoming Yama, it must be the Yama of the *Atharva-Veda* tradition. Logically, in the *Ṛg-Veda,* Yama is not to be overcome, because, as Kane writes,[72] "In Ṛg. IX. 113.8 the poet prays 'make me immortal (in heaven) where dwells the king Vaivasvata, where the sun is confined (i.e., where it never sets) and where the divine waters flow'."

As "Lord of the Fathers" (*pitṛpati*), Yama rules the men who succeed in reaching the world in the Intermediate Space (*antarikṣa*) between earth and heaven[73]—presumably what is later called in Buddhism, the "Realm of Form" (*rūpa-dhātu*) between the "Realm of Desire" (*kāma-dhātu*) and "Formless Realm" (*arūpa-dhātu*). The *pitṛs* have an extensive literature, not always consistent, and here only a brief presentation may be made. Kane points out that the Fathers (*pitṛ*) called Barhiṣadaḥ (who sit on kuśa grass) and the Agniṣvāttāḥ (tasted or licked by Agni) are mentioned in Ṛg. X. 15.3-4, 11.[74] He says,[75] "In Vāyu 72.1 and 73.60, Brahmāṇḍa (Upodhghāta 9.53), Padma V. 9. 2-3, Viṣṇudharmottara I. 138.2-3 and other Purāṇas, the classes of *pitṛs* are said to be seven, three of which are formless (*amūrtimat*) and four have forms (*mūrtimat*) and they and their offspring are described in detail." Presumably the Agniṣvāttāḥ would be the formless (or, "incorporeal") variety since they have been "licked by fire". The ones that sit on *kuśa* grass obviously have not yet been licked by fire. Giving Ṛg-V. references, Kane says,[76] "The *pitṛs* are often said to regale themselves in the company of gods, particularly of Yama... The *pitṛs* are said to be fond of Soma drink... Fire is supposed to take the spirit of a cremated person to the *pitṛs*.... It was supposed that the departed spirit after the cremation of the body was endowed with an ethereal body and became associated with Yama, the gatherer of departed men, and with pitṛs." Again,[77] "The Baud. Dh. S. II.8.14 summarizes a Brāhmaṇa text stating that *pitṛs* move about in the form of birds. The *Auśanasa-smṛti* and Devala quoted by the Kalpataru say the same thing. In the Vāyu-purāṇa, it is stated that at the time of *śrāddha*, the ancestors enter the brāhmaṇas (invited) after assuming an aerial form..." The Skt. passage quoted for the last statement shows that *vāyubhūta* is the original for "assuming an aerial form". Basing himself on the Matsya Purāṇa, Kantawala writes,[78] "Somapa (lit. drinkers of Soma) *pitṛs* of Vedic antiquity, the progeny of Svadhā and the residents of the Mānasa region situated above the universe are eternal and the embodiment of *Dharma par excellence* and are held to be higher than Brahmā. Being proficient in *yoga* and having attained Brahmahood and having discharged the work of creation etc., one and all, they reside in the Mānasa."

The Buddhist texts—with which the writer is most familiar—do not use the "father" (*pitṛ*) terminology as exposed above. The northern Buddhists have a heaven for the faithful called the "Western Paradise", or the "Happy Land" (*sukhāvatī*), ruled by Amitābha, whose name "Immeasurable Light" reveals his solar nature; and recalls King Vaivasvata's heaven "where the sun is confined". On the other hand, the Buddhist Yāma Heaven in the *Kāma-dhātu* has no apparent connection with Yama.[79] In Abhidharma Buddhism, he is the King of the Pretas and his capital is 500 fathoms beneath Jambudvipa.[80] Buddhist texts have much to say about the *dhyāna* heavens in the "Realm of Form" (*rūpa-dhātu*), which is the Buddhist middle region and pre-eminently, the realm of yogic attainment. In some Buddhist schools, it is taught that one becomes a complete Buddha in this Realm of Form as the Sambhogakāya Vairocana, another solar name,[81] but this Vairocana is by no means associated with Yama in Buddhism.

The name "King of the Law" (*dharmarāja*) will be the last one discussed. It not only refers to Yama's popular role as judge of merit and demerit, but in the case of the profound *Kaṭha Upaniṣad* could reasonably include his position as *guru*. The Buddha's *Dharmakāya* is also associated with death in the Buddhist Tantras. Thus, Tsoṅ-kha-pa (1357-1419 A.D.), founder of the Gelugpa school of Tibetan Buddhism, quotes in the Prajñā-jñāna Initiation section of his *Sṅags rim chen mo,* the work *Mukhāgama* regarding the experience of the Dharmakāya in five states (*avasthā*):[82]

> Because one experiences the Dharmakāya,
> Joyful, equal to the sky, for only an instant
> At the time of (1) death, (2) faint,
> (3) Going to sleep, (4) yawning, and (5) coitus...

Coomaraswamy might well have seized on this passage as a point of departure for his extraordinary insight and learning.

When he speaks of "the sacrificial initiation which involves a temporary or symbolic death, and a rebirth"[83] he may also have indicated the relevance of the Dharmakāya of the Buddhist Tantras to the *Kaṭha Upaniṣad*.

II. Interpretation of Yama in the Mythological Pantheon

A simple way of showing Yama's place in the "scheme of things" is by a table of the *lokapāla* prepared from two Tibetan passages.[84]

The word "Seal" (*mudrā*) needs some explanation. This is the variety known as "Symbolic Seal" (*samayā mudrā*). Buddhaguhya writes,[89] "Moreover, the "Symbolic Seals" are the ideas (*saṃjñā*) 'thunderbolt' (*vajra*), 'hook' (*aṅkuśa*), 'arrow' (*śara*), '(?)drum' *nanda,* T. *mñes pa*), and so forth." Thus this particular "Seal" is the idea possessed by the deity in question. For example, the Earth Goddess (*pṛthivī*) has the idea of "water pot", probably filled with water and adorned with young sprouts.[90] When we look upon earth this way, we are thinking in mythological terms. Yama has

Directional Regents (*lokapāla*)	Seal (*mudrā*)	Retinue (*parivāra*)
(E.) Indra	Thunderbolt (vajra)	Gods (deva)
(S.E.) Agni	Hearth (agnikuṇḍa)	Seers (ṛṣi)[85]
(S.) Yama	Club (daṇḍa)	Mothers (mātṛkā)
(S.W.) Nirṛti	Sword (khaḍga)	Demons (rākṣasa)
(W.) Varuṇa	Noose (pāśa)	Serpents (nāga)
(N.W.) Vāyu	Banner (dhvaja)	Flying Wisdom-holders (vidyādhara)[86]
(N.) Kubera, *or* Vaiśravaṇa	Mace (gadā)	Secret Folk (yakṣa)[87]
(N.E.) Īśāna, *or* Īśvara	Trident (triśūla)	Creatures (bhūta)[88]
(Below) Pṛthivī (Earth Goddess)	Water Pot (kumbha or kalaśa)	Local Genii (kṣetrapati)
(Above) Sūrya-Candra (Visible Sun and Moon)	Disk (maṇḍala)	—

the idea of "club", the Skt. word *daṇḍa* also meaning "punishment".

The eight directions of the guardians are standardized in the Hindu Purāṇas—post-Christian literature, although some of their contents are older; and earlier texts vary considerably in the directions ascribed to the guardians as well as in the particular guardians themselves.[91] Coomaraswamy writes.[92] "The earliest assignments of deities to the four quarters are those of YV., I, 8, 7, where we get Agni (E), Yama (S), Savitṛ (W), and Varuṇa (N), Bṛhaspati (Zenith), and *ib.* VI, I, where we find Pathyā Svasti (E), Agni (S), Soma (W), Savitṛ (N), and Aditi (Zenith); *ib.*, II, 4, 14, Indra is guardian of the East." This shows that from the earliest assigning of deities to directions, Yama was in the South in one system, and this assignment won out over alternate possibilities.

Yama's relation with Varuṇa requires some treatment. Kane translates Ṛg. X. 14.7:[93] "Hasten, hasten by the ancient paths (to that place) where our forefathers that went before us passed. May you (the departed) see the two kings Yama and god Varuṇa rejoicing as they will." Kane writes,[94] "In Ṛg. IV. 5.5, it is said that those men who are bereft of *ṛta* and *satya,* being sinful, create a deep place for themselves." Varuṇa was of course, the upholder of *ṛta*: "Durch die Wahrheit schütze du mich, O Varuṇa."[95] Karṇa speaks in MBh. Vana P., edn. of Krishnacarya and Vyasacharya, 303, 6A: "Not so do I fear death as I fear untruth" (*bibhemi na tathā mṛtyor yathā bibhye 'nṛtād aham*), showing that being in disgrace with Varuṇa is more terrible than being in Yama's power. As we come into the

Christian period, "truth" was still of lofty prestige in India under the word *satya* (in modern times, the scholars have discussed the meaning of Varuṇa's *ṛta*, while they do not doubt the meaning of *satya*). The word *dharma* had undoubtedly risen to higher prestige, through being one of the *trivarga* of Hinduism, "righteousness" (*dharma*), "endowment" (*artha*), and 'desire" (*kāma*), and through being one of the *triratna* of Buddhism, Buddha, Dharma, and Saṅgha. So Āryaśūra in the *Jātaka-mālā*, XXXI, "The Story of Sutasoma," while in earlier stanzas (especially No. 22) speaking highly of "truth" (*satya*) has the Bodhisattva say in verse 62: "Who, stationed in righteousness (*dharma*), ought fear from death?" (*dharmasthitaḥ ko maraṇād bibhīyāt*). Varuṇa is out of the picture. The departed will see Yama, "King of Righteousness" (*dharmarāja*).

That brings up the subject of *nirṛti*—the S.W. corner of this deity is translated into Tibetan as *bden bral* "truthless". In Vedic times, Nirṛti is especially the goddess of destruction, but she has a creative side. Renou[96] explains this word as meaning "dis-order" ("dés-ordre", for *nis+ṛti*), implying dis-organisation. "Disintegration" also seems compatible with his interpretation. For him, *ṛta* means "order" rather than "truth". Dandekar[97] explains *ṛta* as "the unbreakable, invulnerable law." Kane says,[98] "In Ṛg. X. 165.4 Yama is identified with Mṛtyu (death) and the owl (an evil omen) or a *kapota* is said to be the *dūta* (harbinger) of Yama." Now, in the *Atharva-Veda*, the owl and the pigeon (*kapota*) are the messengers of the goddess Nirṛti.[99] It should not be concluded that Nirṛti and Mṛtyu are identical: Renou[100] cites examples showing the two in contrast. Further, in the *Śatapathabrāhmaṇa* Nirṛti is the Earth, and the Earth is Yamī, while Yama is Fire.[101] In the latter text (*Mādhyandina*, ed. Weber, VII, 2, 1), "Fire" is of course Agni, and "Earth" is *iyaṃ* ("this"), or *bhūmi*. It follows that when Yamī attempts to seduce her brother Yama, and he resists in Ṛg. X. 10, there is more to this than at first appears. Yama actually refused Nirṛti. Consistent with the etymology, he prefers the Ascendant (*ṛta*) to the Down-fall (*nirṛti*). When in verse 7 of that hymn, she expresses her desire to lie with Yama on the same bed (Geldner III, p. 135), we must remember that she is earth. The ŚBr. says (VII, 2, 1, 11): "This (earth) is Nirṛti. And this (earth) makes him decay who passes away" (*iyaṃ vai nirṛtir iyaṃ vai taṃ nirarpayati yo nirṛchati*). But it also says (*idam*): "Whoever comes into being, comes into being on this (earth)" (*asyāṃ vai sa bhavati yo bhavati*).

When we compare what is said about the goddess Nirṛti with the two lines in the table for Nirṛti and Pṛthivī, it appears that the lines present the destructive and creative aspects, respectively, of the Vedic Nírṛti.

Yama's retinue of Mother (*mātṛkā*) requires some discussion. We might have expected the retinue to consist of Fathers (*pitṛ*), as in MBh. Vana P. 41.9, where the *pitṛs* are called *martyamūrtidhara* ("mortal corporeal"). But, as Bergaigne (II, 98) shows from the Ṛg, he is "le mari des femmes" and "l'amant des filles". Also Yama is the regent of Bharaṇī (either the 27th or 28th asterism), three stars in the shape of the female organ (*bhagasaṃsthāna*).[102] Fausböll tells us from the MBḥ.[103] "His wife is named Dhūmorṇā (XIII, 7637). Daxa [dakṣa] prajāpati gave ten of his daughters to Yama (I, 2577). But in XII, 2522 Çrī is naṃed as being his consort, thus also in I, 2578." Gonda states,[104] "Before being constantly described as specially connected with Viṣṇu—this stage is not reached before the younger parts of the Mahābhārata—Śrī was associated with various gods, all of them assorting well with her. One of them was Kubera.... Another was Dharma, whose wife she is in the Mahābhārata and even in Viṣṇuitic purāṇas like ViP. 1, 7, 21; cf. also Mbh. 1, 66, 13 etc., where Lakṣmī belongs to the thirteen daughters of Dakṣa, who were given in marriage to Dharma, Tuṣṭi "Satisfaction", Puṣṭi "Thriving", Ṛddhi "Growth, Success", Kīrti "Renown" etc. being her sisters and co-wives." Now, Winternitz says,[105] "....in the whole of the Mahābhārata, the idea prevails that *Yama,* the god of death, is one with *Dharma,* the personification of law." A curious feature of this situation is that thirteen daughters of Dakṣa are also stated by the *Mahābhārata* to have been given in marriage to Kāśyapa Prajāpati,[106] who, as the father of Vivasvat is Yama's "grandfather" on his father's side.[107] But in this respect, Yama also resembles his "grandfather" on his mother's side, Tvaṣṭṛ (whose daughter Saraṇyū with Vivasvat gave birth to the twins Yama and Yamī). Macdonell writes,[108] "Probably, because of his creative agency in the womb, Tvaṣṭṛ is closely allied with celestial females (*gnāḥ, janayaḥ*) or the wives of the gods, who are his most frequent attendants (I, 22[9], etc.)."

The group of ten, and group of thirteen daughters of Dakṣa given in marriage to Yama presumably come from among the 27 asterisms (*nakṣatra*) because in the *Mahābhārata,* the 27 Nakṣatras are the daughters of Dakṣa (also the wives of Soma, the moon god).[109] The group of thirteen can be interpreted in one or both of two ways: (1) the 13 Yamanakṣatra, (2) the 13 lunar months that approximate the solar year.

(1) *The 13 Yamanakṣatra.* Macdonell and Keith write,[110] "....the Taittirīya Brāhmaṇa divides the Nakṣatras into two sets, the Deva Nakṣatras and the Yama Nakṣatras, being 1-14 and 15-27 (with the omission of *Abhijit*) respectively. This division corresponds with one in the third book of the Brāhmaṇa, where the days of the light half of the month and those of the dark half are equated with the Nakṣatras. The Brāhmaṇa treats the former series as south, the later as north; but this has no relation to facts and can only be regarded as a ritual absurdity." That division is presumably related to the *Atharva-Veda* teaching, "The gods go to the other world by a path known as *devayāna* and a dead man, a prospective *Pitṛ* by means of a path known as *pitṛyāna*. Ultimately, they reach the same place."[111] This implies Yama's name "Lord of the Fathers" (*pitṛpati*).

(2) *The 13 lunar months that approximate the solar year.* Whitney writes,[112] "Through all the known periods of Indian history, down even to the present, the current appellations of the lunar periods into which the year is divided have been asterismal, and taken in each case from the *nakshatra* in (or near) which the moon, during that particular synodical revolution, reached her full." He further states,[113] ".... even in the earliest of the Brāhmaṇas, the month-date is always given by the same asterism as at present," and goes on to discuss the problem of the year in which (or, for which) the system was established. What is meant is that the Hindus traditionally had a series of 12 solar months, *Pauṣa*, down to *Mārgaśīrṣa*, derivatives from the names, almost all of feminine gender, of the twelve asterisms near which the moon first became full in a certain year: Puṣyā down to Mṛgaśirā. The derivative names are transferred to the lunar months in the Luni-solar Year, with one name (Caitra) repeated in modern practice to make thirteen.[114] Hopkins shows that, while the 30-day month is also Vedic, anciently, beginning with the RV, ten months were the regular ascription to the period of pregnancy.[115] This is not a solar year, which would only rarely begin with such a stipulated full moon. Also a year beginning with a full moon insures thirteen full moons in the year, whereas a solar year more often has only twelve full moons. If Yama's thirteen wives are the corresponding *nakṣatras*, Yama might be the sacrificial year.

The group of ten daughters married to Yama may imply the development in the womb during ten lunar months. This phase of Yama's career was already alluded to when discussing the name "Coagulated Milk" (*dadhna*). He was connected there with the Soma. Sometime in the Vedic period, Soma becomes definitely a name of the moon;[117] but since the latter marries all the twenty-seven daughters of Dakṣa, he cannot be Yama, who marries only ten or thirteen. The solar nature of Yama indicates that he is a kind of "sun by way of the moon". The Soma of the moon is really the contribution of the sun, for as Macdonell points out,[118] "In the post-Vedic literature Soma is a regular name of the moon, which is regarded as being drunk up by the gods and so waning, till it is filled up again by the sun." This is partly implied in Ṛg. I, 105, 1, as cited and translated by Hillebrandt.[119]

> candramā apsv ántár á suparṇó dhāvate divi/
> ná vo hiraṇyanemayaḥ padáṃ vindanti vidyutaḥ–//
> "es läuft der Mond in den Waṣs..rn, ein Vogel am Himmel.
> Nicht findet man euren Ort, O goldgefelgte Blitze."

The moon is a bird, but why "gold-rimmed"? This is not the color of the moon, but of the sun which has descended into the moon and in this guise is in the water. Lüders[120] devotes a chapter to the subject "De Sonne im Wasser", and Brown says,[121] "Possibly the Ādityas knew that the sun was in the water as an embryo...." Macdonell writes,[122] "Soma is described as purified with the hands (9, 86^{34}), by the ten fingers (9, 8^4, 15^8 etc.), or figuratively, by the ten maidens who are sisters (9, 1^7. 6^5) by the daughters (*naptī*) of Vivasvat (9, 14^5)", one of whose daughters is Yamī. Also,[123] "Soma is the drop which grows in the waters (9, 85^{10}, 89^2). Hence he is the embryo of the waters (9, 97^{41}, ŚB. 4, 4, 5^{21}) or their child, for seven sisters as mothers are around the child, the newly born, the Gandharva of the waters (9, 61^4)." As another well-known formulation of Yama's ancestry, Macdonell states,[124] "In their dialogue in the RV (10, 10^4) Yama and Yamī call themselves children of Gandharva and the water nymph (*apyā yoṣā*)," the latter being an *apsara,*[125] who could be called a "divine courtesan" (*divya-veśya*), for Bergaigne (II, 506) points out regarding the mother of the twins (cf. his. II, 98): "Nous avons déjà vu que Saraṇyū est la femelle céleste qui se dérobe à l'attente des hommes."

Ehni informs us,[126] "In späteren Stücken wird Saraṇyu mit der Sindhu (Luftmeer) identifizirt." Wherever this river may be, Law says,[127] "As described in the Ṛg-Veda (X, 75) the Sindhu in might surpassed all the flowing streams." Just as Yama's mother Saraṇyū is a river, so also is his sister Yamī, because Yama was shown to have the name "Brother of Yamunā", and the Yamunā is a river. We need not raise our eyebrows at Yamī's ability to be in one text—the earth and in another a river. After all, Yama is many things; why deny Yamī the right to change her mind? It appears that when Yama and Yamī are co-uterine; she is a "river", and that when he becomes a ploughman, she becomes the earth.

That brings up the topic of rivers, about which Lüders (in the posthumous work already cited) has gathered much material. Childe[128] mentions that among clay tablets of Mohenjo-daro, "one shows a river gushing out of a goddess' womb." In the MBh. Vaitaraṇī is a river in the region of Yama, and in the regions of the Pitṛs the Gaṅgā becomes Vaitaraṇī.[129] The Vaitaraṇī is called a cow (*dhenu*) in the *Garuḍa-Purāṇa.*[130] According to Dhārmika Subhūti, the water current of the river Vaitaraṇī is of blazing copper, and the man whose evil deed sends him into this river is perpetually burned by fire.[131] According to Vasubandhu, on both sides of this river the "policemen of Yama" (*yamarākṣasa*), armed with sharp weapons, prevent any of the hell beings from emerging.[132]

Buddhist doctrine speaks of the three "evil destinies" (*durgati*), hell beings, animals, and *pretas.*[133] Ui Hakuju's *Concise Buddhist Dictionary* (in Japanese), p. 365, mentions a river to be crossed on the seventh day after death. There are three current speeds of this river according to the *karma* of the previous life. The implication here is that the three currents represent the *karma* of the three "evil destinies". If the river can be crossed, presumably one would go to one of the "good destinies" (*sugati*), men and gods.

Asaṅga (4th cent., A.D.) in the *Cintāmayī Bhūmi* of his *Yogācāra-bhūmi,* quotes this verse from the *Kumārikā-praśna-gāthā:*[134]

> /kathaṃ vihārabahulo bhikṣuḥ pañcaughatīrṇas taratīha sasṭham/
> /evaṃ dhyāyī vipulāṃ kāmatṛṣṇāṃ tīrṇobhavaty apratilabdhayoktā//
> "How does the monk with a multiplicity of states of existence,[135]

> Having forded the five turbulent streams, ford here the sixth? And how does the meditator who has not achieved union ford the extensive thirst of desire?"

Asaṅga comments on the six turbulent streams (*ogha*):

> ṣaḍ ime oghāś cakṣur ogho rūpāṇāṃ darśanāya/yāvan mana ogho dharmāṇāṃ vijñapanāya/
> "These are the six turbulent streams: the eye (*cakṣus*) is a turbulent stream through seeing forms (*rūpa*); ....(down to) the mind (*manas*) is a turbulent stream through knowing natures (*dharma*)."

Hence, the five turbulent streams are the five senses through which we perceive the outer world. The meditator has turned away from that world because he is referred to as having "forded the five turbulent streams". But he still has the problem of the mind (*manas*). In order to ford the turbulent stream of the mind, one must "be not aroused, not excited, and be mindful" (*nābhisaṃskaroti/na kupyati/smṛtimāṃś ca bhavati*), expressions which Asaṅga then goes on to explain.

The term *ādānavijñāna* is used for the stream in a celebrated verse of the *Saṃdhinirmocana Sūtra*. The verse runs as follows:

> The profound and subtle Appropriating Perception (*ādānavijñāna*) flows with all its seeds (*bīja*) like a turbulent stream (*ogha*). I did not teach that to the 'children' (*bāla*), indeed, lest they should imagine it to be a self (*ātman*).[136]

The foregoing might appear to be a departure from the subject of Yama. Here the appropriateness of introducing such material appears when considering what happens at the time of death. As to the consciousness at death, the *Abhidharma-kośa* places the *manovijñāna* here.[137] The *manovijñāna* immediately implies a *manas*. The basic fact is the withdrawal of the "stream of consciousness" (*citta-saṃtāna*) from its involvement with the outer senses. This is just what the *yogin* attempts to do. The deceased person must face Yama. The *yogin* may therefore evoke Yama without actually having died. This may be in back of the *Kaṭha Upaniṣad*. Consistent with the *Abhidharma-kośa*, the "Perception based on mind" (*manovijñāna*), no longer having material to work on from the outer senses, continues its work of objectifying. What it objectifies are the natures associated (*saṃprayukta-dharma*) with the *citta*. Consistent with mythology, what is seen is Yama. Still, the mind (*manas*) continues to know the natures (*dharma*), and consequently the mind is a turbulent stream. Perhaps, this is the river to be crossed on the seventh day after death.

Another factor in the situation is that in Buddhism, the fourth member of Dependent Origination (*pratītya-samutpāda*) is called "Name and Form" (*nāma-rūpa*) and understood as the five personality aggregates in the womb.[138] In the Tibetan "Wheel of Life", this member is depicted as two persons in a boat. Vinītadeva, while explaining the drawing of the wheel, says,[139] "Name and form are a woman and a man." In mentioning the "woman" first, there is little doubt that he intends the two forms to correspond in the given order.

For the 'name' there is the mysterious verse of the *Taittirīya Saṃhitā*:[140]

> My name and thine, O all-knower,
> Which like men changing garments we bear,
> Let us exchange again;
> Thou for life, and we to live.

For the 'form', there is the fact that the Buddha Vairocana (a name meaning "sun") is considered to be the intrinsic nature (*svabhāva*) of the personal aggregate "form" (*rūpa*).[141] Each of the five basic winds (*vāyu*) are the intrinsic nature (*svabhāva*) of one of the five Tathāgatas, according to the *Vajramālā*, an Explanatory Tantra (*vyākhyātantra*) of the *Guhyasamāja*. The *Pañcakrama* quotes this verse from the Explanatory Tantra:[142]

> Sarvadehānugo vāyuh sarvaceṣṭāpravartakaḥ
> Vairocanasvabhāvo 'sau mṛtakāyād viniścaret.
> 'The wind that is the intrinsic nature of Vairocana
> Proceeds through the whole body,
> Causing all movements of the limbs,
> And departs (only) from the dead body."

In Tsoṅ-kha-pa's *Sṅags rim chen mo,* where this stanza is part of a lengthy quotation (beginning f. 440b-2 in the Peking edn.) from that Explanatory Tantra, the associated discussion shows that this wind is the one called *vyāna* (T. *Khyab byed*).The identification of Vairocana with the *vyāna* wind may have preserved an ancient doctrine found in the *Śatapatha-brāhmaṇa* (III, 9, 4, 7), as translated by Eggeling:[143] "Now that Upāṃśusavana (stone), forsooth is in reality Āditya Vivasvant (the sun), it is the pervading vital air (*vyāna*) of this (sacrifice)." But if the *rūpa* is the offspring of Vairocana, and Vairocana is equivalent to Vivasvat, who is the father of Yama, it follows that Yama is the "form" (*rūpa*) and Yamī the "name" ("*nāma*). This is consistent with their co-uterine state.

III. The Four Māras

Āryāsaṅga, or Asaṅga has this passage in his Śrāvaka-bhūmi as found in the photographic manuscript of the Bihar Research Society, and a translation follows immediately after the Sanskrit:[144]

> */ tatra catvāro mārāḥ saṃbahulāni mārakarmāṇi / veditavyāni yoginā / yogaprayuktena / tena parijñāya parivarjayitavyāḥ tatra catvāro mārāḥ / tadyathā skandhamāraḥ kleśamāraḥ maraṇamāraḥ devaputramāraś ca / pañcopādānaskandhāḥ / skandhamāraḥ / traidhātukāvacarāḥ kleśāḥ kleśamāraḥ/teṣāṃ teṣāṃ satvānāṃ / tasmāt tasmāt satvanikāyāḥ yan maraṇaṃ kālakriyā maraṇamāraḥ / yo 'sya kuśalapakṣaprayuktasya skandhakleśamṛtyuṃ samatikramāya kāmadhātūpapanno devaputraḥ aiśvaryaprāptaḥ / antarāyam upasaṃharati / vyākṣepakaraṇe / ayam ucyate devaputramāraḥ // tatra yatra ca mriyate / yena ca mriyate / yaś cāsau mṛtyur yena ca mṛtyuṃ na samatikrāmaty antarāyikena vastunā ity etad adhikṛtya catvāro mārā vyavasthāpitāḥ / tatra pañcasūpādāna- skandheṣu jāteṣu vartamāneṣu mriyate / kleśāṃ janayaty āyatyāṃ jātaś ca mriyate / cyutiś ca cyāvanatā satvānāṃ jivitendriyanirodhaḥ / kāla kriyāsvabhāva eva mṛtyuḥ / devaputramāro ('sya?) maraṇam samatikramāya prayuktasyāntarāyam upasaṃharati / yena naiva vā śaknoti maraṇadharmatāṃ samatikramitum / kālāntarena vā samatikrāmati /*
>
> Here there are four Māras, and the *yogin* applied to *yoga* should know the numerous deeds of Māra (*mārakarmāṇī*). Having understood well [the latter], they [i.e. the four Māras] should be avoided. Among those—the four Māras are the *skandha-māra*, the *kleśa-māra*, the *maraṇa-māra*, and the *devaputra-māra*. The *skandha-māra* is the five grasping

> personal aggregates (*skandha*). The *kleśa-māra* is the defilements (*kleśa*) that range in the three worlds. The *maraṇa-māra* is what fixes the time of the various sentient beings for death (*maraṇa*) from the various classes of sentient beings. [As to the *devaputra-māra*:] When someone is applied to the virtuous side for the purpose of transcending the personal aggregates (*skandha*), defilements (*kleśa*), and death (*mṛtyu*), a "Son of the Gods" (*devaputra*) born in the world of desire (*kāma-dhātu*) who has attained lordship brings about an "interruption", so as to swerve that person. This is called *devaputra-māra*. Among those, where does one die, whereby does one die, which is death itself, and by what interruptive element does one not transcend the death? Leading with those questions, the four Māras are well-established. Among those, one dies among the five grasping personal aggregates that having been born, are present. One generates defilements (*kleśa*), and having been subsequently born [thereby], one dies. The decease and passing away of sentient beings is cessation of their life organ; and death is precisely the intrinsic nature of fixing the time [of that]. The "Son of the Gods" Māra brings about an interruption for the one engaged in the purpose of transcending death. Either one is just not able, by reason of that [interruptive element], to transcend the true nature of death; or, at later time he transcends it.[145]

The passage shows that the word *māra* has for Asaṅga is etymological meaning of "death", but employed metaphorically. For example, the tenement of death is the personal aggregates (skandha*)*, so the latter are called *"death" (māra)*. When an ascetic is trying to avoid death by transcending it and the "Son of the Gods" swerves him, the ascetic cannot avoid death, so the "Son of the Gods" is also called "death" (*māra*). Accordingly, while the conventional translation of the word *"māra"* as "the Evil One, the adversary and tempter"[146] may seem suitable in many contexts, when we come to a strict employment of the word, as in the above passage by Asaṅga, it can only mean "death" (understood metaphorically). The word *māra* passes through four metaphorical values of "death" and in one of the values, so to say the "zero value"— the word means the concrete death, the *death* "*death*".

Asaṅga follows the passage quoted above with illustrations of the deeds of Māra, closing with the remark, "Whatever are of the same kind, known as deeds of Māra (*mārakarmāṇī*). Those belong to the four Māras as appropriate" (*itīmāny evaṃbhāgīyāni mārakarmāṇī veditavyāni tāni caturṇāṃ mārāṇāṃ yathāyogaṃ*). He did not classify particular deeds of Māra under one or other of the four Māras, but this would usually not be difficult to do. In the text, the various cravings (*rāga*) are called "nooses of Māra" (*mārapāśa*). Here the deeds of Māra are the various influences that swerve a person attempting to succeed in *yoga*. One example, which has an interest of its own, will be cited:

> Likewise, when one who is occupied in engagement to the practice of staying awake in the former and latter parts of night sinks his thought in the pleasure of sleep, the pleasure of resting, the pleasure of lying on his side—that is known as a deed of Māra (*evaṃ pūrvarātrāpararātraṃ/ jāgarikāyogam anuyuktasya viharataḥ / nidrāsukhe śayanasukhe pākṣasukhe cittaṃ praskandhati / veditavyaṃ mārakarmaitad iti*).[147]

If we should try to relate this "deed of Māra" to one of the four Māras, the solution in terms of the *Atharva-Veda* would probably be the death "*death*" (*maraṇa-māra*), because this attraction to sleep reminds us that in the *Atharva-Veda* sleep is called the child of death: "Thou who art neither alive nor dead, the immortal child of the gods are thou, O sleep! Varuṇāṇī is thy mother, Yama (death) thy father, Araru is thy name."[148] Varadachari points out,[149] "One fact that has to be noted is that the word *svapna* meant two things—the state of sleep as well as what it contains, the dreams." He applies this twofold connotation in his analysis of the *Atharva-Veda* hymn XIX. 56 (trans. Whitney), which begins "Out of Yama's world hast thou come hither; . . ."

In Buddhist doctrine, the "Son of the Gods"—Māra is the king of the Paranirmitavaśavartin gods.[150] In the general Indian tradition, Indra, at least in epic or later times, seems to fill the position, for as Winternitz writes:[151]

> It is even said that asceticism can compel Indra himself to enter the home of Yama (the god of death). And often indeed does Indra have recourse to the proved expedient of allowing

a beautiful Apsaras to seduce a saint who, through his severe austerities threatens to become dangerous to the gods.

This role of Indra is beautifully illustrated in the *Kathāsaritsāgara* version of the Śibi story.[152]

> And likewise, in olden times, there was a king, ascetic (*tapasvin*), compassionate, generous, steadfast, Śibi by name, who gave a feeling of safety to all creatures. In order to deceive him, Indra, having himself adopted the form of eagle (*śyena*), pursued Dharma in the form of an illusory pigeon (*kapota*). (That pigeon, proceeding through fear) went for protection to the lap of Śibi. The eagle then spoke with human speech to the king, "O monarch, this is my food. Surrender the pigeon to me, who is hungry. Otherwise, know me dead. What Dharma would you then have?" Then Śibi said to him, "This, having come to me for protection, is not to be abandoned. Therefore, I shall give you other flesh equal to it." The eagle said, "If that so, offer me your own flesh!" The king, being delighted with that replied "Agreed!" And just as much as that king, cutting off his flesh, lifted up just so much did the pigeon increase the scales. Then the king lifted his whole body to the scales. Thereupon, "Excellent, excellent! That is indeed equal," a divine voice came forth. Then, Indra and Dharma, having abandoned the form of eagle and pigeon, (being satisfied) fashioned that injured body as King Śibi. And having granted him other wishes, they disappeared.

In the popular conception, "This is my food" means not only that the pigeon is the eagle's food, but also that righteousness (*dharma*) is Indra's food. "What Dharma would you then have?" points both to righteousness and to the pigeon. But there is a more profound interpretation of the story. For this, we recall that the deity Dharma is really Yama and that the pigeon (*kapota*)is a messenger of Yama. Then the story can be understood through Asaṅga's remarks about the *devaputra-māra*. King Śibi is practising severe austerities (*tapasvin*), so he may be in danger of death. Indra's food is the death of ascetics for, if they do not die his existence of supremacy will be overthrown. Therefore, Indra contrives an "interruption" for Śibi in the form of the frightened pigeon, and the latter could well be the harbinger of Śibi's death. But the ascetic does not give the pigeon (his death) to Indra. Instead he gives his life. Life alone is the equal of death. Indra cannot refuse Śibi's life, although he prefers his death. Thereby the ascetic defeats the "Son of the Gods" Māra. This interpretation can be compared with the explanation in the *Ārya-Akṣayamatinirdeśa-ṭīkā*:[153]

> The four kinds of Māra are the *devaputramāra*, the *kleśamāra*, the *skandhamāra, and the *mṛtyumāra*. Among them the *devaputramāra* was defeated by the *samādhi* of love (*maitrī*) beneath the Tree of Enlightenment (*bodhi-vṛkṣa*). The *kleśamāra* was defeated at the time of clear comprehension (*abhisamaya*) of Enlightenment. The *skandhamāra* was defeated by the *ālayavijñāna-āśraya-parāvṛtti* at the time of clear comprehension of Enlightenment. Repressing the life motivation (*āyuḥ-saṃskāra*) in Vaiśālī,[154] three months before passing into Nirvāṇa-the **mṛtyumāra* was defeated there by achieving the power over life (*āyur-vaśitā*).

The comments (attributed to Vasubandhu) that the *devaputramāra* is defeated first is consistent with Asaṅga's statement that when someone is trying to surmount the other three Māras, a *devaputramāra* tries to divert him. His order of defeating the Māras will also explain a rather obscure part of Asaṅga's statement. "Either one is just not able, by reason of that, to transcend the true nature of death"—i.e. the *devaputra* Māra has defeated the ascetic; "or, at a later time he transcends it"—that "later time" being the time when he defeats the last Māra to be defeated, the *Death "Death"*.

Now we can return to Yama. As Keith translates the *Taittirīya-Saṃhitā*:[155]

> Yama is Agni, Yamī is this (earth); the sacrificer becomes under a debt to Yama in that he strews the altar with plants; if he were to go away without burning (them), they would drag him about bound by the neck in yonder world.

If we now consider what it might mean in Buddhist terms. The Skt. word *skandha* is equivalent to Pāli *khandha*, which is used for the trunk of a tree or the stem of a palm.[156] Asaṅga said that one dies among the five *skandhas*, so we might say figuratively that they drag him about bound by the neck in yonder world. For, the burning of the *skandhas* we resort to Buddhaguhya's commentary on the *Mahāvairocana* when he discusses the "Inner burnt offering" (T. *naṅ gi sbyin sreg,* S. **ādhyātmika-homa*):[157]

> Moreover, one destroys the five *ātmaka-skandha* in voidness (*śūnyatā*), and also destroys the forms of sense objects (*viṣaya*), such as the external 'hearth' (*agnikuṇḍa*), in Voidness. In the same way one individually destroys the issuances of six-doored perception (*vijñāna*);[158] and when they do not issue and are stopped in the same way, the "thought of enlightenment" (*bodhicitta*) which destroys and stops those is itself stopped by the non-issuing insight (*prajña*); and that abiding in the non-discursive (**avikalpa*) *samādhi* is the Inner Burnt Offering. Hence, one stops the "fire of wind" (*vāyv-agni*) by the non-issuing Insight (*prajña*), and "One makes the burnt offering to fire with the mind (**manas*)". "Stops the fire of wind" means "restrains the *prāṇa* and *āyāma*".[159] "One makes the burnt offering to fire with the mind" means "one burns thoughts immobile (*añinjya* or *āniñjya*)".

Hence the mind is the sacrificer; and this accords with standard Buddhist doctrine that the mind—the *manas* or the *cittasantati*—transmigrates. The fire is first said to be Voidness (*śūnyatā*), then identified with the winds. The mind may be said to be under a debt to the winds, for these support the *skandhas* and the perception of outer objects. Suppose the mind were to leave without having made offering to the fiery wind (or Yama): that would simply be an ordinary death. But if the mind makes the proper offering, it can leave by special permission (*anujña*) with a vehicle given the mind by the winds, as mentioned in the tantras. Presumably the disengagement of the subtle form from the body also takes place in ordinary death. Is this what is meant by the seventh day after death, alluded to in Ui's Dictionary, as cited in Section II, above?

Then where does Yamī fits in? The *Saṃhitā* says, "Yamī is this," and of course Yamī is the altar. When Keith interprets "this" as the *earth*, it is a most proper interpretation for an external sacrifice—also a proper interpretation for an internal sacrifice if "earth" be understood metaphorically. When the sacrifice is made with the mind, the altar is in the mind. Padmavajra quotes[160] "Our own mind (*citta*) is called 'Māra'." This appears consistent with the *Cittamātra* school, also known as Yogācāra or Vijñaptimātra. The external earth, demons, daughters of Māra, and the like are understood as the mental entities.

IV. The Three Yamas

The passages to be translated in this section show how in some Buddhist traditions, the concepts of Yama and Māra have completely merged, and the passages will justify the procedure of treating both these figures in these studies.

In the legend of Yama as set forth by the Dzaya-paṇḍita Blo bzaṅ ḥphrin las[161] not only are three Yamas described, but also their three executioners (Yamāri or Yamāntaka). The initial descriptions of the latter three will be translated, but not the extended descriptions.

Translation

It is said in the *mūlatantra* of the *Kālacakra-* (*tantra*) that at the time when the teacher pronounced the *Kālacakra-tantra* at Śrī-Dhānyakaṭaka, he also pronounced the other Anuttara Tantras.[162] It is said in the 18th section of the *Kṛṣṇayamāri-kalpa*: "At the time, when the teacher was demonstrating on the Diamond Seat (*vajrasana*), the taming of Māra at dusk (*srod*), for the purpose of taming Māra and Yama, he caused Yamāntaka and retinue (*parivāra*) to manifest, as the Tantras say." In accordance with the school that says that, there are three Yamas to be tamed—"external" (*phyi*), "personal" (*naṅ*), and "concealed" (*gsaṅ*).[163] It says in the *Vimala* [*prabhā*]:

> The Departed Spirit (*preta*) dwelling in the place;
> The Lord of Death (*mṛtyu*) dwelling in the body;
> The Defilement (*kleśa*) dwelling in the mind;
> These three are the *karmic* Yamas to be tamed.

Just as that says, there are three Yamas to be tamed. It says in the *Kṛṣṇajāla-Tantra*:

> The "Cycle of Life" (*saṃsāra*) in the three worlds is Yama;
> The King of the Law (*dharmarāja*) is the Master (T. *rje bo*);
> Yamāntaka is his executioner.

This sets forth individually both Yama and Yamāri.[164]

Furthermore, it says in the *Vimala- [prabhā]* Tantra: "As both Yama and Yamāri are individually set forth with respect to taming, there are also three kinds of Yamāri to do the taming:

"(a) By showing the nature (*ṅo bo*) of the Form Body (*rūpa-kāya*) from the nature of the Law Body (*dharma-kāya*), the Departed Spirit (*preta*) dwelling in the place is tamed.

"(b) By manifesting from the joyful Realm *Dharmadhātu,* the True Thought (**cittatā*) Divine Body (**divya-kāya*), which is unpolluted with the illusion of false reflection, the Lord of Death dwelling in the body is tamed.

"(c) By the non-duality of action (*karma*) and knowledge (*jñāna*); by the non-duality, in the pure immensity of True Thought of what is to be tamed and the taming agent: by full comprehension (**avabodha*) introspectively, the defilement (*kleśa*) dwelling in the mind (*citta*) is tamed." Thus, his executioner is also said to be three.[165]

A. The External Yama

First, the Yama that is the departed spirit dwelling in the place. In the southern direction, beneath the seven steps of the underworld (*pātāla*) at the bottom of the great ocean, at the limit of the wind disk (*vāyumaṇḍala*), there is a dark iron castle produced from action (*karma*) and defilement (*kleśa*) without doors of sixteen sides (*kha*) and very sharp edges. Many fresh corpses and hearts are piled up in undulating trenches.[166] A lake of blood clots is greatly agitated with whirlpools and waves. Outside of this is a spread-out scattering of flesh, blood and bones, within which is the delusion in the inner apprehending consciousness, and there is a myriad (*koṭi*) black *preta* Māras produced from the fierce power of the maturation of *karma*.[167]

[Among them] is Gu riṅ.[168] He is also called Yama *pīvasattva* ("mighty being"). He is of black color, naked, with long curly hair, fangs bared, tongue curled, eyes laughing, whites of the eyes inflamed, enveloped in pitch-black fruit [of *karma*(?)]; his eyebrows and eye-lashes bristle; his two hands hold the club and the noose. His thought blazes like the fire of hatred.[169]

His consort is a demoness with the heat of *karma*, Caṇḍā (or Caṇḍālī). She is also called "she attired in an old tattered garment" and also Cāmuṇḍī, the black one (*kalī*). She is naked with long hair; is extremely angry. Her two hands hold a trident (*triśūla*) and a skull dripping with blood. Her thought is agitated like the water of lust.[170]

The offspring of their union is the servants, messengers of *karma*, eight in all: Yama Dharmarāja and the serpent *Phya bsaṅs, Yavati* and *Telapa, Ava glaṅ mgo can* and *Rmig pa, Ral pa tshar dgu* and *Mig dmar po.*[171] Also he has a consort with a hundred feet and nine storied heads, one "*mtshan mo dred kyi ha-ba-śam can*" with many feet and nine storied heads, etc.[172]

Also an innumerable host of male and female Yamas have [respectively] thought blazing like the fire of hatred and agitated like the water of lust. The blackish red and blackish green clouds of the sky above are [thereby] supported in agitation. The one who subjects the life force of the three worlds is called the Lord of Death, Yama.[173] It says in the same work:

> The worldly sentient beings have multiplied the power in the wayward path since the limit of beginningless time,
> And consequently have matured the harsh seed of the cycle of life.

The Māra in general agreement with this is the Karmic Māra.[174]

B. The Personal Yama

The Personal Yama is said to be the Death "Death" (*maraṇa-māra* or *mṛtyu-māra*), who appears in one's own dress to all the people who see (him) from this side and overcomes (those) powerless, but in fact all the four Māras are the manifestation of impure actions (*karma*). He is accompanied by his various ministers, messengers, and servants, and is fearfully ugly. Because he seizes the life of the living beings, he is called *Śrī-svayambhūmāra (Glorious self-originated Māra).[175]

C. The Concealed Yama

In regard to the Yama of defilements (*kleśa*), located in the mind (*citta*), the defilements located in the stream of thought (*citta-santāna*) are called 'Yama'. The reason is that just as the *karmic* Yama severs the life energy of the living beings, so also the defilements of craving and so forth sever the life energy of liberation of [from?] what is to be tamed.[176] Here Yama is something to be overcome.

Discussion of the Yama to be Overcome

The External Yama is called the *karmic* Māra. His surrounding host is presumably the Mārakāyika *pretas* set forth above. Perhaps, the Son-of-the-Gods Māra is also included here. This is the Yama commonly depicted in Tibetan iconography (*Dharmarāja bāhya-sādhana*).[177]

The Personal Yama is the Lord-of-Death Māra and may include also the *skandha*-Māra. It seems to be the epic Yama that appears to the deceased.[178] The idea here, as the writer understands it, is that one's own actions (mental, verbal, and physical) become objectified as a nightmare.

The Concealed Yama is the "Defilement" Māra (*kleśa-māra*). The three principal varieties taken from the list of twenty *citta*, are "thought with craving" (*sarāga-citta)*, "thought with hatred" (*sadveṣa-citta*), and "thought with delusion" (*samoha-citta*).

Conclusion

When one has gathered together so many diverse traditions, it is still not necessary to expect from him some one absolute conclusion regarding the nature of Yama. This is consistent with the primary assumption of the studies: material drawn from texts separated by several thousands of years will not always be saying the same thing; but the staying within a single cultural continuum, and utilizing texts of living, even if not always well-understood tradition is the illuminating approach-both to the old and the new. The writer does not agree with a certain view that the Indian thought has always had the same message, if one is sufficiently profound to detect it; but does hold that many primary ideas of which Indian thought have been passed down through the many centuries and that there were disagreements in the middle and in the end as well as probably in the beginning. By bringing together various and contrasting views on the same general topic, gradually a picture of what is meant presents itself.

It has been exposed that there two strains of Yama: (1) A divine Yama of solar nature—the prototype of immortality; (2) A fearful Yama, personification of the evil in man and his inevitable death—

the principal Epic and Buddhist Yama. Both these Yamas occur in the Vedic literature. The difficulty of further interpretation is that the second kind of Yama gained textual and popular supremacy over the first. But this is the case as long as we discuss the matter using only the name "Yama". The first kind of Yama is by no means forgotten, if we take into consideration other names and then the difficulty is extended to those names.

It seems that the Solar Yama is the Form (*rūpa*) or the fiery Wind when Yamī is the Name (*nāma*) or a river. The four Māras are what obscure the true nature of that Name and Form.

REFERENCES

1. J. Ehni, *Der Vedische Mythus des Yama* (Strassburg, 1890), 41-2.
2. Arthur Berriedale Keith, *The Veda of the Black Yajus School,* HOS Vol. 18, p. 137.
3. Arthur Anthony Macdonell, *The Bṛhad-devatā,* HOS Vol. 6, p. 43.
4. V. Fausbøll, *Indian Mythology* (London, 1902), p. 136.
5. Dpal ḥdzin sde's *Abhidhānaśāstraviśvalocana (ityaparābhidhānamuktāvali)-nāmā,* Derge Tg., *Sna tshogs,* Po. 80a-3, f.:// chos kyi rgyal po pha gśin bdag/ḥtshe baḥi dbaṅ phyug gśin rjeḥi rgyal/źi byed gśin rje mtshuṅs ḥjug daṅ/lho phyogs bdag po mthar byed daṅ/graṅs can/byas mthaḥ/kī-nā-śa/ma-heḥi rgyal mtshan/chad pa ḥdzin/ kun ḥdod/rñiṅ gnas/gśin gyi rgyal/dus ḥdzin/ḥphrog byed/yi dags bdag/dbyug ḥdzin lto bcas ka-li-ndī/ñi maḥi bu daṅ mtshun gyi lha/chad pa can daṅ dgaḥ byed do// ḥdi yi chuṅ ma dud pas ḥgebs//groṅ ni yaṅ dag ḥgog ces bya//mdun paḥi miṅ ni ñi ma can//kā-ṇī-tsī ni rnam spyod pa//pa-ñtsa-ka-tva-gri-sa-nnā-li//sna tshogs sbas pa/yi ge pa//gYog ni/gtum po/gtum chen dag//
6. lho phyogs bdag po la miṅ ñer drug.
7. Cf. Manfred Mayrhofer, *Kurzgefasstes etymoligisches Wörterbuch des Altindischen,* I, 215; F.B.J. Kuiper, "Rigvedic Loanwords", *Studia Indologica* (Festschrift für Willibald Kirfel) (1955), 155-6; H.W. Bailey, "Indo-Iranian Studies-III", *Transactions of the Philogical Society* (1955), 68, where the solution is "ploughshare" (**kina or *kinā*) plus "possessing" or "concerned with" (*–āśa*). The difficulty of analyzing this term was doubtless felt as well by the Tibetan translator as by western scholars: hence the transcription into Tibetan.
8. S. Sörensen, *Index to the Names in the Mahābhārata,* p. 768.
9. Böhtlingk and Roth, *Sanskrit Wörterbuch,* Vol. 3, 496: *daṇḍadhārasya yamasya.*
10. Monier-Williams, *Sanskrit-English Dictionary,* p. 423, equates this word with *jīvitanatha and cites Raghuvaṃśa* xi, 20.
11. Böhtlingk and Roth, *Sanskrit Wörterbuch,* Vol. 2, 252.
12. *Op. cit.,* I, 225.
13. A.A. Macdonell, *Vedic Mythology* (Strassburg, 1897), p. 172.
14. Macdonell and Keith, *Vedic Index,* I, 42, and 470.
15. This is the spelling in Fausboll (*op. cit.*), p. 136, where some names of Yama's kingdom are found. Willibald Kirfel, *Das Purāṇa vom Weltgebäude* (Univ. Bonn,

1954), p. 303, also gives references to Saṃyamanī. In the Tibetan translation of Candragomin's *Uṇādivṛtti* (Derge Tg., *Sgra mdo,* Re, f. 121b-1,2) the transcribed word *Marūkaḥ* is glossed *gśin rjeḥi groṅ* ("city of Yama"); but no verification of this was noticed.

16. This particular entry especially domonstrates how the Tibetan text of the lexicon is often misleading or incomprehensible without the utilization as has been, done of both the *Amarakośa* (in the Skt.-Tib. *Bibl. Ind.* edn.) and a lexicon such as Hemacandra's. The Sarat Chandra Das *Tibetan-English Dictionary,* p. 1249, under *gśin rje* (Yama) repeats this entry as found in a native lexicon which incorporated material from the Tanjur lexica. The T. *mdun pa* is then translated as "minister", but the dictionary does not even list *mdun pa* in its ordinary place (which would be on p. 675), and the word for "minister" is given there as *mdun na ḥdon*. T. *mdun pa* means literally "the one in front" and this suits the usage "doorkeeper". Besides the difficulty with *mdun pa,* the T. *ñi ma can* "solar" would hardly suggest a Sanskrit original of *vaidhyata*. But since doubtless the Tib. did translate that Skt., we must consider the possibility that the doorkeeper here is Viṣṇu, because the latter is stated to be the doorkeeper of the gods in J. Gonda, *Aspects of Early Viṣṇuism* (Utrecht, 1954), p. 93, and it is relevant to our further arguments that "Viṣṇu is requested to guard the soma..." (*ibid.*, p. 95).
17. This word understood to be the original of the Tib. transcription *kā-ṇī-tsī,* is not given this explanation in the Monier-Williams Dictionary, which, however, does record *vicārabhū,* the presumed original of T. *rnam spyod pa*.
18. An Interlinear Tibetan note reads: *dkaḥ. ḥgrel ni mchog dam pa sgrubs.* This is an entirely inadequate translation, but facilitates the restoration from the corrupt transcription of the correct Sanskrit: *pañjikā tv agrasaṃdhānī.* This is because T. *dkaḥ ḥgrel* is the standard translation of *pañjikā* (as a type of commentary), and T. *mchog* frequently translates *agra.* The rest follows easily because *agrasaṃdhānī* is in the Monier-Williams Dict. The term occurs in Böhtlingk and Roth, Vol. I, 42, from Puruṣottama's *Trikāṇḍaśeṣa,* I, 1, 73. Further, the corrupt Sanskrit transcription *pa-ñtsa-ka* (S. pañcaka) "group of five" may have given rise to a spurious name of Yama in the Das Dictionary, p. 1248, T. *lṅa paḥi bdag* "lord of the group of five."
19. This has the alternate form *śirṇapāda*. Böhtlingk and Roth, Vol. 7 cites *Trikāṇḍaśeṣa,* I, 1, 71.
20. J. Scheftelowitz, "Die Zeit als Schicksalsgottheit in der indischen und iranischen Religion," *Beiträge zur indischen Sprachwissenschaft und Religionsgeschichte,* IV (Stuttgart, 1929), pp. 19, 29-30. He cites Baudh. Dharm. 2, 5, 9, 11, and the Utsarjana-prayoga. Cf. Mahāmahopādhyāya Pandurang Vaman Kane, *History of Dharmaśāstra,* Vol. IV (Poona 1953), p. 593.
21. Cf. Emil Abegg, *Der Pretakalpa des Garuḍa-Purāṇa* (Berlin, 1921), p. 54.
22. Cf. the MBh. passage cited in note 28, below.
23. When Yama is identified with Agni: cf. É. Senart, *Essai sur la Légende du Buddha* (Paris, 1882), p. 191.
24. *Śatapatha Brāhmaṇa,* tr. Julius Eggeling, SBE XLI (Oxford, 1894), III, p. 298.
25. *Vedic Mythology,* 172, for the RV references.
26. N.J. Shende, *The Foundations of the Atharvaṇic Religion* (Poona, 1929) 248-63.
27. *Vedic Mythology,* 172.
28. *Śānti P.,* Crit. edn., 169, 1: *atikrāmati kāle'smin sarvabhūtakṣayāvahe.*
29. For example, Maurice Bloomfield, *Hymns of the Atharva-Veda,* SBE XLII (Oxford, 1897), pp. 224-5.
30. *Ibid.,* p. 21.

31. A. Bergaigne, *La Religion Védique* (Paris, 1878 and 1883). I, 274.
32. *Op. cit.*, p. 416.
33. *Śatapatha Brāhmaṇa,* III, p. 256-7.
34. Haṃsarāja, *Vaidikakoṣaḥ* (Lahore, 1926), p. 203: *somo vai dadhi.*
35. Ananda K. Coomaraswamy, *Yakṣas,* Part II (Wash., D.C., 1931), p. 21.
36. The work cited in note 20, above.
37. *Ibid.*, p. 349.
38. *Ibid.*, p. 335. Ludwik Sternbach, reviewing this volume of Kane's work in *JAOS*, 74 (Oct.-Dec. 1954), p. 272, mentions the view of W. Caland "that the motive for *śrāddha* to the dead was merely the fear of the dead (*preta*)..... ."
39. Paul Mus, *La Lumière sur les Six Voies* (Institut d'Ethnologie, XXXV) (Paris, 1939), 250, f. (the note to verse 49).
40. This agrees with K.F. Geldner, *Der Rig-Veda,* III, HOS Vol. 35, p. 157, note to 5d.
41. Kane (*op. cit.*), 185f.; Franklin Edgerton, "The Hour of Death", *Annals of the Bhandarkar Institute,* Vol. VIII (1927), 219-49.
42. *Op. cit.*, p. 68, f.
43. Sörensen (*op. cit.*), p. 768.
44. *Op. cit.*, I, 111; cf. also II, 96.
45. V.M. Apte, "Varuṇa in the Ṛgveda", *NIA,* Vol. VIII (July-Dec. 1946), p. 145.
46. *Op. cit.*, pp. 248-61.
47. Lin Li-kouang, *L'Aide-Mémoire de la Vraie Loi* (Paris, 1949), 16-8.
48. The beginning of the *preta* section in the Tibetan translation is in Derge Kg., Mdo, Vol. Ya, f. 284b-6: *de nas...* The section ends f. 313b-1. Most of the space is given to description of the 36 families, the order of which is followed in my numbering, in agreement with Lin. Preceding the individual descriptions is a list of the 36, with slight irregularities in the order and some alternate misleading trranslations of terms. The Japanese text was made accessible by my wife Hideko, who also makes possible the other Sino-Japanese references in this article. The Japanese translation employed is in the *Kokuyaku Issaikyō,* 1st Ser., Kyō-shū-bu, vol. 8, beginning p. 292 (Japanese numerals).
49. Lin was justified in restoring the Sanskrit as *kapāli,* because after the transcription the word is translated by the logogram meaning the 3-legged vessel. The subsequent description of the particular *preta* family is of the *preta* with no head, arms, or legs, for which one would expect the Sanskrit *kabandha.* The Tib. has *lto gug*"prostrate belly" which suits either *kapāli* or *kabandha.*
50. *Salila* must be the word, verified by the description, which usually involves river water, or running water. However, the Japanese reading *bariraṇ* is justified by the *Taishō* Vol. 17, p. 92b-1 *ba* graph. Lin presumably and justifiably took this as a graphical error for a similar graph (*Ueda Daijiten* No. 10717, pronounced *sa*), but a note by him would have been helpful.
51. However, *āśaka* is given by Lin in a note with a question mark.
52. The original Sanskrit is made certain by Tib. *drag śul spyod pa* = *abhicāra.* Moreover, this completely fits the description of the *preta,* who is bent on bringing harm to people and giving them nightmares. The source of the mistranslation into Chinese, "marchant vite", is probably the fact that the final statement, "That is why he is called "**abhicārapreta*" is immediately preceded by a reference to the *preta*'s fast-going, but that final statement referred to the entire description of the *preta.*
53. The Skt. is decided from the Tib. *glags lta ba.* Lin's *cettāra-preta* cannot be defended.
54. However, the T. *mtsan mo lus rab tu ḥbar ba* "Whose body blazed at night"

suggests a longer Skt. form, perhaps *rātrijvālapreta*.

55. Tib. *mi rnams kyi bus pa la glags lta ba* suggests the Skt. given. This *preta* seeks to take the life of a human infant as soon as it is born.
56. Tib. is *bdud kyi sde*.
57. *Op. cit.*, p. 286, note.
58. *Ibid.*, pp. 307-9.
59. *Dam paḥi chos mṅon pa mdzod kyi don legs par bśad pa rin po cheḥi gru gziṅs*, III, 33b-4, f.:/ ḥo na dmyal baḥi bsruṅ ma de dag sems can yin nam min źe na/ bye brag smra ba ni gaṅ zag tu ḥdod ciṅ/mdo sde pas ḥbyuṅ ba daṅ ḥbyuṅ ḥgyur gyi khyad par las grub paḥi bem por ḥdod do/ dbu sems gñis kyaṅ de daṅ ḥdra/ dmyal baḥi gśin rje ni gaṅ zag yin par thams cad kyis ḥdod do/ The author of this *abhidharma* commenary is considered to be the rebirth of the Jam-yaṅ-zhad-pa referred to by Th. Stcherbatsky, *Buddhist Logic* (photomechanic reprint, 's-Gravenhage, 1958), Vol. I, p. 57. Accordingly, he is called the second Jam-yaṅ-zhad-pa. The "whole library of works" mentioned by Stcherbatsky may well have been written in part by Dkon mchog ḥjigs med dbaṅ po.
60. Cf. Mus (*op. cit.*), "Les Gardes infernaux sont-ils des êtres?" (p. 209-11); and *Abhidharma-kośa* , tr., Chap. III, p. 152-3.
61. This statement shows that the *Ārya-Saddharmasmṛtyupasthāna* is a Vaibhāṣika work, since in its standard way, it gives a presumed offence as a man leading to birth among the *pretas* as a policeman of Yama. "Vaibhāṣika", however, can mean various "Hīnayāna" schools. This agrees with the sub-title of Lin Li-Kouang's work, "Recherches sur un Sūtra Développé du Petit Véhicule".
62. Abegg, *op. cit.*, p. 63.
63. *Vedic Mythology*, 173.
64. *Op. cit.*, p. 404. He has a note to the word "Yama", "In RV. I, 29, 3 the two messengers (dogs) of Yama are personified as females."
65. H.J. Hariyappa, "Ṛgvedic Legends through the Ages", *Bulletin of the Deccan College Research Institute*, Vol. XI (March, 1951), p. 142.
66. Chap. III, p. 155.
67. Sörensen (*op. cit.)*, p. 489.
68. F.W. Thomas in *Indian Antiquary*, 32 (1903).
69. W. Woodville Rockhill, *Udānavarga* (London, 1892), p. 4. N.P. Chakravarti, *L'Udānavarga Sanskrit*, Tome Premier (Paris, 1930), p. 3, Sanskritizes the Tibetan of the second half as follows : *evaṃ vyādhiś ca jarā ca janān mṛtyurājasakāśaṃ nayati*. The Tibetan here does not agree with extant Pāli and Prakrit versions.
70. Mus, p. 68, note, already cited above (note 42).
71. Shende, p. 253.
72. Kane, IV, p. 156.
73. Cf. Kane, 342-3.
74. *Ibid.*, 194-5 and 201.
75. *Ibid.*, 344.
76. *Ibid.*, 341-2.
77. *Ibid.*, 339-40.
78. S.G. Kantawala, "The Cult of Manes as Depicted in the Matsya Purāṇa", *Journal of the Oriental Institute*, Baroda, Vol. V (July 1956), p. 407.
79. Cf. Lin (*op. cit.*), p. 21-2, for a discussion of the three chief personages of the Yāmas, with no suggestion that any of the three is Yama.
80. *Abhidharma-kośa*, Chap. III, commentary on stanza 59.
81. The author's "Contributions regarding the thirty-two characteristics of the Great

Person", *Liebenthal Festschrift; Sino-Indian Studies*, Vol. V, Parts 3 and 4, pp. 245-6.

82. *Sṅags rim*, Peking edn., f. 286b-2:/źal luṅ las/chos sku rab dgaḥ mkhaḥ mñam pa/ śi daṅ brgyal daṅ gñid log daṅ/ glal daṅ ḥkhrig dus skad cig tsam/ myoṅ bar ḥgyur bas/ źes śi ba la sogs pa gnas skabs lṅar chos sku myoṅ bar gsuṅs pa.
83. "Notes on the Kaṭha Upaniṣad", *NIA*, Vol. I (April, 1938), p. 45.
84. The commentary on the *Subāhuparipṛcchā, Tshig gi don bśad paḥi brjed byaṅ* (Tōhoklu Cat. No. 2672), Derge Tg., *Rgyud*, Thu, 71b-3, f.:/ gsaṅ baḥi dkyil ḥkhor las/ ji skad du/ brgya byin gyi ni rdo rjer gsuṅs/ me lhaḥi phyag rgya źugs thab yin/ gśin rjeḥi phyag rgya be con yin/ bden bral gyi ni ral gri yin/ chu bdag gi ni źags par bśad/ rluṅ gi phyag rgya rgyal mtshan yin/ ku-be-ra yi dbyug to yin/ dbaṅ phyug gi ni rtse gsum gsuṅs/ sa yi phyag rgya bum pa yin/ ñi zlaḥi phyag rgya zlum por bya/źes gsuṅs te/. The work *Ḥphags pa drā-bi-daḥi bum paḥi cho ga* (Tōhoku No. 3130), Derge Tg., *Rgyud*, Pu, 240b-3, 4:/ brgya byin gyi ḥkhor ni lha rnams so/ meḥi ḥkhor ni draṅ sroṅ rnams so/ gśin rjeḥi ḥkhor ni ma mo rnams so / bden bral gyi ḥkhor ni srin po rnams so/chu lhaḥi ḥkhor ni klu rnams so/ rluṅ lhaḥi ḥkhor ni rig sṅags ḥchaṅ rnams so/ rnam thos kyi bu ḥkhor ni gnod sbyin rnams so/ dbaṅ ldan gyi ḥkhor ni ḥbyuṅ po rnams so/ saḥi lha mo ḥkhor rnams ni sa bdag rnams so/. The former work gives the entries Kubera and Īśvara; the latter, the entries Vaiśravaṇa and Īśāna.
85. D.R. Patil, *Cultural History from the Vāyu Purāna* (Poona, 1946), p. 22: "It is said that they are called *maharṣis* because they see (*ṛṣanti mahat*)....." "the Brahmarṣis... 'see' Brahman...." "The Devarṣis...'see' Devas...."
86. See the illustrations in Stella Kramrisch, *The Art of India* (New York, 1954): No. 68 "Flying Vidyādhara, on East Wall, Virūpākṣa Temple"; and No. 77 "Vidyādharas flying with lotus bud and mirror, Svarga Brahmā Temple".
87. The translation is a combination of the "good folk" (*puṇyajana*) of the AV as pointed out by Coomaraswamy, *Yakṣas*, II, p. 3; and the "secret one" (*guhyaka*), an epithet of the *yakṣas*.
88. Apart from the direction, this may be the oldest line of all. Īśāna, or Īśvara, i.e., Śiva, with trident, and master of creatures may (as has been postulated) have descended from the horned "lord of animals" (*paśupati*) of Mohenjo-daro.
89. *Tantrārthāvatāra*, Derge Tg., *Rgyud ḥgrel*, Vol. Hi, 6b-3:/ dam tshig gi phyag rgya de dag kyaṅ rdo rje daṅ/ lcags kyu daṅ/mdaḥ daṅ/ mñes pa la sogs par ḥdu śes ste/.
90. Cf. the illustrations of filled vases in Coomaraswamy, *Yakṣas*, Part II, Plates 28, and 29, 31-3.
91. See Jitendra Nath Banerjea, *The Development of Hindu Iconography* (Univ. of Calcutta, 1956), 519-29, for a discussion of the directional guardians.
92. *Yakṣas*, II, 31 (note). In Dr. Subhadra Jha's "Studies in the Paippalādi Atharvaveda", *JBRS*, Vol. XXXIX (Sept. 1953), p. 347, we find in one list Yama in the south, and in another, not containing Yama, Indra in the south.
93. *Op. cit.*, in the translation of X. 14, pp. 191-4.
94. *Ibid.*, p. 154. J. Norman Brown, "The Rigvedic Equivalent for Hell", *JAOS*, 61 (June 1941), p. 79, locates Nirṛti (our next topic) "Personification of Malevolence and Destruction" beneath the earth in a place of non-ṛta (*anṛta*) and non-existence (*asat*).
95. Heinrich Lüders, *Varuṇa*, I: *Varuṇa und die Wasser*. Aus dem Nachlass herausgegeben von Ludwig Alsdorf (Göttingen, 1951), p. 31.
96. Louis Renou, 'Vedique *Nirṛti*', *Indian Linguistics* (Chatterji Jubilee Volume),

Vol. 16 (Nov. 1955), p. 11.

97. R.N. Dandekar, "*Asura Varuṇa*", *Annals of the Bhandarkar Inst.*, Vol. XXI (April-July 1940), p. 184.
98. *Op. cit.*, 159.
99. Bloomfield (*op. cit.*), p. 166-7.
100. *Op. cit.*, p. 13.
101. Eggeling, Part III, "The Altar of Nirṛti" (pp. 319-25).
102. Sujitkumar Mukhopadhyaya, Ed., *Śārdūlakarṇāvadānam* (Shantiniketan, 1954), text p. 51, Cf. Nakṣatra Table in H.T. Colebrooke, *Asiatic Researches*, Vol. IX (1809 reprint), between p. 322 and 323.
103. *Op. cit.*, p. 137.
104. *Op. cit.*, p. 223.
105. M. Winternitz, *A History of Indian Literature* (Univ. of Calcutta, 1927), I, 297.
106. Fausbøll (*op. cit.*) pp. 1-2.
107. John Dowson, *A classical Dictionary of Hindu Mythology*... under Kaśyapa.
108. *Op. cit.*, p. 117.
109. Sörensen (*op. cit.*), p. 496.
110. *Vedic Index*, I, p. 414.
111. Shende (*op. cit.*), p. 253.
112. William Dwight Whitney, *Oriental and Linguistic Studies*, Sec. Ser. (New York, 1874), p. 360 (in his essay "The Lunar Zodiac").
113. *Ibid.*, p. 361.
114. See the convenient tables in L. Renou et J. Filliozat, *L'Inde Classique*, Tome II (Paris, 1953), 729 f.; example in *Sūrya-Siddhānta* translation (Univ. of Calcutta, 1935), p. 34; discussion and bibliography in *Vedic Index*, I, under "Nakṣatra": some recent views in Philip Yampolsky, "The Origin of the Twenty-eight Lunar Mansions", *Osiris* (1950), 62-83.
115. W. Hopkins, "Epic Chronology", *JAOS*, Vol. 24, p. 19.
116. A.B. Keith, HOS Vol. 19, p. 607.
117. Macdonell (*op. cit.*), p. 112.
118. *Idem.*
119. Alfred Hillebrandt, *Vedische Mythologie* (Breslau, 1927), I, 335.
120. *Op. cit.*, 294-307.
121. W. Norman Brown, *JAOS*, Vol. 62 (June 1942), p. 91.
122. *Op. cit.*, 105.
123. *Ibid.*, 107.
124. *Ibid.*, 172.
125. Cf. the entry s.v. in Mayrhofer, *op. cit.*, I, 40-1.
126. *Op. cit.*, p. 18.
127. Bimala Churn Law, *Rivers of India* (Calcutta, 1944), p. 10. The same author's *Historical Geography of Ancient India* (Paris, 1954) is a convenient reference work for the geographical names sacred to Hindu and Buddhist texts.
128. V. Gordon Childe, *New Light on the Most Ancient East*, 4th Edn., p. 195.
129. Sörensen (*op. cit.*), p. 703.
130. Cf. Abegg (*op. cit.*), p. 117-22.
131. Mus (*op. cit.*), p. 237.
132. *Abhi. Kośa*, tr. III, p. 151-2.
133. Cf. W.E. Soothill and Lewis Hodous, *A Dictionary of Chinese Buddhist Terms*, p. 62b, entry on the "three mires".
134. A large part of this *bhūmi* intrudes in the Bihar Society Ms. of the *Śrāvaka-bhūmi*,

which the writer analyzed as a doctoral dissertation at the University of California. The verse is in *Taishō* 30.372c-29 f.

135. The translation "states of existence" for *vihāra* is due to Edgerton, *Buddhist Hybrid Sanskrit Dictionary,* p. 505.
136. Etienne Lamotte, in his edition and translation of the Tibetan text (Louvain, 1935), cites the Tib. and Skt. for the verse on p. 58. His Skt. is presumably the corrected form in Louis de La Vallée Poussin, *Vijñaptimātratāsiddhi* (Paris, 1928), I, 173, further modified by the suggestions of Sylvain Lévi, *Matériaux pour l'Etude du Systême Vijñaptimātra* (Paris, 1932), 103 (note).
137. The *Vijñaptimātratāsiddhi,* I, 195, and 196 (note).
138. Cf. A Wayman, "A Study of the Vedāntic and Buddhist Theory of Nāma-Rūpa," reprinted in the present volume.
139. *Vinayavibhaṅgapadavyākhyāna,* Tib. translation in Derge Tg., *Ḥdul ḥgrel,* Tshu, 149b-4:
 miṅ daṅ gzugs ni bud med daṅ skyes paḥo.
140. Keith, translation of *Taittirīya Saṃhitā,* p. 80.
141. Cf. A. Wayman, *Yoga of the Guhyasamājatantra,* p. 210.
142. L. de la Vallée Poussin, Ed. *Pañcakrama* (Gand, 1896), p. 19. The Vyākhyā Tantras are not considered commentaries, traditionally placed in the Tibetan Tanjur, but are treated as further promulgations (so to say, "telling more") of the Basic Tantra (*mūlatantra*), and hence are placed in the Tibetan Kanjur. The textual history of these works is obscure, but they appear to have been composed at the same time as the Basic Tantras, or soon afterwards. The *Vajramālā* is No. 445 in the Tōhoku Kanjur-Tanjur Catalog. While S.K. De, "The Buddhist Tantric Literature (Sanskrit) of Bengal", *NIA,* Vol. I (April, 1938) 1-23, does not discuss the Vyākhyā Tantras, his article is a useful introduction to Tantric literature. For Buddhist Tantric literature of Tibet, a good introduction is in Giuseppe Tucci, *Tibetan Painted Scrolls* (Roma, 1949), Vol. I.
143. J. Eggeling, *Śatapatha Brāhmaṇa,* Part 2, SBE Vol. 26 (Oxford, 1885), p. 240.
144. Tib. is in Derge Tg., *Sems tsam,* Dzi, 126a-2, f.; Chin. in *Taishō* 30.449a-22, f.; Ja. in *Kokuyaku Daizōkyo,* 2nd Ser. *Yoga* , Vol. 7, p. 56.
145. For the renditions "bring about" for *upasaṃharati* and "at a later time" for *antareṇa,* cf. Edgerton, *BHS Dict.*
146. E.g., Edgerton, *BHS Dict.*
147. For the rendition "sinks" for *praskandhati,* cf. Edgerton, *BHS Dict.*
148. Bloomfield (*op. cit.*), p. 167.
149. K.C. Varadachari, *Sri Ramanuja's Theory of Knowledge; A Study* (Tirupati, 1943), p. 186.
150. Cf. Étienne Lamotte, *Le Traité de la Grande Vertu de Sagesse* (Louvain, 1944), I, 340, and I, 251 (note).
151. *Op. cit.,* I, 393.
152. Cf. Lamotte (*op. cit.*), I, 255 f., for a Buddhist version of the story and for extensive bibliography. The *Kathāsaritsāgara* version (I, 7) is listed under the Brahmanical sources. This version is noteworthy for economy of words and to the writer's mind is more elegant than the Buddhist one. However, a comparison of the two versions is instructive in illustrating the different roles of Indra in Buddhism and in Hinduism. In the Buddhist one, Indra is not charged with a bad intention. He is only going to test the King, who is a Bodhisattva.
153. Derge, *Mdo-ḥgrel,* Vol. Ci, 3b-5f.:/ bdud rnam bźi ni lhaḥi buḥi bdud daṅ/ ñon moṅs paḥi bdud daṅ/ phuṅ poḥi bdud daṅ/ ḥchi bdag gi bdud do/ de la lhaḥi buḥi bdud

ni byaṅ chub kyi śiṅ druṅ du byams paḥi tiṅ ṅe ḥdzin gyis bcom/ñon moṅs pāhi bdud kyaṅ byaṅ chub mṅon par rtogs paḥi tshe bcom/ phuṅ poḥi bdud kyan byaṅ chub mṅon par rtogs paḥi tshe kun gźi rnam par śes pa gnas yoṅs su gyur pas bcom/ ḥchi bdag gi bdud kyaṅ groṅ khyer yaṅs pa can du mya ṅan las ḥdaḥ ba las mi ḥdaḥ bar zla ba gsum du tsheḥi ḥdu byed slar bsnur te/ tshe la dbaṅ thob pas ḥchi bdag gi bdud kyaṅ der bcom mo/.

154. For this event, see, for example. Ernst Waldschmidt. *Das Mahāparinirvāṇasūtra,* Abh. der D. Akad. der Wiss. zu Berlin, Klasse für Sprachen, Literatur und Kunst, 1950, Nr. 2, Teil II, 218-9. We learn there that three months before the *parinirvāṇa,* the Great Earth quakes, for at that time he abandons the life motivation (*āyusaṅkhāraṃ ossajjati* in the *Dīghanikāya* XVI, 3, 19). The Pāli has no equivalent for the Skt. *jīvitasaṃskārān adhiṣṭhāya.* This may well be what the commentary means by "achieving the power over life", if we translate *adhiṣṭhāya* as "superintending", i.e., "superintending the life motivations".

155. HOS 18, p. 261.

156. The Pāli Text Society's Pāli Dictionary, s.v.

157. Derge T., *Rgyud ḥgrel,* Vol. Tu, 115-b2, f.: de yaṅ bdag ñid kyi phuṅ po lṅa stoṅ pa ñid du bśig la/ phyi rol gyi me thab la sogs pa yul gyi gzugs rnams kyaṅ stoṅ par bśig ste/ de bźin du sgo drug gi rnam par śes pa ḥphro ba rnams kyaṅ so sor bśig nas mi ḥphro bar bkag ciṅ de ltar ḥjig ciṅ ḥgog par byed paḥi byaṅ chub kyi sems de yaṅ ḥphro ba med paḥi śes rab kyis bkag pa rnam par mi rtog paḥi tiṅ ṅe ḥdzin la gnas pa ni naṅ gi sbyin sreg ste/ de bas na/ rluṅ gi me yaṅ ḥphro ba med paḥi śes rab kyis bkag ste/ yid kyis me la sbyin sreg byaḥo źes gsuṅs pa yin no/ rluṅ gi me bkag pa ni srog daṅ rtsol ba rab tu bsdams nas źes paḥo/ yid kyis me la sbyin sreg byaḥo/ źes pa ni sems mi gyo bar bsreg go źes paḥo/.

158. This of course means the five *vijñāna* based on the five outer senses, and the *vijñāna* based on mind, the *manovijñāna.*

159. Buddhaguhya states in the *Dhyānottarapaṭalaṭikā,* Derge, *Rgyud ḥgrel,* Thu, 14b-6: "It is said in other texts, '*Prāṇa* is explained as wind (*vāyu*); by *āyāma* is meant Mindfulness (*smṛti*)" (srog ces bya ba rluṅ du bśad/rtsol bas dran pa źes byaḥo/ źes gźan dag las gsuṅs so/). This seems to be admitting that *prāṇāyāma* is interpreted in some Buddhist quarters as a *tatpuruṣa* compound and equivalent to *ānāpāna-smṛti.* But Buddhaguhya's own view, following the particular Tantra tradition of his commentary, is that *prāṇa* is the vital wind passing through the various orifices of the body, and that *āyāma* is the outward-passing mental element, as is shown in Mkhas grub's *Fundamental of the Buddhist Tantras,* translation from Tib. by F.D. Lessing and A. Wayman.

160. *Tantrārthāvatāravyākhyāna,* Derge, *Rgyud ḥgrel,* Ḥi, 235a-3:/ raṅ gi sems ni bdud.

161. In the work *Zab pa daṅ rgya che baḥi rgya che baḥi daṁ paḥi chos kyi thob yig gsal baḥi me loṅ* ("The 'Bright-mirror' *Thob-yig* of the profound and far-reaching illustrious Doctrine"), Peking ed., Vol. I, 272a-2 to 276a-3. This *Thob-yig* (book of received teachings) has four volumes. According to the colophon of Vol. IV, the author was 61 years old when the sixth Dalai Lama was 19 years old (i.e., in A.D. 1702). This seems to be the year he completed the work. He actually sums up Tibetan Buddhism at a turning point in Tibet's political destiny. For the events brewing at that time, and the loss of Tibetan independence, see L. Petech, *China and Tibet in the Early 18th Century,* Monographies du T'oung Pao, Volume I (Leiden, 1950). My supposition that he was a teacher of the Sixth Dalai Lama was supported by the Dilowa Gegen Hutukhtu in a conversation.

In the two volume collection of his essays (*Ṅag rnams phyogs su bsgrigs pa*), there is an auto-biography in Vol. Kha (*Raṅ gi ḥkhor bar spyod paḥi tshul / śin tu gsal baḥi sgron me*), where we learn he was born in *chu pho rta*, therefore in 1642.

162. There are four divisions of the Tantras in the Kanjur: Kriyā-, Caryā-, Yoga-, and Anuttara-Tantra.

163. /ston pas dpal ldan ḥbras spuṅs su/ dus hkhor gyi rgyud gsuṅs paḥi tshe/ bla med kyi rgyud gźan rnams kyaṅ gsuṅs par dus ḥkhor rtsa rgyud las gsuṅs śiṅ/dgra nag gi rtog pa bco brgyad pa las/ ston pas rdo rje gdan du srod la bdud btul baḥi mdzad pa bstan paḥi tshe/ bdud daṅ gśin rje ḥdul baḥi phyir gśin rje gśed kyi lha tshogs sprul te rgyud rnams gsuṅs so/ źes gsuṅs paḥi lugs ltar na/ gdul bya gśin rje la phyi naṅ gsaṅ gsum du yod do/.

164. /dri ma med paḥi luṅ las/ gnas na gnas paḥi yi dvags daṅ/lus la gnas paḥi ḥchi bdag daṅ/sems la gnas paḥi ñon moṅs gsum/ gdul bya las kyi gśin rje yin/ ces gsuṅs pa ltar gdul bya gśin rje gsum du yod ciṅ/ nag po dra ba can gyi rgyud las/ khams gsum ḥkhor ba gśin rje yin/ chos kyi rgyal po rje bo yin/ Ya-mā-nta-ka gśed po yin/ ces gśin rje daṅ gśed gñis so sor gsuṅs/.

165. dri ma med paḥi rgyud las kyaṅ/ ḥdul byed gśin rje daṅ gśed gñis so sor gsuṅs pa ltar/ḥdul byed gśed kyaṅ rnam gsum ste/ chos kyi sku yi ṅo bo las/ gzugs skuḥi ṅo bor bstan pas ni/gnas na gnas paḥi yi dvags ḥdul/chos dbyiṅs bde baḥi ṅaṅ las ni/ log rtog ḥkhrul pas ma bslad ciṅ/ sems ñid lha yi skur snaṅ bas/ lus la gnas paḥi ḥchi bdag ḥdul/ las daṅ ye śes gñis med pas/sems ñid dag paḥi kloṅ du ni/ gdul bya ḥdul byed gñis med pas/ raṅ la gnas par rtogs pas ni/sems la gnas paḥi ñon moṅs ḥdul/źes deḥi gśed kyaṅ gsum du gsuṅs pa las/.

166. Tib. *raṅ roṅ*, according to the explanation in the 3-Vol. Tibetan Chinese Dictionary Bod rgya tshig mdsod chen mo.

167. daṅ po gnas na gnas paḥi yi dvags gśin rje ni/lho phyogs sa ḥog rim pa bdun gyi ḥog/ rgya mtsho chen poḥi gtiṅ/rluṅ gi dkyil ḥkhor gyi mtshams na/ la daṅ ñon moṅs pa las grub paḥi lcags kyi mun khaṅ sgo med bcu drug kha zur kun rno ba/ mi ro gsar sñiṅ maṅ po raṅ roṅ du spuṅs pa/ khrag źag gi rgya mtsho ḥkhyil źin rba kloṅ rab tu ḥkhrugs pa/phyi śa khrag rus paḥi thaṅ mar bdal baḥi naṅ du/ naṅ ḥdzin paḥi śes pa la ḥkhrul ziṅ/las kyi rnam par smin pa drag poḥi mthu las grub paḥi yi dvags kyi bdud nag po bye ba.

168. If this equals *Gu lin*, then per the native dictionary *Brda dag miṅ gsal ba*, it is *dbaṅ phyug chen po* (Maheśvara), but with question mark.

169. gu riṅ źes kyaṅ bya/gśin rje pi-wa-sa-tva źes kyaṅ bya ba mdog nag po gcer bu ral pa can kha gdaṅs pa/mche ba gtsigs pa/ ljags ḥkhril ba/ migrtsa rgod pa/ mig sprin dmar ba/ḥbras bu mthiṅ nag ḥdril ba/ smin ma daṅ rdzi ma gziṅs pa/ lag pa gñis dbyug pa daṅ źags pa ḥdzin pa/sems źe sdaṅ me ltar ḥbar ba.

170. deḥi yum las kyi gtum paḥi srin mo gtum mo/dug hrul gos gyon ma źes kyaṅ bya/ cā-mu-ṇḍi źes kyaṅ bya ba mdog nag mo/gcer mo ral pa can śin tu khros pa lag pa gñis tri śul daṅ/thod rlon khrag daṅ bcas pa ḥdzin pa/ sems la ḥdod chags chur ltar ḥkhrugs pa.

171. See Tucci, *Tibetan Painted Scrolls*, II, p. 582-3, for the description of his Tanka No. 154 (Plate 187), Yama *phyi sgrub*, which includes these entities, which he calls the eight great Yamas. He gives some iconographical description and shows that the cycle has been elaborated in Tibet. Apparently the fierce being Gu-riṅ is represented among the group of eight as Yama Dharmarāja.

172. gñis tshogs paḥi sras/bkaḥ sdod las kyi pho ña/gśin rje chos kyi rgyal po daṅ/sbrul pa phya bsaṅs gñis/ya-va-ti daṅ/te-la-pa gñis/ a-va glaṅ mgo daṅ rmig pa gñis/

ral pa tshar dgu daṅ mig dmar po gñis te brgyad/ deḥi yum yaṅ mgo dgu brtsegs paḥi rkaṅ brgya daṅ/ mtshan mo dred kyi ha ba śam can/ mgo dgu brtsegs paḥi rkaṅ maṅ sogs/.

173. gśin rje pho moḥi tshogs dpag tu med pa de rnams kyaṅ sems la źe sdaṅ me ltar ḥbar pa/ḥdod chags chu ltar ḥkhrugs pa/steṅ gi nam mkhaḥi sprin dmar nag daṅ ljaṅ nag rab tu ḥkhrugs pa la brten bcas/ srid pa gsum gyi tshe srog sdud par byed pa la ḥchi bdag gśin rje źes bya ste.

174. de ñid las/ḥjig rten pa yi sems can rnams/thog ma med paḥi dus mthaḥ nas/log paḥi lam la mthu brtas pas/ḥkhor baḥi sa bon rtsub mor smin/bdud ḥdi spyi mthun las kyi bdud/ ces so/.

175. /naṅ gi gśin rje ni/tshur mthoṅ gi skye bo kun la ḥchi bdag bdud pos raṅ dbaṅ med par ḥjoms pa raṅ chas su yod par gsuṅs la bdud bźi po de kun kyaṅ las ma dag pa rnams kyi snaṅ ba la/so soḥi blon po daṅ pho ña daṅ bran pho mor bcas pa ḥjigs su ruṅ ba bźin mi sdug pa/skye ḥgroḥi srog len pas na/dpal raṅ byuṅ gi bdud ces bya.

176. /sems la gnas paḥi ñon moṅs paḥi gśin rje ni/sems rgyud la gnas pahi ñon moṅs pa rnams la gśin rje źes bya ste las kyi gśin rjes skye ḥgroḥi srog gcod pa ltar/chags sogs ñon moṅs pa rnams kyis gdul byaḥi thar paḥi srog gcod par byed paḥi phyir ro/.

177. Besides the reference in the note 220 to Tucci's monumental work, see Lessing, *Yung-Ho-Kung*, p. 76 and Plate XXII, No. 2 . Also see Grünwedel, *Mythologie du Buddhisme* (French translation, 1900), Fig. 48, p. 64, where the trident held by Yamī is wrongly interpreted as held by Yama, and Yamī's skull bowl is not known to be full of blood.

178. The Yama described in the Mahābhārata: Fausbøll (*op. cit.*), 137.

22

Vedāntic and Buddhist Theory of *Nāma-Rūpa*

The theory of *nāma-rūpa* is of great importance in the development of Indian religion and philosophy, especially for the Vedāntic understanding of the Upaniṣads, and for Buddhism where it occurs as the fourth member of the Dependent Origination formula. Because the early, i.e. Vedic, terms *nāma* and *rūpa* were in separate contexts, it is necessary to treat these two as such. And because they were combined in the well-known compound *nāma-rūpa*, it is also necessary to treat it as such.

It will be shown in the course of this chapter that the name

Reprinted from *Indological and Buddhist Studies*. Faculty of Asian Studies, Canberra, 1982.

(*nāma*) came to indicate the individuality in the human case, and individual things in the case of external entities. *Rūpa* is the matter or its appearance.

The Śaṅkara type of Vedānta is chosen to represent the Vedāntic theory, since his commentary is the earliest extant on the *Brahmasūtra,* which has been much studied, and there are fine reference works.

There are some curious features about this topic. For one thing, the celebrated Vedānta author Śaṅkara had a theory of two kinds of *nāma-rūpa*, although his sources appear to have only one kind. On its part, Buddhism seems unaware of the usages of the terms *nāma* and *rūpa* found in the Vedas and subsequent literature culminating in the great Upaniṣads. Even so, Buddhism appears to have inherited the connotations of these terms and to have adequate explanations for the two in the compound as occurring in its oldest scriptures.

I. *Nāma* and *Rūpa* as Separate Terms

The following should make it clear that the old Vedic usages of the terms *nāma* and *rūpa* were independent—as they were possibly so, in later centuries of the Sanskrit language and were not in terms of the compound *nāma-rūpa*. Thus, while the old Indic word *nāman* is cognate with the English word 'name' through the Latin *nōmen,* it is not necessarily in the Indic usage the 'name' of something. Nor was *rūpa,* usually translated 'form', necessarily employed as the 'form' (e.g. 'shape') of something.

The *Śatapatha-Brāhmaṇa* may well be the earliest text that pairs the two, *nāma* and *rūpa*, while speaking of them in a contrasting manner. This is in XI, 2, 3, 1-6, a passage to be treated later. Here we may observe the explanation (Eggeling's translation): "Whatever has a name, that is name; and that again which has no name, and which one knows by its form, 'This is (of a certain) form', that is form."[2] This contrast was to continue, for Vasubandhu's *Abhidharmakośa,* Chap. III, 30a, has: "*Nāma*—it is the aggregates (*skandha*) that are not *rūpa*".[3] Thus it treats the topic of *nāma* in its Chapter III, while having treated *rūpa* in Chapter I, indicating that the connotations of the terms are independent.

A. INDEPENDENT *NĀMA*

Of great help is Renou's *Études*.[4] The first *ṛṣis* (seers or sages) gave names to things (RV, X, 71,1).[5] The conferring itself is referred to there by *dheya*, as in other RV compounds such as *bhāgadheya*, hence as *nāmadheya* (conferral of name) frequent later, also in *Ch. Up.* (an important usage, *infra*); Renou: in the sense of creating a name.[6] Then, *Taitt. Ār.* (III, 12, 7), as cited twice in Saṅkara's *VS-Bhāṣya*: "The wise one, who having classified[7] all formations and madeup names, sits calling them by their names."[8] The word *nāman* could be used for names of persons and things. Gods like Indra or Agni had an auspicious name (one that is *bhadra*) in common, e.g. Vṛtrahan (slayer of the demon Vṛtra).[9]

The wind deities have a name Marut that deserves worship. This name is not an unreal appearance: the names 'Marut'—they are the Marut (i.e. the wind gods) themselves (RV IV.39, 4, and elsewhere). In some places, according to Geldner, *nāman* is more a characteristic than a name; e.g. "The relationship (*sajātya*) of the Aśvin is a good name (*nāma*)."[10] Perhaps, this is the implication of the 'secret names', such as extra given names to persons in cults, and epithets of the deities.[11]

The *Aitareya Āraṇyaka* (from II, 1, 6): "So by his [i.e. *prāṇa*'s] speech (*vāk*) as cord (*tanti*), and by names (*nāma*) as nooses (or 'loops') (*dāma*), all this is tied (*sita*). For all these are names; and by his speeches, he tells (*vadati*) everything."[12] The *Ch. Up.*'s (Chap. VII) progressive worship of Brahman presents meditation on the name as the first worship. Sanatkumāra tells Nārada, "What it is you have learned, is just the name. Verily, a name is *Ṛgveda* ... (down to) the science of serpents and minor gods... He who meditates on name as Brahman can move as he wishes as far as the name goes."[13] The *Aitareya Upaniṣad* (III, 2) includes a classification of mental functions, all identified as "name-conferrals (*nāmadheya*) of intelligence".

To be compared with the Buddhist tenets is the well-known passage in *Bṛhad-Ār. Up.* (III, 2, 12): " 'Yājñavalkya', said he, 'in whatever [body] this person dies, what does not leave him?' 'The name'."[14] Hence, we mention the Buddhist Abhidharma etymology from *nam-* (to bend, bow), which is a false etymology of the ancient word *nāma*. Thus, both Vasubandhu[15] and Saṃghabhadra[16] in their comments of *Abhidharmakośa* III, 30a, say that the four formless aggregates, which are *vedanā, saṃjñā, saṃskāras*, and *vijñāna*, go toward the objects (*artha*) as though naming them, thus 'bending' toward them. They give a second explanation that these aggregates are called 'name', because when the body disintegrates these aggregates so to say, bend toward another existence. The phrase in Saṃghabhadra's text (Tibetan translation) is worth citing: "because it (i.e. name) causes the bending toward another existence" (*skye ba gźan du gźol bar byed pa'i phyir)*, with *gźol bar byed pa* tantamount to the causative form *namayati.*[17] These Abhidharma explanations of 'name' do not necessarily agree with the *Bṛhad-Ār*. passage above cited, since 'bending towards', even less 'causing the bending towards', does not mean that the 'name' itself transmigrates. Asaṅga, *Viniścayasaṃgrahaṇī* (PTT, Vol. 110, p. 266, p. 266-2-6),[18] when answering the question "Why are the four formless aggregates called 'name'?" leaves out all mention of another existence, his two explanations being first the metaphorical 'naming' and second the primary or literal 'naming': "because bending towards the diversity of consciousness-supports (*ālambana*); and because, relying on conventional names, discursive thought (*vikalpa*) is (derived) from the consciousness-supports" (*dmigs pa sna tshogs la ñe bar gźol ba'i don daṅ / tha sñad las byuṅ ba'i miṅ las brten te dmigs pa las rnam par rtog pa'i don gyis so/*

B. Independent *Rūpa*

There is a surprising possible relationship between the words *rūpa*, *varpas*, and *varṇa*, through an old Indic metathesis ru/var, or hru/hvar, and so also an affiliation with the grammarians' verb root *vṛ-* (to cover).[19] The word *varpas* appears to signify change or metamorphosis of form, even deceptive appearances,[20] in this way practically equivalent in usage to *vivarta*,[21] which however goes with a root *vṛt*-rather than with the mentioned *vṛ-*. The word *varṇa* (the classical word for 'color') seems, according to Renou, to intend a 'category of recognition' in such expressions as *dāsa* or *ārya varṇa* rather than a difference of racial color, although granted that a few passages do suggest that the 'caste' meaning was already emerging in the *Ṛgveda*.[22]

Much later, there was the Buddhist Abhidharma explanation of *rūpa* as of two kinds, shape (*saṃsthāna*) and color (*varṇa*).[23]

Since the word *rūpa,* among the five personality aggregates (*skandha*) equivalent to *nāma-rūpa,* in its Buddhist usage was translated into Chinese regularly as 'color', I am inclined to take this as continuing a well-attested meaning which Renou mentions as frequent for *rūpa* in Vedic passages.[24] But this leaves a problem: How can the 'color' translation be defended, when Buddhism in its formula *nāma-rūpa* says that *rūpa* is the four great elements (*mahābhūta*), namely, fire, wind, water, earth, and their evolutes *(bhautika),* so that translators from the Pāli scriptures render this *rūpa* as 'body', 'corporeality', and the like?[25] I can suggest that the word *rūpa* in this Buddhist context gained the connotation of 'coloring', meaning 'touching up', filling out', 'giving body to', amounting to a verbal noun, even granted that the Chinese rendition by its 'color' character does not permit a verbal usage in Chinese literature.[26] And while in common with other translators, I have in the past rendered *nāma-rūpa* as 'name-and-form', in the light of the foregoing, the rendition should preferably be 'name-and formation'.

The subtle connotation of the term *rūpa,* starting from its initial Vedic setting, inspired some sharp disputes among the Buddhist clergy, accounting for the generous treatment of the topic in the first chapter of Vasubandhu's *Abhidharmakośa.* The simplest case has *rūpa* as the object of the eye and called *rūpāyatana* (form base), namely, in I, 24, with comments giving three reasons for its being *rūpa*: (1) a formation with the character of supplanting (*bādhana*), for example, with a hand (removing something and replacing it), referred to anciently as *sa-pratigha* (with obstacle); (2) a formation showing a place (*deśanidarśana*), indicating it as here or there; (3) a formation popularly referred to (*pratīta*) as 'that *rūpa*', meaning visible shape or color.[27] More troublesome is the *rūpa* in the compound *nāma-rūpa,* and *Abhidharmakośa,* I, 9, presents the Vaibhāṣika listing of formation (*rūpa*), as the five sense organs *(indriya)* the five (external) object (*artha)*, and reticence (*avijñapti*).[28] Vasubandhu defines *avijñapti* in the Vaibhāṣika manner rather than his own Sautrāntika by using the words 'is called' in I, 11: "The continuous series (*anubandha*), whether good or bad, of the distracted (person) and of the unthinking (person) in dependence on the great elements (*mahābhūta*)—is called 'reticence' (*avijñapti*)."[29]

C. *Nāma* and *Rūpa*,—in Contrast

The terms *nāmakāya* and *rūpakāya* occur a number of times in the Pāli Buddhist work *Netti-Pakaraṇa* attributed to Mahākaccāyana, who is not a personal disciple of the Buddha according to the editor, Professor Hardy. The text says: "Name-and-formation is defined as the conjunction of the name-set and the formation-set" (*nāmakāya-rūpakāya-saṃghātalakkhanaṃ nāmarūpam*).[30] The *Paṭisambhidāmagga* in the *Khuddakanikāya* of the Pāli canon defines the two sets this way: "What is the *nāmakāya*? Feelings (*vedanā*), ideas (*sañña*), volitions (*cetanā*), sense contacts (phassa), mental orientations (*manasikāra*); both 'name' and 'set of names' as well as any mental motivations (*cittasaṅkhāra*)—this is *nāmakāya*. What is *rūpakāya*? Both the four great elements (*mahābhūta*) and the formations depending on the great elements, exhalation and inhalation, the sign-source (*nimitta*) as a bondage, as well as any corporeal motivations (*kāyasaṅkhāra*)—this is *rūpakāya*."[31] The list of five from *vedanā* to *manasikāra* is the same as is found in the Dependent Origination (S. *pratītyasmutpāda*) exposition in the *Saṃyuttanikāya* (Nidāna Book, ii, 2) delivered at Sāvatthī, and this scripture also has for its *rūpa* explanation (of *nāma-rūpa*) the same mention of the four great elements and their derivatives.[32] Asaṅga, *Viniścayasaṃgrahaṇī* of *Yogācārabhūmi*, (1st two *bhūmis*), says (PTT, Vol. 110, p. 266-4-2), "Besides, it is what the Bhagavat stated as concomitant (*sahaja*), 'feelings (*vedanā*), ideas (*saṃjñā*) volitions (*cetanā*), and these natures (*dharma*) are mingled."[33] This suggests that the Abhidharma terms *nāmakāya* and *rūpakāya* arose in attempts to define concomitant natures that are not explicit in the standard list of *nāma-rūpa*, feasibly in application to this very *Saṃyuttanikāya* exposition.

Asaṅga himself details five kinds of *nāma* and five kinds of *rūpa* in his *Viniścayasaṃgrahaṇī* on *Śrutamayī bhūmi* (PTT, Vol. 111, p. 21-4-5), as follows: (a) 'name' (*nāma*)—a thought (*citta*), thought associates (*caitta* or *caitasika*), virtuous (*kuśala*), non-virtuous (*akuśala*), and indeterminate (*avyākṛta*). (b) 'formation' (*rūpa*)—elements (*bhūta*), element derivatives (*bhautika*), showing and impeding (*sanidarśana-sapratigha*), not showing but impeding (*asanidarśana-sapratigha*), not showing and not impeding (*asanidarśana-apratigha*). We should note that Asaṅga's five kinds for both *nāma* and *rūpa* assign the better and worse in Buddhist terms (the *kuśala* and *akuśala*) to *nāma*. Previously, we noticed that the disputed term *avijñapti* refers to a special kind of *rūpa* that is good or bad (the *śubha* and *aśubha*). Whatever his attitude towards the *avijñaptirūpa*, still Asaṅga admits the subtle kind of *rūpa* which is neither showing nor impending, and so these five kinds of *rūpa* cover a wider usage than does the *rūpāyatana* (form base as object of visual faculty) which seems to be always *sa-pratigha*. Besides, the term *avyākṛta*, here rendered 'indeterminate' is the same word already rendered 'unevolved' in the *Bṛhad-Ār.* I, 4, 7, and to be rendered 'unevolved' or 'unseparated' in the *Ch. Up.* passage to be discussed in our next section. In a way, these renditions also fit the Buddhist usage, since one may interpret the *avyākṛta* of Asaṅga's passage as 'not separated' into *kuśala* and *akuśala*.

The *Bṛhad-Ār. Up.* (I, 6, 1-3) expounds a theory that this world is a triad of name, formation, and action (*nāma rūpaṃ karma*). Speech (*vāk*) is the recitation (*uktha*) of the names, and said to be their Brahman. The eye (*cakṣus*) is the recitation of formation, and said to be their Brahman. The embodiment (*ātman*) is the recitation of actions, and said to be their Brahman. The breath (*prāṇa*) is the immortal (*amṛta*), veiled (*channa*) by name and formation, which are the real (*satya*,[34] as the 'undeniable').[35]

The usage of *ātman* for 'embodiment' is certainly not general, but attested elsewhere in the Indian literature.[36] We should note that this special usage was carried on in Buddhism by the term *ātmabhāva*. Thus, Asaṅga, in his *Śrāvakabhūmi*: "Only by oneself does the embodiment succeed in those five ways" (*svayam evānena sa ātmabhāva ebhiḥ pañcabhir aṅgaiḥ sampādito bhavati*), where the five mean the list beginning with ' human state' (*manuṣyatva*).[37] A Buddhist continuation of that *Bṛhad-Ār.* attribution to name and formation is in Asaṅga, *Viniścayasaṃgrahaṇī* (PTT, Vol. III, p. 175-4-1): "What is a place of truth? Name-and-formation, called the 'self-presence of a man "(*manuṣyasvabhāva*)" (*bden pa'i gnas gaṅ źe na / miṅ daṅ gzugs ni mi'i raṅ bźin źes bya ba'o/*).

The Buddhist continuation of the Vedic meaning of *rūpa* as 'color', Asaṅga's continuation of the *Bṛhad-Ār.* attribution of *satya* to *nāma-rūpa*, and the various foregoing explanations from Buddhist sources, as well as those to be given in the next section, provide evidence for regarding the early Buddhist canon as a link between the earlier Indian religion and the later developments rather than concluding, as is sometimes done by European writers, that there is no proof of characteristic Buddhist doctrines being in the earliest canon.[38]

The preceding passages about *nāma* and *rūpa* did not take one of these two as superior to the other one. But the *Śatapatha-Brāhmaṇa* does precisely that, XI, 2, 3, in 5: "One of these two is superior: *rūpa* indeed" (*tayor anyataraj jyāyo rūpam eva*). The text points to the reason, XI, 2, 3, in 6: "formation being mind" (*mano vai rūpam*); and "name being speech" (*vāg vai nāma*).[39] To get the point, one must refer to an earlier part of the same work, I, 4, 5, 8-12, which presents a dispute between speech and mind as to which was the better of the two. They appealed to Prajāpati for a decision. When he picked mind, speech henceforth refused to be Prajāpati's oblation-bearer (she does not speak out on such occasions, but only mutters). As *Mahābhārata*'s *Anugītā* expands upon the story, Prajāpati mollified the goddess by declaring that there are two kinds of mind, the stationary (*sthāvara*), which is his own, and the moving (*jaṅgama*), which is in the dominion of the speech goddess.[40] Putting the accounts together, *rūpa* is the stationary mind of Prajāpati.

II. *Nāma-Rūpa* (The Terms in Compound)

A. The Theory of Two Kinds of *Nāma-Rūpa*

The earliest suggestion that *nāma-rūpa* may be of two kinds is presumably that of the *Śatapatha-Brāhmaṇa* (XI, 2, 3, in 4-5): "These, indeed, are the two great monsters (*abhva*) of the Brahman" (*te haite brahmaṇo mahatī abhve*); "These, indeed, are the two great tempting appearances (*yakṣa*) of the Brahman" (*te haite brahmaṇo mahatī yakṣe*).[41] We shall see that the usual occurrences of the term *nāma-rūpa* go with the second one of the two kinds. Certainly such is the case of the Buddhist *nāma-rūpa*, 4th member of Dependent Origination (*pratītya-samutpāda*), explained as the five personality aggregates (*skandha*) in the womb, depicted in the 'Wheel of Life' as two persons in a boat, the two persons noted by Vinītadeva in his Vinaya commentary as a woman and a man.[42] While the Vedāntic author Śaṅkara has a theory of two kinds of *nāma-rūpa*, their authority is attributed to the *Ch. Up.*, where there is no explicit mention of two kinds, as the matter will be discussed below. Of those *Śatapatha-Br.* terms, *abhva* fell into disuse, and *yakṣa* came to mean a kind of minor spirit in Indian folklore, so while its theory of two contrasting descriptions for *nāma-rūpa* might be passed on to subsequent doctrine, these two terms (*abhva* and *yakṣa*) would not be useful in later times for such a context.

It appears that of the two kinds, the second kind is conceivable by man's mind, called the 'moving' (*jaṅgama*) in *Anugītā*'s version as cited at the close of my preceding section. The first kind, said to be the Brahman's two great monsters would be beyond man's ordinary mind. Thus I am reminded of P.T.S. Iyengar's remarks, which may be summarized this way: The *ṛṣis* spoke about the Brahman from ecstatic intuitions after stilling their usual mental activities and passions; such intuitions necessarily lead to contradictory expressions. But the later *ācāryas*, especially the principal commentators of the *Vedānta Sūtras*, and those who founded sects, namely, Śaṅkara, Rāmānuja, and Mādhava, imposed on the various pertinent statements of the Vedas and their continuation literature culminating in the Upaniṣads, mutually different systems, each of which purported to be self-consistent, i.e. logical in human terms. Thus, these system-founders and their squabbling later followers departed more and more from the Vedic intuitions expressed in mystical doctrines that were not mutually consistent, and in particular Śaṅkara's Advaita kind of *māya* was a modern invention foisted upon the ancient Upaniṣads.[43]

Be that as it may, Śaṅkara's *Upadeśasāhasrī* sets forth two kinds of *nāma-rūpa*. These two kinds were his peculiar attempts to solve problems of the *Vedānta-Sūtras* (=*Brahma-sūtras*), namely, the 'unevolved (*avyākṛta*) and the 'evolved' (*vyākṛta*) *nāma-rūpa* mentioned, e.g. in his *VS-Bhāṣya* on I, 4, 9, as the two kinds are rendered in Mayeda's study of the *Upadeśasāhasrī*.[44] This expression 'unevolved' is equivalent to 'unseparated' since the *vi-* in the Sanskrit word frequently means 'separate' or 'apart' in the *Ṛgveda*, where it was a separable prefix, the 'apart, asunder' in Katre's entry,[45] and since this meaning fits.

Śaṅkara justifies his method by the remark, "Deduction of a doubtful passage's meaning by a non-doubtful passage—people deem a rule" (*asaṃdigdhena ca saṃdigdhasya nigamanaṃ nyāyaṃ manyante*).[46] It turns out that the *Śvetāśvatara-Up.* has the non-doubtful passages that can be used to interpret the doubtful passages of other Upaniṣads, especially the *Chāndogya.* The main non-doubtful passage is *Śve,* IV, 10-11: "Know then, Prakṛti is *māyā,* and the great Lord is the holder of *māyā* ... the One who rules over every birth place" (*māyāṃ tu prakṛtiṃ vidyān māyinaṃ tu maheśvaram / ...yo yoniṃ yoniṃ adhitiṣṭhaty eko...).*[47] Śaṅkara claims that this *māyā* is the divine power having the unevolved *nāma rūpa,* that the *Śve* mantra depicts the prior condition of the (evolved) *nāma-rūpa* (*saiva daivī śaktir avyākṛtanāmarūpā nāmarūpayoḥ prāgavasthānenāpi mantreṇa*).[48] Although he does not appeal to *Śatapatha-Br.*'s vocabulary, Śaṅkara's two kinds can be considered as a much later formulation rationalized in a system of the earlier intuition. If we follow through this idea, then what was once called "the two great monsters of the Brahman" became the *māyā* (=Prakṛti) of the great Lord, and what was once called "the two great tempting appearances of the Brahman" became the evolved *nāma-rūpa.* This is not to maintain, however, that the *Śatapatha ṛṣis* would have countenanced Śaṅkara's application of 'avidyā', or that the early sages in their rare usage of the word *māyā* meant by it its pervasive role in Śaṅkara's system.

As to how the Brahman (neuter) can be equivalent to 'great Lord' (*maheśvara*) (masculine), let Śaṅkara tell (*VS Bhāṣya* on I, 2, 14): "The Brahman, while devoid of qualities (*nirguṇa*) is spoken of as possessed of qualities (*saguṇa*) (with qualities contained in *nāma-rūpa*) for the purpose of devotion" (*nirguṇam api sad brahma nāmarūpagatair guṇaiḥ saguṇam upāsanārthaṃ ... uktam eva*).[49] The example given there is *Ch. Up.* I, 6, in 6-7: The sun has a golden beard (*hiraṇya-śmaśru*); his name (*nāma*) is high (*ut*). We can add *Ch. Up.* VIII, 3, 4: "Verily the name of that Brahman is 'true' (*satya*)." Here there are names 'high' and 'true' and there are formations, such as 'golden beard'. Again, there is the verse in the Śibi story of the *Jātakamālā,* showing Lakṣmī in the role in or for the divine king, 'her name according to its meaning' (*yathārthanāma*): "Lakṣmī, who is the scorn of the unrestrained errant, the grievous misfortune of the incompetent, the intoxicating drink of the debased, became her name for him (Śibi) according to its meaning."[50] Her name (Lakṣmī, characteristic) is a lucky name for King Śibi, unlucky for others (the unrestrained errant, etc.). This last appears to illustrate Śaṅkara's further remark (*VS-Bhāṣya* on I, 2, 14): "And for the purpose of apprehending the omnipresent Brahman, it is spoken of by indicating it here and there" (*tatra tatro-padiśyata ity etad apy uktam eva /sarvagatasyāpi brahmaṇa upalabdhyartham*).[51]

Following Mayeda's summary,[52] based on the *Upadeśasāhasrī*, an 'unevolved' name-and-formation is the first emergence from Brahman and amounts to nescience (*avidyā*) or *māyā*. When that first kind became the second kind, it had the name 'space' (*ākāśa*) and its configuration (*ākṛti*). The first *nāṃa-rūpa* is like 'clear water' and the *nāma-rūpa* with the name 'space' is like dirty foam. But, then, how does the first kind become the second kind? The unevolved (=unseparated) Name-and-Formation is the seed of the world (*jagadbījabhūta*), also called Prakṛti. But the second kind of Name-and-Formation pre-exists in the first kind, and is the second kind by what the *Brahmasūtra* (=Vedāntasūtra) calls 'transformation' (*pariṇāma*), although the *Brahmasūtra* does not itself expound two kinds of *nāma-rūpa*. The followers of Śaṅkara did not adopt his terminology of an 'unevolved *nāma-rūpa*', but held that the phenomenal world is a transformation of *avidyā* and in regard to Brahman (the reality) is a *vivarta* (illusion). Mayeda, apparently agreeing with H. Nakamura and P. Hacker that Śaṅkara did not employ the term *vivarta* in this illusionist sense, and also agreeing that Śaṅkara differs in some ways from the *Brahmasūtra*, concludes that Śaṅkara's own position might be styled 'early *vivartavāda*', thus contrasting with the *'pariṇāmavāda'*, and enabling Śaṅkara to avoid the Sāṃkhya role of Prakṛti.

Then what is the 'name' and what the 'formation' in the first and the second kinds of *nāma-rūpa*? The second kind is easier to describe, and so will be treated first.

(a) *The second kind of nāma-rūpa*: Since this *nāma-rūpa* is like dirty foam, the *rūpa* part can be identified with the deceitful *varpas*, and perhaps the word *vivarta* also fits; or else it is the four phenomenal elements.

The 'name' portion of *nāma-rūpa* is not clarified when the *Ch. Up.* (VIII, 14, 1) says: "Verily the one named 'Space' is the evolver (*nirvahitṛ*) (='separator') of name-and-formation" and continues "that within which they are, is the Brahman". The *Ch. Up.* (VI, 3, 2) expresses the same theory with other words: "That divinity thought, 'Well, let me imitate[53] these three divinities with this *jīva-ātman* and evolve (i.e. separate out) the *nāma-rūpa*' " (*seyaṃ devataikṣata—hantāham imās tisro devatā anena jīvenātmanān-upraviśya nāma rūpe vyākaravāṇīti*). Now, 'Space (*ākāśa*), being where they are, is perhaps said metaphorically to evolve name-and-formation; and this interpretation would agree with Buddhism which does not include 'space' among the great elements (*mahābhūta*), because it does not cause the body to develop.[54] The idea of 'imitating' (*anupraviśya*) is to duplicate these three divinities in each given thing that can be referred to as a '*nāma-rūpa*'. The *Jīva-ātman* has the role of doing this imitation. Śaṅkara, citing these *Ch. Up.* lines in several places of his *VS-Bhāṣya* insists that however expressed, it is always the highest Lord (*parameśvara*) that is meant, or else that this *jīva-ātman* is not different from this highest Lord, and so the individual soul (*jīva*) is not meant. Śaṅkara justifies himself under VS II, 4, 20: *saṃjñāmūrtiklptis tu trivṛtkurvata upadeśāt* ("But the fashioning of names and material forms belongs to him rendering threefold, according to the precept"). Interpreting the *saṃjñā-mūrti* as the *nāma-rūpa* of the *Ch. Up.* passages, and the *klpti* as the 'evolving', he insists that this is the work of the highest Lord, who alone can evolve such names-and-formations as mountains, rivers, etc.[55] Now, the *Ch. Up.* itself says (VII, 6, 1): "The earth as though contemplates" (*dhyāyatīva pṛthivī*): "The waters as though contemplate" (*dhyāyantīvāpaḥ*)." Hence, this *nāma-rūpa* does not signify objects like pots which men make and give names to. Śaṅkara is right: They are the natural objects, creatures, lightning, and the rest. Hence, the 'name' in the name-and-formation should be understood as the individual life or self (called in these texts the *jīva*).

(b) *The first kind of nāma-rūpa*: Since Śaṅkara's pupils refrained from this terminology of an 'unevolved *nāma-rūpa*',[56] they did not clarify it. The Sāṃkhya can interpret the dual compound *nāma-rūpa*, when 'unevolved', as their own Puruṣa and Prakṛti—and the Vedānta cannot tolerate this![57] As to the *rūpa*, this is already indicated in the passage already translated, *Ch. Up.* (VI, 3, 2), "That divinity thought, 'Well, let me imitate these three divinities with this *jīva-ātman* ...'" These three divinities are specified in *Ch. Up.* VI, 4, 1-4, as the red heat, the white water and the dark food or earth, and called the three *rūpas*—, which are the only reality in fire, sun, moon, and lightning. The same statements are made for each of these four. Whatever red formation they have is a formation of heat; whatever white is a formation of water; whatever dark is a formation of food (=earth). The fire state has just left the fire, the sun-state the sun, the moon-state the moon, the lightning-state the lightning; (in each case) the modification is a usage of speech and a conferral of name (*nāmadheya*). Only the three formations are real (*satya*). Here the 'names' of the evolved (i.e. separated) name-and-formation are given in the illustrations as 'fire', 'sun', 'moon', and 'lightning'. Hence, the *jīva-ātman* has imitated, or duplicated the three divinities in all the natural entities; but when we strip away the usages of speech and discern the reality of those entities, it turns out to be just the three formations.[58] Thus, the 'unevolved formation' is the three *rūpa* divinities of the *Chāndogya*.

A later *Upaniṣad* called the *Varāha* in the collection called the Yoga Upaniṣads, has this: "For says the Śruti: 'It is, it shines forth, the pleasing, formation, name—these are the five portions. The first three are the nature of Brahman. The two thereafter are the nature of the world."[59] Notice that this tradition accepts only one kind of *nāma-rūpa,* the phenomenal kind, and allots three characters to the nature of Brahman, which appear to agree with the three of the *Chāndogya,* if we take the dark food as the 'It is'; the red heat as the 'It shines forth'; the white water as the 'pleasing';—amounting to the pregenetic triad of 'formation' (*rūpa*). However, the *Brahmasūtra* opposes this view and so does Śaṅkara, i.e. VS, III, 2,14: *arūpavad eva hi tatpradhānatvāt* ("For [Brahman] is indeed devoid of form, as this is salient among those [Upaniṣadic passages]"). Among Śaṅkara's citations is that same *Ch. Up.* VIII, 14, 1, "Verily, the one named 'space'... " since he insists on taking as the highest Lord this 'Space'—claimed to be *per se* devoid of *rūpa.* It is of interest that later Vedānta writers came up with another triad for Brahman, the *sat-cit-ānanda,* which might agree with the *Varāha's* terminology, if we take 'It is' as the *sat,* 'It shines forth' as the *cit,* and 'the pleasing' as the *ānanda.* As we saw, the *Śatapatha Bṛ* takes Prajāpati's mind as *rūpa.*

As to the 'unevolved name', it seems unavoidable that this is the *jīvātman,* the name of the Lord. Perhaps, this is alluded to in the appeal to Agni (the fire god) in the *Taittirīya Saṃhitā* (Keith tr., p. 80): "My name and thine, O all-knower, which like men changing garments we bear, let us exchange again; thou for life, and we to live."[60] My name is *jīva* (individual self); thine is *jīvātman.* Let us exchange them: 'thou for life' with 'Mind, speech, breath' (*infra*); 'we to live' partaking of thy omniscience.

B. The Theory of Entering and Surmounting *Nāma-Rūpa*

The *Śatapathabrāhmaṇa*, XI, 2, 3, 3, says: "Then the Brahman itself went to the remote side (*parārdha*). Having gone to the remote side, it considered, 'Well, now, how can I pass through these worlds in reverse?' It then reversed its course by these two, by formation and by name."[61] The idea seems to be that the Brahman returned to the terrestrial world by these two.

The *Bṛhad-Ār. Up.* (I, 4, 7) states: "At that time, this (world) was unevolved. It became evolved by name and formation... He (the Brahman) entered in here even to the tips of the nails... When breathing, he is called *prāṇa*; when speaking, the voice; when seeing, the eye; when hearing, the ear; when thinking, the mind. These are just the names (*nāma*) of his acts (*karma*)."[62]

The imitation or duplication of the unevolved formation triad is a special feature of the *Chāndogya* description, and it deals with both the human and the objective case. Previously I mentioned *Chāndogya's* exposition of the objective case, the triple reality in fire, sun, moon, lightning, and so on. In the human case, *Ch. Up.* (VI, 5, 4, and later) sets forth a development order of (1) heat becoming speech; (2) water becoming breath; (3) food, becoming mind. While the *Bṛhad-Ār.* (I, 5, 3) has "Mind, speech, breath, these he made for himself,"[63] he being Prajāpati, the creating Lord. This shows the creation of the individual self (*jīva*), thence supplying the 'name' of a separate name-and-formation.

Those passages attribute to name-conferral in the phenomenal world, the power to supply modifications amounting to individuals—in the case of man, individual persons; and in the case of external objects, individual things like fire, etc.

Passing to the Buddhist tradition of *nāma-rūpa*, the *Madhyāntavibhāga*[64] in its *kārikā* (I, 10) assigning a single descriptive term to each of the twelve members of Dependent Origination, refers to the fourth member as 'circumscribing' (*saṃparigraha*), and Vasubandhu comments, "i.e. by name-and-formation's embodiment (*ātmabhāva*)". Notice that this passage treats *nāma* and *rūpa* together, and that the comment 'circumscribing' goes with the Vedāntic term 'space' (*ākāśa*) attributed to the role of 'evolving' (i.e. separating) name-and-formation, since 'circumscribing', like 'space', provides the room, the scope.

To take the Buddhist formula from the beginning, it starts with

(1) nescience (*avidyā*); arising with this as condition is (2) motivations (*saṃskāra*) (=the 'constructed *dharma*' realm); and arising with this as condition is (3) 'perception' (*vijñāna*). Buddhism holds that then there is a reciprocal process: (4) 'name-and-formation' (*nāma-rūpa*) arises with 'perception' as condition; and 'perception' falls in the case of human birth into the *nāma-rūpa*, thus increasing the three 'names' (*nāma*) of *nāma-rūpa*—per Buddhaghosa of the Southern Buddhist tradition[65]—to four by adding its own name *'vijñāna'*. As to the original set of three names, they are feelings (*vedanā*), ideas (*saṃjñā*) and motivations (*saṃskāra*).

In a previous essay,[66] I had compared a creation legend of the *Bṛhad-Ār.* (I, 2, 2) with the first four members of Buddhist Dependent Origination. The *Bṛhad-Ār.* statement begins: "There was nothing whatsoever here in the beginning. Then:

Bṛhadāraṇyaka statement	*Dependent Origination*
"by death indeed was this covered."	1. nescience (*avidyā*)
"or by hunger, for hunger is death."	2. motivations (*saṃskāra*)
"He created the mind, thinking: 'Let me have a self'."	3. perception (*vijñāna*)
"Then he moved about, worshipping. From him, thus worshipping, water was produced."	4. name-and-formation (*nāma-rūpa*) (=*vijñāna* in the womb)

The point of the comparison is that the Buddhist series of twelve ends with 'old age and death' foreshadowing a new life. Determining the new life is the specific nescience and past *karma* (present as the motivations)—these are the contributions from death. The *Bṛhadāraṇyaka* pair 'death' and 'hunger'—the Buddhist pair 'nescience' and 'motivations'—might have prototypes in the two 'monsters' (*abhva*) of the *Śatapatha Brāhmaṇa*.[67] It goes without saying that Buddhism generally talks differently from the Brahmanical way. Still, Buddhism explains death as the breaking-down of the old personality aggregates (*skandha*),[68] the five called name-and-formation and these do not transmigrate but simply mirror their essentials in what does transmigrate.[69] It is of interest that the

Buddhist series manages to represent this contribution from the past by three members preceding No. 4, name-and-formation. According to the Buddhist canon, when the Buddha discovered the twelve members, he worked backward from No.12 'old age and death' (*jarā-maraṇa*); thus, he worked up to name-and-formation, then to *vijñāna*, to *saṃskāra*, and finally to *avidyā*.[70] Thus, he parallels the Brahman in the *Śatapatha* story—who went to the remote side of name-and-formation. The *vijñāna* of the Buddhist list falls into *nāma-rūpa* in the womb, as the Brahman in the Upaniṣadic account enters the *nāma-rūpa*. The Buddhist account goes better with the *Bṛhadāraṇyaka Up.* portrayal ("He [the Brahman] entered in here even to the tips of the nails") than with the various Upaniṣadic passages that emphasise the heart location. It was probably not until the earliest Buddhist Tantras in the classical Sanskrit period that the heart was designated as the chief centre of consciousness, and in the Theravāda the like treatment of a *hadaya-vatthu* (heart basis) is not found until the time of Buddhaghosa.[71] Also, the *Bṛhad-Ār.* (I, 6, 1-3) addition of the *karma* term alongside of *nāma* and *rūpa* makes it more compatible with the Buddhist position.

There are a number of passages in Buddhist literature taking *nāma-rūpa* as the object of false views—so in *Abhidharmakośa* (IV, 71c-d, and Vasubandhu's comment). One could write at length on the ones in the Pāli text *Sutta-Nipāta*, but I shall choose and be brief:

> *anattani attamāniṃ passa lokaṃ sadevakaṃ /*
> *niviṭṭhaṃ nāmarūpasmiṃ idam saccan ti maññati //*[72]
> The world—both men and gods—seeing the non-self as self, devoted to name-and-formation deems this as 'true'.

This citation is not a denial of self, *per se*; rather it is a denial that *nāma-rūpa* is a self as it is mistakenly viewed. Besides, the Buddhist texts are not always taking *nāma-rūpa* as something to escape from, since for the time being it is the apparatus for advancing on the Buddhist path. So, the *Dharmasamuccaya* (X, 49):[73]

> *nāmarūpavināśāya cittanāśāya dehinām /*
> *utpannadoṣajanakaṃ madyaṃ dharmapradūṣakam //*
> The intoxicating drink destroys name-and-formation, destroys the spirit (*citta*) of men, promotes sinful persons, and makes Dharma decline.

This is the next citation from the *Sutta-Nipāta*:

> *accī yathā vātavegena khitto (upasīvāti bhagavā)*
> *attham paleti na upeti saṃkham /*
> *evaṃ munī nāmakāyā vimutto atthaṃ paleti*
> *na upeti saṃkham //*[74]
>
> The Bhagavat responded: "Lo, Upasīva, as a flame blown about by force of wind reaches its goal (i.e. quiescent state) that none can sum, so the silent sage (*muni*), liberated from the set of names (*nāmakāya*), reaches the goal that none can sum."

The commentary clarifies that he had previously been liberated from the 'set of formations' (*rūpakāya*): *pubbeva rūpakāya vimutto.*[75] The verse is intriguing. When a fire goes out, where does it go, i.e., where is it hiding? Likewise, the *muni* is liberated from the set of names, where does he go, i.e., where is he hiding?

A comparable Upaniṣadic passage is that of the *Muṇḍaka Up.* (III, 2, 8):

> *yathā nadyas syandamānās samudre astaṃ*
> *gacchanti nāma-rūpa vihāya/*
> *tathā vidvān nāmarūpād vimuktaḥ parātparaṃ*
> *puruṣam upaiti divyam//*
>
> Just as the flowing streams disappear in the ocean, abandoning name-and-formation, so the knower, liberated from name-and-formation, reaches the divine person, superior to the best.

In this Brahmnic tradition, there is no problem of where one goes—it is to the divine person—but then there is a problem as to the nature of this divine person, since Śaṅkara insists, as was mentioned, that this one is given characteristics just for the sake of devotion.

Asaṅga discusses the matter in his *Cintāmayī Bhūmi* (PTT, Vol. 110, p. 17-1 ff.). He starts by citing a verse from an unnamed source: "The same and the different arose; and the Muni, having equipoised himself with the inward ecstasy, abandoned the life motivation (*bhavasaṃskāra=ayuḥsaṃskāra*), like one born in an egg, breaks the eggshell" (*mtshuṅs daṅ mtshuṅs pa ma yin 'byuṅ ba daṅ / naṅ du dgyes par mdzad ciṅ mñam bźag nas / thub pas srid pa'i 'du byed spaṅs mdzad do / sgo ṅar skyes pas sbubs ni rtol ba bźin/).* Asaṅga explains that the Buddha while a Bodhisattva in his life has the *rūpakāya* adorned with the major and minor marks and then became completely enlightened. Being a Tathāgata (one come the same way), his *rūpakāya* was the same. His *nāmakāya*, being dissimilar, because without flux (*anāsrava*), was different.[76] Upon passing into Nirvāṇa by the *samādhi* of abandoning the life motivation, he broke the *rūpakāya* and *nāmakāya* in the manner of an eggshell. Asaṅga is thus consistent with the *Sūtta-Nipāta,* and refrains from Mahāyāna vocabulary of multiple Buddha bodies.

However, the *Aṅguttara-Nikāya* of the Pāli canon, in the "Book of Eights" speaks of the 'eggshell' as the 'eggshell of nescience' (*avijjaṇḍakosaṃ*)[77]—so also *Mahāvyutpatti,* No. 6963, *avidyāṇḍa-koṣa-paṭalam.* This *avidyā* of the Buddhist text does not appear identifiable with the one which Śaṅkara identifies with the first kind of *nāma-rūpa*. But it is easily the *avidyā* of Buddhist Dependent Origination, preceding the *nāma-rūpa* of the Buddhist formula. In the "Book of Eights" account, it was upon breaking this 'eggshell of nescience' that Gautama awakened to complete enlightenment. Assuming that Asaṅga accepts this position, then it was through elimination of nescience that Gautama was a Tathāgata, his *rūpa-kāya* the 'same'. Asaṅga presumably has this very Sutta[78] in mind, because (PTT, Vol. 110, p. 17-2-2, f) in order to explain the breaking of the *rūpa-kāya* and the *nāma-kāya* upon the Buddha's abandonment of the life motivation, he cites another verse from an unnamed source: "(He is) free from the mud-like lust, free from the demon-like hatred, free from the net-like delusion, free from the rapids-like phenomenal life (*bhava*)" (*'dod pa lta bu'i dam med de / że sdaṅ 'dra ba'i gdon yaṅ med / gti mug 'dra ba'i dra ba med / srid pa 'dra ba'i chu kluṅ med).* Now, in this Sutta of the "Book of Eights", soon before the passage about breaking the eggshell of nescience, the interlocutor Brahmin calls Gotama a '*venayika*' (cf. *BHS Dictionary,* under '*vaināśika*), a "destructionist". And Gotama (S. Gautama) responds that he is indeed such a one, but not in the Brahmin's intention. To show his way, Gotama says: "I teach the doctrine (*dharma*) of destroying lust, hatred, and delusion; I teach the doctrine of destroying the numerous sinful, unvirtuous natures."[79] This goes well with Asaṅga's context, if the 'numerous sinful, unvirtuous natures' are equivalent to the term 'phenomental life' (*bhava*). But Asaṅga continues in a manner absent from the Sutta mentioned. He points out that these four 'lust', etc. cause lack of independence (*asvātantrya*),[80] which in his *Srāvakabhūmi* he says is the sole aspect by which one examines non-self (*anātmaka*) as one of the four aspects of the Noble Truth of Suffering.[81] The implication is that these four, which he calls at the four non-genuine natures' (*chos yaṅ dag pa ma yin pa bźi po*),[82] define respectively the 'non-self' of sentient beings and that their destruction amounts to establishing the true self—referred to as the Buddha's kind of *rūpa-kāya* and *nāma-kāya* and by Asaṅga further on (PTT, Vol. 110, p. 17-5-6) as 'master-like' (*rje bo lta bur gyur pa*). This would be a glorified kind of *ātmabhāva* (embodiment) mentioned previously in citation of Asaṅga. This points to the true gulf between the Brahmanical and the Buddhist positions in these matters, to wit, that the Upaniṣads and their Vedāntic continuators insist on a higher self, the *jīvātman* always, while Buddhism insists there is nothing to be called higher unless man acts higher.

In conclusion, while this topic of *nāma-rūpa* is a large one, and many other passages could be found, it does seem possible to discuss these issues meaningfully in one chapter. Our investigation suggests that a stress on the *ātman*-adherence of the Vedānta, and *anātman*-adherence of Buddhism would have obscured and choked an exposition of *nāma-rūpa*, at least along the lines expressed above.

That the ancient Indian scriptures do have at least rudimentary statements about two kinds of *nāma-rūpa*, I believe this chapter to have established. While Buddhism speaks of only one kind of *nāma-rūpa* (=the five *skandha*), in a way it also has two—the one of the previous life and the one of the present life, since this topic always figures in the discussions of what transmigrates. The relation between these two in the Buddhist case shares a feature of the two in Śaṅkara's Vedānta that man's ordinary mind does not suffice to arrive at solutions. So the Buddhist sects had divergent views on the matter, as found in their scriptures, and Śaṅkara's pupils abandoned his terminology of two kinds.

A rather exciting outcome of these researches is that in the Brahmanical as well as in the Buddhist portrayal of *nāma-rūpa*, this constitutes a kind of dividing line between our commonplace world and the superior world of the gods or of yoga-success.

REFERENCES

1. Very useful is *Word Index to the Brahma-Sūtra-Bhāṣya of Śaṅkara* (University of Madras; Part One, 1971; Part Two, 1973). Besides, there is *Eighteen Principal Upaniṣads*, Vol. I, Ed: by V.P. Limaye and R.D. Vadekar (Vaidika Saṁśodhana Maṇḍala, Poona, 1958). My copy of Śaṅkara's *Bhāṣya* is the edition by Nārāyan Rām Āchārya (Satyabhāmābāi Panduraṅg, for the Nirṇaya Sāgar Press, Bombay, 1948). I shall refer to the *Bhāṣya* as *VS-Bhāṣya* (VS for *Vedānta-sūtra*).
2. Julius Eggeling, tr. *The Śatapatha-Brāhmaṇa, according to the text of the Mādhyandina School*, Part V (SBE, Vol. XLIV), pp. 27-8.
3. Louis de La Vallée Poussin, *L'Abhidharmakośa de Vasubandhu*, Troisième Chapitre (Paris, 1926), p. 94.
4. Louis Renou, *Études sur le Vocabulaire du Rgveda, Première Série* (Institut Francais d'Indologie, Pondichéry, 1958).
5. Renou, *Études*, p. 10, n.
6. Renou, *Études*, p. 10, and n.
7. This rendition for *vicitya* is adapted from Böhtlingk und, Roth, *Sanskrit Wörterbuch*, VI, p. 1012, under *vicit 'adj. sondernd, sichtend'*.
8. *Sarvāṇi rūpāṇi vicitya dhīro nāmāni kṛtvā 'bhivadan yad āste/* (*Bhāṣya's* comments on VS I, 1, 11 and on VS I, 4, 22).
9. Renou, *Études*, p. 10.
10. Renou, *Études*, p. 11, and n.
11. Cf. A.A. Macdonell and A.B. Keith, *Vedic Index of Names and Subjects* (reprint, Varanasi, 1958), entry 'Nāman', pp. 443-4.
12. Arthur B. Keith, *The Aitareya Āraṇyaka* (Oxford University Press, reprint, 1969), text in II, 1, 6, tr. at p. 207. I have modified the translation of the passage which has a suggestion of weaving vocabulary. Curiously, *dāma* goes with *dyáti*, and *sita* with *syáti*, according to M. Mayrhofer, *A Concise Etymological Sanskrit Dictionary*.
13. For the last sentence, *sa yo nāma brahmety upāste/yāvan nāmno gatam tatrāsya yathākāmacāro bhavati/*Eighteen Principal Upaniṣads, p. 148, in VII, 1.5.
14. *Yājñavalkyeti hovāca—yatrāyaṃ puruṣo mriyate kim enaṃ na jahātīti/nāmeti/ Eighteen Principle Upanisads*, p. 216.
15. La Vallée Poussin, Troisième Chapitre, pp. 94-5.
16. This work is the *Abhidharmakósa-śāstra-kārikā-bhāṣya*, PTT. Vol. 116, p. 305-1.
17. Cf. Akira Hirakawa, *Index to the Abhidharmakośabhāṣya*, Part One, Sanskrit-Tibetan-Chinese (Tokyo, 1973), p. 204, entry 'NAM-'.
18. PTT is the abbreviation reference to the Peking Tibetan canon, Japanese photo edition.
19. Renou, *Études*, p. 12
20. Renou, *Études*, pp. 13-4.
21. Cf. Pal Hacker, *Vivarta* (Wiesbaden, 1953).
22. Renou, *Études*, p. 14-5.
23. *Abhidharmakośabhāṣyam of Vasubandhu*, Ed: Pradhan (Patna, 1975), I. 10a: *rūpaṃ dvidhā*, with Vasubandhu's comment: *varṇaḥ. saṃsthānaṃ ca*.

24. Renou, *Études*, p. 13.
25. But Y. Karunadasa, *Buddhist Analysis of Matter* (Colombo, 1976), p. 2, mentions the occurrence of *'rūpa'* in a frequent canonical passage whereby Pāli commentators claimed it to mean 'color' in this context, to wit, *cakkhuñ ca paṭicca rūpe ca uppajjati cakkhuviññānam*. This is the *rūpa* that is the object of the visual faculty.
26. I have garnered this restriction of the Chinese character for 'color' from conversation with Profesor Pei-yi Wu of Queens College, N.Y., and Columbia University. and with Professor Wing-tsit Chan, emeritus of Dartmouth College.
27. La Vallée Poussin, *L'Abhidharmakósa de Vasubandhu*. Premier et deuxième chapitres (Paris, 1923), p. 45.
28. La Vallée Poussin, Premier et deuxième, pp. 14-5.
29. *Abhidharmakośa and Bhāṣya with Sphuṭārtha Commentary*, Part I, Shastri ed. (Varanasi, 1970), pp. 38-41. Vasubandhu (author of the *Bhāṣya*) comments on the words *śubhāśubha* ('whether good or bad') as *kuśalākuśala* (virtuous or unvirtuous); and Yaśomitra (author of the *Sphuṭārtha*) says that the *anubandha* so described is restricted to *kuśala or akuśala*, without possibility of the *avyākṛta* (indeterminate) (*kuśalākuśala evety avadhāraṇam/avyākṛto nāstītyarthaḥ*). Ah-Yueh Yeh, "The Characteristics of 'vijñāna' and 'vijñapti' on the basis of Vasubandhu's *Pañcaskandha-prakaraṇa*", *Annals* (B.O.R. Institute), Vol. LX (Poona, 1979), reports (p.178) that Sthiramati's commentary allows for the positive form *vijñapti* (which I render as 'candor') *kuśala, akuśala*, and *avyākṛta*. She accepts V.V. Gokhale's rendition of *avijñapti-rūpa* as 'concealed form of activity' while I render the *avijñapti* as 'reticence'.
30. E. Hardy, ed., *The Netti-Pakaraṇa* (London, 1961), p. 28.
31. Bhikkhu J. Kashyap, *The Paṭisambhidāmagga* (Pāli Publication Board, 1960), p. 212.10-15.
32. I translated and discussed this *sutta* in my article, "Dependent Origination—the Indo-Tibetan Tradition", Journal of Chinese Philosophy, 7 (1980), 275-300.
33. */ bcom ldan 'das kyis kyaṅ lhan cig skyes pa'i tshor ba daṅ 'du śes daṅ sems pa źes gaṅ gsuṅs pa daṅ /chos 'di dag ni 'dres pa ste.*
34. Cf. H.D. Velankar, *Ṛgveda Maṇḍala*, VII (Bombay, 1963), discussion of *ṛta* and *satya*, pp. iv-x.
35. Eighteen, p. 198.
36. See, for example, the 'ātman' entry, Monier-Williams, *A Sanskrit-English Dictionary*.
37. Alex Wayman, *Analysis of the Śrāvakabhūmi Manuscript* (Berkeley, 1961), p. 60.
38. For example, Maryla Falk, *Nāma-rūpa and Dharma-rūpa* (University of Calcutta, 1934), pp. 136-7, n. 42, agreeing with Mrs. C.A.F. Rhys Davids that the doctrine of the *skandha* pentad, contrasting with the notion of 'self' was introduced in later monk exegesis and does not "belong to the earliest strata of the Buddhist teaching." Besides, one can obtain more evidence of Vedāntic continuation in Buddhist texts from Hajime Nakamura, "The Vedānta Philosophy as was Revealed in Buddhist Scriptures", *Pañcāmṛtam* (Shrī Lāl Bahādur Śāstrī Rāṣṭriya Sanskrit Vidyā Peeṭha, Delhi, 1968), pp. 1-74.
39. *Śatapatha-Brāhmaṇa* Ed: Albrecht Weber (reprint, Varanasi, 1964), pp. 838-9.
40. Cf. A. Wayman, "The Significance of Mantras, from the Veda down to Buddhist Tantric Practice", *Adyar Library Bulletin*, XXXIX, 1975, pp. 66-7.
41. The rendering for *abhva* follows the dictionaries, e.g. the Monier-Williams one. For *yakṣa*, cf. Velankar, *Ṛgveda Maṇḍala*, VII, p. xv, especially "All this would tend to show that *yakṣá* was something that looked very tempting, but inscrutable in its true nature, hence unaceptable to a straightforward man." The contrast

between the two seems to be in terms of the spirits picked—the *abhva* being monstrous, and the *yakṣa* attractive.

42. Cf. A. Wayman, "Studies in Yama and Māra", *Indo-Iranian Journal,* III, 1959, p. 69. The Vinītadeva commentary is the *Vinayavibhaṅgapadavyākhyāna.*
43. P.T. Srinivasa Iyengar, *Outlines of Indian Philosophy* (Theosophical Publishing Society, Benares and London, 1909), especially pp. 84-91.
44. Sengaku Mayeda, *A Thousand Teachings; The Upadeśasāhasrī of Śaṅkara* (University of Tokyo Press, Tokyo, 1979).
45. S.M. Katre, *Dictionary of Pāṇini,* Part II (Deccan College, Poona, 1968), p. 513. Of course, the word *skandha.* used by the Buddhists for the five aggregates of *nāma-rūpa,* anciently meant 'branching out'. Paul Hacker, "Eigentümlichkeiten der Lehre und Terminologie Śaṅkaras", *ZDMG,* 1950, p. 273, opts for 'unevolved' by the word 'das Unentfaltete', for *avyākṛta.*
46. *Bhāṣya's* comments on VS, I, 4, 9, Bombay ed., p. 156.
47. *Bhāṣya's* comments on VS, I, 4, 9, Bombay ed., p. 157.
48. *Bhāṣya's* comments on VS, I, 4, 9, Bombay ed., p. 157.
49. Bombay ed., p. 76.
50. *viḍambanevāvinayoddhatānāṃ durmedhasām āpad ivātikaṣṭā /*
alpātmanāṃ yā madireva lakṣmīr babhūva sā tatra yathārthanāmā //
(ed. Ḥ. Kern, HOS, Vol. One, p. 6.20-21).
51. Bombay ed., p. 76.
52. Mayeda, *A Thousand Teachings,* pp. 18-26.
53. The rendition 'imitation' is in the Monier-Williams Sanskrit Dictionary under *anupraveśa* and attributed to lexicographer(s). The usual translation of *anupraviśya* as 'entering', only takes account of the *viś-*. The *anu-* itself signifies 'after' or 'in conformity with'; the verbal *pra-* is often rendered 'forth'. The *viś-* is employed frequently in metaphorical extensions of 'to enter', hence 'to engage' and the like. Thus, 'engaging forth in conformity' is a clumsy equivalent to 'imitating'. Ananta Charana Sukla, *The Concept of Imitation in Greek and Indian Aesthetics* (Calcutta, 1977) does not mention this Sanskrit expression. He says (p. 154) that Pāṇini and Kālidāsa used the words *anukaraṇa* and *anukṛti* in the sense of an exact likeness or imitation. But we notice in these cases also the prefix *anu-*.
54. The Buddhist Abhidharma position about this is well-presented in Karunadasa, *Buddhist Analysis of Matter,* where p. 16, he mentions that *ākāśa* was listed as a *dhātu* along with the usual four elements, but was always in Buddhism excluded from the list of *mahābhūta,* which generate the *bhautika* (derivative elements). At p. 34, he mentions the important list of six *dhātu,* of which man is composed, the four *mahābhūta* (fire, wind, water, earth), space (*ākāśa*) and *vijñāna* (here probably meaning 'understanding'). Asaṅga, *Viniścayasaṃgrahaṇī* (PTT, Vol. 110, p. 266-4-4), mentions this list as coming from the scripture and claims it does not contradict material he had just given (cf. above, n. 33).
55. *Bhāṣya's* comments on VS II, 4, 20, Bombay ed., p. 322 (top).
56. Mayeda, *A Thousand Teachings,* p. 25.
57. Cf. Mayeda, *A Thousand Teachings,* p. 22.
58. Cf. the discussion of these matters in Madeleine Biardeau, "*Ahaṃkāra,* the Ego Principle in the Upaniṣad", *Contributions to Indian Sociology,* VIII, Oct. 1965, pp. 72-4.
59. "*asti bhāti priyaṃ rūpaṃ nāma cety aṃśapañcakam /*
ādya trayaṃ brahmarūpaṃ jagadrūpaṃ tato dvayam //"
iti śruteḥ /

(*The Yoga Upaniṣads*, with the commentary of Śrī Upaniṣad Brahmayogin Ed: by A Mahadeva Sastri, The Adyar Library and Research Center, Madras, 1968). Cf. also *Lalitā-Sahasranāman* with Bhāskararaya's Commentary, tr. into English by R. Ananthakrishna Sastry (Adyar, Madras, India. ed. of 1951), p. 175. "300. Transcending name and form *(nāmarūpavivarjitā)*... As the latter two, name and form are illusory, she transcends them. 'She' is here the 'supreme Devī' "called Nārāyaṇī, the creator of Nara (men) and women".

60. *mam nāma tava ca jātavedo vāsasī iva vivasānau ye carāvaḥ / āyuṣe tvaṃ jīvase vayaṃ yathāyathaṃ vi pariṃ dadhāvahai punas te //* (*Taittirīya-saṃhitā* of the Kṛṣṇa Yajurveda, publ. at Pāraḍī-nagara, 1957), p. 33 (I, 5, 10). Note that the 'name' is called a garment *(vāsas)*, implying that the one wearing the garment is the *rūpa*. Also, Chitrabhau Sen. *A Dictionary of the Vedic Rituals* based on the Śrauta and Gṛhya Sūtras (Concept Publishing Company, Delhi, 1978), has the entry 'nāma-vyatiṣañjanīya (homa)', the rite 'interchange of names' "between the royal sacrificer and his son (heir apparent)"

61. *atha brahmaiva parārdham agacchat / tat parārdham gatvaikṣata kathaṃ nv imāṃ lokān pratyaveyām iti tad dvābhyām eva pratyavaid rūpeṇa caiva nāmnā ca /.*

62. *Eighteen Principal Upaniṣads,* p. 186, passage beginning *taddhedaṃ tarhy avyākṛtam āsīt/tan nāmarūpābhyām eva vyākriyata.*

63. Eighteen, Principal Upaniṣads p. 192: *mano vācaṃ prāṇaṃ tāny ātmane 'kuruta.*

64. Gadjin Ṃ Nagao, *Madhyāntavibhāga-Bhāṣya* (Tokyo 1964), p. 21.

65. *Visuddhimagga of Buddhaghosācariya,* Ed: H.C. Warren, revised by Dharmananda Kosambi (Harvard University Press, 1950), p. 477 *nāṃan ti ārammanābhimukhaṃ namanato vedanādayo tayo khandhā.* (It is 'name' because bending towards the consciousness-support [*ārammana* = *ālambana*]; it is the three aggregates, feelings, etc. [the remaining two being 'ideas' and 'motivations']).

66. A. Wayman, "The Intermediate-state Dispute in Buddhism", *Buddhist Studies in Honour of I.B. Horner* (Dordrecht, Holland, 1974), p. 230.

67. This is said on the intuitive level, because the *Śatapatha* as was mentioned, referred to *nāma* and *rūpa* as the 'two monsters'. The closest Buddhism comes to this, as far as I know, is in the *Ārya Śālistamba Sūtra* Ed. by N. Aiyaswami Sastri (Adyar Library, 1950), p. 14, mentioning *vijñāna* as the 'seed' *(bīja), karma (=saṃskāra)* as the 'field' *(kṣetra); tṛṣṇā* as the 'moisture' (*sneha*); and *avidyā* as the 'manure' (*pāṣī;* cf. Edgerton's BHS Dictionary for this word, omitted from Sastri's edition, for Tibetan *lud*); and with the conditions mentioned, from the 'seed' *vijñāna* comes the 'shoot' *nāma-rūpa* in the womb. The 'field' *saṃskarā* has the role of the *rūpa* (even though not the *rūpa* of the previous life); and the 'manure' *avidyā* has the role of the *nāma* ('cloak') (even though not the previous *nāma*) (cf. n. 60, above). Then *vijñāna* cast into this field as a 'seed' is a forecast of completing the *nāma-rūpa* in the womb.

68. The Sutta of *Saṃyutta-Nikāya* ii, 2 (cf. n.32, above) includes in the description of 'old age and death' (*jarā-maraṇa*), death in particular, 'break up of the *skandhas*' (*khandhānam bhedo*) (from Bihar edition, 1959).

69. My article "The Intermediate-state Dispute" (n. 66, above) cites the *Pratītyasamutpādahṛdaya-vyākaraṇa* (attributed to Nāgārjuna): "Just as in the case of a flame from a flame, the reflected image in a mirror from a face, ... a sprout from a seed ... a person is not taught to understand that the one is different from the other, so also in the case of reconnection (*pratisaṃdhi*) of the personality aggregates (*skandha*), the wise person will understand that there is no transfer."

70. As one source, there is the Sutta of *Saṃyutta-Nikāya* ii.2, already mentioned above, which portrays the Buddha explaining the twelve members of Dependent Origination by their reverse order. meaning from No. 12 up to No. 1.
71. For the late doctrine of heart basis in the Pāli literature, cf. Karunadasa, *Buddhist Analysis of Matter,* pp. 62-3.
72. *Suttanipāta, Mahā-Vagga* (The Great Chapter), last section *Dūyatānupassanā sutta* (Sermons on Dual viewpoints), in edition by Bhikṣu Dharmaratna (Sarnath, 1951), at p. 164, bottom.
73. *Dharma-Samuccaya* (Compendium de la Loi), 2e Partie (Chapitres Vi à XII), par Lin Li-Kouang, Révision de André Bareau, J.W. de Jong et Paul Demiéville, avec des Appendices par J.W. de Jong (Paris, 1969), p. 316.
74. *Suttanipāta, Pārāyaṇa-Vagga* (chapter on the Final Goal), section on 'Brahman Upasīva's questions', Dharmaratna's ed., p. 226.
75. *The Suttanipāta-Atthakathā,* Ed: Angraj Chaudhary (Nālandā, Bihar, 1975), Vol. II, p. 571.20-1.
76. PTT, Vol. 110, p. 17-1-14: */de bźin gśegs par gyur pa na yaṅ / de'i gzugs kyi sku byuṅ ba de ni mtshuṅs so / miṅ gi sku byuṅ ba de dag ni zag pa med pas mi 'dra ba'i phyir mtshuṅs pa ma yin no /.*
77. *The Aṅguttara Nikāya,* Vol. III (Bihar, 1960), p. 290.1 (VIII, 2, 1).
78. Of course, Asaṅga does not employ the Pāli version, rather what is called the *Ekottara-Āgama.*
79. *The Aṅguttara Nikāya,* Vol. III, p. 289.15-6: *vinayāya dhammaṃ desemi rāgassa dosassa mohassa; anekavihitānaṃ pāpakānaṃ akusalānaṃ dhammānaṃ vinayāya dhammaṃ desemi /.*
80. PTT, Vol. 110, p. 17-2-3, 4: */raṅ dbaṅ med par byed pa'i chos bźi po 'di dag ni...*
81. Cf. Alex Wayman, *Analysis of the Śrāvakabhūmi Manuscript,* pp. 130-1.
82. PTT, Vol. 110, p. 17-2-5.

POST-SCRIPTUM

The author wishes to mention that after writing the above article he traced the verse which Asaṅga cited, namely, "The same and the different . . .", in its comparable Pāli form in *Aṅguttara Nikāya,* iv, 311, also *Saṃyutta Nikāya,* v. 263, namely, "*tulaṃ atulaṃ ca . . ..*" Asaṅga evidently drew the verse from either of those canons in *Āgama* Sanskrit form; or else from *Udānavarga,* XXVI, 30. Besides, since the interpretation of VS III, 2,14, *arūpavad* . . . is very important for Vedānta doctrine, the author wishes to concede that while Śaṅkara insists that *arūpavad* ("does not possess *rūpa*") suggests that Brahman is not *rūpa,* the *Brahmasūtra* by the expression may mean that Brahman does not 'possess' *rūpa* because it 'is' *rūpa.*

23

The 'No-self' of Buddhism within Indian Culture

One can often read in books about Buddhism that it gets its followers to believe that there is no *ātman* in man; and that this position disallows a soul to transmigrate, although accepting the theory of transmigration; and that it accepts no soul to experience, the fruits of virtue and vice, although talking a lot about *karma* and its fruits. To show that such evaluations are wide of the mark, the relevant data will be presented in two sections, I. 'I' and 'mine'; II. 'No-self' and transmigration.

To bring in Indian culture, in both sections certain non-Buddhist works will be consulted to establish a wider context. For this purpose, the writer was inspired by Rasik Vihari Joshi's long article on '*aham-artha*' (the 'I'-sense),[1] although not taking sides in Joshi's acceptance of the Vaiṣṇava position against the Śaivitic Śaṅkara interpretations of the Upaniṣadic *ātman.*

I. 'I' AND 'MINE'

The reason for initially treating in this part certain rival Vedānta traditions is to determine whether the term *ātman* is being employed for the 'I' sense.

Joshi called to my attention that there are two words *aham,* 'I'—a declinable and an indeclinable. The declinable form goes with the grammatical *asmāt,* allowing the accusative *māṃ* ('me') and the genitive *mama* ('mine') and the indeclinable *aham* means the ego. I consulted the work *Avyayakośa,*[2] a treatise on indeclinables and found that the indeclinable *aham* goes with the finite verb *asmin* ('I am') as an indeclinable noun that allows such a Sanskrit word as *asmitā* (rendered 'egotism') in the *Yogasūtras.* Therefore, we must consider the Sāṃkhya system's term *ahaṃkāra,* the well-known evolute from *prakṛti.* According to K.C. Bhattacharyya, *ahaṃkāra* manifests as willing, but it is also a kind of knowing the sensed object as *mine* or to *be mine.*[3] Hence the *aham* of *ahaṃkāra* is the declinable form. Besides, when there are such identifications as, "I am fat," or "I am a man," or "I am a woman," this is because the world keeps reminding the person that the person is like *that;* and this generates the 'me' of the declinable *aham.* In contrast, the heroic utterance "I have found it," or as is illustrated below, "I am first of the world," implicates the indeclinable *aham,* because the statement issues from inner resources that are independent of 'me' and 'mine'. A historical anecdote can be cited to illustrate the latter *aham.* The Greek Philosopher Archimedes, a remarkable inventor, was at the bath-house and observing the overflow of water in his bath, suddenly figured out a perplexing problem of how to decide whether the king's crown was pure gold. He exclaimed, "Eureka," which means "I have found it," and was so oblivious of having no clothes on, that he ran home naked.

The Vaiṣṇava argument against Śaṅkara as regards the self (*ātman*) apparently rests on Śaṅkara's differentiation of the *ātman* from the 'I'-sense, as I notice in his *Viveka-Cūḍāmaṇi,* k. 431, in Swāmī Mādhavānanda's translation:[4]

> The absence of the ideas of "I" and "mine" even in this

> existing body, which follows as a shadow is a characteristic of one liberated-in-life.

Śaṅkara's preceding verses show this condition going with the ascetic's merging the *ātman* in Brahman—the stated goal of various old Upaniṣads. We could presume that Śaṅkara is right in this differentiation on the grounds that the Upaniṣadic *ātman* was supposed to be present in the states called waking, dream, dreamless sleep, and the fourth (*turīya*). In the usual examples of the 'I'—sense, such as the assertions "I know" and "I don't know"; "I like it" and "I don't like it"; even "I'm sacred stiff"—the 'I'-sense is predominately a feature just of the waking state.

But, as I learned from Joshi's article, the Vaiṣṇava commentators, especially Rāmānuja, cannot tolerate Śaṅkara's differentiation of the *ātman* from the 'I'-sense. And I should cite a passage from Veliath's article devoted to Rāmānuja's position on these matters:[5]

> The individual self is basically an immutable entity. Even during the state of sleep, it was a subject of knowledge and it was conscious of pleasure and sorrow, but in the state of deep sleep and in similar states, the self which reveals itself does so as the "I". The "I" so revealed is not to be understood as a mere attribute of the self, because it constitutes the very nature of the self, and it continues even in the state of Final Release. This consciousness of the "I" when it is not sublated by anything else has the *Ātman* for its object, but the consciousness of the "I" that has the body for its object is mere *Avidyā*.

Now turning to Buddhism for the 'I'-sense, we may start with the sentences attributed to the future Buddha upon his birth. According to the Pāli canon,[6] he took seven steps toward the north (*uttara*) and proclaimed: "I am chief in the world" (*aggo ham asmi lokassa*); "I am eldest (first) in the world" (*jeṭṭho ham asmi lokassa*); "I am best in the world" (*seṭṭho ham asmi lokassa*); "This is the last birth" (*ayam antimā jāti*); "There is not now a rebirth" (*natthi dāni punabbhavo*). Notice that there is no indication of "mine" or "me"; and so we may refer to this *aham* as the indeclinable or invariant one. This particular statement seems to agree more with the position of Rāmānuja than with the Śaṅkara one.

The Buddhist texts did not forget this type of language, for in a later work, the *Vairocanābhisaṃbodhi-tantra*, Chap. 10, I translate from Tibetan: "I am called Lord of the World, am first of the world; and teach the Dharma that is supreme, quiescent from the outset and incomparable."[7]

For the Buddhist rejection of 'I' and 'mine', a good passage is in the Pāli Aṅguttara-nikāya, Book of Threes, chapter on messengers of the Devas, namely, Sāriputta's visit to the Buddha, including:[8]

> Then, Sāriputta, you should train in this manner: Toward this body together with its set of perceptions, there should be no clingings of 'I', 'mine', or pride. And toward any external (attractive) objects, there should be no clingings of 'I', 'mine', or pride. Continuing in this (training), one accomplishes (respectively) the liberation by mind (Skt. *cetas*) and the liberation by insight (Skt. *prajñā*).

This passage appears to agree with Śaṅkara's verse presented above. Besides, it brings in 'pride' (*māna*) as a third in this Book of Threes. So also in this important passage of the canonical Majjhima-nikāya, Vol. I, no. 8, the *Sallekhasutta*. Mahācunda asked the Buddha: "Whatever be the views (Skt. *dṛṣṭi*) of various sorts that occur among the people and are involved with theories of the self or are involved with theories of the world—how can there be a rejection of these views, how can there be a renunciation of these views for a monk who would orient his mind from the outset (for the given purpose)?" The Buddha responded this way:[9]

> Wherever these views arise, wherever they resurge, and wherever they are current, it is by seeing them with right insight (Skt. *samyak-prajñā*) as they really are, namely, 'this is not mine,' 'I am not this,' 'this is not my self'—that there is rejection of these views, that there is renunciation of these views.

Horner in her own translation of this scripture cited the commentary: "To think *etaṃ mama,* this is mine, is to be in the grip of craving;" "To think *eso aham asmi,* I am this, is to be in the grip of pride;" "To think *eso me attā,* this is my self, is to be in the grip of wrong views."[10]

The old Buddhist texts had a certain amount of pride-bashing. Thus, the Saṃyutta-nikāya, I, the Brahmin Suttas, has the *Mānatthaddha Sutta.*[11] At Sāvatthī (Skt. Śrāvastī), there was a brahmin with a nickname Pride-stiff (*mānatthaddha*), who did not respect his father, mother, his teacher, or his eldest brother. The Buddha was there teaching a large congregation. Pride-stiff decided to approach Gotama (the clan name of the Buddha), thinking, "If he talks to me, I will talk to him. If not, I won't speak to him." He drew near and stood aside. The Buddha said nothing to him. Pride-stiff thought, "This ascetic Gotama doesn't know anything," and started to leave. The Buddha divined the thoughts in Pride-stiff's mind and spoke this verse:

> A brahmin who is proud does not serve the purpose here. Brahmin, on whose account you have come hither, give just that person your devotion![12]

Pride-stiff realized that the ascetic Gotama had read his mind. He prostrated himself at the Buddha's feet and kissed his feet. The Buddha told him, "That's enough. Since belief in me has arisen in your heart, stand up and take your place in the congregation." So Pride-stiff took a place there and then asked the Buddha to whom one should show humility. The Buddha in a verse told him to show humility to his mother, father, eldest brother, and fourthly his teacher.

Buddhism was so condemnatory of pride that in time had classified it as seven kinds. Genjun Sasaki in a published essay gave the Pāli list from Theravāda sources;[13] and once I noticed the Sanskrit equivalent list in Vasubandhu's *Abhidharmakośa* (V, 10), and translated them as follows: pride (*māna*), haughty pride (*atimāna*), 'I-am' pride (*asmimāna*), assuming pride (*abhimāna*), pride over pride (*mānātimāna*), begrudging pride (*ūnamāna*), and a perverse kind (*mithyāmāna*).[14]

The 'I am' kind of pride was mentioned above by Horner's citation. Sasaki's essay provides important information about it, especially that it implies "to conceive that I am the five aggregates".[15] The five personal aggregates are in Sanskrit *rūpa* (form, the bodily parts), *vedanā* (feelings), *saṃjña* (ideas, notions), *saṃskāra* (motivations, most of the dharmas associated with consciousness), *vijñāna* (the six perceptions, five based on the 'outer' senses, the sixth on the *manas,* i.e., the mind). The comparison of these five personal aggregates as constituting a 'self' with the parts of a chariot as constituting a 'chariot' was presumably made by the early Buddhist nun Vajirā,[16] later taken up in questions of King Milinda, then expanded upon by Candrakīrti in his *Madhyamakāvatāra.* I had to deal with the matter by translating the last part of Tsong-kha-pa's *Lam rim chen mo* from the Tibetan language, wherein there was a lengthy treatment based on Candrakīrti's position.[17] It is an argument that a 'self' as a synthetic union of the five personal aggregates is no more real than is a 'chariot' as a synthetic union of its parts. Suppose we grant this argument. Even so, it does not deny that this 'self' as a synthetic union can grow, study in school, get a job, get married, etc., just as that 'chariot' can be used to transport people from one place to another. Indeed, the Buddhist contemplation of the 'self' in comparison with the 'chariot' is feasibly explainable as a way of getting rid of wrong notions about the 'self' so that the individual may finally realize what is the true Self, presuming that there is such a Self.

There is a problem about the use of the word 'pride', particularly for the 'I am' variety. Sasaki tried to explain this. I think he was on the right track in taking the term 'pride' here as a connotation turning to the "psychological sphere".[18] I would add that it implicates a psychological attitude of turning the 'I am' into 'It's mine'. This was evidently the position of the commentary which Horner cited: "To think *eso me attā,* this is my self, is to be in the grip of wrong views." Indeed, people do not say, "I am this body;" rather, "This is my body;" or, as the wife to her violent husband, "Stop, you're hurting me." In this light, the 'self'—'chariot' discussion may be viewed as a Buddhist attempt to make the contemplator consider the five personal aggregates in an identification manner—and then disprove it—rather than in the possession manner that one would rather enact in commonplace parlance.

That Buddhism was more interested in counteracting the 'mine' than the 'I' is my own conclusion from a study of this field over the years. As S. Radhakrishnan translates the Dhammapada, Chap. 5, on the fool, verse 3:[19]

> The fool is tormented thinking 'these sons belong to me', 'this wealth belongs to me'. He himself does not belong to himself. How then can sons be his? How can wealth be his?

As to the sentence, "He himself does not belong to himself," this is equivalent to the *anātman* term as a qualified negation. Thus, Asaṅga's explanation in the *Śrāvakabhūmi: asvātantrya,* 'not independent';[20] and Vasubandhu's explanation in the *Abhidharmakośa: akāmakārin,* "unable to do as wished".[21] The Dhammapada verse suggests that the fool has sold himself into spiritual slavery.

And there is the story found in the Pāli Vinaya. A group of young men had been picnicking with their wives, except that one of them had brought along his mistress, and she had run off with some of the men's belongings. All of them were looking for her and when encountered the Buddha, asked him if he had seen her. The Buddha replied: "Were it not better ye sought the Self (*attānaṃ gaveseyyātha*), rather than the woman?"[22] The Buddha was suggesting to them that the thieving woman had in a sense done them a favour by reducing their belongings, because they had been in bondage to what they considered was theirs.[23]

According to the tradition, five days after the Buddha delivered his first sermon to the five disciples he delivered another one called the *Anattalakhaṇa Sutta* to those same five disciples.[24] In this sermon, the Buddha pointed out that each of the five personal aggregates (Skt. *skandha*) is not the Self. But never denied a self.

Something else was introduced in this *Anattalakhaṇa Sutta.* It was a peculiar kind of causation that in early and later times was referred to by the Sanskrit word *dharmatā*—a grouping of *dharmas.* In this theory, certain elements, as here, 'suffering', 'impermanence', and 'non-self' are in a *dharmatā* set, such that when there is one of them, one can infer on the others, since they are independent of mental *karma.*[25] Conze realized the importance of the theory and wrote on the three marks of the Truth of Suffering in his book.[26] This sermon also introduced the terminology, noticed above that in regard to the elements of this set, 'suffering', etc. for each of the five personal aggregates, the disciple should contemplate, "This is not mine; I am not this; this is not my Self." In the course of the Buddha's further discourses, a further element was added to this set, namely, 'voidness' (*śūnyatā* in Skt.), but this was more subtle to grasp.

Besides, it is important to notice that this early *Sutta* takes the terms 'suffering', 'impermanence', and 'non-self' each to apply to the five personal aggregates (*skandha*). Hence, when the

Dhammapada 277-79 states: "All *saṃkhāra* (Skt. *saṃskāra*) are impermanent;" "All *saṃkhāra* are suffering (*dukkha*);" "All *dhammas* (Skt. *dharma*) are non-self,"[27] these identifications must apply to each of the five personal aggregates. The motto "All *saṃskāras* (constructions) are impermanent" allows the comparison of the five aggregates to the parts of a chariot, as was previously mentioned. The motto "All *saṃskāras* (motivations) are suffering" relates the five to the four Noble Truths of Buddhism. Then the third motto "All *dharmas* are non-self" must mean that the 'all *dharmas*' are those fitting into the five personal aggregates and that it is these *dharmas* that are non-self. It follows that in the case of the third motto, the term *anātman* would be misconstrued as a denial of *ātman,* since here the meaning is that all these *dharmas* exclude the *ātman*. That *dharma* should be taken as other than *ātman* is also the message of Vasubandhu's *Triṃśikā,* initial verse starting with *ātmadharmopacāro,* upon which Sthiramati comments: *ātmavijñaptir dharmaprajñaptis ca.*[28] According to Sthiramati, Vasubandhu's *ātmopacāra* means 'representation' (*vijñapti*) of *ātman*; the *dharmopacāra* means 'determination' (*prajñapti*) of *dharma.* Thus, *ātman* is something to represent, while *dharma* is something to determine.[29]

Then, as those three, suffering, etc., are in a set implicating each other, the question arises: What happens when suffering is transcended in the attainment of *nirvāṇa*? Otherwise asked, what happens to the impermanence and to the non-self? We would expect the impermanence to flip to permanence, and the *anātman* to flip to *ātman.* It was at this point, we will recall that the Vedānta has two camps in spirited disagreement, since if this *ātman* be the 'I' sense, the Rāmānuja camp says it is there at the time of *mokṣa* (the Hindu equivalent to *Nirvāṇa*), while the Śaṅkara camp denies it. To get to the Buddhist position, we must refer to a celebrated passage of Pāli Buddhism, repeated with minor modifications in Mahāyāna literature, going like this: "Whether Tathāgatas arise or do not arise, there remains this *dharmatā* (continuum) of *dharmas.*"[30] Hence, when impermanence flips to permanence, it turns out to be the permanence of *dharmas.* When *anātman* flips to *ātman,* it cannot be identified with the *dharma* realm since the *dharmas* exclude *ātman*. The *ātman* would have to go with the sentient-being realm, so also with the Tathāgata. That must be why the Tathāgata was called 'Great Person' (*mahāpuruṣa*) and even in Mahāyāna a *mahātman* ('Great Self').[31] So, in part the Buddhists agree with the Rāmānuja camp, but in part not so, because this *ātman* in Buddhism belongs to the process of arising and passing away. In the language suggested by Sthiramati, the *ātman* is to be represented as 'great', 'small', 'restrained', 'unrestrained', etc., while *dharma* is always there to be determined.

In Buddhist sources, we have noticed the 'I' sense to be of two kinds—one which involves pride, which starting with "I am", turns into 'mine'; and the other based on inner resources and is the heroic 'I'. Therefore, Buddhism does not appear to criticize the 'I' sense as much as it does the sense of mine.

The 'I' sense is implicit in the first person form of verbs, and used for pledges and vows in Buddhism. For example, for the three refuges, the verb *gacchāmi* ("I go") is used for the three formulas taken by the person who thus becomes a lay Buddhist. This person says, (in our translation) "I go to the Buddha for refuge. I go to the Dharma for refuge. I go to the Saṅgha for refuge." He repeat these formulas three times.

Later in Tantric Buddhism, the egoistic *aham* can appear in mantras. Thus, *Om svabhāvaśuddhāḥ sarvadharmāḥ svabhāva-śuddho 'ham,* which can be rendered, "Om. All dharmas are intrinsically pure. I am intrinsically pure."[32]

The 'I' consciousness regularly arrogates to itself such attainments of which it is incapable. It claims "I was there." Nāgārjuna, (in a verse cited below), denies this. Granted that there is a kind of continuity in being there and later here, but the 'I' consciousness which claims this attainment is simply the beneficiary of the process and really had nothing to do with it. And most of us, probably have noticed that someone can work on a problem for months, even years; and then upon waking up in the morning one day the answer is there; and the person declares, "I solved it." But, to follow Nāgārjuna's suggestion, the one who says so did not solve it. Some power was working on it while the person slept and did the solving. Buddhist texts have alluded to this power. Thus, Śāntideva, *Bodhicaryāvatāra,* I, 36ab: "I bow to their bodies wherein arises that best jewel of mind." And Tsong-kha-pa in Tibet, in his autobiographical sketch: "Thank you very much, O Venerable Treasure of Wisdom."[33] This power seems to have been referred to in general Indian literature as the *cintāmaṇi* (wish-granting jewel), perhaps also the *kalpavṛkṣa* (wish-granting tree) or the *kāmadhenu* (wish-granting cow).

II. 'NO-SELF' AND TRANSMIGRATION

Both Hindus and the Buddhists had experienced much difficulty in explaining how a transmigrating being manages to arrive at a new birthplace, and making those explanations consistent with their respective authoritative sources. Indeed, the theory of transmigration or reincarnation has been a deeply held belief in India. The medieval commentators had to deal with the issue, and manage to deal with it with sufficient brevity as to avoid having to make decisions on points for which we would want answers. In the case of the Hindus, there are various explanations in commentaries on the *Brahma-sūtras* (also called the *Vedānta-sūtras*). The Buddhist get explanations in the Abhidharma literature. Other Buddhist sources provide further explanations.

Buddhaghosa's *Visuddhimagga* cites this verse:[34]

> The results ('maturations') proceed from *kamma* (Skt. *karma*). Result has *kamma* as source. Regestation occurs from *kamma*. This is how the world goes round.

But *karma*, which is credited with the power to get the transmigrating entity to various destinies in hells or heavens, rebirth in the human kingdom, etc., is not an experiencer. It does not experience itself. A Mahāyāna scripture, the *Pitāputrasamāgama-sūtra* explains: "So, great king, a 'first *vijñāna*' arises having two conditions pertaining to birth—by reason of the 'last *vijñāna*' as predominant condition (*adhipati-pratyaya*) and, by reason of *karma* as support condition (*ārambana-pratyaya*)."[35] Hence, death has a 'death consciousness'—a kind of *vijñāna*; and also a 'death vision'—a kind of *karma* dramatization.

Then we may consult Vasubandhu's *Abhidharmakośa*, Chap. III, k. 18a and read that the *ātman* does not exist. But reading more, we find out that this 'self' is the synthetic one going with the five *skandhas*, which being momentary do not transmigrate to the other world. Thus the *ātman* denial is of a permanent self that would leave behind one set of personal aggregates (*skandha*) and adopt another set later on. But this text does admit that the five aggregates are succeeded by another set that exists during the intermediate state even in the absence of this synthetic 'self'.[36] Of these five, one is called *vijñāna*; and we have noticed that there is the terminology of a 'last one' which is a cause of the 'first one' at the moment of rebirth. The *vijñāna* at least for those believing in an 'intermediate-state' (*antarābhava*) has to all intents and purposes, fallen asleep or has fainted for the interval. One faculty that still seems to be active after death was mentioned in Ratnākaraśānti's commentary on a *Kṛṣṇayamāri-tantra* for the deceased's imagination of Yama (Lord of the Dead): "Thus, the person's volitional thinking (*cetanā*) imagines the Yama holding a club, his eye looking askew and with inflamed membrane, his face with furious laughter."[37]

Granted though, the Buddhists had their problems in justifying the memory of past lives which was credited to the Buddha. We read in the Jākata literature of Buddhism at the ends of these tales, where the Buddha says to his disciples that he was the so-and-so of the story, his present wife (of his early years) Yaśodharā was so-and-so. This topic is treated in detail in Candrakīrti's *Madhyamakāvatāra*, the part as was translated within the book *Calming the Mind and Discerning the Real.* Here, the example stems from a Buddhist account found in the Mūla-Sarvāstivāda Vinaya. In this story the Teacher, the Buddha was reported to say, "In that life, at that time I was the King Māndhātṛ."[38] In this case, there is no way to prove a non-memory or wrong memory, because while we all know of cases where someone remembers wrongly, it must be acknowledged that some persons have astonishingly good memories. Some persons wondered if the scriptural statement meant an identity of the Teacher and Māndhātṛ. The reply, as I once translated it, goes this way: "This pronouncement denies a difference in their stream of consciousness (*saṃtāna*), but it does not teach a (mere) identity." For this, Nāgārjuna's *Madhyamaka-kārikā,* chap. XXVII, 3, is cited: "The statement, 'I was born in a former time,' is not valid. For whatever (self-person) was in previous lives, precisely that (self-person) is not this (self-person)."[39] It means that the Teacher, Śākyamuni, is not a clone of King Māndhātṛ; and yet this tradition claims a non-difference of their stream of consciousness, or of whatever this term *saṃtāna* (also in the form *saṃtati*) means. The identity could not be of the five personal aggregates, because these are declared to be impermanent, changing constantly. While those words (*saṃtāna, saṃtati*) can mean lineal descent with the Sanskrit words *gotra,* etc., the *gotra-saṃtati* is apparently denied by the story of when Śākyamuni first returned to his native place; because when told that his lineage was the kṣatriya one which never practiced begging, he replied that his own lineage was the Buddha lineage of Dīpaṅkara and others, "who gained their livelihood by begging."[40] The *nānārtha* lexicon definitions for *saṃtati* and *saṃtāna* need not be cited, since their information is precisely what is available under those words in such a dictionary as the Monier-Williams Sanskrit-English dictionary. But worth mentioning is that the term *saṃtati* is used to define *syūti,* a form of words meaning 'sewing' and which the Monier-Williams dictionary states is only lexical. The lexicons *Medinīkośa, Viśvaprakāśa,* and *Viśvalocana* agree in defining *syūti* as *sīvana* (sewing) and *saṃtati.*[41] The *saṃtati* entry is surely why the Monier-Williams dictionary (p. 1273c) puts 'lineage, offspring' under *syūti:* but I would explain it differently. The term *saṃtati* seems to mean a 'stitched continuity' for the Buddhist usage, thus not an unchanging continuity. Besides, according to Surya Kanta, the term *sūtra* as a 'thread' has the same verb root *syū-, 'to sew'.*[42] There is an implication of the 'thread' or 'cord' sense for the Buddhist discussions.

Maryla Falk wrote a long article "Nairātmya and Karman" discussing this life-long problem of Louis de La Vallée Poussin's thought. The French scholar is well-known for his remarkable scholarship in Buddhism and he loved Buddhism while he was as well a fervent Christian. For years, he thought the resolution of the problem lay in the usage of this word *saṃtāna,* and that this term in the Buddhist Abhidharma is a perfect equivalent to the *puruṣa* of the Sāṃkhya. He also believed that Buddhism had the term *vijñāna* in an older meaning and in a later meaning, but that modern students of these topics usually take the term in the later meaning.[43] Of course, the present essay can do little more about these views than to mention them. But I would certainly agree about the term *vijñāna* (or its Pāli form).

Buddhism is not alone in setting forth apparently incompatible positions. Let us see what the Śaṅkara commentary on the *Brahma- sūtras* tells us of the Higher Self and the Lower Self.[44] Thus, the Thibaut translation, Part I, p. 116 (I, 2, 9): "The eater (is the highest Self) since what is movable and what is immovable is mentioned (as his food)." Then go to p. 159-60 (I, 3, 7): And on account of the two conditions of standing and eating (of which the former is characteristic of the highest Lord, the latter of the individual soul). The reference is to the *Muṇḍaka Upaniṣad* (III, 1, 1) about the two selves called birds that are on the same tree, one "that eats the sweet fruit"—the lower self, and the other which 'looks on without eating"—the higher self. Śaṅkara goes to the *Muṇḍaka* text, 'Two birds, inseparable friends,' etc., and explains: "This passage describes the two states of mere standing, i.e., mere presence and of eating, the clause, 'One of them eats the sweet fruit,' referring to the eating, i.e., the fruition of the results of works, and the clause, 'The other one looks on without eating,' describing the condition of mere inactive presence." Returning to the first place, starting p. 116, we wish to learn how the lower self there is referred to. After ploughing through much verbiage, we learn (on I, 2, 11), p. 120, that the individual soul is the *vijñānātman*. The higher self is also intelligent, because it is of the same nature (as the lower self). Checking with the Sanskrit text,[45] I find that *cetana*, the masculine gender is the word translated 'intelligent'; while the Buddhists use the feminine *cetanā*, mental *karma*. So now it is clear that the Buddhist *vijñāna* (the last one, at the time of death, which could be said to 'eat' the *karma*) is what Śaṅkara refers to as the *vijñānātman*. There seems to be no Buddhist equivalent to Śaṅkara's highest self, the eater, but which also looks on without eating, i.e., the non-dual lord.

Anyway, Buddhism in its early Mahāyāna form spoke of two kinds of passing away in a way that appears to go back to the genesis myth. The earliest form of this myth is in the Dīgha-nikāya, the scripture called *Aggañña Sutta*. In the first eon, these beings were in a body made of mind (*manomaya-kāya*) and fed on joy. Their kind of birth was by transformation (*upapāduka*). Vasubandhu's *Abhidharmakośa* (II, 9bc) says that the beings with this type of birth are the hell-beings, the beings in the intermediate state, and the gods. Then the beings began to subsist on a subtle kind of food. As their food became progressively coarse, their exterior body also became more and more substantial and coarse. Then the distinguishing characteristics of male and female appeared.[46] The two kinds of passing away are set forth in the scripture *The Lion's Roar of Queen Śrīmālā*:[47]

> Because, there are two kinds of passing away—[the ordinary] discontinuous passing away and the passing away which is the inconceivable transference. The discontinuous passing

away belongs to the sentient beings, who have reconnection (*pratisaṃdhi*) [with sense organs]. The passing away which is the inconceivable transference belongs to the bodies made of mind (*manomaya-kāya*) of Arhats, Pratyekabuddhas, and of Bodhisattva great beings, who have attained power, up to their reaching the terrace of enlightenment.

It is a significant feature of this scripture that it does not mention this 'body made of mind' for ordinary persons, who have the 'discontinuous passing away, and then goes on to mention this kind of body in the case of these advanced beings called Arhats, etc. The scripture thereby suggests that in the usual cases, the original 'body made of mind' which these beings had in the first eon had become so mixed up with coarser matter, including the male and female organs with all the differences brought in, that these beings cannot live in a separate 'body made of mind'. And it also suggests that those advanced beings called Arhats, etc. had so managed to separate this 'body made of mind' from the coarser matter that those beings could indeed live in their 'body made of mind'. In this sense, these advanced beings, Arhats, etc. are of course not like the beings of the first eon, but perhaps have something in common with those beings when they subsisted on subtle food.

For the purpose of this essay I read—in fact, re-read the chapter "The Doctrine of No-soul: *anatta*" in Walpola Rahula's book *What the Buddha taught*. He quoted H. von Glasenapp, "The negation of an imperishable *Ātman* is the common characteristic of all dogmatic systems of the Lesser as well as the Great Vehicle, and, there is, therefore, no reason to assume that Buddhist tradition which is in complete agreement on this point has deviated from the Buddha's Original teaching."[48] I must agree wholeheartedly with this statement. But those who talk this way seems to think it is the most important thing to say to characterize Buddhism.

If this—which they call the 'doctrine of no-soul'—is so important and so consistent with the Buddha's teaching, then why is it that we do not find among the passages cited by Rahula, or among the ones I have so far cited from the Pāli canon in this essay, or among any other sūtras which one might read, any dialogue of the following theoretical kind: A disciple asks the Buddha, "O Bhagavat, could you please tell me what I should *believe* about the five personal aggregates of man?" And the Buddha responds: "That is indeed a good question. You should *believe* that there is no more to man than the five aggregates; take those five away and there is nothing left; and you should *believe* that each one of those five is a non-self (or non-soul) (*anatta*; or in Sanskrit, *anātman*)." Until someone can point to such a passage in the canon, I must declare: They are promulgators of misinformation on Buddhism, who represent these *anātman* statements as matters to be believed in by the Buddhists; and that having believed them, they do indeed have an insight into Buddhism. Rather, what was set forth in the passage I cited, also in those which Rahula cites; and in the numerous other passages on such topics in the Pāli canon is that the Buddha was telling his disciples how they should contemplate the personal aggregates; so with right insight, 'this is not mine', 'I am not this', 'this is not my self'. In the light of the other information I have provided above, it is a reasonable conclusion that the Buddha insisted on such *anātman* contemplations, because it is a way of disengaging coarser matter from the 'body made of mind'. Thus, by such contemplations, one may eventually be an Arhat, etc. Whereas by simply believing that Buddhism has the doctrine of no-soul, one may have the pride of thinking one understands; but this gets one nowhere.

We should now, if only briefly speak of how Buddhism would explain the part of transmigration consisting in birth, or rebirth in the human kingdom. That same scripture, *The Lion's Roar of Queen Śrīmālā* states: "Lord, 'perished' and 'born' are conventional terminology for the world (*loka*). 'Perished' is the loss of the senses. 'Born' is the renewal of the senses."[49] Thus, rebirth is shown by the first seven members of dependent origination, in translation, (1) nescience; (2) motivations; (3) perception; (4) name-and-form; (5) six sense bases; (6) sense contact; and (7) feelings. In Asaṅga's school, the first three are the cause of dharmas; the next four, dharmas.[50] Asaṅga said that there are two kinds of nescience (*avidyā*), defiled and undefiled.[51] And Vasubandhu in his commentary on the *Mahāyānasaṃgraha,* explained no. 3 perception (*vijñāna*) as the 'defiled mind' (*kliṣṭamanas*).[52] Thus, Vasubandhu's explanation depends on *avidyā* being the defiled kind. It is no. 3, (*vijñāna*) which is said to fall into the womb. It is by being ruled by defilement that the usual birth takes place that way, for which the scripture previously cited explained their perishing as the discontinuous passing away. But when *avidyā* is undefiled, it has a special power and is called in Sanskrit *avidyā-vāsa-bhūmi*, rendered 'nescience entrenchment'.[53] That scripture (*The Lion's Roar*) announces the mysterious theory of rebirth of those mentioned three bodies made of mind with that kind of *avidyā* as a condition and nonfluxional action (*karma*) (i.e., a special kind of no. 2, motivations) (*saṃskara*), as the basic cause[54] hence making this 'body made of mind' virtually a substitute for no. 3, *vijñāna*, going with the 'inconceivable transference'.

Concluding Considerations

Recently, I was reading Paṇḍita Sukhalalji's *Essence of Jainism*, the chapter on the Nirgrantha cult; and the Paṇḍita's conclusion is well worth citing: "The real and authentic form of the beliefs of any cult can possibly be known only from its own works and tradition."[55] That is why one cannot find out what Śaṅkara is talking about from his rival Vedāntins Rāmānuja and Madhva; or learn about these other Vedāntins in truth from the followers of Śaṅkara. And it is no use in trying to find out the real attitudes of Buddhism from the opponents like Kumārila. Otherwise, it is seemingly an endless classroom with the student in row 2 during the test peeking over the shoulder of the student in front and copying that persons's wrong answer; the student in row 3 doing the same over the shoulder of the one in row 2, and so on and on. Until someone adds up all the answers, and finds that incorrect answer so numerous as to deserve a conclusion that it must be the correct answer because so many persons say that.

Then if we look at the Buddhist scriptures and what its Buddhist followers say about it, we also find a certain amount of disparity. Thus, while the 'non-self' expressions of Buddhist scriptures were expressed by the Buddha as a guru telling how the disciple is to do it, various of those followers converted this into a doctrine—something that one learns and repeats, but does not do.

A brilliant Sanskritist, who frequently compared Indian and Western Philosophy, and who was recently cruelly snatched by death, believed that he could understand these Buddhist topics through the works of opponents of Buddhism such as Śālikanātha and Jayanta. This modern author appealing to such Hindu writers said: "Dignāga's theory of perception and language stands and falls along with the Buddhist theory of non-soul and the doctrine of momentariness." He also correctly pointed out that what he refers to as the "momentariness doctrine" is a logical development of the old Buddhist 'impermanence' which he also refers to as a 'doctrine'.[56] I would not fault him for the evaluation, even though the premises are suspect. The reason is that the modern followers of Buddhism themselves refer to such features of Buddhism as 'doctrines'. But when we revert to what the Buddha taught, in contrast to what the modern exponents assert, we find that the Buddha put the *anātman* in a set with 'suffering' and 'impermanence'. For the Buddha, suffering is not a doctrine: it is a *satya.* H.D. Velankar, explaining the word *satya* as used in the Veda informs us that the term means that which when uttered cannot be undone or falsified by anyone.[57] In short, the Buddha never announced suffering as a doctrine to be believed in, but as an undeniable fact. Therefore when he announced 'impermanence' and *anātman* in the same set, these also could not be doctrines. When modern defenders of Buddhism call these 'doctrines', such persons bring on the doctrinal refutations which indeed happened.

Some scholars have wondered what is the meaning of *ātman* in the negative compound *anātman.* It was already mentioned that Asaṅga took the negative term to mean 'non-independence'. Vasubandhu's explanation 'unable to do as wished' suggests a positive meaning 'able to do as wished'. The second explanation is probably the more important of the two. It agrees with a description of the 'body made of mind' (*manomaya-kāya*) in the Buddhist *Mahāvastu,* describing the beings of the 'first eon'.[58] Among the attributes there given is that they go where they wish (*yenakāmamṃgatāḥ*). We may therefore conclude that the positive term *ātman* for Vasubandhu's *anātman* explanation is the 'body made of mind' that was previously referred to.

This 'body made of mind' may well be the *ātman* meant by Śaṅkara's verse of the *Viveka-Cūḍāmaṇi* cited above, wherein it is mentioned that this existing body follows as a shadow. The following explanation is my own and differing from others I have noticed. This 'shadow' is not said in deprecation; since persons may wait for hours to get a glimpse (*darśana*) of a saint emerging from his hut, a glimpse namely of his 'shadow body' as Śaṅkara would call it. The description of the 'body made of mind' in Pāli (*Aggañña-sutta, Dīgha-nikāya* III) has the term *sayaṃpabhā;* the

Mahāvastu (Vol. I) Sanskrit version, has *svayaṃprabhā,* 'self-luminous'[59]—thus like the sun with its own light. Śaṅkara may well have implied this luminous quality of the *ātman*;[60] and so would refer to the physical body that lacks this luminous quality in a metaphorical sense as a 'shadow'. In this sense, the Buddhist account appears compatible with the Śaṅkara one.

On the other hand, the Buddhist vows, such as the legendary one of the Buddha long ago to become a Buddha-named Śākyamuni, thus sticking to the vow through many lives, is the continuity of the heroic 'I', agreeing with the Rāmānuja approach to the Vedānta. My investigations has shown the superiority of the *anātman* insistence by the Buddha. This is because the negation in Sanskrit cuts down the possible interpretations of the positive term.[61] Therefore, it was easy for me to relate the positive term *ātman* (i.e., the positive for the negation) to the 'body made of mind'. In contrast, the Hindu positive term *ātman* has a remarkable range of meanings, starting with its usage in the Veda. One may refer to the comprehensive book *The Concept of Ātman* to see the range of meanings of *ātman* when uncontrolled by the negation.[62]

Certainly among the Upaniṣadic meanings and those given in the lexicons for *ātman*[63] a very important one for the Śaṅkara *Vedānta* is *paravyāvartanam* (exclusion of the others) accounting for the emphasis on what *ātman* is not. The Rāmānuja approach probably goes well with the definition *brahman* (ulitmate reality), and in this approach it is not necessary to stress what *ātman* is not.

Finally, none of the foregoing passages from Buddhist sources seems inconsistent with the important passage of the *Cūḷa-suññatā-sutta* in the Pāli canon: "When there is liberation, there is the knowledge, [I] am liberated."[64] This is the 'I' of certainty.

REFERENCES

1. R.V. Joshi, "The Doctrine of 'Aham-Artha'" (*Researches in Indian and Buddhist Philosophy*; Volume in honor of Professor Alex Wayman, Ed. Ram Karan Sharma; Motilal Banarsidass, Delhi, 1993). This is a continuation of R.V. Joshi's essay, "Identity of 'I-cognition' and 'Self'" in his *Studies in Indian Logic and Metaphysics* (Bharatiya Vidya Prakashan, Delhi, 1979), 127-64.

2. V. Srivatsankacharya, *Avyaya Koša; a Dictionary of Indeclinables* (Mylapore, Madras, 1971).
3. Krishnachandra Bhattacharyya, *Studies in Philosophy,* Vol. I, Ed. Gopinath Bhattacharyya (Calcutta, 1956), p. 194.
4. This particular edition and translation is published by Advaita Ashrama, 12th impression, Nov. 1989; k. 431 in its counting:
vartamāne 'pi dehe 'smiñ chāyāvad/anuvartini/
ahantā-mamatā' bhāvo jīvanmuktasya lakṣaṇam//
5. Cyril Veliath, "Rāmānuja's Concept of the Individual Soul and Human Freedom," in *Sambhāṣā* 12 (Dept. of Indian Philosophy, University of Nagoya, 1991), p. 11.
6. I use the account in the *Acchariyabbhutadhammasutta* of the Majjhima-nikāya, Vol. III, in the edition of the Pāli series, Bihar Government, 1958.
7. *The Enlightenment of Vairocana; Book One: Study of the Vairocanābhisambodhitantra,* by Alex Wayman; *Book Two: Study of the Mahāvairocanasūtra,* by R. Tajima (Motilal Banarsidass, Delhi, 1992), p. 2, 143-4 (n. 18).
8. Bihar edn. of *Aṅguttara-nikāya,* Vol. I, p. 124.7-10: "tasmāt iha, sāriputta, evam sikkhatabbaṃ—'imasmiṃ ca saviññānake kāye ahaṅkāramamākāramānānusayā na bhavissanti, bahiddhā ca sabbanimittesu ahaṅkāramamakāramānānusayā na bhavissanti, yaṃ ca cetovimuttiṃ paññāvimuttim upasampajja viharato'."
9. Bihar edn. of *Majjhima-nikāya,* Vol. I, p. 54.10-14: yattha cetā diṭṭhiyo uppajjanti yattha ca anusenti yattha ca samudācaranti taṃ 'netaṃ mama, nesoham asmi, na meso attā' ti—evam etaṃ yathābhūtaṃ sammappaññāya passato evam etāsaṃ diṭṭhīnaṃ pahānaṃ hoti, evam etāsaṃ diṭṭhīnaṃ paṭinissaggo hoti.
10. I.B. Horner, *The Collection of the Middle Length Sayings,* Vol. I (London, 1967), p. 52, notes.
11. Cf. in translation, Mrs. Rhys Davids, *The Book of Kindred Sayings,* Part I (London, 1917), pp. 224-6.
12. Bihar edn. of *Saṃyutta-nikāya,* Vol. I, p. 177.17-18: "na mānaṃ brāhmaṇa sādhu, atthikassīdha brāhmaṇa/yena atthena āgacchi, tam evam anubrūhaye".
13. Genjun H. Sasaki, *Linguistic Approach to Buddhist Thought* (Motilal Banarsidass, Delhi, 1986), p. 51.
14. Alex Wayman, *Yoga of the Guhyasamājatantra* (Motilal Banarsidass, Delhi, 1977), p. 110.
15. Sasaki, p. 53.
16. Cf. G.P. Malalasekera, *Dictionary of Pāli Proper Names,* Vol. II, p. 809.
17. Cf. Alex Wayman, *Calming the Mind and Discerning the Real* (Columbia University Press, New York, 1978), pp. 336-47.
18. Sasaki, p. 54.
19. S. Radhakrishnan, *The Dhammapada* (Oxford University Press, London, 1950).
20. Alex Wayman, *Analysis of the Śrāvakabhūmi Manuscript* (University of California Press, Berkeley, 1961), pp. 130-1.
21. The term occurs in Vasubandhu's auto-commentary on *Abhidharmakośa* VII, 13a.
22. Adapted from Ananda K. Coomaraswamy and I.B. Horner, *Gotama the Buddha* (Cassell, London, 1948), p. 5.
23. The two above passages from the *dhammapada* and the Pāli Vinaya were also presented in A. Wayman, "The position of women in Buddhism," *Studia Missionalia,* Vol. 40, 1991, but in contexts differing from the present one.
24. Cf. G.P. Malalasekera, *Dictionary of Pāli Proper Names,* Vol. I, pp. 62-3. The scripture is located in the Saṃyutta Nikāya (iii, 66f).

25. This theory is expounded in *The Enlightenment of Vairocana* (n. 7, above), pp. 57-62, where it is shown to be a kind of causation based on 'place', so the symbolism in the *Lankāvatāra-sūtra* where it is referred to as an 'ancient road'. But in fact this theory is all through the Pāli canon, even when not using the word *dhammatā*. For example, see F.L. Woodword, *The Book of Kindred Sayings*, Part V (Mahā-vagga), p. 1 (One need not search for the passages): "The Exalted One said: 'When ignorance leads the way, by the reaching of states unprofitable, shamelessness and recklessness follow in its train.' "
26. Edward Conze, *Buddhist Thought in India* (London, 1962), pp. 34-9.
27. According to Daw Mya Tin, *The Dhammapada; Verses and Stories* (reprint of 1986 Burma Pitaka Association publication by Central Institute of Higher Tibetan Studies, Sarnath, Varanasi, 1990), *Dhammapada* verses 277-9 were separately presented by the Buddha at the Jetavana monastery. In the case of verse 279 on 'non-self', the Buddha is reported to explain that the five personal aggregates "are not subject to one's control" thus accounting for Asaṅga's explanation in the *Śrāvakabhūmi*.
28. Sylvain Levi, *Vijñaptimātratāsiddhi* (Paris, 1925), p. 15.
29. I have discussed this distinction between *ātman* and *dharma* in an essay "Core Teachings" and in the section on Dharma 'Dharma the other one'. See in the present essay collection.
30. Cf. *The Enlightenment of Vairocana* (n. 7, above), pp. 61-2, for a discussion of this passage in the *Vairocanābhisaṃbodhitantra* and in the *Laṅkāvatārasūtra*.
31. For the *mahātman, Mahāyāna-Sūtrālaṃkāra*, IX. 23: "After attaining the path and selflessness in pure voidness, the Buddhas having purified the self are in the *mahātma* state of the self."
32. Cf. Mkhas Grub Rje's *Fundamentals of the Buddhist Tantras*, tr. by Ferdinand D. Lessing and Alex Wayman (The Hague, 1968), p. 160, n. 12.
33. See *Ethics of Tibet; Bodhisattva Section of Tsong-kha-pa's Lam Rim Chen Mo* (State University of New York Press, Albany, 1991), tr. by Alex Wayman, p. 32 for the Śāntideva citation, and p. 17f for the autobiographical sketch of Tsong-kha-pa.
34. *Visuddhimagga of Buddhaghosācariya*, Ed. Henry Clarke Warren, revised by Dharmananda Kosambi (Harvard University Press, Cambridge, 1950), p. 516, para. 18.
35. A. Wayman, "The religious meaning of concrete death in Buddhism," *Studia Missionalia*, Vol. 31, 1982, p. 281.
36. Cf. Louis de La Vallée Poussin, *L'Abhidharmakośa de Vasubandhu*, Troisiéme Chapitre (Paris, 1926), pp. 56-7.
37. A. Wayman, "Eschatology in Buddhism," *Studia Missionalia*, Vol. 32, 1983, p. 80. The Tantric work being commented upon is the *Kṛṣṇayamārimahātantrarāja*.
38. Wayman, tr. *Calming the Mind* (n. 17, above), p. 349. Cf. George N. Roerich, *The Blue Annals*, Part One (Calcutta, 1949), starting with the story extracted from the Tibetan Vinaya on origin of the Śākyas, p. 4, for the mention of Māndhātṛ with the information that during his time men became known as Mānavas ('mind-born'). For the account in Sanskrit about Māndhātṛ, see Raniero Gnoli, *The Gilgit Manuscript of the Saṅghabhedavastu*, Part I (Roma, 1977), p. 16.
39. Wayman, tr. *Calming the Mind*, p. 350.
40. A. Wayman, "Śākyamuni, founder of Buddhism," *Studia Missionalia*, Vol. 33, 1984, p. 89.
41. For the first two mentioned lexicons, cf. Anundoram Borooah, *Nānārtha-saṃgraha* (Guwahati, Assam, 1969), p. 360. The *Viśvalocana* has been edited in Sanskrit and

Tibetan, along with an English translation by Lozang Jamspal and Alex Wayman. (Narita, Japan, 1992, 1994, 1995).

42. Surya Kanta, *A Grammatical Dictionary of Sanskrit (Vedic)*; I-Phonetics (Delhi. 1989), p. 271.
43. See the *Indian Historical Quarterly*, Vol. XVI, 3 (Sept. 1940), pp. 647-82.
44. Cf. George Thibaut, tr., *The Vedānta Sūtras* of Bādarāyana with the commentary by Śaṅkara, in two parts (Dover edition).
45. My text of the Śaṅkara *Bhaṣya* is that of the Nirnaya Sagar Press, Bombay, 1948; and here p. 72.12 for the word *cetana*.
46. The present writer's first dealing with this topic was with an essay "Buddhist Genesis and the Tantric Tradition." *Oriens Extremus*, 9:1, 1962, pp. 127-1 1.
47. Alex Wayman and Hideko Wayman, *The Lion's Roar of Queen Śrīmālā* (New York, 1974; or Delhi, 1990), p. 82.
48. The second and enlarged edition of 1967 in 1972 reprint (Gordon Fraser, Bedford), p. 55.
49. *The Lion's Roar* (n. 47, above), p. 104.
50. Cf. A. Wayman's essay "Dependent Origination—the Indo-Tibetan Tradition," in *Buddhist Insight:* Essay by Alex Wayman, Ed: George R. Elder (Motilal Banarsidass, Delhi, 1984), pp. 171-3.
51. Cf. A. Wayman's essay "Nescience and Insight According to Asaṅga," in *Buddhist Insight*, pp. 198-9.
52. A. Wayman, "Vasubandhu—Teacher Extraordinary," *Studia Missionalia*, Vol. 37. 1988, p. 264 and n. 50. In this essay collection.
53. The expression was used several times in the scripture *The Lion's Roar* (n. 47. above) in important passages; and since one of those passages was cited in the Tathāgatagarbha manual *Ratnagotravibhāga* (called in Tibetan tradition the *Uttaratantra*) and this was edited in Sanskrit (by E.H. Johnston) the original Sanskrit term is certain.
54. *The Lion's Roar*, p. 85.
55. This work published by L.D. Institute of Indology, Ahmedabad, 1988, was rendered from the original Hindi by R.S. Betai; cf. p. 48.
56. Bimal K. Matilal, *Epistemology, Logic and Grammar in Indian Philosophical Analysis* (Mouton, The Hague, 1971), p. 79.
57. H.D. Velankar, *Ṛgveda Maṇḍala VII* (Bharatiya Vidya Bhavan, Bombay, 1963), Introduction, p. vi.
58. Radhagovinda Basak, ed. *Mahāvastu Avadāna*, Vol. I (Sanskrit College, Calcutta, 1963), p. 442.
59. Basak, ed., Vol. I, p. 441.
60. Cf. Velankar, tr. (n. 57, above), hymn to the Vasiṣṭhas, p. 85: "Their (inner) light (of knowledge) is like the rising splendour of the sun."
61. Cf. Alex Wayman, "The Negative A-/An- Prefix in Sanskrit," in *Sanskrit and Related Studies*, eds. Bimal Krishan Matilal and Purushottama Bilimoria (Satguru, Delhi, 1990), pp. 21-2.
62. Baldev Raj Sharma, *The Concept of Ātman in the Principal Upaniṣads* (Dinesh Publications, New Delhi, 1972).
63. Sharma, *The Concept of Ātman*, p. 11.
64. From the *sutta* in the Majjhima-nikāya, Part III (Bihar Govt., 1958), p. 172.13-14: / *vimuttasiṃ vimuttam iti ñāṇaṃ hoti*/.

24

Nescience and Omniscience

A. The Meaning of Nescience (*Avidyā*)

The word *avidyā* is crucial in Indian philosophy. It is usually translated into English as "ignorance". Some might ask concerning my rendition as "nescience"[1]—why is this any better; indeed, what is meant by the word "nescience"? The very question implies the superiority of the latter translation. People think they understand "ignorance". They would not ask, "What is the meaning of the word 'ignorance'?" But the word "*avidyā*" is not understood at the outset. How much better is to translate it by a word that might arouse the question, "What is the meaning of the word "nescience"?

A. Reprinted from *Philosophy East and West*, VII, Nos. 1 and 2, 1957.

I. The First Kind of Nescience

In the *Buddhacarita*, Aśvaghoṣa cast in poetical form the visit of the future Buddha to the sage Arāḍa, who imparts his Sāṃkhya doctrines to the resolute youth who has left home for the ascetic life and is destined to become a religious genius.[2] Presumably Aśvaghoṣa believes these doctrines to ante-date Buddhism. Whether he is correct in this view or not, it is certain that for Aśvaghoṣa, who lived in either the first or second century, A.D., these doctrines were ancient ones. In Canto XII, verses 33-7, the sage describes the five varieties of nescience: darkness, delusion, great delusion, obscuration, and blind obscuration, and these are explained, respectively, as torpor, birth and death, passion, fury, and weariness.

The *Śrīmadbhāgavata* (the *Bhāgavata-purāṇa),* III. vii. 2, calls those five varieties the modes of non-knowledge (*ajñāna-vṛtti*) and represents them as of primordial creation. The *Maitri Upaniṣad* (also called the *Maitrāyaṇi Upaniṣad*) states, "Verily, in the beginning this world was Darkness (*tamas*) alone. That, of course, would be in the Supreme. When impelled by the Supreme, that goes on to differentiation."[3] The *Kālacakra* school[4] sets the zodiac in correspondence with the twelve members of the Buddhist doctrine of Dependent Origination, and labels each with one of the three "virtualities" (*guṇa*)-darkness (*tamas*), excitement (*rajas*), and lucidity (*sattva*); and here nescience, the first member of Dependent Origination corresponds to Makara (Capricornus) and is labelled "darkness". In the language of the *Guhyasamāja* school, nescience is the balanced merger of instrument (*upāya*) and insight (*prajñā*), symbolized by the junction of day and night.[5] According to the *Lalitavistara*, "By the wrong procedure engendered by [former] discursive thought and imagination, nescience arises; and there is no one who is its producer," while this nescience member of Dependent Origination does not constitute a transmigration.[6]

Since the *Bhāgavata-purāṇa*, as cited above, refers to the fivefold nescience as the modes of non-knowledge, this permits an immediate passage to the Vedānta explanations. Dasgupta, in his exposition of the Śaṁkara school of Vedānta, writes, "Ajñāna, the cause of all illusions is defined as that which is beginningless, yet positive and removable by knowledge,"[7] However, "Ajñāna is not a positive entity (*bhāva*) like any other positive entity, but it is called positive simply because it is not a mere negation (*abhāva*)."[8] Again, "Ajñāna defined as the indefinite, which is neither positive nor negative is also directly experienced by us in such perceptions as 'I do not know, or I do not know myself or anybody else,' or 'I do not know what you say,' or more particularly 'I had been sleeping so long happily and did not know anything.' Such perceptions point to an object which has no definite characteristics, and which cannot properly be said to be either positive or negative."[9]

Considering all those accounts, the first kind of nescience is a passive something, the original cause of illusion, darkness to our understanding, and alluded to by the recollection "I was in deep sleep and did not know anything."

II. The Second Kind of Nescience

Dasgupta[10] shows that the *Majjhima Nikāya* of the Pāli Buddhist canon sets forth a fourfold "ignorance" (*avijjā*), "ignorance of the four Noble Truths. As is well-known, these Truths are, Suffering, the Source of Suffering, the Cessation of Suffering, and the Path Leading to that Cessation. He continues, "The avidyā, which is equivalent to the Pāli word avijjā, occurs in the Upaniṣads also, but there it means ignorance about the ātman doctrine, and it is sometimes contrasted with vidyā or true knowledge about the self (*ātman*)."

Nescience (*avidyā*) is defined in Patañjali's *Yoga Sūtra* (II.5) as follows: Nescience is taking impermanence, impurity, suffering, and non-*ātman* to be respectively, permanence, purity, bliss, and *ātman.*" Patañjali's explanation of nescience is precisely the four varieties of "waywardness" (*viparyāsa*), an ancient doctrine of Buddhism, *vipallāsa* in Pāli.[11]

The four varieties are discussed in Āryāsaṅga's *Yogācārabhūmi*. In stages VIII-IX, "With thought and without thought" (*sacittikā bhūmi, acittikā bhūmi*), he has a section entitled "Establishment of Thought Delusion and Non-Delusion" *(cittabhrānti-vyavasthāna)* where he states,[12] "Any thought deluded by one of the four waywardness has Thought Delusion." He had stated earlier[13] the four waywardnessses and exactly the same as the standard list in the order of impermanence, suffering, impurity, and non-*ātman.* In the commentarial portion of the *Yogācārabhūmi*, Āryāsaṅga writes,[14]

"In the *Srāvakabhūmi,* it is expounded that the Four Truths are observed under sixteen aspects. In that case, why is the Truth of Suffering observed under four aspects? It is said: as the adversary for the four forms of waywardness. Among those one aspect is the adversary for one waywardness. One aspect is the adversary for two waywardnesses. The two last aspects are the adversary for the last waywardness. He means that of the four aspects of the Truth of Suffering, "There is impermanence" is the adversary for the waywardness that impermanence is permanence; "There is suffering," for the waywardness that suffering (*duḥkha*) is bliss (*sukha*)[15] and that impurity is purity; "There is voidness" and "There is non-*ātman,*" for the waywardness that non-*ātman* is *ātman.*

It follows that Patañjali's "nescience" is in Buddhist terminology, nescience concerning the truth of suffering in its four aspects. This use of the word nescience is fully consistent with the Upaniṣadic usage of false knowledge, contrasted with true knowledge about the self.

The second kind of nescience is the positive impediment of false knowledge. The individual is deluded, misled, thinks that he knows but does not know.

III. The Buddha and the Complete Buddha

When commenting of the expression *saṅs rgyas* (the Tibetan translation for *Buddha*) as occurring in the *Vajravidāraṇā-dhāraṇī* Jñānavajra writes,[16] "Regarding the terms *saṅs,* having eliminated all the hindrances of defilement and of the knowable, he has awakened (*Buddha*) from the sleep of the nescience, for which reason he is called "awakened" (*saṅs, Buddha*). He is like a person awakened from sleep. Regarding the term *rgyas,* his knowledge (*jñāna*) has been expanded (*vibuddha*) to all the knowable for which reason he is called "expanded" (*rgyas, vibuddha*). He is like the expanded (or, full-blown) Kumuda flower. He has the perfection of elimination and of knowledge."[17]

Now, this question is obvious: "Is the nescience from which he has awakened (*Buddha*) one or both of the two nesciences already expounded?" The key words are "elimination" and "knowledge". Briefly answering the question, only the second kind of nescience affords something to be actively eliminated. Otherwise stated: to whatever extent the first kind of nescience offers anything to be eliminated, this elimination cannot take place through effort. In the case of this first kind, it is simply a matter of knowing everything in the situation where formerly one recognized that he did not know anything.

But the topic warrants more explanation. Early Buddhism, now represented most completely, but not exclusively by the Pāli texts amounts to the four Noble Truths in their extensive exposition. Here, by following the Noble Eightfold Path, one attains the Cessation of the Sources of Suffering. This is the basic path of "elimination", later rewritten with additions, as the *Bodhisattva* path. Recalling that the aspect of the Truth of Suffering "There is Suffering" is the adversary for both the waywardness that suffering is bliss and that impurity is purity, the familiar lotus symbolism becomes relevant. The lotus takes its rise from mud, and, becoming cleansed in the intermediate space of water, presents the sun with a pure flower, which the sun opens. In terms of some Chinese Buddhist schools—although they might not look at the matter in this light—the path of purification of the lotus is the "gradual path"; the full expansion of the flower is "the sudden enlightenment". To speak of "sudden enlightenment" without the "gradual path" amounts to teaching that a flower can open without support of a stem that takes its rise from roots in soil. Thus, those Buddhists who rejected the "gradual path" had rejected the bulk of the Buddha's teachings as well.

In terms of the Indian situation, one might explain the Buddhist reform by the example of baking a cake. Instead of the way of exposition that dwells on the loveliness and tastiness of the cake, the Buddha wrote a cook-book prosaically stating how to bake the cake. Or, rather than spend time expanding the topic of heaven's glories, he showed the ladder that enables the candidate to transcend earth. In short, the Buddha showed the way of becoming a Buddha by the method now called "elimination". This method is sometimes called "works" (*karma*) as contrasted with "knowledge" (*jñāna*), and it is frequently set forth in terms of "merit" (*puṇya*). Because Buddhism has fully treated this phase, one may understand that Patañjali's *Yoga Sūtra* has borrowed from Buddhism in the matter of a certain "nescience"—the second kind.

On the other hand, the borrowing goes the other way in the matter of the opening of the flower, or complete Buddhahood. The broad treatment of this topic in the Mahāyāna Buddhist texts cannot be traced to the Pāli scriptures, except perhaps in stray and rare passages that were not stressed in Pāli Buddhism. The Upaniṣads provide abundant information about this; and one may tentatively state that these and the Purāṇic literature, added to early Buddhism and recast in language have resulted in Mahāyāna Buddhism.

Apparently with good reason Aśvaghoṣa expressed the "fivefold nescience" the first kind of nescience in the words of the sage Arāḍa. In my view, Buddhism has not contributed, although it contains and has elaborated the instruction of the particular knowledge or the knowledge that replaces the fivefold nescience.

B. The Meaning of Omniscience

There is a considerable source of information on the topic of omniscience in the traditions of India. A rather brief exposition, but good in its way is that of Jadunath Sinha, a chapter on "supernormal perceptions" and another on "divine perception".[18] A whole book, and useful is the effort of Ramjee Singh: *The Concept of Omniscience in Ancient Hindu Thought.*[19] In Buddhist literature, there is the *Tattvasaṃgraha*, by Śāntarakṣita with commentary by Kamalaśīla, the Chap. XXVI, examination of the 'person of supernormal vision'.[20] Of course, there are other works, but those are a good start on the topic.

Sinha gives a good summary: "Almost all schools of Indian philosophers believe in supernormal perceptions. Only the materialist Cārvāka cannot believe in any other source of knowledge than sense perception. And the Mīmāṃsaka also denies the possibility of supernormal perceptions, because according to him—the past, the future, the distant, and the subtle can be known only through the injunctions of the Vedas. But the Nyāyā Vaiśeṣika, the Sāṁkhya-Pātañjala, the Vedāntist, the Buddhist, and the Jaina believe in supernormal perception, though they give different accounts of them."[21]

Singh puts it iṇ terms of belief in a supreme deity like the Īśvara: "all the theistic systems believe in the existence of omniscience of some form or the other, e.g. the Nyāya, Vaiśeṣika, and the Yoga. Put negatively, all the non-believers in omniscience like the Lokāyats, the Indian sceptics, the Agnostics, and the Mīmāṃsakas, are also non-believers in God. But the converse of this rule is, however, not true because all *sarvajñavādins* (believers in omniscience) are not Īśvaravādins (theists), like the Buddhists, the Jainas, the Sāṃkhyas, and the Advaitins. Negatively, all atheists are not necessarily *asarvajñavādins*. This shows that the category of omniscience is wider than that of belief in god".[22]

Singh starts out by mentioning the words used for this 'omniscience'. After referring to a variety of lexicons, he gives the expression *sarvajña* (omniscient) defined as *sarvavid*. For the noun form he gives *sarvajñatā*. He apparently did not come across the form found in the tradition of the *Vairocanābhisaṃbodhī-tantra*, a scripture of esoteric Buddhism, namely *sarvajña-jñāna* (omniscient knowledge)[23]—thus contrasting with mundane knowledge (*laukika-jñāna*) and perhaps also with supramundane knowledge (*lokottara-jñāna*) [cf. below, on *sarvajñā* and *sarvajñajñā*]. Besides, the Buddhists use an expression *prajñāpāramitā* (perfection of insight), which represents the feminine side of omniscience. The Jainas have the expression *kevala-jñāna*, which also means 'omniscient knowledge'[24]

Now 'omniscience' can be discussed either positively or negatively. When positively, it is omniscience about this or that or about everything. When negatively, what must be rid of in order that there be omniscience; otherwise stated, the states or entities that are avoided, or as in a list to be presented below, the 'non-companions'.

The omniscience or perfect knowledge about particular things was a feature of Vedic deities. For example, Agni (the fire god) is frequently called *jātavedas*, which can be interpreted as 'knowing all the created beings.[25] Varuṇa, with the sun as his eye was said to observe all the doings of mankind, and to be 'thousand-eyed'. Mitra's and Varuṇa's spies are said to be undeceived and wise.[26] Pūṣan knows the far paths, and so can conduct the dead to the Fathers.[27] Indra is the eye of all that moves and sees.[28] Prajāpati knows all places and beings, and alone gives the names to the gods (so must know all the names).[29] The Gandharvas know the plants.[30] According to the author Airi, the goddess Sarasvatī went through an evolution, and in the *Yajurveda* came to comprise in her person the Vedic lore; it was about the time she became identified with Vāk (speech goddess).[31]

The Veda also had a legend of beings, who were not originally gods, namely, the Ṛbhus, who had such extraordinary ability to fashion things, even Indra's steeds, that they became "Indra-like", like a "new Indra".[32] Thus, they are in a sense the prototype of the ascetic who threatens to become the new Indra, leader of the gods.

The arguments in the *Tattvasaṃgraha* show that the term 'omniscient' (*sarvajña*) has its difficulties, especially when applied to humans who started schools of Indian philosophy and religion. This is because, "knowing all" could be applied to a part of the whole, as for example, when a brahmin learns all of the *Ṛg-Veda*, thus knowing it all, yet does not know the other Vedas. The text (k. 3148), as Jha translates it, should make the point clear: "When there are many omniscient persons, preaching mutually contradictory doctrines,—the grounds of reliability being the same in all,—which one of these should be accepted as reliable?" Kamalaśīla comments that there are many teachers, to wit, Buddha, Kapila, Kaṇada, Gautama and so on, whose respective devotees wish to prove as being 'omniscient'; and yet which one of them is truly reliable?[33]

Such arguments clarify the problem of attributing 'omniscience' to a human, while there seemed no problem in such attribution to a deity. Eventually, such challenges prompted the Buddhists to attribute several bodies to the Buddha—a Dharmakāya that is omniscient, but does not speak; and one or more bodies that can appear to sentient beings and teach them. Yet even that 'omniscience' is not intended to cover all the mundane dates of historical events, names of medical products, and the like. It is rather an 'omniscience' about the truth of the world and of man; which can realize all the 'paths' in an instant.[34]

Now, an attentiveness to the statements made above for Vedic deities, and to other statements about them that could be made, should show that sometimes the 'omniscience' was expressed in knowing everything about a topic, or of an area of the world, and sometimes, it is expressed in seeing everything in some scope—as when Pūṣan knows the far paths, and as when Varuṇa uses the sun to see all of mankind's doings. Both the Jainas and the Buddhists continued this contrast by the words *jñāna* and *darśana*.

Jñāna and Darśana

The *Lalitavistara* Buddha's biography when setting forth the first sermon reports that the Buddha told his disciples of what arose in him as he sat under the Bodhi-tree and thought of each of the four Noble Truths. "There is suffering," and so on. The sequence of terms is headed by *jñānaṃ utpannaṃ cakṣur utpannaṃ* ("knowledge arose: vision arose"). The set of five supernormal faculties (*abhijñā*) are classified under those two in Vasubandhu's commentary on the *Daśabhūmika-sūtra*, namely, one is vision (*darśana*)—the divine eye (*divyacakṣus*), which sees the passing away of beings to various destinies; and the other four are knowledge—remembering past lives (*pūrvanivāsānusmṛti*), magical power (*ṛddhi-vidhi*), divine hearing (*divyaśrotram*), and knowing others' minds (*paracittajñāna*).[35]

As to the Jaina account, Tatia mentions that *jñāna* is *sākāra,* which I render 'with image', while *darśana* is *anākāra,* which I render 'without image'.[36] Furthermore, the Jaina Āgamas insist that even the Kevalins (the omniscient ones) cannot have these two activities simultaneously. This would follow from the fact that one is *sākāra,* the other *anākāra*. However, there were some differences of opinion about this matter among the later Jaina authorities, and some of the most eminent among these claimed that an omniscient one could have these activities simultaneously.[37]

Asaṅga, in his *Yogācārabhūmi*, presents nine cases of 'knowledge' (*Jñana*) and vision (*darśana*), generally in contrast, and clarifies that each are aspects of 'insight' (*prajñā*), the one being its cognitive side, the other being its visionary side.[38] In the latter case, there is the terminology 'eye of prajñā'.

Knowledge	*Vision*
1. Any insight (*prajñā*) that has as object one that is past or future or remote	1. Any (insight) that has a present-time object
2. Any with consciousness-support (*ālambana*) in the apprehensible (i.e. future)	2. Any with consciousness-support in the (on-going) apprehending
3. Any (insight) consisting of hearing (*śruta*) or of pondering (*cintā*)	3. Any one consisting of contemplation-cultivation (*bhāvanā*)
4. One which eliminates defilement (*kleśa*)	4. Any insight that directly realizes liberation after ending defilement.
5. Any with consciousness-support in an individual character (*svalakṣaṇa*) e.g. earth's hardness	5. Any consciousness-support in a generalizing character (*sāmānya-lakṣaṇa*) e.g. impermanence
6. With recourse to name-conferral, any insight with consciousness-support in these and those knowable inner and outer motivations (*saṃskāra*), namely, 'I', 'being' (*sattva*), 'god' (*deva*), 'serpent' (*nāga*) . . . 'forest', 'mountain', etc.	6. Any with apprehending of individual and generalizing characters of the knowable inner and outer *saṃskāra*, but without name-conferral

Knowledge	*Vision*
7. Any with search of *dharmas*	7. Any discriminating (insight) of any that have been searched out
8. One with consciousness-support in reflected image without constructive thought	8. One with consciousness-support in reflected image with constructive thought
9. One with consciousness-support in reflected image of knowable that is formless	9. One with consciousness-support in reflected image of knowable that has form

The Jaina view seems to accord with no. 5 of the list, by taking *darśana* with the *sāmānya-lakṣaṇa* (my 'generalizing character'; Tatia's 'universal characteristic'), and taking *jñāna* with the *svalakṣaṇa* (Buddhist accepted term) or with the *viśeṣa* (the Jaina term).[39] And there is also an accord by Asaṅga's no. 6 under 'vision' that allows both characters to the scope of 'vision' in a transcendental situation.

Yüan-t'se's great commentary on the *Saṃdhinirmocana-sūtra*, which I utilize in its Tibetan version, Peking Tanjur, has a long treatment of *jñāna-darśana* there.[40] The expression is explained pursuant to the third of the three degrees of *prajñā*, the one 'consisting of contemplation-cultivation' (*bhāvanāmayī*). At p. 219-4, the author gives from a Prajñāpāramitā commentary, four cases of 'knowledge and vision': (1) When there is knowledge, but no vision; and this is any knowledge of a phenomenon (Tib. *ji snyed*),[41] as well as any *dharmas* of insight outside of (or, excluding) right mundane view and the five views.[42] (2) When there is vision, but no knowledge; and this is the five views and right mundane view,[43] as well as the 'eight forbearances' (*kṣānti*).[44] (3) When there is both; and this is the non-fluxional *prajñā* which can be called both 'knowledge' and 'vision'. (4) When there is neither; and this is any *dharmas* other than (in the explanations of) 'knowledge' and 'vision'. Yüan-t'se cites an important difference between 'knowledge' and 'vision': "Any seeing and imagining of a formation (*rūpa*) without (its) name (*nāma*)—that is vision (*darśana*). Any knowing, "The names of the gods are such-and-such"; "their lineages are such-and-such"—that is knowledge.[45] This goes with Asaṅga's no. 6.

As to which of the two precedes, it is clear from Asaṅga's list that sometimes it is the one and sometimes the other. For example, the insight with present-time object probably precedes the one with past or future object, so 'vision' precedes 'knowledge'. On the other hand, any insight with search of *dharmas* would precede the one that discriminates the *dharmas* that have been searched out; so knowledge' precedes 'vision'. This last mentioned, no. 7 in Asaṅga's list, about search, is the pair I used in explanation of the celebrated Heart Sūtra.[46]

The Non-Companions for Omniscience

The preceding exposition treats the subject of divine knowledge or divine realization in a positive way. The religious systems of India frequently employ negative teachings; for example, when telling the disciple what bad companions to avoid, and what mental natures to drop off. The preceding portion of this essay on "the meaning of nescience" has already set forth five varieties of nescience, and made the distinction of deviant nescience as contrasted with the nescience of simply not knowing something. There are various other ways of referring to the impediment to omniscience. Often the word *āvaraṇa* is employed for the hindrance. In Jainism, this is due to the inrush of material *karmas,* which build up the ordinary self, which should be eliminated. Sometimes the opponent is represented mythologically, e.g. Indra's foe Vṛtra; and the Buddha had Māra and his troops as the enemy of spiritual life. The Yoga systems have purifying practices called *yama,* especially non-injury to any living being, not lying, not stealing, sexual restraint, and not collecting inessentials.[47] In the Śaṅkara school of Vedānta, salvation (*mukti*) meant a dissociation of the self—both from the subjective psychosis and from the objective world of superimpositions.[48] So also, a Mahāyāna Buddhist scripture, the *Akṣayamatinirdeśa* in its large *prajña* section tells the 'sixteen non-companions' of *Prajñāpāramitā* (perfection of Insight). I have studied the entire list in the Peking Kanjur, PTT, Vol. 34, p. 51-4-7, ff.; and the commentary (ascribed to Vasubandhu, but not by him) in PTT, Vol. 104, p. 188-4-5, ff. However, it is not necessary here to give the full list with commentary, so I shall tell the list and in a few cases give more information because of the inherent interest. So the sixteen non-companions: I. The twelve members of Dependent Origination (*pratītyasamutpāda*); II. The twenty reifying views (*satkāyadṛṣṭi*) and the 62 (wrong) views (*dṛṣṭi*); III. The eight worldly natures (*loka-dharma*); IV. The defilement troop (*upakleśa*), totalling 21; V. The defilements (*kleśa*), which are lust (*rāga*), hatred (*dveṣa*), and delusion (*moha*)—that can be subtle, gross; tiny, middling, or great; VI. The caul of nescience, which is the darkness of delusion, the caul of darkness, obscuration, over-covering; VII. The four Māras, and the acts of Māra, which are the distinct powers (*guṇa*) of the five sense objects, and quarrel; VIII. The clinging (*abhiniveśa*) to *pudgala*-notion; IX. The hindrances (*āvaraṇa*) which are interruptions, namely, to recognizing *karma*, to hearing the Dharma, to be prevented by defilement (*kleśa*), to be misled by wrong views (*dṛṣṭi*); to not acknowledge the danger of bad destiny (*gati*), to be misled by good destiny, and to not know rightly, namely, the 'hindrance of the knowable' (*jñeya-āvaraṇa*); X. The knots which are 'construction' (*kalpa*), 'constructive thought' (*vikalpa*), and 'thorough construction' (*parikalpa*), and the superimpositions (*āropa*) by way of sign (*nimiita*), consciousness-support (*ālambana*), seeing and hearing, non-distinction (aviśeṣa*),* and representation (*vijñapti*); XI. The waywardnesses, namely, the four classical *viparyāsa;*[49] XII. The *dharma-skandha* amounting to 24,000 natures (*dharma*); XIII. The detraction to the perfections—greed, spoiling the 'perfection of giving' (*dāna-pāramitā*), an immoral act spoiling the 'perfection of morality' (*śīla-p.*), hostility spoiling the 'perfection of forbearance' (*kṣānti-p.*), laziness detracting from the 'perfection of striving' (*vīrya-p.*), straying of mind detracting from the 'perfection of meditation' (*dhyāna-p.*) and from the 'perfection of insight' (*prajñā-p.*); XIV. Opposing camps of *dharmas,* namely, the usually opposed dharmas, e.g. 'genuine' (*samyak*) and 'wrong' (*mithyā*); XV. Attention to differences (*bheda*), such as different vehicles (*yāna*), different doctrines (*dharma*); XVI. All mental orientation (*manasikāra*) to signs, namely to those of ignorance, knowing, perceiving, convention (*saṃvṛti*), absolute (*paramārtha*). The *Akṣayamatinirdeśa-sūtra* summarizes: "*Prajñā* does not move, is incorporeal (*anaṅga*), without character (*alakṣaṇa*), without mark (*animitta*), unconstructed (*asaṃskṛta*)."[50] Thus divine knowledge must avoid a lot of bad companions.

It follows that omniscience in this sense must avoid even the separate and distinct 'knowledge' and 'vision'. Prominent Jaina authorities say the same thing.[51]

A Note on 'Proof of Omniscience'

There is at hand two brief Buddhist treatises on *sarvajñāsiddhi*—

a separate work by Jñānaśrīmitra;[52] and a chapter in Bhavya's *Madhyamaka-hṛdaya-kārikā*.[53]

Bhavya's 14 verses on the topic—Sanskrit is available only for the last 2—seem to construe 'proof' (*siddhi*) of an 'omniscient person' (*sarvajña*), not by a formal syllogism, but by an appeal to the physical appearance of Gautama Buddha, by his 'acts'—for example, conquering Māra, appearing with subdued senses, training many disciples, displaying 'miracles'. Even the failed attempt of Devadatta to provoke schism is considered part of the 'proof'. Thus the life of Gautama Buddha is the proof.

The Jñānaśrīmitra work purports to refute the Mīmāṃsā rejection of the 'ominiscient person' as well as to establish Gautama Buddha as the 'ominiscient person'. Even so, this 'proof' seems to be along the lines of the Bhavya kind of proof. There is an appeal to the life situations (*daśā*) as in the Sanskrit fragments which Steinkellner has published. This is his fragment 4 with my own translation:

> ityabhyāsabalāt parisphuṭadaśākoṭiḥ sphuratsambhavī
> heyādeyatāṅgalakṣaṇaguṇaḥ sarvajñatā saiva naḥ //
> By dint of repeated contemplation of those (causes of *saṃsāra*), the 'peak' (i.e. foremost) of very clear life situations distinctly coming together; (also) the characteristics and the virtuality of 'taking' and 'rejecting' and their 'limbs'—only this we take to be omniscience.

Apparently such proofs involve pointing to the actual case of the person who pronounced the four Noble Truths; preached what one should accept and what reject in order to proceed on the path—and who in his own life displayed the authority and majesty of a Buddha. Thus, the proof consists in referring to the concrete example. It is a kind of *svabhāvahetu,* as in my re-translation of Dharmakīrti's *Nyāyabindu*:[54]

> Svabhāvaḥ svasattamātrabhāvini sādhyadharme hetuḥ/
> Individual-presence is a reason when the thesis feature has a presence that amounts to the existence of itself.
> yathā vṛkṣo 'yaṃ śiṃśapātvād iti /
> as e.g. "This is a tree, because it is an Aśoka."

So these authors assert the same type of proposition, to wit,

> This is an omniscient person, because he is Buddha.

But such proofs require a community of concord, namely, of followers who are so convinced.

Āryaśūra, *Jātakamālā*, no. XXIX, acknowledges that the concrete appearance of the superior person is not convincing, as I cited in my essay on prophecy,[55] namely, in the case of the disbelieving Videha king Aṅgadinna, whom the Bodhisattva, then dwelling in the Brahmaloka, sought to change in attitude. The Bodhisattva descended in front of the king, displaying a lightning-like brilliance, and introduced himself as having come from a different world. Even his own presence in this remarkable manner did not swerve the king. So the Bodhisattva had to resort to other tactics, independent of his own auspicious presence.

Omniscience (*sarvajñā*) and Ominiscient Knowledge (*sarvajña-jñāna*)

My work on the *Vairocanābhisambodhi-tantra*, from which comes the term *sarvajña-jñāna* (omniscient knowledge) should help explain a rather astonishing statement by Buddhaghosa in his commentary on the Pāli *Aṅguttaranikāya* called *Manorathapūraṇī*, while explaining the scripture's portrayal of the five dreams portending enlightenment. These five dreams are not only in the *Aṅguttaranikāya*, Vol. III, but in the *Mahāvastu*, Vol. II, and in the Buddha's Mahāyāna biography, the *Lalitavistara* (its *svapnaparivarta*). I shall here give just the gist of the five dreams, with comments of my own: Before the Tathāgata had awakened to full enlightenment, among his five dreams the first shows his five limbs upon the entire earth—the first of the non-movings; the second shows the grass *kṣīrikā* planted at his navel and going up to the sky—the vegetable kind of non-moving; the third is the dream that reddish creatures with black heads covered him from the soles of his feet up to his kneecaps—moving life but of the underworld; the fourth is that four vultures of different colors came from the four quarters, kissed the soles of his feet and departed all white—the moving life of the intermediate space, the future defeat of the four Māras, and the healing of all illness by the becoming 'white'; the fifth that he walked all over a mountain of dung without being soiled by it—living among the men of the upon-world without being contaminated. The five dreams show the reaching out to the 'receptacle world' (*bhājana-loka*) and to the sentiency world' (sattva-loka)—hence the overcoming of the 'hindrance of the knowable' (*jñeya-āvaraṇa*). Now for Buddhaghosa's remark:[56]

> Ime pana pañca mahāsupine n' eva lokiyamahājano passati na mahārājāno na cakkavattirājāno na aggasāvakā na paccekabuddha na sammāsambuddha, eko sabbaññu-bodhisatto yeva passati.
>
> Furthermore, neither the world's crowd sees these five great dreams, nor does a great king, nor wheel-turning king, nor the best disciples, nor the Pratyekabuddhas, nor a Right Completed Buddha. Alone an omniscient Bodhisattva is who sees them.

In my work on the *Vairocanābhisambodhi-tantra,* an introductory chapter "Beings and their minds" cites the scripture's definition of Buddha:[57]

> Who having accomplished the Tenth Stage, realizes the ten powers; comprehends the *dharmas* as void and illusory; omniscient in this life, while knowing the mundane rules—he is called 'Buddha'.

Buddhaguhya's commentary points out the Bodhisattvas of the Tenth Stage are called 'Buddhas' (but not Complete Buddhas); and that here 'Buddha' means the Nirmāṇakāya going through the 'Buddha acts', as birth as son of Śuddhodana, etc. This agrees with Buddhaghosa's remark, even though he is not a Mahāyānist. In Mahāyāna terms, the being going through the 'acts of a Buddha' had the five dreams as an omniscient Bodhisattva.

The corollary to the above finding is that a Complete Buddha, or as the scriptures state it, a Right Complete Buddha (*Samyaksambuddha*), does not have these dreams—as Buddhaghosa points out—and also his 'omniscience' must differ. Indeed, in the terminology of the Vairocana scripture, it is to be called 'omniscient knowledge' (*sarvañajñāna*). The term 'knowledge' actually refers to the set of five; and in this case, I generally render the term 'wisdom'. Buddhaguhya's concise commentary on the *Vairocanābhisambodhi-tantra* (Photo ed., p. 88-4-1) states that the Sameness Wisdom (*samatā-jñāna*) is the first instant of complete enlightenment; and p. 88-3-7, that the other three Wisdoms follow as forms of omniscient knowledge. These three are the Mirror-like Wisdom (*ādarśa-j.*), the Discriminative Wisdom (*pratyavekṣaṇā-j.*), and the Procedure-of-Duty Wisdom (*kṛtyānuṣṭhāna-j.*). This account leaves out mention of the Dharmadhātu-j., which commentaries explain to be the basis of the other four.[58]

In the Mādhyamika tradition of the five wisdoms, they are the transformation (*parāvṛtti*) of the five personal aggregates (*skandha*).[59] Citing many tantric authorities, the Tibetan author Tsong-kha-pa, in his commentary *de nyid rab tu gsal ba* on the meaning of initiation (*abhiṣeka*) (in Photo edition of Tibetan canons, extra vol. 160, pp. 110-11), explains the order of the five wisdoms in correlation with the order of the flask initiations of the Anuttarayoga-tantra. At p. 110-3-5, he states by way of the water initiation, there is transformation of aggregate of perceptions (*vijñāna-sk.*), yielding the direct vision of Dharmadhātu Wisdom. Hence, this is the meaning of the 'omniscient Bodhisattva' who has the five prophetic dreams. Continuing, at p. 111-1-1, by transformation of the feelings aggregate (*vedanā-sk.*) there is realization of the Sameness Wisdom. At p. 111-2-2, by transformation of the ideations aggregate (*saṃjñā-sk.*) there is realization of Discriminative Wisdom. At p. 111-3-2, by transformation of the motivations aggregate (*saṃskāra-sk.*) there is Procedure-of-Duty Wisdom. Finally, at p. 111-5-3, by transformation of the formations aggregate (*rūpa-sk.*) one realizes the Mirror-like Wisdom. Hence, these subsequent four Wisdoms amount to the 'omniscient knowledge'. In fact, the foregoing materials come from the section of Tsong-kha-pa's work treating the "Initiation rite of a complete Buddha" (*rdsogs pa'i sangs rgyas kyi dbang bskur ba'i cho ga*), so it is quite proper to interpret these correlations as relevant to the distinction of 'omniscience' and 'omniscient knowledge'.

This theory of the order of Wisdoms seems to stem from the Prajñāpāramitā scripture, esp. the *Saptaśatikā* as interpreted by Vimalamitra's commentary.[60] The scripture, after the introductory paragraph, says: "Then you should know, Mañjuśrī, the youth at the time of the morning twilight, leaving his own dwelling, went where the Tathāgata was dwelling, and approaching the dwelling, stood outside the door so as to behold the Tathāgata, praise him, reverence him. Then the venerable Śāradvatīputra, leaving his own dwelling, went where the Tathāgata was dwelling, so as to behold the Lord, praise him, reverence him. (So also, the other great *Śrāvakas*.) Then, you should know, the Lord, being aware of the coming, converging, and congregating of the great Śrāvakas, left his own abode and seated himself on a seat that was arranged (*prajñapta*) at one side outside the door. And being seated, the Lord, although knowing, addressed the venerable Śāradvatīputra, why coming right at dawn (*kalyam*), are you standing at the door of the Tathāgata's dwelling?" According to Vimalamitra, p. 170-2-2, when the Lord went outside his dwelling, he transcended time and place; thus was inconceivable. According to Vimalamitra, p. 170-1-5, 6, that dawn had four colors, sky-blue (Tib. *mthon ka*), yellow (*ser po*), red (*dmar po*), and the sun's color (=white). The sky-blue is the phase when objects still have the same color, so this is the Sameness Wisdom. Then the colors yellow, red, and white, seem to symbolize the Discriminative Wisdom, the Procedure-of-Duty Wisdom, and the Mirror-like Wisdom. The Tathāgata himself was representing the Dharmadhātu Wisdom, because Vimalamitra says, p. 170-2-7, 8:[61] "The Buddha's body is understood (here) as the Dharmakāya; and his body is 'seen' as included in the Dharmadhātu; while those who 'see' it, (in fact) do not see it."

The poet Aśvaghoṣa, *Buddhacarita*, XII, 117, represents the 'omniscient Bodhisattva' in this manner, as the serpent Kāla declares: "Since, O muni, the earth repeatedly roars, as it were, pressed by thy feet, and since your light shines like the sun, surely today you will experience the desired fruit." The fruit meant is enlightenment, the gaining of the 'omniscient knowledge'. The group of five followers who deserted him just prior to this event thought they saw him, but did not really see him.

The associations of those dawn colors with the respective wisdoms is aided by information given in Vitapāda's *Mukhāgama-vṛtti* (Photo ed., PTT, Vol. 65, p. 54-4-5, 6). Thus, he says that "hair of head loose" is the symbol (*rtags*) for Discriminative Wisdom;[62] and this may implicate the color yellow by the Uṣas (Dawn) Hymn, *Ṛg-Veda*, IV, 52, 7: "Uṣas, you stretch with beams the broad, favorite intermediate space to the sky, along with your bright radiance"—possibly to be construed as the goddess's letting her hair down. Vitapāda explicitly brings in the red color, saying that the red complexion and red eyes symbolize the Procedure-of-Duty Wisdom.[63] He might also help in associating the color white with the Mirror-like Wisdom, when saying, "The expression 'heart trembles, and memory is lost' is a symbol of the Mirror-like

Wisdom."[64] This is because the loss of memory appears to implicate a clean slate without memory tracings, hence the color white is able to represent the Mirror-like Wisdom.

The preceding information concerns the complete Buddha. It may be that the different explanation by the *Yogācāra* school has to do just with the human candidate. This school explains the set of four Wisdoms by transformation of its various vijñānas. Thus, the Mirror-like Wisdom appears as soon as the 'store consciousness' (*ālayavijñāna*) ceases by the 'diamond-like *samādhi*' (*vajropamas*), yielding the 'immediate path' (*ānantarya-mārga*), meaning that the Bodhisattva is ushered into the first Bodhisattva stage. Then, with the 'path of vision' (*darśana-mārga*), he has the second wisdom, the 'sameness', through the transformation of, or by exchange with the 'defiled mind' (*kliṣṭamanas*). Next to occur is the 'discriminative wisdom' through exchange with the 'mental perception' (*manovijñāna*), said to go with the path of creative contemplation (*bhāvanā-mārga*). Finally, the procedure-of-duty wisdom goes with the 'path beyond training' (*aśaikṣa-mārga*) through the 'knowledge obtained afterwards' (*pṛṣṭhalabdha-j.*) in a transformation of the five outer-sense perceptions.[65]

With the preceding information on the five wisdoms, is it feasible to show them as the adversaries or triumph over the five varieties of nescience or modes of non-knowledge as told from the *Buddhacarita*? While there need be no underlying association, it is possible to glean a few correspondences. It does seem that the Dharmadhātu Wisdom is necessary to combat the first variety, called 'darkness'; and the fifth one, 'blind obscuration' explained as 'weariness' seems to be overcome by the Mirror-like Wisdom, according to Vitapāda's comment. Besides, 'obscuration', dubbed 'fury', seems combatted by Vitapāda's red complexion and red eyes, the Procedure-of-Duty Wisdom. Then 'great delusion', explained as 'passion' does seem to go with hair loosely hanging, the Discriminative Wisdom. That would leave as the last solution, the 'delusion' claimed to mean 'birth and death' to go with the Sameness Wisdom.

Final Note

After completing the foregoing assessment, I am in receipt of the book in Japanese by Shinjō Kawasaki, *Issaichi Shiso no Kenkyu* (Tokyo, 1992), which he renders "A Study of the Omniscient Being (*sarvajña*) in Buddhism." This work earned him the Ph.D. degree at the University of Tokyo, and in 1994 election to the Japanese Akademy of Science.

REFERENCES

1. In the original version of this paper, Philosophy East and West, VII, Nos. 1 and 2, 1957, I have used the rendition 'unwisdom' as previously in my "Notes on the Sanskrit term Jñāna," *Journal of the American Oriental Society*, Vol. 75, No. 4 (October-December, 1955), 253-68. This will be referred to as "Notes".
2. E.H. Johnston, *The Buddhacarita: or, Acts of the Buddha*, Punjab University Oriental Publication Nos. 31 and 32 (Calcutta: Baptist Mission Press, 1935 and 1936). I Sanskrit Text, and II, Translation.
3. *Maitri Upaniṣad* V. 2, in Robert Ernest Hume, *The Thirteen Principal Upanishads* (Oxford University Press, Madras 1949), p. 423.
4. I have first found these correspondences neatly set forth in a native Tibetan work on astrology, the Bstan risis by Blo bzaṅ tshul khrims rgya mtsho, in the section entitled "Rtsis ḥgrel". Later, I have traced out the places of presentation in the *Kālacakra* commentary *Vimalaprabhā* (Derge Tanjur, No. 1347, in Vols. Tha and Da of *Rgyud*). For example, correspondence of Makara (Tibetan: *cbu srin*) with *avidyā*, (Tibetan: ma *rig pa*, etc., Vol. Tha. 212b—4, f.; correspondence of the zodiac with the *guṇas*, Vols. Da, 206, f.; discussion of Dependent Origination and in relation to the zodiac, Vol. Da, 261-1, f.
5. "Notes," p. 260.
6. *Ibid.*, pp. 266-7n.
7. Surendranath Dasgupta, *A History of Indian Philosophy* (Cambridge: the University Press, 1932), Vol. I, p. 452.
8. *Ibid.*, p. 453.
9. *Ibid.*, p. 454.
10. *Ibid.*, p. 111.
11. This has been pointed out by Louis de La Vallée Poussin, "Le Buddhism et le Yoga de Patañjali," *Mélanges Chinois et Bouddbiques*, V (1936-37), 233. The oldest reference he gives is to the *Aṅguttara Nikāya* of the Pāli canon.
12. The original Sanskrit for these two brief stages is on a folio which intruded into the Bihar manuscript of the *Śrāvakabhūmi*, which I have edited and published.
13. *Yogacārabhūmi*, "Bahubhūmika" section, Derge Tanjur, *Sems isam*, Tshi, 7a-2, 3.
14. *Yogacārabhūmi*, "*Viniścayasaṃgrahanī*" section, *Sems isam*, Zhi, 66b-5 6.
15. Since *duḥkha* is contrasted with *sukha* both in Patañjali's *Yoga Sūtra* and in Buddhism, one cannot translate *duḥkha* with such a rendering as "uneasiness," and the like, without also finding some comparable contrasting translation for *sukha*. The fallacy of such a translation as "uneasiness" is that the translator assumes that a word ceases to have its ordinary concrete significance, because it is employed in a metaphysical context. The metaphorical language "He eats up the cash" still leaves "eats up" in its concrete meaning.
16. The commentary *Bhāṣyavṛttipradīpa*, No. 2687 in the Derge Tanjur, *Rgyud*, Thu, 246b-3, f.; saṅs zhes bya ba ni / ñon moṅs pa daṅ / śes byaḥi sgrib pa mthaḥ dag

spaṅs nas / ma rig paḥi gñid las saṅs pas na saṅs zhes byaḥo / dper na skyes bu gñid las saṅs pa bzhin no / rgyas zhes bya ba ni / śes bya mthaḥ dag la ye śes rgyas pa na rgyas zhes gsuṅs so / dper na ku-mū-da rgyas pa lta buḥo / spaṅs pa daṅ ye śes phun sum tshogs paḥo /

17. For further information on the material of this passage, see "Notes," pp. 257-8n, and Nils Simonsson, *Indo-tibetische Studien* (Uppsala: Almqvist & Wiksells Boktryckeri Ab, 1957), pp. 265-6.
18. Jadunath Sinha, *Indian Psychology; Perception* (London, 1934).
19. Oriental Publishers & Distributors, New Delhi (author's date: 1979).
20. Ganganatha Jha's translation has been reprinted in two volumes by Motilal Banarsidass, 1986.
21. Sinha, p. 335.
22. Singh (n. 19, above), p. 15.
23. The term appears in the indexes to Wayman and Tajima, *The Enlightenment of Vairocana*, Motilal Banarsidass, Delhi, 1992); see Omniscience, 'Omniscient knowledge'.
24. Nathmal Tatia, *Studies in Jaina Philosophy* (P.V. Research Institute, Varanasi, 1951), pp. 69-70.
25. Singh, p. 58.
26. A.A. Macdonell, *The Vedic Mythology* (Indian ed., Varanasi, 1963), p. 23.
27. Macdonell, p. 35.
28. Macdonell, p. 58.
29. Macdonell, p. 118.
30. Macdonell, p. 136.
31. Raghunath Airi, *Concept of Sarasvatī* (Delhi, 1977), p. 23.
32. Macdonell, p. 131.
33. Jha, tr. *Tattvasaṃgraha* (n. 20, above), p. 1401.
34. Cf. E. Obermiller, "The Doctrine of Prajnā-pāramitā as exposed in the Abhisamayalaṃkara of Maitreya," *Acta Orientalia*, Vol. XI (reprint, dated 1932), p. 62, where the special omniscience of a Buddha is in a single moment of "all the aspects (*ākāra*)" whether phenomenal or noumenal. The omniscience of both the Hīnayāna and Mahāyāna paths is credited to the Buddha and also to the Bodhisattva, who has entered the 'path of vision' (*darśana-mārga*). The omniscience in regard to given things (*vastu*) of our world is possessed by the Buddha; and also by the saints of the three vehicles, namely, the Śrāvaka, the Pratyekabuddha, and the Bodhisattva, insofar as they realize non-self of the given things.
35. Cf. Wayman's essay, "The Buddhist theory of Vision," reprinted in *Buddhist Insight*, pp. 153-4.
36. Tatia, pp. 70-1.
37. Tatia, pp. 72-4.
38. This is in PTT, Vol. 111, part of Vastusaṃgrahaṇī, subsection on analysis of *saṃskāra*, p. 130-2-6 to 130-3-6, in the Tibetan Tanjur.
39. Tatia, p. 73.
40. This is in PTT, Vol. 106, p. 218-2-2, ff.
41. Cf. Alex Wayman, tr., *Calming the Mind and Discerning the Real* (New York, 1978), p. 105, for the information that the 'phenomenal end' is all the constructed natures comprised in the five personal aggregates (*skandha*), in the eighteen realms (*dhātu*), and in the twelve sense bases (*āyatana*), as well as all the knowable entities comprised in the four (noble) truths.

42. According to Yüan-t'se, p. 219-1-3, the five views are of defiling (*saṃkleśa*) and purifying (*vyavadāna*).
43. According to Abhayākaragupta in his *Munimatālaṃkāra*, PTT, Vol. 101, p. 196-2-4, "right mundane view" means those as a member of the eightfold noble path of Buddhism, i.e. *samyagdṛṣṭi*; and he explains it as "non-fluxional *prajñā*" (Tib. *zag pa med pa'i śes rab*).
44. The eight forbearances are technical language of what is called the Śrāvaka's path of Vision (*darśana-mārga*). They are forbearances, i.e. tacit acceptances toward the four Noble Truth, first, four "forbearances of the knowledge of doctrine" (*dharmajñānakṣānti*); then four "following forbearances of the knowledge" (*anvayajñānakṣānti*). Despite the word 'knowledge', according to Abhayākaragupta, *Munimata*, p. 221-3-3, they are eight 'visions' directed toward suffering (and the other truths), agreeing with their placement on the Śrāvaka's 'Path of Vision'. They amount to four visions of the four truths, and then four subsequent visions of those truth; cf. Alfonso Verdu, *Early Buddhist Philosophy, in the Light of the Four Noble Truths* (Motilal Banarsidass Delhi, 1985), chart, p. 156.
45. PTT, Vol. 106, p. 219-4-5, 6 (where the reading *mig med par* is a mistake for *ming med par*).
46. This essay was reprinted in *Buddhist Insight*; cf. pp. 314-5, and there the fnt. 16.
47. Surendranath Dasgupta, *A History of Indian Philosophy*, Vol. I (Cambridge, 1932), p. 270.
48. S. Dasgupta, Vol. I, p. 440.
49. Described in my essay on 'Core Doctrine', subsection on 'Suffering', the "third misery".
50. PTT, Vol. 34, p. 52-2-5: / śes rab ni gang rgyu ba med pa / lus med pa/ mtshan nyid med pa / mtshan ma med pa 'dus ma byas pa ste /.
51. Tatia, pp. 75-9.
52. Cf. Ernest Steinkellner, "Jñānaśrīmitra's *Sarvajñasiddhiḥ*," in the Conze volume, Berkeley Buddhist Studies Series, 1977, pp. 383-93. Steinkellner discussed also the implications of this text and others in an essay, Yogische Erkenntnis als Problem im Buddhismus," within a volume, *Transzendenzerfahrung, Vollzugshorizont des Heils,* Wien, 1978, pp. 121-34.
53. Shinjō Kawasaki, "The Mimamsa Chapter of Bhavya's *Madhyamaka-hṛdaya-kārikā*—Sanskrit and Tibetan texts—with the Sarvajña Chapter," *Tetsugaku shisōronshū* (Published by Tsukuba University), No. 13, 1987, pp. 42.
54. Part of my manuscript, readied for publication, A Millennium of Buddhist Logic, Vol. One.
55. This Jātaka is alluded to in my essay "Prophecy for persons in Buddhism", in this volume.
56. *Manorathapūraṇī*; Commentary on the Aṅguttara Nikāya, Vol. III (London, 1936), p. 318. I came to know of this passage from a dissertation on dreams in Buddhist biography which was completed by Serinity Young at Columbia University.
57. This information is drawn from A. Wayman and R. Tajima, *The Enlightenment of Vairocana* (Motilal Banarsidass, Delhi, 1992).
58. Lessing, F.D. and Wayman, A., *Mkhas grub rje's Fundamentals of the Buddhist Tantras* (1968), p. 222, n. 17.
59. Cf. Alex Wayman, *Yoga of the Guhyasamājatantra* (Delhi, 1977), references to five jñāna under 'Knowledge' in the Index, and referring to a derivation of five

wisdoms from the five personal aggregates (*skandha*).

60. I employ this scripture in the PTT, Vol. 21, p. 231, ff. for the Tibetan version. The first part of the text was edited in Sanskrit by J. Masuda, *Journal of Taisho University*, Vols. VI-VII, Part II, Tokyo, 1930; .and reprinted in P.L. Vaidya, *Mahāyāna-Sūtra-Saṃgraha* (Darbhanga, 1961). Vimalamitra's commentary is in PTT, Vol. 94, pp. 167, ff.
61. /sangs rgyas kyi sku yang chos kyi sku yin par rtogs / rang gi lus kyang chos kyi dbyings kyi nang du gtogs par mthong / mthong pa rnams kyang yin par ma mthong/
62. Vitapāda, p. 54-4-5: / spyi bo skra grol zhes pa ni so sor kun tu rtog pa /
63. Vitapāda, p. 54-4-6: / mdog dmar ba dang mig dmar ba ni bya ba la nan tan te /
64. Vitapāda, p. 54-4-5: / snying ni 'dar zhing dran pa nyams zhes pa ni me long lta bu'i ye shes /
65. Cf. Louis de La Vallée Poussin, *Vijñaptimātratāsiddhi*, Tome II (Paris, 1929), chap. La Mahābodhi (pp. 681-92).

Bibliography

Abbreviations: *BEFEO*—Bulletin de l'école Francaise d'Extreme-Orient
BSOAS—Bulletin of Oriental and African Studies
HOS—Harvard Oriental Series
JAOS—Journal of the American Oriental Society
NIA—New Indian Antiquary
PEW—Philosophy East and West
WZKS—Wiener Zeitschrift für die Kunde Südasiens

Note: The entries for authors with three or more citations are ordered by date. PTT means: the Peking Tibetan Tripitaka, reprinted by Otani University, Kyoto, Vols. 1-168 (Tokyo-Kyoto: Tibetan Tripitaka Research Institute, 1955-61).

Abegg, Emil, *Der Pretakalpa des Garuḍa-Purāṇa* (Berlin, 1921).

Abhayākaragupta, *Munimatālaṃkāra*, Peking edn. of Tibetan Tanjur (PTT, Vol. 101).

Abhidhānaśāstraviśvalocanam, by Śrīdharasena, Derge edn. of Tanjur, Sna tshogs, Vol. Po.

Abhidharmakośa and-*bhāṣya*, by Vasubandhu; and *Sphuṭārtha* commentary, by Yaśomitra, Ed: D. Shastri (Varanasi, 1970). Text of *kārikā* publ. by V.V. Gokhale, *Journal of the Bombay Branch of the Royal Asiatic Society*, Vol. 22, 1946, pp. 73-102. *Abhidharmakośabhāṣya of Vasubandhu*, Ed: P.Pradhan (Patna, 1975). *Abhidharmakośaṭīkopāyikānāma, by* Śamathadeva, in Tibetan Tanjur (PTT, Vol. 118). tr. of *Abhidharmakośa* and —*bhāṣya* by Louis de La Vallée Poussin, Chaps. 1-2 (Paris, 1923), Chap. 3 (Paris, 1926), Chap. 7 (Paris, 1925).

Abhidharmakośaśāstrakārikābhāṣya, by *Saṃghabhadra (PTT, Vol. 116).

Abhisamayālaṃkārā-prajñāpāramitā-upadeśaśāstra, Ed: Th. Stcherbatsky and E. Obermiller (1970 reprint of 1929 edition). *Abhisamayālaṃkāravṛtti de Ārya-Vimuktasena;* Primo Abhisamaya, Ed: Corrado Pensa (Rome, 1967). Tibetan commentary *Legs bshad gser phreng* by Tsong-kha-pa ('Dharamsala, 1970).

Abhyankar, K.V. and Shukla, J.M., *A Dictionary of Sanskrit Grammar* (Baroda: Oriental Institute, 1977).

Acchariyabbhutadhammasutta in Majjhima-nikāya, Vol. III (Bihar Govt., 1958).

Agni-Purāṇa, Ānandāśrama Sanskrit Series, 41 (Poona, 1900).

Agrawala, Vasudeva S., *Vedic Lectures* (Varanasi, 1960).

—*The Wheel Flag of India* (Varanasi, 1964).

Airi, Raghunath. *Concept of Sarasvatī* (Delhi, 1977).

Aiyangar, Narayan, *Essays on Indo-Aryan Mythology,* Part II (Madras, 1901).

Akṣayamatinirdeśa-sūtra, Peking edn. of Tibetan Kanjur (PTT, Vol. 34); *-ṭīkā* by unknown author (PTT, Vol. 104).

Anacker, Stefan, *Seven Works of Vasubandhu* (Delhi: Motilal Banarsidass, 1984).

Aṅguttara-nikāya, Vols. I, II, III (Bihar Govt., 1960).

Altekar, A.S. *The Position of Women in Hindu Civilization* (Delhi: Motilal Banarsidass, 1962).

Amitāyus-Sūtropadeśa in *Selected Texts of Shin Buddhism* (Kyoto, Japan: Honpo Hongwanji, 1953).

Apte, V.M., "Varuṇa in the Ṛgveda," *NIA,* Vol. VIII (July-Dec., 1946).

Āryabhadracaripraṇidhānarāja (Sikkim: Namgyal Institute of Tibetology, 1961).

Ārya-Mahāvajrameruśikhara-kuṭāgara-dhāraṇī, Derge edn. of Tibetan Kanjur, Rgyud 'bum', Vol. Dsa.

Ārya Śālistamba Sūtram, Ed: Aiyaswami Sastri (Madras: Adyar Library, 1950).

Āryavinayaviniścaya-upāli-paripṛcchā, Peking Tibetan Kanjur (PTT, Vol. 24).

Asaṅga, *Abhidarmasamuccaya,* Ed: Prahlad Pradhan (Santiniketan, 1950). Tibetan commentary by Rgyal tshab rje, Labrang edition, Vol. Ga, "Chos mngon".

—*Cintāmayī bhūmi* (PTT, Vol. 110).

—*Mahāyāna-Sūtrālaṃkāra,* Ed: Sylvain Lévi (Paris, 1911).

—*Paryāyasaṃgrahaṇī* (PTT, Vol. 111).

—*Yogācārabhūmi* [first part], Ed: Vidhushekhara Bhattacharya (University of Calcutta, 1957).

—*Vastusaṃgrahaṇī* (PTT, Vol. 111).

Ashikaga, Ensho, "The Festival for the Spirits of the Dead in Japan," *Western Folklore,* IX:3, July, 1950.

—"Notes on Urabon," *JAOS,* 71:1, 1951.

Asmussen, Peter. *The Khotanese Bhadracaryādeśanā* (Denmark, 1961).

Aśvaghoṣa, *Fifty Verses of Guru Devotion,* translated (Dharamsala, India: Library of Tibetan Works and Archives, 1975)

Bailey, H.W., "Indo-Iranian Studies-III," *Transactions of the Philological Society* (1955).

Banerjea, Jitendra Nath, *The Development of Hindu Iconography* (University of Calcutta, 1956).

Bapat, P.V., "The Arthapadasūtra Spoken by the Buddha, *Visva-Bharati Annals,* Vol. I, 1945; Vol. III, 1950.

—*Vimuttimagga and Visuddhimagga: A Comparative Study* (Calcutta, 1937).

—and Hirakawa, A., trs. *Shan-Chien-P'i-P'o-Sha;* a Chinese version by Saṅghabhadra of *Samantapāsādika* (Poona: Bhandarkar Oriental Research Institute, 1970).

Bareau, André, "La date du Nirvāṇa," *Journal Asiatique,* 1953.

—*Les premier conciles boudhiques* (Paris: Presses Universitaires de France, 1955).

—*Les sectes bouddhiques du Petit Véhicule* (Saigon, 1955).

—*Researches sur la biographie du Buddha dans les*

—*Sūtrapiṭaka et les Vinayapiṭaka anciens* (Paris: E'cole Francaise d'Extreme -*Orient,* 1963).

—"La composition et les étapes de la formation progressive du

Mahāparinirvaāna-sūtra ancien," *BEFEO,* LXVI, 1979.

—"Les Massacre des Śākya; Essai d'interpétation," *BEFEO,* LXIX, 1981.

Basham, A.L., *History and Doctrines of the Ājīvakas* (London: Luzac & Co., 1951).

—*The Wonder that was India* (New York: Grove Press, from the original 1954 edition).

Bechert, Heinz, "Die Lebenszeit des Buddhā-das älteste feststehende Datum der indischen Geschichte?" *Nachrichten der Academie der Wissenschaften in Göttingen;* 1. Philologisch-Historische Klasse, 4 (1986).

—"Remarks on the Date of the Historical Buddha," in *Buddhist Studies (Bukkyō Kenkyū),* Vol. XVII, March 1988.

—"The Problem of the Determination of the date of the historical Buddha," *Wiener Zeitschrift für die Kunde Südasiens,* Vol. XXXIII, 1989.

Bendall, Cecil. Ed., *Subhāṣita-saṃgraha,* Part I, *Le Muséon,* Nouvelle Série, Vol. 4. 1903.

Bergaigne, A., *La Religion Vēdique* (Paris, 1878 and 1883).

Bhattacharya, Benoytosh. See *Sādhanamālā.*

Bhattacharya, K., *et al. The Dialectical Method of Nāgārjuna (Vigrahavyāvartinī)* (Delhi, 1978).

Bhattacharyya, Krishnachandra, *Studies in Philosophy,* Vol. I, Ed: Gopinath Bhattacharyya (Calcutta, 1956).

Bhikṣuṇī-karmavācana. Ed: Ridding and La Vallée Poussin, *BSOS,* Vol. 1, Part 3 (1920).

Biardeau, Madeleine. "Ahaṃkāra, the Ego Principle in the Upaniṣad" *Contributions to Indian Sociology,* VIII, Oct. 1965.

Blo bzang tshul khrims rgyal mtsho. Author of a native Tibetan work on historical calculation, the *Bstan rtsis,* which I consulted in the Tibetan collection in what was called the East Asian Library, University of California, Berkeley, California.

Bloomfield, Maurice, *Hymns of the Atharva-Veda, SBE,* XLII (Oxford, 1897).

Bod rgya tshig mdzod chen mo, three vols. (Peking: Mi rigs dpe skrun khang, 1985).

Bodhicaryāvatāra, by Śāntideva (Darbhanga, 1960).

Bodhisattvabhūmi, by Asaṅga. Ed: N. Dutt (Patna, 1966). Ed: Unrai Wogihara, two vols. (Tokyo, 1936).

Böhtlingk, Otto von and Roth. Rudolph. *Sanskrit Wörterbuch* (St.

Petersburg, 1855-75).

Bond, George D., "Theravada Buddhism's Meditations on Death and the Symbolism of Initiatory Death," *History of Religions,* 19:3, Feb. 1980.

Borooah, Anundoram, *Nānārthasaṃgraha* (Gauhati, Assam, 1969).

Bowlby, John, *Child Care and the Growth of Love* (Baltimore: Penguin Books, 1965).

Boyd, James W. "Symbols of Evil in Buddhism," *The Journal of Asian Studies,* XXXI, No. 1 (Nov., 1971).

Brahmasūtrabhāṣya, Word Index to the Brahma-Sūtra Bhāṣya of Śaṅkara (University of Madras; Part I, 1971; Part II, 1973).

Bronkhorst, Johannes, *The Two Traditions of Meditation in Ancient India* (Stuttgart: Franz Steiner Verlag, 1986).

Brough, John, Ed., *The Gāndhārī Dharmapāda* (Oxford University Press, 1962).

Brown, Norman J., "The Rigvedic Equivalent for Hell," *JAOS,* 61 (June, 1941).

— "The Creation Myth of the Rig Veda," *JAOS,* 62 (June 1942).

Buddhacarita, Skt. text and tr. by E.H. Johnston (Calcutta: Baptist Mission Press, 1555-56)

Buddhadatta Thera, *The Clarifier of the Sweet Meaning (Madhuratthavilāsinī).* Tr. I.B. Horner (London: The Pāli Text Society, 1978).

Buddhaghosa, See: *Visuddhimagga.*

Buddhaguhya, See: *Dhyānottarapaṭala-ṭīkā, Tantrāvatāra,* and *Vairocanābhisambodhi-tantra* (Commentary).

Buddhapālita, commentary on *Madhyamakakārikā* (of Nāgārjuna). Derge edn. of Tibetan version in Tanjur.

Burlingame, Eugene Watson. *Buddhist Legends,* Part 2 (Cambridge, Mass.: Harvard University Press, 1921).

Bu-ston, *History of Buddhism,* Part II, Tr. E. Obermiller (Heidelberg, 1932).

Carakasaṃhitā, Vimāṇasthāna. Tr. by R.K. Sharma and Bhagwan Dash, Vol II (Varanasi: Chowkhamba Press, 1977).

Chakravarti, Tapo Nath. "Food and Drink in Ancient Bengal," *Journal of the Department of Letters,* University of Calcutta, new series, Vol. 2, Part 2 (1958).

Ch'an, Chu, *The Sūtra of 42 Sections and Two Other Scriptures of the Mahāyāna School* (London, 1947).

Chanana, Dev Raj, "The Vinaya Piṭaka and Ancient Indian Jurisprudence," *Journal of the Bihar Research Society*, XLIV, Mar.-June, 1958.

Chang, Chen-chi, *The Practice of Zen* (New York, 1959).

Chau, Thich Minh, *The Chinese Madhyama Āgama and the Pāli Majjhima Nikāya* (Delhi: Motiial Banarsidass, 1991).

Chaudhary, Radhakrishna. *Vrātyas in Ancient India* (Varanasi, 1964).

Childe, V. Gordon, *New Light on the Most Ancient East*, 4th edn.

Conze, Edward. *Aṣṭasāhasrikā Prajñāpāramitā*, tr. into English (Calcutta, 1958).

— *Buddhist Thought in India* (London, 1962).

— *The Gilgit Manuscript of the Aṣṭadaśasāhasrikā Prajñāpāramitā* (Rome, 1962).

— *The Prajñāpāramitā Literature*, 2nd edn. (Tokyo, 1978).

Colebrooke, H.T., *Asiatick Researches*, Vol. IX (1809 reprint).

Coomaraswamy, A.K., *Yakṣas*, Part II (Washington, D.C., 1931).

— "Notes on the Kaṭha Upaniṣad," *NIA*, Vol. I (April, 1938).

— *The Transformation of Nature in Art* (New York: Dover, 1956).

— and Horner, I.B., *The Living Thoughts of Gotama the Buddha* (London: Cassell, 1948).

Cornford, Francis M., *Plato's Cosmology* (New York: The Liberal Arts Press, 1957).

Cox, Collett, *Disputed Dharmasi: Early Buddhist Theories on Existence*, Studia Philologica, Buddhica (Tokyo: The International Institute for Buddhist Studies, 1995).

Csoma de Körös, Alexander, "Origin of the Shakya Race. . .," Translated in E.D. Ross, ed., *Tibetan Studies* (Calcutta, 1912).

Cūḷa-suññatā-sutta. Majjhima-nikāya, III (Bihar Govt., 1958).

Dam pa'i chos mngon pa mdzod kyi don legs pa bśad pa rin po che'i gru gzings, III, by Jam yang zhad pa (the 2nd), a Peking blockprint edn.

Daṃṣṭṛsena, his *Bṛhaṭṭīkā* (on the large Prajñāpāramitā scriptures), Peking edn. of the Tibetan Tanjur (PTT, Vol. 93, in Tibetan Vol. Pha).

Dandekar, R.N. "Asura Varuṇa," *Annals of the Bhandarkar Institute*, Vol. XXI (April-July 1940).

— "Vaiṣṇavism and Śaivism," in *Ramakrishna Gopal Bhandarkar as arIndologist* (Poona:Bhandarkar Oriental Research Institute, 1976).

Daśabhūmikaśutra, Ed: J. Rahder (Paris, 1926).
Daśabhūmisśvaro nāma mahāyānasūtram, Ed: Ryūko kondo (Tokyo, 1936).
Dasgupta, Surendranath, *A History of Indian Philosophy* (Cambridge: the University Press, 1932), Vol. I.
Davies, C. Collin, *An Historical Atlas of the Indian Peninsula* (Oxford University Press, 1959).
Dayal, Har, *The Bodhisattva Doctrine in Buddhist Literature* (London, 1942).
De Jong, J.W., "L'Episode d'Asita dans le Lalitavistara," *Asiatica; Festschrift Friedrich Weller* (Leipzig: Otto Harrassowitz, 1934).
— *Cinq Chapitres de la Prasannapadā* (Paris, 1949).
— "Emptiness," *Journal of Indian Philosophy,* 2 (1972).
— "The Problem of the Absolute in the Madhyamaka school," *Journal of Indian Philosophy,* 2 (1972).
Demiéville, Paul, "La Yogācārabhūmi de Saṅgharakṣa," *BEFEO,* 44 (1954).
— "Le Bouddhisme et la guerre," *Mélanges publiés par l'Institut des hautes études chinoises,* XI (Paris, 1957).
De, S.K., "The Buddhist Tantric Literature (Sanskrit) of Bengal," *NIA,* Vol. I (April 1938).
De Visser, M.W., *The Bodhisattva Akāśagarbha (Kokūzō) in China and Japan* (Amsterdam, 1931).
Dhammapada, Tr. by S. Radhakrishnan (London, 1950). *(The) Dhammapada: Verses and Stories* (Sarnath, Varanasi: Central Institute of Higher Tibetan Studies, 1990).
Dharmasaṃgraha, Ed. by Kenjiu Kasawara and F. Max Müller (New Delhi, 1981).
Dharmasamuccaya, 2nd part by Lin Li-kouang, revised by André Bareaü, *et al* (Paris, 1969); *Dharmasamuccaya,* 3rd part (Paris, 1973).
Dhyānottarapaṭalaṭīkā, by Buddhaguhya, Derge Tanjur, Rgyud 'grel, Vol. Thu.
Dīgha-nikāya, Vols. II and III (Bihar Govt., 1958).
Divyāvadānam, Ed: P.L. Vaidya (Darbhanga, 1959).
Dowson, John, *A Classical Dictionary of Hindu Mythology* (London: Routledge & Kegon Paul, 1950).
Dube, S.A., *Cross Currents in Early Buddhism* (New Delhi: Manohar, 1980).
Durt, H. "La 'Visite aux laboureurś et la 'Meditation sous l'arbre

Jambu' dans lls biographies sanskrites et chinoises du Buddha," *Indological and Buddhist Studies* (Canberra, 1982).

Dutt, Nalinaksha. "Buddhism in Kashmir" in his *Gilgit Manuscripts*, Vol. I (Srinagar, 1939).

— *Gilgit Manuscripts*, Vol. IV (Calcutta, 1959).

Edgerton, Franklin, *Buddhist Hybrid Sanskrit Dictionary, Buddhist Hybrid Sanskrit Grammar; Buddhist Hybrid Sanskrit Reader* (New Haven, 1953).

— "The Hour of Death," *Annals of the Bhandarkar Institute*, Vol. III (1927).

Eggeling, See: *Śatapathabrāhmaṇa*.

Eggermont. P.H. in *Persica*, No. VIII (1979).

Ehni, J., *Der Vedische Mythus des Yama* (Strassburg: K.J. Trübner, 1890).

Eighteen Principal Upaniṣads, Vol. I Ed: V.P. Limaye and R.D. Vadekar (Poona: Vaidika Samśodhana Maṇḍala, 1958).

Emmerick, R.E., Ed. and tr. *The Book of Zambasta* (London, 1968).

(An) Encyclopaedic Dictionary of Sanskrit, Vol. One, Part III (Poona, 1978).

Evans-Wentz, W.Y. *Tibetan Yoga and Secret Doctrines* (London, 1935).

Falk, Maryla, "Nairātmya and Karman," *Indian Historical Quarterly*, XVI:3 (Sept. 1940).

— *Nāma-rūpa and Dharma-rūpa* (University of Calcutta, 1943).

Fausball, V. *Indian Mythology* (London, 1902).

Foucher, A, *The Beginnings of Buddhist Art* (Paris: Paul Geuthner, 1917).

Frauwallner, Erich. "Landmarks in the History of Indian Logic," *Wiener Zeitschrift für die Kunde Süd- und Ostasiens*, Band V, 1961.

— *On the Date of the Buddhist Master of the Law Vasubandhu*, Serie Orientale Roma, III (Rome, 1951).

Gāyaśīrṣa, Aṅguttara-nikāya, Book of Eights (Bihar Govt., 1960); and Vasubandhu's commentary, Derge edn., Mdo 'grel, Vol. Ngi.

Geiger, Wilhelm, *The Mahāvaṃsa* (Colombo: The Ceylon Government, 1950).

Geldner, K.F. *Der Rig-Veda*, III, Harvard Oriental Series, Vol. 35.

Gnoli, Raniero, *The Gilgit Manuscript of the Saṅghabhedavastu,* Part I (Rome, 1977).

Gombrich, Richard, "'Merit Transference' in Sinhalese Buddhism: A Case Study of the Interaction between Doctrine and Practice," *History of Religions,* 11:2, 1971.

Gonda, J., *Aspects of Early Vishnuism* (Utrecht, 1954).

Gopalachari, K. in *A Comprehensive History of India,* Vol. Two (Calcutta, 1957).

Grünwedel, *Mythologie du Buddhisme* (the French translation, 1900).

Guenther, Herbert V., *The Life and Teaching of Nāropa* (Oxford University Press paperback, 1971).

Guhyasamājatantra, Ed: Benoytosh Bhattacharya (Baroda, 1931): its explanatory tantra *Vajramālā;* and *Pañcakrama,* q.v. And see Wayman, *Yoga of* . . . (1977).

Hacker, Paul, *Vivarta* (Wiesbaden, 1953).

Hahn, Michael, *Indica et Tibetica; Nāgārjuna's Ratnāvalī,* Vol. 1 (Bonn, 1982).

— "Vararucis Gāthāśataka—einer Analyse," in *Documenta Barbarorum; Festschrift für Walter Heissig* (Wiesbaden, 1984).

Hakeda, Yoshito S., *Kukai; Major Works* (New York, 1972).

Haṃsarāja, *Vaidikakoṣa* (Lahore, 1926).

Hanayama, Shinsho, *A History of Japanese Buddhism* (Tokyo: The CIIB, 1985).

Hare, E.M., tr. *The Book of Gradual Sayings,* Vol. III (London, 1952); Vol. IV (London, 1955).

Haribhadra, his *Āloka* commentary on the *Aṣṭasāhasrikā-Prajñāpāramitā,* Ed: U. Wogihara (Tokyo: Toyo Bunko, 1932-35).

Hariyappa, "Ṛgvedic Legends through the Ages," *Bulletin of the Deccan College Research Institute,* Vol. XI (March 1951).

Hattori, Masaaki, *Dignāga, On Perception* (Cambridge, Mass., 1968).

Hikata, Ryusho, "On the Period of the Lifetime of Śākyamuni," in his *Studies in Buddhism and Buddhist Culture* (Narita: Naritasan Shinshoji, 1985).

— Ed. *Suvikrāntavikrāmi-paripṛcchā Prajñāpāramitāsūtra* (Kyoto: Rinsen Book Co., 1983).

Hillebrandt, Alfred, *Vedische Mythologie* (Breslau, 1927), Vol. I.

Hirakawa, Akira, "The Rise of Mahāyāna Buddhism and its Relationship to the Worship of Stūpas," *Memoirs of the Research Department of the Toyo Bunko,* No.22 (Tokyo, 1963).

— *Index to the Abhidharmakośabhāṣya,* Part One (Tokyo, 1973).

— *Monastic Discipline for the Buddhist Nuns* (Patna: Kashi Prasad Jayaswal Research Institute, 1982).

— "The Meaning of 'Dharma' in the Concept of the 'Jewel of the Dharma' (Dharmaratna), *Amalā Prajñā; Aspects of Buddhist Studies* (Delhi, 1989).

Hoernle, A.F. Rudolf, Ed. "The Bower Manuscript," *Archaeological Survey of India,* n.i.s. Vol. 22.

Hopkins, W., "Epic Chronology," *JAOS,* Vol. 24.

Horner, I.B., *The Book of Discipline,* Vol. I (London, 1949).

— Tr. *The Collection of the Middle Length Sayings,* Vol. I (London, 1967); Vol. III (London Luzac & Co., 1959).

— *Women Under Primitive Buddhism* (Delhi: Motilal Banarsidass, 1975).

Horsch, Paul, "The Wheel; An Indian Pattern of World Interpretation," *Sino-Indian Studies, Liebenthal Festschrift,* Ed: Kshitis Roy (Santiniketan: Visvabharati, 1957).

Hume, Robert Ernest, *The Thirteen Principal Upanishads* (London, 1934; Madras, 1949).

Huntington, Susan L. *The Art of Ancient India* (New York and Tokyo, 1985).

Inada, Kenneth, Ed: *East-West Dialogues in Aesthetics* (Buffalo, N.Y., 1978).

Iyengar, P.T. Srinivasa. *Outlines of Indian Philosophy* (Benares and London: Theosophical Publishing Society, 1909).

Jaini, Padmanabh S., "On the Theory of Two Vasubandhus," *BSOAS,* 21:1, 1958.

— "The Sautrāntika Theory *Bīja,*" *BSOAS,* Vol. 22, 1959.

— "Ed. *Abhidharmadīpa* with *Vibhāṣāprabhāvṛtti* (Patna, 1969).

— *The Jaina Path of Purification* (Delhi, 1979).

Jamspal, Lozang, Tr. *Ārya-Bodhisattvagocaropāyaviṣaya-vikurvāṇanirdeśa-nāma-Mahāyānasūtra* (a doctoral dissertation, Middle East Department, Columbia University, 1991).

— *Nāgārjuna's Letter to King Gautamīputra* [sic.] (Delhi, 1978).

Jan, Yün-hua. "Buddhist Self-immolation in Medieval China," *History of Religions,* 4:2, Winter, 1965.

Jātakamālā, Ed: Hendrick Kern (Cambridge, Mass.: The Harvard University Press, 1943).

Jha, Subhadra, "Studies in the Paippalādi Atharva-veda," *Journal of the Bihar Research Society,* XXXIX, Sept. 1953.

Johnston, E.H., Ed. *The Buddhacarita,* Sanskrit text (Calcutta: Baptist Mission Press, 1935).

Jones, J.J. See *Mahāvastu.*

Joshi, Rasik Vihari, *Studies in Indian Logic and Metaphysics* (Delhi: Bharatiya Vidya Prakashan, 1979).

— "The Doctrine of 'Aham-Artha'," in *Researches in Indian and Buddhist Philosophy,* Ed: Ram Karan Sharma (Delhi: Motilal Banarsidass, 1993).

Kajiyama, Yuichi, *An Introduction to Buddhist Philosophy;* an annotated translation of the *Tarkabhāṣā* of Mokṣākaragupta (Memoirs of the Faculty of Letters, Kyoto University, No. 10, 1966).

Kālidāsa, *Śakuntalā,* Tr. by M.B. Emeneau from the Bengali recension (Berkeley, California, 1962).

Kalupahana, David J., *Nāgārjuna: The Philosophy of the Middle Way* (Albany, N.Y., 1986).

Kane, P.V., *History of Dharmaśāstra,* Vol. IV (Poona, 1953).

Kantawala, S.G., "The Cult of Manas as Depicted in the Matsya Purāṇa," *Journal of the Oriental Institute,* Baroda, Vol. V (July, 1956).

Karetsky, Patricia Eichenbaum, "The Act of Pilgrimage and Guptan Steles with Scenes from the Life of the Buddha," *Oriental Art,* XXXIII, 1987.

Karunadasa, Y., *Buddhist Analysis of Matter* (Colombo, 1967).

Katre, S.M., *Dictionary of Pāṇini,* Part II (Poona Deccan College, 1968).

Katsura, Shoryu, "A Synopsis of the Prajnāparamitopadeśa of Ratnākaraśānti," *Journal of Indian Buddhist Studies,* XXV. No. 1, Dec. 1976.

Kawasaki, Shinjō, "The Mīmāṃsā Chapter of Bhavya's *Madhyamakahṛdaya-kārikā,*" in *Tetsugaku Shisōronshū* (Tsukuba University), No. 13, 1987.

Keith, Arthur B., Tr. *The Aitareya Āraṇyaka* (Oxford: at the University Press, reprint, 1969).

— Tr. *The Veda of the Black Yajus School,* Part 1 (*HOS,* Vol. 18),

1914, Delhi re issue 1967; Part 2 (*HOS,* Vol. 19), 1914, Delhi re issue 1967.

Kennedy, Jean and Gehman, Henry S., Trs. *The Minor Anthologies of the Pāli Canon,* Part IV (London, 1942).

Khuddaka-nikāya, (selections), The Pāli Text Society, Translation Series, No. 32 (London, 1960).

Kerfel, Willibald, *Das Purāṇavom Weltgebäude*(University Bonn, 1954).

Kloetzli, Randy, *Buddhist Cosmology* (Delhi: Motilal Banarsidass, 1983).

Kochumuttom, Thomas A, *A Buddhist Doctrine of Experience* (Delhi: Motilal Banarsidass, 1982).

Kojima, Bonpo, "Some Thoughts on Buddha's Footprints," *Journal of Indian and Buddhist Studies,* X:2, March 1962.

Kokuyaku Daizōkyō [Japanese collection of popular scriptures, with scholarly introductions], Rọmmbu, VI.

Kokuyaku Issaikyō [Japanese rendition of the whole Chinese canon of Scriptures], Ist Ser. Kyō-shū-bu, Vol. 8.

Kosambi, D.D., *Ancient India* (New York: World Publ. Co., 1969).

Kramrisch, Stella, *The Art of India* (London: Phaidon Press, 1954; also New York, 1954).

— *History of Religions,* 2:1 (Summer, 1963) and 2:2 (Winter, 1963).

Krishan, Y., "*Puṇyadāna* or transference of merit—a fiction," *Journal of Indian Council of Philosophical Research,"* VII:2, Jan.-April 1990.

Kubo, Tsugunari, *On the Saddharmapuṇḍarīka* [Japanese with an English summary] (Tokyo, 1987).

Kuiper, F.B.J., "Rigvedic Loanwords," in *Studia Indologica* (Festschrift für Willibald Kirfel) (1955).

Lai, Whalen W., "Non-duality of the Two Truths in Sinitic Mādhyamika: Origin of the 'Third Truth'," *The Journal of the International Association of Buddhist Studies,* 2:2 (1979).

Lalitavistara, Ed: S. Lefmnn (Halle, 1902).

Lalitā-Sahasranāman, with Bhāskararāya's Commentary. Tr. into English by R. Ananthakrishna Sastry (Adyar, Madras: The Theosophical Publishing House, 1951).

Lamotte, Étienne, See: *Saṃdhinirmocana Sūtra.*

— Tr. *La Somme du Grand Vehicule* (Louvain, 1938).

— Tr. *Le Traité de la Grande Vertu de Sagesse,* Tome I (Louvain: Bureau du Muséon, 1944); Tome III (Louvain, 1970).

— "Le légende du Buddha," *Revue de l'histoire des religions*, Vol. 134 (1948).

— *Histoire du bouddhisme indien* (Louvain, 1958).

— Tr. *La Concentration de la Marche Héroïque* (Śūraṃgamasamādhisūtra) (Bruxelles, 1965).

Lam rim chen mo, See: Tsong-kha-pa.

Lancaster, Lewis R. "The Chinese translation of the Aṣṭasāhasrikā-Prajñāpāramitā-Sūtra attributed to Chih Ch'ien," *Monumenta Serica*, Vol. XXVIII, 1969.

Laṅkāvatāra-sūtra. Ed: Bunjiu Nanjio (Kyoto, 1956).

La Vallée Poussin, Louis de, *Vijñaptimātratāsiddhi* (Paris, 1928).

— [partial translation of Saṃghabhadra's *Nyāyānusārā*], *Mélanges Chinoises et Bouddhiques*, II (1933-34).

— "Le Bouddhisme et le Yoga de Patañjali," *Mélanges Chinoises et Bouddhiques*, V (1936-37).

— *The Buddhist Councils* (Calcutta: K.P. Bagchi & Co., 1976).

La Vallée Poussin, See *Abhidharmakośa*.

Law, Bimala Charan, *Designation of Human Types* (Puggala-Paññatti), (London, 1922).

— *Rivers of India* (Calcutta, 1944).

— *Historical Geography of Ancient India* (Paris, 1954).

— *Heaven and Hell in Buddhist Perspective* (Varanasi, 1973).

Lessing, Ferdinand D., *Yung-Ho-Kung: An Iconography of the Lamaist Cathedral in Peking* (Stockholm, 1942).

— "Calling the Soul; A Lamaist Ritual," *Semitic and Oriental Studies, University of California Publications in Semitic Philology*, XI, 1951.

— "The Eighteen Worthies Crossing the Sea" (Stockholm: Statens Etnografiska Museum, 1954).

Lessing, F.D., See Mkhas grub rje.

Lévi, Sylvain, Ed. *Vijñaptimātratāsiddhi* (Paris, 1925).

— "Autour d'Aśvaghoṣa," *Journal Asiatique*, 1929.

— *Materiaux pour l'Etude du Systeme Vijñaptimātra* (Paris, 1932).

— See: *Mahāyāna-Sūtrālaṃkāra*.

Lin Li-Kouang, *L'Aide-Mémoire de la Vrai Loi* (Paris, 1949).

Lin Li-Kouang, See *Dharmasamuccaya*.

Lindtner, Chr., *Nagarjuniana: Studies in the Writings and Philosophy of Nāgārjuna* (Copenhagen, 1982).

Lüders, Heinrich, *Varuṇa, I: Varuṇa und die Wasser* (Göttingen: Ludwig Alsdorf, 1951).

Macdonell, A.A., *The Vedic Mythology* (Strassburg, 1897; Varanasi, 1983).

— Ed: and Tr. *The Bṛhad-Devatā (HOS,* Vols. 5, 6), 1904; Delhi reissue, 1965.

— *A History of Sanskrit Literature* (Delhi: Motilal Banarsidass, 1952).

— and Keith, A.B., *Vedic Index* (I and II) (Varanasi, 1958).

Madhyāntavidbhāgabhāṣya, See: Gadjin M. Nagao.

Mahathera, Paravahera Vajiranāṇa, *Buddhist Meditation in Theory and Practice* (Colombo, 1962).

Mahāvastu Avadāna, Ed: Radhagovinda Basak (Calcutta: Sanskrit College, 1963, 1964, 1968); Tr. by J.J. Jones, Vol. I (London, 1949).

Mahāyāna-Sūtrālaṃkāra, Ed: Sylvain Lévi (Paris: Librairie Honoré Champion, 1907).

Majjhima-nikāya, Vols. I, II, III (Bihar Govt. 1958).

Majumdar, Girija Prasanna, "Food [Man's Indebtedness to Plants]," *Indian Culture,* Jan. 1935.

Majumdar, Ramesh Chandra, *The Classical Accounts of India* (Calcutta, 1960).

— and Altekar, Anant Sadashiv, *The Vākāṭaka-Gupta Age* (Delhi: Motilal Banarsidass, 1986).

Malalasekera, G.P., *Dictionary of Pāli Proper Names* (London: Luzac & Co., 1960), two volumes.

— "'Transference of Merit' in Ceylonese Buddhism," *Philosophy East and West,* XVII: 1-4.

Maloney, Calarence, Ed: *The Evil Eye* (New York, 1976).

Manorathapūraṇī, Commentary on the Aṅguttara-nikāya, Vol. III (London, 1936).

Masuda, Jiryo, *Origin and Doctrines of Early Indian Buddhist Schools* (Leipzig, 1925).

Matilal, Bimal K., *Epistemology, Logic, and Grammar in Indian Philosophical Analysis* (The Hague: Mouton, 1971).

May, Jacques. "Madhyamaka Philosophy," *Journal of Philosophy,* Vol. 6, 1978.

Mayeda, Sengaku, *A Thousand Teachings: The Upadeśasāhasrī of Śaṅkara* (Tokyo: University of Tokyo Press, 1979).

Mayrhofer, Manfred. *Kurtzgefasstes etymologisches Wörterbuch des Altindischen* (Heidelber Carl Winter, 1953-1980)

Mehendale, Madhukar Anant, *Nirukta Notes,* Series I (Poona: Deccan College, 1965).

Meyer, Johann Jacob, *Sexual Life in Ancient India* (New York, 1953).

Mishra, Yogendra, *An Early History of Vaiśalī* (Delhi: Motilal Banarsidass, 1962).

Mitra, Debala, *Buddhist Monuments* (Calcutta, 1971).

Mkhas grub rje's Fundamentals of the Buddhist Tantras, Tr. by Ferdinand D. Lessing and Alex Wayman (The Hague: Mouton, 1968).

Mookerji, Radhakumud, *The Gupta Empire* (Delhi: Motilal Banarsidass, 1973).

— in *A Comprehensive History of India,* Vol. II, The Mauryas and Satavahanas (Calcutta: Orient Longmans, 1956).

Mukhāgama-vṛtti by Vitapada. Peking Tibetan Tanjur (PTT, Vol. 65).

Munimatālaṃkāra. By Abhayākaragupta (PTT, Vol. 101).

Murti, T.R.V., *The Central Philosophy of Buddhism* (London, 1955).

Murty, K.S., *Nāgārjuna* (Delhi, 1978).

Mus, Paul, *La Lumière sur les Six Voies* (Paris: Institut d'Ethnologie, 1939).

Nagao, Gadjin M., *Index to the Mahāyāna-Sūtrālaṃkāra,* Part One (Tokyo, 1958).

— Ed: *Madhyāntavibhāgabhaāṣya* (Tokyo: Suzuki Research Foundation, 1964).

Nāgārjuna, "Friendly Epistle", Tr. by Heinrich Wenzel, *Journal of the Pāli Text Society,* 1886; *Nāgārjuna's Letter to King Gautamaputra* [sic.], Tr. by Lozang Jamspal *et al.* (Delhi: Motilal Banarsidass, 1978).

— *Madhyamaka-kārikā,* within the *Prasannapadā-nāma-mādhyamika-vṛtti,* Ed: Louis de La Vallée Poussin (St. Petersbourg, 1903-14); and Ed: Jan de Jong (Madras: The Adyar Library and Research Center, 1977).

Nakamura, Hajime, "The Influence of Confucian Ethics on the Chinese Translations of Buddhist Sūtras," *Liebenthal Festschrift; Sino-Indian Studies,* Vol. 5, parts 3-4 (Santiniketan, 1957).

— *Shakuson no Kotoba* (Japanese) (Tokyo, 1958).

— "The Vedānta Philosophy as was revealed in Buddhist Scriptures," *Pañcāmṛtam* (Delhi: Shri Lāl Bahādur Śāstrī Rāṣṭrīya Sanskrit Vidyā Peeṭha, 1968).

Ñāṇamoli, Bhikkhu, *The Life of the Buddha according to the Pāli Canon* (Kandy, Ceylon: Buddhist Publication Society, 1972).

Nanjio, Bunyiu, *A Catalogue of the Chinese Translation of the Buddhist Tripitaka* (reprint, San Francisco, 1975).

Narain, A.K. and Lancaster, Lewis R., *Studies in Buddhist Art and Archaeology* [no further data available].

Nāro-pā, Author, *Sekoddesa-ṭīkā,* Ed: Mario E. Carelli (Baroda: Oriental Institute, 1941).

Netti-Pakaraṇa, Ed: E. Hardy (London, 1961).

Nāyanatilaka, *Buddhist Dictionary* (Colombo, 1950).

Obermiller, E, "The Doctrine of Prajñāpāramitā as exposed in the Abhisamayālaṃkāra of Maitreya," *Acta Orientalia,* Vol. XI (reprint, 1932).

O'Flaherty, Wendy Doniger, Ed: *Karma and Rebirth in Classical Indian Traditions* (Berkeley, 1980; Delhi, 1983).

Pañcakrama, Ed: Louis de La Vallée Poussin (Gand, 1896).

Pañcasutta, In Saṃyutta-nikāya, III (Bihar Govt., 1959).

Pal, Pratapaditya, "South Indian Sculptures in the Museum," *Bulletin of the Los Angeles County Museum of Art,* 1976.

Pāli Tripitakam Concordance, Vol. II by F.L. Woodward *et al.* (London: Pāli Text Society, 1973).

Parinibbāna-sutta. In Dīgha-nikāya, II (Bihar Govt., 1958).

Patañjali, *Vyākaraṇa-Mahābhāṣya,* Kārakāhnika, Tr. by S.D. Joshi and J.A.F. Roodbergen (Poona, 1975).

Patil, D.R., *Cultural History from the Vāyu Purāṇa* (Poona, 1946).

Paṭisambhidāmagga, Ed: Bhikkhu J. Kashyap (Bihar Govt., 1960); Ed: (previously) by Arnold C. Taylor, Vol. II (London, 1907): Tr. by Ñānamoli, *The Path of Discrimination* (London: The Pāli Text Society, 1982).

Pedersen, Kusumita Priscilla, Doctoral Dissertation (Columbia University, 1976), "The *Dhyāna* Chapter of the *Bodhisattva-piṭaka-sūtra."*

Pensa, Corrado, See *Abhisamayālaṃkāra.*

Petech, L., *China and Tibet in the Early 18th Century,* Monographies du T'oung Pao, Vol. I (Leiden, 1950).

Pezzali, Amalia, "Vasubandhu, l'autore dell'Abhidharmakośa," *Studia Missionalia,* Vol. 36, 1987.

'Phags pa drā-bi-da'i bum pa'i cho ga, Derge Tanjur, Rgyud, Vol. Pu.

Pillai, P.K. Narayana, *Non-Ṛgvedic Mantras in the Marriage Cer-*

emonies (Trivandrum, 1958).

Pitāputrasamuccaya-sūtra, Peking Kanjur (PTT, Vol. 23).

Prajñāpāramitā-ratnaguṇa-saṃcaya-gāthā, Sanskrit and Tibetan texts Ed: E. Obermiller, *Bibliotheca Buddhica* XXIX, 1937; Reprinted with a Sanskrit-Tibetan-English index, by Edward Conze ('S-Gravehage, 1960). [Same title] Sanskrit Recension A, Ed: Akira Yuyama along with a Tunhuang Tibetan version (London, 1976). Tr. by Edward Conze, *Indo-Asian Studies,* Part I (New Delhi: International Academy of Indian Culture, 1962).

Price, A.F., *The Jewel of Transcendental Wisdom* (the Diamond Sūtra) (London, 1947).

Przyluski, Jean, *Le Parinirvāṇa et les Funerailles du Buddha* (Paris: Paul Geuthner, 1920).

Rahula, Walpole Sri, *What the Buddha Taught* (Bedford, England, 1972 reprint).

Randhava, M.S., "The Cult of Tree and Tree Worship in Buddhist-Hindu Sculpture," *Roopa Lekha,* XXIII, Nos. 1 and 2.

Ratnagotravibhāga Mahāyānottaratantraśāstra, Ed: E.H. Johnston (Patna, 1950).

Ratnākaraśānti, *Prajñāpāramtopadeśa,* Peking Tanjur (PTT, Vol. 114).

Raychaudhuri, H.C. In: *Age of the Nandas and Mauryas,* Ed: K. A. Nilakanta Sastri (Delhi, 1967).

— In: *Ancient India,* Part I of *An Advanced History of India* (London, 1960).

Renou, Louis, "Védique *Nirṛti,*" *Indian Linguistics* (Chatterji Jubilee Volume), Vol. 16 (1955).

— *Études sur le Vocabulaire du Ṛgveda,* 1st Series (Pondicherry: Institut francais d'Indologie, 1958).

— and Filliozat, J. *L'Inde* Classique, Tome II (Paris, 1953).

Ṛgveda. Tr. by R.T.H. Griffith, 2 Vols. (India reprint, Varanasi: Chowkhamba, 1963).

Rhys Davids, C.A.F. Mrs. *Psalms of the Early Buddhists,* I; Psalms of the Sisters (London, 1909).

— *The Book of the Kindred Sayings,* Part I (London, 1917).

Rhys Davids, T.W. and Rhys Davids, C.A.F., Trs. *Dialogues of the Buddha;* Part I (London, 1956), Part II (London, 1956), Part III (London, 1957).

Rhys Davids and Stede, William, *Pali-English Dictionary* (London: The Pali Text Society, 1921, with reprints).

Robinson, Richard H., *Early Madhyamaka in India and China* (Madison: The University of Wisconsin Press, 1967).

Rockville, W. Woodville, See *Udānavarga*.

Roerich, George N., Tr. *The Blue Annals* (Calcutta: The Asiatic Society, 2 vols. 1949, 1953).

Ruegg, David Seyfort, *The Literature of the Mādhyamika School of Philosophy in India* (Wiesbaden, 1981).

—"Towards a Chronology of the Madhyamaka School," in *Indological and Buddhist Studies,* Ed: L.A. Hercus *et al.* (Canberra, 1982).

Saddharmapuṇḍarīka-sūtra, Tr. by Leon Hurvitz, *Scripture of the Lotus Blossom of the Fine Dharma* (New York: Columbia University Press, 1976).

Sādhanamālā, Ed: B. Bhattacharya (Baroda: Oriental Institute, 1968).

Samantabhadracaryā-praṇidhānarāja, Ed: Sushama Devi (New Delhi: International Academy of Indian Culture, 1958); Tibetan commentary by Lcang skya Khutukhtu Lalitavajra, Ed: Lokesh Chandra (Sikkim: Namgyal Institute of Tibetology, 1963).

Saṃdhinirmocana-sūtra, Tibetan text Ed. (Tr.): by Étienne Lamotte (Louvain and Paris, 1935); the great commentary by Yüan-t'se, Peking Tanjur, Sems tsam (PTT, Vol. 106).

Sampuṭa-tantra, the commentary *Āmnāyamañjari.* By Abhayākaragupta (PTT, Vol. 111).

Samtani, N.H., Ed: *The Arthaviniścaya-sūtra and its commentary (Nibandhana)* (Patna, 1971).

Saṃyutta-nikāya, Vols. I, II, IV, V. Ed: Bhikku Kashyap ed. (Bihar Govt., 1959).

Sankalia, N.H., *The University of Nalanda* (Delhi: Oriental Publishers, 1972).

Sanskrit Studies of M.B. Emeneau; Selected Papers, Ed: B.A. Van Nooten (Berkeley: Center for South and Southeast Asia Studies, University of California, 1988).

Saptaśatikā Prajñāpāramitā (PTT, Vol. 21); its commentary by Vimalamitra (PTT Vol. 94).

Śārdūlakarṇāvadānam, Ed: Sujitkumar Mukhopadhyaya (Santiniketan, 1954).

Sarkar, H. and Misra, R.N., *Nagarjunakonda* (New Delhi: Archaelogical Suvey of India, 1980).

Sarup, Lakshman, *The Nighaṇṭu and the Nirukta* (Delhi: Motilal Banarsidass, 1984).

Sarvadurgatipariśodhana-tantra, Commentary ascribed to Buddhaguhya (PTT, Vol. 76); Commentary by Vajravarman, *Vyākhya-sundarālaṃkāranāma*

Sasaki, Genjun, "The three aspects of truth in Buddhist epistemology," *Journal of the Oriental Institute,* Baroda, XIV, 3-4, March-June, 1965.

—"The Time Concept in Abhidharma," *Proceedings of the Twenty-Sixth International Congress of Orientalists,* [New Delhi, 1964]. (Poona: Bhandarkar Oriental Research Institute, 1969). Vol. III, Part 1.

—*Linguistic Approach to Buddhist Thought* (Delhi: Motilal Banarsidass, Delhi, 1986).

Sastri, Nilakanta, *A History of South India* (Oxford University Press, 1958).

Śatapathabrāhmaṇa, Ed: Albrecht Weber (Varanasi, 1964); Tr. by Julius Eggeling in five Volumes, Nos. 12, 26, 41, 43, 44. of *Sacred Books of the East,* Ed: Max Müller (now reprinted in Delhi, Motilal Banarsidass).

Scheftelowitz, J., "Die Zeit als Schicksalsgottheit in der indischen und iranischen Religion," *Beiträge zur indischen Sprachwissenschaft und Religionsgeschichte,* IV (Stuttgart, 1929).

Schlingloff, Dieter, 'Ein Zyklus des Buddhalebens in Ajanta," *WZKS,* XXVII, 1983.

—"Die Meditation unter dem Jambu-Baum," *WZKS,* XXX, 1987.

—"Die Bedeutung der Symbole in der Altbuddhistichen Kunst," in *Hinduism und Buddhismus; Festschrift für Ulrich Schneider* (Freiburg, 1987).

Schmid, Toni, *The Cotton-Clad Mila* (Stockholm, 1952).

Schmithausen, Lambert. *Der Nirvāṇa-Abschnitt in der Viniścayasaṃgrahaṇi der Yogācārabhūmi* (Wien: Osterr. Ak. d. Wissens., 1969).

—"Zu den Rezensionen des Udānavargaḥ," *Archiv für Indische Philosophie, WZKS,* 14, 1970.

—*Ālayavijñāna,* Part I (Text), Part II (Notes) (Tokyo: The International Institute for Buddhist Studies, 1987).

Senart, É, *Essai sur la Légende du Buddha* (Paris, 1882).

Sgrub thabs kun btus; a collection of sādhanas and related texts of the Vajrayāna traditions of Tibet (Dehradun, 1970), Vol. II (Kha).

Sharma, Baldev Raj, *The Concept of Ātman in the Principal Upaniṣads* (New Delhi: Dinesh Publications, 1972).

Shende, N.J., *The Foundations of the Atharvanic Religion* (Bulletin of the Deccan Research Institute, IX, 3-4) (Poona, 1929).

Shukla, N.S., Ed: *The Buddhist Hybrid Sanskrit Dharmapada* (Patna, 1979).

Śikṣāsamuccaya, by Śāntideva, Ed: P.L. Vaidya (Darbhanga, 1961); Tr: Cecil Bendall and W.H.D. Rouse (London, 1922).

Silva-Vigier, Anil de, *The Life of the Buddha Retold from Ancient Sources* (London: The Phaidon Press, 1955).

Simonsson, Nils, *Indo-Tibetische Studien* (Uppsala: Almqvist & Wiksells Boktryckeri Ab, 1957).

Singh, Madan Mohan, "Authenticity of the Buddhist Pāli Canon for the Cultural History of Pre-Maurya Bihar," *The Journal of the Bihar Research Society,* Vol. XLVI, Pts. i-iv, 1960.

Singh, Ramjee, *The Concept of Omniscience in Ancient Hindu Thought* (New Delhi: Oriental Publishers, 1979).

Sinha, Jadunath, *Indian Psychology; Perception* (London, 1934).

Sivaramamurti, C., *Amaravati Sculptures in the Madras Government Museum* (Madras, 1956).

—"Buddha as a Mahāpurusha," *Bulletin of Tibetology,* IX:3 (Gangtok, Sikkim, 1972).

Smidt, H., *Eine populäre Darstellung der Shingon-lehre* (Berlin: Oesterheld & Co., 1918).

Smith, Helmer, *Saddanīti,* Vol. 1 (Lund, 1954).

Sngags rim chen mo. See: Tsong kha pa.

Sorensen, S., *Index to the Names in the Mahābhārata* (Delhi: Motilal Banarsidass, 1978).

Śrīmālādevīsiṃhanāda, See Wayman, Alex and Wayman, Hideko.

Śrīvatsankacharya, *Avyaya Kośa: A Dictionary of Indeclinables* (Mylapore, Madras, 1971).

Stcherbatsky, Th., *The Conception of Buddhist Nirvāṇa* (Leningrad, 1927; reprint Shanghai, China, 1940).

—*Buddhist Logic,* 2 vols. ('s-Gravenhage, 1958).

—*The Central Conception of Buddhism* (Calcutta: Susil Gupta, 1961).

Steinkellner, Ernst. "Wirklichkeit und Begriff bei Dharmakīrti," *WZKS*

15 (1971).

—"Jñānaśrīmitra's *Sarvajñasiddhiḥ,*" Conze Vol., Berkeley Buddhist Studies Series, 1977.

—"Yogische Eerkenntnis als Problem im Buddhismus," in a volume *Transzendenzerfahrung Vollzugshorizont des Heils* (Wien, 1978).

Stone, Elizabeth, *The Buddhist Art of Nāgārjunakoṇḍa* (Delhi: Motilal Banarsidass, 1994).

Streng, Frederick J., *Emptiness: A Study in Religious Meaning* (Nashville, 1967).

Subāhuparipṛcchā, its commentary by Buddhaguhya, *Tshig gi don bśad pa'i brjed byang,* Derge edn. of Tanjur, Rgyud, Vol. Thu.

Subramanyam, K.N., *The Anklet Story: Silappadhikaaraṁ of Ilango Adigal* (Delhi: Agam Prakashan, 1977).

Sukhalalji, Pandit, *Essence of Jainism* (translated from Hindi by R.S. Betai) (Ahmedabad: L.D. Institute of Indology, 1988).

Sukla, Ananta Charana, *The Concept of Imitation in Greek and Indian Aesthetics* (Calcutta, 1977).

Sūrya Kānta, *A Grammatical Dictionary of Sanskrit* (Vedic) (Delhi, 1989).

Sūrya-siddhānta, Translated (University of Calcutta, 1935).

Suttaṇipāta, Ed: Bhikshu Samgharatna (Sarnath, Varanasi, 1951).

Suttanipāta-Aṭṭhakathā, Ed: Angraj Chaudhary (Nālandā-Bihar, 1975), Vol. II.

Taittirīya-Saṃhitā, See Keith, A.B. for translation,

—of the Kṛṣṇa Yajurveda. Ed. (Pāraḍī-nagara, 1957).

Takakusu, J. "The Date of Vasubandhu, the Great Buddhist Philosopher," in *Indian Studies in honor of Charles Rockwell Lanman* (Cambridge, Mass., 1929).

—"The Life of Vasubandhu by Paramārtha (A.D. 499-569)," *T'oung Pao,* Ser. II, 5.

Takasaki, Jikido, *A Study of the Ratnagotravibhāga* (Roma: Instituto Italiano per il Medio ed Estremo Oriente, 1966).

—in *Journal of Indian and Buddhist Studies* (Tokyo), Vol. 22, No. 2, 1974.

Tambiah, S.J., *Buddhism and the Spirit Cults in Northeast Thailand* (Cambridge: University Press, 1970).

Tantrārthāvatāra, by Buddhaguhya, Derge Tanjur, Rgyud 'grel, Vol. 'I.

Tantrārthāvatāra-vyākhyāna, by Padmavajra, Derge Rgyud 'grel, Vol. 'I.

Tāranātha's History of Buddhism in India, Tr. from the Tibetan by Lama Chimpa and Debiprasad Chattopadhyaya (Simla, 1970).

Tathāgata-guhya-sūtra, Derge edn. of Kanjur, Vol. 39.

Tatia, Nathmal, *Studies in Jaina Philosophy* (Varanasi: P.V. Research Institute, 1951).

Tattvasaṃgraha, by Śāntarakṣita with commentary by Kamalaśīla, Ed: Dwarikadas Shastri, 2 vols. (Varanasi: Buddha Bharati, 1968): Tr. by Ganganatha Jha (Delhi: Motilal Banarsidass, 1986).

Temple, Richard, *et al., Shivaji and the Rise of the Mahrattas* (Calcutta: Susil Gupta, 1953) [a booklet].

Thomas, Edward J., *The Life of Buddha as Legend and History* (New York: Barnes and Noble, 1952).

—*The History of Buddhist Thought* (London, 1963).

Thomas, F.W., Tr. *Mahārājakaniṣka-lekha,* in *Indian Antiquary,* 32, 1903.

Tibetan Kanjur, Japanese photo edition (PTT, Vol. 5).

Tiwari, Kapil N., *Suffering: Indian Perspectives* (Delhi: Motilal Banarsidass, 1986).

Tsong-kha-pa, *Lam rim chen mo* (Tashilunpo edition).

—*Sngags rim chen mo* (Peking blockprint).

Tucci, Giuseppe, *On Some Aspects of the Doctrines of Maitreyanātha and Asaṅga* (University of Calcutta, 1930).

—[portions of *Ratnāvalī* with English translation] *Journal of the Royal Asiatique Society,* 1934.

—*Tibetan Painted Scrolls* (Roma: La Libreria dello Stato, 1949).

—*Minor Buddhist Texts,* Part I (Roma: Serie Orientale, 1956).

Udānavarga, Ed: Franz Bernhard (Göttingen, 1965-1968); Ed: N.P. Chakravarti, *L'Udānavarga Sanskrit,* Tome Premier (Paris, 1930); Tibetan text Ed: H. Beckh (Berlin: George Reimer, 1911); Tr. from Tibetan by W. Woodville Rockhill (London: Kegan Paul, 1892).

Udānavarga-Vivaraṇa, by Prajñāvarman, (Tibetan) Ed: Michael Balk (Bonn, 1984).

Ui, Hakuju, *Concise Buddhist Dictionary* [in Japanese, Tokyo, 1938].

Uṇādivṛtti, by Candragomin, Derge Tanjur, Sgra mdo, Vol. Re.

Underwood, Fred, Doctoral dissertation in Religion Department, Columbia University: "Buddhist Insight: The Nature and Function of Paññā in the Pāli Nikāyas."

Upadhyaya, B.C., *India in Kālidāsa* (Allahabad: Kitabistan, 1947).

Vaidya, P.L., Ed: *Mahāyāna-sūtra-saṃgraha* (Darbhanga, 1961).

Vairocanābhisambodhi-tantra, Buddhaguhya's commentary, Derge Tanjur, Rgyud 'grel, Vol. Tu.

Vajravidāraṇa-dhāraṇī, the commentary *Bhāṣyavṛttipradīpa,* by Jñānavajra, Derge Tanjuir, Rgyud 'gel, Vol. Thu.

Varadachari, *Sri Ramanuja's Theory of Knowledge; A Study* (Tirupati, 1943).

Varaha-Upaniṣad, in collection *Yoga Upaniṣads,* q.v.

Velankar, H.D., *Ṛgveda Maṇḍala VII* (Bombay, 1963).

Veliath, Cyril, "Rāmānuja's Concept of the Individual Soul and Human Freedom," in *Sambhāṣā* 12 (Department of Indian Philosophy, Universty of Nagoya, 1991).

Verdu, Alfonsa, *Early Buddhist Philosophy in the Light of the Four Noble Truths* (Delhi: Motilal Banarsidass, 1985).

Vetter, Tilmann, "A Comparison between the Mysticism of the older Prajñā Pāramitā literature and the Mysticism of the Mūla-Madhyamaka-kārikās of Nāgārjuna," *Acta Indologica,* VI (Naritasan Shinshoji, 1984).

— *The Ideas and Meditative Practices of Early Buddhism* (Leiden: E.J. Brill, 1988).

Viennot, Odette, *Le Culte de l'Arbre dans l'Inde Ancienne* (Presses Universities de France, 1954).

Vijñaptimātratāsiddhi, Ed: Sylvain Lévi (Paris, 1925); Tr. by Louis de La Vallée Poussin. Tome I (Paris, 1928), Tome II (Paris, 1929).

Vimalaprabhā (on the *Kālacakra*), Derge Tanjur, Rgyud 'grel, Vols. Tha and Da.

Vinayavibhaṅgapadavyākhyāna, by Vinītadeva, Tibetan translation in Derge Tanjur, 'Dul 'grel, Vol. Tshu.

Vilāsavajra, *Namamantrārthāvalokinī,* in Tibetan Tanjur (PTT, Vol. 74).

Visuddhimagga of Buddhaghosácariya, Ed: Henry Clarke Warren; revised by Dharmananda Kosambi (Cambridge, Mass.: Harvard University Press, 1950); Tr. by Bhikku Ñāṇamoli, *The Path of Purification* (Colombo, 1956).

Viveka-Cūḍāmaṇi by Śaṅkara, Tr. by Swāmī Mādhavānanda (Advaita Ashrama, 1989).

Vogel, J. Ph., *Indian Serpent Lore* (Delhi: reprint Indological Book House, 1972).

Waldschmidst, Ernst, *Die Überlieferung vom Lebensende des Buddha.*

—Abhandlungen der Akademie der Wissenschaften in Göttingen, Phil.-Hist. Kl. 3. Folge, 1944-48.

—*Das Mahāparinirvāṇasūtra, Abh. der D. Akad. der Wiss. zu Berlin, Klasse für Sprachen, Literatur und Kunst,* 1950, No. 2, Teil II.

—"A Fragment from the *Saṃyuktāgama,*" *The Adyar Library Bulletin,* Vol. 20 (1956).

Walleser, M., *The Life of Nāgārjuna from Tibetan and Chinese Sources* (Delhi, 1979).

Warder, A.K., *Indian Buddhism* (Delhi, 1970).

—"Is Nāgārjuna a Mahāyānist?" in *The Problem of Truths in Buddhism and Vedānta,* Ed: M. Sprung (Dordercht, 1973).

Warren, Henry Clarke, *Buddhism in Translations* (Cambridge, Mass.: Harvard University Press, 1947).

Watters, Thomas, *On Yuan Chwang's Travels in India,* Vol. I (London, 1904), Vol. II (London, 1905).

—*The Way of the Buddha* (Publications Division, Government of India; 2500th anniversary of the Mahāparinirvāṇa).

Wayman, Alex, "Notes on the Sanskrit term Jñāna," *JAOS,* 75:4, 1955.

—"Contributions regarding the thirty-two characteristics of the Great Person," *Sino-Indian Studies; Liebenthal Festschrift* (Visvabharati, 1957).

—"The Meaning of Unwisdom (*avidyā*), PEW, 7:1-2, 1957.

—"Studies in Yama and Mara," *Indo-Iranian Journal,* 3:1-2, 1959.

—The Twenty-one Praises of Tārā, a Syncretism of Śaivism and Buddhism," *Journal of the Bihar Research Society,* 45:1-4, 1959.

—"The Sacittikā and Acittikā Bhūmi and the Pratyekabuddhabhūmi (Sanskrit texts)," *Journal of Indian and Buddhist Studies* (Tokyo), 7:1, 1960; reprinted in Wayman, *Buddhist Insight* (1984).

—*Analysis of the Śrāvakabhūmi Manuscript,* University of California Publications in Classical Philology, Vol. 17, Berkeley, California, 1961.

"The Buddhist 'Not this, not this,' " *PEW,* 11:3, 1961.

—"Buddhist Genesis and the Tantric Tradition," *Oriens Extremus,* 9:1, 1962/

—"The Yogācāra Idealism," [a review article] *PEW,* 15:1, 1965.

—"Climactic Times in Indian Mythology and Religion," *History of Religions,* 4:;2, 1965.

—"The Hindu-Buddhist Rite of Truth—an Interpretation," in *Studies in Indian Linguistics* (Linguistic Society of India, Poona), 1968.

—"Contributions to the Mādhyamika School of Buddhism," [a review article] *JAOS,* 89:1, 1969.

—"The Buddhist Theory of Vision," *Añjali: A Felicitation Volume* (Peradeniya: University of Ceylon, 1970); reprinted in Wayman, *Buddhist Insight* (1984).

—"Buddhism," in *Historia Religionum,* Vol. II (Leiden: E.J. Brill, 1971).

—*The Buddhist Tantras: Light on Indo-Tibetan Esotericism* (New York: Samuel Weiser, 1973).

—"The Intermediate-State Dispute in Buddhism," *Buddhist Studies in Honor of I.B. Horner,* Ed: L. Cousins, *et al.* (Dordrecht: D. Reidel, 1974); reprinted in Wayman, *Buddhist Insight* (1984).

—"The Mirror as a Pan-Buddhist Metaphor-Simile,"*History of Religions,* 13:4, 1974.

—"Purification of Sin by Vision and Confession," in *A Study of Kleśa,* Ed: G.H. Sasaki (Tokyo, 1975).

—"The Significance of Mantras, from the Veda down to Buddhist Tantric Practice," *Adyar Library Bulletin,* XXXIX, 1975.

—"Meditation in Theravāda and Mahīśāsaka," *Studia Missionalia,* Vol. 25, 1976.

—"Secret of the Heart Sūtra," in *Prajñāpāramitā and Related Systems,* Ed: L. Lancaster (Berkeley: Berkeley Buddhist Series, 1977).

—*Yoga of the Guhyasamājatantra: The Arcane Lore of Forty Verses* (Delhi: Motilal Banarsidass, 1977).

—*Calming the Mind and Discerning the Real,* from the *Lam rim chen mo* of Tsong-kha-pa (New York: Columbia University Press, 1978); Indian edition, Delhi, 1979.

—"Ancient Buddhist Monasticism," *Studia Missionalia,* Vol. 28, 1979.

—"Yogācāra and the Buddhist Logicians," *The Journal of the International Association of Buddhist Studies,* II:1, 1979.

—"The Twenty Reifying Views (*sakkāyadiṭṭhi), Studies in Pāli and Buddhism,* Ed: A.K. Narain (Delhi: B.R. Publishing Corpn., 1979); reprinted in Wayman, *Buddhist Insight* (1984).
—"Buddha as Savior," *Studia Missionalia,* Vol. 29, 1980.
—"Dependent Origination--the Indo-Tibetan Tradition," *Journal of Chinese Philosophy* 7, 1980; reprinted in Wayman, *Buddhist Insight* (1984).
—"Nescience and insight according to Asaṅga's Yogācārabhūmi," *Buddhist Studies in Honor of Walpola Rahula* (London: Gordon Frazer, 1980); reprinted in Wayman, *Buddhist Insight,* (1984).
—"A Report on the *Akṣayamatinirdeśa-sūtra,*" in *Studies in Indo-Asian Art and Culture,* Vol. 6, Ed: Lokesh Chandra (New Delhi: International Academy of Indian Culture, 1980).
—"Some Accords with the Sāṃkhya Theory of Tanmātra," in *A Corpus of Indian Studies* (Calcutta: Sanskrit Pustak Bhandar, 1980).
—"The samādhi lists of the *Akṣayamatinirdeśasūtra* and the *Mahāvyutpatti," Acta Orientalia Academiae Scientiarum Hung.,* XXXIV, 1:3, 1980.
—"The Religious Meaning of concrete death in Buddhism," *Studia Missionalia,* Vol. 31, 1982.
—"A Study of the Vedāntic and Buddhist Theory of Nāma-rūpa," in *Indological and Buddhist Studies* (Canberra: Faculty of Asian Studies, 1982).
—"Eschatology in Buddhism," *Studia Missionalia,* Vol. 32, 1983.
—*Buddhist Insight: Essays by Alex Wayman,* Ed: George E. Elder (Delhi: Motilal Banarsidass, 1984).
—"The Interlineary-type Commentary in Tibetan," in *Tibetan and Buddhist Studies,* Ed: Louis Ligeti, Vol. 2 (Budapest: Akademiai Kiado, 1984).
—"The Metaphysics of Cooking in the Satyartha Prakash and in the Indian Tradition," in *World Perspectives on Swami Dayanand Saraswati* by Ganga Ram Garg (New Delhi: Concept Publishing Company, 1984).
—"Śākyamuni, Founder of Buddhism," *Studia Missionalia,* Vol. 33, 1984.
—*Chanting the Names of Mañjuśrī,* translation of the *Mañjuśrī-namā-saṃgīti* (Boston: Shambala Publications, 1985).
—"Nāgārjuna: Moralist Reformer of Buddhism," *Studia Missionalia,* Vol. 34, 1985.

—"The Gait (*gati*) and the Path (*mārga*)—Reflections on the Horizontal," *JAOS,* 105:3, 1985.

—"Some observations on dualistic mirror symbolism in Western Philosophy and in the Upaniṣads," *Aligarh Journal of Oriental Studies,* II, 1-2 (1985).

—"The Vedic Three Worlds in Early and Later Times," *Adyar Library Bulletin,* Vol. 50 (1986).

—"The Guru in Buddhism," *Studia Missionalia,* Vol. 36, 1987.

—"A Prajñāpāramitā Scripture within a Tantra," in *Śramaṇa Vidyā* (Sarnath, Varanasi: Central Institute of Higher Tibetan Studies, 1987).

—"The Mathurā Set of Aṣṭamaṅgala (Eight Auspicious Symbols) in Early and Later Times" in *Mathurā: The Cultural Heritage,* Ed: Doris Meth Srinivasan, *et al.* (New Delhi: American Institute of Indian Studies, 1988).

—"The Tathāgata chapter of Nāgārjuna's Mūla–Madhyamaka-kārikā," *PEW,* XXXVIII: 1, 1988.

—"Vasubandhu—Teacher Extraordinary," *Studia Missionalia,* Vol. 37, 1988.

—"Dcotrinal Affiliation of the Buddhist Master Asaṅga," in *Amala Prajñā: Aspects of Buddhist Studies,* Ed: N.H. Samtani and H.S. Prasad (Delhi, 1989).

—"The negative a-/an- prefix in Sanskrit," Ed: B.K. Matilal and P. Bilimoria (Delhi, 1990).

—"The Position of Women in Buddhism," *Studia Missionalia,* Vol. 40, 1991.

Wayman, Alex and Wayman, Hideko, Trs., *Śrīmālādevīsiṃhanāda-sūtra:*
The Lion's Roar of Queen Śrīmālā: A Buddhist Scripture on the Tathāgatagarbha Theory (New York: Columbia University Press, 1974); reprinted (Delhi, 1990).

Wayman, Alex and Tajima, R., *The Enlightenment of Vairocana,* Book One: *Study of the Vairocanābhisambodhi-tantra,* by A. Wayman; Book Two: *Study of the Mahāvairocana-sūtra,* by R. Tajima (Delhi: Motilal Banarsidass, 1992).

Wayman, Alex, See Mkhas grub rje.

Whitney, William Dwight, "The Lunar Zodiac," in his *Oriental and Linguistic Studies,* Sec. Ser. (New York, 1874).

—*The Roots, Verb-Forms, and Primary Derivatives of the Sanskrit Language* (Leipzig, 1885).

Willetts, William, *Chinese Art,* I (Penguin Books, 1958).
Willis, Janice D., "Nuns and Benefactresses: The Role of Women in the Development of Buddhism," in *Women, Religion, and Social Change,* Ed: Yvonne Yazbeck Haddad and Ellison Banks Findly (Albany: State University of New York Press, 1985).
Winternitz, Maurice, *A History of Indian Literature,* Vol. I (Calcutta, 1927); Vol. II (Calcutta, 1933).
Woodword, F.L., Tr., *The Book of Gradual Sayings,* Vol. II (London, 1952).
—Tr., *The Book of Kindred Sayings,* Vol. V (Mahāvagga) (London, 1956).

Yampolsky, Philip, "The Origin of the Twenty-eight Lunar Mansions," *Osiris* (1950).
Yeh, Ah-Yueh, "The Characteristics of 'vijñāna' and 'vijñapti' on the basis of Vasubandhu's *Pañcaskandhaprakaraṇa,*" *Annals* (B.O.R. Institute), Vol. LX (Poona, 1979).
—"The Theories of the Bodhisattva's '*avaraṇa*' and '*karaṇa*' in the *Madhyāntāvibhāgabhāṣya,*" *Philosophical Review* (Taiwan), Jan. 1987.
Yetts, W. Perceval, "Notes on the Disposal of Buddhist Dead in China," *Journal Royal Asiatic Society,* 1911.
Yoga Upaniṣads, with the commentary of Śrī Upaniṣad-Brahmayogin, Ed: by A. Mahadeva Sastri (Madras: The Adyar Library and Research Center, 1968).

Zab pa dang rgya che ba'i dam pa'i chos kyi thob yig gsal ba'i me long, Peking edition, Vol. I.
Zukan, Butsuzö. *Hito no maki* [Japanese].
Zurcher, E., *The Buddhist Conquest of China* (Leiden, 1959).

Index

In the following, when a page number is for a section of notes (that are at the ends of chapters), an extra number is given in parentheses, with abbreviation 'n.' meaning "note number". *Up.* = *Upaniṣad*.